PEARSON CUSTOM LIBRARY

COMMUNICATION

Pearson Custom Publishing

New York   Boston   San Francisco
London   Toronto   Sydney   Tokyo   Singapore   Madrid
Mexico City   Munich   Paris   Cape Town   Hong Kong   Montreal

Senior Vice President, Editorial and Marketing: Patrick F. Boles
Senior Sponsoring Editor: Natalie Danner
Development Editor: Mary Kate Paris
Editorial Assistant: Jill Johnson
Operations Manager: Eric M. Kenney
Database Product Manager: Jennifer Berry
Production Project Manager: Troy Lilly
Rights Manager: Jennifer Lerman
Art Director: Renée Sartell
Cover Designers: Kristen Kiley and Tess Mattern

Cover Art: "Amperstand Stencil" courtesy of Rob Szajkowski/iStockphoto, "Interview Microphones" courtesy of Valerie Loiseleux/iStockphoto, "Telephone Made Out of Cans" courtesy of Photodisc Photography/Veer Images, "Speech Balloon" courtesy of iStockphoto, "Road Markings" courtesy of iStockphoto.

Printed in the United States of America.

Please visit our websites at *www.pearsoncustom.com*.

Attention bookstores: For permission to return any unsold stock, contact us at *pe-uscustomreturns@pearson.com*.

**Pearson
Custom Publishing**
is a division of

www.pearsonhighered.com
ISBN 10: 0-558-17926-6
ISBN 13: 978-0-558-17926-7

Contents

Chapter 1

Preliminaries to Human Communication

Preliminaries to Human Communication

MAJOR TOPICS

The Benefits, Forms, and Purposes of Human Communication

The Elements of Human Communication

The Principles of Human Communication

Special Features

Values of a Human Communication
Course: Mark Hickson III

What Do You Believe about Communication?

What Is Media Literacy?

The Areas of Ethics

Understanding Communication Theories

Understanding Communication Research

Skills Distinguishing Content from
Relationship Messages

Skills Resolving Ambiguity

© image 100/CORBIS

Of all the knowledge and skills you have, those concerning communication will prove the most useful. Your ability to communicate will always influence and play a crucial part in how effectively you live your personal and professional lives. It's vital to your success to learn how communication works and to master its most essential skills.

In this unit you'll learn about:
- the benefits, forms, and purposes of human communication.
- the major elements in the human communication process.
- the essential principles that explain how communication works.

You'll learn to:
- communicate with a clear understanding of the essential elements and how they relate to one another.
- use the essential principles of human communication to increase your own effectiveness in interpersonal, small group, and public speaking.

Let's begin this unit with a clear explanation of what you'll get out of this course and what forms of communication you'll study.

THE BENEFITS, FORMS, AND PURPOSES OF HUMAN COMMUNICATION

You'll benefit greatly from studying the forms of communication covered in this course. So let's begin our exploration with an introduction of these benefits. Next we'll preview the forms of human communication you'll cover and look at some of the purposes served when you communicate.

The Benefits of Human Communication

A perfectly legitimate question to ask before beginning your study of any subject is "why?" You may ask yourself, "Why should I learn about human communication? What will it do for me? What will I be able to do after taking this course that I wasn't able to do before? In short, how will I benefit from the study of human communication presented in this course and in this text?"

Actually, you'll benefit in lots of ways. Your knowledge of human communication and your mastery of many of its skills will enable you to better:

- **Present yourself as a confident, likable, approachable, and credible person.** Your effectiveness in just about any endeavor depends heavily on your *self-presentation*—your ability to present yourself in a positive light, through your verbal and nonverbal messages. Incidentally, it is also largely through your skills of self-presentation (or lack of them) that you display negative qualities as well.

- **Build friendships, enter into love relationships, work with colleagues, and interact with family members.** These are the *interpersonal and relationship skills* for initiating, maintaining, repairing, and sometimes dissolving relationships of all kinds. And unless you're going to be living totally alone, these are skills you'll use every day, in every encounter. These are the skills that businesses of all kinds have on their lists of most important competencies for organizational success; they are an essential part of business competence (Bassellier & Benbasat, 2004).

- **Interview to gain information, to successfully present yourself to get the job you want, and to participate effectively in a wide variety of other interview types.** *Interviewing skills* will help get you the job you want and ultimately the career you're preparing for in college.

- **Participate effectively in relationship and task groups—informative, problem-solving, and brainstorming groups, at home or at work.** These *group interaction and leadership skills* will help you both as a group member and as a leader. In a workplace world that operates largely on group interaction, these skills are increasingly essential if you are to be an effective organizational member and will help you rise in the organization. After all, people in power will often come to know you best through your group (that is, communication) performance.

- **Communicate information to and influence the attitudes and behaviors of small and large audiences.** These *presentation* or *public speaking skills* will enable you to manage your fear and make it work for you rather than against you.

3

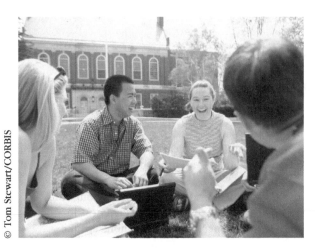

© Tom Stewart/CORBIS

COMMUNICATION CHOICE POINTS

Throughout this text you'll find marginal items, labeled What Do You Say? that identify a communication choice point, a point at which you need to make a decision and say something (or, of course, decide to remain silent). These What do you say? items are designed to encourage you to apply the skills discussed in the text to a wide variety of communication situations.

Effective public speaking is essential in leadership positions of all kinds; whether in politics, business, education, or medicine, leaders speak publicly.

■ **Use the media critically and with awareness of the techniques media use to influence you.** *Media literacy skills* will make you a more informed and empowered user of the many media that you encounter on a daily basis. Without such skills, you risk being used by the media for their ends alone. Much as a lack of media literacy will disempower you, competence in media literacy—the aim of discussions of media literacy—will empower you and put you in charge. A Media Watch boxes appears later in this chapter and explains in more detail what media literacy is.

You'll learn these skills and reap the benefits as you learn the various areas or forms of communication, to which we now turn.

The Forms of Human Communication

The forms of human communication vary from one-person communication (in which you talk to yourself) to communication with millions (as in public speaking, mass communication, and computer-mediated communication). Here we look briefly at each of these forms.

Intrapersonal Communication

Intrapersonal communication is communication you have with yourself. Through intrapersonal communication you talk with, learn about, and judge yourself. You persuade yourself of this or that, reason about possible decisions to make, and rehearse messages that you plan to send to others. In intrapersonal communication you might, for example, wonder how you did in an interview and what you could have done differently. You might conclude you did a pretty good job but that you need to be more assertive when discussing salary. Increasing your self-awareness, your mindfulness, and your ability to think critically about all types of messages will aid you greatly in improving your own intrapersonal communication. And this information—on the self, perception, listening, and verbal and nonverbal messages—will provide a foundation for learning about the various forms of human communication.

Interpersonal Communication

Interpersonal communication is communication between two persons or among a small group of persons. Most often, the communication emphasized in the study of interpersonal communication is communication of a continuing personal (rather than temporary and impersonal) nature; it's communication between or among intimates or those involved in close relationships—friends, romantic partners, family, and coworkers, for example. These relationships are interdependent, meaning that the actions of one person have some impact on the other person; whatever one person does influences the other person. Sometimes interpersonal communication is pleasant, but sometimes it erupts into conflict, making each person's communication especially significant for the other.

Interpersonal communication can take place face-to-face as well as through electronic channels (as in e-mail, instant messaging, or chat rooms, for example) or even via traditional letter-writing. Whether you e-mail your friends or family about your plans for the weekend, ask someone in class for a date, or confront a colleague's racist remarks at the water cooler, you're communicating interpersonally.

Interviewing

Interviewing is communication that proceeds by question and answer. Through interviewing you learn about others and what they know; you counsel or get counseling from others; or you get or don't get the job you want. Today much interviewing (especially initial interviews) takes place through e-mail and (video) phone conferencing.

Small Group Communication

Small group communication is communication among members of groups of about 5 to 10 people. Small group communication serves both *relationship needs* such as those for companionship, affection, or support and *task needs* such as balancing the family budget, electing a new chairperson, or designing a new ad campaign. Through small group communication you interact with others, solve problems, develop new ideas, and share knowledge and experiences. You live your work and social life largely in groups, from school orientation meetings to executive board meetings, from informal social groups to formal meetings discussing issues of local or international concern. You also may live a good part of your life in online chat rooms, where you may interact with people from different cultures living thousands of miles away, and in social network chat (for example, MyFace, MySpace, Facebook, Xanga) where you learn about and chat with others.

Organizational Communication

Organizational communication is communication that takes place within an organization among members of the organization. Conferencing with colleagues, working in teams, talking with a supervisor, or giving employees directions are just a few examples of organizational communication. The study of organizational communication offers you guidelines for improving your own formal and informal communication in an organizational setting.

Public Speaking

Public speaking, also termed *public communication* or *presentational speaking*, is communication between a speaker and an audience. Audiences range in size from several people to hundreds, thousands, and even millions. Through public communication others inform and persuade you. And you, in turn, inform and persuade others—to act, to buy, or to think in a particular way.

Much as you can address large audiences face-to-face, you also can address such audiences electronically and through the mass media. Through newsgroups, blogs, or social networks, for example, you can post a "speech" for anyone to read and then read their reactions to your message. And with the help of the more traditional mass media of radio and television, you can address audiences in the hundreds of millions as they sit alone or in small groups scattered throughout the world.

Computer-Mediated Communication

The term **computer-mediated communication** refers to communication between people that takes place through some computer connection. E-mail, chat room, newsgroup, instant messaging, website, and blog communication are all examples of computer-mediated communication, often abbreviated CMC. In large part, the principles of face-to-face and computer-mediated communication are similar; if you're effective in one mode, you're likely to be effective in others. The principles and skills we'll discuss will prove applicable to all forms of communication. Table 1 presents a summary of some of the ways in which computer-mediated communication differs from face-to-face communication. As you continue reading about these elements in this chapter, you may want to return to this table and add your own ideas to those presented here.

Table 1   Face-to-Face and Computer-Mediated Communication

Throughout this text, face-to-face and computer-mediated communication are discussed, compared, and contrasted. Here is a brief summary of some communication concepts and some of the ways in which face-to-face and computer-mediated communication are similar and different.

Human Communication Element	Face-to-Face Communication	Computer-Mediated Communication
Sender [presentation of self, impression management, speaking turn]	• Visual appearance communicates who you are; personal characteristics (sex, approximate age, race, etc.) are overt and open to visual inspection; receiver controls the order of what is attended to; disguise is difficult.	• You present the self you want others to see; personal characteristics are covert and are revealed when you want to reveal them; speaker controls the order of revelation; disguise or anonymity is easy.
	• You compete for the speaker's turn and time with the other person(s); you can be interrupted.	• It's always your turn; speaker time is unlimited; you can't be interrupted.

Human Communication Element	Face-to-Face Communication	Computer-Mediated Communication
Receiver [number, interests, third party, impression formation]	• One or a few who are in your visual field. • Limited to those you have the opportunity to meet; often difficult to find people who have the same interests you do especially in isolated communities with little mobility. • Your messages can be overheard by or repeated to third parties, but not verbatim and not with the same accuracy as online. • Impressions are based on the verbal and nonverbal cues receiver perceives.	• One, a few, or as many as you find in a chat room, have on your e-mail list, or who read your bulletin board posts. • Virtually unlimited; you can more easily and quickly find people who match your interests. • Your messages can be retrieved by others or forwarded verbatim to a third party or to hundreds of third parties (with or without your knowledge). • Impressions are based on text messages (usually) receiver reads.
Context [physical, temporal]	• Where you both are; together in essentially the same physical space. • As it happens; you have little control over the context once you're in a communication situation. • Communication is *synchronous*—messages are exchanged at the same time.	• Where you and receiver each want to be, separated in space. • You can more easily choose the timing—when you want to respond. • Communication may be synchronous, as in chat rooms and instant messaging, or *asynchronous*—messages are exchanged at different times, as in e-mail and bulletin board postings.
Channel	• Auditory plus visual plus tactile plus proxemic (related to distance) • Two-way channel enabling immediate interactivity.	• Visual for text (though auditory and visual for graphics and video are available). • Two-way channels, some enabling immediate and some delayed interactivity.
Messages [verbal, nonverbal, permanence]	• Spoken words along with gestures, eye contact, accent, paralinguistic (vocal but nonverbal) cues, space, touch, clothing, hair, and all the other nonverbal cues. • Temporary unless recorded; speech signals fade rapidly. • Rarely are abbreviations verbally expressed.	• Written words in purely text-based CMC, though that's changing. • Messages are permanent unless erased. • Limited nonverbal cues; some can be created with emoticons or words, and some (like smells and touch) cannot. • Use lots of abbreviations.
Feedforward	• Conveyed nonverbally and verbally early in the interaction.	• In e-mail it's given in the headings and subject line, as well as in the opening sentences.
Ethics and Deception	• Presentation of false physical self is more difficult, though not impossible; presenting false psychological and social selves is easier. • Nonverbal leakage cues often give you away when you're lying.	• Presentation of false physical self as well as false psychological and social selves is relatively easy. • Can probably lie more easily.

Mass Communication

Mass communication is communication from one source to many receivers, who may be scattered throughout the world. Mass communication takes place via at least the following media outlets:

- *newspapers*
- *television*
- *radio*
- *film and video*
- *music*
- *the Internet, the Web, and blogs*

The coverage of mass communication in this book focuses on media literacy and aims to help you to become a wiser, more critical user of the media (see the Media Watch box below).

As you can see if you glance through your college catalogue, each of these forms of communication is likely to be covered in separate and more detailed courses in public speaking, small group communication, interpersonal communication, mass communication, and so on. In this course, the essentials of these communication forms are introduced, giving you the knowledge and skills to become a more effective communicator, and at the same time the background to move on to more detailed study, whether in more in-depth courses or in your own reading. Table 2 gives you an overview of these varied forms of human communication.

Through these varied forms of communication, you'll accomplish a number of different purposes. Let's take a look at several of these purposes.

The Purposes of Human Communication

The purposes of human communication may be conscious or unconscious, recognizable or unrecognizable. And although communication technologies are changing rapidly and drastically—we send e-mail, work at computer terminals, and telecommute, for example—the purposes of communication have remained essentially the same throughout the computer revolution and are likely to continue

WHAT IS MEDIA LITERACY?

[I]t is precisely because they [the mass media] are so familiar that we need to study them. Familiarity, for example, may blind us to the distinct kind of communication that takes place through the mass media, and especially to the processes by which they influence us.

—Kathleen Hall Jamieson and Karlyn Kohrs Campbell

Media literacy—as you'll discover in this Media Watch box—covers a range of skills that are vital to dealing with the mass media. Because these skills are so important, Media Watch boxes are presented throughout the text, reminding you that the media are influencing you in ways you need to be aware of.

Media literacy may be defined as your ability to understand, analyze, evaluate, and produce mass communication messages (television, film, music, radio, billboards, advertising, public relations, newspapers and magazines, books, websites and blogs, newsgroups and chat rooms).

Because the media influence you in numerous ways (only some of which you may be conscious of), it's crucial that you learn how this influence is exerted so that you, rather than the media, can determine what influences you and what doesn't. Looked at in this way, media literacy is a form of empowerment. It can help you to use the media more intelligently; to understand, analyze, and evaluate media messages more effectively; to influence the messages that the media send out; and to create your own mediated messages.

Increasing Media Literacy

Increase your sensitivity to media by examining your own use of media. If possible, keep a record or log of all the time you spend on media in one day, the media you use most often, the purposes you use the media for, the rewards you get from the media, and especially the ways in which the media might be influencing you. Also, increase your sensitivity by supplementing these Media Literacy boxes with visits to some interesting websites; try, for example, Citizens for Media Literacy at **www.main.nc.us/cml** *and the Media Education Foundation at* **www.mediaed.org.**

Table 2 Forms of Human Communication

This table identifies and arranges the forms of communication in terms of the number of persons involved, from one (on intrapersonal communication) to thousands and millions (in mass communication). It also previews (in general) the progression of topics in this book.

Forms of Human Communication	Some Common Purposes	Some Theory-Related Concerns	Some Skills-Related Concerns
Intrapersonal: communication with the self	To think, reason, analyze, reflect	How does a person's self-concept develop? How does the self-concept influence communication? How can problem-solving and analyzing abilities be improved and taught? What is the relationship between personality and communication?	Enhancing self-esteem, increasing self-awareness, improving problem-solving and analyzing abilities, increasing self-control, reducing stress, managing intrapersonal conflict
Interpersonal: communication between two persons	To discover, relate, influence, play, help	What is interpersonal effectiveness? Why do people develop relationships? What holds friends, lovers, and families together? What tears them apart? How can relationships be repaired?	Increasing effectiveness in one-to-one communication, developing and maintaining effective relationships (friendship, love, family), improving conflict resolution abilities
Interviewing: communication that proceeds through questions and answers	To learn, evaluate, influence	What are the legal issues in interviewing? How can interview responses be analyzed? What is the role of nonverbal communication?	Phrasing questions to get at the information you want, presenting your best self, writing résumés and cover letters
Small group: communication within a small group of persons	To share information, generate ideas, solve problems, help	What makes a leader? What type of leadership works best? What roles do members play in groups? What do groups do well, and what do they fail to do well? How can groups be made more effective?	Increasing effectiveness as a group member, improving leadership abilities, using groups to achieve specific purposes (for example, solving problems, generating ideas)
Organizational: communication within an organization	To inform, persuade, relate	What leadership styles work best in organizations? How and why do organizations grow and deteriorate? What role does culture play in the organization?	Transmitting information, motivating workers, dealing with feedback, dealing with the grapevine, increasing satisfaction

Public: communication of speaker with audience 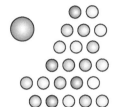	To inform, persuade, entertain	What kinds of organizational structure work best in informative and persuasive speaking? How can audiences be most effectively analyzed and adapted to? How can ideas be best developed for communication to an audience?	Communicating information more effectively; increasing persuasive abilities; developing, organizing, styling, and delivering messages with greater effectiveness
Computer-mediated: communication between people through computers	To discover, relate, influence, play, help	Are there gender differences? In what ways is CMC more efficient? How can modalities be combined?	Increasing security in e-communications, combining CMC with face-to-face communication
Mass: communication addressed to an extremely large audience, mediated by audio and/or visual means	To entertain, persuade, and inform	What functions do the media serve? How do the media influence us? How can we influence the media? In what ways is information censored by the media for the public? How does advertising work?	Improving your ability to use the media to greater effectiveness, increasing our ability to control the media, avoiding being taken in by advertisements and tabloid journalism

through whatever revolutions follow. Five general purposes of communication can be identified: To discover, to relate, to help, to persuade, and to play (see Figure 1).

To Discover

One of the major purposes of communication concerns personal discovery. When you communicate with another person, you learn about yourself as well as about the other person. In fact, your self-perceptions result largely from what you've learned about yourself from others during communications, especially your interpersonal encounters. Communication also helps you discover the external world—the world of objects, events, and other people. Communication enables you to reduce your uncertainty about people and about the world, and reducing uncertainty in turn enables you to communicate more effectively.

To Relate

You probably spend much of your communication time and energy establishing and maintaining social relationships. You communicate with your close friends in school, at work, on the phone, and over the Internet. You talk with your parents, children, and brothers and sisters. You interact with your relational partner. All told, this takes a great deal of your time and attests to the importance of the relational purpose of communication.

To Help

You fulfill the helping purpose when you constructively criticize, express empathy, work with a group to solve a problem, or listen attentively and supportively to a public speaker. Not surprisingly, obtaining and giving help are among the major functions of Internet communication and among the major reasons people use the Internet (Meier, 2000, 2002).

To Persuade

In your everyday interpersonal and group encounters, you often try to persuade—to change the attitudes and behaviors of others. You try to get people to vote a particular way, try a new diet, buy a particular item, see a movie, visit a website, take a specific course, believe that something is true or false, value or devalue some idea, and so on. In interviews, you may try to persuade a company to hire you; in public speaking, you may try to persuade your audience that you should be elected to hold a certain office or position. Some researchers, in fact, argue that all communication is persuasive and that all our communications seek some persuasive goal (Canary, Cody, & Manusov, 2000).

To Play

Communication as play includes motives of pleasure, escape, and relaxation (Barbato & Perse, 1992; Rubin, Perse, & Barbato, 1988). You tell jokes, say clever things, and relate interesting stories largely for the pleasure it gives to you and your listeners. Similarly, you may communicate because it relaxes you, allowing you to get away from pressures and responsibilities.

These five purposes are the reasons you communicate. The next section will help explain *how* you communicate by exploring the elements involved in the communication act.

THE ELEMENTS OF HUMAN COMMUNICATION

Before examining the definition of the term *communication* and its various elements, take a moment to think about your beliefs about communication by taking the self-test on the next page.

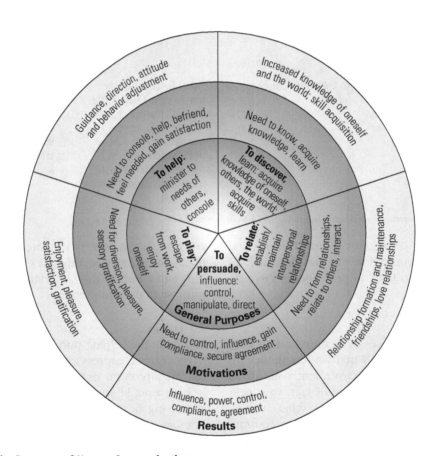

FIGURE 1 The Purposes of Human Communication

Shown here are the five general purposes of communication—but the aims of communication also can be looked at from at least two other perspectives. First, purposes may be seen as motives for engaging in communication. That is, you engage in communication to satisfy your need for knowledge or to form relationships. Second, these purposes may be viewed in terms of the results you want to achieve. That is, you engage in interpersonal communication to increase your knowledge of yourself and others or to exert influence or power over others. Any communication act serves a unique combination of purposes, is prompted by a unique combination of motives, and can produce a unique combination of results. A similar typology of purposes comes from research on motives for communicating. In a series of studies, Rubin and her colleagues (Rubin & Martin, 1998; Rubin, Fernandez-Collado, & Hernandez-Sampieri, 1992; Rubin & Martin, 1994; Rubin, Perse, & Barbato, 1988; Rubin & Rubin, 1992; Graham, 1994; Graham, Barbato, & Perse, 1993) have identified six primary motives for communication: pleasure, affection, inclusion, escape, relaxation, and control. How do these compare to the five purposes discussed here?

ASK THE RESEARCHER

Values of a Human Communication Course

I'm taking this course in human communication. I am not certain what practical uses this course will have for me. Why should I be taking this course? You interact with others every day in a variety of contexts. In most contexts, you have a purpose in mind: To learn or to persuade. In job interviews, you need to know what factors the employers are seeking in nonverbal behavior, language use, attitude, level of knowledge, amount of enthusiasm, and personal motivation. In learning situations, you need to know when to ask a question as well as how to frame your question. As a manager of others, you need to know what kinds of messages will motivate your subordinates to perform at their highest levels. Human communication is significant for every aspect of your life from learning at school to obtaining positions in corporations to soliciting a salary increase. Socially, human communication is at the core of what makes relationships work or fail. This course and this book may be among the most important instruments in developing you as a more sensitive and effective person.

For further information: Hickson, M., III, Stacks, D. W., & Padgett-Greely, M. (1998). *Organizational communication in the personal context: From interview to retirement.* Boston: Allyn & Bacon.

Mark Hickson III (Ph.D., Southern Illinois University) is a professor of communication studies at the University of Alabama at Birmingham. He teaches courses in communication theory, nonverbal communication, and organizational communication.

TEST YOURSELF

What Do You Believe about Communication?

Respond to each of the following statements with T (true) if you believe the statement is usually true or F (false) if you believe the statement is usually false.

__F__ 1. Good communicators are born, not made.

__T__ 2. The more a couple communicates, the better their relationship will be.

__F__ 3. When two people are in a close relationship for a long period of time, one person should not have to communicate his or her needs and wants; the other person should know what these are.

__T__ 4. Complete openness should be the goal of any meaningful interpersonal relationship.

__F__ 5. Interpersonal or group conflict is a reliable sign that the relationship or group is in trouble.

__F__ 6. Like good communicators, leaders are born, not made.

__F__ 7. Fear of speaking in public is detrimental and must be eliminated.

HOW DID YOU DO? As you may have figured out, all seven statements are generally false. As you read this text, you'll discover not only why these beliefs are false but also the trouble you can get into when you assume they're true. Briefly, here are some of the reasons why each of the statements is generally false:

1. Effective communication is a learned skill; although some people are born brighter or more extroverted than others, all can improve their abilities and become more effective communicators.

2. If you practice bad communication habits, you're more likely to grow less effective than to become more effective; consequently, it's important to learn and follow the principles of effectiveness.

3. This assumption is at the heart of many interpersonal difficulties: People aren't mind readers, and to assume that they are merely sets up barriers to open and honest communication.

4. Although you may feel ethically obligated to be totally honest, this is generally not an effective strategy. In fact, "complete" anything is probably a bad idea.

5. Interpersonal conflict does not have to involve a winner and a loser; both people can win.

6. Leadership, like communication and listening, is a learned skill that you'll develop as you learn the principles of human communication in general and of group leadership in particular.

7. Most speakers are nervous; managing, not eliminating, the fear will enable you to become effective regardless of your current level of fear.

WHAT WILL YOU DO? Consider how these beliefs about communication influence the way you communicate. Then, as you read this book and participate in class discussions and activities, reexamine your beliefs about communication and consider how new beliefs would influence the way you communicate. The theories and research discussed in this text will help you reconsider your own beliefs about communication, and the skill-building activities will help you practice new ways of communicating. Three excellent websites containing a variety of self-tests on emotional intelligence, personality, knowledge, relationships, careers, and more are **www.allthetests.com, www.queendom.com/ tests,** and **www.psychologytoday.com.**

Defining Communication

Communication occurs when one person (or more) sends and receives messages that are distorted by noise, occur within a context, have some effect, and provide some opportunity for feedback. Figure 2 illustrates the elements present in all communication acts, whether intrapersonal, interpersonal, small group, public speaking, or mass communication—or whether face-to-face, by telephone, or over the Internet: (1) context, (2) sources–receivers, (3) messages, (4) channels, (5) noise, and (6) effects. In addition, we'll examine the role of ethics in communication.

Communication Context

All communication takes place in a **context** that has at least four dimensions: (1) physical, (2) social-psychological, (3) temporal, and (4) cultural (Figure 3). The *physical context* is the tangible or concrete environment in which communication takes place—the room or hallway or park. This physical context exerts some influence on the content of your messages (what you say) as well as on the form (how you say it).

The *social-psychological context* includes, for example, the status relationships among the participants, the roles and the games that people play, and the cultural rules of the society in which people are communicating. It also includes the friendliness or unfriendliness, formality or informality, and seriousness or humorousness of the situation. For example, communication that would be permitted at a graduation party might not be considered appropriate at a funeral.

The *temporal (or time) context* includes the time of day as well as the time in history in which the communication takes place. For many people, the morning is not a time for communication. For others, the morning is ideal. Historical context is no less important—because the appropriateness and impact of messages depend, in part, on the time in which they're uttered. Consider, for example, how messages on racial, sexual, or religious attitudes and values would be differently framed and responded to in different times in history. Still another aspect of time is how a message fits into the sequence of communication events. For example, consider the varied meanings a "simple" compliment paid to a friend would have depending on whether you said it immediately after your friend paid you a compliment, immediately before you asked your friend for a favor, or during an argument.

The *cultural context* has to do with your (and others') **culture**: the beliefs, values, and ways of behaving that are shared by a group of people and passed down from one generation to the next. Cultural factors affect every interaction and influence what you say and how you say it. As you'll see throughout this book, the communication strategies and principles that work with members of one culture may not work with members of other cultures. Further, research shows that you lose approximately 50 percent of information communicated in an *inter*cultural situation (communication between members of different cultures) and only 25 percent in an *intra*cultural situation (communication between members of the same culture) (Li, 1999). These are just some reasons why **intercultural communication** is so difficult and why culture is so crucial to communication.

These four dimensions of context interact with one another. For example, arriving late for an appointment (temporal context) might violate a cultural rule, which might lead to changes in the social–psychological context, perhaps creating tension and unfriendliness,

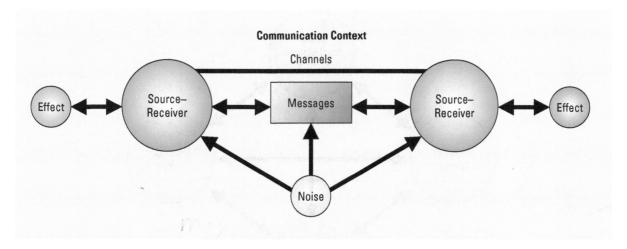

FIGURE 2 The Elements of Human Communication

This is a simplified view of the elements of human communication and their relationship to one another. Messages (including feedforward and feedback) are sent simultaneously through a variety of channels from one source-receiver to another. The communication process takes place in a context (physical, cultural, social-psychological, and temporal) and is subjected to interference by noise (physical, psychological, and semantic). The interaction of messages with each source–receiver leads to some effect.

which in turn might lead to changes in the physical context—for example, choosing a less intimate restaurant for your lunch meeting.

Sources–Receivers

The compound term *sources-receivers* emphasizes that each person involved in communication is both a **source** (or speaker) and a **receiver** (or listener). You send messages when you speak, write, gesture, or smile. You receive messages in listening, reading, smelling, and so on. As you send messages, however, you're also receiving messages. You're receiving your own messages (you hear yourself, you feel your own movements, you see many of your own gestures), and you're receiving the messages of the other person—visually, aurally, or even through touch or smell. As you assign meaning to these verbal and nonverbal signals, you're performing receiving functions.

Source–Receiver Encoding–Decoding

The act of producing messages—for example, speaking or writing—is called **encoding**. By putting your ideas into sound waves or into a computer program you're putting these ideas into a **code**, hence encoding. The act of receiving messages—for example, listening or reading—is called **decoding**. By translating sound waves or words on a screen into ideas you take them out of code, which is decoding. Thus, speakers or writers are called **encoders**, and listeners or readers, **decoders**.

As with sources-receivers, the compound term *encoding-decoding* emphasizes that you perform these functions simultaneously, at least in face-to-face communication. As you speak (encoding), you're also deciphering the responses of the listener (decoding). In computer communication this simultaneous exchange of messages occurs only sometimes. In e-mail (as well as snail mail) and newsgroup communication, for example, the sending and receiving may be separated by several days or much longer. In chat groups and instant messaging, on the other hand, communication takes place in real time; the sending and receiving take place (almost) simultaneously.

Source–Receiver Competence

The term **communication competence** refers to your knowledge of the social aspects of communication (Rubin, 1982, 1985; Spitzberg & Cupach, 1989). Communication competence includes knowledge of such factors as the role of context in influencing the content and form of communication messages—for example, the knowledge that in certain contexts and with certain listeners one topic is appropriate and another is not. Knowledge about the rules of nonverbal behavior—for example, the appropriateness of touching, vocal volume, and physical closeness—is also part of communication competence.

Communication competence also includes your ability to apply this knowledge in communicating. So when you read about communication competence,

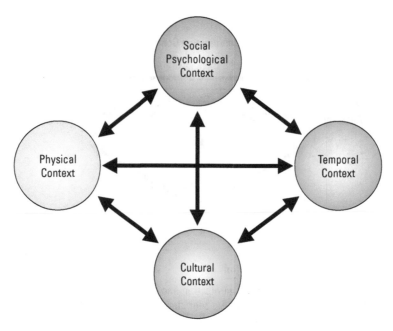

FIGURE 3   The Communication Context

This figure is intended to illustrate that the communication context is not a single entity but consists of a variety of contexts that affect communication—and, perhaps most important, to remind you that each dimension of context influences each other dimension.

realize that it includes both an understanding of how communication works, *and* the ability to use this understanding in communicating effectively. Keep in mind, however, that communication competence is culture specific; the way communication works and the elements that make it effective differ from one culture to another.

Messages

Communication **messages** take many forms. You send and receive messages through any one or any combination of sensory organs. Although you may customarily think of messages as being verbal (oral or written), you also communicate nonverbally. Everything about you communicates. For example, the clothes you wear and the way you walk, shake hands, tilt your head, comb your hair, sit, and smile all communicate messages.

In face-to-face communication the actual message signals (the movements in the air) are evanescent; they fade almost as they're uttered. Some written messages, especially computer-mediated messages such as those sent via e-mail, are unerasable. E-mails that are sent among employees in a large corporation, for example, are often stored on disk or tape.

Two special types of messages include *feedback* (the messages you send that are reactions to other messages) and *feedforward* (the messages you send as

preface to your "main" messages). Both feedback and feedforward are **metamessages**—messages that communicate about other messages. Such communication about communication, or **metacommunication**, may be verbal ("I agree with you" or "Wait until you hear this one") or nonverbal (a smile or a prolonged pause). Or, as is most often the case, it's some combination of verbal and nonverbal signals.

Feedback Messages

Throughout the listening process, a listener gives a speaker **feedback**—messages sent back to the speaker reacting to what is said. Feedback tells the speaker what effect he or she is having on the listener(s). This can take many forms: A frown or a smile, a yea or a nay, a pat on the back or a punch in the mouth are all types of feedback. Sometimes feedback is easy to identify, but sometimes it isn't (Skinner, 2002).

Part of the art of effective communication is the ability to discern feedback and to adjust messages on the basis of that feedback. For example, on the basis of feedback, a speaker may adjust messages by strengthening, deemphasizing, or changing the content or form of the messages. These adjustments then serve as feedback to the receiver—who, in response, readjusts his or her feedback messages. The process is circular, with one person's feedback serving as the stimulus for the other person's

© Charles Gupton/Stock Boston

NEGATIVE COMMUNICATION EFFECTS

An e-mail that you wrote to a close friend in anger (but never intended to send) was sent. You want to reduce the negative effects of such an e-mail.

WHAT DO YOU SAY?

feedback, just as any message serves as the stimulus for another person's message.

Another type of feedback is the feedback you get from listening to yourself: You hear what you say, you feel the way you move, you see what you write. On the basis of this self-feedback you adjust your messages; for example, you may correct a mispronunciation, shorten your story, or increase your volume.

You can view feedback in terms of five important dimensions: positive–negative, person focused–message-focused, immediate–delayed, low-monitored–high-monitored, and supportive–critical.

- *Positive–negative.* **Positive feedback** (smiles, applause, and head nods signifying approval) tells the speaker that the message is being well received and that he or she should continue speaking in the same general mode. **Negative feedback** (frowns, boos, puzzled looks, gestures signifying disapproval) tells the speaker that something is wrong and that some adjustment needs to be made.
- *Person-focused–message-focused.* Feedback may center on the person ("You're sweet," "You've got a great smile") or on the message ("Can you repeat that phone number?" "Your argument is a good one").
- *Immediate–delayed.* In interpersonal situations feedback is most often conveyed immediately after the message is received. In other communi-

cation situations, however, the feedback may be delayed; for example, feedback from an interview may come weeks after the interview took place. In media situations some feedback comes immediately—for example, through Nielsen ratings; other feedback comes much later, through consumers' viewing and buying patterns.

- *Low-monitored–high-monitored.* Feedback varies from the spontaneous and totally honest reaction (low-monitored feedback) to the carefully constructed response designed to serve a specific purpose (high-monitored feedback). In most interpersonal situations you probably give feedback spontaneously; you allow your responses to show without any monitoring. At other times, however, you may be more guarded, as when your boss asks you how you like your job or when your grandmother asks what you think of her holiday fruitcake.
- *Supportive–critical.* Supportive feedback confirms the worth of a person and of what that person says; it occurs when, for example, you console another or when you encourage the other to talk; it often involves **affirmation** of the person's self-definition. Critical feedback, on the other hand, is evaluative. When you give critical feedback you judge another's performance—as in, for example, evaluating a speech or coaching someone learning a new skill.

Each feedback opportunity, then, presents you with choices along at least these five dimensions. To use feedback effectively, you need to make educated choices along these dimensions. Realize that these categories are not exclusive. Feedback does not have to be either critical or supportive; it can be both. For example, in teaching someone how to become a more effective interviewer, you might critically evaluate a practice interview but you might also express support for the effort. Similarly, you might respond to a friend's question immediately and then after a day or two elaborate on your response.

Feedforward Messages

Feedforward is information you provide before sending your primary messages; it reveals something about the messages to come (Richards, 1951). Feedforward includes such diverse examples as the preface or the table of contents in a book, the opening paragraph of a chapter, movie previews, magazine covers, and introductions in public speeches. Feedforward has four major functions: (1) to open the channels of communication, (2) to preview the message, (3) to altercast, and (4) to disclaim.

■ **To open the channels of communication**. Often we preface our messages with comments whose only function is to open the channels of communication (Malinowski, 1923; Lu, 1998). The infamous "opening line" ("Do you come here often?" or "Haven't we met before?") is a clear example of this type of feedforward. Another type of feedforward serving this function of opening the channels is **phatic communication** or "small talk." It's the "how are you" and "nice weather" greetings that are designed to maintain rapport and friendly relationships (Placencia, 2004; Burnard, 2003). Similarly, listeners' short comments that are unrelated to the content of the conversation but that indicate interest and attention may also be considered phatic communication in that they keep the channels of communication open (McCarthy, 2003).

■ **To preview future messages**. Feedforward messages frequently preview other messages. Feedforward may, for example, preview the content ("I have news for you"), the importance ("Listen to this before you make a move"), the form or style ("I'll be brief"), or the positive or negative quality of subsequent messages ("You're not going to like this, but here's what I heard").

■ **To altercast**. The type of feedforward known as **altercasting** asks the receiver to approach your message in a particular role or even as someone else (McLaughlin, 1984; Weinstein & Deutschberger, 1963; Johnson, 1993; Pratkanis, 2000). For example, you might ask a friend, "As a single mother, what do you think of the new child care proposals?" This question casts your friend into the role of single mother (rather than that of teacher, Democrat, or Baptist, for example). It asks your friend to assume a particular perspective.

■ **To disclaim**. A **disclaimer** is a statement that aims to ensure that your message will not reflect negatively on you. Disclaimers entice the listener to hear your message as you wish it to be heard rather than through some assumption that might reflect negatively on you (Hewitt & Stokes, 1975). For example, to ensure that people listen to you fairly, you might disclaim any thought that you're biased against one gender: "I'm no sexist, but. . . ."

Channels

The communication **channel** is the medium through which the message passes. Communication rarely takes place over only one channel; you may use two, three, or four different channels simultaneously. For example, in face-to-face interactions you speak and listen (vocal channel), but you also gesture and receive signals visually (visual channel). In chat groups, you type and read words and use various symbols and abbreviations to communicate the emotional tone of the message. If your computer system is especially sophisticated, you may communicate via the Internet through audio and visual means as well. In addition, in face-to-face communication you emit and detect odors (olfactory channel). Often you touch another person, and this too communicates (tactile channel).

At times, one or more channels may be damaged. For example, in individuals with visual difficulties, the visual channel is impaired, and so adjustments have to be made. Table 3 gives you an idea of how such adjustments between those with and without visual impairments can make communication more effective.

Noise

Noise is anything that interferes with your receiving a message. At one extreme, noise may prevent a message from getting from source to receiver. A roaring noise or line static can easily prevent entire messages from getting through to your receiver. At the other extreme, with virtually no noise interference, the message of the source and the message received are almost identical. Most often, however, noise distorts some portion of the message a source sends as it travels to a receiver. Like messages that may be auditory or visual, noise comes in both auditory and visual forms. Four types of noise are especially relevant:

■ *Physical noise* is interference that is external to both speaker and listener; it interferes with the physical transmission of the signal or message. Examples include the screeching of passing cars, the hum of a computer, sunglasses, extraneous messages, illegible handwriting, blurred type or fonts that are too small or difficult to read, misspellings and poor grammar, and popup ads.

■ *Physiological noise* is created by barriers within the sender or receiver such as visual impairments, hearing loss, articulation problems, and memory loss.

■ *Psychological noise* is mental interference in speaker or listener and includes preconceived ideas, wandering thoughts, biases and prejudices, closed-mindedness, and extreme emotionalism. You're likely to run into psychological noise when you talk with someone who is closed-minded or who refuses to listen to anything he or she doesn't already believe.

Table 3 Interpersonal Communication Tips

Between People with and People without Visual Impairments

People vary greatly in their visual abilities; some people are totally blind, some are partially sighted, and some have unimpaired vision. Ninety percent of individuals who are "legally blind" have some vision. All of us, however, have the same need for communication and information. Here are some tips for making communication between blind and sighted people more effective.

If you're the sighted person and are talking with a blind person:

1. *Identify yourself.* Don't assume the blind person will recognize your voice.

2. *Face your listener; you'll be easier to hear.* At the same time, don't shout. People who are visually impaired are not hearing impaired. Speak at your normal volume.

3. Because your gestures, eye movements, and facial expressions cannot be seen by the visually impaired listener, *encode into speech all the meanings-both verbal and nonverbal-that you wish to communicate.*

4. *Use audible turn-taking cues.* When you pass the role of speaker to a person who is visually impaired, don't rely on nonverbal cues; instead, say something like "Do you agree with that, Joe?"

5. *Use normal vocabulary, and discuss the same kinds of topics you would discuss with sighted people.* Don't avoid terms like "see" or "look" or even "blind." Don't avoid discussing a television show, or a painting, or the way your new car looks; these are normal conversational topics for all people.

If you are a visually impaired person and are interacting with a sighted person:

1. *Help the sighted person meet your special communication needs.* If you want your surroundings described, ask. If you want the person to read the road signs, ask.

2. *Be patient with the sighted person.* Many people are nervous talking with people who are visually impaired for fear of offending. Put them at ease in a way that also makes you more comfortable.

These suggestions were drawn from www.cincyblind.org/what_do_you_do_.htm and www.rnib.org/uk/ (both accessed October 23, 2004).

Semantic noise is created when the speaker and listener have different meaning systems; it includes language or dialectical differences, the use of jargon or overly complex terms, and ambiguous or overly abstract terms whose meanings can be easily misinterpreted. You see this type of noise regularly—for example, in the medical doctor who uses "medicalese" without explanation or in the insurance salesperson who speaks in the jargon of the insurance industry.

As you can see from these examples, all communications contain noise. Noise cannot be totally eliminated, but its effects can be reduced. Making your language more precise, sharpening your skills for sending and receiving nonverbal messages, and improving your listening and feedback skills are some ways to combat the influence of noise.

Communication Effects

Communication always has some **effect** on one or more persons involved in the communication act. For every communication act, there is some consequence. Generally three types of effects are distinguished.

- **Intellectual (or cognitive) effects** are changes in your thinking. When you acquire information from a class lecture, for example, the effect is largely intellectual.

- **Affective effects** are changes in your attitudes, values, beliefs, and emotions. Thus, when you become frightened when watching the latest horror movie, its effect is largely affective. Similarly, after a great experience with, say, a person of another culture, your feelings about that culture may change. Again, the effect is largely affective (but perhaps also intellectual).

- **Psychomotor effects** are changes in overt behaviors such as, for example, learning new bodily movements such as how to throw a curve ball or how to paint a room or learning to use different verbal and nonverbal behaviors.

These effects are not as separate as they might at first seem. In many cases, a single message—say a public speech on homelessness—may inform you (intellectual effect), move you to feel differently (affective effect), and lead you to be more generous when you come upon a homeless person (psychomotor effect).

Ethics

Because communication has consequences, it also involves questions of **ethics**, of right and wrong (Bok, 1978; Jaksa & Pritchard, 1994). For example, while it might be (temporarily) effective to exaggerate or even lie in order to sell a product or get elected, it would not be ethical to do so.

The ethical dimension of communication is complicated because ethics is so interwoven with our personal philosophy of life and with the culture in which we have been raised that it's difficult to propose general guidelines for specific individuals. Nevertheless, ethical responsibilities need to be considered as integral to any communication act. The decisions you make concerning communication must be guided by what you consider right as well as by what you consider effective.

In thinking about the ethics of communication, you can take the position that ethics is objective or that it's subjective. In an *objective view* you'd claim that the morality of an act—say, a communication message—is absolute and exists apart from the values or beliefs of any individual or culture. This objective view holds that there are standards that apply to all people in all situations at all times.

In this way of thinking, if lying, advertising falsely, using illegally obtained evidence, and revealing secrets, for example, are considered unethical, then they'll be considered unethical regardless of the circumstances surrounding them or of the values and beliefs of the culture in which they occur.

In a *subjective view* you'd claim that the morality of an act depends on the culture's values and beliefs as well as on the particular circumstances. Thus, from a subjective position you would claim that the end might justify the means—a good result can justify the use of unethical means to achieve that result. You would further argue that lying is wrong to win votes or sell cigarettes, but that lying can be ethical if the end result is positive (such as trying to make someone who is unattractive feel better by telling them they look great, or telling a critically ill person that they'll feel better soon).

To emphasize the central role of ethics in all aspects of communication, each unit of this text includes a Reflections on Ethics box. The first such discussion continues explaining the nature of ethics and discusses the three major areas of ethics (below).

REFLECTIONS ON ETHICS

The Areas of Ethics

According to the Internet Encyclopedia of Philosophy (www.iep.utm.edu/e/ethics.htm), the field of ethics consists of three areas:

- *Metaethics* concerns itself with the origins of ethical principles (where they come from—God? Social conventions? Cultural norms?) and with the meanings of various ethical concepts (What is responsibility? What is right? What is wrong?).
- *Normative ethics* concerns itself with articulating the standards of right and wrong; this is the area that proposes specific ethical principles (for example, Don't lie; Don't willfully hurt another person). It is from normative ethics that we learn the principles governing what is ethical and what is unethical.
- *Applied ethics* concerns itself with the ethical implications of controversial issues (Is capital punishment ethical? Is preventing marriage by same-sex couples ethical? Is it ethical to engage in war?).

These three areas often intersect. For example, the ethics of capital punishment is clearly *applied ethics*, as it focuses on a controversial issue. But this topic also draws on the insights of *metaethics* (Where do the rights to kill another person come from? Who has the right to kill another human being?) and on *normative ethics* (By what standard does one person claim the right to kill another person? Under what conditions might it be justifiable to kill another person?).

Ethical Choice Point

In a class discussion of ethics, your instructor presents the following possible ethical guidelines: (1) Behavior is ethical when you feel in your heart that you're doing the right thing; (2) Behavior is ethical when it is consistent with your religious beliefs; (3) Behavior is ethical when it's legal within the society; (4) Behavior is ethical when the majority of people would consider it ethical; and (5) Behavior is ethical when the end result is in the interest of the majority. How would you respond to these guidelines? Would you accept any as an accurate statement of what constitutes ethical behavior? Would you reject any? Why?

The Elements in Transaction

Communication is **transactional**, which means that the elements in communication are interdependent. Each person in the communication act is both speaker and listener; each person is simultaneously sending and receiving messages (see Figure 4 below) (Barnlund, 1970; Watzlawick, 1977, 1978; Watzlawick, Beavin, & Jackson, 1967; Wilmot, 1987).

There are several implications and ramifications of this transactional view.

■ First, "transactional" means that *communication is an-ever changing process*. It's an ongoing activity; all the elements of communication are in a state of constant change. You're constantly changing, the people with whom you're communicating are changing, and your environment is changing. Nothing in communication ever remains static.

Linear View

Interactional View

Transactional View

FIGURE 4   Three Views of Communication

The top diagram represents a linear view of communication, in which the speaker speaks and the listener listens. The middle diagram represents an interactional view, in which speaker and listener take turns speaking and listening; A speaks while B listens, then B speaks while A listens. The bottom diagram represents a transactional view. This is the view that most communication theorists hold. In the transactional view, each person serves simultaneously as speaker and listener; at the same time that you send messages, you're also receiving messages from your own communications and also from the messages of the other person(s).

■ Second, in any transactional process, *each element relates integrally to every other element*; each exists in relation to the others. For example, there can be no source without a receiver. There can be no message without a source. There can be no feedback without a receiver. Because of this interdependence, a change in any one element of the process produces changes in the other elements. For example, you're talking with a group of your friends when your mother enters the group. This change in "audience" will lead to other changes. Perhaps you or your friends will adjust what you're saying or how you say it. The new situation may also influence how often certain people talk, and so on. Regardless of what change is introduced, other changes will be produced as a result.

■ Third, *each person in a communication transaction acts and reacts on the basis of a multitude of factors*. For example, the way you act in a communication situation will naturally depend on the immediate context, which in turn is influenced by your history, past experiences, attitudes, cultural beliefs, self-image, future expectations, emotions, and a host of related issues. One implication of this is that actions and reactions in communication are determined not only by what is said, but also by the way each person interprets what is said. Your responses to a movie, for example, don't depend solely on the words and pictures in the film but also on your previous experiences, present emotions, knowledge, physical well-being, and other factors. Similarly, two people listening to the same message will often derive two very different meanings. Although the words and symbols are the same, each person interprets them differently because each is influenced differently by their history, present emotions, and so on.

THE PRINCIPLES OF HUMAN COMMUNICATION

Here we'll explore several important principles that govern how communication works and that have important implications for your own communication effectiveness: (1) Communication is a package of signals; (2) communication is a process of adjustment; (3) communication involves content and relationship dimensions; (4) communication is ambiguous; (5) communication sequences are punctuated; (6) communication involves symmetrical and complementary transactions; and (7) communication is inevitable, irreversible, and unrepeatable. Before

19

reading these principles, take a look at the Understanding Theory and Research box on "Communication Theories".

Communication Is a Package of Signals

Communication behaviors, whether they involve verbal messages, gestures, or some combination thereof, usually occur in "packages" (Pittenger, Hockett, & Danehy, 1960). Usually, that is, verbal and nonverbal behaviors reinforce or support each other. All parts of a message system normally work together to communicate a particular meaning. You don't express fear with words while the rest of your body is relaxed. You don't express anger through your posture while your face smiles. Your entire body works together—verbally and nonverbally—to express your thoughts and feelings.

In any form of communication, whether interpersonal, small group, public speaking, or mass media, you probably pay little attention to this "packaging." It goes unnoticed. But when there's an incongruity—when the weak handshake belies the confident verbal greeting, when the nervous posture belies the focused stare, when the constant preening belies the verbal expressions of being comfortable and at ease—you take notice. Invariably you begin to question the credibility, the sincerity, and the honesty of the individual.

Often, contradictory messages are sent over a period of time. Note, for example, that in the following interaction the employee is being given two directives—use initiative and don't use initiative. These **mixed messages** place the employee in a "double bind"—regardless of what he or she does, rejection will follow.

> EMPLOYER: You've got to learn to take more initiative. You never seem to take charge, to take control.
>
> EMPLOYEE: [Takes the initiative, makes decisions.]
>
> EMPLOYER: You've got to learn to follow the chain of command and not do things just because you want to.
>
> EMPLOYEE: [Goes back to old ways, not taking any initiative.]
>
> EMPLOYER: Well, I told you. We expect more initiative from you.

Contradictory messages may be the result of the desire to communicate two different emotions or feelings. For example, you may like a person and want to communicate a positive feeling, but you may also feel resentment toward this person and want to communicate a negative feeling as well. The result is that you communicate both feelings; for example, you say that you're happy to see the person but your facial expression and body posture communicate your negative feelings (Beier, 1974). In this example, and in many similar cases, the socially acceptable message is usually communicated verbally while the less socially acceptable message is communicated nonverbally.

Communication Is a Process of Adjustment

Communication can take place only to the extent that the communicators use the same system of signals (Pittenger, Hockett, & Danehy, 1960). You will not be able to communicate with another person to the extent that your language systems differ. In reality, however, no two persons use identical signal systems, so a process of **adjustment** is relevant to all forms of communication. Parents and children, for example, not only have largely different vocabularies but also have different meanings for the terms they do share. Different cultures, even when they use a common language, often have greatly different nonverbal communication systems. To the extent that these systems differ, meaningful and effective communication will not take place.

Part of the art of communication is identifying the other person's signals, learning how they're used, and understanding what they mean. Those in close relationships will realize that learning the other person's signals takes a great deal of time and often a great deal of patience. If you want to understand what another person means (by smiling, by saying "I love you," by arguing about trivia, by making self-deprecating comments), rather than simply acknowledging what the other person says or does, you have to learn that person's system of signals.

This principle of adjustment is especially important in intercultural communication, largely because people from different cultures use different signals—and sometimes also use the same signals to signify quite different things. Focused eye contact means honesty and openness in much of the United States. But in Japan and in many Hispanic cultures, that same behavior may signify arrogance or disrespect if, say, engaged in by a youngster with someone significantly older.

Communication Accommodation

Generally, you're likely to view someone who is similar to you more positively and to see that person as more attractive than someone who is dissimilar. For example, in one study roommates who had similar communication attitudes (both were high in their willingness to communicate and low in their verbal aggressiveness) liked each other better and were more satisfied with their status as roommates than those with dissimilar attitudes (Martin & Anderson, 1995). Similarly, you're likely to judge a speaker as more believable when his or her language intensity is similar to your own (Aune & Kikuchi, 1993). And you're likely to see those whose speech rate is similar to yours as more sociable and intimate than those

---

Theory and Research   Communication Theories

UNDERSTANDING

A **theory** is a generalization that explains how something works—for example, gravity, blood clotting, interpersonal attraction, or communication. In academic writing, the term *theory* is usually reserved for a well-established system of knowledge about how things work or how things are related. A theory is still fundamentally a generalization, but it's often supported by research findings and other well-accepted theories.

The theories you'll encounter try to explain how communication works—for example, how you accommodate your speaking style to your listeners, how communication works when relationships deteriorate, how friends self-disclose, how problem-solving groups communicate, how speakers influence audiences, and how the media affect people. As you can see from even these few examples, theories provide general principles that help you understand an enormous number of specific events.

One great value of communication theories is that they help you predict future events. Because theories summarize what's been found, they can offer reasonable predictions for events that you've never encountered. For example, theories of persuasion will help you predict what kinds of emotional appeals will be most effective in persuading a specific audience. Or theories of conflict resolution will enable you to predict what strategies would be effective or ineffective in resolving differences.

Despite their many values, theories don't reveal truth in any absolute sense. Rather, theories reveal some degree of accuracy, some degree of truth. In the natural sciences (such as physics and chemistry), theories are extremely high in accuracy. If you mix two parts of hydrogen to one part of oxygen, you'll get water—every time you do it. In social and behavioral sciences such as communication, sociology, and psychology, the theories are far less accurate in describing the way things work and in predicting how things will work.

This failure to reveal truth, however, does not mean that theories are useless. In increasing your understanding and your ability to predict, theories are extremely helpful. Theories often have practical implications as you work on developing your own communication skills. For example, theories of interpersonal attraction offer practical insights into how to make yourself more attractive to others; theories of leadership offer practical advice on how you can more effectively exert your own leadership. This interrelationship between theories and skills is a theme you'll find throughout this book. The more you know about how communication works (that is, the theories and research), the more likely you'll be able to use it effectively (that is, build your communication skills).

Working with Theories and Research

Log on to one of the academic databases to which you have access and browse through issues of Quarterly Journal of Speech, Communication Monographs, *or* Communication Theory *(or scan similar journals in your own field of study); you'll be amazed at the breadth and depth of academic research and theory.*

© Royalty-Free/CORBIS

who speak much more slowly or more rapidly than you do (Buller, LePoire, Aune, & Eloy, 1992). In interethnic interactions, people who saw themselves as similar in communication styles were attracted to each other more than to those they perceived as having different communication styles (Lee & Gudykunst, 2001). These findings, and many more like them, support **communication accommodation theory**, the theory that you adjust to or accommodate to the speaking style of your listeners in order to gain a variety of benefits—not only believability and likeability, as already noted, but also general social approval and even communication efficiency (Giles, Mulac, Bradac, & Johnson, 1987).

Communication Involves Content and Relationship Dimensions

Communications, to a certain extent at least, refer to the real world, to something external to both speaker and listener. At the same time, however, communications also refer to the relationships between the parties (Watzlawick, Beavin, & Jackson, 1967). In other words, communication has both **content and relationship dimensions**.

For example, an employer may say to a worker, "See me after the meeting." This simple message has a content aspect and a relational aspect. The **content message** refers to the behavioral response expected—namely, that the worker see the employer after the meeting. The **relationship message** tells how the communication is to be dealt with. For example, the use of the simple command says that there's a status difference between the two parties: The employer can command the worker. This aspect is perhaps seen most clearly if you imagine the worker giving this command to the employer; to do so would be awkward and out of place, because it would violate the expected relationship between employer and worker.

In any communication situation, the content dimension may stay the same but the relationship aspect may vary. For example, the employer could say to the worker either "You had better see me after the meeting" or "May I please see you after the meeting?" In each case, the content is essentially the same; that is, the message being communicated about the behaviors expected is the same. But the relationship dimension is very different. The first example signifies a definite superior–inferior relationship and even a put-down of the worker. In the second, the employer signals a more equal relationship and shows respect for the worker.

Similarly, at times the content may be different but the relationship essentially the same. For example, a teenager might say to his or her parents, "May I go away this weekend?" or "May I use the car tonight?" The content of the two messages is clearly very different. The relationship dimension, however, is essentially the same. It clearly denotes a superior–inferior relationship in which permission to do certain things must be secured.

Ignoring Relationship Dimensions

Problems may arise when the distinction between the content and relationship levels of communication is ignored. Consider a couple arguing over the

Theory and Research — Communication Research
UNDERSTANDING

Research is usually conducted on the basis of some theory and its predictions—although sometimes the motivation to conduct research comes from a simple desire to answer a question. Communication research is a systematic search for information about communication, the very information that is discussed throughout this text; for example, information about perception and listening, verbal and nonverbal messages, interpersonal interactions, small group encounters, and public speaking situations.

Some research is designed to explore what exists; for example, *What do people say after getting caught in a lie?* Other research is designed to describe the properties of some communication behavior; for example, *What are the various types of excuses?* Still other research aims to predict what will happen in different situations; for example, *What types of excuses will work best in a business relationship?* Research findings bearing on these questions help explain how communication works and suggest ways to use communication more effectively.

In evaluating communication research (or any kind of research), ask yourself three questions:

- **Are the results reliable?** In establishing reliability, a measure of the extent to which research findings are consistent, you ask if another researcher, using the same essential tools, would find the same results. Would the same people respond in the same way at other times? If the answer to such questions is yes, then the results are reliable. If the answer is no, then the results may be unreliable.

- **Are the results valid?** Validity is a measure of the extent to which a measuring instrument measures what it claims to measure. For example, does your score on an intelligence test really measure what we think of as intelligence? Does your score on a test of communication apprehension measure what most people think of as constituting apprehension?

- **Do the results justify the conclusion?** Results and conclusions are two different things. Results are objective findings such as "men scored higher than women on this test of romanticism." Conclusions are the researcher's (or reader's) interpretation of the results and might include, for example, "Men are more romantic than women."

Working with Theories and Research

What question about communication would you like answered? Research the question and find out if the question has already been answered. If not, how might you go about conducting your own research to secure the answer?

---

fact that Pat made plans to study with friends during the weekend without first asking Chris if that would be all right. Probably both would have agreed that to study over the weekend was the right choice to make. Thus the argument is not at all related to the content level. The argument centers on the relationship level. Chris expected to be consulted about plans for the weekend. Pat, in not doing so, rejected this definition of the relationship.

Let me give you a personal example. My mother came to stay for a week at a summer place I had. On the first day she swept the kitchen floor six times,

though I had repeatedly told her that it did not need sweeping: I would be tracking in dirt and mud from outside, so all her effort would be wasted. But she persisted in sweeping, saying that the floor was dirty and should be swept. On the content level we were talking about the value of sweeping the kitchen floor. But on the relationship level we were talking about something quite different. We were each saying, "This is my house." When we realized this (though only after considerable argument), I stopped complaining about the relative usefulness of sweeping a floor that did not need sweeping, and she stopped sweeping it.

© Richard Lord/PhotoEdit

For another insight consider the following inter-change:

THOM: I'm going bowling tomorrow. The guys at the plant are starting a team. [He focuses on the content and ignores any relational implications of the message.]

SOFIA: Why can't we ever do anything together? [She responds primarily on a relational level, ignoring the content implications of the message and expressing her displeasure at being ignored in his decision.]

THOM: We can do something together anytime; tomorrow's the day they're organizing the team. [Again, he focuses almost exclusively on the content.]

This example reflects research findings that show that men tend to focus more on content messages, whereas women focus more on relationship messages (Pearson, West, & Turner, 1995). Once we recognize this gender difference, we may be able to develop increased sensitivity to the opposite sex.

Recognizing Relationship Dimensions

Here's essentially the same situation but with added sensitivity to relationship messages:

THOM: The guys at the plant are organizing a bowling team. I'd sure like to be on the team. Do you mind if I go to the organizational meeting tomorrow? [Although he focuses on content, he shows awareness of the relational dimensions by asking if

this would be a problem. He also shows this in expressing his desire rather than his decision to attend this meeting.]

SOFIA: That sounds great, but I'd really like to do something together tomorrow. [She focuses on the relational dimension but also acknowledges his content message. Note too that she does not respond as if she has to defend herself or her emphasis on relational aspects.]

THOM: How about you meet me at Luigi's for dinner after the organizational meeting? [He responds to the relational aspect without abandoning his desire to join the bowling team—and seeks to incorporate it into his communications. He attempts to negotiate a solution that will meet both Sofia's and his needs and desires.]

SOFIA: Perfect. I'm dying for spaghetti and meatballs. [She responds to both messages, approving of both his joining the team and their dinner date.]

Arguments over content are relatively easy to resolve. You can look something up in a book or ask someone what actually took place. Arguments on the relationship level, however, are much more difficult to resolve, in part because you (like me in the example with my mother) may not recognize that the argument is in fact about your relationship. The accompanying Building Communication Skills box, Distinguishing Content and Relationship Messages, provides additional insight into this important distinction.

Distinguishing Content from Relationship Messages

Deborah Tannen, in *You're Wearing That?* (2006), gives examples of content and relationship communication and the problems that can result from different interpretations. For example, the mother who says, "Are you going to wear those earrings?" may think she's communicating solely a content message. To the daughter, however, the message is largely relational and is a criticism of the way she intends to dress. (Of course, the mother may have intended criticism.) Often, questions that may appear to be objective and focused on content are perceived as attacks, as in the title of Tannen's book. Identify the possible content and relational messages that a receiver might get in being asked the following questions:

- *You're* calling me?
- Did you say, *you're* applying to *medical* school?
- You're in *love*?
- You paid a *hundred dollars* for that?
- And that's *all* you did?

Content and relationship messages serve different communication functions. Being able to distinguish between these functions is a prerequisite for using and responding to messages effectively.

Communication Is Ambiguous

Ambiguous messages are messages with more than one potential meaning. Sometimes this **ambiguity** occurs because we use words that can be interpreted differently. Informal time terms offer good examples; *soon, right away, in a minute, early, late,* and similar terms often mean different things to different people. The terms are ambiguous. A more interesting type of ambiguity is grammatical ambiguity. You can get a feel for this type of ambiguity by trying to paraphrase—rephrase in your own words—the following sentences:

1. What has the cat in its paws?
2. Visiting relatives can be boring.
3. They are flying planes.

You can interpret and paraphrase each of these in at least two different ways:

1. What monster has the cat in its paws? What does the cat have in its paws?
2. To visit relatives can be boring. Relatives who visit can be boring.
3. Those people are flying planes. Those planes are for flying.

Although these examples are particularly striking—and are the work of linguists, or specialists who analyze language—some degree of ambiguity exists in all communication; all messages are ambiguous to some degree. In other words, when you express an idea, you never communicate your meaning exactly and totally; rather, you communicate your meaning with some reasonable accuracy—enough to give the other person a reasonably clear sense of what you mean. Sometimes, of course, you're less accurate than you anticipated: Your listener "gets the wrong idea," or "gets offended" when you only meant to be humorous, or "misunderstands your emotional meaning." Because of this inevitable uncertainty, you may qualify what you're saying, give an example, or ask, "Do you know what I mean?" These tactics help the other person understand your meaning and reduce uncertainty (to some degree).

Similarly, all relationships contain uncertainty. Consider a close relationship of your own and ask yourself the following questions. Answer on a scale ranging from 1 (completely or almost completely uncertain) to 6 (completely or almost completely certain). How certain are you about:

- what you can or cannot say to each other in this relationship? Do you know what the sore spots are or what topics are best avoided?
- whether or not you and your partner feel the same way about each other? Would you each describe your relationship similarly?
- the future of the relationship? Do you each see your future and the relationship's future in the same way?

Very likely you were not able to respond to all four questions with 6s, and it's equally likely that your relationship partner would be unable to respond with all 6s. These questions from a relationship uncertainty scale (Knobloch & Solomon, 1999)—and other similar tests—illustrate that you probably experience some degree of uncertainty about the norms that govern your relationship communication (question 1), the degree to which each of you defines the relationship in similar ways (question 2), and the relationship's future (question 3).

Any communication situation can be ambiguous. In small group or organizational situations, you may be unsure of how you or your ideas are being evaluated. You may be unsure of the hierarchy in the organization. You may be unsure of what style of leadership will prove effective and what style will cause resentment. In public speaking you probably face the greatest ambiguity; namely, how your audience will respond to your speech. Will they be in favor of what you're advocating or against it? Will they understand certain technical terms, or will you have to define them? Will they be willing to pay attention?

By developing the skills of communication presented in this text, you'll be able to reduce ambiguity and make your meanings as unambiguous as possible. In this connection take a look at the accompanying Building Communication Skills box, Resolving Ambiguity.

Communication Is Punctuated

Communication events are continuous transactions. There's no clear-cut beginning or ending. As a participant in or an observer of the communication act, you engage in punctuation: You divide up this continuous, circular process into causes and effects, or **stimuli** and **responses**. That is, you segment this continuous stream of communication into smaller pieces. You label some of these pieces causes or stimuli and others effects or responses.

Consider an example: The students are apathetic; the teacher does not prepare for classes. Figure 5 (a) illustrates the sequence of events, in which there's no absolute beginning and no absolute end. Each action (the students' apathy and the teacher's lack of preparation) stimulates the other. But there's no initial stimulus. Each of the events may be regarded as a stimulus and each as a response, but there's no way to determine which is which.

Consider how the teacher might divide up this continuous transaction. Figure 5 (b) illustrates the teacher's perception of the situation. From this point of view, the teacher sees the students' apathy as the stimulus for his or her lack of preparation, and the lack of preparation as the response to the students' apathy. In Figure 5 (c) we see how the students might divide up the transaction. The students might see this "same" sequence of events as beginning with the teacher's lack of preparation as the stimulus (or cause) and their own apathy as the response (or effect).

Take another example: Pat cooks; Chris criticizes the cooking. Pat begins to exert less effort, Chris criticizes more, Pat exerts still less effort, Chris continues to criticize, and so on. Pat may see the argument as beginning with Chris's negative comments—the criticism is the cause and exerting less effort is the effect. Chris may see the argument as beginning with Pat's lousy cooking—lack of effort is the cause and justifiable criticism is the effect.

FIGURE 5 **Punctuation and the Sequence of Events**

Try using this three-part figure, discussed in the text, to explain what might go on when Pat complains about Chris's nagging and Chris complains about Pat's avoidance and silence.

(a) The sequence of events punctuated by the teacher

(b) The sequence of events punctuated by the students

This tendency to divide up the various communication transactions in sequences of stimuli and responses is referred to as **punctuation of communication** (Watzlawick, Beavin, & Jackson, 1967). People punctuate the continuous sequences of events into stimuli and responses for ease of understanding and remembering. And, as both the preceding examples illustrate, people punctuate communication in ways that allow them to look good and that are consistent with their own self-image.

If communication is to be effective, if you're to understand what another person means from his or her point of view, then you have to see the sequence of events as punctuated by the other person. Further, you have to recognize that your punctuation does not reflect what exists in reality. Rather, it reflects your own unique but fallible perception.

Communication Involves Symmetrical and Complementary Transactions

Relationships can be described as either symmetrical or complementary (Watzlawick, Beavin, & Jackson, 1967). In a **symmetrical relationship** the two individuals mirror each other's behavior. The behavior of one person is reflected in the behavior of the other. If one member nags, the other member responds in kind. If one member expresses jealousy, the other member expresses

jealousy. If one member is passive, the other member is passive. The relationship is one of equality, with the emphasis on minimizing the differences between the two individuals.

Note, however, the problems that can arise in this type of relationship. Consider the situation of a husband and wife, both of whom are aggressive. The aggressiveness of the husband fosters aggressiveness in the wife; the anger of the wife arouses anger in the husband. As this escalates, the aggressiveness can no longer be contained, and the relationship is consumed by aggression.

In a **complementary relationship**, in contrast, the two individuals engage in different behaviors. The behavior of one serves as the stimulus for the complementary behavior of the other. In complementary relationships the differences between the parties are maximized. One partner acts as the superior and the other as the inferior, one is passive and the other active, one strong and the other weak. At times cultures establish such relationships—as, for example, the complementary relationship between teacher and student or between employer and employee. Early marriages are likely to be complementary relationships in which each person tries to complete himself or herself. When these couples separate and form new partnerships, the new relationships are likely to be symmetrical and to involve a kind of reconfirmation of each partner's own identity (Prosky, 1992). Generally, research finds that complementary couples have a lower marital adjustment level than do symmetrical couples (Main & Oliver, 1988; Holden, 1991; McCall & Green, 1991).

A problem in complementary relationships—familiar to many college students—is the situation created by extreme rigidity. Whereas the complementary relationship between a nurturing and protective mother and a dependent child is at one stage vital and essential to the life of the child, a **rigid complementarity** when the child is older can become a handicap to further development, if the change so essential to growth is not allowed to occur.

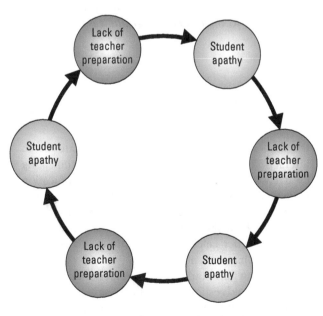

(c) The sequence of events as it exists in reality

Communication Is Inevitable, Irreversible, and Unrepeatable

Communication is a process that is inevitable, irreversible, and unrepeatable. Communication messages are always being sent (or almost always), can't be reversed or uncommunicated, and are always unique and one-time occurrences. Let's look at these qualities in more detail.

Building Communication Skills   Resolving Ambiguity

Here are a few ambiguous situations; for each, indicate what you would say to resolve the ambiguity. If possible, try to share your responses with others in a small group and perhaps combine responses to come up with the ideal way to reduce the ambiguity. Or responses from a larger group can be written on index cards (anonymously), collected, and read aloud for the entire group to evaluate.

1. You've been dating Pat on and off for the past six months. Today, Pat asks you to come to dinner and meet the parents. You're not sure if this means that Pat wants to get more serious (which you do not want) or if it's a simple dinner invitation with no additional motives. How might you disambiguate this dinner invitation message?

2. At an appraisal interview, your supervisor says that your work over the last six months has improved considerably—then smiles and says, "But there's always more that we need to do," and then nonverbally indicates that the interview is over and you can return to work. Since you're considering other job offers, you want to know in more detail how your current employer sees you and your prospects for advancement. How might you disambiguate this job appraisal?

3. You receive a written invitation to address the eighth-grade class of your local middle school on careers in communication. The invitation said little more than that a conference on careers is planned and that they are hoping you'll be one of the speakers. This is too ambiguous for you; you need to know in more detail what will be expected of you. How might you disambiguate this invitation to speak?

4. You've been invited to a colleague's house for dinner. Around two hours before you're scheduled to leave for the dinner, it begins to snow, and your colleague calls to say that you shouldn't feel you have to come to dinner in the snow; the roads may get dangerous. The snow is only a light dusting, and your SUV would have no trouble getting there. You wonder what your colleague was really saying—whether it's "I'd like to cancel the dinner and I'm using the snow as an excuse" or "I'm concerned about your safety and I don't want you to travel in potentially dangerous weather just because of this dinner." What do you say?

Messages and relationships are often ambiguous; instead of assuming one interpretation is right and another wrong, it may be useful to try to disambiguate the message and find out exactly what the speaker means.

Inevitability

In many instances communication takes place even though one of the individuals does not think he or she is communicating or does not want to communicate. Consider, for example, the student sitting in the back of the classroom with an expressionless face, perhaps staring out the window. Although the student might claim not to be communicating with the teacher, the teacher may derive any of a variety of messages from this behavior; for example, that the student lacks interest, is bored, or is worried about something. In any event, the teacher is receiving messages even though the student may not intend to communicate. In an interactional situation, you can't avoid communicating (Watzlawick, Beavin, & Jackson, 1967); communication is inevitable. This principle of **inevitability** does not mean, of course, that all behavior is communication. For example, if the student looked out the window and the teacher failed to notice this, no communication would have taken place.

Further, when you're in an interactional situation you can't avoid responding to the messages of others. For example, if you notice someone winking at you, you must respond in some way. Even if you don't

IRREVERSIBILITY

Without thinking you make some culturally insensitive remarks and even though everyone laughs politely, you want to explain that you're really not the kind of person who normally talks this way.

WHAT DO YOU SAY?

© Lara Jo Regan/Getty Images

respond actively or openly, that lack of response is itself a response, and it communicates. Again, if you don't notice the winking, then obviously communication has not occurred.

Irreversibility

Notice that you can reverse the processes of only some systems. For example, you can turn water into ice and then the ice back into water. And you can repeat this reversal process as many times as you wish. Other systems, however, are irreversible. You can turn grapes into wine, but you can't turn the wine back into grapes—the process can go in only one direction. Communication is such an irreversible process. Once you say something, once you press the send key on your e-mail, you can't uncommunicate it. You can of course try to reduce the effects of your message by saying, for example, "I really didn't mean what I said" or "I was so angry I couldn't think straight." But regardless of how you try to negate or reduce the effects of a message, the message itself, once it has been sent and received, can't be reversed.

Because of **irreversibility** (and unerasability), be careful not to say things you may be sorry for later. Especially in conflict situations, when tempers run high, avoid saying things you may later wish to withdraw. Commitment messages—"I love you" messages and their variants—also need to be monitored. And in group and public communication situations, when messages are received by many people, it's crucial to recognize their irreversibility. Similarly, online messages that could be interpreted as sexist, racist, homophobic, or ageist, which you thought were private or erased from your computer, may

later be recalled and retrieved by others, creating all sorts of problems for you and your organization.

As a result of the differences between the permanency of electronic communication and the evanescence of face-to-face communication, you may wish to be cautious in your electronic messages. E-mail is probably your most common form of computer communication, though these cautions also apply to all other forms of electronic communication, including newsgroup postings, instant messages, and website messages. In an organizational context, it's important to find out what the e-mail policy of the company is. One survey found that 75 percent of companies had written e-mail policies but that less than half of all companies surveyed trained their workers in e-mail policies (Coombes, 2003).

- E-mails are difficult to destroy. Often e-mails you think you deleted will remain on servers and workstations and may be retrieved by a clever hacker.

- E-mails can readily be made public; the ease of forwarding e-mails to others or of posting your comments on websites makes it especially important that you consider carefully what you write. The message that you intend for one person may actually be received by many others, too.

- E-mails are not privileged communication and can easily be used against you, especially in the workplace. Criticizing a colleague may one day leave you open to accusations of discrimination. Passing along sexist, racist, homophobic, or ageist "jokes" to a friend may one day fuel accusations of a hostile working environment and cost your employer millions, as such "jokes" cost Chevron a few years ago.

- E-mails provide permanent records: They make it impossible for you to say, for example, "That's not exactly what I said," because exactly what you said will be there in black and white.
- E-mail files may be accessed by others, such as a nosy colleague at the next desk or a visiting neighbor, and can then be sent to additional outsiders.

Unrepeatability

The reason for the **unrepeatability** of communication is simple: Everyone and everything is constantly changing. As a result, you can never recapture the exact same situation, frame of mind, or relationship dynamics that defined a previous communication act. For example, you can never repeat meeting someone for the first time, making a first impression in an interview, or resolving a specific group problem.

You can, of course, try again, as when you say, "I'm sorry I came off so forward, can we try again?" But even after you say this, you have not erased the initial impression. Instead you try to counteract this initial and perhaps negative impression by going through the motions again.

SUMMARY: PRELIMINARIES TO HUMAN COMMUNICATION

This unit explained the benefits, forms, and purposes of human communication; the major elements of human communication, and several functional principles that explain how human communication works.

1. Communication is the act, by one or more persons, of sending and receiving messages that occur within a context, are distorted by noise, have some effect (and some ethical dimension), and provide some opportunity for feedback.

2. The major skills to be learned here include self-presentation, relationship, interviewing, group interaction and leadership, and presentation.

3. The major types of human communication are intrapersonal, interpersonal, small group, organizational, public, computer-mediated, and mass communication.

4. Communication is multipurposeful; we use communication to discover, to relate, to help, to persuade, and to play.

5. The universals of communication—the elements present in every communication act—are the context, including culture; source–receiver sending or encoding processes and receiving or decoding processes; messages; channels; noise; feedback and feedforward; effects; and ethics.

6. The communication context has at least four dimensions: physical, social–psychological, temporal, and cultural.

7. Culture consists of the collection of beliefs, attitudes, values, and ways of behavior shared by a group of people and passed down from one generation to the next through communication rather than genes.

8. Communication competence is knowledge of the elements and rules of communication, which vary from one culture to another.

9. Communication is a transactional process in which each person simultaneously sends and receives messages.

10. Noise is anything that distorts a message; it's present to some degree in every communication transaction and may be physical, physiological, psychological, or semantic in origin.

11. Feedback is information or messages that are sent back to the source. It may come from the source itself or from the receiver, and may be characterized along such dimensions as positive and negative, person-focused and message-focused, immediate and delayed, low-monitored and high-monitored, and supportive and critical.

12. Feedforward messages preface other messages and may be used to open the channels of communication, to preview future messages, to disclaim, and to altercast.

13. Communication messages may be of varied forms and may be sent and received through any combination of sensory organs. The communication channel is the medium through which the messages are sent.

14. Communication always has an effect. Effects may be cognitive, affective, or psychomotor.

15. Ethics in communication consists of the rightness or wrongness—the morality—of a communication transaction. Ethics is integral to every communication transaction.

16. Communication is normally a package of signals, each reinforcing the other. Opposing communication signals from the same source result in contradictory messages.

17. The double bind, a special kind of contradictory message, may be created when contradictory messages are sent simultaneously.

18. Communication is a process of adjustment and takes place only to the extent that the communicators use the same system of signals.

19. Communication involves both content dimensions and relationship dimensions.

20. Communication is ambiguous and often can be interpreted in different ways.

21. Communication sequences are punctuated for processing. Different people divide up the communication sequence into stimuli and responses differently.

22. Communication involves symmetrical and complementary transactions.

23. In any interaction situation, communication is inevitable; you can't avoid communication, nor can you not respond to communication.

24. Communication is irreversible. You can't uncommunicate.

25. Communication is unrepeatable. You can't duplicate a previous communication act.

KEY TERMS IN PRELIMINARIES TO HUMAN COMMUNICATION

Here are the essential terms used in this unit and the pages on which they are introduced. Many of these terms are also defined in the glossary at the end of the text. In addition, flash cards are available online at MyCommunicationLab (www.mycommunicationlab.com) to help you further master the vocabulary of human communication.

adjustment
affirmation
altercasting
ambiguity
channel
code
communication
communication accommodation theory
communication competence
complementary relationship
computer-mediated communication
content and relationship dimensions
content messages

context
culture
decoder
decoding
disclaimer
effect
encoder
encoding
ethics
feedback
feedforward
inevitability
intercultural communication
interpersonal communication

interviewing
intrapersonal communication
irreversibility
mass communication
messages
metacommunication
metamessages
mixed messages
negative feedback
noise
organizational communication
phatic communication
positive feedback
public speaking

punctuation of communication
receiver
relationship messages
responses
rigid complementarity
small group communication
source
stimuli
symmetrical relationship
theory
transactional
unrepeatability

THINKING CRITICALLY ABOUT PRELIMINARIES TO HUMAN COMMUNICATION

1. **Reading Feedback.** Based on your own experiences, do you find that instructors who accurately read and respond to student feedback are better liked than instructors who can't read feedback as accurately? Is there a relationship between the ability to read feedback and the ability to communicate information or to motivate or persuade an audience? In what ways might the ability to give effective feedback influence the growth or deterioration of a relationship?

2. **Feedforward.** In this book there are several examples of feedforward; for example, (1) the cover, (2) the "Welcome" section, (3) the tables of contents, (4) each unit's opening page, (5) each unit's opening paragraph,

and (6) the section headings within units. What more specific purposes do each of these serve?

3. **Online and Off-line Activities.** A report dated August 11, 2004, by the Pew Internet and American Life Project (The Internet and Daily Life, www.pewinternet.org/PPF/r/131/report_display.asp, accessed February 10, 2005) noted that people are more likely to "get news, play games, pay bills, send cards, look up phone numbers and addresses, buy tickets, check sports scores, listen to music, schedule appointments, and communicate with friends" off-line than online. Why do you think this is the case? Do you think the items on this list will change over the next 5 years? Over the next 20 years?

4. **Synchronous and Asynchronous Messaging.** In face-to-face and chat room communication, messages are exchanged with virtually no delay; communication is synchronous. In other forms of communication—for example, snail or e-mail and blog posts—the messages may be exchanged with considerable delay; communication here is asynchronous. What differences in communication style can you attribute to synchronicity and asynchronicity?

5. **Inevitability, Irreversibility, and Unrepeatability.** Identify one or two or three rules or guidelines that the concepts of inevitability, irreversibility, and unrepeatability would suggest for each of the following situations: (a) the first day at a new job, (b) asking for a date, (c) a face-to-face job interview, (d) chatting in an online group, (e) meeting with a dying friend, (f) popping the question, (g) introducing yourself in class, (h) arguing with your romantic partner, (i) seeing an old friend after many years, (j) giving a speech to regain the goodwill of the people, and (k) leading a group of colleagues in a brainstorming session.

LogOn! MyCommunicationLab
WWW.MYCOMMUNICATIONLAB.COM

MyCommunicationLab will provide you with a broad collection of materials that will help you master the theory and skills of this course and this text; it will also make your experience in this course more enjoyable and more varied. There are practice tests, crossword puzzles, videos, and figures and tables from a variety of books; all of these will prove useful supplements for each unit in the text. At the end of each unit you'll find a brief note of just some of the materials available on MCL that are relevant to the unit.

For Unit 1, visit MCL for such exercises as the following: Using Communication Channels, Modeling Human Communication, Responding to Contradictory Messages, Symmetrical and Complementary Relationships, Applying the Principles, Analyzing an Interaction, Principles of Communication, and Communication Competence.

While in MCL click on the Research Navigator tab and you'll find a wealth of research materials that you can use throughout this course and especially in the public speaking section.

References

Aune, R. K., & Kikuchi, T. (1993). Effects of language intensity similarity on perceptions of credibility, relational attributions, and persuasion. *Journal of Language and Social Psychology, 12* (September), 224-238.

Barbato, C. A., & Perse, E. M. (1992). Interpersonal communication motives and the life position of elders. *Communication Research, 19*, 516-531.

Barnlund, D. C. (1970). A transactional model of communication. In J. Akin, A. Goldberg, G. Myers, & J. Stewart (Eds.), *Language behavior: A book of readings in communication*. The Hague: Mouton.

Bassellier, G., & Benbasat, I. (2004). Business competence of information technology professionals: Conceptual development and influence on IT-business partnerships. *MIS Quarterly 28* (December), 673-694.

Beier, E. (1974). How we send emotional messages. *Psychology Today, 8* (October), 53-56.

Bok, S. (1978). *Lying: Moral choice in public and private life.* New York: Pantheon.

Bok, S. (1998). *Mayhem: Violence as public entertainment.* Reading, MA: Perseus Books.

Buller, D. B., LePoire, B. A., Aune, K., & Eloy, S. (1992). Social perceptions as mediators of the effect of speech rate similarity on compliance. *Human Communication Research, 19* (December), 286-311.

Burnard, P. (2003). Ordinary chat and therapeutic conversation: Phatic communication and mental health nursing. *Journal of Psychiatric and Mental Health Nursing, 10*(December), 678-682.

Canary, D. J., Cody, M. J., & Manusov, V. L. (2000). *Interpersonal communication: A goals-based approach* (2nd ed.). Boston: Bedford/St. Martins.

Coombes, A. (2003). E-termination: Employees are getting fired for e-mail infractions. CBSMarketWatch.Com (accessed 9/3/04).

Giles, H., Mulac, A., Bradac, J. J., & Johnson, P. (1987). Speech accommodation theory: The first decade and beyond. In M. L. McLaughlin (Ed.), *Communication yearbook 10* (pp. 13-48). Thousand Oaks, CA: Sage.

Graham, E. E. (1994). Interpersonal communication motives scale. In R. B. Rubin, P. Palmgreen, & H. E. Sypher (Eds.), *Communication research measures: A sourcebook* (pp. 211-216). New York: Guilford.

Graham, E. E., Barbato, C. A., & Perse, E. M. (1993). The interpersonal communication motives model. *Communication Quarterly, 41*, 172-186.

Hewitt, J., & Stokes, R. (1975). Disclaimers. *American Sociological Review, 40*, 1-11.

Holden, J. M. (1991). The most frequent personality priority pairings in marriage and marriage counseling. *Individual*

Psychology Journal of Adlerian Theory, Research, and Practice, 47 (September), 392-398.

Jaksa, J. A., & Pritchard, M. S. (1994). *Communication ethics: Methods of analysis* (2nd ed.). Belmont, CA: Wadsworth.

Johnson, S. A. (1993). *When "I love you" turns violent: Emotional and physical abuse in dating relationships.* Far Hills, NJ: New Horizon Press.

Knobloch, L. K., & Solomon, D. H. (1999). Measuring the sources and content of relational uncertainty. *Communication Studies, 50* (Winter), 261-278.

Lee, C., & Gudykunst, W. B. (2001). Attraction in initial interethnic interactions. *International Journal of Intercultural Relations, 25* (July), 373-387.

Li, H. Z. (1999). Communicating information in conversations: A cross-cultural comparison. *International Journal of Intercultural Relations, 23* (May), 387-409.

Lu, S. (1998, October 9). *Critical reflections on phatic communication research: schematizations, limitations and alternatives.* Paper delivered at the New York State Speech Communication Association, Monticello, New York.

Main, F., & Oliver, R. (1988). Complementary, symmetrical, and parallel personality priorities as indicators of marital adjustment. *Individual Psychology Journal of Adlerian Theory, Research, and Practice, 44* (September), 324-332.

Malinowski, B. (1923). The problem of meaning in primitive languages. In C. K. Ogden & I. A. Richards, *The meaning of meaning* (pp. 296-336). New York: Harcourt Brace Jovanovich.

Martin, M. M., & Anderson, C. M. (1995). Roommate similarity: Are roommates who are similar in their communication traits more satisfied? *Communication Research Reports, 12* (Spring), 46-52.

McCall, D. L., & Green, R. G. (1991). Symmetricality and complementarity and their relationship to marital stability. *Journal of Divorce and Remarriage, 15,* 23-32.

McCarthy, M. (2003). Talking back: Small interactional response tokens in everyday conversation. *Research on Language and Social Interaction 36* (January), 33-63.

McLaughlin, M. L. (1984). *Conversation: How talk is organized.* Thousand Oaks, CA: Sage.

Meier, A. (2000). Offering social support via the Internet: A case study of an online support group for social workers. *Journal of Technology in Human Services, 1,* 237-267.

Meier, A. (2002). An online stress management support group for social workers. *Journal of Technology in Human Services, 20,* 107-132.

Pearson, J. C., West, R., & Turner, L. H. (1995). *Gender and communication* (3rd ed.). Dubuque, IA: William C. Brown.

Pittenger, R. E., Hockett, C. F., & Danehy, J. J. (1960). *The first five minutes.* Ithaca, NY: Paul Martineau.

Placencia, M. E. (2004). The Online Disinhibition Effect. *Journal of Sociolinguistics 8* (May), 215-245.

Pratkanis, A. R. (2000). Altercasting as an influence tactic. In D. J. Terry & M. A. Hogg (Eds.), *Attitudes, behavior, and social context: The role of norms and group membership* (pp. 201-226). Mahwah, NJ: Erlbaum.

Prosky, P. S. (1992). Complementary and symmetrical couples. *Family Therapy, 19,* 215-221.

Richards, I. A. (1951). Communication between men: The meaning of language. In H. von Foerster (Ed.), *Cybernetics, transactions of the eighth conference.*

Rubin, R. B. (1982). Assessing speaking and listening competence at the college level: The communication competency assessment instrument. *Communication Education, 31* (January), 19-32.

Rubin, R. B. (1985). The validity of the communication competency assessment instrument. *Communication Monographs, 52,* 173-185.

Rubin, R. B., Fernandez-Collado, C., & Hernandez-Sampieri, R. (1992). A cross-cultural examination of interpersonal communication motives in Mexico and the United States. *International Journal of Intercultural Relations, 16,* 145-157.

Rubin, R. B., & Martin, M. M. (1994). Development of a measure of interpersonal communication competence. *Communication Research Reports, 11,* 33-44.

Rubin, R. B., & Martin, M. M. (1998). Interpersonal communication motives. In J. C. McCroskey, J. A. Daly, M. M. Martin, & M. J. Beatty (Eds.), *Communication and personality: Trait perspectives* (pp. 287-307). Cresskill, NJ: Hampton Press.

Rubin, R. B., Perse, E. M., & Barbato, C. A. (1988). Conceptualization and measurement of interpersonal communication motives. *Human Communication Research, 14,* 602-628.

Rubin, R. B., & Rubin, A. M. (1992). Antecedents of interpersonal communication motivation. *Communication Quarterly, 40,* 315-317.

Skinner, M. (2002). In search of feedback. *Executive Excellence* (June), 18.

Spitzberg, B. H., & Cupach, W. R. (1989). *Handbook of interpersonal competence research.* New York: Springer.

Tannen, D. (2006). *You're wearing that? Understanding mothers and daughters in conversation.* New York: Random House.

Watzlawick, P. (1977). *How real is real? Confusion, disinformation, communication: An anecdotal introduction to communications theory.* New York: Vintage.

Watzlawick, P. (1978). *The language of change: Elements of therapeutic communication.* New York: Basic Books.

Watzlawick, P., Beavin, J. H., & Jackson, D. D. (1967). *Pragmatics of human communication: A study of interactional patterns, pathologies, and paradoxes.* New York: Norton.

Weinstein, E. A., & Deutschberger, P. (1963). Some dimensions of altercasting. *Sociometry, 26,* 454-466.

Wilmot, W. W. (1987). *Dyadic communication* (3rd ed.). New York: Random House.

Chapter 2

Culture and Communication

MAJOR TOPICS

What Is Culture?

Cultural Differences

Intercultural Communication

Special Features

Culture Talk, Melbourne S. Cummings

What Are Your Cultural Beliefs and Values?

What's Your Cultural Orientation?

How Ethnocentric Are You?

Cultural Imperialism

Culture and Ethics

Understanding Cultural Theories

Understanding Language and Thought

Skills Exploring Cultural Attitudes

Skills Confronting Intercultural Difficulties

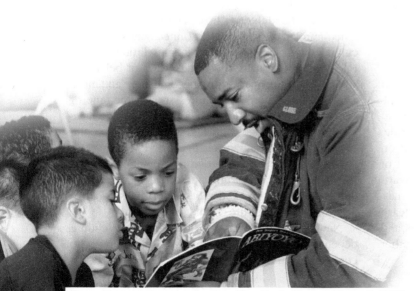

© Kathy McLaughlin/The Image Works

When you speak or listen, you're doing so as a member of a particular and unique culture—you're greatly influenced by the teachings of your religion, your racial and national history, the social expectations for your gender, and a host of other factors. This unit explores this topic of culture and its relationship to human communication.

In this unit you'll learn about:
- culture's role in human communication.
- the ways cultures differ from one another.
- the forms and principles of intercultural communication.

You'll learn to:
- send and receive messages with a recognition of cultural influences and differences.
- communicate successfully in intercultural situations.

WHAT IS CULTURE?

Culture consists of (1) relatively specialized elements of the lifestyle of a group of people (2) that are passed on from one generation to the next through communication, not through genes.

(1) Included in a social group's "culture" is everything that members of that group have produced and developed—their values, beliefs, artifacts, and language; their ways of behaving and ways of thinking; their art, laws, religion, and, of course, communication theories, styles, and attitudes.

(2) Culture is passed on from one generation to the next through communication, not through genes. Thus, the term *culture* does not refer to color of skin or shape of eyes, as these are passed on through genes, not communication. But because members of a particular race or country are often taught similar beliefs, attitudes, and values, it's possible to speak of "Hispanic culture" or "African American culture." It's important to realize, however, that within any large group—especially a group based on race or nationality—there will be enormous differences. The Kansas farmer and the Wall Street executive may both be, say, German American, but may differ widely in their attitudes, beliefs, and lifestyles. In some ways the Kansas farmer may be closer in attitudes and values to a Chinese farmer than to the New York financier.

In ordinary conversation *sex* and *gender* are often used synonymously. In academic discussions of culture, they're more often distinguished. **Sex** refers to the biological distinction between male and female; sex is determined by genes, by biology. **Gender**, on the other hand, refers to the "social construction of masculinity and femininity within a culture" (Stewart, Cooper, Stewart, with Friedley, 2003). Gender (masculinity and femininity) is what boys and girls learn from their culture; it's the attitudes, beliefs, values, and ways of communicating and relating to one another that boys and girls learn as they grow up.

Thus, gender—although partly transmitted genetically and not by communication—may be considered a cultural variable, largely because cultures teach boys and girls different attitudes, beliefs, values, and ways of communicating and relating to one another. Thus, you act like a man or a woman in part because of what your culture has taught you about how men and women should act. This is not, of course, to deny that biological differences also play a role in the differences between male and female behavior. In fact, research continues to uncover biological roots of male/female differences we once thought were entirely learned (McCroskey, 1997).

Culture is transmitted from one generation to another through **enculturation**, the process by which you learn the culture into which you're born (your native culture). Parents, peer groups, schools, religious institutions, and government agencies are the main teachers of culture.

A somewhat different process of learning culture is **acculturation**, the process by which you learn the rules and norms of a culture different from your native culture. In acculturation your original or native culture is modified through direct contact with or exposure to a new and different "host" culture. For example, when immigrants settle in the United States (the host culture), their own culture becomes influenced by U.S. culture. Gradually, the values, ways of behaving, and beliefs of the host culture become more and more a part of the immigrants' culture. At the same time, of course, the host culture changes, too, as it interacts with the immigrants' culture. Generally, however, the culture of the immigrant changes more. The reasons for this are that the host country's members far outnumber the immigrant group and that the media are largely dominated by and reflect the values and customs of the host culture (Kim, 1988).

New citizens' acceptance of the new culture depends on many factors (Kim, 1988). Immigrants who come from cultures similar to the host culture will

Theory and Research   Cultural Theories

UNDERSTANDING

Consider two very different theories of culture: cultural evolution and cultural relativism. The theory of *cultural evolution* (often called social Darwinism) holds that much as the human species evolved from lower life forms to Homo sapiens, cultures also evolve. Consequently, some cultures may be considered advanced and others primitive. Most contemporary scholars reject this view, because the judgments that distinguish one culture from another have no basis in science and are instead based on individual values and preferences as to what constitutes "advanced" and what constitutes "primitive."

The *cultural relativism* approach, on the other hand, holds that all cultures are different but that no culture is either superior or inferior to any other (Berry, Poortinga, Segall, & Dasen, 1992). This view is generally accepted today and guides the infusion of cultural materials into contemporary textbooks on all academic levels (Jandt, 2004). But this position does not imply that all cultural practices are therefore equal or that you have to accept all cultural practices equally. As noted in the text, there are many cultural practices popular throughout the world that you may find, quite logically and reasonably, unacceptable.

Working with Theories and Research

Explore these two positions more fully by consulting one or more of the references cited in this unit, or by logging on to your favorite search engine or database and searching for such concepts as "cultural relativism," "cultural evolution," and "social Darwinism." What might you add to the brief discussion presented here?

become acculturated more easily. Similarly, those who are younger and better educated become acculturated more quickly than do older and less well educated people. Personality factors also play a part. Persons who are risk takers and open-minded, for example, have greater acculturation potential. Also, persons who are familiar with the host culture before immigration—through interpersonal contact or through media exposure—will be acculturated more readily.

Before exploring further the role of culture in communication, consider your own cultural values and beliefs by taking the self-test on page 36. This test illustrates how your own cultural values and beliefs may influence your interpersonal, small group, and public communications—both the messages you send and the messages to which you listen.

The Importance of Culture in Communication

There are many reasons for the current cultural emphasis in the field of communication. Because of (1) demographic changes, (2) increased sensitivity to cultural differences, (3) economic interdependency, (4) advances in communication technology, and (5) the fact that communication competence is specific

to a culture (what works in one culture will not necessarily work in another), it's impossible to communicate effectively without being aware of how culture influences human communication.

Demographic Changes

Most obvious, perhaps, are the vast demographic changes taking place throughout the United States. Whereas at one time the United States was largely a country populated by northern Europeans, it's now a country greatly influenced by the enormous number of new citizens from Central and South America, Africa, and Asia. And the same is true to an even greater extent on college and university campuses throughout the United States. With these changes have come different customs and the need to understand and adapt to new ways of looking at communication.

Consider these facts (*The New York Times Almanac 2005*; *The World Almanac and Book of Facts 2005*): The foreign-born population of the United States is increasing dramatically. In 1980, the foreign-born population was 14 million (about 6.2 percent of the total population), in 1990 it was 19.8 million (7.9 percent), and in 2000 it was 28.4 million (10.4 percent). Increasingly, frequent communication in a multicultural context is inevitable.

TEST YOURSELF

What Are Your Cultural Beliefs and Values?

Here the extremes of eight cultural differences are identified. For each characteristic indicate your own values:

a. If you feel your values are very similar to the extremes, then select 1 or 7.

b. If you feel your values are quite similar to the extremes, then select 2 or 6.

c. If you feel your values are fairly similar to the extremes, then select 3 or 5.

d. If you feel you're in the middle, then select 4.

Men and women are equal and are entitled to equality in all areas.	**Gender Equality** 1 2 3 4 ⑤ 6 7	Men and women are very different and should stick to the specific roles assigned to them by their culture.
You should enjoy yourself as much as possible.	**Hedonism** 1 2 3 4 ⑤ 6 7	You should work as much as possible.
Religion is the final arbiter of what is right and wrong; your first obligation is to abide by the rules and customs of your religion.	**Religion** 1 ② 3 4 5 6 7	Religion is like any other social institution; it's not inherently moral or right just because it's a religion.
Your first obligation is to your family; each person is responsible for the welfare of his or her family.	**Family** 1 ② 3 4 5 6 7	Your first obligation is to yourself; each person is responsible for himself or herself.
Romantic relationships, once made, are forever.	**Relationship Permanency** ① 2 3 4 5 6 7	Romantic relationships should be maintained as long as they're more rewarding than punishing and dissolved when they're more punishing than rewarding.
People should express their emotions openly and freely.	**Emotional Expression** 1 ② 3 4 5 6 7	People should not reveal their emotions, especially those that may reflect negatively on them or others or make others feel uncomfortable.
Money is extremely important and should be a major consideration in just about any decision you make.	**Money** 1 2 ③ 4 5 6 7	Money is relatively unimportant and should not enter into life's really important decisions, such as what relationship to enter or what career to pursue.

HOW DID YOU DO? This test was designed to help you explore the possible influence of your cultural beliefs and values on communication. If you visualize communication as involving choices, then your beliefs will influence the choices you make and thus how you communicate and how you listen and respond to the communications of others. For example, your beliefs and values about gender equality will influence the way in which you communicate with and about the opposite sex. Your group and individual orientation will influence how you perform in work teams and how you deal with your peers at school and at work. Your degree of hedonism will influence the kinds of communications you engage in, the books you read, and the television programs you watch. Your religious beliefs will influence the ethical system you follow in communicating. Review the entire list of characteristics and try to identify one specific way in which each characteristic influences your communication.

WHAT WILL YOU DO? Are you satisfied with your responses? If not, how might you get rid of your unproductive or unrealistic beliefs? What beliefs would you ideally like to substitute for these?

In your more immediate environment, consider the number of foreign students who come to the United States to continue their education. For the years 2002-2003, according to the Institute of International Education (www.parstimes.com/news/archive/2003/washfile028.html, accessed February 8, 2005) there were 586,323 international students studying in the United States. The number of students from the top 10 countries, along with the percentage of increase or decrease from the previous year, were:

- India, 74,603 (up 12 percent)
- China, 64,7575 (up 2 percent)
- South Korea, 51,519 (up 5 percent)
- Japan, 45,960 (down 2 percent)
- Taiwan, 28,017 (down 3 percent)
- Canada, 26,513 (unchanged)
- Mexico, 12,801 (up 2 percent)
- Turkey, 11,601 (down 4 percent)
- Indonesia, 10,432 (down 10 percent)
- Thailand, 9,982 (down 14 percent)

Students from the Middle East—especially from Saudi Arabia, Kuwait, and the United Arab Emirates—declined the most, although the absolute numbers were still quite high: from 38,545 during the previous year to 34,803 for 2002-2003.

As you can see from even these few figures, frequent intercultural communication is an inevitable part of college life today.

Cultural Sensitivity

As a people we've become increasingly sensitive to cultural differences. American society has moved from an *assimilationist perspective* (which holds that people should leave their native culture behind and adapt to their new culture) to a perspective that values *cultural diversity* (which holds that people should retain their native cultural ways). And, with some notable exceptions—hate speech, racism, sexism, homophobia, and classism come quickly to mind—we're more concerned with communicating respectfully and ultimately with developing a society where all cultures can coexist and enrich one another. At the same time, the ability to interact effectively with members of other cultures often translates into financial gain and increased employment opportunities and advancement prospects.

Economic Interdependency

Today most countries are economically dependent on one another. Our economic lives depend on our ability to communicate effectively across different cultures. Similarly, our political well-being depends in great part on that of other cultures. Political unrest in any part of the world—South Africa, eastern Europe, or the Middle East, to take a few examples—affects our security in the United States. So interdependent have nations become that a new phrase, "spaghetti bowl," has come into use to refer to "the interconnected and tangled economic relationships of a group of nations" (*New York Times*, December 24, 2006, Section 4, p. 4).

U.S. corporations, too, are becoming more and more interculturally oriented. Increasingly you see large and small corporations expanding into foreign countries. Manufacturing, media, information technology, and farming interests depend on foreign markets. Business opportunities, therefore, have an increasingly international dimension, making cultural awareness and intercultural communication competence essential skills for professional success.

Communication Technology

The rapid spread of communication technology has brought foreign and sometimes very different cultures right into our living rooms. News from foreign countries is commonplace. You see nightly—in vivid color—what is going on in remote countries. Technology has made intercultural communication easy, practical, and inevitable. Daily the media bombard you with evidence of racial tensions, religious disagreements, sexual bias, and all the other problems caused when intercultural communication fails. And, of course, the Internet has made intercultural communication as easy as writing a note on your computer. You can now communicate by e-mail just as easily with someone in Europe or Asia, for example, as with someone in another city or state.

Communication Competence

Communication competence is specific to a given culture; what proves effective in one culture may be ineffective in another. For example, in the United States corporate executives get down to business during the first several minutes of a meeting. In Japan, however, business executives interact socially for an extended period and try to find out something about one another. Thus, the communication principle influenced by U.S. culture would advise participants to get down to the meeting's agenda during the first five minutes. The principle influenced by Japanese culture would advise participants to avoid dealing with business until everyone has socialized sufficiently and feels well enough acquainted to begin negotiations. Each principle seems effective within its own culture and ineffective outside its own culture. For example, Asians often find that the values they have learned—values that discourage competitiveness and assertiveness—work against them in Western cultures that endorse competition and outspokenness (Cho, 2000).

© Bloomimage/CORBIS

The Aim of a Cultural Perspective

Because culture permeates all forms of communication, it is necessary to understand its influences if you are to understand how communication works and master its skills. Culture influences communications of all types (Moon, 1996). It influences what you say to yourself and how you talk with friends, lovers, and family in everyday conversation. It influences how you interact in groups and how much importance you place on the group versus the individual. It influences the topics you talk about and the strategies you use in communicating information or in persuading. And it influences how you use the media and the credibility you attribute to them.

A cultural emphasis helps distinguish what is *universal* (true for all people) from what is *relative* (true for people in one culture but not for people in other cultures) (Matsumoto, 1994). The principles for communicating information and for changing listeners' attitudes, for example, will vary from one culture to another. If you are to understand communication, then you need to know how its principles vary and how the principles must be qualified and adjusted on the basis of cultural differences.

And, of course, this cultural understanding is necessary to communicate effectively in a wide variety of intercultural situations. Success in communication—on your job and in your social life—will depend on your ability to communicate effectively with persons who are culturally different from yourself.

Cultural differences exist across the communication spectrum—from the way you use eye contact to the way you develop or dissolve a relationship (Chang & Holt, 1996). But these should not blind you to the great number of similarities that also exist among even the most widely separated cultures. Close interpersonal relationships, for example, are common in all cultures, though they may be entered into for very different reasons by members of different cultures. Further, when reading about cultural differences, remember that these are usually matters of degree. Thus, most cultures value honesty, but not all value it to the same degree.

An emphasis on cultural awareness does not imply that you should accept all cultural practices, or that all cultural practices are equal (Hatfield & Rapson, 1996). For example, cockfighting, foxhunting, and bullfighting are parts of the culture of some Latin American countries, England, and Spain, but you need not find these activities acceptable or equal to cultural practices in which animals are treated kindly. Further, a cultural emphasis does not imply that you have to accept or follow even the practices of your own culture. For example, even if the majority in your culture finds cockfighting acceptable, you need not agree with or follow the practice. Similarly, you can reject your culture's values and beliefs; its religion or political system; or its attitudes toward the homeless, the handicapped, or the culturally different. Of course, going against your culture's traditions and values is often very difficult. But it is important to realize that although culture influences you, it does not determine your values or behavior. Often, for example, personality factors (such as your degree of assertiveness, extroversion, or optimism) will prove more influential than culture (Hatfield & Rapson, 1996).

In sum, cultural beliefs exert powerful (often unconscious) influences on your communication. Becoming aware of these beliefs will help you deal more effectively with their influences on your communication interactions, especially when you are communicating with people holding widely different beliefs.

CULTURAL DIFFERENCES

For effective communication to take place in a global world, goodwill and good intensions are helpful—but they are not enough. If you're going to be effective, you need to know how cultures differ and how these differences influence communication. Research supports five major cultural distinctions that have an impact on communication. Cultures differ in terms of their (1) individualist or collectivist orientation, (2) emphasis on context (whether high or low), (3) power structure, (4) masculinity-femininity, and (5) tolerance for ambiguity. Each of these dimensions of difference has significant impact on all forms of communication (Hofstede, 1997; Hall & Hall, 1987; Gudykunst, 1994). Before reading about these dimensions, take the self-test on the next page; it will help you think about your own cultural orientations and will personalize the text discussion and make it more meaningful.

Individual and Collective Orientation

Cultures differ in the way in which they promote individualist and collectivist thinking and behaving. An **individualist culture** teaches members the importance of individual values such as power, achievement, hedonism, and stimulation. Examples include the cultures of the United States, Australia, United Kingdom, Netherlands, Canada, New Zealand, Italy, Belgium, Denmark, and Sweden (Hofstede, 1997; Singh & Pereira, 2005). A **collectivist culture** teaches members the importance of group values such as benevolence, tradition, and conformity. Examples of such cultures include Guatemala, Ecuador, Panama, Venezuela, Colombia, Indonesia, Pakistan, China, Costa Rica, and Peru (Hofstede, 1997; Singh & Pereira, 2005). Americans generally have a preference for individualist values; in contrast, many Asian cultures have a preference for collectivist values (Kapoor, Wolfe, & Blue, 1995; Hofstede, 1997).

One of the major differences between these two orientations is the extent to which an individual's goals or the group's goals are given greater importance. Of course, these goals are not mutually exclusive; you probably have both individualist and collectivist tendencies. For example, you may compete with other members of your basketball team for the most baskets or most valuable player award (and thus emphasize individual goals). At the same time, however, you will—in a game—act in a way that will benefit the entire team (and thus emphasize group

goals). In actual practice, both individual and collective tendencies will help you and your team each achieve your goals. Yet most people and most cultures have a dominant orientation; they're more individually oriented or more collectively oriented in most situations, most of the time. In an individualist culture members are responsible for themselves and perhaps their immediate family. In a collectivist culture members are responsible for the entire group.

In some instances these tendencies may come into conflict. For example, do you shoot for the basket and try to raise your own individual score, or do you pass the ball to another player who is better positioned to score and thus benefit your team? You make this distinction in popular talk when you call someone a team player (collectivist orientation) or an individual player (individualist orientation).

Success, in an individualist culture, is measured by the extent to which you surpass other members of your group; you take pride in standing out from the crowd. And your heroes—in the media, for example—are likely to be those who are unique and who stand apart. In a collectivist culture success is measured by your contribution to the achievements of the group as a whole; you take pride in your similarity to other members of your group. Your heroes are more likely to be team players who don't stand out from the rest of the group's members.

In an individualist culture you're responsible to your own conscience, and responsibility is largely an individual matter; in a collectivist culture you're responsible to the rules of the social group, and responsibility for an accomplishment or a failure is shared by all members. Competition is fostered in individualist cultures, whereas cooperation is promoted in collectivist cultures. In small group settings in an individualist culture, you may compete for leadership; there will likely be a very clear distinction between leaders and members. In a collectivist culture leadership will often be shared and rotated; there will likely be little distinction between leader and members. These orientations also influence the kinds of communication members consider appropriate in an organizational context. For example, individualist organization members favor clarity and directness; in contrast, collectivists favor "face-saving" and the avoidance of hurting others or arousing negative evaluations (Kim & Sharkey, 1995).

Distinctions between in-group members and out-group members are extremely important in collectivist cultures. In individualistic cultures, which prize each person's individuality, the distinction is likely to be less important.

Today the nightly news brings stories of suicide bombers—people who will give up their own life in support of a cause in which they believe. In individualistic cultures this is something difficult to understand;

it's so foreign to everything such cultures teach and value. But for those from collectivist cultures, the larger social group is more important than the individual; giving up an individual life for the life of the group is entirely consistent with their cultural orientation.

TEST YOURSELF

What's Your Cultural Orientation?

For each of the items below, select either *a* or *b*. In some cases, you may feel that neither *a* nor *b* describes yourself accurately; in these cases simply select the one that is closer to your feeling. As you'll see when you read this next section, these are not *either/or* preferences, but *more-or-less* preferences.

1. Success, to my way of thinking, is better measured by
   a. the extent to which I surpass others.
   b. my contribution to the group effort.

2. My heroes are generally
   a. people who stand out from the crowd.
   b. team players.

3. Of the following values, the ones I consider more important are:
   a. achievement, stimulation, enjoyment.
   b. tradition, benevolence, conformity.

4. Generally, in my business transactions, I feel comfortable
   a. relying on oral agreements.
   b. relying on written agreements.

5. If I were a manager, I would likely
   a. reprimand a worker in public if the occasion warranted.
   b. always reprimand in private regardless of the situation.

6. In communicating, it's generally more important to be
   a. polite rather than accurate or direct.
   b. accurate and direct rather than polite.

7. I'd enjoy working in most groups where
   a. there is little distinction between leaders and members.
   b. there is a clearly defined leader.

8. As a student (and if I feel well informed) I'd feel
   a. comfortable challenging a professor.
   b. uncomfortable challenging a professor.

9. In choosing a life partner or even close friends, I'd feel more comfortable
   a. with just about anyone, not necessarily one from my own culture and class.
   b. with those from my own culture and class.

10. Of the following characteristics, the ones I value more highly are
    a. aggressiveness, material success, and strength.
    b. modesty, tenderness, and quality of life.

11. In a conflict situation, I'd be more likely to
    a. confront conflicts directly and seek to win.
    b. confront conflicts with the aim of compromise.

12. If I were a manager of an organization I would stress
    a. competition and aggressiveness.
    b. worker satisfaction.

13. Generally, I'm
    a. comfortable with ambiguity and uncertainty.
    b. uncomfortable with ambiguity and uncertainty.

14. As a student, I'm more comfortable with assignments in which
    a. there is freedom for interpretation.
    b. there are clearly defined instructions.

15. Generally, when approaching an undertaking with which I've had no experience, I'd feel
    a. comfortable.
    b. uncomfortable.

HOW DID YOU DO?

- Items 1–3 refer to the **individualist–collectivist orientation; a** responses indicate an individualist orientation, and **b** responses indicate a collectivist orientation.

- Items 4–6 refer to the **high- and low-context** characteristics; **a** responses indicate a high-context focus, and **b** responses indicate a low-context focus.

- Items 7–9 refer to the **power distance** dimension; **a** responses indicate greater comfort with a low power distance, and **b** responses indicate comfort with a high power distance.

- Items 10–12 refer to the **masculine–feminine** dimen-sion; **a** responses indicate a masculine orienta-tion; **b** responses, a feminine orientation.

- Items 13–15 refer to the **tolerance for ambiguity** or uncertainty; **a** responses indicate high tolerance, and **b** responses indicate a low tolerance.

WHAT WILL YOU DO? Understanding your preferences in a wide variety of situations as culturally influenced (at least in part) is a first step to controlling them and to changing them should you wish to do so. This understanding also helps you modify your behavior as appropriate for greater effectiveness in certain situations. The remaining discussion in this section further explains these orientations and their implications.

Theory and Research — Understanding — Language and Thought

The linguistic relativity hypothesis claims (1) that the language you speak influences the thoughts you have, and (2) that therefore, people speaking widely differing languages will see the world differently and will think differently.

Theory and research, however, have not been able to find much support for this claim. A more modified hypothesis currently seems supported: The language you speak helps you to talk about what you see and perhaps to highlight what you see. For example, if you speak a language that is rich in color terms (English is a good example), you will find it easier to talk about nuances of color than will someone from a culture that has fewer color terms (some cultures, for example, distinguish only two, three, or four parts of the color spectrum). But this doesn't mean that people see the world differently, only that their language helps (or doesn't help) them to talk about certain variations in the world and may make it easier (or more difficult) for them to focus their thinking on such variations.

Nor does it mean that people speaking widely differing languages are doomed to misunderstand one another. Translation enables you to understand a great deal of the meaning in any foreign language message. And, of course, you have your communication skills; you can ask for clarification, for additional examples, for restatement. You can listen actively, give feedforward and feedback, use perception checking, and employ a host of other skills you'll encounter throughout this course.

Language differences don't make for very important differences in perception or thought. Difficulties in intercultural understanding are due more often to ineffective communication than to differences in languages.

Working with Theories and Research

Based on your own experience, how influential do you find language differences to be in perception and thought? Can you recall any misunderstandings that might be attributed to a particular language's leading its speakers to see or interpret things differently?

High- and Low-Context Cultures

Cultures also differ in the extent to which information is made explicit, on the one hand, or is assumed to be in the context or in the persons communicating, on the other. In a **high-context culture** much of the information in communication is in the context or in the person—for example, information that was shared through previous communications, through assumptions about each other, and through shared experiences. The information is thus known by all participants but it is not explicitly stated in the verbal message.

In a **low-context culture** most of the information is explicitly stated in the verbal message. In formal transactions it will be stated in written (or contract) form.

To appreciate the distinction between high and low context, consider giving directions:

High-Context Situation

A person who knows the neighborhood asks you: "Where's the voter registration center?"

You answer: "Next to the laundromat on Main Street" or "The corner of Albany and Elm."

Low-Context Situation

A newcomer to your city asks you: "Where's the voter registration center?"

You answer: "Make a left at the stop sign. Then go two blocks and turn right. The office is next to a wash-and-dry service called Green's Laundromat."

With someone who knows the neighborhood (a high-context situation), you can assume the person knows local landmarks (like the laundromat). With a newcomer (a low-context situation), you cannot assume the person shares any information with you. So you have to use directions that a stranger will understand; you have to be more explicit and include more information than you would in a high-context situation, where you can assume that you have neighborhood information in common.

High-context cultures are also collectivist cultures (Gudykunst, Ting-Toomey, & Chua, 1988; Gudykunst & Kim, 1992). These cultures (Japanese, Arabic, Latin American, Thai, Korean, Apache, and Mexican are examples) place great emphasis on personal relationships and oral agreements (Victor, 1992). Low-context cultures are also individualist cultures. These cultures (German, Swedish, Norwegian, and American are examples) place less emphasis on personal relationships and more emphasis on verbalized, explicit explanation—for example, on written contracts in business transactions.

Members of high-context cultures spend lots of time getting to know one another interpersonally and socially before any important transactions take place. Because of this prior personal knowledge, a great deal of information is shared by the members and therefore does not have to be explicitly stated. Members of low-context cultures spend a great deal less time getting to know one another and hence don't have that shared knowledge. As a result everything has to be stated explicitly.

A frequent source of intercultural misunderstanding that can be traced to the distinction between high- and low-context cultures can be seen in **face-saving** (Hall & Hall, 1987). People in high-context cultures place a great deal more emphasis on face-saving. For example, they're more likely to avoid argument for fear of causing others to lose face, whereas people in low-context cultures (with their individualist orientation) will use argument to win a point. Similarly, in high-context cultures criticism should take place only in private. Low-context cultures may not make this public-private distinction. Low-context managers who criticize high-context workers in public will find that their criticism causes interpersonal problems—and does little to resolve the difficulty that led to the criticism in the first place (Victor, 1992).

Members of high-context cultures are reluctant to say no for fear of offending and causing the person to lose face. So, for example, it's necessary to understand when the Japanese executive's yes means yes and when it means no. The difference is not in the words used but in the way in which they're used. It's easy to see how the low-context individual may interpret this reluctance to be direct—to say no when you mean no—as a weakness or as an unwillingness to confront reality.

Power Distances

In some cultures power is concentrated in the hands of a few, and there's a great difference between the power held by these people and the power of the ordinary citizen. These are called **high-power-distance cultures**; examples are Malaysia, Panama, Guatemala, the Philippines, Venezuela, Mexico, China, the Arab world, Indonesia, and Ecuador (Hofstede, 1997; Singh & Pereira, 2005). In **low-power-distance cultures** power is more evenly distributed throughout the citizenry; examples include Austria, Israel, Denmark, New Zealand, Ireland, Norway, Sweden, Finland, Switzerland, and Costa Rica (Hofstede, 1997; Singh & Pereira, 2005). These differences impact communication in numerous ways. For example, in high-power-distance cultures there's a great power distance between students and teachers; students are expected to be modest, polite, and totally respectful. In low-power-distance cultures (and you can see this clearly in U.S. college classrooms) students are expected to demonstrate their knowledge and command of the subject matter, participate in discussions with the teacher, and even challenge the teacher—something many high-power-distance culture members wouldn't even think of doing.

Friendship and dating relationships also will be influenced by the power distance between groups (Andersen, 1991). In India, for example, such relationships are expected to take place within your cultural class. In Sweden a person is expected to select friends and romantic partners on the basis not of class or culture but of individual factors such as personality, appearance, and the like.

In low-power-distance cultures you're expected to confront a friend, partner, or supervisor assertively; there is in these cultures a general feeling of equality that is consistent with assertive behavior (Borden, 1991). In high-power-distance cultures, direct confrontation and assertiveness may be viewed negatively, especially if directed at a superior.

Consider, for example, the war in Iraq. Put in terms of power distance, the United States and some allies are trying to change Iraq from a high-power-distance culture, in which those few in authority made the decisions for the many, to a low-power-distance culture, in which people are relatively equal (that is, a democracy). Yet even in democracies where everyone is equal under the law (or should be), there are still great power distances between those in authority—the employers, the police, the politicians—and the ordinary citizen, as there are between those who are rich and those who are poor.

Masculine and Feminine Cultures

Especially important for self-concept is the culture's attitude about gender roles; that is, about how a man or woman should act. In fact, a popular classification of cultures is in terms of their masculinity and femininity (Hofstede, 1997, 1998). When denoting cultural orientations, the terms *masculine* and *feminine*, and used by G. Hofstede (1997) to describe this cultural difference, should be taken not as perpetuating stereotypes but as reflecting some of the commonly held assumptions of a sizable number of people throughout the world. In a highly **masculine culture**, people value male aggressiveness, material success, and strength. Women, on the other hand, are valued for their modesty, focus on the quality of life, and tenderness. A highly **feminine culture** values modesty, concern for relationships and the quality of life, and tenderness in both men and women. On the basis of Hofstede's (1997, 1998) research, the 10 countries with the highest masculinity score are (beginning with the highest) Japan, Austria, Venezuela, Italy, Switzerland, Mexico, Ireland, Jamaica, Great Britain, and Germany. The 10 countries with the highest femininity score are (beginning with the highest) Sweden, Norway, the Netherlands, Denmark, Costa Rica, Yugoslavia, Finland, Chile, Portugal, and Thailand. Of the 53 countries ranked, the United States ranks 15th most masculine.

Masculine cultures emphasize success and so socialize their members to be assertive, ambitious, and competitive. For example, members of masculine cultures are more likely to confront conflicts directly and to fight out any differences competitively; they're more likely to emphasize win–lose conflict strategies. Feminine cultures emphasize the quality of life and so socialize their members to be modest and to highlight close interpersonal relationships. Feminine cultures, for example, are more likely to utilize compromise and

negotiation in resolving conflicts; they're more likely to seek win–win solutions.

Similarly, organizations can be viewed as masculine or feminine. Masculine organizations emphasize competitiveness and aggressiveness. They stress the bottom line and reward their workers on the basis of their contributions to the organization. Feminine organizations are less competitive and less aggressive. They emphasize worker satisfaction and reward their workers on the basis of need; those who have large families, for example, may get better raises than single people, even if they haven't contributed as much to the organization.

Try exploring your own cultural attitudes and ways of looking at things with the accompanying Building Communication Skills box below.

High-Ambiguity-Tolerant and Low-Ambiguity-Tolerant Cultures

Levels of **ambiguity tolerance** vary widely among cultures. In some cultures people do little to avoid uncertainty, and they have little anxiety about not knowing what will happen next. In some other cultures, however, uncertainty is strongly avoided and there is much anxiety about uncertainty.

High-Ambiguity-Tolerant Cultures

Members of high-ambiguity-tolerant cultures don't feel threatened by unknown situations; uncertainty is a normal part of life, and people accept it as it

---

Building Communication Skills   Exploring Cultural Attitudes

One of the best ways to appreciate the influence of culture on communication is to consider the attitudes people have about central aspects of culture. In a group of five or six—try for as culturally diverse a group as you can find—discuss how you think most of the students at your school feel (not how you feel) about each of the following. Use a five-point scale: 5 = most students strongly agree; 4 = most students agree; 3 = students are relatively neutral; 2 = most students disagree; 1 = most students strongly disagree.

_____ 1. Most feminists are just too sensitive about sexism.

_____ 2. Both females and males are victims of sexism.

_____ 3. Gay rights means gay men and lesbians demanding special privileges.

_____ 4. All men and women have a choice to be homosexual or not.

_____ 5. Racism isn't going to end overnight, so minorities need to be patient.

_____ 6. Minorities have the same opportunity as whites to succeed in our society.

Attitudes strongly influence communication. Understanding your cultural attitudes is prerequisite to effective intercultural communication.

Source: These statements were taken from the Human Relations Attitude Inventory (Koppelman, with Goodhart, 2005). The authors note that this inventory is based on an inventory developed by Flavio Vega.

comes. Examples of such low-anxiety cultures include Singapore, Jamaica, Denmark, Sweden, Hong Kong, Ireland, Great Britain, Malaysia, India, the Philippines, and the United States.

Because high-ambiguity-tolerant cultures are comfortable with ambiguity and uncertainty, they minimize the importance of rules governing communication and relationships (Hofstede, 1997; Lustig & Koester, 2006). People in these cultures readily tolerate individuals who don't follow the same rules as the cultural majority, and may even encourage different approaches and perspectives.

Students from high-ambiguity-tolerant cultures appreciate freedom in education and prefer vague assignments without specific timetables. These students want to be rewarded for creativity and readily accept an instructor's lack of knowledge.

Low-Ambiguity-Tolerant Cultures

Members of low-ambiguity-tolerant cultures do much to avoid uncertainty and have a great deal of anxiety about not knowing what will happen next; they see uncertainty as threatening and as something that must be counteracted. Examples of such low-ambiguity-tolerant cultures include Greece, Portugal, Guatemala, Uruguay, Belgium, El Salvador, Japan, Yugoslavia, Peru, France, Chile, Spain, and Costa Rica (Hofstede, 1997).

Low-ambiguity-tolerant cultures create very clear-cut rules for communication that must not be broken. For example, students from strong-uncertainty-avoidance cultures prefer highly structured experiences with little ambiguity; they prefer specific objectives, detailed instructions, and definite timetables. An assignment to write a term paper on "anything" would be cause for alarm; it would not be clear or specific enough. These students expect to be judged on the basis of the right answers and expect the instructor to have all the answers all the time (Hofstede, 1997).

With these five cultural distinctions in mind, let's now examine intercultural communication.

MEDIA WATCH

CULTURAL IMPERIALISM

The theory of *cultural imperialism* affords an interesting perspective on the influence of media, especially the impact of Western media on the cultures of developing countries (Becker & Roberts, 1992; DeZoysa & Newman, 2002). The theory argues that media from developed countries such as those of North America and western Europe dominate the cultures of countries importing such media. This cultural dominance is also seen in computer communication, in which the United States and the English language dominate.

Media products from the United States emphasize the country's dominant attitudes and values—for example, the preference for competition, the encouragement of individual expression, the promotion of capitalism and democracy, and the quest for financial success. An extreme form of the theory of cultural imperialism argues that the attitudes and values of the dominant media culture will eventually become the attitudes and values of the rest of the world.

Television programs, films, and music from the United States and western Europe are so popular and so in demand in developing countries that they may actually inhibit the growth of the native culture's own talent. So, for example, instead of pursuing their own vision by creating an original television drama or film, native writers in developing countries may find it easier to work as translators for products from more developed countries. And native promoters may find it more lucrative to sell, say, U.S. rock groups' CDs than to cultivate native talent. Similarly, the popularity of U.S. and western European media may also lead artists in developing countries to imitate Western cultural artifacts rather than developing their own styles—styles more consistent with their native culture. From another perspective, however, some people might argue that media products from the United States are superior to those produced elsewhere and hence serve as a standard for quality work throughout the world. Also, it might be argued that such products introduce new trends and perspectives and hence enrich the importing cultures.

Increasing Media Literacy

What do you think of the influence that media from the United States and western Europe are having on native cultures throughout the world? How do you evaluate this trend? Do you see advantages? How does this influence what you believe and feel about cultures other than your own?

INTERCULTURAL COMMUNICATION

Regardless of your own cultural background, you will surely come into close contact with people from a variety of other cultures—people who speak different languages, eat different foods, practice different religions, and approach work and relationships in very different ways. It doesn't matter whether you're a longtime resident of a country or a newly arrived immigrant: You are or you soon will be living, going to school, working, and forming relationships with people who are from very different cultures. Your day-to-day experiences are sure to become increasingly intercultural. Here we look first at the nature and forms of intercultural communication and second at guidelines for improving your own intercultural interactions.

The Nature and Forms of Intercultural Communication

The term *intercultural communication* refers to communication between persons who have different cultural beliefs, values, or ways of behaving. The model in Figure 1 illustrates this concept. The larger circles represent the culture of the individual communicators. The inner circles symbolize the communicators (the sources–receivers). In this model each communicator is a member of a different culture. In some instances, the cultural differences are relatively slight—say, between persons from Toronto and New York. In other instances, the cultural differences are great—say, between a farmer from Borneo and a surgeon in Germany.

All messages originate from within a specific and unique cultural context, and that context influences the messages' content and form. You communicate as you do largely as a result of your culture. Culture (along with the processes of enculturation and acculturation) influences every aspect of your communication experience.

The following types of communication may all be considered "intercultural" and, more important, subject to the varied barriers and gateways to effective communication identified in this unit:

■ Communication between people of different national cultures—for example, between Chinese and Portuguese individuals, or between French and Norwegian.

■ Communication between people of different races (sometimes called *interracial communication*)—for example, between African Americans and Asian Americans.

© Bernard Lang/Getty Images

DATING AN ETHNOCENTRIC

You've been dating this wonderful person for the last few months but increasingly are discovering that your "ideal" partner is extremely ethnocentric and sees little value in other religions, other races, other nationalities, in short, a bigot. You want to educate your possible life partner.

WHAT DO YOU SAY?
In what context?

■ Communication between people of different ethnic groups (sometimes called *interethnic communication*)—for example, between Italian Americans and German Americans.

■ Communication between people of different religions—for example, between Roman Catholics and Episcopalians, or between Muslims and Jews.

■ Communication between nations (sometimes called *international communication*)—for example, between the United States and Argentina, or between China and Italy.

■ Communication between smaller cultures existing within the larger culture—for example, between doctors and patients, or between research scientists and the general public.

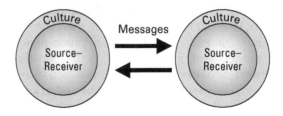

FIGURE 1   A Model of Intercultural Communication

This basic model of intercultural communication is designed to illustrate that culture is a part of every communication transaction. What other ways can you think of to illustrate the process of intercultural communication?

47

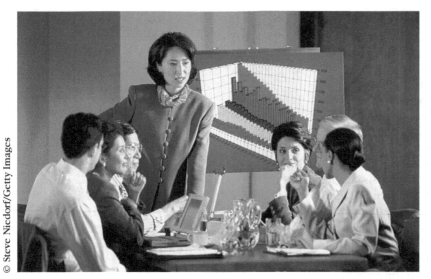

GETTING YOUR FOOT OUT OF YOUR MOUTH

At work you tell a homophobic joke only to discover that it was resented and clearly violated the organizational norms for polite and unbiased talk. You want to make this situation a little less awkward and potentially damaging to your work experience.

WHAT DO YOU SAY?

■ Communication between a smaller culture and the dominant culture—for example, between homosexuals and heterosexuals, or between older people and the younger majority.

■ Communication between genders—between men and women. Because gender roles are largely learned through culture, it seems useful to consider male-female communication as intercultural (Tannen, 1994a, b; Payne, 2001). Further, you can view male-female communication as cross-cultural because of the numerous differences in the way men and women speak and listen (Eckstein & Goldman, 2001).

Improving Intercultural Communication

Murphy's law ("If anything can go wrong, it will") is especially applicable to intercultural communication. Intercultural communication is, of course, subject to all the same barriers and problems as are the other forms of communication discussed throughout this text. In this section, however, we'll consider some suggestions designed to counteract the barriers that are unique to intercultural communications (Barna, 1997; Ruben, 1985; Spitzberg, 1991).

Above all, intercultural communication depends on the cultural sensitivity of both individuals. **Cultural sensitivity** is an attitude and way of behaving in which you're aware of and acknowledge cultural differences. Cultural sensitivity is crucial on a global scale, as in efforts toward world peace and economic growth; it's also essential for effective interpersonal communication and for general success in life (Franklin & Mizell, 1995). Without cultural sensitivity there can be no effective interpersonal communication between people

who are different in gender or race or nationality or affectional orientation. So be mindful of the cultural differences between yourself and the other person. For example, the close physical distance that is normal in Arab cultures may prove too familiar or too intrusive in much of the United States and northern Europe. The empathy that most Americans welcome may be uncomfortable for most Koreans (Yun, 1976).

The following guidelines can help you achieve cultural sensitivity: (1) Prepare yourself, (2) reduce your ethnocentrism; (3) confront your stereotypes; (4) be mindful; (5) avoid overattribution; (6) recognize differences; and (7) adjust your communication. We'll take a look at each guideline in turn.

Prepare Yourself

There's no better preparation for intercultural communication than learning about the other culture. Fortunately, there are numerous sources to draw on. View a video or film that presents a realistic view of the culture. Read what members of the culture as well as "outsiders" write about the culture. Scan magazines and websites from the culture. Talk with members of the culture. Chat in international chat rooms. Read blogs from members of the culture. Read materials addressed to people who need to communicate with those from other cultures. The easiest way to do this is to search the online bookstores (for example, Barnes and Noble at **www.bn. com**, Borders at **www.borders.com**, and Amazon at **www.Amazon.com**) for such keywords as *culture, international,* and *foreign travel.*

Another part of this preparation is to recognize and face fears that may stand in the way of effective intercultural communication (Gudykunst, 1994; Stephan & Stephan, 1985). For example, you may

ASK THE RESEARCHER

Culture Talk

I'm going to work abroad in a firm where most of the people are members of a culture very different from mine. I know culture is important; what I don't know is when it's appropriate to discuss cultural differences and when it's not. Any general guidelines I could follow? I don't want to do anything stupid, at least not during my first few weeks.

Your recognizing that culture is important is the first sign that you'll do well abroad. Intercultural communication as an academic discipline developed because of our (Americans') oblivion to other people's cultures, even as guests in their country.

We earned the "ugly American" title because we assumed that American culture was superior to others, and that despite where we visited or worked, people from the host culture had to acquiesce to our desires. Before you move to a foreign country, learn as much about its culture and people as you can; it will help you accept, appreciate, and respect difference.

Talking about cultural difference is inevitable. It's how you do it. When you notice difference, ask, respectfully, about it; for example, "I noticed that your head is always covered, I've never seen your hair. Is there some cultural or religious reason for it?" Instead of, "Why don't you take that scarf off your head, I get tired of looking at it."

For further information: Calloway-Thomas, C., Cooper, P. J., & Blake, C. (1999). *Intercultural communication: Roots and routes.* Boston: Allyn & Bacon and Samovar, L. A., & Porter, R. E. (2003). *Intercultural communication: A reader* (10th ed.). Belmont, CA: Wadsworth.

Melbourne S. Cummings (Ph.D., University of California, Los Angeles) is a professor of communication at Howard University and teaches courses in African American communication, nonverbal communication, and intercultural communication.

fear for your self-esteem. You may be anxious about your ability to control the intercultural situation, or you may worry about your own level of discomfort. You may fear saying something that will be considered politically incorrect or culturally insensitive and thereby losing face.

You may fear that you'll be taken advantage of by a member of the other culture. Depending on your own stereotypes, you may fear being lied to, financially duped, or made fun of.

You may fear that members of this other group will react to you negatively. You may fear, for example, that they will not like you or will disapprove of your attitudes or beliefs or perhaps even reject you as a person. Conversely, you may fear negative reactions from members of your own group. They might, for example, disapprove of your socializing with culturally different people.

Some fears, of course, are reasonable. In many cases, however, fears are groundless. Either way, you need to assess your concerns logically and weigh their consequences carefully. Then you'll be able to make informed choices about your communications.

Reduce Ethnocentrism

As you learn your culture's ways, you develop an **ethnic identity**—that is, a commitment to the beliefs and philosophy of your culture (Chung & Ting-Toomey, 1999). The degree to which you identify with your cultural group can be measured by your responses to such questions as the following (from Ting-Toomey, 1981). Using a scale ranging from 1 (strongly disagree) to 5 (strongly agree), indicate how true about you the following statements are:

- I am increasing my involvement in activities with my ethnic group.
- I involve myself in causes that will help members of my ethnic group.
- It feels natural being part of my ethnic group.
- I have spent time trying to find out more about my own ethnic group.
- I am happy to be a member of my ethnic group.
- I have a strong sense of belonging to my ethnic group.
- I often talk to other members of my group to learn more about my ethnic culture.

High scores (5s and 4s) indicate a strong commitment to your culture's values and beliefs; low numbers (1s and 2s) indicate a relatively weak commitment.

A different type of cultural identification is ethnocentrism. Before reading about this important concept, examine your own cultural thinking by taking the self-test below.

TEST YOURSELF

How Ethnocentric Are You?

Here are 18 statements representing your beliefs about your culture. For each statement indicate how much you agree or disagree, using the following scale: Strongly agree = 5, agree = 4, neither agree nor disagree = 3, disagree = 2, strongly disagree = 1.

_____ 1. Most cultures are backward compared to my culture.

_____ 2. My culture should be the role model for other cultures.

_____ 3. Lifestyles in other cultures are just as valid as those in my culture.

_____ 4. Other cultures should try to be like my culture.

_____ 5. I'm not interested in the values and customs of other cultures.

_____ 6. People in my culture could learn a lot from people in other cultures.

_____ 7. Most people from other cultures just don't know what's good for them.

_____ 8. I have little respect for the values and customs of other cultures.

_____ 9. Most people would be happier if they lived like people in my culture.

_____ 10. People in my culture have just about the best lifestyles of anywhere.

_____ 11. Lifestyles in other cultures are not as valid as those in my culture.

_____ 12. I'm very interested in the values and customs of other cultures.

_____ 13. I respect the values and customs of other cultures.

_____ 14. I do not cooperate with people who are different.

_____ 15. I do not trust people who are different.

_____ 16. I dislike interacting with people from different cultures.

_____ 17. Other cultures are smart to look up to my culture.

_____ 18. People from other cultures act strange and unusual when they come into my culture.

HOW DID YOU DO? This test was presented to give you the opportunity to examine some of your own cultural beliefs, particularly those cultural beliefs that contribute to ethnocentrism. The person who is low in ethnocentrism would have high scores (4s and 5s) for items 3, 6, 12, and 13, and low scores (1s and 2s) for the other items. The person who is high in ethnocentrism would have low scores for items 3, 6, 12, and 13, and high scores for the other items.

WHAT WILL YOU DO? Use this test to bring to consciousness your own cultural beliefs so that you can examine those beliefs logically and objectively. Ask yourself if your beliefs are productive; will they help you achieve your professional and social goals? Or are they counterproductive; will they actually hinder your achieving your goals?

Source: This test is taken from James W. Neuliep, Michelle Chaudoir, and James C. McCroskey (2001). A cross-cultural comparison of ethnocentrism among Japanese and United States college students. *Communication Research Reports*, 18 (Spring), 137-146. Used with permission of Eastern Communication Association.

As you've probably gathered from taking this test, **ethnocentrism** is the tendency to see others and their behaviors through your own cultural filters, often as distortions of your own behaviors. It's the tendency to evaluate the values, beliefs, and behaviors of your own culture as more positive, superior, logical, and natural than those of other cultures. So although ethnocentrism may give you pride in your own culture and its achievements and may encourage you to sacrifice for that culture, it also may lead you to see other cultures as inferior and may foster an unwillingness to profit from the contributions of other cultures. For example, recent research shows a "substantial relationship" between ethnocentrism and homophobia (Wrench & McCroskey, 2003).

Ethnocentrism exists on a continuum. People are not either ethnocentric or not ethnocentric; rather, most are somewhere between these polar opposites. And, of course, your degree of ethnocentrism varies depending on the group on which you focus. For example, if you're Greek American, you may have a low degree of ethnocentrism when dealing with Italian Americans, but a high degree when dealing with Turkish Americans or Japanese Americans. Your degree of ethnocentrism (and we're all ethnocentric to at least some degree) will influence your communication in all its forms, an influence illustrated throughout this text.

Confront Stereotypes

Stereotypes, especially when they operate below the level of conscious awareness, can create serious communication problems. Originally, *stereotype* was a printing term that referred to the plate that printed the same image over and over. A sociological or psychological **stereotype** is a fixed impression of a group of people. Everyone has attitudinal stereotypes—of national groups, religious groups, or racial groups, or perhaps of criminals, prostitutes, teachers, or plumbers. Ask yourself, for example, if you have any stereotypes of, say, bodybuilders, the opposite sex, a racial group different from your own, members of a religion very different from your own, hard drug users, or college professors. It is very likely that you have stereotypes of several or perhaps all of these groups. Although we often think of stereotypes as negative ("They're lazy, dirty, and only interested in getting high"), they may also be positive ("They're smart, hardworking, and extremely loyal").

If you have these fixed impressions, you might, upon meeting a member of a particular group, see that person primarily as a member of that group. Initially, a stereotype may provide you with some helpful orientation. However, it creates problems when you apply to a person all the characteristics you assign to members of that person's group without examining the unique individual. If you meet a politician, for example, you may tend to apply to the person a series of stereotypical "politician" images. To complicate matters further, you may see in the person's behavior the manifestation of various characteristics that you would not see if you did not know that this person was a politician. In online communication, because there are few visual and auditory cues, it's not surprising to find that people form impressions of their online communication partner with a heavy reliance on stereotypes (Jacobson, 1999).

Consider another kind of stereotype: You're driving along a dark road and are stopped at a stop sign. A car pulls up beside you and three teenagers jump out and rap on your window. There may be a variety of reasons for this: They may need help, they may want to ask directions, or they may be planning a carjacking. Your self-protective stereotype may help you decide on "carjacking" and may lead you to pull away and into the safety of a busy service station. In doing that, of course, you may have escaped being carjacked, or you may have failed to help innocent people who needed your help.

Stereotyping can lead to two major barriers. First, you will fail to appreciate the multifaceted nature of all people and all groups. The tendency to group a person into a class and to respond to that person primarily as a member of that class can lead you to perceive that a person possesses those qualities

(usually negative) that you believe characterize the group to which he or she belongs. For example, consider your stereotype of an avid computer user. Very likely it's quite different from the research findings—which show that such users are as often female as male and are as sociable, popular, and self-assured as their peers who are not into heavy computer use (Schott & Selwyn, 2000).

Second, stereotyping also can lead you to ignore the unique characteristics of an individual; you therefore fail to benefit from the special contributions each person can bring to an encounter.

Increase Mindfulness

Being mindful rather than mindless is generally helpful in intercultural communication situations (Burgoon, Berger, & Waldron, 2000). When you're in a mindless state, you behave on the basis of assumptions that would not normally pass intellectual scrutiny. For example, you know that cancer is not contagious, and yet you may still avoid touching cancer patients. You know that people who are blind generally don't have hearing problems, yet you may use a louder voice when talking to persons without sight. When the discrepancies between behaviors and available evidence are pointed out and your mindful state is awakened, you quickly realize that these behaviors are not logical or realistic.

You can look at this textbook and your course in human communication as means of awakening your mindful state about the way you engage in interpersonal, group, and public communication. After completing this course, you should be much more mindful and much less mindless about all your communication behavior.

Avoid Overattribution

Overattribution is the tendency to attribute too much of a person's behavior or attitudes to one of that person's characteristics (she thinks that way because she's a woman; he believes that because he was raised as a Catholic). In intercultural communication situations, overattribution appears in two ways. First, it's the tendency to see too much of what a person believes or does as caused by the person's cultural identification. Second, it's the tendency to see a person as a spokesperson for his or her particular culture—to assume that because a person is, say, African American, he or she is therefore knowledgeable about the entire African American experience; or that the person's thoughts are always focused on African American issues. People's ways of thinking and ways of behaving are influenced by a wide variety of factors; culture is just one of them.

REFLECTIONS ON ETHICS

Culture and Ethics

Throughout history there have been numerous cultural practices that most people today would judge unethical and might well wish to make illegal. Sacrificing virgins to the gods and sending children to fight wars are obvious examples. And even today there are practices woven deep into the fabric of different cultures that many Americans would find unethical. Consider a few examples:

- Some cultures support bronco-riding events at which the bull's testicles are tied so that it will experience pain and try to throw off the rider.

- Some cultures support female circumcision, whereby part or all of a young girl's genitals are surgically altered so that she can never experience sexual intercourse without extreme pain, a practice designed to keep her a virgin until marriage.

- Some cultures support the practice of wearing fur. In some cases this means catching wild animals in extremely painful traps; in others it involves raising captive animals so they can be killed when their pelts are worth the most money.

Ethical Choice Point

Imagine that you're talking with a group of work colleagues about cultural differences and diversity. During the discussion one or another of your colleagues expresses approval of each of the above practices, arguing that each culture has a right to its own practices and beliefs and that no one has the right to object to cultural traditions. Given your own beliefs about these issues and about cultural diversity in general, what ethical obligations do you have to respond? What would you say?

Recognize Differences

To communicate interculturally you need to recognize the differences between yourself and people from other cultures, the differences within the other cultural group, and the numerous differences in meaning.

Differences between Yourself and the Culturally Different.

A common barrier to intercultural communication occurs when you assume that similarities exist and that differences do not. This is especially true of values, attitudes, and beliefs. You might easily accept different hairstyles, clothing, and foods. In basic values and beliefs, however, you may assume that deep down all people are really alike. They aren't. When you assume similarities and ignore differences, you'll fail to notice important distinctions and when communicating will convey to others that your ways are the right ways and that their ways are not important to you. Consider this example. An American invites a Filipino coworker to dinner. The Filipino politely refuses. The American is hurt and feels that the Filipino does not want to be friendly. The Filipino is hurt and concludes that the invitation was not extended sincerely. Here, it seems, both the American and the Filipino assume that their customs for inviting people to dinner are the same when, in fact, they aren't. A Filipino expects to be invited several times before accepting a dinner invitation. When an invitation is given only once, it's viewed as insincere.

Here's another example. An American college student hears the news that her favorite uncle has died. She bites her lip, pulls herself up, and politely excuses herself from the group of foreign students with whom she is having dinner. The Russian thinks: "How unfriendly." The Italian thinks: "How insincere." The Brazilian thinks: "How unconcerned." To many Americans, it's a sign of bravery to endure pain (physical or emotional) in silence and without any outward show of emotion. To members of other groups, such silence is often interpreted negatively to mean that the individual does not consider them friends who can share such sorrow. In other cultures, people are expected to reveal to friends how they feel.

Differences within the Culturally Different Group.

Within every cultural group there are vast and important differences. As all Americans are not alike, neither are all Indonesians, Greeks, Mexicans, and so on. When you ignore these differences—when you assume that all persons covered by the same label (in this case a national or ethnic label) are the same—you're guilty of stereotyping. A good example of this is seen in the use of the term "African American." The term stresses the unity of Africa and of those who are of African descent and is analogous to "Asian American" or "European American." At the same time, it ignores the great diversity within the African continent when, for example, it's used as analogous to "German American" or "Japanese American." More analogous terms would be

PRIVILEGED LANGUAGE

In discussing your friendship with members of another race, you use terms that members of the race use among themselves but which are normally considered negative. The people you're talking to, however, take offense at your use of these terms. You want to lessen this negative reaction and to let the group know that you don't normally use such racial terms.

WHAT DO YOU SAY?

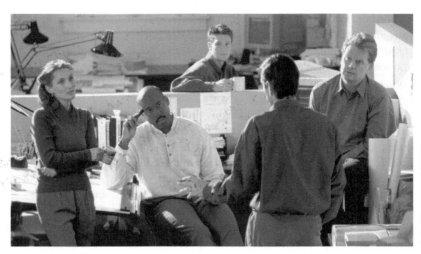

© R. W. Jones/CORBIS

"Nigerian American" or "Ethiopian American." Within each culture there are smaller cultures that differ greatly from each other and from the larger culture.

Differences in Meaning. Meaning exists not in words but in people. Consider, for example, the differences in meaning that exist for words such as woman to an American and a Muslim, religion to a born-again Christian and an atheist, and lunch to a Chinese rice farmer and a Madison Avenue advertising executive. Even though the same word is used, its meanings will vary greatly depending on the listeners' cultural definitions.

Nonverbal differences in meaning also exist. For example, a left-handed American who eats with the left hand may be seen by a Muslim as obscene. To the Muslim, the left hand isn't used for eating or for shaking hands but to clean oneself after excretory functions. So using the left hand to eat or to shake hands is considered insulting and obscene.

Adjust Your Communication

Intercultural communication (in fact, all communication) takes place only to the extent that you and the person you're trying to communicate with share the same system of symbols. Your interaction will be hindered to the extent that your language and nonverbal systems differ. Therefore, it's important to adjust your communication to compensate for cultural differences.

Building Communication Skills — Confronting Intercultural Difficulties

How might you deal with any one or two of the following obstacles to intercultural communication? If you have the opportunity, share your responses with others in the class. You'll gain a wealth of practical insights.

1. You're in an interracial, interreligious relationship. Your partner's family ignores your "couplehood." For example, you and your partner are never invited to dinner as a couple or included in any family affairs. You decide to confront your partner's family.

2. Your parents persist in holding stereotypes about other religious, racial, and ethnic groups. These stereotypes come up in all sorts of conversations. You're really embarrassed by these attitudes and feel you must tell your parents how incorrect you think these stereotypes are.

3. George, a colleague at work, recently underwent a religious conversion. He now persists in trying to get everyone else—you included—to undergo this same religious conversion. You decide to tell him that you find this behavior offensive.

Confronting cultural insensitivity is not an easy task; most people do not see their own insensitivity. So approach these situations carefully; rely on all the communication skills presented throughout this text and in your course.

Furthermore, you have to share your own system of signals with others so that they can better understand you. Although some people may know what you mean by your silence or by your avoidance of eye contact, others may not. You cannot expect others to decode your behaviors accurately without help.

Communication accommodation theory, holds that speakers will adjust or accommodate to the communication style of their listeners in order to interact more pleasantly and efficiently (Giles, Mulac, Bradac, & Johnson, 1987). As you adjust your messages, recognize that each culture has its own rules and customs for communication (Barna, 1997; Ruben, 1985; Spitzberg, 1991). These rules identify what is appropriate and what is inappropriate. Thus, for example, in U.S. culture you would call a person you wished to date three or four days in advance. In certain Asian cultures you might call the person's parents weeks or even months in advance. In U.S. culture you say, as a general friendly gesture and not as a specific invitation, "come over and pay us a visit sometime." To members of other cultures, this comment is sufficient to prompt the listeners actually to visit at their convenience. Table 1 presents a good example of a set of cultural rules—guidelines for communicating with an extremely large and important culture that many people don't know.

Table 1 Communication Tips

Between People with and without Disabilities

The suggestions offered here are considered appropriate in the United States, though not necessarily in other cultures. For example, although most people in the United States accept the phrase "person with mental retardation," it's considered offensive to many in the United Kingdom (Fernald, 1995).

If you're the one without such a disability:

1. *Avoid negative terms and terms that define the person as disabled such as "the disabled man" or "the handicapped child."* Instead say "person with a disability," always emphasizing the person rather than the disability. Avoid terms that describe the person with a disability as abnormal; for example, when you refer to people without disabilities as "normal," you in effect say that a person with a disability isn't normal.

2. *Treat assistive devices such as wheelchairs, canes, walkers, or crutches as the personal property of the user.* Be careful not to move these out of your way; they're for the convenience of the person with the disability. Avoid leaning on a person's wheelchair, for example; it's similar to leaning on a person.

3. *Shake hands with the person with the disability if you shake hands with others in a group.* Don't avoid shaking hands if an individual's hand is crippled, for example.

4. *Avoid talking about the person with a disability in the third person.* For example, avoid saying, "Doesn't he get around beautifully with the new crutches." Always direct your comments directly to the individual.

5. *Don't assume that people who have a disability are intellectually impaired.* Slurred speech—such as may occur with people who have cerebral palsy or cleft palate—should never be taken as indicating a low-level intellect. Be especially careful not to talk down to such people as, research shows, many people do (Unger, 2001).

6. *When you're not sure of how to act, ask.* For example, if you're not sure if you should offer walking assistance, ask: "Would you like me to help you into the dining room?" And, even more important, accept the person's response. If he or she says no, then that means no; don't insist.

7. *Maintain similar eye level.* If a person is in a wheelchair, for example, it might be helpful for you to sit down or kneel down to get onto the same eye level.

If you're the one with a disability:

1. *Let the other person know if he or she can do anything to assist you in communicating.* For example, if you want someone to speak in a louder voice, ask. If you want to relax and have someone push your wheelchair, say so.

2. *Be patient and understanding.* Many people mean well but may simply not know how to act or what to say. Put them at ease as best you can.

3. *Demonstrate your own comfort.* If you detect discomfort in the other person, you might talk a bit about your disability to show that you're not uncomfortable and that you understand that others may not know how you feel. But don't feel this is something you should or have to do; you're under no obligation to educate the public.

These suggestions are based on a wide variety of sources; for example, www.empowermentzone.com/etiquet.txt (the website for the National Center for Access Unlimited), www.dol.gov/dol/top/disability/index.htm, www.dissvcs.uga.edu/com-peodis.html, and www.ucpa.org/ucp_generaldoc.cfm (all accessed October 23, 2004).

SUMMARY: CULTURE AND COMMUNICATION

This unit introduced the study of culture and its relationship to communication and considered how cultures differ and some of the theories developed to explain how culture and communication affect each other. In addition, the unit introduced the study of intercultural communication and its nature and principles.

1. Culture consists of the relatively specialized lifestyle of a group of people—their values, beliefs, artifacts, ways of behaving, and ways of communicating—that is passed on from one generation to the next through communication rather than through genes.

2. Enculturation is the process by which culture is transmitted from one generation to the next.

3. Acculturation involves the processes by which one culture is modified through contact with or exposure to another culture.

4. Cultures differ in terms of individualist or collectivist orientations, high and low context, high and low power distance, masculinity and femininity, and tolerance of ambiguity.

5. Individualist cultures emphasize individual values such as power and achievement, whereas collectivist cultures emphasize group values such as cooperation and responsibility to the group.

6. In high-context cultures much information is in the context or the person; in low-context cultures information is expected to be made explicit.

7. In high-power-distance cultures there are large differences in power between people; in low-power-distance cultures power is more evenly distributed throughout the population.

8. Masculine cultures emphasize assertiveness, ambition, and competition; feminine cultures emphasize compromise and negotiation.

9. High-ambiguity tolerant cultures feel little threatened by uncertainty; it's accepted as it comes. Low-ambiguity tolerant cultures feel uncomfortable with uncertainty and seek to avoid it.

10. Intercultural communication is communication among people who have different cultural beliefs, values, or ways of behaving.

11. Ethnocentrism, which exists on a continuum, is our tendency to evaluate the beliefs, attitudes, and values of our own culture positively and those of other cultures negatively.

12. Stereotyping is the tendency to develop and maintain fixed, unchanging impressions of groups of people and to use these impressions to evaluate individual members of these groups, ignoring unique individual characteristics.

13. Among guidelines for more effective intercultural communication are: prepare yourself, recognize and reduce your ethnocentrism, confront your stereotypes, be mindful, avoid overattribution, recognize differences, and adjust your communication.

KEY TERMS IN CULTURE AND COMMUNICATION

acculturation	ethnic identity	high-context culture	low-power-distance
ambiguity tolerance	ethnocentrism	high-power-distance	cultures
collectivist culture	face-saving	cultures	masculine culture
cultural sensitivity	feminine culture	individualist culture	sex
enculturation	gender	low-context culture	stereotype

THINKING CRITICALLY ABOUT CULTURE AND COMMUNICATION

1. **Cultural Differences.** Cultural differences underlie some of the most hotly debated topics in the news today. For example, consider the following questions. How would you answer these? How do your cultural attitudes, beliefs, and values influence your responses?

   • Should Christian Scientist parents be prosecuted for preventing their children from receiving life-saving medical procedures such as blood transfusions?

   • Should cockfighting be permitted or declared illegal in all states as "cruelty to animals"? Some Latin Americans have argued that cockfighting is a part of their culture and should be permitted even though it's illegal in most of the United States.

   • Should same-sex marriages be legalized? Right now, only one state (Massachusetts) permits same-sex marriage, but other states such as New York have it on their agenda.

2. **Choosing a Mate.** Men and women from different cultures were asked the following question: "If a man (woman) had all the other qualities you desired, would you marry this person if you were not in love with him (her)?" (LeVine, Sato, Hashimoto, & Verma, 1994). Fifty percent of the respondents from Pakistan, 49 percent from India, and 19 percent from Thailand said yes. At the other extreme were respondents from Japan (only 2

percent said yes), the United States (3.5 percent), and Brazil (4 percent). How would you answer this question? How is your answer influenced by your culture?

3. **Sexual Relations.** Some cultures frown on sexual relationships outside of marriage; others consider sex a normal part of intimacy. Intercultural researchers (Hatfield & Rapson, 1996) recall a discussion between colleagues from Sweden and the United States on ways of preventing AIDS. When researchers from the United States suggested promoting abstinence, their Swedish counterparts asked, "How will teenagers ever learn to become loving, considerate sexual partners if they don't practice?" "The silence that greeted the question," note Hatfield and Rapson (1996, p. 36), "was the sound of two cultures clashing." How have your cultural beliefs and values influenced what you consider appropriate relationship behavior?

4. **What's in a Name?** Some researchers prefer to use the term *subculture* to refer to smaller cultures within larger cultures; other researchers do not use the term, feeling that it implies that some cultures are less important than others. Some researchers prefer to use the term *co-culture* to refer to a variety of cultures coexisting side by side, whereas others think this term is imprecise, because all cultures coexist (Lustig & Koester, 2006); these theorists prefer simply to refer to all cultures as *cultures*. How do you feel about the terms "subculture," "co-culture," and just plain "culture"?

5. **Cell Phone Etiquette.** Cell phone users vary widely in how they use their phones in public places, and rules of cell phone etiquette abound (for example, www.microsoft.com/smallbusiness/resources/technology/communications/cell_phone_etiquette_10_dos_and_donts.mspx and www.dmwmedia.com/news/2006/12/14/12-unwritten-rules-of-cell-phone-etiquette, accessed May 2, 2007). What rules of cell phone etiquette do you follow? Where are you most likely to turn off your cell phone? In what public situations are you likely to leave it on?

LogOn! MyCommunicationLab
WWW.MYCOMMUNICATIONLAB.COM

Among the materials you'll find on MCL relevant to the discussion of culture and human communication are two self-tests (What's Your Cultural Awareness? and How Open Are You Interculturally?) and exercises including Going from Culture to Gender, The Influence of Cultural Beliefs, and Sources of Your Cultural Beliefs. Also, take a look at American Fact Finder and watch the videos Bikes & Spikes, Vietnamese Culture, Cultural Background, and Tonya in the Classroom.

References

Andersen, P. (1991). Explaining intercultural differences in nonverbal communication. In L. A. Samovar & R. E. Porter (Eds.), *Intercultural communication: A reader* (6th ed., pp. 286–296). Belmont, CA: Wadsworth.

Barna, L. M. (1997). Stumbling blocks in intercultural communication. In L. A. Samovar & R. E. Porter (Eds.), *Intercultural communication: A reader* (7th ed., pp. 337–346). Belmont, CA: Wadsworth.

Becker, S. L., & Roberts, C. L. (1992). *Discovering mass communication* (3rd ed.). New York: HarperCollins.

Berry, J. W., Poortinga, Y. H., Segall, M. H., & Dasen, P. R. (1992). *Cross-cultural psychology: Research and applications*. New York: Cambridge University Press.

Borden, G. (1991). *Cultural orientation: An approach to understanding intercultural communication*. Englewood Cliffs, NJ: Prentice-Hall.

Burgoon, J. K., Berger, C. R., & Waldron, V. R. (2000). Mindfulness and interpersonal communication. *Journal of Social Issues, 56*, 105–127.

Chang, H.-C., & Holt, G. R. (1996). The changing Chinese interpersonal world: Popular themes in interpersonal communication books in modern Taiwan. *Communication Quarterly, 44* (Winter), 85–106.

Cho, H. (2000). Asian in America: Cultural shyness can impede Asian Americans' success. *Northwest Asian Weekly, 19* (December 8), 6.

Chung, L. C., & Ting-Toomey, S. (1999). Ethnic identity and relational expectations among Asian Americans. *Communication Research Reports, 16* (Spring), 157–166.

DeZoysa, R., & Newman, O. (2002). Globalization, soft power and the challenge of Hollywood. *Contemporary Politics, 8*, 185–202.

Eckstein, D., & Goldman, A. (2001). The couple's gender-based communication questionnaire (CGCQ). *Family Journal: Counseling and Therapy for Couples and Families 9*, 62–74.

Fernald, C. D. (1995). When in London ...: Differences in Disability Language Preferences Among English-Speaking Countries. *Mental Retardation, 33* (April), 99–103.

Franklin, C. W., & Mizell, C. A. (1995). Some factors influencing success among African-American men: A preliminary study. *Journal of Men's Studies, 3*, 191–204.

Giles, H., Mulac, A., Bradac, J. J., & Johnson, P. (1987). Speech accommodation theory: The first decade and beyond. In M. L. McLaughlin (Ed.), *Communication yearbook 10* (pp. 13–48). Thousand Oaks, CA: Sage.

Gudykunst, W. B. (1994). *Bridging differences: Effective intergroup communication* (2nd ed.). Thousand Oaks, CA: Sage.

Gudykunst, W. B., & Kim, Y. Y. (1992). *Communicating with strangers: An approach to intercultural communication* (2nd ed.). New York: Random House.

Gudykunst, W. B., & Ting-Toomey, S., with Chua, E. (1988). *Culture and interpersonal communication.* Thousand Oaks, CA: Sage.

Hall, E. T., & Hall, M. R. (1987). *Hidden differences: Doing business with the Japanese.* New York: Doubleday.

Hatfield, E., & Rapson, R. L. (1996). *Love and sex: Cross- cultural perspectives.* Boston: Allyn & Bacon.

Hofstede, G. (1997). *Cultures and organizations: Software of the mind.* New York: McGraw-Hill.

Hofstede, G. (Ed.). (1998). *Masculinity and femininity: The taboo dimension of national cultures.* Thousand Oaks, CA: Sage.

Jacobson, D. (1999). Impression formation in cyberspace: Online expectations and offline experiences in text-based virtual communities. *Journal of Computer-Mediated Communication, 5,* n.p.

Jandt, F. E. (2004). *Intercultural communication* (4th ed.). Thousand Oaks, CA: Sage.

Kapoor, S., Wolfe, A., & Blue, J. (1995). Universal values structure and individualism–collectivism: A U.S. test. *Communi cation Research Reports, 12* (Spring), 112–123.

Kim, M.-S., & Sharkey, W. F. (1995). Independent and interdependent construals of self: Explaining cultural patterns of interpersonal communication in multi-cultural organizational settings. *Communication Quarterly, 43* (Winter), 20–38.

Kim, Y. Y. (1988). Communication and acculturation. In L. A. Samovar & R. E. Porter (Eds.), *Intercultural communication: A reader* (4th ed., pp. 344–354). Belmont, CA: Wadsworth.

Koppelman, K. L., with Goodhart, R. L. (2005). *Understanding human differences: Multicultural education for a diverse America.* Boston: Allyn & Bacon.

LeVine, R., Sato, S., Hashimoto, T., & Verma, J. (1994). Love and marriage in eleven cultures. Unpublished manuscript. California State University, Fresno. Cited in Hatfield & Rapson (1996).

Lustig, M. W., & Koester, J. (2006). *Intercultural competence: Interpersonal communication across cultures* (5th ed.). New York: Longman.

Matsumoto, D. (1994). *People: Psychology from a cultural perspective.* Pacific Grove, CA: Brooks/Cole.

McCroskey, J. C. (1997). *Introduction to rhetorical communication* (7th ed.). Englewood Cliffs, NJ: Prentice-Hall.

Moon, D. G. (1996). Concepts of "culture": Implications for intercultural communication research. *Communication Quarterly, 44* (Winter), 70–84.

Payne, K. E. (2001). *Different but equal: Communication between the sexes.* Westport, CT: Praeger.

Ruben, B. D. (1985). Human communication and cross-cultural effectiveness. In L.A. Samovar & R. E. Porter (Eds.), *Intercultural communication: A reader* (4th ed., pp. 338–356). Belmont, CA: Wadsworth.

Schott, G., & Selwyn, N. (2000). Examining the "male, antisocial" stereotype of high computer users. *Journal of Educational Computing Research, 23,* 291–303.

Singh, N., & Pereira, A. (2005). *The culturally customized Web site.* Oxford, UK: Elsevier Butterworth-Heinemann.

Spitzberg, B. H. (1991). Intercultural communication competence. In L. A. Samovar & R. E. Porter (Eds.), *Intercultural communication: A reader* (pp. 353–365). Belmont, CA: Wadsworth.

Stephan, W. G., & Stephan, C. W. (1985). Intergroup anxiety. *Journal of Social Issues, 41,* 157–175.

Stewart, L. P., Cooper, P. J., Stewart, A. D., with Friedley, S. A. (2003). *Communication and gender,* 4th ed. Boston: Allyn & Bacon.

Tannen, D. (1994a). *Gender and discourse.* New York: Oxford University Press.

Tannen, D. (1994b). *Talking from 9 to 5: How women's and men's conversational styles affect who gets heard, who gets credit, and what gets done at work.* New York: Morrow.

Ting-Toomey, S. (1981). Ethnic identity and close friendship in Chinese-American college students. *International Journal of Intercultural Relations, 5,* 383–406.

Victor, D. (1992). *International business communication.* New York: HarperCollins.

Wrench, J. S., & McCroskey, J. C. (2003). A communibiological examination of ethnocentrism and homophobia. *Communication Research Reports, 20,* 24–33.

Yun, H. (1976). The Korean personality and treatment considerations. *Social Casework, 57,* 173–178.

Chapter 3

Public Speaking Topics, Audiences, and Research

MAJOR TOPICS

Introducing Public Speaking

Apprehension in Public Speaking

Step 1: Select Your Topic and Purpose

Step 2: Analyze Your Audience

Step 3: Research Your Topic

Special Features

Nervousness: Virginia Peck Richmond

How Apprehensive Are You in Public Speaking?

How Well Do You Know Your Audience?

 The Diffusion of Innovations

 Plagiarism

 Performance Visualization

 Systematic Desensitization

 Limiting a Topic

 Using Cultural Beliefs as Assumptions

 A Speech of Introduction

© Bill Aron/PhotoEdit

As you move up the hierarchy in your personal and professional lives, you'll find an ever greater need for public speaking. At the same time, learning the skills of public speaking will enable you to reap important benefits both now and in the future.

In this unit you'll learn about:
- the nature of public speaking.
- the very normal nervousness that most people feel.
- the first three steps for preparing a public speech.

And you'll learn to:
- manage your own anxiety and not let it prevent you from developing and presenting effective speeches.
- select an appropriate speech topic and purpose.
- analyze and adapt to your audiences.
- research your topic.

Public speaking is one of the essential skills people need to function effectively in today's society. The higher you move in any chain of command—say, from intern, to junior analyst, to manager, to CEO—the more important public speaking becomes. This chapter explains these essential skills, the skills you'll need to prepare and present effective public speeches. As you'll see, these skills will also prove useful to you in a variety of other situations as well.

INTRODUCING PUBLIC SPEAKING

Although public speaking principles were probably developed soon after our species began to talk, it was in ancient Greece and Rome that our Western tradition of public speaking got its start. This Greco-Roman tradition has been enriched by the experiments, surveys, field studies, and historical studies that have been done since classical times and that continue to be done today.

Aristotle's *Rhetoric*, written some 2,300 years ago in ancient Greece, was one of the earliest systematic studies of public speaking. It was in this work that the three kinds of persuasive appeals—*logos* (or logical proof), *pathos* (emotional appeals), and *ethos* (appeals based on the character of the speaker)—were introduced. This three-part division is still followed today.

Roman rhetoricians added to the work of the Greeks. Quintilian, who taught in Rome during the first century, built an entire educational system—from childhood through adulthood—based on the development of the effective and responsible orator. Over the following 2,000 years, the study of public speaking continued to grow and develop.

Contemporary public speaking—the kind discussed in this text—builds on this classical heritage but also incorporates insights from the humanities, the social and behavioral sciences, and computer science and information technology. Likewise, perspectives from different cultures are being integrated into our present study of public speaking. Table 1 shows some of the contributors to contemporary public speaking and illustrates the wide research and theory base from which the principles of this discipline are drawn.

The Benefits of Public Speaking

Here are just a few of the benefits you'll derive from this section of the text and from your course work in public speaking.

Improve Your Personal and Social Abilities

Public speaking provides training in a variety of personal and social competencies. For example, you'll learn to manage your fear of communication situations, develop greater self-confidence and self-presentation skills, enhance your own personal and interpersonal power and influence, and regulate and adapt your listening to the specific situation.

Improve Your Academic and Career Skills

As you learn public speaking, you'll also learn a wide variety of academic and career skills, many of which are largely communication skills (as you can tell from reading the employment ads, especially for middle management positions in just about every field you can name). For example, you will learn to:

- conduct research efficiently and effectively, using the latest and the best techniques available.

Tablex 1   Growth and Development of Public Speaking

Academic Roots	Contributions to Contemporary Public Speaking
Classical rhetoric	Emphasis on substance; ethical responsibilities of the speaker; use of a combination of logical, ethical, and emotional appeals; the strategies of organization
Literary and rhetorical criticism	Approaches to and standards for evaluation; insights into style and language
Philosophy	Emphasis on the logical validity of arguments; continuing contribution to ethics
Public address	Insights into how famous speakers dealt with varied purposes and audiences to achieve desired effects
Psychology	How language is made easier to understand and remember; principles of attitude and behavior change; emphasis on speech effects
General semantics	Emphasis on using language to describe reality accurately; techniques for avoiding common thinking errors that faulty language usage creates
Communication theory	Insights on information transmission; the importance of viewing the whole of the communication act; the understanding of such concepts as feedback, noise, channel, and message
Computer science and information technology	The virtual audience; design, outlining, and presentation software; search tools for research; easily accessed databases
Interpersonal communication	Transactionalism; emphasis on mutual influence of speaker and audience.
Sociology	Data on audiences' attitudes, values, opinions, and beliefs and how these influence exposure to and responses to messages
Anthropology	Insights into the attitudes, beliefs, and values of different cultures and how these influence communication in general and public speaking in particular

- critically analyze and evaluate arguments and evidence from any and all sources.

- understand human motivation and make effective use of your insights in persuasive encounters.

- develop an effective communication style (whether for conversation or for that important job interview) that you feel comfortable with.

- give and respond appropriately to criticism so as to increase your insight into your own strengths and weaknesses.

- communicate your competence, character, and charisma to make yourself believable.

Improve Your Public Speaking Abilities

Speakers aren't born; they're made. Through instruction, exposure to different speeches, experience with diverse audiences, feedback on your own speeches, and individual learning experiences, you can become an effective speaker. Regardless of your present level of competence, you can improve through proper training.

At the end of your public speaking training, you'll be a more competent, confident, and effective public speaker. You'll also be a more effective listener—more open yet more critical, more empathic yet more discriminating. And you'll emerge a more competent and discerning critic of public communication. You'll learn to organize and explain complex concepts and processes clearly and effectively to a wide variety of listeners. You'll learn to support an argument with all the available means of persuasion and to present a persuasive appeal to audiences of varied types.

As a leader (and in many ways you can look at this course as training in leadership skills), you'll need the skills of effective communication to help preserve a free and open society. As a speaker who wants your message understood and accepted, as a listener who needs to evaluate and critically analyze ideas and arguments before making decisions, and as a critic who needs to evaluate and judge the thousands of public communications you hear every day, you will draw on the public speaking skills you'll learn here.

Beliefs about Public Speaking

A good way to begin your study of public speaking is to examine your own beliefs about public speaking and public speakers. Compare some common beliefs with the research and theory that bear on these beliefs:

Belief: Good public speakers are born, not made.

Research finds that effective public speaking is actually a learned skill. Although some people are born brighter or more extroverted—which will certainly help in public speaking—all people can improve their abilities and become more effective public speakers.

Belief: The more speeches you give, the better you'll become at it.

Research finds that this is true only if you practice effective skills. If you practice bad habits, you're more likely to grow less effective than to become more effective; consequently, it's important to learn and follow the principles of effectiveness.

Belief: You'll never be a good public speaker if you're nervous giving speeches.

Research finds that most speakers are nervous; managing, not eliminating, the fear will enable you to become effective regardless of your current level of anxiety. In fact, your fear may actually encourage you to prepare more thoroughly and to practice more often, which will contribute to more effective speaking.

MEDIA WATCH

THE DIFFUSION OF INNOVATIONS

Mass media audiences are even more diverse and varied than public speaking audiences. One of the most interesting theories to illustrate this diversity is the theory of the *diffusion of innovations*, which focuses on the ways in which mass communications influence people to adopt something new or different. *Diffusion* refers to the spread of new information or innovation through society. The innovation may be of any type—soft contact lenses, laptop computers, PDAs, PowerPoint software for public speaking. In this theory the word *adoption* refers to people's positive reactions to and use of the innovation. Research distinguishes five types of adopters:

- The *innovators* are the first to adopt the innovation. They are not necessarily the originators of the new idea, but they're the ones who take the innovation to the point that others become aware of it.

- The early adopters, sometimes called the "influentials," legitimize the idea and make it acceptable to large numbers of people.

- The early majority follows the influentials and further legitimates the innovation.

- The late majority adopts the innovation after about half the population has adopted it.

- The laggards are the last group to adopt the innovation and may take the lead from any of the preceding groups.

One last group, the *diehards*, never adopt the innovation. These include accountants who continue to do tax returns without the aid of tax-preparation software and lawyers and doctors who don't avail themselves of computerized databases.

Increasing Media Literacy

Where would you position yourself on this diffusion of innovation curve? In what ways do the media influence you to adopt innovations? Which media are most influential with you? With your friends?

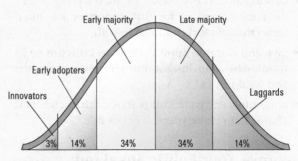

The Five Types of Adopters

Source: Reprinted with permission of The Free Press, a Division of Simon & Schuster, Inc., from The Diffusion of Inventions, Fourth Edition, by Everett M. Rogers. Copyright © 1995 by Everett M. Rogers, Copyright © 1962, 1971, 1983 by The Free Press.

Belief: It's best to memorize your speech, especially if you're fearful.

Research finds that memorizing your speech is one of the worst things you can do; there are easier ways to deal with fear.

Belief: The skills of public speaking are similar throughout the world.

Research finds that they are not; the techniques of public speaking are culture specific. In other words, what proves effective with an Asian audience may not work with audiences in the United States or in Latin America, and vice versa.

A Definition of Public Speaking

In *public speaking*, a speaker presents a relatively continuous message to a relatively large audience in a unique context (see Figure 1). Like all forms of communication, public speaking is transactional (Watzlawick, Beavin, & Jackson 1967; Watzlawick 1978): Each element in the public speaking process depends on and interacts with all other elements. For example, the way in which you organize a speech will depend on such factors as the speech topic, the specific audience, the purpose you hope to achieve, and a host of other variables—all of which are explained in the remainder of this unit and in the units to follow.

Especially important is the mutual interaction and influence between speaker and listeners. True, when you give a speech, you do most of the speaking and the listeners do most of the listening.

However, the listeners also send messages in the form of feedback—for example, applause, bored looks, nods of agreement or disagreement, and attentive glances. The audience also influences how you'll prepare and present your speech. It influences your arguments, your language, your method of organization, and, in fact, every choice you make. You would not, for example, present the same speech on saving money to high school students as you would to senior citizens.

APPREHENSION IN PUBLIC SPEAKING

Being fearful of giving a public speech is perfectly normal. Everyone experiences some degree of fear in the relatively formal public speaking situation. After all, in public speaking you're the sole focus of attention, and you are usually being evaluated for your performance.

Although you may at first view apprehension as harmful, it's not necessarily so. In fact, apprehension can work for you. Fear can energize you. It may motivate you to work a little harder to produce a speech that will be better than it might have been. Further, the audience cannot see the apprehension that you may be experiencing. Even though you may think that the audience can hear your heart beat faster and faster, they can't. They can't see your knees tremble. They can't sense your dry throat—at least not most of the time.

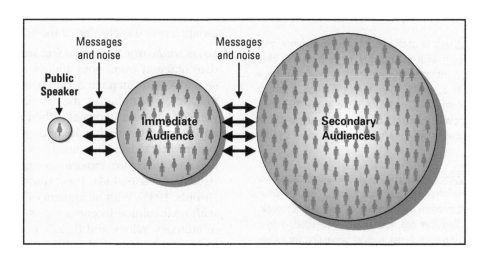

FIGURE 1   **Process and Elements of Public Speaking**

This diagram is designed to illustrate the interplay of elements in the public speaking process and to emphasize that there are a variety of audiences of public speaking: (1) the immediate audience—the audience that hears the speaker as he or she is speaking, whether in person, on television, on the Internet, or even via cell phone—and (2) the additional audiences that get the material second hand; for example, people who read the speech, read about the speech, or hear from those who heard the speech, from those who heard about the speech from immediate audience members, or from those who heard about the speech from those who heard about the speech.

Before beginning the actual speech preparation process, let's look first at fear of public speaking, or what is now called **communication apprehension**. People experience apprehension in all forms of communication, but public speaking apprehension is the most common (Richmond & McCroskey, 1998; Daly, McCroskey, Ayres, Hopf, & Ayres, 1997). Take the following apprehension test to measure your own fear of speaking in public.

TEST YOURSELF

How Apprehensive Are You in Public Speaking?

This questionnaire consists of six statements concerning your feelings about public speaking. Indicate the degree to which each statement applies to you, using the following scale: 1 = strongly agree; 2 = agree; 3 = are undecided; 4 = disagree; 5 = strongly disagree. There are no right or wrong answers. Don't be concerned that some of the statements are similar to others. Work quickly; just record your immediate response.

_____ 1. I have no fear of giving a speech.

_____ 2. Certain parts of my body feel very tense and rigid while giving a speech.

_____ 3. I feel relaxed while giving a speech.

_____ 4. My thoughts become confused and jumbled when I am giving a speech.

_____ 5. I face the prospect of giving a speech with confidence.

_____ 6. While giving a speech, I get so nervous that I forget facts I really know.

HOW DID YOU DO? To obtain your public speaking apprehension score, begin with the number 18 (selected so that you won't wind up with negative numbers) and add to it the scores for items 1, 3, and 5. Then, from this total, subtract the scores from items 2, 4, and 6. A score above 18 shows some degree of apprehension. Most people score above 18, so if you scored relatively high, you're among the vast majority of people.

WHAT WILL YOU DO? As you read the suggestions for reducing apprehension in the text that follows, consider what you can do to incorporate these into your own public speaking experiences. Consider too how these suggestions might be useful in reducing apprehension more generally; for example, in social situations and in small groups and meetings.

Source: From James C. McCroskey, *An Introduction to Rhetorical Communication* (9th ed.). Published by Allyn & Bacon, Boston, MA. Copyright © 2006 by Pearson Education. Adapted by permission of the publisher.

Reducing Your Apprehension

The following suggestions will help you overcome communication apprehension in public speaking as well as in small group and interpersonal communication situations (Beatty, 1988; Richmond & McCroskey, 1998).

- *Gain experience:* New and different situations such as public speaking are likely to make you anxious, so try to reduce their newness and differentness. The best way to do this is to get as much public speaking experience as you can. With experience, your initial fears and anxieties will give way to feelings of control, comfort, and pleasure. Try also to familiarize yourself with the public speaking context. For example, try to rehearse in the room in which you will give your speech.

- *Think positively:* When you see yourself as inferior—when, for example, you feel that others are better speakers or that they know more than you do—anxiety increases. Therefore, think positive thoughts and build your confidence through preparation. At the same time, maintain realistic expectations for yourself. Fear increases when you feel that you can't meet your own or your audience's expectations (Ayres, 1986).

- *See public speaking as conversation:* When you are the center of attention (as you are in public speaking), you feel especially conspicuous, and this often increases anxiety. It may help to think of public speaking as another type of conversation (some theorists call it "enlarged conversation"). Or, if you're comfortable talking in small groups, visualize your audience as an enlarged small group; it may dispel some of the anxiety you feel.

- *Stress similarity:* When you feel similar to (rather than different from) your audience, your anxiety should lessen (Stephan & Stephan, 1992). Therefore, try to emphasize the likenesses between yourself and your audience. When cultural differences exist between you and your audience, you're likely to feel less similarity with your listeners and therefore experience greater anxiety (Gudykunst & Nishida, 1984; Gudykunst, Yang, & Nishida, 1985). With all audiences, but especially with multicultural listeners, stress commonalities in attitudes, values, and beliefs; it will make you feel more at one with your listeners.

- *Prepare and practice thoroughly:* Much of the fear you experience is a fear of failure. Practice and preparation will lessen the possibility of failure and the accompanying apprehension. Because apprehension is greatest at the beginning of the speech, try memorizing the first few sentences of

Theory and Research — Performance Visualization

UNDERSTANDING

The theory of **performance visualization** argues that you can reduce the outward signs of apprehension and the negative thinking that often creates anxiety through a few simple techniques (Ayres & Hopf, 1992, 1993; Ayres, Hopf, & Ayres, 1994).

First, develop a positive attitude and a positive self-perception. Visualize yourself in the role of the effective public speaker. Visualize yourself walking to the front of the room—fully and totally confident, fully in control of the situation. The audience pays rapt attention to your talk and bursts into wild applause as you finish. Throughout this visualization, avoid all negative thoughts. As you visualize yourself as this effective speaker, take note of how you walk, look at your listeners, handle your notes, and respond to questions; especially, think about how you feel about the public speaking experience.

Second, model your performance on that of an especially effective speaker. View a particularly competent public speaker on video, for example, and make a mental "movie" of it. As you review the actual video and mental movie, shift yourself into the role of speaker; become this speaker.

Working with Theories and Research

Try performance visualization as you rehearse for your next speech. Did it help reduce your apprehension?

your speech. If there are complicated facts or figures, be sure to write these out; plan to read them so as to remove your worries of forgetting them.

■ *Move about and breathe deeply:* Physical activity —large bodily movements as well as small movements of the hands, face, and head—lessens apprehension. Using a presentation aid, for example, will temporarily divert attention from you and will allow you to get rid of your excess energy. Also, try breathing deeply a few times before getting up to speak. Your body will relax, and this will help you overcome your initial fear of walking to the front of the room.

■ *Avoid chemicals as tension relievers:* Unless prescribed by a physician, chemical means for reducing apprehension are not a good idea. Tranquilizers, marijuana, or artificial stimulants are likely to create problems rather than reduce them. They're likely to impair your ability to remember the parts of your speech, to accurately read audience feedback, and to regulate the timing of your speech. And, of course, alcohol does nothing to reduce public speaking apprehension (Himle, Abelson, & Haghightgou, 1999).

With the nature of public speaking and its benefits in mind and with an understanding of communication apprehension and some ways for managing it, we can look at the essential steps for preparing an

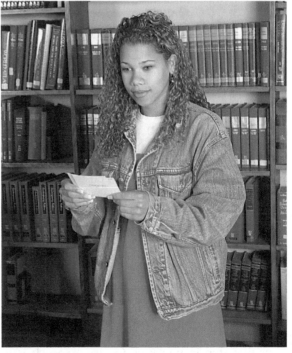

© Michael Newman/PhotoEdit

APPREHENSION MANAGEMENT

This is your first experience with public speaking and you're very nervous. You're afraid you'll forget your speech or stumble somehow so you're wondering if it would be a good idea to alert your audience to your nervousness.

WHAT DO YOU SAY?

Theory and Research   Systematic Desensitization

UNDERSTANDING

The theory of **systematic desensitization** holds that you can reduce fear through a process of gradually adapting to lesser and then successively greater versions of the thing you fear. This technique has been used to deal with many kinds of fear, including public speaking fears (Wolpe 1957; Goss, Thompson, & Olds, 1978; Richmond & McCroskey, 1998). In the case of public speaking, the general idea of systematic desensitization is to create a hierarchy of behaviors leading up to the desired but feared behavior. One specific hierarchy might look like this:

5.   Giving a speech in class

4.   Introducing another speaker to the class

3.   Speaking in a group in front of the class

2.   Answering a question in class

1.   Asking a question in class

You begin at the bottom of this hierarchy and rehearse behavior number 1 mentally over a period of days until you can clearly visualize asking a question in class without any uncomfortable anxiety. Once you can accomplish this, move to the second level. Here you visualize a somewhat more threatening behavior: answering a question. Once you can do this, move to the third level, and so on until you get to the desired behavior.

Working with Theories and Research

Create a hierarchy for dealing with communication apprehension. Use small steps to help you get from one step to the next more easily.

---

effective public speech (Figure 2): (1) Select your topic and purpose; (2) analyze your audience; (3) research your topic; (4) develop your thesis and main points; (5) support your main points; (6) organize your speech materials; (7) construct your conclusion, introduction, and transitions; (8) outline your speech; (9) word your speech; and (10) rehearse and deliver your speech. The first three of these steps are discussed in this unit.

STEP 1: SELECT YOUR TOPIC AND PURPOSE

Your first step in preparing to give a speech is to select your topic and purpose.

Your Topic

As you begin to think about public speaking, and especially about your own speech, perhaps the first question you have is "What do I speak about?"—that is,

what **topic** would be appropriate? The answer to this question will change as your life situation changes; in the years ahead you'll most likely speak on topics that grow out of your job or your social or political activities. In the classroom, however, where your objective is to learn the skills of public speaking, there are literally thousands of subjects to talk about. Nevertheless, the question remains: "What do I speak about?" To answer this question, focus on three related questions: "What makes a good topic?" "How do I find such a topic?" and "How do I focus or limit my topic?"

A Good Public Speaking Topic

A good public speaking topic is one that deals with matters of substance, is appropriate to you and the audience, and is culturally sensitive. These three characteristics suggest some guidelines for selecting a good topic. Let's consider each briefly.

Substantive. The most important criterion of a good topic is that it be *substantive*—that it deal with matters of substance. Select a topic that is important enough to merit the time and attention of

66

a group of intelligent people. Ask yourself: Would this topic engage the attention of my classmates? Would a reputable newspaper cover such a topic? Would students find this topic relevant to their social or professional lives?

Appropriate. Select a topic that is *appropriate to you as the speaker*. For example, if you're male, it probably isn't a good idea to give a speech on the stages of childbirth. On the other hand, if you're female and have just given birth, this might be a good topic. If you've never been incarcerated, then a speech on what life is like in prison is probably not going to ring true to your audience. If you're known to be a big spender, then giving a speech on how to eke by on $3

a day is not likely to be well received by your listeners. The best way to look at this criterion is to ask if— given what the audience already knows about you and what you'll tell them during your speech—your listeners will see you as a knowledgeable and believable spokesperson on this topic. If the answer is yes, then you have a topic appropriate to you as a speaker. If the answer is no, then it will probably be useful to continue your search for an appropriate topic. (The next section will focus on this issue.)

Also, select a topic that is *appropriate to your audience in terms of their interests and needs*. Giving a speech to students in your class on the need to have a computer would be inappropriate, simply because they already know the importance of

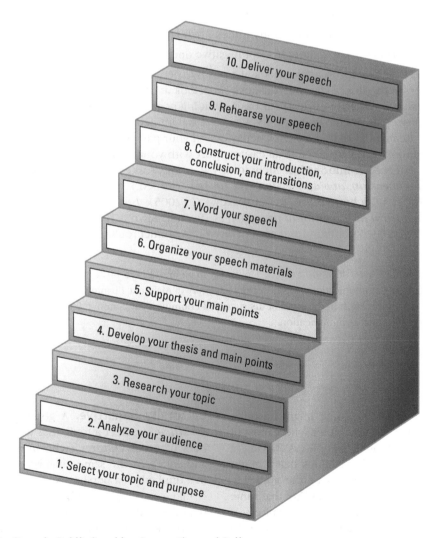

FIGURE 2 **The Steps in Public Speaking Preparation and Delivery**

Speakers differ in the order in which they follow these steps. Some speakers, for example, prefer to begin with audience analysis; they ask themselves what the audience is interested in and then select the topic and purpose. Some speakers prefer to identify their main points before conducting extensive research, whereas others prefer to allow the points to emerge from the research. The order presented here will prove useful to most speakers for most situations, but you can vary the order to serve your purposes. As long as you cover all steps, you should be in good shape.

THE RESEARCHER

Nervousness

I'm nervous giving speeches, and I feel this comes through to the audience and I'm not as effective as I'd like to be. What can I do to help reduce and manage my apprehension? Is there anything I can do to hide the symptoms of nervousness from the audience?

Feeling anxious and nervous prior to a presentation is normal. Try these ideas before a presentation:

1. Know your subject matter better than the audience.
2. Dress and look like a competent communicator.
3. Spend time in the room in which you are to give the presentation and practice.
4. Relax and reassure yourself that you have the knowledge and skills to give a successful presentation.
5. Review videos of previous students who have given presentations.
6. Think positive thoughts, not negative ones, and attempt to relax.

During the presentation, look at a positive person first. Looking at this one positive person can lower your nervousness. Next, look at other members of the audience. Scan the audience on a regular basis, avoiding negative persons (e.g., the person who is asleep or yawning). Practice your nonverbal immediacy skills.

Remember that immediacy behaviors on your part will generate a positive audience response and can generate an easy rapport with your audience.

For further information: Richmond, V. P., & McCroskey, J. C. (1998). *Communication: Apprehension, avoidance, and effectiveness* (5th ed.). Boston: Allyn & Bacon. And Mottet, T., Richmond, V. P., & McCroskey, J. C. (2005). *Instructional communication: Rhetorical and relational perspectives*. Boston: Allyn & Bacon. Or go to www.virginiapeckrichmondphd.com or www.jamescmccroskey.com.

Virginia Peck Richmond (Ph.D., University of Nebraska) is a professor and chair of the department of Communication Studies at the University of Alabama, Birmingham, where she teaches and conducts research in the areas of instructional communication, nonverbal communication, and organizational communication.

the computer. But that same topic might be quite appropriate if given at a senior center where most of the members did not own computers. Giving a speech advocating a specific religious belief might well prove insulting to members of the audience who didn't share your religious beliefs. Yet that same speech might be very well received by members of a particular religious congregation. Always look to your audience when thinking about a topic, and try to gauge their reaction to it. After all, your audience is giving you their time and attention; selecting a topic that is responsive to their needs and interests seems only fair.

Culturally Sensitive. A good topic is *culturally sensitive*, so select a topic that will not offend members of other cultures (who may even be in your audience). At the same time, recognize that we live in a time when a person's level of cultural sensitivity is taken as a sign of education and sophistication, qualities that can only help a speaker.

To take one example, in many Arab, Asian, and African cultures, discussing sex in an audience of both men and women would be considered obscene and offensive. In Scandinavian cultures, on the other hand, sex is expected to be discussed openly and without embarrassment or discomfort. Here are some

TOPIC APPROPRIATENESS

Stephen, a 20-year-old student, gave a speech on flower arranging—a topic so unexpected that members of the audience giggled and avoided eye contact with the speaker throughout the speech. You're called upon to offer a critique of the speech.

WHAT DO YOU SAY?

© JupiterImages/BananaStock/Alamy

additional examples of topics that intercultural experts recommend that visiting Americans avoid. These **taboo** topics change with the times, however, so what is true today may not be true tomorrow (Axtell, 1993; Allan & Burridge, 2006):

- In the Caribbean, avoid discussions of race, local politics, and religion.
- In Colombia, avoid politics and the criticism of bullfighting.
- In Egypt, avoid Middle Eastern politics.
- In Japan, avoid discussion of World War II.
- In Mexico, avoid talking about the Mexican-American War and illegal aliens.
- In the Philippines, avoid discussing politics, religion, corruption, or foreign aid.
- In South Korea, don't talk about internal politics or voice criticism of the government, socialism, or communism.
- In Spain, avoid discussions of family, religion, or jobs, and refrain from making negative comments on bullfighting.

Finding Topics

Here are five ways to find topics: *yourself, brainstorming, surveys, news items,* and *topic lists.*

Yourself. Perhaps your first step in thinking about appropriate speech topics is to look at yourself. What are you interested in? What engages your time and interest? If you were in a bookstore, what book topics would encourage you to flip through a book?

What titles of magazine articles would entice you to thumb through a magazine? In short, think about your own interests; they may be similar to your audience's.

As you consider your interests, also consider your own unique experiences. Have you been a part of well-known events or lived in different places? Do you have special talents? Are you knowledgeable about odd or different topics? What are your hobbies? If you're a philatelist, a speech on unique stamps or the value of stamps or the way in which stamps are printed might prove interesting. If you're a spelunker, perhaps a speech on caves—how they form and what they mean to the ecology—might prove interesting.

If you plan a speech on a topic that you're interested in and want to learn more about, you'll enjoy and profit from the entire experience a great deal more. The research that you do for your speech, for example, will be more meaningful; the facts you uncover will be more interesting. At the same time, your enthusiasm for your topic is likely to make your delivery more exciting, less anxiety provoking, and more engaging to the audience. All around, you win by selecting a topic in which you're especially interested or to which you have a special connection.

Brainstorming. Another useful method for finding a topic is *brainstorming*, a technique designed to enable you to generate lots of topics in a relatively short time (DeVito, 1996; Osborn, 1957). To apply brainstorming to your public speaking "problem"—namely, "What will I talk about?"—you first record any and all ideas that occur to you. Allow your mind to free-associate. Don't censor yourself;

instead, allow your ideas to flow as freely as possible. Record all your thoughts, regardless of how silly or inappropriate they may seem. Write them down or record them on tape. Try to generate as many ideas as possible. The more ideas you think of, the better your chances of finding a suitable topic in your list. After you've generated a sizable list—it should take you no longer than five minutes—read over the list or replay the tape. Do any of the topics on your list suggest other topics? If so, write these down as well. Can you combine or extend your ideas? Which ideas seem workable?

Surveys. Look at some of the national and regional *surveys* concerning what people think is important—polls that identify the significant issues, the urgent problems. Survey data are now easier than ever to get, because many of the larger poll results are available on the Internet. For example, the Gallup Organization maintains a website at http://www.gallup.com that includes national and international surveys on political, social, consumer, and other issues speakers often talk about. The Polling Report website also will prove useful; it provides a wealth of polling data on issues such as political science, business, journalism, health, and social science (www.pollingreport.com). Other sources are search directories, such as Hotbot or Yahoo!, where you can examine the major directory topics and any subdivisions of those you'd care to pursue—a process that's explained later in this unit. Many search engines and browsers provide lists of "hot topics," which are often useful starting points. These topics are exactly the topics that people are talking about and therefore often make excellent speech topics.

Or you can conduct a survey yourself. Roam through the nonfiction section of your bookstore (online, if you prefer—for example, at Amazon, www.amazon.com; Barnes & Noble, www.bn.com; or Borders, www.borders.com) and you'll quickly develop a list of the topics book buyers consider important. A glance at your newspaper's best-seller list will give you an even quicker overview.

News Items. Other useful starting points are *news items* in newspapers and newsmagazines. Here you'll find the important international and domestic issues, the financial issues, and the social issues all conveniently packaged in one place. The editorial page and the letters to the editor also are useful indicators of what people are concerned about.

Newsmagazines such as *Time* and *Newsweek* and financial magazines such as *Forbes*, *Money*, and *Fortune* (in print or online) will provide a wealth of suggestions. Similarly, news shows such as *20/20, 60*

Minutes, and *Meet the Press* and even the ubiquitous talk shows (and their corresponding websites) often identify the very issues that people are concerned with and on which there are conflicting points of view.

Topic Lists. One of the easiest ways to examine and select a potential topic is to look at some of the *topic lists* that are available. For example, The Dictionary of Topics (available at www.myspeechlab.com) lists hundreds of appropriate topics for informative and persuasive speeches. It's simply a dictionary-like listing of subjects, within which each topic is broken down into several subtopics. These subtopics should begin to suggest potential subjects for your informative and persuasive speeches. A small sample of this dictionary is presented in Table 2. There are also useful topic lists that have been compiled by various communication and English instructors. For example, the University of Hawaii maintains a website, Topic Selection Helper, which lists hundreds of topics (www.hawaii.edu/mauispeech/html/infotopichelp.html). Similarly, Cincinnati State Technical and Community College has lists for informative and persuasive speeches at http://faculty.cinstate.cc.oh.us/gesellsc/publicspeaking/topics.html.

Some websites contain topic generators where you can repeatedly press a button and view a wide variety of topics. For example, WritingFix (www.writingfix.com) helps you with topics for writing (which can often, though not always, be adapted for public speaking). And McMaster eBusiness Research Center (http://merc.mcmaster.ca/mclaren/ebiztopics.html) maintains a topic generator for business topics.

There is another class of websites that will sell you speeches and term papers for a fee, and in searching for topics you're likely to run across these sites. Avoid these websites. Many colleges now have software to identify plagiarism, so it's easy to get caught; and considering that the consequences are often severe, it's not worth going there. Finally, using such sites and services will keep you from learning critical skills that you'll need in your professional life.

Limiting Topics

Many beginning speakers make the error of trying to cover a huge topic in too short a period of time. The inevitable result is that such speakers cannot cover anything in depth; they touch on everything superficially. To be suitable for a public speech, a topic must be limited in scope; it must be narrowed down so as to fit the time restrictions and yet permit some depth of coverage.

Another reason to narrow your topic is that it will help you focus your collection of research materials.

Table 2 The Dictionary of Topics

This table presents just a few general topics to illustrate how you can use existing lists as ideas for speech topics. Lists like these will stimulate you to think of subjects dealing with topics you're interested in but may not have thought of as appropriate to a public speech. Each topic is broken down into several subtopics that should stimulate you to see these as potential ideas for your informative and persuasive speeches. Just a small sampling of topics is presented here; a much more extensive "dictionary of topics" may be found at **www.mycommunicationlab.com**.

Abortion arguments for and against; techniques of; religious dimension; legal views; differing views of

Academic freedom nature of; censorship; teachers' role in curriculum development; and government; and research; restrictions on

Acupuncture nature of; development of; current practices in; effectiveness of; dangers of

Adoption agencies for; procedures; difficulties in; illegal; concealment of biological parents; search for birth parents

Advertising techniques; expenditures; ethical; unethical; subliminal; leading agencies; history of; slogans

Age ageism; aging processes; aid to the aged; discrimination against the aged; treatment of the aged; different cultural views of aging; sex differences

Aggression aggressive behavior in animals; in humans; as innate; as learned; and territoriality

Agriculture science of; history of; in ancient societies; technology of; theories of

Alcoholism nature of; Alcoholics Anonymous; Al-Anon; abstinence; among the young; treatment of

Amnesty in draft evasion; in criminal law; and pardons; in Civil War; in Vietnam War; conditions of

Animals experimentation; intelligence of; aggression in; ethology; and communication

If your topic is too broad, you'll be forced to review a lot more research material than you're going to need. If you narrow your topic, you can search for research materials more efficiently. Here are three methods for narrowing and limiting your topic: *topoi*, *tree diagrams*, and *search directories*.

Topoi, the System of Topics.

Topoi, the system of topics, is a technique that originated with the classical rhetorics of ancient Greece and Rome but today is used more widely as a stimulus to creative thinking (DeVito, 1996). Using this method of **topoi**, you ask yourself a series of questions about your general subject. The process will help you see divisions of your general topic on which you might want to focus. Table 3 provides an example; the column on the left contains seven general questions (Who? What? Why? When? Where? How? and So?) and a series of subquestions (which will vary depending on your topic). The right column illustrates how some of the questions on the left might suggest specific aspects of the general subject of "homelessness."

Tree Diagrams.

Tree diagrams help you to divide your topic repeatedly into its constituent parts. Starting with the general topic, you divide it into its parts. Then you take one of these parts and divide it into its

parts. You continue with this dividing process until the topic seems manageable—until you believe you can reasonably cover it in some depth in the time allotted.

For example, suppose you begin with the topic of mass communication and choose television programs as the first general subtopic. Television programs, without some limitation, would take a lifetime to cover adequately. So you might divide this topic into such subtopics as comedy, children's programs, educational programs, news, movies, reality programs, soap operas, game shows, and sports. You might then take one of these topics, say comedy, and divide it into subtopics. Perhaps you might consider it on a time basis and divide television comedy into its significant time periods: pre-1960, 1961–1999, 2000 to the present. Or you might focus on situation comedies. Here you might examine a topic such as women in situation comedies, race relations in situation comedies, or family relationships in situation comedies. The resulting topic is at least beginning to look manageable. Figure 3 illustrates a tree diagram, showing another way of subdividing the general topic of television programs.

Search Directories.

A more technologically sophisticated way of both selecting and limiting your topic is to let a **search directory** do some of the

Table 3 Topoi: The System of Topics

These questions should enable you to use general topics to generate more specific ideas for your speeches. Try this system on any one of the topics listed in the Dictionary of Topics at **www.mycommunicationlab.com**. You'll be amazed at how many topics you'll be able to find. Your problem will quickly change from "What can I speak on?" to "Which one of these should I speak on?" Here's an example on the topic of homelessness.

General Questions	Subject-Specific Questions
Who? Who is he or she? Who is responsible? To whom was it done?	Who are the homeless? Who is the typical homeless person? Who is responsible for the increase in homelessness? Who cares for the homeless?
What? What is it? What effects does it have? What is it like? What is it different from? What are some examples?	What does it mean to be homeless? What does homelessness do to the people themselves? What does homelessness do to the society in general? What does homelessness mean to you and me?
Why? Why is there homelessness? Why does it happen? Why does it not happen?	Why are there so many homeless people? Why did this happen? Why does it happen in the larger cities more than in smaller towns? Why is it more prevalent in some countries than in others?
When? When did it happen? When will it occur? When will it end?	When did homelessness become so prevalent? When does it occur in the life of a person?
Where? Where did it come from? Where is it going? Where is it now?	Where is homelessness most prevalent? Where is there an absence of homelessness?
How? How does it work? How is it used? How do you do it? How do you operate it? How is it organized?	How does someone become homeless? How can we help the homeless? How can we prevent others from becoming homeless?
So? What does it mean? What is important about it? Why should I be concerned with this? Who cares?	Why is homelessness such an important social problem? Why must we be concerned with homelessness? How does all this affect me?

work for you. A search directory is a nested list of topics. You go from the general to the specific by selecting a topic, then a subdivision of that topic, then a subdivision of that subdivision. Eventually you'll be directed to relatively specific areas and websites that will suggest topics that may be suitable for a classroom speech.

Your Purpose

The *purpose* of your speech is the goal you want to achieve; it identifies the effect that you want your speech to have on your audience. In constructing your speech you'll first identify your general purpose and then your specific purpose.

General Purposes

Since you're now in a course in learning public speaking skills, your general purpose will likely be chosen for you. In this way, the classroom is like the real world. The situation, the audience you'll address, the nature of your job will dictate your **general purpose**; that is, whether your speech is to be informative or persuasive. If you're a lawyer giving a closing at a trial, you're speech must be persuasive. If you're an engineer explaining blueprints to clients, your speech must be informative. If you're a college professor, your speeches will be largely informative; if you're a politician, they will be mostly persuasive.

To inform and to persuade are the two general purposes of most public speeches. Another purpose is to serve some special occasion function—to toast, to bid farewell, to present an award. Special occasion speeches are in many ways combinations of informative and persuasive purposes.

In the **informative speech** (for example, a speech composed to inform your audience about a career seminar), you seek to create understanding: to clarify, to enlighten, to correct misunderstandings, to demonstrate how something works. In this type of speech, you'll rely most heavily on materials that amplify—examples, illustrations, definitions, testimony , visual aids, and the like.

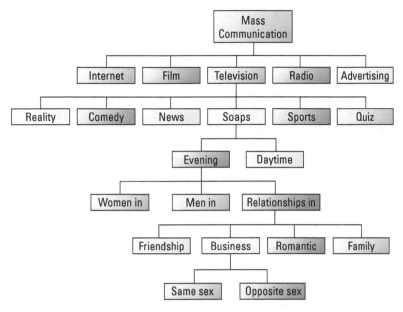

FIGURE 3 A Tree Diagram for Limiting Speech Topics

How would you draw a tree diagram for limiting topics beginning with such general subjects as immigration, education, sports, transportation, or politics? An alternative method for limiting topics with the "fishbone diagram" may be found at **www.mycommunicationlab.com.**

In the **persuasive speech** (for example, a speech aimed at persuading your audience to vote in the next election), you try to influence attitudes or behaviors; you seek to strengthen or change existing attitudes or to get the audience to take some action. In this type of speech, you'll rely heavily on materials that offer proof—on evidence, argument, and psychological appeals, for example.

In the **special occasion speech**, which contains elements of information and persuasion, you might, for example, introduce another speaker or a group of speakers, present a tribute, try to secure the good-

---

B u i l d i n g   C o m m u n i c a t i o n   S k i l l s   Limiting a Topic

Here are some overly general speech topics. Limit each of these topics to a subtopic that would be reasonable for a 5- to 10-minute speech.

1. Dangerous sports
2. Race relations
3. Parole
4. Censorship on the Internet
5. Ecological problems
6. Problems faced by college students
7. Morality
8. Health and fitness
9. Ethical issues in politics
10. Urban violence

As a general rule, focus on depth rather than breadth; avoid trying to cover too much in short speeches.

will of the listeners, toast your friends' anniversary, or "just" entertain your listeners.

Specific Purposes

Once you have chosen your general purpose, develop your **specific purpose** by identifying more precisely what you aim to accomplish. For example, in an informative speech, your specific purpose will identify the information you want to convey to your audience. Here are a few examples on the topic of stem cell research:

General purpose: To inform.

Specific purposes: To inform my audience of the differences between embryonic and adult stem cell research.

To inform my audience of two areas of stem cell research progress.

To inform my audience of the current federal regulations for funding stem cell research.

You may find it helpful to view your specific informative purposes in behavioral terms, identifying how you want the audience to demonstrate what they've learned from your speech. Here are a few examples:

- After listening to my speech, listeners should be able to describe the procedures for systematic desensitization.
- After listening to my speech, listeners should be able to define the three major differences between communism and capitalism.
- After listening to my speech, listeners should be able to demonstrate the five steps of active listening.

In a persuasive speech, your specific purpose identifies what you want your audience to believe, to think, or perhaps to do. Here are a few examples:

General purpose: To persuade.

Specific purposes: To persuade listeners to use systematic desensitization to reduce their apprehension.

To persuade listeners to believe that capitalism is superior to communism.

To persuade listeners to use active listening more often.

As you formulate your specific purposes, follow these five guidelines: Use an infinitive phrase; focus your purpose on your audience; limit it to one idea;

limit it to what you can reasonably expect to achieve; and use specific terms.

Use an Infinitive Phrase. Begin the statement of each specific purpose with your general purpose (to inform, to persuade) and then elaborate on your general purpose. For example:

- To inform my audience of the new registration procedures.
- To persuade my audience to contribute a book for the library fund-raiser.
- To introduce the main speaker of the day to my audience.

Focus on the Audience. Right now, your audience is your public speaking class, and it may at first seem unnecessary to include reference to them in each specific purpose statement. Actually, however, including the words "my audience" is crucial, because it keeps you focused on the people you want to inform or persuade; it's a reminder that everything you do in your speech needs to be directed by the purpose you want to achieve with this specific audience. Your speech purpose must be relevant to your audience. And in your career in years to come, you'll probably address a variety of different audiences; you need to keep each unique and distinct audience clearly in focus.

Limit Your Specific Purpose to One Idea. Try not to accomplish too much in too short a time. For example, consider the following statement of a specific purpose:

To persuade my audience of the prevalence of date rape in our community and that they should attend the dating seminars offered on campus.

This statement contains two specific purposes: (1) informing my audience of the prevalence of date rape in our community and (2) persuading my audience to attend the dating seminars offered on campus. This speaker needs to limit the specific purpose statement by selecting one specific purpose or the other. As you construct your specific purpose statement, beware of the word *and*—it's often a sign that your statement contains more than one specific purpose.

Limit Your Specific Purpose to What Is Reasonable. Limit your specific purposes to what you can reasonably develop and achieve in the allotted time. Specific purposes that are too broad are useless. Note how broad and overly general are such purposes as *To inform my audience about clothing design* or *To persuade my audience to improve their health*. You couldn't hope to cover such topics in one speech. It would be much more reasonable to have such purposes as *To inform my audience of the importance of color in clothing design* or *To persuade my audience to exercise three times a week.*

Use Specific Terms. Phrase your specific purposes with specific terms. The more precise your specific purpose statement, the more effectively it will guide you in the remaining steps of preparing your speech. Notice that the purposes used as examples of covering too much are also overly general and very unspecific ("clothing design" can mean hundreds of things, as can "improve your health"). Instead of the overly general *To persuade my audience to help the homeless,* consider the more specific *To persuade my audience to donate a few hours a month to make phone calls for the Homeless Coalition.*

STEP 2: ANALYZE YOUR AUDIENCE

The characteristic that seems best to define an audience is common purpose: A public speaking **audience** is a group of individuals gathered together to hear a speech. If you're to be a successful speaker, then you must know your audience. This knowledge will help you in selecting your topic; phrasing your purpose; establishing a relationship between yourself and your audience; and choosing examples, illustrations, and logical and emotional appeals.

Your first step in **audience analysis** is to construct an audience profile in which you analyze audience members' sociological or demographic characteristics. These characteristics help you estimate the attitudes, beliefs, and values of your audience. If you want to effect changes in these attitudes, beliefs, and values, you have to know what they are.

Attitudes, Beliefs, and Values

An **attitude** is a tendency to act for or against a person, object, or position. If you have a positive attitude toward the death penalty, you're likely to argue or act in favor of the death penalty (for example, vote for a candidate who supports the death penalty). If you have a negative attitude toward the death penalty, then you're likely to argue or act against it. Attitudes toward the death penalty will influence how favorably or unfavorably listeners will respond to a speaker who supports or denounces capital punishment.

A **belief** is the confidence or conviction you have in the truth of some proposition. For example, you may believe that there is an afterlife, that education is the best way to rise from poverty, that democracy is the best form of government, or that all people are

born equal. If your listeners believe that the death penalty is a deterrent to crime, for example, then they will be more likely to favor arguments for (and speakers who support) the death penalty than will listeners who don't believe in the connection between the death penalty and deterrence.

The term **value** refers to your perception of the worth or goodness (or worthlessness or badness) of some concept or idea. For example, you probably attribute positive values to financial success, education, and contributing to the common welfare. At the same time, you probably place negative values on chemical weapons, corrupt politicians, and selling drugs to children. Because the values an audience holds will influence how it responds to ideas related to those values, it's essential that you learn the values of your specific audience. For example, if the people in your audience place a high positive value on child welfare, then they are likely to vote for legislation that protects children or allocates money for breakfasts and lunches in school—and they might consider signing a petition, volunteering their time, or donating their money to advance the welfare of children. If you find that your audience places a negative value on big business, you may want to reconsider using the testimony of corporate leaders or the statistics compiled by corporations.

Analyzing the Sociology of the Audience

In analyzing an audience, be careful not to assume that people covered by the same label are necessarily all alike. As soon as you begin to think about a sociological characteristic in terms of an expressed or implied "all," consider the possibility that you may be stereotyping. Don't assume that all women or all older people or all highly educated people think or believe the same things. They don't.

Nevertheless, there are characteristics that seem to be more common among one group than another, and it is these characteristics that you want to explore in your sociological analysis of your audience. Let's look at four major sociological or demographic variables: (1) cultural factors, (2) age, (3) gender, and (4) religion and religiousness.

Cultural Factors

Cultural factors such as nationality, race, and cultural identity are crucial in audience analysis. Largely because of different training and experiences, the interests, values, and goals of various cultural groups will differ. Further, cultural factors will influence each of the remaining sociological factors; for example, attitudes toward age and gender will differ greatly from one culture to another. Perhaps the primary

---

Building Communication Skills — Using Cultural Beliefs as Assumptions

Evaluate each of the cultural beliefs listed below in terms of how effective each would be if used as a basic assumption by a speaker addressing your public speaking class. Use the following scale:

A = The audience would accept this assumption and would welcome a speaker with this point of view.

B = Some audience members would listen receptively and others wouldn't.

C = The audience would reject this assumption and would not welcome a speaker with this point of view.

1. A return to religious values is the best hope for the world.

2. The welfare of our country must come first, even before our own individual interests.

3. Sex outside of marriage is wrong and sinful.

4. Winning is all-important; it's not how you play the game, it's whether or not you win that matters.

There are probably few topics that the audience has not been culturally influenced about. So don't neglect cultural analysis regardless of your specific topic or audience.

---

question to ask is "Are the cultural beliefs and values of the audience relevant to your topic and purpose?" That is, might the cultural background(s) of your audience members influence the way they see your topic? If so, find out what these beliefs and values are and take these into consideration as you build your speech.

Age

Different age groups have different attitudes and beliefs, largely because they have had different experiences in different contexts. Take these differences into consideration in preparing your speeches. For example, let's say that you're an investment counselor and you want to persuade your listeners to invest their money to increase their earnings. Your speech to an audience of retired people (say in their 60s) would be very different from an address to an audience of young executives (say in their 30s). In considering the age of your audience, ask yourself if the age groups differ in goals, interests, and day-to-day concerns that may be related to your topic and purpose. Graduating from college, achieving corporate success, raising a family, and saving for retirement are concerns that differ greatly from one age group to another.

Gender

Gender is one of the most difficult audience variables to analyze. In recent decades rapid social changes have made it difficult to pin down the effects of gender. As you analyze your audience in

terms of gender, ask yourself if men and women differ in the values they consider important insofar as these values are related to your topic and purpose. For example, traditionally, men have been found to place greater importance on theoretical, economic, and political values. Traditionally, women have been found to place greater importance on aesthetic, social, and religious values. In framing appeals and in selecting examples, take into account the values your audience members consider most important.

Ask too if your topic will be seen as more interesting by one gender or the other. Will men and women have different attitudes toward the topic? Men and women do not, for example, respond in the same way to such topics as abortion, rape, and equal pay for equal work. Select your topics and supporting materials in light of the gender of your audience members.

Religion and Religiousness

The religion and religiousness of your audience often will influence their responses to your speech. Religion permeates all topics and all issues. On a most obvious level, such issues as attitudes toward birth control, abortion, and divorce are often connected to religion. Similarly, people's views on premarital sex, marriage, child rearing, money, cohabitation, responsibilities toward parents, and thousands of other issues are frequently influenced by religion. Religion also influences many people's ideas concerning such topics as obedience to authority; responsibility to government; and the usefulness of such qualities as honesty, guilt, and happiness.

UNFAVORABLE AUDIENCE

From their initial reactions you immediately see that your audience is totally against your thesis and are tuning you out.

WHAT DO YOU SAY?

© A. Ramey/PhotoEdit

Ask yourself if your topic or purpose might be seen as an attack on the religious beliefs of any segment of your audience. If so, then you might want to make adjustments—not necessarily to abandon your purpose, but to rephrase your arguments or incorporate different evidence.

In analyzing the religiousness of your audience, also consider whether members identify themselves as being a part of a secular or a sacred culture. Secular cultures are those in which religion does not dominate the attitudes and views of the people or greatly influence political or educational decisions (Hofstede, 1997; Dodd, 1995). Liberal Protestant cultures such as those of the Scandinavian countries would be clearly secular. Sacred cultures, on the other hand, are those in which religion and religious beliefs and values dominate everything a person does and influence politics, education, and just about every topic or issue imaginable. Islamic cultures would be traditional examples of sacred cultures. Technically, the United States would be a secular culture (the Constitution, for example, expressly separates church and state); but in some areas of the country, religion exerts a powerful influence on schools (from prayers to condom distribution to sex education) and in politics (from the selection of political leaders to concern for social welfare to gay rights legislation).

Analyzing the Psychology of the Audience

In addition to looking at the sociological characteristics of audience members, it's often useful to consider their psychological characteristics—particularly their willingness to listen to you, their favorableness to your purpose, and their background knowledge.

How Willing Is Your Audience?

Your immediate concern in a public speaking class, of course, is with audience willingness on the part of your fellow students. Do they come to hear your speech because they have to, or do they come because they're interested in what you'll say? If they're a willing group, then you have few problems. And even if they're an unwilling group, all is not lost; you just have to work a little harder in preparing your speech. The unwilling audience demands special and delicate handling. Here are a few suggestions to help change your listeners from unwilling to willing:

- Secure their interest and attention as early in your speech as possible, and reinforce their interest throughout the speech by using little-known facts, quotations, startling statistics, examples, narratives, audiovisual aids, and the like.

- Reward the audience for their attendance and attention. Let the audience know you're aware they're making a sacrifice in coming to hear you speak. Tell them you appreciate it.

- Relate your topic and supporting materials directly to your audience's needs and wants. Show the audience how they can—for example—save time, make money, solve important problems, or become more popular.

How Favorable Is Your Audience?

Audiences vary in the degree to which their ideas and attitudes will be favorable or unfavorable toward you, your topic, or your point of view. You may wish to examine your ability to predict audience favor toward various topics or beliefs by taking the following self-test.

77

TEST YOURSELF

How Well Do You Know Your Audience?

Here are some statements of beliefs that members of your class may agree or disagree with—and which you might want to use as basic theses (propositions) in your in-class speeches. Try predicting how favorable or unfavorable you think your class members would be to each of these beliefs. Use a 10-point scale ranging from 1 (extremely unfavorable) through 5 (relatively neutral) to 10 (extremely favorable).

_____ 1. The welfare of the family must come first, even before your own.

_____ 2. Sex outside of marriage is wrong and sinful.

_____ 3. In a heterosexual relationship, a wife should submit graciously to the leadership of her husband.

_____ 4. Individual states should be allowed to fly the Confederate flag if they wish.

_____ 5. Intercultural relationships are OK in business but should be discouraged when it comes to intimate or romantic relationships; generally, the different ethnic groups should be kept "pure."

_____ 6. Money is good; the quest for financial success is a perfectly respectable (even noble) one.

_____ 7. Immigration into the United States should be curtailed, at least until current immigrants are assimilated.

_____ 8. Parents who prevent their children from receiving the latest scientific cures because of a belief in faith healing should be prosecuted.

_____ 9. Same-sex marriage should be legalized.

_____ 10. Medicinal marijuana should be readily available.

_____ 11. Physician-assisted suicide should be legalized.

_____ 12. Male and female prostitution should be legalized and taxed like any other job that produces income.

HOW DID YOU DO? After you've indicated your predictions, discuss these with the class as a whole. How accurate were you in guessing your audience's beliefs?

WHAT WILL YOU DO? Practice adapting a thesis to both the favorable and the unfavorable audience. Select a thesis (one of those listed in this self-test or one of your own) toward which your audience would be highly favorable, and indicate how you'd adapt your speech to them. Then try the more difficult task: Select a thesis toward which your audience would be highly unfavorable, and indicate how you'd adapt to them.

If you conclude that your audience will be unfavorable to your chosen topic or viewpoint, the following suggestions should help:

- Clear up any possible misapprehensions that may be causing disagreement. For example, if they believe that the new parking regulations are the first step to higher parking fees, but that isn't true, mention it. Say, quite directly, "I understand that some people believe that these new regulations will lead to higher parking fees, but they won't; in fact, they will save money."

- Build on commonalities; stress what you and the audience share as people, as interested citizens, as fellow students. When audience members see similarity or common ground between themselves and you, they become more favorable to both you and your speech.

- Organize your speech inductively. Try to build your speech from areas of agreement, through areas of slight disagreement, up to the major differences between the audience's attitudes and your position. Once areas of agreement are established, it's easier to bring up differences.

- Strive for small gains. Don't try, in a five-minute speech, to convince a pro-life group to contribute money for a new abortion clinic or to persuade a pro-choice group to vote against liberalizing abortion laws. Be content to get the audience to listen fairly and to see some validity in your position.

- Acknowledge the differences explicitly. If it's clear to the audience that they and you are at opposite ends of an issue, you might want to acknowledge this fact and use it as a takeoff point to stress what you both agree on. You might say, for example, "I know that our differences on this issue are great, but what I also know is that we have the same ultimate goal."

How Knowledgeable Is Your Audience? Listeners differ greatly in the knowledge they have. Some listeners will be quite knowledgeable about a given topic; others will be almost totally ignorant. Mixed audiences are the most difficult to address. Treat audiences that lack knowledge of your topic very carefully. Never confuse a lack of audience knowledge with a lack of ability to understand.

- Don't talk down to your audience. No one wants to listen to a speaker putting them down.

- Don't confuse a lack of knowledge with a lack of intelligence. An audience may have no knowledge of your topic but be quite capable of following a clearly presented, logically developed argument. Try especially hard to use concrete examples,

78

audiovisual aids, and simple language. Fill in background details as required. Avoid jargon and other specialized terminology that may not be clear to someone new to the subject.

- Let the audience know that you're aware of their knowledge and expertise. Try to do this as early in the speech as possible. Emphasize that what you have to say will be relevant and valuable. Tell them that you'll be presenting recent developments or new approaches. In short, let them know that they will not be wasting their time listening to your speech.
- Emphasize your credibility, especially your competence in this general subject area.

Analyzing and Adapting during the Speech

In addition to analyzing your audience and making adaptations in your speech *before* delivering your speech, devote attention to analysis and adaptation *during* the speech. Although this during-the-speech analysis is especially important when you know little of your audience or find yourself facing a very different audience than you expected, it is always crucial to public speaking success. Here are a few suggestions:

Focus on Listeners as Message Senders

As you're speaking, look at your listeners. Remember that just as you're sending messages to your audience, they're also sending messages to you. Pay attention to these messages; and on the basis of what they tell you, make whatever adjustments are necessary.

You can make a wide variety of adjustments to each type of audience response. For example, if your audience shows signs of boredom, increase your volume, move closer to them, or tell them that what you're going to say will be of value to them. If your audience shows signs of disagreement or hostility, stress a similarity you have with them. If your audience looks puzzled or confused, pause a moment and rephrase your ideas, provide necessary definitions, or insert an internal summary. If your audience seems impatient, say, for example, "my last argument . . ." instead of your originally planned "my third argument . . ."

Ask "What If" Questions

As you prepare your speech, it's helpful to ask "what if" questions. These will help you make any necessary on-the-spot adjustments and adaptations. For example, let's say you have been told that you're to explain the opportunities available to the nontradi-

tional student at your college. You've been told that your audience will consist mainly of working women in their 30s and 40s who are just beginning college. As you prepare your speech with this audience in mind, ask yourself "what if" questions. For example:

- What if the audience has a large number of men?
- What if the audience consists of women much older than 40?
- What if the audience members also come with their spouses or their children?

Keeping such questions in mind will force you to consider alternatives as you prepare your speech. Then you'll have ideas readily available if you face a new or different audience.

Address Audience Responses Directly

Another way of dealing with audience responses is to confront them directly. To those who are giving disagreement feedback, for example, you could say something like:

You may disagree with this position, but all I ask is that you hear me out and see if this new way of doing things will not simplify your accounting procedures.

Or, to those who seem puzzled, you might say:

I know this plan may seem confusing, but bear with me; it will become clear in a moment.

Or, to those who seem impatient, you might respond:

I know this has been a long day, but give me just a few more minutes and you'll be able to save hours recording your accounts.

By responding to your listeners' reactions and feedback, you acknowledge your audience's priorities. You let them know that you hear them, that you're with them, and that you're responding to their very real needs.

STEP 3: RESEARCH YOUR TOPIC

Throughout the process of preparing your public speeches, you'll need to find information to use as source material in your speech. This means doing research. Through research you'll find examples, illustrations, and definitions to help you inform your listeners; testimony, statistics, and arguments to support your major ideas; personal anecdotes, quotations, and stories to help you bring your topics to life.

Research, however, also serves another important function: It helps you persuade your listeners, because it makes you appear more believable. For example, if your listeners feel you've examined lots of research, they'll be more apt to see you as competent and knowledgeable and therefore more apt to believe what you say. And of course, presenting the research is itself convincing. When you present research to your listeners, you give them the very reasons they need to draw conclusions or decide on a course of action.

In this section we'll consider research in some depth: (1) general principles, (2) taking research notes, (3) the major sources of information, (4) evaluating research, (5) integrating research into your speech, (6) citing research sources, and lastly the dreaded topic of plagiarism.

General Research Principles

Here are a few principles to help you research your speeches more effectively and more efficiently.

Examine What You Know

Begin your search by examining what you already know. For example, write down relevant books, articles, or websites that you're familiar with or people who might know something about the topic. Also consider what you know from your own personal experiences and observations. In this way you can attack the problem systematically and not waste effort or time.

Begin with a General Overview

Continue your search by getting an authoritative but general overview of the topic. An encyclopedia article, book chapter, or magazine article in print or online will serve this purpose well. This general overview will help you see the topic as a whole and understand how its various parts fit together.

Consult Increasingly Specific Sources

Follow up the general overview with increasingly more detailed and specialized sources. Fortunately, many of the general articles contain references or links to direct this next stage of your search for more specific information.

Research Time Management

Because a great deal of your time—in this course and in numerous others—will be spent on research, learn to use your research time efficiently. Here are a few suggestions:

- *Multitask.* Combine your research tasks and do them simultaneously. For example, when going to the library or logging on to the Internet, have more than one task in mind. If you know the topics of your next few speeches, or if you're writing a sociology paper on a related topic, do the research for both at the same time.

- *Watch detours.* When you are searching the Net, it's easy to get lured into taking long detours. These are often excellent learning experiences and are not necessarily detrimental. For purposes of time management, however, it will help if you keep your purpose clearly in mind—even to the point of writing it down—as you surf the Net or lurk among the chat groups.

- *Access your library from home.* If possible, access your college library's online catalog of books from home; it will save you time if you can go to the library with your searches already completed. If your library subscribes to full text databases that can be accessed from your home computer (ProQuest and Lexis-Nexis are popular examples), you may be able to do all your research from the comfort of your home.

- *Consult your librarian.* One useful but often overlooked research resources is your librarian. Librarians are experts in the very researching issues that may be giving you trouble. They'll be able to help you access biographical material, indexes of current articles, materials in specialized collections at other libraries, and a wide variety of computerized databases.

Research Notes

The more accurate your research notes are, the less time you'll waste going back to sources to check on a date or a spelling. Accurate records also will prevent you from going to sources you've already consulted but may have forgotten about. The following suggestions may prove helpful to you as you take notes during the research process.

Create Folders

If you want to collect your material on paper, loose-leaf notebooks or simple manila folders work well to keep everything relating to a speech or article in the same place. If you want to file your material electronically, create a general folder and subfolders as you need them. This will work especially well if you can scan into your folder material you find in print. In this notebook or folder, you can consolidate the sources consulted, quotations, ideas, arguments,

REFLECTIONS ON ETHICS

Plagiarism

The term **plagiarism** refers to passing off the work (ideas, words, illustrations) of others as our own. It is not the act of using another's ideas—we all do that. Plagiarism is using another's ideas without acknowledging that they are the ideas of this other person; it is presenting the ideas as if they were ours.

Plagiarism exists on a continuum, ranging from appropriating an entire term paper or speech written by someone else to using a quotation or research finding without citing the author.

Plagiarism also includes situations in which, for example, a student gets help from a friend without acknowledging this assistance. In some cultures—especially in collectivist cultures (cultures that emphasize the group and mutual cooperation) such as those of Korea, Japan, and China—teamwork is strongly encouraged. Students are taught to help other students with their work. But in the United States and in many other individualist cultures (cultures that emphasize individuality and competitiveness), teamwork without acknowledgment is considered plagiarism.

In U.S. institutions of higher education, plagiarism is a serious violation of the rules of academic honesty and carries serious penalties, sometimes even expulsion. And it's interesting to note that instructors are mobilizing and educating themselves in the techniques for detecting plagiarism. Further, as with all crimes, ignorance of the rules is not an acceptable defense against charges of plagiarism. This last point is especially important because a good deal of plagiarism is committed through a lack of information as to what does and what does not constitute plagiarism. Here are just a few reasons why plagiarism is wrong.

Why Plagiarism Is Unacceptable

Plagiarism is unacceptable for a variety of reasons:

- Plagiarism is a violation of another's intellectual property rights. Much as it would be wrong to take another person's watch without permission, it's wrong to take another person's ideas without acknowledging that you did it.
- You're in college to develop your own ideas and ways of expressing them; plagiarism defeats this fundamental purpose.
- Evaluations (everything from grades in school to promotions in the workplace) assume that what you present as your work is in fact your work.

Avoiding Plagiarism

Let's start with the easy part. You do not have to—and should not—cite sources for common knowledge: information that is readily available in numerous sources and is not likely to be disputed. For example, the population of Thailand, the amendments to the U.S. Constitution, the actions of the United Nations, or the way the heart pumps blood are all common knowledge, and you would not cite an almanac or political science text from which you got this information. On the other hand, if you were talking about the attitudes of people from Thailand or the reasons constitutional amendments were adopted, then you'd need to cite your sources, because this information is not common knowledge and may well be disputed.

For information that is not common knowledge, you need to acknowledge your source. Here are a few rules that will help you avoid even the suggestion of plagiarism:

1. Acknowledge the source of any ideas you present that are not your own. If you learned of an idea in your history course, then cite the history instructor or history textbook. If you read an idea in an article, then cite the article.

2. Acknowledge the words of another. It's obvious what to do when you're quoting another person exactly; you need to cite the person you're quoting. You should also cite others even when you paraphrase their words, because you are still using others' ideas; but when paraphrases need to be credited may not always be so clear. To help with this question, some of the plagiarism websites established by different universities include exercises and extended examples; see, for example, Indiana University's site at **www.indiana.edu/∼uts/ wts/plagiarism.html** or Purdue University's at **http://owl.english.purdue.edu/handouts/ print/reseach/r-plagiar.html**. The same is true when you use the organizational structure of another person; just say, for example, "I'm following the line of reasoning proposed by Andrew Rancer in his comparison of aggression and argument."

3. Acknowledge help from others. If your roommate gave you examples or ideas or helped you style your speech, acknowledge the help.

Ethical Choice Point

While listening to an impressive speech in your class, you recognize that you've read this exact same material in an obscure online publication. You're annoyed that this student has not done the work that everyone else has done and yet will probably earn a high grade. However, you wonder if you want to or should take on being the ethical conscience of your class. What is your ethical obligation in this case? What would you do?

suggested references, preliminary outlines, and material you've printed or downloaded.

Key Your Notes

Notes are most effective when they're keyed to specific topics. For example, let's say that your speech is to be on animal experimentation. Your notebook or major folder might be titled *Animal Experimentation*. The notebook divisions or subfolders might then be labeled "Basic Information" (statistics on animal experimentation, people to contact, organizations involved in this issue), "Arguments for Animal Experimentation," and "Arguments against Animal Experimentation." Taking notes with reference to your preliminary outline will help focus your research and will remind you of those topics for which you need more information. It will also help you keep the information logically organized.

Take Complete Notes

Make sure your notes are complete (and legible). If you have to err, then err on the side of too much detail. You can always cut the quotation or select one example out of the three at a later time. As you take notes, be sure to identify the source of the material—so that you can find that reference again should you need it, and so that you can reference it in your speech outline. When you use material from a Web source, be sure to print out or save to folder the Web page, noting the URL and the date you accessed this site. This way you'll be able to cite a source even if the Web page disappears, a not unlikely possibility.

The resources available to you today are rich and varied. A brief survey follows.

Libraries and Bookstores

Libraries, the major depositories of stored information, have evolved from a concentration on print sources to their current focus on computerized databases. Starting your research at the library (and with the librarian's assistance) is probably a wise move.

Here are a few online libraries that you'll find especially helpful.

- Quick Study, the University of Minnesota's Library Research Guide (http://tutorial.lib.umn.edu), will help you learn how to find the materials you need and will answer lots of questions you probably have about research.

- For a list of library catalogs that will help you find the location of the material you need, try www.libdex.com/. By clicking on "library-type index"

you'll get a list of categories of libraries; for example, government or medical or religious.

- The largest library in the United States is the Library of Congress, which houses millions of books, maps, multimedia, and manuscripts. Time spent at this library (begin with www.loc.gov) will be well invested. The home page will guide you to a wealth of information.

- Maintained by the National Archives and Records Administration, the presidential libraries may be accessed at www.archives.gov/.

- The Virtual Library is a collection of links to 14 subject areas; for example, agriculture, business and economics, computing, communication and media, and education. Visit this at www.vlib.org.

- If you're not satisfied with your own college library, visit the libraries of some of the large state universities, such as the University of Pennsylvania (www.library.upenn.edu/cgi-bin/res/sr.cgi) or the University of Illinois (http://gateway.library.uiuc.edu).

- The Internet Public Library (www.ipl.org) is actually not a library; it's a collection of links to a wide variety of materials. But it will function much like the reference desk at any of the world's best libraries.

Also visit some of the online bookstores, such as Amazon (www.amazon.com), Barnes & Noble (www.bn.com), or Borders (www.Borders.com) and their brick-and-mortar counterparts. In addition, other useful sites include: http://aaupnet.org/ (the Association of American University Presses) and http://www.cs.cmu.edu/Web/People/spok/banned-books.html (contains links to texts of books that have been banned in the United States and elsewhere). Some online bookstores now enable you to search some of their books for specific topics and read a paragraph or so on each topic reference.

Of course, you'll also go to a brick-and-mortar library, because it houses materials that are not on the Net and/or that you want to access in print. Because each library functions somewhat differently, your best bet in learning about a specific library—such as your own college library—is to talk with your librarian about what the library has available, what kinds of training or tours it offers, and how materials are most easily accessed.

Interviewing for Information

One research activity that you'll often find helpful is interviewing people who have special information that you might use in your speech. For example, you might want to interview a veterinarian for

ASKING A FAVOR

You're preparing a speech on the architectural ideas for rebuilding Ground Zero and you want to ask some of the famous architects a few questions so you can integrate their most recent thoughts (and interject a more personalized note) into your speech.

WHAT DO YOU SAY?
In what channel?

© DiMaggio/Kalish/CORBIS

information on proper diet for household pets, a meteorologist for information on living through a hurricane, or average people for information on their opinions on politics, religion, or any of a wide variety of topics. In these informational interviews, a great part of your effectiveness will hinge on your ability to listen actively, for total meaning, with empathy, with an open mind, and ethically, all of which are covered in this chapter. Here are a few additional suggestions to help you use interviewing to find needed information.

- *Select the person you wish to interview.* You might, for example, look through your college catalog for an instructor teaching a course that involves your topic. Or visit newsgroups and look for people who have posted articles on your topic. If you want to contact a book author, you can always write to the author in care of the publisher or editor (listed on the copyright page), though many authors are now including their e-mail addresses. You often can find the address and phone number of a professional person in the *Encyclopedia of Associations*, or you can write to the person via the association's website. Newsgroup and listserv writers are of course the easiest to contact, as their e-mail addresses are included with their posts. To find an expert, try *The Yearbook of Experts, Authorities, and Spokespersons* or any of a variety of websites, such as www.experts.com or http://uscnews3.usc.edu/experts/.

- *Secure an appointment.* Phone the person or send an e-mail requesting an interview. State the purpose of your request and say that you hope to conduct a brief interview by phone or that you'd like to send a series of questions by e-mail.

- *Develop your questions.* Generally, ask questions that provide the interviewee with room to dis-

cuss the issues you want to raise. Fore example, asking, "Do you have formal training in the area of family therapy?" may elicit a simple yes or no, which will not be very informative. On the other hand, asking, "Can you tell me something of your background in this field?" is open-ended, allowing the interviewee to talk in some detail. Ask questions phrased in a neutral manner. Try not to lead the interviewee to give the answers you want.

- *Establish rapport with the interviewee.* Open the in-person, telephone, e-mail, or chat-group interview by thanking the person for making the time available and again stating your purpose. You might say something like: "I really appreciate your making time for this interview. As I mentioned, I'm preparing a speech on XYZ, and your experience in this area will help a great deal."

- *Ask for permission to tape or print the interview.* It's a good idea to keep an accurate record of the interview, so ask permission to tape the interview if it's in person or by telephone. Taping will eliminate your worry about taking notes and having to ask the interviewee to slow down or repeat. It will also provide you with a much more accurate record of the interview than will handwritten notes. But always ask permission first. Similarly, if the interview is by e-mail or via chat group and you want to quote the interviewee's responses, ask permission first. An agreement to be interviewed does not include permission to print or distribute the interview or even parts of it.

- *Close with an expression of appreciation, and follow up with a thank-you note.* Thank the person for making the time available for the interview and for being informative, cooperative, helpful, and so forth. Follow up the interview with a note of thanks. Or perhaps you might send the person you interviewed a copy of your speech (e-mail would work well here), again with a note of thanks.

Primary and Secondary Sources

As a researcher, be sure to distinguish between primary and secondary source material, whether your materials come from print or online. **Primary sources** include, for example, an original research study reported in an academic journal, a corporation's annual report, or an eyewitness report of an accident. With primary sources there is nothing (or very little) standing between the event (say, an accident) and the reporting of it (the eyewitness testimony). **Secondary sources** include, for example, a summary of research appearing in a popular magazine, a television news report on a corporation's earnings, or a report by someone who talked to someone who witnessed an accident. With secondary sources someone stands between the actual event and the report; for example, a science reporter reads the scientist's monograph (primary source), then writes up a summary for the popular press (secondary source).

As a listener and speaker you'll hear and use both types of source material. Yet there are important differences that you should keep in mind. Above all, secondary source material is less reliable than primary source material, because it is a step removed from the actual facts or events. The writer of secondary material may have forgotten important parts, may be biased and so may have slanted the reporting to reflect his or her attitudes, or may have distorted the material because he or she misunderstood the data.

On the other hand, the writer may have been able to express complicated scientific data in simple language—often making it easier for a nonscientist to understand than the original report. In any case, when using or listening to secondary sources, examine the information for any particular spin the writer may be giving the material. If possible, check the primary source material itself to see if anything was left out or if the conclusions are really warranted on the basis of the primary evidence.

General Reference Works

General reference works are excellent starting points for researching your topic. One of the best general reference works is the standard encyclopedia. Any good encyclopedia will give you a general overview of your subject and suggestions for additional reading. The most comprehensive and the most prestigious is the *Encyclopaedia Britannica*, available in print, on CD-ROM, and online. A variety of other encyclopedias also are available in print, on CD-ROM, or online. The best way to search for these is to visit Freeality.com (www.freeality.com//encyclop.htm) and search through the available general and specific encyclopedias.

Perhaps the most widely known online encyclopedia, and a resource that you'll find extremely useful, is Wikipedia (www.wikipedia.com). This encyclopedia is a bit different from those mentioned above. The articles in Wikipedia—some brief and some extremely long and detailed—are written by people who are not necessarily experts. Therefore, although many of the articles are reviewed, updated, and corrected periodically, Wikipedia doesn't have the authority of the more traditional encyclopedias. Some universities have even banned the use of this source because of some inaccuracies, so you may want to check on the acceptance of referencing such work. If you do use Wikipedia, you'll need to check its facts and statistics—most of which you'll find easy to do because of the extensive hotlinks written into each article and the list of additional sources provided for most articles.

News Sources

Often you'll want to read reports on scientific breakthroughs, political speeches, congressional actions, obituaries, financial news, international developments, United Nations actions, or any of a host of other topics. Or you may wish to locate the date of a particular event and learn something about what else was going on in the world at that particular time. For this type of information, you may want to consult one or more of the many *news sources* available. Especially relevant are newspaper indexes, newspaper and newsmagazine websites, news wire services, and broadcast news networks.

- *Newspaper indexes.* One way to start a newspaper search is to consult one of the newspaper indexes, such as those at www.all-links.com/newscentral, www.newspapers.com, www.newslink.org/menu.html, and www.newspaperlinks.com. At sites like these you'll find hot links to thousands of national and local newspapers.

- *Newspaper and newsmagazine websites.* Most newspapers and magazines maintain their own websites from which you can access current and past issues. Here are a few to get you started: www.latimes.com/ (*Los Angeles Times*), www.usatoday.com/ (*USA Today*), www.wsj.com (Wall Street Journal), www.nytimes.com (the *New York Times*), and www.washingtonpost.com (the *Washington Post*).

- *News wire services.* Four wire services should prove helpful. The Associated Press can be accessed at www.ap.org/, Reuters at www.reuters.com/, United Press International at www.upi.com, and PR Newswire at www.prnewswire.com/.

- *News networks online.* All of the television news stations maintain extremely useful websites. Here are some of the most useful: Access CNN at www.cnn.com/, ESPN at http://espn.sportszone.com/, ABC News at www.abcnews.com/newsflash, CBS News at www.cbs.com/news/, or MSNBC News at www.msnbc.com/news.

You'll find it helpful to compare the news available on one of the major newspapers' websites (for example, the *Washington Post* site or the *New York Times* site) with the news presented by a wire service such as the Associated Press (www.ap.org) or Reuters (www.reuters.com). Which seems the more reliable? The more complete? The more impartial?

Biographical Material

As a speaker you'll often need information about particular individuals. For example, in using the testimony of experts in various fields, it's helpful to stress their qualifications, which you can easily learn about from even brief biographies. Or you may want to look up authors of books or articles to find out something about their education, their training, or their other writings. Or you may wish to discover if there have been critical evaluations of their work—such as, say, book reviews or articles about them or their writings. Knowing something about your sources enables you to more effectively evaluate their competence, convey their credibility to the audience, and answer audience questions about them.

One of the most enjoyable and useful biography sites is maintained by The Biography Channel (www.biography.com) and contains biographies of some 25,000 individuals from all walks of life. Another great source is the Biography and Genealogy Master Index, which indexes several hundred biographical sources. Online versions of this are maintained by a variety of colleges; one of the best is Arizona State University Libraries (www.asu.edu/lib/resources/db/biogr.htm). This master index will send you to numerous specialized works.

Other excellent general resources include the Biography Almanac available at Infoplease (www.infoplease.com), which lists some 30,000 biographies; the University of Michigan's Internet Public Library (http://ipl.sils/umich.edu), which contains a great list of biography websites; and the Biograph-

ical Dictionary (http://s9.com/biography), which covers some 28,000 men and women.

The Government

Governmental bodies and agencies throughout the United States (at the federal, state, and municipal levels) publish an enormous amount of information that you're sure to find useful in speeches on almost any topic. One excellent starting point is Google's government search (www.usgov.google.com). This engine covers all websites in the *.gov* domain. The amount of information you'll find, however, may at first be daunting. For example, if you search for "publications," you find more than 4 million websites; for "education," more than 11 million; and for "health," more than 24 million. You'll definitely need to limit your search. One way to do this is of course to include additional terms (for example, health + drugs + teenagers) or to use phrases in quotations ("teenage drug use").

Another way is to visit one or more of the 13 relevant departments of the federal government (these are the Departments of Agriculture, Commerce, Defense, Education, Energy, Health and Human Services, Housing and Urban Development, Interior, Justice, Labor, State, Treasury, and Transportation). All issue reports, pamphlets, books, and assorted documents dealing with their various concerns. Here are a few of the topics on which some of the departments have information that you'll find useful in researching your speeches.

- Department of the Treasury (www.ustreas.gov): taxes, property auctions, savings, economy, financial markets, international business, and money management.

- Department of Housing and Urban Development (www.hud.gov): home buying, selling, renting, and owning; fair housing; foreclosures; consumer information; FHA refunds; homelessness; and information for tenants, landlords, farm workers, senior citizens, and victims of discrimination.

- Department of Defense (www.defenselink.mil/): news releases, speech texts, military pay and benefits, casualty reports.

- Department of Justice (www.usdoj.gov): drugs and drug enforcement; Patriot Act information; trafficking in persons; inmate locator; Americans with Disabilities Act; sentencing statistics; and information from the Bureau of Alcohol, Tobacco, Firearms, and Explosives.

- Department of Health and Human Services (www.hhs.gov): aging, AIDS, disease, safety issues, food and drug information, disaster and emergency

A Speech of Introduction

Throughout these six public speaking units, you'll find Public Speaking Sample Assistant boxes. These boxes present complete speeches or outlines with annotations; they will help you to see the public speech as a whole and to ask critical questions about structure, support, language, and numerous other public speaking factors we consider in these units.

One of the first speeches you may be called upon to make is the speech in which you introduce yourself or (as illustrated in this particular speech) some other person. This speech also will let you see a public speech as a whole and will give you reference points for examining each of the 10 steps for preparing and delivering a public speech.

Introduction

It's a real pleasure to introduce Joe Robinson to you. I want to tell you a little about Joe's background, his present situation, and his plans for the future.

In this introduction, the speaker accomplishes several interrelated purposes: to place the speech in a positive context, to explain the purpose of the speech and orient the audience, to tell them what the speech will cover and that it will follow a time pattern—beginning with the past, moving to the present, and then ending with the proposed future. What other types of opening statements might be appropriate? In what other ways might you organize a speech of introduction?

Transition

Let's look first at Joe's past.

This transitional statement alerts listeners that the speaker is moving from the introduction to the first major part of what is called the "body" of the speech.

Body, first main point (the past)

Joe comes to us from Arizona, where he lived and worked on a small ranch with his father and grandparents—mostly working with dairy cows. Working on a farm gave Joe a deep love and appreciation for animals that he carries with him today and into his future plans.

Joe's mother died when he was three years old, and so he lived with his father most of his life. When his father, an air force lieutenant, was transferred to Stewart Air Force Base here in the Hudson Valley, Joe thought it would be a great opportunity to join his father and continue his education.

Joe also wanted to stay with his father to make sure he eats right, doesn't get involved with the wrong crowd, and meets the right woman to settle down with.

The speaker here gives us information about Joe's past that makes us see him as a unique individual. We also learn something pretty significant about Joe, namely that his mother died when he was very young. The speaker continues here to answer one of the questions that audience members probably have; namely, why this somewhat older person is in this class and in this college. If this were a longer speech, what else might the speaker cover here? What else would you want to know about Joe's past?

Here the speaker shows that Joe has a sense of humor in his identifying why he wanted to stay with his father, the very same things that a father would say about a son. Can you make this more humorous?

Transition

So Joe and his father journeyed from the dairy farm in Arizona to the Hudson Valley.

Here's simple transition, alerting the audience that the speaker is moving from the first main point (the past) to the second (the present). In what other ways might you state such a transition?

Second main point (the present)

Right now, with the money he saved while working on the ranch and with the help of a part-time job, Joe's here with us at Hudson Valley Community College.

Like many of us, Joe is a little apprehensive about college and worries that it's going to be a difficult and very different experience, especially at 28. Although an avid reader—mysteries and biographies are his favorites—Joe hasn't really studied, taken an exam, or written a term

Here the speaker shifts to the present and gives Joe a very human dimension by identifying his fears and concerns about being in college and taking this course and his concern for animals. The speaker also explains some commonalities between Joe and the rest of the audience (for example, being apprehensive in a public speaking class is something shared by nearly everyone). Some textbook writers would suggest that telling an audience that a speaker has apprehension about speaking is a bad idea. What do you think of its disclosure here?

The Public Speaking Sample Assistant

A Speech of Introduction *(Continued)*

paper since high school, some 10 years ago. So he's a bit anxious, but at the same time he's looking forward to the changes and the challenges of college life.

And, again, like many of us, Joe's a bit apprehensive about taking a public speaking course.

Joe is currently working for a local animal shelter. He was especially drawn to this particular shelter because of their no-kill policy; lots of shelters will kill the animals they can't find adopted homes for, but this one sticks by its firm no-kill policy.

Transition

But it's not the past or the present that Joe focuses on, it's the future.

This transition tells listeners that the speaker has finished talking about the past and present and is now moving on to the future.

Third main point (the future)

Joe is planning to complete his AB degree here at Hudson Valley Community and then to move on to the State University of New Paltz, where he intends to major in communication with a focus on public relations.

His ideal job would be to work for an animal rights organization. He wants to help make people aware of the ways in which they can advance animal rights and stop so much of the cruelty to animals common throughout the world.

From the present, the speaker moves to the future and identifies Joe's educational plans. This is the one thing that everyone has in common and something that most in the class would want to know. The speaker also covers Joe's career plans: again, something the audience is likely to be interested in. In this the speaker also reveals important aspects of Joe's interests and belief system—his concern for animals and his dedication to building his career around this abiding interest. What kinds of information might this speech of introduction give you about the attitudes and beliefs of its listeners?

Transition, internal summary

Joe's traveled an interesting road from a dairy farm in Arizona to the Hudson Valley, and the path to New Paltz and public relations should be just as interesting.

This transition (a kind of internal summary) tells you that the speaker has completed the three-part discussion (past, present, and future) and offers a basic summary of what has been discussed.

Conclusion

Having talked with him for the last few days, I'm sure he'll do well—he has lots of ideas, is determined to succeed, is open to new experiences, and enjoys interacting with people. I'd say that gives this interesting dairy farmer from Arizona a pretty good start as a student in this class, as a student at Hudson Valley Community, and as a soon-to-be public relations specialist.

In this concluding comment the speaker appropriately expresses a positive attitude toward Joe and summarizes some of Joe's positive qualities. These qualities are then tied to the past–present–future organization of the speech. Although the speaker doesn't say "thank you"—which can get trite when 20 speakers in succession say this—it's clear that this is the end of the speech from the last sentence, which brings Joe into his future profession. How effective do you think this conclusion is? What other types of conclusions might the speaker have used?

---

protection, families and children, disabilities, homelessness, and immigration.

- Department of Education (**www.ed.gov**): teaching resources in science, math, history, and language arts; innovations in education; reports on performance and accountability, "no child left behind," at-risk and gifted students, the Pell grant program, and religious expression in the schools.

- Deparment of Labor (**www.dol.gov**): pensions, unemployment, wages, insurance, and just about any other topic even remotely related to labor.

At each of these departments, you'll be able to find statistics appropriate to the topics covered, but an easier way is to log on to FedStats (**www.fedstats.gov**). Here you'll find statistics from more than 100 federal agencies, including statistical profiles of each

© PhotoDisc/Getty Images

CORRECTING ERRORS

In your speech you say that over 70 percent of the students favored banning alcohol. Toward the end of the speech, you realize that you mixed up the figures (only 30 percent favored banning alcohol). During the question-and-answer period no one asks about the figures.

WHAT DO YOU SAY?

state, county, and city as well as statistics on crime, population, economics, mortality, and energy, along with comparisons with other countries.

Databases

A database is simply an organized collection of information. Today there are a wide variety of research database packages available from an increasing number of vendors. These databases contain resources that you most likely will not be able to find on the Web without paying a fee. ProQuest, EBSCO, Info-Trac, WilsonWeb, and Search Premier are some of the names you'll probably run across in your exploration of databases. All of these vendors package databases in different ways. Your college library has no doubt purchased certain of these packages and makes them available to students and faculty for access from home or from the library without charge.

Some databases focus on specific areas; for example, history (America: History and Life, Historical Abstracts), health (Medline, Health Source), or communication (Communication & Mass Media Complete, Sage: Communication Studies Collection). Some databases are combinations of a variety of specific databases and contain a variety of publications from the major disciplines. Some databases focus on scholarly articles published in professional journals by academic researchers and scientists. Other databases focus on popular articles in magazines and newspapers. There is almost surely to be a database on just about any topic you'll want to research.

Integrating and Citing Research

Even the best and most extensive research would count for little if you didn't integrate it into your speech. By integrating and acknowledging your sources of information in your speech, you'll give fair credit to those whose ideas and research findings you're using, and you'll lessen the risk that anything you say can be intepreted as plagiarism. At the same time, you'll help establish your own reputation as a responsible researcher and thus increase your own credibility. Here are a few suggestions for integrating your research into your speech (additional suggestions are presented in Table 4).

Mention the Sources in Your Speech

Cite at least the author; if appropriate, cite the publication and the date. Check out some of the speeches reprinted in this book and any of the many public speaking sites on the Internet, and note how the speakers integrate their sources in their talks. In your written preparation outline, give the complete bibliographical reference.

Here is an example of how you might cite your source:

My discussion of the causes of anorexia nervosa is based on the work of Dr. Peter Rowan of the Priory Hospital in London. In an article titled "Introducing Anorexia Nervosa," which I last accessed on October 5, 2007, Rowan notes that "this is a disorder of many causes that come together." It's these causes that I want to cover in this talk.

Although it's possible to overdo oral source citations—to give more information than listeners really need—there are even greater dangers in leaving out potentially useful source information. Because your speeches in this course are learning experiences, it will be better to err on the side of being more rather than less complete.

Avoid Unnecessary Lead-In Expressions

Comments such as "I have a quote here" or "I want to quote an example" serve no persuasive purpose. Let the audience know that you're quoting by pausing before the quote, taking a step forward, or—to read an extended quotation—referring to your notes. If you want to state more directly that this is a quotation, you might do it this way:

Recently, Mary Kay Ash put this in perspective: "A woman can no more duplicate the male style of leadership than an American businessman can exactly reproduce the Japanese style."

In addition to the oral citation, you'll most likely want to include a listing of your references in your preparation outline. In citing references, first find out what style manual is used in your class or at your school. Generally, it will be a style manual developed by the American Psychological Association (APA), the Modern Language Association (MLA), or the University of Chicago (*The Chicago Manual of Style*). Different colleges and even different departments within a given school often rely on different formats for citing research, which, quite frankly, makes a tedious process even worse.

Fortunately, a variety of websites provide guides to the information you'll need to cite any reference in your speech. For example, Purdue University offers an excellent site that covers APA and MLA style formats and provides examples for citing books, articles, newspaper articles, websites, e-mail, online postings, electronic databases, and more (http://owl.english .purdue.edu/handouts/research). Another excellent website is Capital Community College's Guide for Writing Research Papers (http://ccc.commnet.edu/ apa/apa_index.htm). Guidelines for using *The Chicago Manual of Style* may be found at Ohio State's website (www.lib.ohio-state.edu/). This site provides guidance for citing all types of print and electronic sources. Another valuable source is the *Columbia Guide to Online Style* (www.columbia .edu/cu/cup/cgos/idx_basic.html), which provides detailed instructions and examples for citing e-mail, listserv, and newsgroup communications and even software programs and video games.

Evaluating Internet Resources

As you research your topic, keep in mind that anyone can "publish" on the Internet, making it essential that you subject everything you find on the Net to critical analysis. An article on the Internet can be written by world-renowned scientists or by elementary school students; by fair and objective reporters or by people who would spin the issues to serve their own political, religious, or social purposes. It's not always easy to tell which is which. Here are a few questions to ask in evaluating Internet resources (or in evaluating information from print sources, from interpersonal interaction, or from the media):

■ *Is the author qualified?* Does the author have the necessary credentials? For example, does the author have sufficient background in science or medicine to write authoritatively on health issues?

Do an Internet search using the biography sites already discussed, or simply enter the author's name in your favorite search engine and check on the author's expertise.

■ *Is the information current?* When was the information published? When were the sources cited in the article written? Generally, the more recent the material, the more useful it will be. With some topics—for example, unemployment statistics; developments in AIDS research; tuition costs; stem cell research; or attitudes toward the Iraq war, same-sex marriage, or organized religion—the currency of the information is crucial to its usefulness, simply because these things change so rapidly. Other topics—for example, historical or literary topics—may well rely on information that was written even hundreds of years ago. Even here, however, new understanding frequently sheds light on events that happened in the far distant past.

■ *Is the information fair?* Does the author of the material present the information objectively, or is there a bias favoring one position? Some websites, although seemingly objective on the surface, are actually organs of political, religious, or social organizations, so it's often useful to go to the home page and look for information on the nature of the organization sponsoring the website. Reviewing a range of research in the area will help you see how other experts view the issue. It will also enable you to see if this author's view of the situation takes into consideration all sides of the issue and if these sides are represented fairly.

■ *Is the information sufficient to substantiate your claim?* The opinion of one dietitian is insufficient to support the usefulness of a particular diet; statistics on tuition increases at five elite private colleges are insufficient to illustrate national trends in tuition costs. Generally, the broader your conclusion, the greater the information you'll need to meet the requirements for sufficiency. If you want to claim the usefulness of a diet for all people, then you're going to need a great deal of information from different populations—men and women, old and young, healthy and sickly, and so on.

■ *Is the information accurate?* Determining accuracy is not easy, but the more you learn about your topic, the more able you'll be to judge accuracy. Is the information primary or secondary? If it's secondary information, you may be able to locate the primary information (often provided as a hot link in the Internet article or in a reference at the end of a printed text). Check to see if the information is consistent with information found in other sources and if the recognized authorities in the field accept this information.

89

Table 4   The Oral Citation

Here are a few examples and notes on citing your sources in your speech. The written citations would be included at the end of your preparation outline in a list of references. Additional help is available on Research Navigator (**www.mycommunicationlab.com**), which provides guidance for citing sources in reference lists and bibliographies using all major style manuals; the American Psychological Association (APA) style is used here.

Source to Be Cited and Written Citation	Oral Citation	Tips for Success
Book		
Brownell, J. (2006). *Listening: Attitudes, principles, and skills* (3rd ed.). Boston: Allyn & Bacon.	Judi Brownell, an authority on listening and a professor at Cornell University, in *Listening: Attitudes, Principles, and Skills*, argues that listening is . . .	Try to establish the importance of the book or the author to add weight to your argument.
Magazine Article		
Cloud, J. (2007, February 5). Yep, they're gay. *Time*, 169 (6), 54.	A February 2007 article in *Time* magazine notes, and here I'm quoting the author, John Cloud, "Zoologists have known for many years that homosexuality isn't uncommon among animals."	If the magazine is well known, as is *Time*, it's sufficient to name the magazine. If it were less well known, then you might establish its credibility for your listeners by noting, for example, its reputation for fairness, its longevity, its well-known authors.
Newspaper Article		
Whitlock, C. (2007, March 12). Terrorists proving harder to profile. Retrieved March 12, 2007, from www.washingtonpost.com, p. A1. If a letter to the editor or an editorial, then insert [Letter to the Editor] or [Editorial] after the article title.	A news report dated March 12, 2007, in the online *Washington Post*, one of the world's great newspapers, reports that . . .	It sometimes helps to establish the credibility of the newspaper—some are more reputable than others. And always include reference to the date of the article. You should also indicate whether it was a regular news item or a letter to the editor or an editorial.
Encyclopedia		
Feminism (2007). In *Encyclopaedia Britannica*. Retrieved March 12, 2007, from Encyclopedia Britannica Online: http://www.britannica.com/search?query=feminism&CT=.	The online version of the *Encyclopaedia Britannica*, accessed March 7, 2007, defines feminism as "the belief in the social, economic, and political equality of the sexes."	It isn't necessary to say "www.britannica.com." Your audience will know how to access the encyclopedia—especially if they're in this course.
Research Study		
Andrejevic, M. (2006). The discipline of watching: Detection, risk, and lateral surveillance. *Critical Studies in Media Communication, 23* (December), 391–407.	In the December 2006 issue of *Critical Studies in Media Communication*, one of the official journals of the National Communication Association, a research study conducted by Mark Andrejevic found that . . .	In citing a research study, make it clear that what you're reporting is from the primary source and not from a popular magazine's summary of the research (that is, a secondary source)
Website		
New developments (2008, March 22). Retrieved May 14, 2008, from www.texas.gov. If an author is identified, then: Smith, C. (2008, March 17). The truth. Retrieved April 5, 2008, from www.hhhsmith.org.	The official State of Texas website, which you can access at www.texas.gov, contains the full text of the speeches on this issue; they all are in favor of . . .	Like blogs, websites vary in accuracy and credibility. Some are designed to sell a product or service, so their information may be suspect. (It also may be quite accurate, of course.) Government (.gov domain), educational (.edu domain), and organizational (.org domain) websites are usually more reliable and are more likely to be believed by an educated audience.

Blog

Sullivan, A. (2007, January 28). The Webb factor. Retrieved January 30, 2007, from http:time.blogs.com/daily_dish.

Andrew Sullivan, the author of *The Conservative Soul*, in an article posted on January 28, 2007, to his blog *The Daily Dish*—one of the most widely read blogs on the Internet—had this to say about Webb . . .

Anyone can maintain a blog. If the blog is used for more than examples or illustrations, you need to establish the authority of the blogger and the date of the post you're citing.

Chat Room Conversation

Seabiscuit. (2008, May 4). Happiness. Retrieved June 8, 2008, from www.myheart.com.

One important insight on this issue was posted this week in a chat room by Seabiscuit.

Chat room conversation can give you good examples or ideas. Even if the conversation is no longer available, you need to credit the writer and indicate where you got the idea.

News Broadcast

Charlie Rose. (2008, May 4). Interview with C. A. Smith, broadcast on PBS.

In August of this year, Charlie Rose interviewed Smith on *The Nation* on PBS, and Smith agreed that . . .

It's helpful to name the network (rather than just saying "a television news show said . . .") as well as the specific news show, the person being interviewed and perhaps the interviewer. By naming all these, you create a clearer picture in the minds of your listeners and at the same time ensure accuracy.

Personal Interview

Because personal interviews are not retrievable, they are not included in the references list.

In an e-mail interview I conducted in September of this year with James Wilder, the sheriff of Forest County, Wilder wrote that . . .

State how the interview was conducted—in person, by telephone, or through e-mail—and when it took place. Again, the currency of the date is more important than the specific date, so it's fine to say either "September of this year" or, for example, "September 22."

Classroom Lecture

Smith, R. (2007, September 16). History of American Public Address at Queens College, City University of New York.

In a lecture last week in History of American Public Address, Professor Russel Smith noted that . . .

Citations to classroom lectures should include the professor's name, the course, and the approximate time the comment was made.

Statistics

Hurricane Information. (2006, June 7). Retrieved January 29, 2007, from www.FedStats.gov.hurricane2.html

FedStats—the U.S. federal government's online statistics website, which I accessed on Wednesday—provides sobering statistics on the devastation of Katrina and Rita.

Stress the authority of the source that collected the statistics (.gov sites are more reliable than .com sites) and the recency of the statistics. Providing information on when you accessed the website will further help you establish the statistics' currency.

Major textbook and trade book publishers go to enormous effort to ensure the accuracy of what appears in print or on their websites, so the information they provide is generally reliable. Some publishers, however, are arms of special interest groups with specific agendas. If this is the case with one of the sources you have selected, try to balance this publisher's perspective with information that represents other views of the issue. If an article appears in a journal sponsored by a major academic organization such as the American Psychological Association or the National Communication Association, you can be pretty sure that experts in the field have carefully reviewed the article before publication. Again, if an article appears in a well-respected major newspaper like the *New York Times*, the *Washington Post*, or the *Wall Street Journal*, or in any of the major newsmagazines or news networks (or online on their websites), you can be pretty sure that the information is accurate. Do realize that these claims of accuracy are generalizations and that errors do occur. Both academic journals and newspapers have printed fraudulent articles, though these instances are rare.

SUMMARY: PUBLIC SPEAKING TOPICS, AUDIENCES, AND RESEARCH

This unit introduced the nature of public speaking and covered selecting and limiting the topic and purpose, analyzing and adapting to your audience, and researching your speech.

1. Public speaking also provides training to improve your personal and social competencies, academic and career skills, and general communication abilities.

2. Apprehension in public speaking is normal and can be managed by reversing the factors that cause anxiety, practicing performance visualization, and systematically desensitizing yourself.

3. The preparation of a public speech involves 10 steps: (1) select the topic and purpose; (2) analyze the audience; (3) research the topic; (4) formulate the thesis and identify the main points; (5) support the main points; (6) organize the speech materials; (7) construct the conclusion, introduction, and transitions; (8) outline the speech; (9) word the speech; and (10) rehearse and deliver the speech. The first three of these steps were discussed in this unit; the remaining seven are discussed in the next two units.

4. Speech topics should deal with significant issues that interest the audience. Subjects and purposes should be limited in scope.

5. In analyzing an audience, consider the audience members' attitudes, beliefs, and values.

6. In analyzing the audience, also consider age, gender, cultural factors, religion and religiousness, the occasion, and the specific context.

7. Also analyze and adapt to your audience's willingness to hear your speech, how favorable the audience is to your point of view, and the knowledge that your audience has of your topic.

8. Research the topic, beginning with general sources and gradually exploring more specific and specialized sources.

9. Useful sources of information include libraries, interviews, scholarly articles, popular publications, reference works, news media, biographical material, government publications, electronic databases, and more.

10. Integrate research into your speech by mentioning the sources, providing smooth transitions, and avoiding useless expressions such as "I have a quote."

11. Avoid plagiarism by clearly acknowledging the source of any words or ideas you use that are not your own.

12. Critically evaluate your research by asking if the research is current, if it is fair and unbiased, and if the evidence is sufficient and accurate.

KEY TERMS IN PUBLIC SPEAKING TOPICS, AUDIENCES, AND RESEARCH

attitude	general purpose	search directory	topic
audience	informative speech	secondary sources	topoi
audience analysis	performance visualization	special occasion speech	tree diagrams
belief	persuasive speech	specific purpose	value
communication apprehension	plagiarism	systematic desensitization	
	primary sources	taboo	

THINKING CRITICALLY ABOUT SPEAKING TOPICS, AUDIENCES, AND RESEARCH

1. **Listservs and newsgroups.** Using L-soft's Catalist of listserv lists (**www.lsoft.com/lists/listref.html**), explore the listservs that deal with topics related to your next speech. How many can you find? Using Google (**http://groups.google.com/**), investigate the available newsgroups dealing with topics related to your next speech. Try to find at least three.

2. **Winning over the unwilling.** Jack is scheduled to give a speech on careers in computer technology to a group of high school students who have been forced to go to a Saturday "career day" and to attend at least three of the speeches. The audience is definitely an unwilling group. What advice can you give Jack to help him deal with this type of audience?

3. **Biographical information.** Jill wants to give a speech on television talk shows and wants to include biographical information on some of the talk show hosts. What sources might Jill go to in order to get authoritative and current information on these hosts? What sources might she go to in order to get "fan" type information?

What advice would you give Jill for distinguishing the two types of sources and information?

4. **Two-minute speeches.** Prepare and deliver a two-minute speech in which you do one of the following:
   - evaluate the topics of recent talk shows against the criteria for a worthwhile and appropriate topic
   - explain the cultural factors operating in this class that need to be taken into consideration by the speaker selecting a topic and purpose
   - explain a particularly strong belief that you hold
   - describe members of your class in terms of how willing, favorable, and knowledgeable you believe them to be about any specific topic or speaker
   - describe the audience of a popular magazine or television show or movie
   - explain the value of one reference book, website, database, listserv, or newsgroup for research in public speaking

5. **Accessing the Internet.** According to one survey, approximately 23 percent of Internet users in the United States (about 30 million people) accessed the Internet from a place other than home or office. The leading places were school (27 percent), a friend's or neighbor's house (26 percent), and libraries (26 percent) (Use of the Internet in Places other than Home or Work: A PIP Data Memo, **www.pewinternet.org/ PPF/r/115/report_ display.asp**, dated March 3, 2004, accessed February 10, 2005). Where do you use the Internet, and does the location make a difference in your Internet activities?

LogOn! MyCommunicationLab
WWW.MYCOMMUNICATIONLAB.COM

Visit MCL for a variety of useful resources. For this unit it contains two self-tests on satisfaction with public speaking and knowledge of research; discussions titled Historical Roots of Public Speaking, Growth and Development of Public Speaking, Apprehension, Developing Confidence in Public Speaking, and The Dictionary of Topics (suitable for your classroom speeches); and the exercises Analyzing and Adapting to Your Audience during the Speech, Seeking Audience Information, and Fishbone Diagram for Limiting Topics.

Several useful speeches and speech excerpts are available. Select one of the student speeches and examine it in terms of the topic, intended audience, and research, as discussed in this unit. Also visit **www.ablongman/pubspeak**. Examine the material under the Access, Research, and Analyze tabs; it will provide another perspective on the discussion presented in this unit.

References

Allan, K., & Burridge, K. (2006). *Forbidden words*. Cambridge: Cambridge University Press.

Axtell, R. E. (1993). *Do's and taboos around the world* (3rd ed.). New York: Wiley.

Ayres, J. (1986). Perceptions of speaking ability: An explanation for stage fright. *Communication Education, 35*, 275-287.

Ayres, J., & Hopf, T. S. (1992). Visualization: Reducing speech anxiety and enhancing performance. *Communication Reports, 5*, 1-10.

Ayres, J., & Hopf, T. S. (1993). *Coping with speech anxiety*. Norwood, NJ: Ablex.

Ayres, J., Hopf, T. S., & Ayres, D. M. (1994). An examination of whether imaging ability enhances the effectiveness of an intervention designed to reduce speech anxiety. *Communication Education, 43* (July), 252-258.

Beatty, M. J. (1988). Situational and predispositional correlates of public speaking anxiety. *Communication Education, 37*, 28-39.

Daly, J. A., McCroskey, J. C., Ayres, J., Hopf, T., & Ayres, D. M. (1997). *Avoiding communication: Shyness, reticence, and communication apprehension* (2nd ed.). Cresskill, NJ: Hampton Press.

DeVito, J. A. (1996). *Brainstorms: How to think more creatively about communication (or about anything else)*. New York: Longman.

Dodd, C. H. (1995). *Dynamics of intercultural communication* (4th ed.). Dubuque, IA: William C. Brown.

Goss, B., Thompson, M., & Olds, S. (1978). Behavioral support for systematic desensitization for communication apprehension. *Human Communication Research, 4*, 158-163.

Gudykunst, W., & Nishida, T. (1984). Individual and cultural influence on uncertainty reduction. *Communication Monographs, 51*, 23-36.

Gudykunst, W., Yang, S., & Nishida, T. (1985). A cross-cultural test of uncertainty reduction theory: Comparisons of acquaintance, friend, and dating relationships in Japan, Korea, and the United States. *Human Communication Research, 11*, 407-454.

Himle, J. A., Abelson, J. L, & Haghightgou, H. (1999). Effect of alcohol on social phobic anxiety. *American Journal of Psychiatry, 156* (August), 1237-1243.

Hofstede, G. (1997). *Cultures and organizations: Software of the mind*. New York: McGraw-Hill.

Osborn, A. (1957). *Applied imagination* (Rev. ed.). New York: Scribners.

Richmond, V. P., & McCroskey, J. C. (1998). *Communication: Apprehension, avoidance, and effectiveness* (5th ed.). Boston: Allyn & Bacon.

Stephan, W. G., & Stephan, C. W. (1992). *Improving intergroup relations*. Thousand Oaks, CA: Sage.

Watzlawick, P. (1978). *The language of change: Elements of therapeutic communication*. New York: Basic Books.

Watzlawick, P., Beavin, J. H., & Jackson, D. D. (1967). *Pragmatics of human communication: A study of interactional patterns, pathologies, and paradoxes*. New York: Norton.

Wolpe, J. (1957). *Psychotherapy by reciprocal inhibition*. Stanford, CA: Stanford University Press.

Chapter 4

The Informative Speech

MAJOR TOPICS

Goals of Informative Speaking

Principles of Informative Speaking

Speeches of Description

Speeches of Definition

Speeches of Demonstration

Special Features

Communicating and Teaching:
Timothy P. Mottet

How Satisfying Is Your Public Speaking?

The Knowledge Gap

Speaking Ethically

Understanding Information Theory

Understanding Signal-to-Noise Ratio

Skills Climbing the Abstraction
Ladder

Skills Preparing an Informative
Speech

Public Speaking A Poorly Constructed
Informative Speech

Public Speaking An Excellent Informative
Speech

n Van Etten/PhotoEdit

Many of the speeches you'll deliver will be informative speeches, in which you'll explain to an audience how something works or how to do something.

In this unit, you'll learn about:
- the goals and principles for communicating information.
- the types of informative speeches.

You'll learn to:
- use the principles for communicating information more effectively and efficiently.
- prepare a variety of informative speeches—speeches of description, definition, and demonstration.

This unit looks at informative speaking. More specifically, this unit considers the general goals of informative speaking, the principles for communicating information, and the varied types of informative speeches and how you can develop these most effectively.

Before beginning this journey into these three types of speeches—or after giving your next speech—you may want to examine your own satisfaction as a public speaker by taking the self-test "How Satisfying Is Your Public Speaking?"

TEST YOURSELF

How Satisfying Is Your Public Speaking?

Respond to each of the following statements by recording the number best representing your feelings after a recent speech, using this scale: 1 = strongly agree; 2 = moderately agree; 3 = slightly agree; 4 = neutral; 5 = slightly disagree; 6 = moderately disagree; and 7 = strongly disagree.

_____ 1. The audience let me know that I was speaking effectively.

_____ 2. My speech accomplished nothing.

_____ 3. I would like to give another speech like this one.

_____ 4. The audience genuinely wanted to get to know me.

_____ 5. I was very dissatisfied with my speech.

_____ 6. I was very satisfied with the speech.

_____ 7. The audience seemed very interested in what I had to say.

_____ 8. I did not enjoy the public speaking experience.

_____ 9. The audience did not seem supportive of what I was saying.

_____ 10. The speech flowed smoothly.

HOW DID YOU DO? To compute your score, follow these steps:

1. Add the scores for items 1, 3, 4, 6, 7, and 10.

2. Reverse the scores for items 2, 5, 8, and 9 so that 7 becomes 1, 6 becomes 2, 5 becomes 3, 4 remains 4, 3 becomes 5, 2 becomes 6, and 1 becomes 7.

3. Add the reversed scores for items 2, 5, 8, and 9.

4. Add the totals from steps 1 and 3 to yield your communication satisfaction score.

You may interpret your score along the following scale:

10	20	30	40	50	60	70
Extremely satisfying	Quite satisfying	Fairly satisfying	Average	Fairly unsatisfying	Quite unsatisfying	Extremely unsatisfying

How accurately do you think this scale captures your public speaking satisfaction?

WHAT WILL YOU DO? As you become a more successful and effective public speaker, your satisfaction is likely to increase. What steps can you take to increase your satisfaction?

Source: This test was adapted for public speaking on the basis of the conversational satisfaction test developed by Michael Hecht (1978), "The Conceptualization and Measurement of Interpersonal Communication Satisfaction," *Human Communication Research*, 4, 253–264, and is used by permission of the author and International Communication Association.

GOALS OF INFORMATIVE SPEAKING

An *informative speech*, is a speech in which the speaker tells the audience something it didn't already know. This is the most general goal of all informative speaking. But there are a variety of other more specific goals that can motivate informative speaking. Reviewing these will help explain further the nature and purpose of the informative speech.

One goal of informative speaking may be to *introduce* topics that are totally new to the audience. A sales representative might demonstrate new surgical tools to a group of medical doctors, or an inventor might explain an entirely new toy.

Another goal may be to *clarify* misconceptions that people have about a topic; say, about how an automobile or a cell phone works, or about the ways in which graduate and professional schools select students, or about the criteria for promotion of college professors—all topics that many people assume they understand but about which they actually have lots of misconceptions.

Still another goal may be to *demonstrate* how to use information; the popular cooking shows are good examples of this type of speech. Many of the infomercials on television spend lots of time showing you how to use their new product—whether it's George Foreman's Grilling Machine, Joy Mangano's clothes hangers, or Ron Popeil's slow cooker, baldness fix, or roaster.

Perhaps the most popular goal is to *communicate information* about topics the audience knows something about but not a great deal; your goal here will be to expand on knowledge your listeners already

THE RESEARCHER

Communicating and Teaching

I'm planning to become a high school history teacher, and I'm wondering if there's anything I can start doing now to become a really successful instructor. Are there particular communication skills I should focus on or emphasize?

Effective teachers are also effective informative speakers. Three informative speechmaking skills that will enhance your ability to teach are learning how to create relevant messages, learning how to make messages clear, and learning how to adapt to your audience.

- *Make messages relevant.* Show students how history will benefit their personal development and professional work lives. Relate history to your audience members' experiences and interests. Be prepared and ready to share yourself with your audience. Explain why you find history fascinating.

- *Make messages clear.* Use language and examples that your audience will understand and find interesting. Teaching history is storytelling. Be prepared to explain and illustrate in a vivid manner the historical context, the setting, the characters, and then pull your students through the story.

- *Adapt to your audience.* Carefully interpret your students' nonverbal behavior. Are they following you? Anticipate confusion, and be prepared to offer multiple examples to illustrate your content. Be prepared to make abstract terms and concepts more concrete.

For further information: See Mottet, T. P., Richmond, V. P., & McCroskey, J. C. (Eds.). (2006). *Handbook of instructional communication: Rhetorical and relational perspectives.* Boston: Allyn and Bacon.

Timothy P. Mottet (Ed.D., West Virginia University) holds the Hauser Chair in Communication at the University of Texas–Pan American in Edinburg, Texas. He teaches courses in instructional communication, training and development, and leadership. His research examines the role of communication, personality, and cognition in teaching and learning. He is available to answer your questions at (956) 381-3583.

have. Speeches on such topics as the way pop-ups work or the rules of soccer would likely include information that the audience does not yet know.

As I write this, Microsoft's Vista operating system is making its debut and provides a good example to illustrate that the same topic can be pursued with different goals in mind. So let's say you want to give an informative speech on Vista.

- To an audience of dedicated Mac users, the information might be entirely new, so your goal would be to introduce topics unknown to the audience.

- To an audience of dedicated Mac users who thought there was no or only little difference between the systems, you'd be clarifying misconceptions.

- To an audience of students using Windows, you might demonstrate, for example, the ways in which they could use Vista to accomplish a variety of tasks more efficiently.

- To an audience of Windows XP users, you'd be building on topics they knew a lot about and describing what was new in Vista.

As you can appreciate, your speech on Vista for the dedicated Mac users would have to be different from the speech for the XP users. Though both speeches would cover similar and in some cases the same material, you'd have to approach it very differently depending on the knowledge and experience of your listeners. With this basic principle in mind— a principle you see in operation every time you hear an effective classroom lecture, as you see the principle in violation with every ineffective lecture—we can look at several principles for communicating information.

PRINCIPLES OF INFORMATIVE SPEAKING

When you communicate "information," you tell your listeners something new, something they don't know. You may tell them about a new way of looking at old things or an old way of looking at new things. You may discuss a theory not previously heard of or a familiar theory not fully understood. You may discuss events that the audience may be unaware of or may have misconceptions about. Regardless of what type of informative speech you intend to give, the following guidelines should help.

In addition, the Public Speaking Sample Assistant boxes illustrate some of the pitfalls you'll want to avoid in a poorly constructed informative speech (below) and some of the principles you'll want to follow in an excellent informative speech.

Public Speaking Sample Assistant   **A Poorly Constructed Informative Speech**

This poorly constructed informative speech was written by the author to demonstrate some of the faults that beginning speakers sometimes make and that you'll want to avoid.

Three Jobs

Three Jobs

In general, don't use your title as your opening words. This title seems adequate, though it's not terribly exciting. After reading the speech, try to come up with a more appealing title.

Well, I mean, hello. Er . . . I'm new at public speaking, so I'm a little nervous. I've always been shy. So don't watch my knees shake.

The speaker's nervous opening remarks reveal an anxiety that's understandable but is probably best not shared with the listeners. After all, you don't want the audience to be uncomfortable for you.

Ehm, let me see my notes here. [Mumbles to self while shuffling notes: "One, two, three, four, five—oh, they're all here."] Okay, here goes.

Going through your notes makes the audience feel that you didn't prepare adequately and may be wasting their time.

Three Jobs. That's my title and I'm going to talk about three jobs.

This is the speaker's orientation. Is this sufficient? What else might the speaker have done in the introduction?

Public Speaking Sample Assistant

A Poorly Constructed Informative Speech (Continued)

The Health Care Field. This is the fastest-growing job in the country, one of the fastest, I guess I mean. I know that you're not interested in this topic and that you're all studying accounting. But there are a lot of new jobs in the health care field. The *Star* had an article on health care and said that health care will be needed more in the future than it is now. And now, you know, like they need a lot of health care people. In the hospital where I work—on the west side, uptown—they never have enough health aides and they always tell me to become a health aide, like, you know, to enter the health care field. To become a nurse. Or maybe a dental technician. But I hate going to the dentist. Maybe I will.

I don't know what's going to happen with the president's health plan, but whatever happens, it won't change the need for health aides. I mean, people will still get sick; so it really doesn't matter what happens with health care.

The Robotics Field. This includes things like artificial intelligence. I don't really know what that is but it's like growing real fast. They use this in making automobiles and planes and I think in computers. Japan is a leading country in this field. A lot of people in India go into this field, but I'm not sure why.

The Computer Graphics Field. This field has a lot to do with designing and making lots of different products, like CAD and CAM. This field also includes computer-aided imagery—CAI. And in movies, I think. Like *Star Wars* and *Terminator 2*. I saw *Terminator 2* four times. I didn't see *Star Wars* but I'm gonna rent the video. I don't know if you have to know a lot about computers or if you can just like be a designer and someone else will tell the computer what to do.

I got my information from a book that Carol Kleiman wrote, *The 100 Best Jobs for the 1990s and Beyond*. It was summarized on the Internet somewhere.

My Conclusion. These are three of the fastest-growing fields in the U.S. And in the world, I think—not in Third World countries, I don't think. China and India and Africa. More like Europe and Germany. And the U.S.—the U.S. is the big one. I hope you enjoyed my speech. Thank you.

I wasn't as nervous as I thought I'd be. Are there any questions?

Such expressions of uncertainty make us question the speaker's competence.

And we begin to wonder, why is the speaker talking about this to us?

Stories in the *Star* may be entertaining, but they don't necessarily constitute evidence. What does this tabloid reference do to the credibility you ascribe to the speaker?

Everything in the speech must have a definite purpose. Asides such as comments about not liking to go to the dentist are probably best omitted.

Here the speaker had an opportunity to connect the topic with important current political events but failed to say anything that was not obvious.

Introducing each topic this way is clear but probably not very interesting. How might the speaker have introduced each of the three main points more effectively?

Notice how vague the speaker is—"includes things like," "and I think in computers," "I'm not sure why." Such statements communicate very little information to listeners and leave them with little confidence that the speaker knows what he or she is talking about.

Again, this part of the speech offers little specific information. CAD and CAM are not defined, and CAI is explained merely as "computer-aided imagery." Unless we already knew what these were, we would have no idea even after hearing the speaker. And again the speaker inserts personal notes (for example, seeing *Terminator 2* four times) that have no meaningful connection to the topic.

The speaker uses only one source and, to make matters worse, doesn't even go to the original source but relies on a summary "somewhere" on the Internet. Especially with a topic like this, listeners are likely to want a variety of viewpoints and additional reliable sources.

Note too that the speech lacked any statistics. This is a subject where statistics are essential. Listeners will want to know how many jobs will be available in these fields, what these fields will look like in 5 or 10 years, how much these fields pay, and so on.

Using the word *conclusion* to signal that you're concluding is not a bad idea, but work it into the text instead of using it as if it were a heading in a book chapter.

Once more, this lack of certainty makes us question the speaker's competence and preparation.

Again, personal comments are best left out.

An Excellent Informative Speech

This is an excellent informative speech, given by University of Texas at Austin student Jillian Collum.

When Bangladesh achieved its independence in 1971, Vanderbilt University doctoral student Muhammad Yunus decided that it was time to go home. He soon found himself at Chittagong University, teaching complex economic theories involving the transfer of billions of dollars. However, as Yunus explained to Whole Foods Market team members in a March 2006 address, he couldn't help but notice the intense poverty that existed right outside the university's walls. So, Yunus decided to do something about it, and in 1976 he struck his first blow in the battle against poverty, lending 42 people a combined total of $27.

The recipients used their loans so effectively that Yunus decided to start his own bank, called Grameen, which would give small loans to poor families for income-generating activities, such as buying a cow to sell its milk. Bahrain's *Gulf Daily News* of February 5, 2007, reports that 58 percent of the bank's borrowers have used their loans to rise out of poverty, a success rate so astonishing that it allowed Grameen to launch a global revolution.

The *New York Times* of October 14, 2006, asserts that microcredit, or the concept of giving small loans to individuals so that they can work to lift themselves out of poverty, now helps over 100 million of the world's most destitute people in more than 130 countries. And even the Nobel committee was impressed. In an October 13, 2006, press release, the committee awarded Muhammad Yunus the 2006 Nobel Peace Prize, noting that microcredit is an essential and powerful instrument in the worldwide fight against poverty. Because the *Toronto Star* of December 8, 2006, reveals that microcredit leaders plan to use the technique to help half a billion people rise out of poverty by the year 2015, we must examine how this macrorevolution in microcredit is changing the world.

To do so, we will first explore the development of microcredit; next, discuss its rationale; and finally, look at the implications of this approach that is transforming lives a few dollars at a time.

MacLean's of November 27, 2006, states that two-thirds of the world's population is too poor to secure funds from traditional banks, which fear that poor borrowers won't repay loans. Muhammad Yunus set out to prove that this view of the poor was completely wrong. In his previously cited speech, Yunus explains that Grameen looks at what a conventional bank does, and then does the opposite. Instead of rich customers, the bank seeks poor ones. Instead of big loans, it gives small ones. And instead of men, the bank more often chooses to lend to women, believing that

Using a specific story is a good way to gain attention; we all seem interested in personal stories, especially when they're dramatic, like this one.

Did the story gain your attention? In what other ways might the speaker have gained attention?

The speaker makes the point that a large group (58 percent) used the money to rise out of poverty. In what other ways might you have illustrated the fact that such a large group used the money to rise from poverty?

Here the speaker establishes the importance of the topic. Did this part of the introduction convince you that the topic the speaker was about to cover was worth your effort to listen? What specifically convinced you?

In this third part of the introduction, the speaker provides an orientation to what will follow in the rest of the speech. You know from this that there will be three main parts of the speech: the development of microcredit, its rationale, and its implications.

Here the speaker explains her first main point: the development of microcredit. This gives those in the audience who didn't know much about this approach to loans and lending a better idea of what microcredit is and how it operates.

Throughout this speech the speaker uses a wide variety of sources. What source material do you find especially helpful? What types of source material would you have liked to see included here?

Public Speaking Sample Assistant

An Excellent Informative Speech *(Continued)*

money given to women is more likely to directly benefit families. According to the *International Herald Tribune* of October 14, 2006, today, Grameen serves 6.6 million poor people in Bangladesh and enjoys a 98.5 percent repayment rate, almost twice as high as the average rate for traditional Bengali banks. Borrowers use their loans for income-generating activities, such as operating a small food stand or selling handmade crafts. And most astonishingly, *BusinessWeek* of November 27, 2006, notes that Grameen has reached this level of success even though it hasn't accepted any donations since 1995. Grameen remains self-sustaining much the same way traditional banks do—by taking in deposits and issuing loans.

While Muhammad Yunus's initial $27 loans to 42 Bengalis didn't amount to much, the microcredit revolution that this small act launched has changed the lives of millions. To better understand the rationale for this phenomenon, we'll discuss microcredit's driving principles and why the technique is so necessary.

Canada's Hamilton Spectator of November 13, 2006, reports that there are now more than 3,100 microcredit institutions worldwide. These groups provide average loans of $150, and more than 97 percent of the money they lend out is repaid. According to the *Arizona Daily Star* of November 3, 2006, this high repayment rate can be attributed to the group loan principle, in which five people from the community serve as one another's guarantors. Individual borrowers must repay their loans, or the entire group becomes ineligible for more funding. This provides a powerful incentive for individuals to pay on time and help each other meet their obligations. But the true genius of microcredit is that loans are given for income-generating activities that improve the lives of every member of the family. For example, the *Atlanta Journal-Constitution* of November 13, 2006, tells the story of Susan Wangui from Kenya. Abandoned by her parents and her husband after she contracted HIV, Wangui was forced to work as a prostitute to support her two children. But with a series of loans from a local microcredit institution, Wangui was able to start a clothes-mending business, a venture that has been profitable enough to allow her to move her children out of a slum and into a house with a floor and running water.

Microcredit is necessary because for many of its recipients, no reasonable alternatives exist. For example, the *New Yorker* of October 30, 2006, reveals that Latin America's largest microcredit institution, Compartamos, serves 500,000 people in Mexico, a country where over 70 percent of the population lacks access to traditional banks. In the absence of microcredit, poor individuals are forced to rely on loan sharks. The Allentown, Pennsylvania, *Morning Call* of December 7, 2006, explains that microcredit groups offer interest rates

Here the speaker provides a transition from the first to the second main point. As a listener, you now know that you'll hear the rationale for microcredit, and specifically that you'll hear about it in two parts: the program's driving principles and the reason this approach is so necessary.

You've been prepared to hear about the principles of microcredit. After reading this section on the principles, can you now identify the specific principles discussed by the speaker? If you can, what did the speaker do to help you remember them? If you can't, what might the speaker have done to ensure that you would remember the principles?

This section also provides a good example of explaining a concept in terms of abstract and general statements (for example, the fact that 97 percent of the money is repaid) and then following these with specifics (for example, the story of Susan Wangui). This is almost always a useful technique for helping listeners see the issue as a generalization and as uniquely personal as well.

Here the necessity for microcredit is considered, the second part of the second main idea. Notice that the speaker uses similar words in introducing these concepts as in previewing them in the introduction. This similarity in wording will help the audience follow the speaker.

101

Public Speaking Sample Assistant

An Excellent Informative Speech *(Continued)*

between 20 and 30 percent, compared to the 100 percent interest rates local moneylenders charge. In this way, microcredit provides a source of capital that families can actually afford to pay back, allowing them to improve their lives without getting trapped in an unmanageable cycle of debt.

Muhammad Yunus claims that one day the world will only see poverty in museums. While microcredit could make this a reality, it raises several implications for our views on social welfare, the economic role of women, and poverty.

Microcredit could alter our outlook on social welfare. In his 1980 book *Free to Choose*, Nobel Prize–winning economist Milton Friedman argues that the poor benefit more by being empowered to make their own decisions than they do from government handouts. The previously cited *International Herald Tribune* article notes that microcredit reinforces Friedman's belief in free market capitalism by giving the poor control over how they generate income. The success of this approach could provide ammunition to those who rally against social welfare, strengthening attempts to abolish the so-called welfare state and the safety nets that it currently provides.

Additionally, microcredit may not have the expected positive impact on women. According to an April 3, 2006, press release from the United Nations Department of Public Information, 80 percent of microcredit borrowers are women. Microcredit groups seek out female borrowers because they hope to empower women in traditionally patriarchal societies. However, the February 10, 2007, edition of India's *Economic and Political Weekly* argues that sometimes women are forced to hand their loans over to their husbands. The wife ends up worse off than when she started, because she is responsible for repaying the loan but has not received any of its benefits. Thus, microcredit offers women a road to economic empowerment, but if male dominance in a given community is too deeply entrenched, microcredit may not be able to deliver on its promise.

Finally, microcredit could change our understanding of poverty. The 2005 documentary *Small Fortunes: Microcredit and the Future of Poverty* explains that one long-standing perception about the poor is that they just need to work harder. Yet Pakistan's *The Nation* of December 6, 2006, states that microcredit's central message is that people are poor not because they lack ambition, but rather because traditional banking systems are "discriminatory and anti-poor." As microcredit continues to gain legitimacy, it could shift blame away from the impoverished and refocus our attention on the root causes of poverty—the very systems that perpetuate destitution in the first place.

When awarding Muhammad Yunus the Nobel Prize, the committee noted, "Lasting peace can not be achieved

Here the speaker provides a transition to the third major point, this one dealing with the implications of microcredit. As you can easily tell, the speaker will cover three implications: those pertaining to social welfare, the role of women, and poverty.

The first implication concerns social welfare. Notice that the speaker effectively establishes the credibility of her source, Milton Friedman, by recalling that he was a Nobel Prize–winning economist. In what other ways does the speaker establish credibility—her own as well as that of her sources?

Here we're jolted a bit. We assume that all microcredit is going to be positive, but here the speaker notes a negative impact—it may make women more vulnerable, not more empowered. Of course, this is an informative speech; it isn't designed to persuade you but to inform you.

We now know the speaker has come to the final point of the speech ("finally"), this one dealing with the implications of microcredit on poverty.

Here the speaker concludes the speech by clearly summarizing the main points of the speech: the development, rationale,

Public Speaking Sample Assistant

An Excellent Informative Speech *(Continued)*

unless large population groups find ways in which to break out of poverty."

After examining the development of microcredit, its rationale, and the implications of this movement, it seems that this poverty-fighting technique may be a step toward a more peaceful world. In the meantime, Yunus and other microcredit lenders will continue to spread the message that the poor are creditworthy. But the real challenge, in their eyes, is to continue to build banks that are people-worthy.

and implications of microcredit. The speaker then stresses the importance of microcredit by calling it a poverty-fighting technique and suggesting that it may be a step toward a more peaceful world.

The speaker then recalls the introduction by getting back to Yunus and closes by noting the real challenge.

Limit the Amount of Information

Resist the temptation to overload your listeners with information. Limit the breadth of information you communicate; instead, expand its depth. Limiting the amount of information lets you present a few items of information and explain these with examples, illustrations, and descriptions rather than presenting a wide array of items without this needed amplification. The speaker who attempts to discuss the physiological, psychological, social, and linguistic differences between men and women, for example, is clearly trying to cover too much and is going to be

Theory and Research   Information Theory

UNDERSTANDING

In the 1940s, engineers working at Bell Telephone Laboratories developed the mathematical theory of communication—which became known as information theory. This theory defined **information** as that which reduces uncertainty. For example, if I tell you my name and you already know it, then I haven't communicated information—because my message (my name) didn't reduce uncertainty; you already knew my name and so had no uncertainty in this connection. If, on the other hand, I tell you my salary or my educational background or my fears and dreams, that constitutes information, because these are things you presumably didn't know. Although this theory doesn't explain many of the complexities of human communication very well, it is helpful when you are thinking about the purpose of the informative speech: to communicate information, to tell the members of the audience something they didn't already know, or to send messages that reduce the uncertainty of your listeners about your speech topic. If you don't communicate enough information, the audience will be bored (they'll already know what you're saying). But if you communicate too much information, they'll be overwhelmed. The art of the effective speaker is to strike an appropriate balance.

Working with Theories and Research

Review the speech you're working on now. How much is information? How much does the audience already know? Is this the appropriate balance, or do you need to make adjustments?

© Chip Simons/Getty Images

UNEXPECTED EVENTS

You're going to speak on the newest Microsoft operating system that you've been using the last few weeks. Unfortunately, the previous speaker turns out to be a Microsoft program designer who gives a speech on exactly your topic.

WHAT DO YOU SAY?

forced to cover these areas only superficially, with the result that little new information will be communicated. Even covering one of these areas is likely to prove too broad. Instead, select one subdivision of one area—say, language development or differences in language problems—and develop that in depth.

Adjust the Level of Complexity

As you know from attending college classes, information can be presented in a very simplified form or in an extremely complex form. Adjusting the level of complexity on which you communicate is key and should be guided by a wide variety of factors we have already considered: the level of knowledge your audience has, the time you have available, the purpose you hope to achieve, the topic on which you're speaking, and so on. If you simplify a topic too much, you risk boring or, even worse, insulting your audience. If your talk is too complex, you risk confusing your audience and failing to communicate the desired information.

Generally, however, beginning speakers err on the side of being too complex and do not realize that a

5- or 10-minute speech does not allow much time to introduce sophisticated concepts or make an audience understand how a complicated process works. At least in your beginning speeches, try to keep it simple rather than complex. For example, make sure the words you use are familiar to your audience—or, if they're not, explain and define the terms as you use them. Remember too that jargon and technical vocabulary of specialized fields often will need translation. Always see your topic from the point of view of the members of the audience; ask yourself how much they know about your topic and its unique language.

Stress Relevance and Usefulness

Listeners will remember your information best when they see it as useful and relevant to their own needs of goals. Notice that as a listener you regularly follow the principle of stressing relevance and usefulness. For example, in class you may attend to and remember the stages in the development of language in children simply because you know you'll be tested on the information and you want to earn a high grade. Or you may attend to the information because it will help you make a better impression in your job interview, make you a better parent, or enable you to deal with relationship problems.

Like you, listeners attend to information that will prove useful to them. So if you want the audience to listen to your speech, relate your information to their needs, wants, or goals (Frymier & Shulman, 1995). Throughout your speech, but especially in the beginning, make sure your audience knows that the information you're presenting is relevant and useful to them now—or will be in the immediate future. For example, you might say something like:

> We all want financial security. We all want to be able to buy those luxuries we read so much about in magazines and see every evening on television. Wouldn't it be nice to be able to buy a car without worrying about where you're going to get the down payment or how you'll be able to make the monthly payments? Actually, that is not an unrealistic goal, as I'll demonstrate in this speech. In fact, I will show you several methods for investing your money that will enable you to increase your income by at least 20 percent.

Relate New Information to Old

Listeners will learn information more easily and retain it longer when you relate it to what they already know. In relating new information to old, link the unfamiliar to the familiar, the unseen to the seen, the untasted to the tasted. Here, for example,

Theory and Research — Signal-to-Noise Ratio

UNDERSTANDING

A useful way of looking at information is in terms of its **signal-to-noise ratio**. *Signal* in this context refers to information that is useful to you, information that you want. *Noise*, on the other hand, is what you find useless; it's what you do not want. So, for example, if a mailing list or newsgroup contained lots of useful information, it would be high on signal and low on noise; if it contained lots of useless information, it would be high on noise and low on signal. Spam is high on noise and low on signal, as is static that interferes with radio, television, or telephone transmission.

From the public speaker's point of view, noise is anything that diverts audience attention away from the speech (the signal)—pictures on the walls, writing on the chalkboard, people talking in the hallways, the rustle of newspapers, and so on. The speaker's task is to keep the audience's focus on the speech instead of the noise.

Working with Theories and Research

Look around the classroom in which you give your speeches. What sources of potential noise can you identify? What can you do to prevent the audience from focusing on the noise instead of your speech?

Teresa Jacob, a student at Ohio State University (Schnoor, 1999, p. 97), relates the problems of drug interactions (the new) to mixing chemicals in the school lab (the old or familiar):

During our high school years, most of us learned in a chemistry class the danger of mixing harmless chemicals in lab. Add one drop of the wrong compound and suddenly you've created a stink bomb, or worse, an explosion. Millions of Americans run the same risk inside their bodies each day by combining drugs that are supposed to help restore or maintain good health.

Vary the Levels of Abstraction

You can talk about freedom of the press in **abstractions**—for example, by talking about the importance

Building Communication Skills — Climbing the Abstraction Ladder

For each of the terms listed below, indicate at least four possible terms that indicate increasing specificity. The first example is provided as an illustration:

Level 1	Level 2 more specific than 1	Level 3 more specific than 2	Level 4 more specific than 3	Level 5 more specific than 4
Building	*Masonry building*	*Masonry office building*	*Office skyscraper*	*Chicago's Sears Tower*
Transportation				
Communication				
Toy				
Sport				

Words exist at different levels of abstraction. As you get more specific, you more clearly communicate your own meanings and more easily direct the listeners' attention to what you wish.

TECHNICAL PROBLEMS

You've prepared a great slide show for your informative speech. Unfortunately, the equipment that you need to show the slides never arrives. But you have to give your speech and you have to (or do you?) explain something of what happened.

WHAT DO YOU SAY?

of getting information to the public, by referring to the Bill of Rights, and by relating a free press to the preservation of democracy. That is, you can talk about the topic on a relatively high **level of abstraction**. But you can also talk about freedom of the press by citing specific examples: how a local newspaper was prevented from running a story critical of the town council or how Lucy Rinaldo was fired from the *Accord Sentinel* after she wrote a story critical of the mayor. In other words, you can

talk about the topic on a relatively low level of abstraction, a level that is specific and concrete.

Varying the levels of abstraction—combining the abstract and the specific—seems to work best. Too many high abstractions without specifics or too many specifics without high abstractions will generally prove less effective than a combination of the two approaches.

Here, for example, is an excerpt from a speech on the issue of homelessness. Note that in the first

REFLECTIONS ON ETHICS

Speaking Ethically

One interesting approach to ethics that has particular relevance to public speaking identifies four key rules for speakers (Wallace, 1955; Johannesen, 2001). As an ethical speaker, you should be guided by the following principles:

- Have a thorough knowledge of the topic, an ability to answer relevant questions, and an awareness of the significant facts and opinions bearing on the issues you discuss.

- Present both facts and opinions fairly, without bending or spinning them to personal advantage. You must allow listeners to make the final judgment.

- Reveal the sources of these facts and opinions, and help listeners evaluate any biases and prejudices in the sources.

- Acknowledge and respect opposing arguments and evidence; advocate a tolerance for diversity.

Ethical Choice Point

You're giving an informative speech to explain how the new condom machines on campus will work. Among the important items that should logically be covered is their cost, which is going to come from an increase in student fees. Since you are very in favor of these machines, you'd like to eliminate discussing cost largely because the students may vote against installing the machines if they knew their fees would be raised. You figure you don't have time to include all issues, that it's really the responsibility of the audience to ask where the money is coming from, and that the machines will help prevent sexually transmitted diseases. What is your ethical obligation in this situation? What would you do?

paragraph we have a relatively abstract description of homelessness. In the second paragraph, we get into specifics. In the last paragraph, the abstract and the concrete are connected.

> Homelessness is a serious problem for all metropolitan areas throughout the country. It's currently estimated that there are more than 200,000 homeless people in New York City alone. But what is this really about? Let me tell you what it's about.
>
> It's about a young man. He must be about 25 or 30, although he looks a lot older. He lives in a cardboard box on the side of my apartment house. We call him Tom, although we really don't know his name. All his possessions are stored in this huge box. I think it was a box from a refrigerator. Actually, he doesn't have very much, and what he has easily fits in this box. There's a blanket my neighbor threw out, some plastic bottles he puts water in, and some Styrofoam containers he picked up from the garbage from Burger King. He uses these to store whatever food he finds.
>
> What is homelessness about? It's about Tom and 200,000 other "Toms" in New York and thousands of others throughout the rest of the country. And not all of them even have boxes to live in.

Now that we've considered these guidelines for informative speaking, let's look at the kinds of informative speeches that you may be called upon to present. Researchers on public speaking have developed numerous classification systems for information speeches, but in this text we'll focus on three broad types: speeches of (1) description, (2) definition, and (3) demonstration. We turn now to the first of these categories: the speech of description.

SPEECHES OF DESCRIPTION

In a **speech of description**, you're concerned with explaining an object, person, event, or process. Examples of speeches in which you describe an object or person might include "The Structure of the Brain," "The Contributions of Thomas Edison," "The Parts of a Telephone," "The Layout of Philadelphia," "The Hierarchy of a Corporation," or "The Components of a Computer System."

Examples of speeches in which you describe an event or process might include "The Attacks of September 11, 2001"; "The Events Leading to the Iraq War"; "Organizing a Body-Building Contest"; "How a Newspaper Is Printed"; "Purchasing Stock Online"; or "How a Child Acquires Language."

Thesis

The thesis of a speech is your single most important concept; it is what you most want your audience to remember. The thesis of a speech of description simply states what you'll describe in your speech; for example, "The child acquires language in four stages," or "There are three steps to purchasing stock online," or "Four major events led to the Iraq war."

Main Points

The main points of your speech of description are the major subdivisions of the thesis. You derive your main points from the thesis by asking strategic questions. For example, "What are the four stages in child language acquisition?" "What are the three steps to purchasing stock online?" "What events led to the Iraq war?"

SPEECH OF DESCRIPTION

You're giving a speech of description on how children acquire language and you notice a woman with a child of the age you're talking about in the audience.

WHAT DO YOU SAY?

© Michael Newman/PhotoEdit

Support

Obviously, you don't want simply to list your main points but rather to flesh them out and to make them memorable, interesting, and most of all clear. You do this by using a variety of materials that amplify and support your main ideas—the examples, illustrations, testimony, statistics, and the like, that have already been explained. So, for example, in describing the babbling stage of language learning, you might give examples of babbling, the age at which babbling first appears, the period of time that babbling lasts, or the differences between the babbling of girls and boys.

Because this is a speech of description, give extra consideration to the types of description you might use in your supporting materials. Try to describe the object or event with lots of different descriptive categories. With physical categories, for example, ask yourself questions such as these: What color is it? How big is it? What is it shaped like? How much does it weigh? What is its volume? How attractive/unattractive is it? Also consider social, psychological, and economic categories. In describing a person, for example, consider such categories as friendly/unfriendly, warm/cold, rich/poor, aggressive/meek, and pleasant/unpleasant.

Consider how you might use presentation aids. In describing an object or a person, show your listeners a picture; show them the inside of a telephone, pictures of the brain, the skeleton of the body. In describing an event or process, show them a diagram or flowchart to illustrate the stages or steps; for example, the steps involved in buying stock, in publishing a newspaper, in putting a parade together.

Organization

Consider using a spatial or a topical organization when describing objects and people. Consider using a temporal pattern when describing events and processes. For example, if you were to describe the layout of Philadelphia, you might start from the north and work down to the south (using a spatial pattern). If you were to describe the contributions of Thomas Edison, you might select the three or four major contributions and discuss each of these equally (using a topical pattern).

If you were describing the events leading up to World War II, you might use a temporal pattern, starting with the earliest and working up to the latest. A temporal pattern would also be appropriate for describing how a hurricane develops or how a parade is put together.

Consider the 5W (who? what? where? when? and why?) pattern of organization discussed. These journalistic categories are especially useful when you want to describe an event or a process. For example, if you're going to describe how to purchase a house, you might want to consider the people involved (who?), the steps you have to go through (what?), the places you'll have to go (where?), the time or sequence in which the steps have to take place (when?), and the advantages and disadvantages of buying the house (why?).

Here are two examples of the main components a descriptive speech might contain. In this first example, the speaker describes four suggestions for reducing energy bills. Notice that the speaker derives the main points from asking a question of the thesis.

General purpose: To inform.

Specific purpose: To describe how you can reduce energy bills.

Thesis: Energy bills can be reduced. (How can energy bills be reduced?)

    I. Caulk window and door seams.
    II. Apply weather stripping around windows and doors.
    III. Insulate walls.
    IV. Install storm windows and doors.

In this second example, the speaker describes the way in which fear works in intercultural communication.

General purpose: To inform.

Specific purpose: To describe the way fear works in intercultural communication.

Thesis: Fear influences intercultural communication. (How does fear influence intercultural communication?)

    I. We fear disapproval.
    II. We fear embarrassing ourselves.
    III. We fear being harmed.

In delivering such a speech, a speaker might begin by saying:

Three major fears interfere with intercultural communication. First, we fear disapproval—from members of our own group as well as from members of the other person's group. Second, we fear embarrassing ourselves, even making fools of ourselves, by saying the wrong thing or appearing insensitive. And third, we may fear being harmed—our stereotypes of the other group may lead us to see its members as dangerous or potentially harmful to us.

Let's look at each of these fears in more detail. We'll be able to see clearly how they influence our own intercultural communication behavior. Consider, first, the fear of disapproval. [The speaker would then amplify and support this fear of disapproval, giving examples of disapproval seen in his or her own experience, the testimony of communication theorists on the importance of such fear, research findings on the effects that such fear might have on intercultural communication, and so on.]

SPEECHES OF DEFINITION

What is leadership? What is a born-again Christian? What is the difference between sociology and psychology? What is a cultural anthropologist? What is safe sex? These are all topics for informative **speeches of definition**.

A *definition* is a statement of the meaning or significance of a concept or term. Use definitions when you wish to explain difficult or unfamiliar concepts or when you wish to make a concept more vivid or forceful.

In giving a speech of definition, you may focus on defining a term, defining a system or theory, or pinpointing the similarities and/or differences among terms or systems. A speech of definition may be on a subject new to the audience or may present a familiar topic in a new and different way.

Examples of speeches in which you define a term might include "What Is a Smart Card?" "What Is Machismo?" "What Is Creativity?" "What Is Affirmative Action?" "What Is Multiculturalism?" "What Is Political Correctness?"

Examples of speeches in which you'd define a system or theory might include "What Is the Classical Theory of Public Speaking?" "What Are the Parts of a Generative Grammar?" "Confucianism: Its Major Beliefs," "What Is Expressionism?" "What Is Futurism?" "The 'Play Theory' of Mass Communication."

Examples of speeches in which you'd define similar and dissimilar terms or systems might include "Football and Soccer: What's the Difference?" "What Do Christians and Muslims Have in Common?" "Oedipus and Electra: How Do They Differ?" "Genetics and Heredity," "Animal and Human Rights," and "Key-Word and Directory Searches."

Thesis

The thesis in a speech of definition is a statement identifying the term or system and your intention to define it or to contrast it with other terms; for example, "Christianity and Islam have much in common" or "You can search for information through key words or through a directory."

Main Points

You derive the main points for your speech of definition by asking questions of your thesis; for example, "What do Christianity and Islam have in common?" "How do text and online dictionaries differ?" Your main points will then consist of, say, the factors that Christianity and Islam have in common or the several ways in which text and online dictionaries differ.

Support

Once you have each of your main points, you'll support them with examples, testimony, and the like. For example, one of your main points in the Christianity-Islam example might be that both religions believe in the value of good works. You might then quote from the New Testament and from the Quran to illustrate

DEFINING

In visualizing your next speech, in which you plan to define the basic tenets of your religion, you know that some members of your audience will have a negative view of your religion while others will hold positive views. You want to acknowledge your understanding of these attitudes.

WHAT DO YOU SAY?

© Bruce Ayres/Getty Images

this belief, or you might give examples of noted Christians and Muslims who exemplified this characteristic, or you might cite the testimony of religious leaders who talked about the importance of good works.

Because this is a speech of definition, you'll want to give special attention to different types of definitions.

Organization

In addition to the obvious organizational pattern of multiple definitions, consider using a topical order, in which each main idea is treated equally. In either case, however, proceed from the known to the unknown. Start with what your audience knows and work up to what is new or unfamiliar. This will help the audience to bring to consciousness the material you want to build on. Let's say you want to explain the concept of phon-emics (with which your audience is totally unfamiliar). The specific idea you wish

to get across is that each phoneme stands for a unique sound. You might proceed from the known to the unknown and begin your definition with something like this:

> We all know that in the written language each letter of the alphabet stands for a unit of the written language. Each letter is different from every other letter. A *t* is different from a *g* and a *g* is different from a *b*, and so on. Each letter is called a "grapheme." In English we know we have 26 such letters.
>
> We can look at the spoken language in much the same way. Each sound is different from every other sound. A *t* sound is different from a *d* and a *d* is different from a *k*, and so on. Each individual sound is called a "phoneme."
>
> Now, let me explain in a little more detail what I mean by a "phoneme."

Here are two examples of how you might go about constructing a speech of definition. In this

MEDIA·WATCH

THE KNOWLEDGE GAP

The term *knowledge gap* refers to the difference in knowledge between one group and another; it's the division between those who have a great deal of knowledge about some subject and those who have significantly less. Much of the research in this area has focused on the influence of the media in widening this knowledge gap—a concept known as the knowledge gap hypothesis (Tichenor, Donohue, & Olien, 1970; Severin, 1988; Viswanath & Finnegan, 1995).

Information is valuable; it brings wealth and it gives power. It gives you the means you need to get a high-paid job, to live a healthy life, to plan for retirement, or to accomplish just about any task you set for yourself (Mastin, 1998).

But information is expensive, and not everyone has equal access to it. This is especially true as we live more of our lives in cyberspace. The new communication technologies—computers, CDs, DVDs, high-speed Internet connections, satellite and cable television, for example—are major ways for gaining information. Better-educated people have the money to own and the skills to master the new technologies and thus acquire more information. Less-educated people don't have the money to own or the skills to master the new technologies and thus cannot acquire more information. Thus,

the educated have the means for becoming even better educated, and the gap widens.

You also see the knowledge gap hypothesis when you compare different cultures. Developed countries, for example, have the new technologies in schools and offices, and many people in these countries can afford to buy their own computers and satellite systems. Access to the new technologies helps these countries develop even further. Undeveloped countries, with little or no access to such technologies, cannot experience the same gain in knowledge and information as those with this technological access.

Even the language of a culture may influence the extent of the knowledge gap. For example, English dominates the Internet; so the Internet is more easily accessible to people in English-speaking countries, as well as to people in non-English-speaking countries who speak English as a second language.

Increasing Media Literacy

Do you see the knowledge gap operating in your community or school? Can you see it in different cultures with which you're familiar?

first example, the speaker explains the parts of a résumé and follows a spatial order, going from the top to the bottom of the page.

General purpose: To inform.

Specific purpose: To define the essential parts of a résumé.

Thesis: There are four major parts to a résumé. (What are the four major parts of a résumé?)

    I. Identify your career goals.
    II. Identify your educational background.
    III. Identify your work experience.
    IV. Identify your special competencies.

In this second example, the speaker selects three major types of lying for discussion and arranges these in a topical pattern.

General purpose: To inform.

Specific purpose: To define lying by explaining the major types of lying.

Thesis: There are three major kinds of lying. (What are the three major kinds of lying?)

    I. Concealment is the process of hiding the truth.
    II. Falsification is the process of presenting false information as if it were true.
    III. Misdirection is the process of acknowledging a feeling but misidentifying its cause.

In delivering such a speech, a speaker might begin the speech by saying:

A lie is a lie is a lie. True? Well, not exactly. Actually, there are a number of different ways we can lie. We can lie by concealing the truth. We can lie by falsification, by presenting false information as if it were true. And we can lie by misdirection, by acknowledging a feeling but misidentifying its cause.

Let's look at the first type of lie—the lie of concealment. Most lies are lies of concealment. Most of the time when we lie we simply conceal the truth. We don't actually make any false statements. Rather we simply don't reveal the truth. Let me give you some examples I overheard recently.

SPEECHES OF DEMONSTRATION

In a **speech of demonstration** (or in using demonstration within a different type of speech), you show the audience how to do something or how something operates. Examples of speeches in which you demonstrate how to do something might include "How to Give Mouth-to-Mouth Resuscitation," "How to Drive Defensively," "How to Mix Paint Colors," "How to Ask for a Raise," "How to Burglarproof Your House," or "How to Use PowerPoint in Business Meetings."

Examples of speeches in which you demonstrate how something operates might include "How the Body Maintains Homeostasis," "How Perception Works," "How Divorce Laws Work," "How E-Mail Works," "How a Hurricane Develops," or "How a Heart Bypass Operation Is Performed."

DEMONSTRATING

You want to demonstrate to your audience how some new technology works. Your audience is probably mixed in terms of their knowledge of technology generally—some know a great deal and others know very little. You want to make sure that all audience members will give you their attention and you'd like to accomplish that right at the start of your speech.

WHAT DO YOU SAY?

© Jeff Greenburg/PhotoEdit

Thesis

The thesis for a speech of demonstration identifies what you will show the audience how to do, or how something operates; for example, "E-mail works through a series of electronic connections from one computer to a server to another computer," or "You can burglarproof your house in three different ways," or "Three guidelines will help you get that raise."

Main Points

You can derive the main points for your speech of demonstration by asking a simple How or What question of your thesis—"How do these electronic connections work?" "What are the methods you can use to burglarproof your house?" "What are the guidelines for asking for a raise?"

Support

Support each of your main ideas with a variety of materials. For example, you might show diagrams of houses that use different burglarproofing methods, demonstrate how various locks work, or show how different security systems work.

Presentation aids are especially helpful in speeches of demonstration. A good example of this is the signs in restaurants demonstrating the Heimlich maneuver. These signs demonstrate the sequence of steps with pictures as well as words. The combination of verbal and graphic information makes it easy for restaurant-goers to understand this important process. In a speech on this topic, however, it would be best to use only the pictures so that the written words would not distract your audience from your oral explanation.

Organization

In most cases a temporal pattern will work best in speeches of demonstration. Demonstrate each step in the sequence in which it's to be performed. In this way you'll avoid one of the major difficulties in demonstrating a process—backtracking. Don't skip steps even if you think they're familiar to the audience. They may not be. Connect each step to the next with appropriate transitions. For example, in explaining the Heimlich maneuver, you might say,

Now that you have your arms around the choking victim's chest, your next step is to....

Assist your listeners by labeling the steps clearly; for example, "the first step," "the second step," and so on.

Begin with an overview. It's often helpful when demonstrating to give a broad general picture and then present each step in turn. For example, suppose you were talking about how to prepare a wall

for painting. You might begin with a general overview to give your listeners a general idea of the process, saying something like this:

In preparing the wall for painting, you want to make sure that the wall is smoothly sanded, free of dust, and dry. Sanding a wall isn't like sanding a block of wood. So let's look at the proper way to sand a wall.

Here are two examples of the speech of demonstration. In this first example, the speaker explains the proper way to paint a wall by rag rolling. As you can see, the speaker uses a temporal organizational pattern and covers three stages in the order in which they would be performed.

General purpose: To inform.

Specific purpose: To demonstrate how to rag roll.

Thesis: Rag rolling is performed in three steps. (What are the three steps of rag rolling?)

  I. Apply the base coat of paint.
  II. Apply the glaze coat.
  III. Roll a rag through the wet glaze.

In the next example, the speaker identifies and demonstrates how to listen actively.

General purpose: To inform.

Specific purpose: To demonstrate three techniques of active listening.

Thesis: We can engage in active listening. (How can we engage in active listening?)

  I. Paraphrase the speaker's meaning.
  II. Express understanding of the speaker's feelings.
  III. Ask questions.

In delivering the speech, the speaker might begin by saying:

Active listening is a special kind of listening. It's listening with total involvement, with a concern for the speaker. It's probably the most important type of listening you can engage in. Active listening consists of three steps: paraphrasing the speaker's meaning, expressing understanding of the speaker's feelings, and asking questions.

Your first step in active listening is to paraphrase the speaker's meaning. What is a paraphrase? A paraphrase is a restatement in your own words of the speaker's meaning. That is, you express in your own words what you think the speaker meant. For example, let's say that the speaker said....

Building Communication Skills — Preparing an Informative Speech

Consult the Dictionary of Topics (www.mycommunicationlab.com) for suggestions for informative speech topics. Select a topic and develop a preparation outline:

- Formulate a thesis and a specific purpose suitable for an informative speech of approximately 10 minutes;
- Analyze this class as your potential audience, and identify ways that you can relate this topic to their interests and needs;
- Generate at least two main points from your thesis;
- Support these main points with examples, illustrations, definitions, testimony, and so on;
- Construct a conclusion that summarizes your main ideas and brings the speech to a definite close; and
- Construct an introduction that gains attention and orients your audience.

Discuss these outlines in small groups or with the class as a whole. Try to secure feedback from other members on how you can improve these outlines.

Working repeatedly with the process of preparing a speech will ultimately make the process easier, more efficient, and more effective.

As mentioned earlier, this three-part classification of information speeches into speeches of demonstration, definition, and description is only one way of looking at informative speeches. You may be interested in some alternative classifications of information speeches that other writers in public speaking have devised.

Stephen Lucas (2007), in *The Art of Public Speaking*, uses a four-part classification:

- Speeches about objects, persons, places, or things (for example, the contributions of a noted scientist or philosopher);
- Speeches about processes or series of actions (for example, an explanation of how to do something);
- Speeches about events or happenings (the story of your first date); and
- Speeches about concepts, beliefs, or ideas (for example, a review of theories of economics).

George Grice and John Skinner (2007), in *Mastering Public Speaking*, offer an eight-part system:

- Speeches about people (Cesar Chavez, Margaret Mead);
- Speeches about objects (electric cars, the Great Wall of China);
- Speeches about places (Ellis Island, the Nile);
- Speeches about events (the sinking of the *Titanic*, Woodstock festivals);
- Speeches about processes (cartooning, waterproofing);
- Speeches about concepts (liberty, nihilism);
- Speeches about conditions (McCarthyism, the civil rights movement);
- Speeches about issues (the use of polygraph tests, fetal tissue research).

Rudolph and Kathleen Verderber, in *The Challenge of Effective Speaking* (2006), present a five-part system:

- Speeches of description (speeches about objects, geographical features, settings, or images—a light bulb, a hologram);
- Speeches of definition (speeches that explain something by identifying its meaning—vegetarianism, plane);
- Speeches of comparison and contrast (speeches explaining how something is similar to or different from other things—vegans and vegetarians);
- Speeches of narration (speeches explaining something by recounting events—becoming a vegetarian); and
- Speeches of demonstration (speeches that explain how something is done, the stages of a process, or how something works—how to iron a shirt, the workings of a nuclear reactor).

SUMMARY: THE INFORMATIVE SPEECH

This unit focused on the informative speech, examining the goals of informative speaking, the guidelines to follow in informing others, and the various types of informative speeches.

1. Informative speaking may have a variety of goals, among them: to introduce new topics, to clarify misconceptions, to demonstrate how to do something, and to expand on information the audience already has.

2. Informative speeches are more likely to be effective when they adhere to the following principles of informative speaking: Limit the amount of information you

communicate, adjust the level of complexity, stress the relevance and the usefulness of the information to your audience, relate new information to old, and vary the levels of abstraction.

3. Speeches of description describe a process or procedure, an event, an object, or a person.

4. Speeches of definition define a term, system, or theory or explain similarities and/or differences among terms.

5. Speeches of demonstration show how to do something or how something operates.

KEY TERMS IN THE INFORMATIVE SPEECH

abstractions	level of abstraction	speech of description	speech of demonstration
information	signal-to-noise ratio	speech of definition	

THINKING CRITICALLY ABOUT THE INFORMATIVE SPEECH

1. **Communicating Unknown Concepts.** You want to give an informative speech on virtual reality simulation, but most of your audience members have never experienced it. How would you communicate this concept and this experience to your audience?

2. **Informative Strategies.** You're planning to give an informative speech on the history of doctor-assisted suicide and are considering the strategies that you might use. What organizational pattern would be appropriate? What types of presentation aids might you use? How would you define "doctor-assisted suicide"? How would you introduce your speech?

3. **Same-Topic Speech.** You're scheduled to be the third speaker in a series of six presentations today. Unfortu-

nately, the first speaker presented a really excellent speech on the same topic you're speaking on—how the Internet works. What should you do?

4. **Speaking on Technical Issues.** Visit the Society for Technical Communication at **www.stc-va.org/** for guides for writing and speaking on technical matters.

5. **Two-Minute Speech.** Prepare a two-minute informative speech on one of the following:
   - Explain a card game.
   - Explain a board game.
   - Explain food preparation.
   - Explain a sport.

LogOn! MyCommunicationLab
WWW.MYCOMMUNICATIONLAB.COM

An earlier version of the informative speech on microcredit included in a Public Speaking Sample Assistant box in this unit is available at MCL. You might find it interesting to compare the two versions. Which do you prefer? Watch the speech "Contemporary Education" and examine it in terms of the principles of informative speaking considered in this chapter. Also view one or both of the demonstration speeches ("Baking a Cake" and "CPR"). The "Hybrid Electric Vehicle" speech provides a good example of the speech of description. Also explore the Definitions activity and visit the suggested websites.

REFERENCES

Frymier, A. B., & Shulman, G. M. (1995). "What's in it for me?": Increasing content relevance to enhance students' motivation. *Communication Education, 44* (January), 40–50.

Grice, G. L., & Skinner, J. F. (2007). *Mastering public speaking* (6th ed.). Boston: Allyn & Bacon.

Johannesen, R. L. (2001). *Ethics in human communication* (6th ed.). Prospect Heights, IL: Waveland Press.

Lucas, S. (2007). *The art of public speaking* (9th ed.). New York: McGraw-Hill.

Mastin, T. (1998). Employees' understanding of employer-sponsored retirement plans: A knowledge gap perspective. *Public Relations Review, 24* (Winter), 521–534.

Schnoor, L. G. (Ed.). (1999). *Winning orations of the interstate oratorical association*. Mankato, MN: Interstate Oratorical Association.

Severin, W. J., with Tankard, J. W., Jr. (1988). *Communication theories* (2nd ed.). New York: Longman.

Tichenor, P. J., Donohue, G. A., & Olien, C. N. (1970). Mass media flow and differential growth in knowledge. *Public Opinion Quarterly, 34*, 159–170.

Verderber, R. (2006). *The challenge of effective speaking* (13th ed.). Belmont, CA: Wadsworth.

Viswanath, K., & Finnegan, J. R., Jr. (1995). The knowledge-gap hypothesis: Twenty-five years later. In B. R. Burleson (Ed.), *Communication yearbook 19*. Thousand Oaks, CA: Sage.

Wallace, K. (1955). An ethical basis of communication. *Communication Education, 4* (January), 1–9.

Chapter 5

Supporting and Organizing Your Speech

Supporting and Organizing Your Speech

MAJOR TOPICS

Step 4: Formulate Your Thesis and Main Points

Step 5: Support Your Main Points

Step 6: Organize Your Speech

Step 7: Construct Your Introduction, Conclusion, and Transitions

Special Features

The Motivated Sequence:
Bruce E. Gronbeck

Product Placement

Communicating in Cyberspace

 Primacy and Recency

 Culture and Speech
Organization

 Generating Main Points

 Constructing Conclusions
and Introductions

 A Slide Show Speech

Here the discussion of public speaking continues.

In this unit you'll learn about:
- the main idea or thesis of the speech and its main points.
- the nature of support.
- the organizational patterns, introductions, and conclusions for speeches of all types.

And you'll learn to:
- formulate a clear thesis statement.
- support your ideas with interesting and persuasive materials (examples, testimony, statistics).
- organize your thoughts so that your speech is easy to follow and maintains your audience's interest and attention.

STEP 4: FORMULATE YOUR THESIS AND MAIN POINTS

Your **thesis** is your main assertion; it's what you want the audience to absorb from your speech. The thesis of the *Rocky* movies is that the underdog can win; the thesis of the Martin Luther King Jr. "I Have a Dream" speech is that true equality must be granted to African Americans and to all people. From your thesis you'll be able to derive your main points, the major ideas that you will explore in order to prove or support your thesis.

Your Thesis

In an informative speech, the thesis statement focuses on what you want your audience to learn. For example, a thesis for an informative speech on jealousy might be: "There are two main theories of jealousy." In a persuasive speech, your thesis is what you want your audience to believe as a result of your speech. For example, a thesis for a persuasive speech against using animals for experimentation might be: "Animal experimentation should be banned." Notice that in informative speeches the thesis is relatively neutral and objective. In persuasive speeches, however, the thesis statement puts forth a point of view, an opinion; it's an arguable, debatable proposition.

Be sure to limit the thesis statement to one central idea. A statement such as "Animal experimentation should be banned, and companies engaging in it should be prosecuted" contains not one but two basic ideas.

Word your thesis as a simple declarative sentence: "Animal experimentation should be banned." This will help you focus your thinking, your collection of materials, and your organizational tasks.

Use the thesis statement to help you generate your main points. Each thesis contains within it an essential question, and it is this question that allows you to explore and subdivide the thesis. Your objective is to find this question and ask it of your thesis. For example, let's say your thesis is: "The Hart bill provides needed services for senior citizens." Stated in this form, the thesis suggests the obvious question "What are they?" The answers to this question suggest the main points of your speech; for example, health care, food, shelter, and recreational services. These four areas then become the four main points of your speech.

Use the thesis to help focus the audience's attention on your central idea. In some cases you may wish to state your thesis early in your speech. In other cases, such as situations in which your audience may be hostile to your thesis, it may be wise to give your evidence first and gradually move the audience into a more positive frame of mind before stating your thesis. Here are a few guidelines to help you make the right decision about when to introduce your thesis:

- In an informative speech, state your thesis early and state it clearly and directly.

- In a persuasive speech before a neutral or positive audience, state your thesis explicitly and early in your speech.

- In a persuasive speech before an audience that is hostile to your position, delay revealing your thesis until you've moved your listeners closer to your point of view.

- Recognize that there are cultural differences in the way a thesis should be stated. In some Asian cultures, for example, making a point too directly or asking directly for audience compliance may be considered rude or insulting.

119

Here, for example, is how student Stephanie Cagniart of the University of Texas at Austin expressed her thesis, along with a clear preview of the main points she would cover in her speech:

> The commerce clause is being used by the federal government to dictate social issues—from gun control to same-sex marriage—in a way that threatens our individual liberties and undermines states' rights. So let's first, examine why the commerce clause has broadened; second, explore this abuse's dangers; and finally, investigate how we can scale back what the October 20, 2005, *Wanderer* magazine calls "the clause that ate the Constitution."

Main Points

If your speech were a play, the main points would be its acts. Let's look at how you can select and word your main points and how you can logically arrange them.

As we discussed earlier, you can develop your main points by asking strategic questions. To see how this works in detail, imagine that you are giving a speech on the values of a college education to a group of high school students. Your thesis is: "A college education is valuable." You then ask, "Why is it valuable?" From this question you generate your main points. Your first step might be to brainstorm this question and generate as many answers as possible without evaluating them. You might come up with answers such as the following:

1. It helps you get a good job.
2. It increases your earning potential.
3. It gives you greater job mobility.
4. It helps you secure more creative work.
5. It helps you appreciate the arts more fully.
6. It helps you understand an extremely complex world.
7. It helps you understand different cultures.
8. It allows you to avoid taking a regular job for a few years.
9. It helps you meet lots of people and make new friends.
10. It helps you increase your personal effectiveness.

Theory and Research — UNDERSTANDING — Primacy and Recency

Let's say that you have three points that you intend to arrange in topical order. How will you determine which to put first? The theory and research on primacy and recency offer help. The rule of primacy tells you that what an audience hears first will be remembered best and will have the greatest effect. The rule of recency tells you that what the audience hears last (or most recently) will be remembered best and will have the greatest effect. Research findings on these seemingly incompatible "rules" offer a few useful general suggestions.

- The middle is remembered least and has the least general effect. Thus, if you have a speech with three points, put the weakest one in the middle.

- If your listeners are favorable or neutral, lead with your strongest point. In this way you'll strengthen the conviction of those who are already favorable and you'll get the neutrals on your side early.

- If your audience is hostile or holds very different views than you, put your most powerful argument last and work up to it gradually—assuming, that is, that you can count on the listeners' staying with you until the end.

Research on memory tells us that the audience will remember very little of what you say in a speech. Therefore, repeat your main assertions—whether you put them first or last in your speech—in your conclusion.

Working with Theories and Research

Examine your previous speech or the speech you're currently working on in terms of the order of the main points. What insights does primacy–recency theory give you for ordering your main points?

Building Communication Generating Main Points

Try generating two or three main points (suitable for an informative or persuasive speech) from any one of the following thesis statements by asking strategic questions of each. Try following the general format illustrated in the text in the example of the values of a college education.

1. Property owned by religious organizations should be taxed.
2. Adoption agencies should be required to reveal the names of birth parents to all children when they reach 18 years of age.
3. The growing of tobacco should be declared illegal.
4. Medicinal marijuana should be legalized.
5. Gay men and lesbians should be granted full equality in the military.

The more main points you generate, the more likely you'll find ones that will be especially appropriate for your thesis and audience.

There are, of course, many other possibilities—but for purposes of illustration, these 10 possible main points will suffice. But not all 10 are equally valuable or relevant to your audience, so you should look over the list to see how to make it shorter and more meaningful. Try these suggestions:

■ Eliminate those points that seem least important to your thesis. On this basis you might want to eliminate number 8, as this seems least consistent with your intended emphasis on the positive values of college.

■ Combine those points that have a common focus. Notice, for example, that the first four points all center on the value of college in terms of jobs. You might, therefore, consider grouping these four items into one proposition: A college education helps you get a good job. This main point and its elaboration might look like this in your speech outline:

 I. A college education helps you get a good job.
   A. College graduates earn higher salaries.
   B. College graduates enter more creative jobs.
   C. College graduates have greater job mobility.

Note that A, B, and C all relate to aspects or subdivisions of a "good job."

■ Select the points that are most relevant or interesting to your audience. You might decide that high school students would be interested in increasing personal effectiveness, so you might select point 10 for inclusion as a second main point.

■ In general, limit the number of main points. For your class speeches, which will generally range from 5 to 15 minutes, use two, three, or four major ideas. Too many main points will result in a speech that is confusing, contains too much information and too little amplification, and proves difficult for listeners to remember.

■ Word each of your main points in the same (parallel) style. When outlining, phrase points labeled with Roman numerals in a similar (parallel) style. Likewise, phrase points labeled with capital letters and subordinate to the same Roman numeral (for example, A, B, and C under point I or A, B, and C under point II) in a similar style. In item 2 above, parallel style was used in the example on college education and getting a good job. This parallel styling helps the audience follow and remember your speech.

■ Develop your main points so they are separate and discrete; don't allow them to overlap one another. Each section labeled with a Roman numeral should be a separate entity.

STEP 5: SUPPORT YOUR MAIN POINTS

Now that you've identified your main points—and having learned how to search for information—you can devote attention to your next step: supporting your main points. Supporting materials (such as examples, statistics, and presentation aids) are essential to the public speaker: They give life to the main points; they help maintain attention; and they contribute to your purpose, whether that is to inform or to persuade. Presenting examples of homelessness, for instance, helps you show your listeners what homelessness is, how it happens, and how it affects people. Presenting statistics on the new health insurance plans helps your listeners understand why they should make certain decisions and not make others. Showing slides of your main points will help your listeners remember the most important parts of your speech.

Among the most important sources of support are examples, narratives, analogies, definitions, testimony, statistics, and presentation aids, all of which this section will cover in depth.

Examples

Examples are specific instances that are explained in varying degrees of detail. Examples are useful when you wish to make an abstract concept or idea concrete. It's easier for an audience to understand what you mean by, say, "love" or "friendship" if you provide a specific example along with your definition.

In using examples, keep in mind that their function is to make your ideas vivid and easily understood. Examples are useful for explaining a concept; they're not ends in themselves. Make them only as long as necessary to ensure that your purpose is achieved.

Also, use only enough examples to make your point. Make sure that the examples are sufficient to re-create your meaning in the minds of your listeners, but be careful not to use so many that the audience loses the very point you are making.

Show the audience exactly how your example relates to the assertion or concept you are explaining. Here, for example, former New York mayor Rudolph Giuliani, in his address to the United Nations after the World Trade Center attack of September 11, 2001, gave relevant examples to support his point that we are a land of immigrants and must continue to be so (www.nyc.gov/html/rwg/html/96/united.html, accessed September 17, 2007).

I am stoopid.

MEDIA WATCH
PRODUCT PLACEMENT

Let advertisers spend the same amount of money improving their product that they do on advertising, and they wouldn't have to advertise it.

—*Will Rogers*

James Bond's Aston Martin and E.T.'s Reese's Pieces were early examples of **product placement**—the insertion of brand-name products in movies. Today, the practice of product placement for a fee is becoming increasingly popular throughout all media. The reason is that it means big money to the media producers and effective advertising for the product. For example, *Tomorrow Never Dies*, one of the Bond movies, earned $34 million for placing in the movie such products as BMW, Omega watches, Heineken beer, Avis rental cars, and Bollinger champagne (Rodman, 2001).

In 2005 *The Contender*, a reality boxing show on NBC, had 7,502 product placements (including the presence of the product and/or its mention), from Gatorade to a Toyota truck: more placements than any other show. In 2004 the total number of product placements in television was 81,739; in 2005 it rose to 107,839 (*New York Times*, March 20, 2006, p. C3). In televised sports, products are advertised not only during commercial breaks but on billboards, in the names of the stadiums, or on the players' sneakers.

It's estimated that in 2005 magazines will have earned some $160.9 million and newspapers approximately $65 million for product placements—for advertising products without telling readers that these were in fact advertisements designed to sell the products (Lamb, 2005).

The use of product placement in news shows has created the most debate. For example, *Good Morning America* broadcast one of its shows from a Norwegian Cruise Line ship. Although no fees were paid for the product placement, the Cruise Line reportedly did pay for the airfare, room, and board for 300 contest winners on a cruise to the West Indies. And the *New York Times* has already agreed to allow "watermark" ads to appear behind news and editorial articles (Mandese, 2006).

Increasing Media Literacy

Product placements will surely increase over the coming years and will invade all media forms. When you see a product in a movie or television show, keep in mind that advertisers paid heavily for its being there.

New York City was built by immigrants and it will remain the greatest city in the world as long as we continue to renew ourselves with and benefit from the energizing spirit from new people coming here to create a better future for themselves and their families. Come to Flushing, Queens, where immigrants from many lands have created a vibrant, vital commercial and residential community. Their children challenge and astonish us in our public school classrooms every day. Similarly, you can see growing and dynamic immigrant communities in every borough of our city: Russians in Brighton Beach, West Indians in Crown Heights, Dominicans in Washington Heights, the new wave of Irish in the Bronx, and Koreans in Willow Brook on Staten Island.

Narratives

Narratives, or stories, are often useful as supporting materials in a speech. Narratives give the audience what it wants: a good story. They help you maintain your audience's attention, because listeners automatically perk up when a story is told. Narratives allow you to bring an abstract concept down to specifics. Following Clella Jaffe, we can distinguish three types of narrative: explanatory, exemplary, and persuasive.

- *Explanatory narratives* explain the way things are. The biblical book of Genesis, for example, explains the development of the world from a particular religious viewpoint. An eyewitness report might explain the events leading up to an accident.

- *Exemplary narratives* provide examples of excellence (or its opposite)—examples to follow or admire (or to avoid following). The stories of the lives of saints and martyrs are exemplary narratives, as are the Horatio Alger success stories. Similarly, many motivational speakers often include exemplary narratives in their speeches and will tell stories of what they were like when they were out of shape or on drugs or deep in debt.

- *Persuasive narratives* try to strengthen or change beliefs and attitudes. When Sally Struthers tells us of the plight of starving children, she's using a persuasive narrative. The parables in religious writings are persuasive in urging listeners to lead life in a particular way.

Keep your narratives relatively short and few in number. In most cases, one or possibly two narratives should be sufficient in a short 5- to 15-minute speech. Make explicit the connection between your story and the point you are making. If the people in the audience don't get this connection, you lose not only the effectiveness of the story but also their attention (as they try to figure out why you told that story).

Analogies

Analogies are comparisons that are often extremely useful in making your ideas clear and vivid to your audience. Analogies may be of two types: figurative and literal.

Figurative Analogies

Figurative analogies compare items from different classes—for example, the flexibility afforded by a car with the freedom of a bird, a college degree with a passport to success, playing baseball with running a corporation. Figurative analogies are useful for illustrating possible similarities; they provide vivid examples that are easily remembered.

Literal Analogies

Literal analogies compare items from the same class, such as two cars or two cities. For example, in a literal analogy you might argue (1) that two companies are similar—both are multinational, multibillion-dollar pharmaceutical companies, both have advertising budgets in the hundreds of millions of dollars, and so on; and (2) that therefore the advertising techniques that worked for one company will work for the other.

In evaluating your literal analogies, ask yourself two questions:

- Are the cases compared (the companies in this case) alike in essential respects? Or do the two cases differ from each other in ways that might weaken the comparison? For example, do they differ in the location of their headquarters? Do the two companies differ in the types of drugs they manufacture? Do the companies differ in their pricing of drugs?

- Do the differences make a difference? Obviously, not all differences are significant. Very likely a difference in the headquarters location is not a difference that will bear on the type of advertising that will prove effective. On the other hand, differences in the types of drugs they sell or in pricing may well prove significant. These differences may have an impact on the type of advertising that will prove most effective; advertising techniques used to sell over-the-counter painkillers like aspirin may not prove effective in selling drugs for cancer or diabetes patients.

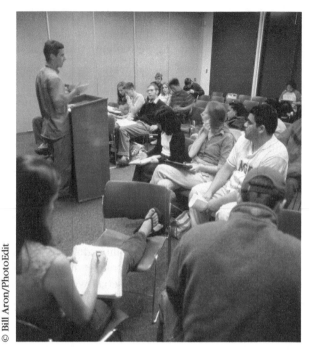

USING DEFINITIONS

You want to define vegan and vegetarian and distinguish between them using a variety of types of definitions.

WHAT DO YOU SAY?

Definitions

A **definition** is a statement of the meaning of a term or concept; it explains what something is. Use definitions when you wish to explain difficult or unfamiliar concepts or when you wish to make a concept more vivid or forceful.

As you can appreciate, definitions are often helpful when you are explaining a concept that the audience may be unfamiliar with or may have misconceptions about. If the purpose of the definition is to clarify, then it must do just that. This would be too obvious to mention if not for the fact that many speakers, perhaps for want of something to say, define terms that don't need extended definitions. Some speakers use definitions that don't clarify and that, in fact, complicate an already complex concept. Make sure your definitions define only what needs defining.

As you think of terms to define, or after you've selected your term, take a look at the OneLook Dictionary Search website at www.onelook.com. This website will enable you to search a wide variety of dictionaries at the same time. There are, of course, many other useful online dictionaries; search for "dictionary," "definitions," or "thesaurus" and you'll find a wealth of material for speeches of definition.

Here are some of the most important approaches you might use to define a term.

Definition by Etymology

One way to define a term is to trace its *etymology*—its historical or linguistic development. In defining the word *communication*, for example, you might note that it comes from the Latin *communis*, meaning "common"; in "communicating" you seek to establish a commonness, a sameness, a similarity with another individual. And *woman* comes from the Anglo-Saxon *wifman*, which meant literally a "wife man," with the word *man* applied to both sexes. Through phonetic change *wifman* became *woman*. Most large dictionaries and, of course, etymological dictionaries will help you find useful etymological definitions.

Or you might define a term by noting not its linguistic etymology, but how it came to mean what it now means. For example, you might note that the word *spam*, meaning junk messages on the Net, comes from a *Monty Python* television skit in which every item on the menu contained the product Spam. And much as the diner was forced to get Spam, so the Net surfer gets spam—even when he or she wants something else.

Definition by Authority

You can often clarify a term by explaining how a particular *authority* views it. You might, for example, define lateral thinking by authority and say that Edward deBono, who developed the concept of lateral thinking, has noted that "lateral thinking involves moving sideways to look at things in a different way. Instead of fixing on one particular approach and then working forward from that, the lateral thinker tries to find other approaches" (deBono, 1973). Or you might use the authority of cynic and satirist Ambrose Bierce and define love as nothing but "a temporary insanity curable by marriage" and friendship as "a ship big enough to carry two in fair weather, but only one in foul."

Definition by Negation

You also might define a term by noting what the term is not; that is, define it by *negation*. "A wife," you might say, "isn't a cook, a cleaning person, a babysitter, a seamstress, a sex partner. A wife is . . ." or "A teacher isn't someone who tells you what you should know but rather one who . . ."

Here Michael Marien (1992) defines futurists first negatively and then positively:

> Futurists do not use crystal balls. Indeed, they're generally loath to make firm predictions of what will happen. Rather, they make forecasts of what is probable, sketch scenarios of what is possible,

and/or point to desirable futures—what is preferable and what strategies we should pursue to get there.

Definition by Direct Symbolization

You also might define a term by *direct symbolization*—by showing the actual thing or a picture or model of it. For example, a sales representative explaining a new computer keyboard would use an actual keyboard in the speech. Similarly, a speech on magazine layout or types of fabrics would include actual layout pages and fabric samples.

Testimony

The term **testimony** refers to the opinions of experts or the accounts of witnesses. Testimony helps to amplify your speech by adding a note of authority to your arguments. For example, you might want to use the testimony of a noted economist to support your predictions about inflation, or the testimony of someone who spent two years in a maximum-security prison to discourage young people from committing crimes.

When you cite testimony, stress first the competence of the person, whether that person is an expert or a witness. For example, citing the predictions of a world-famous economist of whom your audience has never heard will mean little unless you first explain the person's competence. You might say something like "This prediction comes from the world's leading economist, who has successfully predicted all major financial trends over the past 20 years." Now the audience will be prepared to lend credence to what this person says.

Second, stress the unbiased nature of the testimony. If the audience perceives the testimony to be biased—whether or not it really is—it will have little effect. You want to check out any possible biases in a witness so that you can present accurate information. But you also want to make the audience see that the testimony is in fact unbiased.

Third, stress the recency of the testimony. If an audience has no way of knowing when the statement was made, it has no way of knowing how true this statement is today.

Statistics

Let's say you want to show that significant numbers of people are now getting their news from the Internet, that the cost of filmmaking has skyrocketed over the last 20 years, or that women buy significantly more books and magazines than men. To communicate these types of information, you'd use

statistics—summary numbers that help you communicate the important characteristics of an otherwise complex set of numbers. Statistics help the audience see, for example, the percentage of people getting their news from the Internet, the average cost of films in 2007 versus previous years, or the difference between male and female book and magazine purchases. Excellent aids for using and interpreting statistics may be found at http://nilesonline.com/stats/. This site will assist you in understanding and evaluating research results and in using statistics in your own speeches. Some general guidelines for employing statistics:

- *Make the statistics clear to your audience.* Remember, they'll hear the figures only once. Round off figures so they are easy to understand and retain.

- *Make the statistics meaningful.* When you are using statistics, it's often helpful to remind the audience of what the statistic itself means. For example, if you say, "The median price of a co-op apartment in San Francisco is $875,000," remind the audience that this means the middle price—that half the prices are above $875,000 and half are below. Also, present numbers so that the audience can appreciate the meaning you want to convey. To say, for example, that the Sears Tower in Chicago is 1,559 feet tall doesn't help your hearers visualize its height. So consider saying something like "The Sears Tower is 1,559 feet tall. Just how tall is 1,559 feet? Well, it's as tall as the length of more than five football fields. It's as tall as 260 six-foot people standing on each other's heads."

- *Connect the statistics with your point.* Make explicit the connection between the statistics and what they show. A statement, for example, that college professors make an average of $85,000 per year needs to be related specifically to the proposition that teachers' salaries should be raised—or lowered, depending on your point of view.

- *Use statistics in moderation.* Most listeners' capacity for numerical data presented in a speech is limited, so in most cases statistics should be used sparingly.

- *Visually (and verbally) reinforce the statistics.* Numbers are difficult to grasp and remember when they are presented without some kind of visual reinforcement, so it's often helpful to complement your oral presentation of statistics with some type of presentation aid—perhaps a graph or a chart.

Here is a good example of how U.S. Senator Barack Obama (Illinois) used statistics in his speech to the

2006 Global Summit on AIDS and the Church (http://obama.senate.gov, accessed January 14, 2007):

> You know, AIDS is a story often told by numbers. Forty million infected with HIV. Nearly 4.5 million this year alone. Twelve million orphans in Africa. Eight thousand deaths and 6,000 new infections every single day. In some places, 90 percent of those with HIV do not know they have it. And we just learned that AIDS is set to become the third leading cause of death worldwide in the coming years. These are staggering, these numbers, and they help us understand the magnitude of this pandemic.

Presentation Aids

When you're planning a speech, consider using some kind of **presentation aid**—a visual or auditory means for clarifying ideas. Ask yourself how you can represent visually (or via audio) what you want your audience to remember. How can you reinforce your ideas with additional media? If you want your audience to grasp increases in the sales tax, consider showing them a graph of rising sales taxes over the last 10 years. If you want them to see that Brand A is superior to Brand X, consider showing them a comparison chart identifying the superior qualities of Brand A.

Types of Presentation Aids

Among the presentation aids you have available are the actual object, models of the object, graphs, word charts, maps, people, photographs and illustrations, and tapes and CDs.

As a general rule (to which there are many exceptions), the best presentation aid is *the object itself*; bring it with you if you can. Notice that infomercials sell their product not only by talking about it but also by showing it to potential buyers. You see what George Foreman's Lean Mean Grilling Machine looks like and how it works. You see the jewelry, the clothing, and the new mop from a wide variety of angles and in varied settings. If you want to explain some tangible thing and you can show it to your audience, do so.

Models—replicas of actual objects—are useful for a variety of purposes. For example, if you wanted to explain complex structures such as the hearing or vocal mechanism, the brain, or the structure of DNA, you would almost have to use a model. You may remember from science classes that these models (and the pictures of them in the textbooks) make a lot more sense than verbal explanations alone. Models help to clarify relative size and position and how each part interacts with each other part. Large

models can be used to help listeners visualize objects that are too small (or unavailable) to appreciate otherwise. In other cases, small models of large objects—objects that are too large to bring to your speech—are helpful. For example, in a speech on stretching exercises, one student used a 14-inch wooden artist's model.

Graphs are useful for showing differences over time, for showing how a whole is divided into parts, and for showing different amounts or sizes. Figure 1 shows different types of graphs that can be drawn freehand or generated with the graphics capabilities of any word-processing or presentation software.

Word charts (which can also contain numbers and even graphics) are useful for lots of different types of information. For example, you might use a word chart to identify the key points that you cover in one of your propositions or in your entire speech—in the order in which you cover them, of course. Slide 4 in the Public Speaking Sample Assistant box is a good example of a simple word chart listing the major topics discussed in the speech. Or you could use word charts to identify the steps in a process; for example, to summarize the steps in programming a VCR, dealing with sexual harassment, or installing a new computer program. Another use of charts is for presenting information you want your audience to write down. Emergency phone numbers, addresses to write to, or titles of recommended books and websites are examples of the type of information that listeners will welcome in written form.

Maps are useful for illustrating a wide variety of concepts. If you want to show the locations of cities, lakes, rivers, or mountain ranges, maps will obviously prove useful as presentation aids. Maps are also helpful for illustrating population densities, immigration patterns, varied economic conditions, the spread of diseases, and hundreds of other issues you may wish to develop in your speeches. For example, in a talk on natural resources, one speaker used maps to illustrate the locations of large reserves of oil, gas, and precious metals. Another speaker used maps to illustrate concentrations of wealth; still another used maps to show worldwide differences in mortality rates.

You also can use maps to illustrate numerical differences. For example, you might use a map to show the wide variation in literacy rates throughout the world. You could color the countries with 90 to 100 percent literacy red, the countries with 80 to 89 percent literacy green, and so on. When you use maps in this way, it's often helpful to complement them with charts or graphs that, for example, give the specific literacy rates for the specific countries on which you want to concentrate.

126

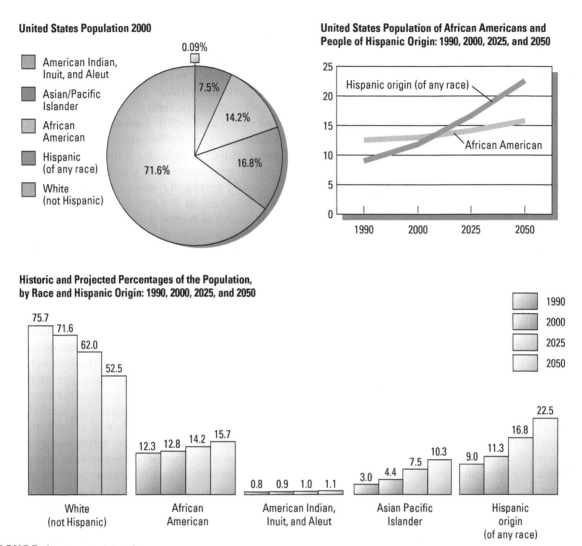

FIGURE 1 Assorted Graphs

Notice that each of the graphs serves a somewhat different purpose. The *pie chart* is especially useful if you want to show how some whole is divided into its parts and the relative sizes of the parts. From the pie chart you can easily see the relative percentages of the different groups in the U.S. population. Pie charts are especially helpful when you have three to five values to illustrate; any more than five creates a pie that is difficult to read at a glance. The *line graph* shows how comparisons can be visualized with a very simple illustration. Notice that the graph is especially clear because it focuses on only 2 groups. Had it focused on 8 or 10 groups, it would have been difficult for an audience to understand. The *bar graph* presents the same information as the pie chart but for four different time periods. You might have used four pie charts—with each pie representing a different year—but comparisons would not have been as easy for an audience to make.

People can also function effectively as "presentation aids." For example, if you wanted to demonstrate the muscles of the body, you might use a bodybuilder. If you wanted to discuss different voice patterns, skin complexions, or hairstyles, you might use people as your aids. Aside from the obvious assistance they provide in demonstrating their muscles or voice qualities, people help to secure and maintain the attention and interest of the audience.

And don't overlook yourself as a (kind of) presentation aid. For example, if you are giving a speech on boxing strategies, exercise techniques, or sitting and standing postures that can lead to backaches, consider demonstrating them yourself. As an added plus, going through these demonstrations is likely to reduce your apprehension and make you more relaxed.

Photographs and illustrations are useful aids for a variety of purposes. Speeches on types of trees, styles of art or architecture, or types of exercise machines would profit greatly from a few well-chosen photographs or illustrations. If you want to show these but don't have the opportunity to put them onto slides, you may try simply holding them up as you refer to them. There are many hazards involved in using this type of aid, however, so pictures are recommended only with reservations. If the image is large enough for all members of the audience to see clearly (say, poster size); if it clearly illustrates what you want to illustrate; and if it's mounted on cardboard, then use it. Otherwise, don't.

Do not pass pictures around the room. This only draws attention away from what you are saying: Listeners will look for the pictures before the pictures circulate to them, will wonder what the pictures contain, and meanwhile will miss a great deal of your speech.

Tapes, CDs, and *DVDs* can be useful for many types of speeches as well. For a speech on advertising, for example, actual samples of commercials as played on radio or television would go a long way in helping the audience see exactly what you are talking about. These aids also provide variety by breaking up the oral presentation.

The Media of Presentation Aids

Once you've decided on the type of presentation aid you'll use, you need to decide on the medium you'll use to present it. The decisions you make concerning which types of media to use should be based on the message you want to communicate and on the audience to whom you'll be speaking.

Some presentation media are low tech—for example, chalkboards, transparencies, and flip charts. These media are generally more effective in smaller, more informal situations, and especially for presentations that arise without prior notice, for which you simply don't have the time to prepare high-tech resources. Low-tech devices are also useful for highly interactive sessions; for example, the flip chart is still one of the best ways to record group members' contributions.

More high-tech media such as slides and videotapes are generally more effective with larger, more formal groups, in which you do most of the talking and the audience does most of the listening. High-tech materials also may be your only choice if the material you have to communicate is extremely complex or if the norms of your organization simply require that you use high-tech presentation formats.

The *chalkboard* or *whiteboard* is the easiest to use, but not necessarily the most effective. All classrooms have such boards, and you have seen them used by teachers with greater or lesser effect; in some way, you've had "experience" with them. Boards may be used effectively to present key terms or important definitions or even to outline the general structure of your speech. But don't use these boards if you can present the same information with a prepared chart or model. It takes too long to write out anything substantial. If you do write on a board, be careful not to turn your back to the audience. In this brief time you can easily lose their attention.

Chartboards (large pieces of semiflexible cardboard that can be held up for an audience to read, placed on an easel or bulletin board, or taped to a chalkboard) are useful when you have just one or two relatively simple charts that you want to display during your speech. If you want to display your charts for several minutes, be sure you have a way of holding them up. For example, bring masking tape if you intend to secure them to the wall, or enlist the aid of an audience member to hold them up. Use a light-colored board; white generally works best. Write in black; it provides the best contrast and is the easiest for people to read.

Flip charts, charts on large pads of paper (usually about 24 by 24 inches) mounted on a stand, can be used to record many types of information, which you reveal by flipping the pages as you deliver your speech. For example, if you were to discuss the various departments in an organization, you might have the key points relating to each department on a separate page of your flip chart. As you discussed the advertising department, you would show the advertising department chart. When you moved on to discuss the personnel department, you would flip to the chart dealing with personnel. You may find this device useful if you have a large number of word charts that you want to have easy control over. Make sure that the flip chart is positioned so that everyone in the audience can see it clearly and that the folding legs are positioned securely so it doesn't collapse when you flip the first page. Make sure you write large enough so that the people in the back can read your material without straining their eyes.

Flip charts also are especially useful for recording ideas at small group meetings. Unlike the chalkboard, the flip chart enables you to retain a written record of the meeting; should you need to, you can easily review the group's contributions.

Slides and transparency projections are helpful for showing a series of visuals that may be of very different types; for example, photographs, illustrations, charts, or tables. The slides can easily be created with many popular computer programs (see "Computer-Assisted Presentations"). To produce actual 35mm slides, you'll need considerable lead time; be sure to build this into your preparation time.

If you don't have access to a slide projector or don't have the time needed to construct slides, consider somewhat less sophisticated transparencies. You can create your visual in any of the word-processing or spreadsheet programs you normally use and probably can find a printer that will enable you to print transparencies. Another alternative is to use a copier that will produce transparencies.

An advantage of transparencies is that you can write on the transparencies (and on slides in computer presentations, as we discuss later) while you're speaking. You can circle important items, underline key terms, and draw lines connecting different terms.

When using any presentation aid, but especially with slides and transparencies, make sure that you have the proper equipment; for example, a projector, a table, a working outlet nearby, control over the lighting in the room, and whatever else you'll need to have the audience see your projections clearly.

Videos may serve a variety of purposes in public speaking. Basically, you have two options. First, you can tape a scene from a film or television show with your VCR and show it at the appropriate time in your speech. Thus, for example, you might record examples of sexism in television sitcoms, violence on television talk shows, or types of transitions used in feature films and show these excerpts during your speech. As you can see, however, this type of video takes a great deal of time and preparation, so if you are going to use such excerpts you must plan well in advance.

Second, you can create your own video with a video camera. One student created a video of ethnic store signs to illustrate the "interculturalization" of the city. With the help (and agreement to be recorded) of a few friends, another student created a three-minute video of religious holidays as celebrated by members of different religions and carefully coordinated each segment with her discussion of the relevant holiday.

In using videos, do make sure that they don't occupy too much of your speaking time; after all, your main objective is to learn the principles of public speaking.

Handouts, or printed materials that you distribute to members of the audience, are especially helpful in explaining complex material and also in providing listeners with a permanent record of some aspect of your speech. Handouts are also useful for presenting information that you want your audience to refer to throughout the speech. Handouts encourage listeners to take notes, especially if you leave enough white space or even provide a specific place for notes—and this keeps your listeners actively involved in your presentation. Handouts also reward the audience by giving them something for their attendance and attention. A variety of handouts can be easily prepared with many of the computer presentation packages that we'll consider in the last section of this unit.

You can distribute handouts at the beginning of, during, or after your speech; but realize that whichever system you use has both pros and cons. If you distribute materials before or during your speech, you run the risk of your listeners' reading the handout and not concentrating on your speech. On the other hand, if the listeners are getting the information you want to communicate—even if primarily from the handout—that isn't too bad. And, in a way, handouts allow listeners to process the information at their own pace.

You can encourage your audience to listen to you when you want them to, and to look at the handout when you want them to, by simply telling them: "Look at the graph at the top of page two of the handout; it summarizes recent census figures on immigration" or "We'll get back to the handout in a minute; now, however, I want to direct your attention to this next slide [or the second argument]."

If you distribute your handouts at the end of the speech, they will obviously not interfere with your presentation—but they may not be read at all. After all, listeners might reason, they heard the speech; why bother going through the handout? To counteract this very natural tendency, you might include additional material in the handout and mention this to your audience, saying something like "This handout contains all the slides shown here and three additional slides that provide economic data for Thailand, Cambodia, and Vietnam, which I didn't have time to cover. When you look at the data, you'll see that they mirror exactly the data provided in my talk on the other countries." When you provide additional information on your handout, it's more likely that it will get looked at and thus provide the reinforcement you want.

Preparing Presentation Aids

In preparing presentation aids, make sure that they add clarity to your speech, that they're appealing to the listeners, and that they're culturally sensitive. *Clarity* is the most important consideration, and you can achieve it by following these simple guidelines:

1. Use colors that will make your message instantly clear; light colors on dark backgrounds or dark colors on light backgrounds provide the best contrast and seem to work best for most purposes. Be cautious about using yellow, which is often difficult to see, especially if there's glare from the sun.

2. Use direct phrases (not complete sentences); use bullets to highlight your points or your support (see the slides in the Public Speaking Sample Assistant box). Just as you phrase your main points in parallel style whenever possible, try to phrase your bullets in parallel style, usually by using the same part of speech (for example, all nouns or all infinitive phrases). And make sure that the meaning or relevance of any graphic is immediately clear. If it isn't, explain it.

129

3. Use the aid to highlight a few essential points; don't clutter it with too much information. A maximum of four bullets on a slide or chart, for example, are as much information as you should include.

4. Use typefaces that can be read easily from all parts of the room. For a chart of typefaces available with most word-processing programs and suggestions for their use, see Table 1.

5. Give the slide or chart or transparency a title—a general heading—to further guide your listeners' attention and focus.

Create presentation aids so that they're *appealing* to your audience. Presentation aids should be attractive enough to engage the attention of the audience, but not so attractive that they're distracting.

An almost nude body draped across a car may be effective in selling underwear, but it will probably detract if your objective is to explain the profit-and-loss statement of General Motors.

Make sure your presentation aids are *culturally sensitive* and can be easily interpreted by people from other cultures. Just as your words will be interpreted within a cultural framework, so too will the symbols and colors you use in your aids. For example, when speaking to international audiences, you need to use universal symbols or explain those that are not universal. Be careful that your icons don't reveal an ethnocentric bias: Using the American dollar sign to symbolize "wealth" might be quite logical in your public speaking class, but it could be interpreted as ethnocentric if used with an audience of international visitors.

Table 1 Some Typefaces

You have an enormous number of typefaces to choose from. Generally, select typefaces that are easy to read and that are consistent in tone with the message of your speech.

Typeface	Comments
Palatino Century Schoolbook Garamond Times	Serif typefaces retain some of the cursive strokes found in handwriting. The cursive stroke is illustrated especially in the *m* and *n*, which begin with a slight upsweep. Serif styles are easy to read and useful for blocks of text.
Helvetica Bauhous Avant Garde Futura	Sans-serif typefaces (a style that is more bold and doesn't include the serif or upsweep) are useful for titles and headings but make reading long text difficult.
Serif Gothic Black **STENCIL** **Gill Sans Ultra Bold**	These extremely bold typefaces are tempting to use; but, as you can see, they're not easy to read. They're most appropriate for short titles.
Akzidenz Grotesk BETON COMPRESSED BOLD Franklin Gothic	These compressed typefaces are useful when you have to fit a lot of text into a small space. They are, however, difficult to read and so should generally be avoided (or at least used sparingly) in slides. It would be better to use an easier-to-read typeface and spread out the text over additional slides.
CASTELLAR ROSEWOOD JAZZ ASHLEY INLINE Linotext	Decorative styles like these, although difficult to read for extended text, make great headings or titles. Be careful, however, that the originality of your typefaces doesn't steal attention away from your message.
Mistral Brush Script Freestyle Script Pepita	Script typefaces are interesting and will give your presentation a personal look, as if you wrote it longhand. But they'll be difficult to read. If you're going to read the slides aloud word for word, then typefaces that are a bit more difficult to read may still be used with considerable effect.

Using Presentation Aids

Keep the following guidelines clearly in mind when using presentation aids.

- Know your aids intimately. Be sure you know in what order they are to be presented and how you plan to introduce them. Know exactly what goes where and when.

- Test the aids before using them. When testing the presentation aids ahead of time, be certain that they can be seen easily from all parts of the room.

- Rehearse your speech with the presentation aids incorporated into the presentation. Practice your actual movements with the aids you'll use. If you're going to use a chart, how will you use it? Will it stand by itself? Can you tape it somewhere? Do you have tape with you?

- Integrate your aids seamlessly into your speech. Just as a verbal example should flow naturally into the text and seem an integral part of the speech, so should the presentation aid. It should appear not as an afterthought but as an essential part of the speech.

- Don't talk to your aid. Both you and the aid should be focused on the audience. Know your aids so well that you can point to what you want without breaking eye contact with your audience. Or, at most, break audience eye contact for only a few seconds at a time.

- Use the aid when it's relevant: Show it when you want the audience to concentrate on it, then remove it. If you don't remove it, the audience's attention may remain focused on the visual when you want them to focus on your next point.

Computer-Assisted Presentations

There are a variety of presentation software packages available: PowerPoint, Corel Presentations, and Lotus Freelance are among the most popular and are very similar in what they do and how they do it. The Public Speaking Sample Assistant box illustrates what a set of slides might look like; the slides were constructed in PowerPoint, though a similar slide show could be produced with most presentation software programs. Also, realize that you can easily import photographs and have slides of these inserted into your slide show; or you can add video clips. As you review the speech in the Public Speaking Sample Assistant box, try to visualize how you would use a slide show in presenting your next speech.

After you read the following material, which applies PowerPoint technology to public speaking, take one of the many available PowerPoint tutorials available online. A tutorial may be on your own computer or may be available somewhere on your campus. If not, visit one of the excellent tutorials from different colleges that are available to everyone; for example, visit Florida Gulf Coast University at www.fgcu.edu/support/office2000/ppt/, the University of Rhode Island at http://einstein.cs.uri.edu/tutorials/csc101/powerpoint/ppt.html, or Indiana–Purdue University at www.science.iupui.edu/SAC98/pp.htm. If you need more advanced training, try the University of Northern Iowa's advanced tutorial at www.uni.edu/plschool/index/profdev/briley/Advppt.html.

Ways of Using Presentation Package Software.

Computer presentation software enables you to produce a variety of aids; the software will produce what you want. For example, you can construct slides on your computer, save them on a disk, and then have 35mm slides developed from the disk. To do this, you need access to a slide printer—or you can send your files out (you can do this via modem) to a lab specializing in converting electronic files into 35mm slides. There may be a slide printer at your school, so check there first. Similarly, your local office supply store or copy shop, such as Staples, OfficeMax, or Kinko's, may have exactly the services you need.

Or you can create your slides and then show them on your computer screen. If you are speaking to a very small group, it may be possible to have your listeners gather around your computer as you speak. With larger audiences, however, you'll need a computer projector or an LCD projection panel. Assuming that you have a properly equipped computer in the classroom, you can copy your entire presentation to a floppy disk and bring it with you on the day of the speech.

Computer presentation software also enables you to print out a variety of handouts:

- the slides shown during your speech, as well as additional slides that you may not have time to include in the speech but that you nevertheless want your listeners to look at when they read your handout (as in the Public Speaking Sample Assistant box)

- the slides plus speaker's notes, the key points that you made as you showed each of the slides (see Figure 2)

- the slides plus places for listeners to write notes next to each of them (see Figure 3)

- an outline of your talk

- any combination of the above

Overhead transparencies also can be created from your computer slides. To make overheads on

A Slide Show Speech

This PowerPoint speech is intended to illustrate the general structure of a slide show speech and is derived from the speech in the Public Speaking Sample Assistant box; you may find it helpful to look ahead to that speech to consider how you might improve this purposely sparse slide show. This PowerPoint presentation is available online at MyCommunicationLab. Copy it to your computer and try altering this basic outline as you learn more about PowerPoint or similar presentation software.

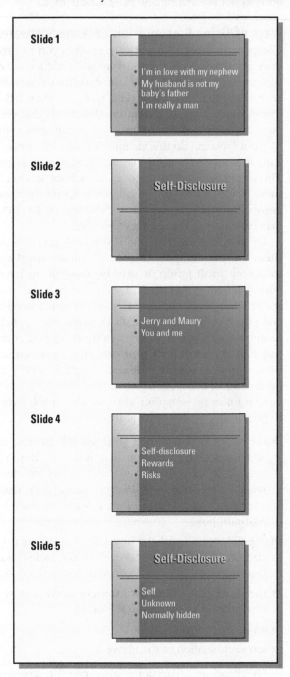

Slide 1

- I'm in love with my nephew
- My husband is not my baby's father
- I'm really a man

This first slide aims to gain attention with these provocative confessions. These three bullets would come up one at a time, with the speaker pausing for (with luck) some laughter. After you review the entire list of slides, try inserting graphics where you think they'd be appropriate.

Slide 2

Self-Disclosure

This second slide introduces the topic of the speech, self-disclosure.

Slide 3

- Jerry and Maury
- You and me

This slide recalls the popular confessions heard on the *Jerry Springer Show* and *Maury* but also relates the process of self-disclosure to the speaker and the audience, establishing an S-A-T connection.

Slide 4

- Self-disclosure
- Rewards
- Risks

This slide orients the audience by identifying the three main ideas to be discussed in the speech: the nature of self-disclosure, its rewards, and its risks. As with slide number 1, these three bullets should come up one at a time to give the speaker a chance to elaborate on each item and to give the audience a chance to digest the informatiion. Note that this slide show does not contain transitions; if you think they might help, insert transitions.

Slide 5

Self-Disclosure

- Self
- Unknown
- Normally hidden

This fifth slide focuses on the first major idea, the nature of self-disclosure as communication about the self, about something previously unknown, and about something that is normally kept hidden. Note here that very few words are used in the actual slide; the speaker will elaborate on each of these items in the actual speech. The words on the slide are best thought of as tags you want the audience to hang on to as you explain each point.

132

Public Speaking Sample Assistant

A Speech of Introduction *(Continued)*

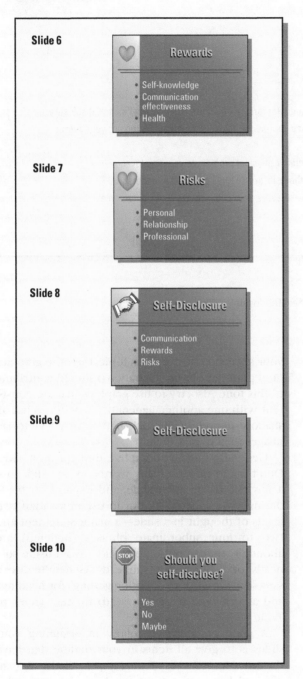

Slide 6

This sixth slide focuses on the second main idea: the rewards of self-disclosure. Those rewards include better self-knowledge, greater communication effectiveness, and improved health. Again, these "rewards" should come up on the screen one at a time, rather than all together.

Slide 7

This is the third main idea: the risks of self-disclosure (personal, relationship, and professional risks). What types of graphics might make this slide more interesting and yet not take attention away from the main ideas?

Slide 8

This slide begins the conclusion and summarizes the three main points of the speech: the nature of self-disclosure, the rewards, and the risks.

Slide 9

While this slide, which contains only the term "Self-Disclosure," is on screen, the speaker would likely motivate the audience to learn more about self-disclosure. Take a look at the speech from which this slide show was derived and create slides for the specific suggestions for learning more about self-disclosure.

Slide 10

This slide closes the speech by repeating the theme of the speech, namely that self-disclosure is both rewarding and risky and that the pros and cons need to be weighed in any decision to self-disclose.

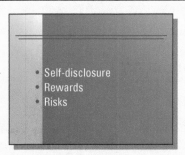

PAUSE!

SCAN AUDIENCE!

Today I'd like to discuss an extremely interesting and significant form of communication. It's called self-disclosure. S-Disclosure can be greatly **rewarding**. You might disclose your secret love and find that you too are your secret lover's secret lover.

S-Disclosure can also be **risky**. You might disclose a mental or physical problem to your employer, only to find yourself without a job. Because the rewards and the risks are so high, we need to understand this unique form of communication. Before discussing the rewards and risks, we need to understand a little more about the nature of S-D.

PAUSE!

FIGURE 2 Slide with Speaker Notes

This example is from slide number 4, the orientation, in the "Self-Disclosure" speech.

many printers and most copiers, simply substitute transparency paper for computer or copy paper. If you create your slides with a computer presentation package, you'll be able to produce professional-looking transparencies.

Suggestions for Using Presentation Software.

The templates and the suggestions of the program "wizards" will parallel the suggestions offered here. Nevertheless, it's important to understand the qualities of effective slides in case you want to make changes in the suggested formats or even want to start from scratch.

In developing your slides, strive for clarity and consistency. For example, choose typeface styles, sizes, and colors that clearly distinguish the main points from the supporting materials. At the same time, use a consistent combination of fonts, colors, backgrounds, and graphics throughout your slides to give your presentation unity.

Use color (of type and background) and graphics sparingly. Remember that clarity is your goal; you want your audience to remember your ideas and not just the fact that all your slides were red, white, and blue. Likewise, too many graphics will distract your audience's attention from your verbal message. Also, be sure to choose graphics that support your tone. If

your speech is on a serious topic, then the graphics (and photographs or illustrations) should contribute to this tone. Also, try to use graphics that are consistent with one another; generally, it's better to use all shadow figures or all stick figures or all Victorian images than to mix them.

Generally, put one complete thought on a slide. Don't try to put too many words on one slide; use a few words on each slide, and expand on these during your speech. Try not to use more than two levels of thought in a slide—a major statement and two to four subordinate phrases (bulleted) are about all you can put on one slide. Avoid using subheads of subheads of subheads. Generally, use a sans-serif type (more attention-getting) for headings and a serif type (easier to read) for text (refer to Table 1).

A good guideline to follow in designing your slides is to give all items in your outline that have the same-level heads (for example, all the Roman numeral heads) the same typeface, size, and color throughout your presentation. Similarly, use the same font for all the A, B, C subheads, and so on. This will help your listeners follow the organization of your speech. Notice that this principle is followed for the most part in the slides in the Public Speaking Sample Assistant box. The rule is broken in one case,

FIGURE 3   Slides with Space for Listeners' Notes

however: The introduction and conclusion are set apart by being in a color and typeface different from the rest of the slides.

Consider using graphs, charts, and tables; you have a tremendous variety of graph and chart types (for example, pie and bar graphs and cumulative charts) and tables to choose from. If you are using presentation software that's part of a suite, then you'll find it especially easy to import files from your word processor or spreadsheet.

If there's a question-and-answer period following your speech, consider preparing a few extra slides to support responses to questions you anticipate being asked. Then, when someone asks you a predicted question, you can say: "I anticipated that someone might ask that question; it raises an important issue. The data I've been able to find are presented in this chart." You then show the slide and explain it more

fully. This is surely going the extra mile, but it can easily make your speech a real standout.

Use transitions wisely. Just as verbal transitions help you move from one part of your speech to another, presentational transitions help you move from one slide to the next with the desired effect—for example, blinds folding from left or right or top or bottom, or a quick fade.

Generally, consistency works best. Don't try to use too many different transitions in the same talk; it will detract attention from what you are saying. Generally, use the same transitions for all the slides in a single presentation. You might vary this a bit by, say, having the last slide introduced by a somewhat different transition; but any more variation is likely to work against the listeners' focusing on your message. In choosing transitions select one that's consistent with your speech purpose; don't use a frivolous black-and-yellow

Theory and Research Culture and Speech Organization

Members of low-context cultures are usually direct in their messages and appreciate directness in others. But directness may be unnecessary or even insulting to the high-context cultural member. Conversely, the indirectness of the high-context member may appear vague or even dishonest to a member of a low-context culture.

High-context cultures prefer indirectness. Speakers in Japan, to take one well-researched example, need to be careful lest they make their point too obvious or too direct and insult the audience. Speakers in Japan are expected to lead their listeners to the conclusion through example, illustration, and various other indirect means (Lustig & Koester, 2006). In contrast, in the United States (a low-context culture) speakers are encouraged to be explicit and direct—to tell the listeners, for example, exactly what the speaker wants them to do.

Another cultural difference influences how focused the speech ought to be. For example, in the United States, each main point of a speech or written composition should be developed by itself. Only when one point is fully developed and finalized does the speaker or writer move on to the next. Hindu culture, however, is less rigid and allows for many ideas being considered in the same paragraph of an essay or in the same part of a speech (Lustig & Koester, 2006).

Working with Theories and Research

As a listener, what type of organization do you prefer? For example, do you prefer a speaker who is direct or indirect? Do you prefer speakers who clearly separate the main points or who consider several points together?

checkerboard transition in a speech on child abuse, for example.

Consider using sound effects with your transitions; but again, go easy. Overdoing it is sure to make your speech seem carelessly put together.

Build effects with bulleted items to focus your listeners' attention. For example, you can have each bulleted phrase fly from the top of the screen into its position; with the next mouse click, the next bullet flies into position. Or you can have your bullets slide in from right to left or from left to right, and so on.

In listing four or five bulleted items, consider the value of hiding or dimming the previous bullet as you introduce the next one. Making the previous bullet disappear or fade into a lighter color when the next bullet appears further enables you to focus your listeners' attention on exactly the point you're discussing. Do be careful that you allow the audience time to read each bullet; otherwise they'll be frustrated when it disappears.

Use the spell-checker. You don't want to show professional-looking slides with misspellings; it can ruin your credibility and seriously damage the impact of your speech.

STEP 6: ORGANIZE YOUR SPEECH

When you organize your ideas, you derive a variety of benefits. First, organization will help you prepare the speech. For example, as you organize your speech you'll be able to see if you have adequately and fairly supported each of your main points and if you are devoting approximately equal time to each main idea. Organization also makes your speech easy to understand and remember. When you organize perhaps 30 pieces of specific information (such as statistics, statement of thesis, examples, illustrations, testimonials, transitions) into, say, three or four or five chunks, you're making it much easier for the audience to remember what you want them to remember. An added bonus here is that organization will also help you remember your speech. You'll be less likely to forget a carefully organized speech than you would a disorganized one. Organization will also contribute to your credibility. The audience is more likely to see the well-organized speaker as more competent, more knowledgeable, and more in control of the information in the speech.

Once you've identified the main points you wish to include in your speech, you need to devote attention to how you'll arrange these points in the **body**, or main part, of your speech. When you follow a clearly identified organizational pattern, your listeners will be able to see your speech as a whole and will be able to grasp the connections and relationships among your various pieces of information. Should they have a momentary lapse in attention— as they surely will at some point in just about every speech—you will be able to refocus their attention.

Consider each of the following organizational patterns in terms of the topics to which it's most applicable and the ways in which you can arrange your main points and supporting materials. The introduction, conclusion, and transitions are considered in depth under Step 7 in this unit.

Temporal Pattern

Organization on the basis of some temporal (time) relationship is a pattern listeners will find easy to follow. Generally, when you use a **temporal pattern**, you organize your speech into two, three, or four major parts, beginning with the past and working up to the present or the future—or beginning with the present or the future and working back to the past.

The temporal (sometimes called "chronological") pattern is especially appropriate for informative speeches in which you wish to describe events or processes that occur over time. It's also useful when you wish to tell a story, demonstrate how something works, or examine the steps involved in some process. The events leading up to the Civil War, the steps toward a college education, or the history of writing would all be appropriate for temporal patterning. A speech on the development of language in the child might be organized in a temporal pattern and could be broken down something like this:

I. Babbling occurs around the 5th month.
II. Lallation occurs around the 6th month.
III. Echolalia occurs around the 9th month.
IV. "Communication" occurs around the 12th month.

Spatial Pattern

You can also organize your main points on the basis of space. The **spatial pattern** is especially useful when you wish to describe objects or places. Like the temporal pattern, it's an organizational pattern that listeners will find easy to follow as you progress— from top to bottom, from left to right, from inside to outside, or from east to west, for example. The structure of a place, an object, or even an animal is easily placed into a spatial pattern. You might describe the layout of a hospital, a school, or a skyscraper, or perhaps even the structure of a dinosaur, with a spatial pattern of organization. Here's an example of an outline describing the structure of the traditional textbook and using a spatial pattern:

I. The front matter contains the preface and the table of contents.
II. The text proper contains the chapters or units.
III. The back matter contains the glossary, bibliography, and index.

Topical Pattern

When your topic conveniently divides itself into subdivisions, each of which is clear and approximately equal in importance, the **topical pattern** is most useful. A speech on important cities of the world might be organized into a topical pattern, as might be speeches on problems facing the college graduate, great works of literature, the world's major religions, and the like. The topical pattern would be an obvious choice for organizing a speech on the powers of the government. The topic itself divides into three parts: legislative, executive, and judicial. A sample outline might look like this:

I. The legislative branch is controlled by Congress.
II. The executive branch is controlled by the president.
III. The judicial branch is controlled by the courts.

Problem–Solution Pattern

The **problem–solution pattern** is especially useful in persuasive speeches in which you want to convince the audience that a problem exists and that your solution would solve or lessen the problem. Let's say that you believe that jury awards for damages have gotten out of hand. You may want to persuade your audience, then, that jury awards for damages should be limited. A problem–solution pattern might be appropriate here. In the first part of your speech, you'd identify the problem(s) created by these large awards; in the second part, you'd propose the solution. A sample outline for such a speech might look something like this:

I. Jury awards for damages are out of control. [the general problem]
    A. These awards increase insurance rates. [a specific problem]

137

B. These awards increase medical costs. [a second specific problem]

C. These awards place unfair burdens on business. [a third specific problem]

II. Jury awards need to be limited. [the general solution]

 A. Greater evidence should be required before a case can be brought to trial. [a specific solution]

 B. Part of the award should be turned over to the state. [a second specific solution]

 C. Realistic estimates of financial damage must be used. [a third specific solution]

Here, for example, is how one student, Ashley Hatcher of the University of Texas at Austin, organized her problem-solution speech on issues in military recruitment—an organization clearly revealed in her introduction:

> Because of this [which the speaker had already covered in the speech], we must first, delve into the problems of recruiter wrongdoings; next, examine the underlying causes as to why these travesties occur; and finally, develop solutions that will ensure that, as the Albuquerque *Tribune* of November 29, 2006, writes, we and those wielding weapons "are satisfied that they made the right decision for the right reasons at the right time."

As you can see from this example, a problem-solution speech often has an additional main point—sometimes an explanation of the development of the problem or a review of some historical background. Sometimes, as in the case of the above excerpt, the speaker provides added discussion of the problem by discussing the causes of the problems. In this speech the speaker has three main points: (1) the problems, (2) the causes of the problems, and (3) the solution.

Cause–Effect/Effect–Cause Pattern

Similar to the problem-solution pattern is the cause-effect or effect-cause pattern. This pattern is useful in persuasive speeches in which you want to convince your audience of the causal connection existing between two events or elements. In the **cause–effect pattern** you divide the speech into two major sections: causes and effects. For example, a speech on the reasons for highway accidents or birth defects might lend itself to a cause-effect pattern. Here you might first consider, say, the causes of highway accidents or birth defects, then turn to some of the effects; for example, the number of deaths, the number of accidents, and so on.

Or suppose you wanted to demonstrate the causes for the increase in AIDS in your state. In this case you might use an **effect–caus pattern** that might look something like this:

I. AIDS is increasing. [general effect]

 A. AIDS is increasing among teenagers. [a specific effect]

 B. AIDS is increasing among IV drug users. [a second specific effect]

 C. AIDS is increasing among women. [a third specific effect]

II. Three factors contribute to this increase. [general causal statement]

 A. Teenagers are ignorant about how the HIV virus is transmitted. [a specific cause]

 B. IV drug users exchange contaminated needles. [a second specific cause]

 C. Women are not practicing safe sex. [a third specific cause]

As you can see from this example, this type of speech is often combined with the problem-solution type. For example, after identifying the causes, the speaker might then treat the causes as problems and offer solutions for each problem/cause (for example: education for teens, free needle exchange programs, and education on safer sex for men and women).

The Motivated Sequence

The **motivated sequence** is an organizational pattern in which you arrange your information so as to motivate your audience to respond positively to your purpose (McKerrow, Gronbeck, Ehninger, & Monroe, 2000). In contrast to the previous organizational patterns, which provided ways of organizing the main ideas in the body of the speech, the motivated sequence is a pattern for organizing the entire speech. Here the speech (introduction, body, and conclusion) is divided into five parts or steps: (1) attention, (2) need, (3) satisfaction, (4) visualization, and (5) action.

1. The attention step makes the audience give you their undivided *attention*. If you execute this step effectively, your audience should be ready and eager to hear what you have to say. You can gain audience attention through a variety of means; examples include asking a question (rhetorical or actual) or making reference to audience members. These methods are presented in the "Introduction" discussion in the Step 7 section of this unit.

2. In the second part of your speech, you establish that a *need* exists for some kind of change. The audience should feel that something has to be learned or something has to be done because of this demonstrated need.

3. You satisfy the need by presenting the answer or the solution to the need you demonstrated in step 2 of the motivated sequence. On the

ASK THE RESEARCHER

The Motivated Sequence

What's so special about the motivated sequence, and how can I use it in preparing to speak on the job?

Alan Monroe originally adapted the motivated sequence from 1920s sales workshops he'd attended, when motivational psychology was all the rage. Since then, it's been thought about more as a convenient organizational form, but one that still makes motivational appeals central to persuasion: Unless I can make you want to act, you won't. Since the '20s, motivational psychology, thanks particularly to Professor David McClelland, has gotten more sophisticated, for he groups motivational appeals into three clusters: (1) affiliation (appeals to positive relationships with others), (2) achievement (appeals to individual success), and (3) power (appeals to dominance or defense). McClelland's work guides your selection of specific appeals for specific audiences, while the motivated sequences provide an easy-to-use organizational pattern for any speech. Get decision-makers' attention, convince them it's in their self-interest to listen, make your pitch, depict the results vividly, and clinch the deal—that's it! It works!

For further information: visit **www.ablongman.com/german15e**. On motivational psychology, see Hoyenga, K. B., & Hoyenga, H. (1984). *Motivational explanations of behavior: Psychological and cognitive ideas*. Monterey, CA: Brooks/Cole.

Bruce E. Gronbeck (Ph.D., University of Iowa) is A. Craig Baird Distinguished Professor of Public Address. As director of the University of Iowa Center for Media Studies and Political Culture, he studies the impact of television and the Internet on political public address. Every four years, he becomes one of the national experts on the Iowa caucuses, doing newspaper, radio, and television interviews on presidential candidates' performances (bruce-gronbeck@uiowa.edu). Used with the permission of Bruce Gronbeck.

basis of this *satisfaction* step, the audience should now believe that what you are informing them about or persuading them to do will satisfy the need.

4. *Visualization* intensifies the audience's feelings or beliefs. In this step you take the people in the audience beyond the present time and place and enable them to imagine the situation as it would be if the need were satisfied as you suggested in step 3. You might, for example, demonstrate the benefits that people would receive if your ideas were put into operation— or perhaps demonstrate the negative effects that people would suffer if your plan were not put into operation.

5. Tell the audience what *action* they should take to ensure that the need (step 2) is satisfied (step 3) as visualized (step 4). Here you want to move the audience in a particular direction— for example, to contribute free time to read to the blind. You can accomplish this step by stating what the audience members should do,

using a variety of supporting materials and logical, emotional, and ethical appeals.

Additional Organizational Patterns

The six patterns just considered are the most common and the most useful for organizing most public speeches. But there are other patterns that might be appropriate for different topics:

Structure–Function. The **structure–function pattern** is well suited to informative speeches in which you want to discuss how something is constructed (its structural aspects) and what it does (its functional aspects). This pattern might be useful, for example, in a speech to explain what an organization is and what it does, the parts of a university and how they operate, or the sensory systems of the body and their various functions. This pattern also might be useful in a discussion of the nature of a living organism: its anatomy (that is, its structures) and its physiology (that is, its functions).

Comparison and Contrast. Arranging your material in a **comparison-and-contrast pattern** is useful in informative speeches in which you want to analyze, for example, two different theories, proposals, departments, or products in terms of their similarities and differences. In this type of speech, you would be concerned not only with explaining each theory or proposal but also with clarifying how they're similar and how they're different.

Pro and Con, Advantages and Disadvantages. The **pro-and-con pattern**, sometimes called the advantages–disadvantages pattern, works well in informative speeches in which you want to explain objectively the advantages (pros) and the disadvantages (cons) of, say, a plan, method, or product.

Claim and Proof. The **claim-and-proof pattern** is especially appropriate in a persuasive speech in which you want to prove the truth or usefulness of a particular proposition. It's the pattern that you see frequently in trials: The prosecution claims that the defendant is guilty and that the proof is the varied evidence—for example, evidence that the defendant had a motive, the defendant had the opportunity, and the defendant had no alibi. In this pattern your speech would consist of two major parts. In the first part, you'd explain your claim (tuition must not be raised, library hours must be expanded, courses in Caribbean studies must be instituted). In the second part, you'd offer your evidence or proof as to why, for example, tuition must not be raised.

Multiple Definition. The **multiple-definition pattern** is often helpful for explaining specific concepts: What is a born-again Christian? What is a scholar? What is multiculturalism? In this pattern each major heading consists of a different type of definition or way of looking at the concept. Earlier, this unit looked at a variety of definition types.

Who? What? Why? Where? When? The **5W pattern** is the pattern of the journalist and is useful when you wish to report or explain an event such as a robbery, political coup, war, ceremony, or trial. In this pattern you'd have five major parts to the body of your speech, each dealing with the answers to one of these five questions.

Fiction–Fact. The **fiction–fact pattern** may be useful when you wish to clarify certain misconceptions that people have about various things. For example, if you were giving a speech on fiction and fact about flu viruses, you might use this pattern. You first would give the fiction (for example, you can get the flu from a flu shot, or antibiotics can help the

REFLECTIONS ON ETHICS

Communicating in Cyberspace

Because of the explosion in computer communication, the ethics of Internet communication (sometimes referred to as *nethics*) has become an important part of ethical communication. Of course, the same principles that govern ethical public speaking should also prevail when you communicate on the Internet. Here, however, are a few ethical principles with special relevance to computer communication. It is unethical to:

- Invade the privacy of others. Reading the files of another person or breaking into files that you're not authorized to read is unethical.

- Harm others or their property. Creating computer viruses; publishing instructions for making bombs; and creating websites that promote racism, heterosexism, ageism, or sexism are some examples of unethical computer use.

- Spread falsehoods. Lying on the Internet—about other people, the powers of medical or herbal treatment, or yourself—is just as unethical as it is in other forms of communication.

- Plagiarize. Appropriating the work of another as your own—whether the original work appeared on the Internet or in a book or journal—is unethical.

- Steal passwords, PINs, or authorization codes that belong to others.

- Copy software programs that you haven't paid for.

Ethical Choice Point

As an experiment, you develop a computer virus that can destroy websites. Recently, you've come across a variety of websites that market child pornography. You wonder if you can ethically destroy these websites. Indeed, you wonder if not destroying them is actually more unethical than using your newly developed virus. What is your ethical obligation in this situation? What would you do?

INTRODUCTIONS

You're scheduled to give a speech on careers in computer technology to students who have been forced to attend this career day on Saturday. If you don't win over this unwilling audience in your introduction, you figure you're finished.

WHAT DO YOU SAY?

© Paul Conklin/PhotoEdit

flu, or older people spread the flu most often) and then follow it with the fact (you can't get the flu from a flu shot; antibiotics are useful only against bacteria, not against viruses; children, rather than older people, spread the flu most often and most easily).

STEP 7: CONSTRUCT YOUR INTRODUCTION, CONCLUSION, AND TRANSITIONS

Now that you have the body of your speech organized, devote your attention to the introduction, conclusion, and transitions that will hold the parts of your speech together.

Introduction

Begin collecting suitable material for your introduction as you prepare the entire speech, but wait until all the other parts are completed before you put the introduction together. In this way, you'll be better able to determine which elements should be included and which should be eliminated.

Together with your general appearance and your nonverbal messages, the introduction gives your audience its first impression of you and your speech. Your introduction sets the tone for the rest of the speech; it tells your listeners what kind of a speech they'll hear.

Your **introduction** should serve three functions: It should (1) gain attention, (2) establish a speaker-audience-topic connection, and (3) orient the audience as to what is to follow. Let's look at each of these functions and at the ways you can serve these functions.

Gain Attention

In your introduction, gain the attention of your audience and focus it on your speech topic. (Then, of course, maintain that attention throughout your speech.) You can secure attention in numerous ways; here are just a few of them.

- Ask a question. Questions are effective because they are a change from declarative statements and call for an active response from listeners.

- Refer to audience members. Talking about the audience makes them perk up and pay attention, because you are involving them directly in your talk.

- Refer to recent happenings. Citing a previous speech, recent event, or prominent person currently making news helps you gain attention, because the audience is familiar with this current event and will pay attention to see how you are going to connect it to your speech topic.

- Use humor. A clever (and appropriate) anecdote is often useful in holding attention.

- Stress the importance of the topic. People pay attention to what they feel is important to them and ignore what seems unimportant or irrelevant. If your topic focuses on the interests of the audience, you might begin by referring directly to the audience.

- Use a presentation aid. Presentation aids are valuable because they are new and different. They engage our senses and thus our attention.

- Tell the audience to pay attention. A simple, "I want you to listen to this frightening statistic," or "I want you to pay particularly close attention to . . . ," used once or twice in a speech, will help gain audience attention.

© Barbara Stitzer/PhotoEdit

AROUSING THE AUDIENCE

You notice that your audience doesn't seem to pay much attention to those who have spoken before you. And your speech topic, at least on first acquaintance, isn't one with a lot of audience appeal. You need to gain their attention early in your introduction.

WHAT DO YOU SAY?

- Use a quotation. Quotations are useful because the audience is likely to pay attention to the brief and clever remarks of someone they've heard of or read about. Do make sure, however, that the quotation relates directly to your topic.

- Cite a little-known fact or statistic. Little-known facts or statistics will help perk up an audience's attention. For example, headlines on unemployment statistics, crime in the schools, and political corruption sell newspapers because they gain attention.

- Use an illustration or dramatic story. Much as we are drawn to soap operas, so are we drawn to illustrations and stories about people. Here's a good example of using a dramatic illustration to gain attention; it was given by U.S. Senator (California) Dianne Feinstein (2006) in a speech on gang violence (http://feinstein.senate.gov/public/index):

> On September 24 of this year, Los Angeles experienced a new low. Three-year-old Kaitlyn Avila was shot point-blank by a gang member who mistakenly thought her father was a member of a rival gang. The gang member shot and wounded her father, then intentionally fired into little Kaitlyn's chest. This is the first time law enforcement officials remember a young child being "targeted" in a gang shooting.

Establish a Speaker–Audience–Topic Relationship

In addition to gaining attention, your introduction should establish connections among yourself as the speaker, the audience members, and your topic. Try to answer your listeners' inevitable question: Why should we listen to you speak on this topic? You can establish an effective **speaker–audience–topic connection**, or S-A-T connection, in many different ways.

- Refer to others present. Not only will this help you to gain attention; it will also help you to establish a bond with the audience.

- Refer to the occasion. Often your speech will be connected directly with the occasion. By referring to the reason the audience has gathered, you can establish a connection between yourself, the audience, and the topic.

- Express your pleasure or interest in speaking.

- Establish your competence in the subject. Show the audience that you are really interested in and knowledgeable about the topic.

- Compliment the audience. Complimenting the audience is a commonly used technique to establish an S-A-T connection in much professional public speaking. In the classroom this technique may seem awkward and obvious, so it is probably best avoided here. But it's important to realize that in other settings paying the audience an honest and sincere compliment (though never overdoing it) will not only encourage your listeners to give you their attention, but also help make them feel a part of your speech. In some cultures—Japan and Korea are good examples—the speaker is expected to compliment the audience, the beauty of the country, or its culture. It's one of the essential parts of the introduction. In this example, musician Billy Joel compliments his audience, the graduating class of the Berklee College of Music, directly and honestly (www.berklee.edu/commencement/past/bjoel.html, accessed February 6, 2004):

> I am truly pleased that the road has twisted and turned its way up the East Coast to Boston. The Berklee College of Music represents the finest contemporary music school there is, and I am honored to be here with you this morning to celebrate.

- Express similarities with the audience. By stressing your own similarity with members of the audience, you create a relationship with them and become an "insider" instead of an "outsider."

Orient the Audience

The introduction should orient the audience in some way as to what is to follow in the body of the speech. This **orientation** can take various forms.

You can preview for the audience what you are going to say, as in "Tonight I'm going to discuss nuclear waste"; give a detailed preview, perhaps outlining your major propositions; or identify your goal by, for example, stating your thesis.

Here Texas governor Rick Perry, in a speech to the Border Governors Conference on August 25, 2006 (www.governor.state.tx.us/divisions/press/speeches, accessed January 14, 2007), orients the audience by briefly identifying the three main points he will cover in his speech:

> In signing this declaration, we commit our resources and our resolve to making the border healthier, better educated, and more secure.

And here a student, Tapashya Ghosh of the University of Texas at Austin, similarly orients by identifying the main ideas to be covered, after explaining the nature and danger of the Stand Your Ground Law:

> To rectify this dangerous and unnecessary situation, it is imperative that we first study the problems of this law, next see how these laws came about, and finally explore solutions to change a situation that ABC News of May 24, 2006, calls the law that gives us the "right to commit murder."

Conclusion

Your **conclusion** is especially important, because it's often the part of the speech that the audience remembers most clearly. It's your conclusion that in many cases determines what image of you is left in the minds of the audience. Devote special attention to this brief but crucial part of your speech. Let your conclusion serve three major functions: to (1) summarize, (2) motivate, and (3) provide closure.

Summarize

The **summary** function is particularly important in an informative speech; it is less so in persuasive speeches or in speeches to entertain. You may summarize your speech in a variety of ways:

- Restate your thesis or purpose. In this type of brief summary, you restate the essential thrust of your speech, repeating your thesis or perhaps the goals you hoped to achieve.
- Restate the importance of the topic. Tell the audience again why your topic or thesis is so important.
- Restate your main points. That is, restate both your thesis and the major points you used to support it.

Motivate

A second function of the conclusion—most appropriate in persuasive speeches—is to motivate the people in the audience to do what you want them to do. In your conclusion you have the opportunity to give the audience one final push in the direction you wish them to take. Whether it's to buy stock, vote a particular way, or change an attitude, you can use the conclusion for a final **motivation**, a final appeal. Here are two excellent ways to motivate:

- Ask for a specific response. Specify what you want the audience to do after listening to your speech.
- Provide directions for future action. Spell out, most often in general terms, the direction you wish the audience to take.

Close

The third function of your conclusion is to provide **closure**. Often your summary will accomplish this, but in some instances it will prove insufficient. End your speech with a conclusion that is crisp and definite. Make the audience know that you have definitely and clearly ended. Some kind of wrap-up, some sort of final statement, is helpful in providing this feeling of closure. You may achieve closure through a variety of methods:

- Use a quotation. A quotation is often an effective means of providing closure.
- Refer to subsequent events. You may also achieve closure by referring to future events—events taking place either that day or soon afterwards.
- Refer back to the introduction. It's sometimes useful to connect your conclusion with your introduction.
- Pose a challenge or question. You may close your speech by leaving the audience with a provocative question to ponder or a challenge to consider. Or, you can pose a question and answer it by recapping your thesis and perhaps some of your major arguments or propositions.
- Thank the audience. Speakers frequently conclude their speeches by thanking the audience for their attention or for their invitation to address them.

Here, for example, a student, Nicole Kreisberg from the University of Texas at Austin, concludes her speech on alternative existence with a provocative thought that tells you the speech is over:

> And while the idea of living an alternative existence may seem a little absurd, as Kurt Vonnegut contends: So is real life.

Transitions

Transitions are words, phrases, or sentences that connect the various parts of your speech. They provide the audience with guideposts that help them follow the development of your thoughts and arguments. Use transitions in at least the following places:

- between the introduction and the body of the speech
- between the body and the conclusion
- between the main points in the body of the speech

Here are the major transitional functions and some stylistic devices that you might use to serve these functions.

To announce the start of a major proposition or piece of evidence: First, . . ., A second argument . . ., A closely related problem . . ., If you want further evidence, look at . . ., Next . . ., Consider also. . ., An even more compelling argument . . ., My next point. . . .

To signal that you're drawing a conclusion from previously given evidence and argument: Thus, . . ., Therefore, . . ., So, as you can see . . ., It follows, then, that. . . .

To alert the audience to your introduction of a qualification or exception: But, . . ., However, also consider. . . .

To remind listeners of what has just been said and of its connection with another issue that will now be considered: In contrast to . . .; Consider also . . .; Not only . . . but also . . .; In addition to . . . we also need to look at . . .; Not only should we . . ., we should also. . . .

To signal the part of your speech you're approaching: By way of introduction . . .; In conclusion . . .; Now, let's discuss why we're here today . . .; So, what's the solution? What should we do?

To signal your organizational structure: I'll first explain the problems with jury awards and then propose a workable solution.

To summarize what you've already discussed. Consider using a special kind of transition: the internal summary. It's a statement that usually summarizes some major subdivision of your speech. Incorporate several internal summaries into your speech—perhaps working them into the transitions connecting, say, the major parts of your speech. An internal summary that also serves as a transition might look something like this:

> Inadequate recreational facilities, poor schooling, and a lack of adequate role models seem to be the major problems facing our youngsters. Each of these, however, can be remedied and even eliminated. Here's what we can do.

This brief passage reminds listeners of what they've just heard and previews what they'll hear next. The clear connection in their minds will fill in any gaps that may have been created through inattention, noise, and the like.

You can enhance your transitions by pausing between your transition and the next part of your speech. This will help the audience realize that a new part of your speech is coming. You might also take a step forward or to the side after saying your transition. This will also help to reinforce the movement from one part of your speech to another.

Building Communication Skills — Constructing Conclusions and Introductions

Prepare a conclusion and an introduction to a hypothetical speech on one of the topics listed below, making sure that in your conclusion you (a) review the speech's main points and (b) provide closure, and that in your introduction you (a) gain attention and (b) orient the audience. Be prepared to explain the methods you used to accomplish each of these functions.

1. Proficiency in a foreign language should be required of all college graduates.
2. All killing of wild animals should be declared illegal.
3. Suicide and its assistance by qualified medical personnel should be legalized.
4. Gambling should be legalized by all states.
5. Maximum sentences should be imposed for hate crimes.
6. Alcoholic beverages should be banned from campus.

Because the conclusion and introduction are often what listeners remember best, give these opening and closing remarks careful attention.

Pitfalls in Introductions, Conclusions, and Transitions

In addition to understanding the principles of effective pubic speaking, it often helps to become aware of common mistakes. Here, then, are some of the common mistakes you'll want to avoid.

In your introduction:

- Don't apologize (generally). In the United States and western Europe, an apology may be seen as an excuse and so is to be avoided. In certain other cultures (those of Japan, China, and Korea are good examples), however, speakers are expected to begin with an apology. It's a way of complimenting the audience.

- Avoid promising something you won't deliver. The speaker who promises to tell you how to make a fortune in the stock market or how to be the most popular person on campus (and fails to deliver such insight) quickly loses credibility.

- Avoid gimmicks that gain attention but are irrelevant to the speech or inconsistent with your treatment of the topic. For example, slamming a book on the desk or telling a joke that bears no relation to your speech may accomplish the limited goal of gaining attention, but quickly the audience will see that they've been fooled, and they'll resent it.

- Don't introduce your speech with ineffective statements such as "I'm really nervous, but here goes" or "Before I begin my talk, I want to say...." These statements will make your audience uncomfortable and will encourage them to focus on your delivery rather than on your message.

In your conclusion:

- Don't introduce new material. Instead, use your conclusion to reinforce what you've already said and to summarize.

- Don't dilute your position. Avoid being critical of your own material or your presentation. Saying, for example, "The information I presented is probably dated, but it was all I could find" or "I hope I wasn't too nervous" will detract from the credibility you've tried to establish.

- Don't drag out your conclusion. End crisply.

In your transitions:

- Avoid too many or too few transitions. Either extreme can cause problems. Use transitions to help your listeners, who will hear the speech only once, to understand the structure of your speech.

- Avoid transitions that are out of proportion to the speech parts they connect. If you want to connect the two main points of your speech, you need something more than just "and" or "the next point." In contrast, if you want to connect two brief examples, then a simple "another example occurs when ..." will do.

SUMMARY: SUPPORTING AND ORGANIZING YOUR SPEECH

This unit covered ways of supporting and organizing your main thoughts and introducing and concluding your speech.

1. Formulate the thesis of the speech. Develop your main points by asking relevant questions about this thesis.

2. Reinforce your main points with a variety of materials that support them. Suitable supporting materials include examples, narratives, analogies, definitions, testimony, statistics, and presentation aids as well as such devices as quotations, comparisons, statements of facts, and repetition and restatement.

3. Among the presentation aids you might consider are the actual object, models of the object, graphs, word charts, maps, people, photographs and illustrations, and tapes and CDs. These can be presented with a variety of media; for example, the chalkboard, chartboards, flip charts, slides and transparency projections, videotapes, and handouts. Presentation aids work best when they add clarity to your speech, are appealing to listeners, and are culturally sensitive.

4. Computer-assisted presentations such as PowerPoint, which have become extremely popular, allow you to communicate lots of information in an interesting format, to print handouts to coordinate with your speech, and to create an outline and speaker's notes for your speech.

5. Organize the speech materials into a clear, easily identifiable thought pattern. Suitable organizing principles include temporal, spatial, topical, problem–solution, cause–effect/effect–cause, motivated sequence, structure–function, comparison-and-contrast, pro-and-con, claim-and-proof, multiple-definition, and who-what-why-where-when (5W) patterns.

6. Introductions should gain attention, establish a speaker–audience–topic (S-A-T) connection, and orient the audience as to what is to follow.

7. Conclusions should summarize the main ideas, provide a final motivation, and provide a crisp closing to the speech.

8. Transitions and internal summaries help connect and integrate the parts of the speech; they also help the listeners to better remember the speech.

KEY TERMS IN SUPPORTING AND ORGANIZING YOUR SPEECH

analogies

body

cause–effect pattern

claim-and-proof pattern

closure

comparison-and-contrast
pattern

conclusion

definition

effect–cause pattern

example

fiction–fact pattern

5W pattern

introduction

models

motivated sequence

motivation

multiple-definition pattern

narrative

orientation

presentation aid

pro-and-con pattern

problem–solution pattern

product placement

spatial pattern

speaker–audience–topic
connection

statistics

structure–function pattern

summary

temporal pattern

testimony

thesis

topical pattern

transitions

THINKING CRITICALLY ABOUT SUPPORTING AND ORGANIZING YOUR SPEECH

1. **Strategies of Arrangement.** What strategies of arrangement would you use if you were giving a pro-choice speech to a pro-life audience? What strategies would you use if you were giving a speech in favor of domestic partnership insurance to gay rights leaders?

2. **Vivid Support.** Jamie, a student at a community college in Texas, wants to give a speech on the cruelty of cockfighting. Most people in the predominantly Hispanic audience come from Mexico, where cockfighting is a legal and popular sport. Among the visuals Jamie is considering are extremely vivid photographs of cocks literally torn to shreds by their opponents, which have razor blades strapped to their feet. Would you advise Jamie to use these photographs if the listeners were, say, moderately in favor of cockfighting? What if they were moderately against cockfighting?

3. **Quotations.** Visit one of the websites for quotations; for example, try **www.bartleby.com** or **http://us .imdb.com/** (a database of quotations from films). Select a quotation suitable for use with the slide show

of the speech on self-disclosure in the Public Speaking Sample Assistant box, and explain how you would use this on a slide.

4. **Presentation Aids.** Shana wants to illustrate the rise and fall in the prices of 12 stocks over the last 10 years to show that her investment club should sell 3 stocks and keep the other 9. This is the first time Shana will be using visual aids, and she needs advice on what aids best serve her purpose. What suggestions do you have for Shana?

5. Prepare and deliver a two-minute speech in which you do any one of the following:
   - Tell a personal story to illustrate a specific point.
   - Explain a print ad that relies on statistics, and show how the advertiser uses statistics to make a point.
   - Describe the events portrayed in a recently seen television program, using a temporal pattern.
   - Discuss a recent newspaper editorial or op-ed letter, using a problem–solution or cause–effect pattern.
   - Explain how television commercials get your attention.

LOG ON! MYCOMMUNICATIONLAB

WWW.MYCOMMUNICATIONLAB.COM

Visit MCL for a self-test on culture-specific icons and discussions of evaluating testimony and arranging supporting materials. A video illustrates principles of PowerPoint presentations and presents techniques for public speaking. View the videos of Writing Position Papers, one of which uses visual aids and one of which doesn't. Which do you find most effective? Explore the material on statistics, transitions, connecting key ideas, and organization. Template outlines are available, as is a scrambled outline exercise. View one or more of the video speeches and consider how these speakers organized their speeches and what you might do differently.

REFERENCES

deBono, E. (1973). *Lateral thinking: Creativity step by step.* New York: Harper Paperbacks.

Hayakawa, S. I., & Hayakawa, A. R. (1990). *Language in thought and action* (5th ed.). New York: Harcourt Brace Jovanovich.

Lustig, M. W., & Koester, J. (2006). *Intercultural competence: Interpersonal communication across cultures* (5th ed.). New York: Longman.

Mandese, J. (2006). When product placement goes too far. Retrieved March 30, 2006, from http://www.broadcastingcable.com.

Marien, M. (1992). *Vital Speeches of the Day* (March 15), 340–344.

McKerrow, R. E., Gronbeck, B. E., Ehninger, D., & Monroe, A. H. (2000). *Principles and types of speech communication* (14th ed.). Boston: Allyn & Bacon.

Rodman, G. (2001). *Making sense of media: An introduction to mass communication.* Boston: Allyn & Bacon.

Chapter 6

Style and Delivery in Public Speaking

MAJOR TOPICS

Step 8: Outline Your Speech

Step 9: Word Your Speech

Step 10: Rehearse and Present Your Speech

Criticizing Speeches

Special Features

Making Myself Clear: Joseph Chesebro

Can You Distinguish between Commonly Confused Words?

What's Wrong with These Critical Evaluations?

 Hate Speech

Criticizing Ethically

 One-Sided versus Two-Sided Messages

 Speech Rate

 Checking Your Pronunciation

 Responding Strategically and Ethically

 A Preparation Outline (Topical Organization)

A Preparation Outline (Motivated Sequence Organization)

A Template Outline

A Phrase/Key-Word Presentation Outline

© JupiterImages/Comstock Images/Alamy

Here the last three steps in public speaking are discussed.

In this unit, you'll learn about:
- the kinds of outlines used in public speaking.
- language and how it influences us.
- ways that speakers use to rehearse and deliver their speeches.

You'll learn to:
- outline your speeches.
- use language to best achieve your purposes.
- rehearse your speech efficiently and deliver your speech with maximum impact.

STEP 8: OUTLINE YOUR SPEECH

The **outline** is a blueprint for your speech; it lays out the elements of the speech and their relationship to one another. With this blueprint in front of you, you can see at a glance all the elements of organization—the functions of the introduction and conclusion, the transitions, the main points and their relationship to the thesis and purpose, and the adequacy of the supporting materials. And, like a blueprint for a building, the outline enables you to spot weaknesses that might otherwise go undetected.

Begin outlining when you first begin constructing your speech. In this way, you'll take the best advantage of one of the major functions of an outline—to tell you where change is needed. Change and alter the outline as necessary at every stage of the speech construction process.

Outlines may be extremely detailed or extremely general. But because you're now in a learning environment whose objective is to make you a more proficient public speaker, a detailed full-sentence outline will serve best. The more detail you put into the outline, the easier it will be for you to examine the parts of the speech for all the qualities and characteristics that make a speech effective.

Constructing the Outline

After you've completed your research and mapped out an organizational plan for your speech, put this plan (this blueprint) on paper. Construct a "preparation outline" of your speech, using the following guidelines.

Preface the Outline with Identifying Data. Before you begin the outline proper, identify the general and specific purposes as well as your thesis. This prefatory material should look something like this:

Title: What Media Do

General purpose: To inform.

Specific purpose: To inform my audience of four major functions of the mass media.

Thesis: The mass media serve four major functions.

These identifying notes are not part of your speech proper. They're not, for example, mentioned in your oral presentation. Rather, they're guides to the preparation of the speech and the outline. They're like road signs to keep you going in the right direction and to signal when you've gone off course. One additional bit of identifying data should preface the statements of purposes and thesis: the title of your speech.

Outline the Introduction, Body, and Conclusion as Separate Units. The introduction, body, and conclusion of the speech, although intimately connected, should be labeled separately and should be kept distinct in your outline. Like the preliminary identifying data, these labels are not spoken to the audience but are further guides to your preparation.

By keeping the introduction, body, and conclusion separate, you'll be able to see at a glance if they do in fact serve the functions you want them to serve. You'll be able to see where further amplification and support are needed. In short, you'll be able to see where there are problems and where repair is necessary.

At the same time, do make sure that you examine and see the speech as a whole—how the introduction leads to the body, and how the conclusion summarizes your propositions and brings your speech to a close.

Insert Transitions. Insert [using square brackets, like these] transitions between the introduction and the body, the body and the conclusion, the main points of the body, and wherever else you think they might be useful.

Include a List of References. Some instructors require that you include a list of references in your preparation outline. If this is requested, then do so at the end of the outline or on a separate page. Some instructors require that only sources cited in the speech be included in the list of references, whereas others require that the full list of sources consulted be provided (those mentioned in the speech as well as those not mentioned).

Your research and references will prove most effective with your audience if you carefully integrate them into the speech. It will count for little if you consulted the latest works by the greatest authorities but never mention this to your audience. So, when appropriate, weave into your speech the source material you've consulted. In your outline, refer to the source material by author's name, date, and page in parentheses and then provide the complete citation in your list of references.

Theory and Research   UNDERSTANDING   **One-Sided versus Two-Sided Messages**

When you're presenting persuasive arguments, should you devote all your time to your side of the case—or should you also mention the other side and show why that side is not acceptable? Originally studied during the 1940s, this question continues to engage the attention of researchers. Early studies found that one-sided presentations were more effective with less-educated audiences, whereas two-sided presentations were more effective with more-educated listeners. One-sided presentations also were more effective with people who were already in favor of the speaker's point of view, whereas two-sided presentations were more persuasive with those who were initially opposed to the speaker's position.

Whether you choose to use a one-sided or a two-sided persuasive approach will depend on your topic (are there two competing positions?), the time you have available (limited time may prevent you from covering both sides), your audience's existing attitude (if they already reject the other position, there may not be a need to include it), and perhaps other factors as well.

If you do decide to present both sides, here are a few points to consider:

1. Using a two-sided presentation generally helps establish your credibility; by mentioning the other side, you demonstrate your knowledge of the entire area and by implication tell the audience that you understand both positions.

2. In a two-sided presentation, be sure to demonstrate the superiority of your position and the reasons why the other position is not as good as yours (O'Keefe, 1999). If you merely mention the other position without pointing out its flaws, then you risk creating doubt in minds of your listeners about the superiority of your position.

3. If your audience is aware of an alternative position, then you need to demonstrate that you too are aware of it but that it's not as good as your position.

4. Demonstrate that you have analyzed the alternative position as carefully and thoroughly as the position you're supporting.

Working with Theories and Research

Take a look at print, television, or Internet ads and identify a few ads that use a two-sided approach (Brand A is better than Brand X). What makes a two-sided advertisement effective?

In your actual speech, a source citation might be phrased something like this:

According to John Naisbitt, author of the nation-wide best-seller *Megatrends*, the bellwether states are California, Florida, Washington, Colorado, and Connecticut.

Regardless of what specific sourcing system is required (find out before you prepare your outline), make certain to include all sources of information, not just written materials. Personal interviews, information derived from course lectures, and data learned from television should all be included in your list of references.

Use a Consistent Set of Symbols.

The following is the standard, accepted sequence of symbols for outlining:

I.
  A.
    1.
      a.
        (1)
          (a)

Begin the introduction, the body, and the conclusion with Roman numeral I. Treat each of the three major parts as a complete unit.

Use Visual Aspects to Reflect the Organizational Pattern.

Use proper and clear indentation. The outlining function of word-processing programs has many of these suggestions built into them.

Not this:

I. Television caters to the lowest possible intelligence.
II. Talk shows illustrate this.
III. *General Hospital*

This:

I. Television caters to the lowest possible intelligence.
  A. Talk shows illustrate this.
    1. *Montel*
    2. *Maury*
    3. *The Jerry Springer Show*
  B. Soap operas illustrate this.
    1. *As the World Turns*
    2. *General Hospital*
    3. *The Young and the Restless*

Use One Discrete Idea per Symbol.

If your outline is to reflect the organizational pattern structur-ing the various items of information, use just one discrete idea per symbol, and make sure each item does not overlap with any other item. Instead of the overlapping "Education might be improved if teachers were better trained and if students were better motivated," break this statement into two propositions: "I. Education would be improved if teachers were better trained" and "II. Education would be improved if students were better motivated."

Use Complete Declarative Sentences.

Phrase your ideas in the outline in complete declarative sentences rather than as questions or as phrases. This will further assist you in examining the essential relationships. It's much easier, for example, to see if one item of information supports another if both are phrased in the declarative mode. If one is a question and one is a statement, this will be more difficult.

Sample Outlines

Now that the principles of outlining are clear, let's look at some specific examples to illustrate how those principles are put into operation in specific outlines. We'll look first at preparation outlines with two different organizational patterns; then at a template outline, a kind of skeletal pattern for a speech; and finally at a delivery outline, the type of outline you might take with you when you deliver your speech.

The Preparation Outline

Two **preparation outlines** are presented in the Public Speaking Sample Assistant boxes on pages 359–363. One uses a topical organizational pattern, perhaps the most common pattern among public speeches; the other uses the motivated sequence, an extremely popular pattern both for informative talks and for persuasive speeches.

These full-sentence outlines are similar to the written materials you might prepare in constructing your own speeches. The side notes in the boxes are designed to clarify both the content and the format of full-sentence outlines.

Template Outline

Another useful type of outline is the **template outline**. Much as a template in PowerPoint guides you to fill in certain information in particular places, the template outline serves a similar function; it ensures that you include all the relevant material in reasonable order. At the same time, it also helps you see your speech as a whole—perhaps with gaps that

Public Speaking Sample Assistant

A Preparation Outline (Topical Organization)

Self-Disclosure

General purpose: To inform.
Specific purpose: To inform my audience of the advantages and disadvantages of self-disclosing.
Thesis: Self-disclosure has advantages and disadvantages.

Generally, the title, thesis, and general and specific purposes of the speech are prefaced to the outline. When the outline is an assignment that is to be handed in, additional information may be requested.

Introduction

I. We've all heard them:

Note the general format for the outline: the headings (introduction, body, and conclusion) are clearly labeled, and the sections are separated visually.

Notice that the introduction serves the three functions discussed in the text: it gains attention (by these extreme confessions); establishes an S-A-T connection (by noting that all of us, speaker and audience, have had this experience); and orients the audience (by identifying the three major ideas of the speech).

A. I'm in love with my nephew.

Note how the indenting helps you to see clearly the relationship that one item bears to another. For example, in Introduction I, the outline format helps you to see that A, B, and C are explanations (amplification and support) for I.

B. My husband is not my baby's father.
C. I'm really a woman.
II. We've all disclosed.
  A. Sometimes it was positive, sometimes negative, but always significant.
  B. Knowing the potential consequences will help us make better decisions.
III. We look at this important form of communication in three parts:
  A. First, we look at the nature of self-disclosure.
  B. Second, we look at the potential rewards.
  C. Third, we look at the potential risks.
[Let's look first at the nature of this type of communication.]

These brief statements are designed to get attention, perhaps a laugh or two, but also to introduce the nature of the topic.

Here the speaker seeks to establish a speaker-audience-topic connection.

Here the speaker orients the audience and explains the three parts of the speech. The use of guide phrases (first, second, third) helps the audience fix clearly in mind the major divisions of the speech.

This transition cues the audience that the speaker will consider the first of the major parts of the speech. Notice that transitions are inserted between all major parts of the speech. Although they may seem too numerous in this abbreviated outline, transitions will be appreciated by your listeners, because they will help them follow and understand your speech.

Body

I. Self-disclosure is a form of communication (Petronio, 2000).
  A. S-D is about the self.
    1. It can be about what you did.
    2. It can be about what you think.

Public Speaking Sample Assistant

A Preparation Outline
(Topical Organization) *(Continued)*

B. S-D is new, previously unknown information.

C. S-D is normally about information usually kept hidden.
  1. It can be something about which you're ashamed.
  2. It can be something for which you'd be punished in some way.

[Knowing what self-disclosure is, we can now look at its potential rewards.]

This transition helps the audience see that the speaker is finished discussing what self-disclosure is and will now consider the potential rewards.

II. Self-disclosure has three potential rewards.
  A. It gives us self-knowledge.
  B. It increases communication effectiveness (Schmidt & Cornelius, 1987).
  C. It improves physiological health (Sheese, Brown, & Graziano, 2004).

[Although these benefits are substantial, there are also risks.]

Notice the parallel structure throughout the outline. For example, note that II and III in the body are phrased in similar style. Although this may seem unnecessarily redundant, it will help your audience follow your speech more closely and will also help you in logically structuring your thoughts.

III. Self-disclosure has three potential risks.
  A. It can involve personal risks.
    1. This happened to a close friend.
    2. This also happened with well-known celebrities.
  B. It can involve relationship risks (Petronio, 2000).
    1. This happens on *Jerry Springer* five times a week.
    2. It also happened to me.
  C. It can involve professional risks (Korda, 1975; Fesko, 2001).
    1. This occurred recently at work.
    2. There are also lots of political examples.

[Let me summarize this brief excursion into self-disclosure.]

Note that the referencese are integrated throughout the preparation outline just as they would be in a term paper. In the actual speech, the speaker might say something like: "Communication theorist Sandra Petronio presents evidence to show that. . . ."

These examples would naturally be recounted in greater detail in the actual speech. One of the values of outlining these examples is that you'll be able to see at a glance how many you have and how much time you have available to devote to each of these examples. Examples, especially personal ones, have a way of growing beyond their importance to the speech.

Note that each statement in the outline is a complete sentence. You can easily convert this outline into a phrase or keyword outline for use in presentation (see Public Speaking Sample Assistant box, page 365). The full sentences, however, will help you see more clearly the relationships among items.

Conclusion

I. Self disclosure is a type of communication.
  A. It's about the self, concerns something new, and concerns something that you usually keep hidden.
  B. Self-disclosure can lead to increased self-knowledge, better communication, and improved health.

This first part of the conclusion summarizes the major parts of the speech. The longer the speech, the more extensive the summary should be.

Public Speaking Sample Assistant

A Preparation Outline (Topical Organization) *(Continued)*

C. Self-disclosure can also create risks to your personal, relational, and professional lives.

II. Self-disclosure is not only an interesting type of communication; it's also vital.

    A. You may want to explore this further by simply typing "self-disclosure" in your favorite search engine.

    B. If you want a more scholarly presentation, take a look at Sandra Petronio's *Balancing the Secrets of Private Disclosures* in the library or online.

III. The bottom line, of course: Should you self-disclose?

    A. Yes.

    B. No.

    C. Maybe.

References

Korda, M. (1975). *Power! How to get it, how to use it.* New York: Ballantine.

Petronio, S. (Ed.). (2000). *Balancing the secrets of private disclosures.* Mahwah, NJ: Erlbaum.

Schmidt, T. O., & Cornelius, R. R. (1987). Self-disclosure in everyday life. *Journal of Social and Personal Relationships, 4,* 365–373.

Sheese, B. E., Brown, E. L, & Graziano, W. G. (2004). Emotional expression in cyberspace: Searching for moderators of the Pennebaker disclosure effect via e-mail. *Health Psychology, 23* (September), 457–464.

Notice that the Introduction's III A, B, and C correspond to the Body's I, II, and III, and to the Conclusion's I A, B, and C. This pattern will help you emphasize the major ideas in your speech—first in the orientation, second in the body of the speech, and third in the conclusion's summary.

This step, in which the speaker motivates the listeners to continue learning about self-disclosure, is optional in informative speeches. In persuasive speeches, you'd use this step to encourage listeners to act on your purpose—to vote, to donate time, to give blood, and so on.

This step provides closure; it makes it clear that the speech is finished. It also serves to encourage reflection on the part of the audience as to their own self-disclosing communication.

This reference list includes just those sources that appear in the completed speech.

need to be filled or items that are discussed at too great a length. In some sense the template outline is mechanical (some might say too mechanical), but it's an extremely useful device for organizing a speech. As you become more familiar with the public speaking process, as with PowerPoint, you'll develop your speech, and your slides, without any template or wizard. As you review the template outline in the Public Speaking Sample Assistant box on page 364, the phrases printed in light ink will remind you of the functions of each outline item.

The Phrase/Key-Word Presentation Outline

Now that you've constructed a preparation outline, perhaps using a template outline for guidance, you need to construct a presentation outline. Resist the temptation to use your preparation outline to deliver the speech. If you use your preparation outline, you'll tend to read from the out-line instead of presenting a seemingly extemporaneous speech in which you attend to and respond to audience feedback. Instead, construct a brief

A Preparation Outline
(Motivated Sequence Organization)

This outline illustrates how you might construct an outline and a speech using the motivated sequence. This outline focuses on the establishment of a youth center as a means of combating juvenile crime. In a longer speech, if you wanted to persuade an audience to establish a youth center, you might include two or three issues and not limit yourself to the single issue of reducing juvenile crime.

As you will see, in the motivated sequence outline, five steps (attention, need, satisfaction, visualization, and action) take the place of the Introduction, Body, and Conclusion structure of the topical organization in the Public Speaking Sample Assistant box.

The Youth Center

General purpose: To persuade.
Specific purpose: To persuade my listeners to vote in favor of Proposition 14, which would establish a community youth center.
Thesis: A youth center will reduce juvenile crime.

I. If you could reduce juvenile crime by some 20 percent by just flipping a lever, would you do it?
   A. Thom's drugstore was broken into by teenagers.
   B. Loraine's video store windows were broken by teenagers.

Step 1: Attention
The speaker asks a question to gain attention and follows it with specific examples of juvenile crime that audience members have experienced. The question and the specific examples focus on one single issue: the need to reduce juvenile crime. If the speech were a broader and longer one and included other reasons for the youth center, then it would have been appropriate to preview them here as well.

II. Juvenile crime is on the rise.
   A. The overall number of crimes has increased.
      1. In 2002 there were 32 juvenile crimes.
      2. In 2004 there were 47 such crimes.
      3. In 2006 there were 63 such crimes.
   B. The number of serious crimes also has increased.
      1. In 2004 there were 30 misdemeanors and 2 felonies.
      2. In 2007 there were 35 misdemeanors and 28 felonies.

Step 2: Need
The speaker states directly and clearly the need and shows that a problem exists. The speaker then demonstrates that the rise in crime is significant both in absolute numbers and in the severity of the crimes. To help the listeners understand these figures, the speaker could display these figures on a chalkboard, on a prepared chart, or on PowerPoint slides. In a longer speech, other needs might also be identified in this step; for example, teenagers' needs for vocational and social skills.

III. A youth center will help reduce juvenile crime.
   A. Three of our neighboring towns reduced juvenile crime after establishing a youth center.
      1. In Marlboro there was a 20 percent decline in overall juvenile crime.
      2. In both Highland and Ellenville the number of serious crimes declined 25 percent.

Step 3: Satisfaction
In this step, the speaker shows the listeners that the proposal to establish a youth center offers great benefits and no significant drawbacks.
The speaker argues that the youth center will satisfy the need to reduce juvenile crime by showing statistics from neighboring towns. The speaker also preemptively answers any objections about increased taxes. If the speaker had reason to believe that listeners had other possible objections, these concerns too should be addressed in this step.

A Preparation Outline (Motivated Sequence Organization) *(Continued)*

B. The youth center will not increase our tax burden.
   1. New York State grants will pay for most of the expenses.
   2. Local merchants have agreed to pay any remaining expenses.

IV. Juvenile crime will decrease as a result of the youth center.
   A. If we follow the example of our neighbors, our juvenile crime rates are likely to decrease by 20 to 25 percent.
   B. Thom's store would not have been broken into.
   C. Loraine's windows would not have been broken.

V. Vote yes on Proposition 14.
   A. In next week's election you'll be asked to vote on Proposition 14, establishing a youth center.
   B. Vote yes if you want to help reduce juvenile crime.
   C. Urge your family members, your friends, and your work colleagues also to vote yes.

Step 4: Visualization
Here the speaker visualizes what the town would be like if the youth center were established, using both the statistics developed earlier and the personal examples introduced in the beginning of the speech.

Step 5: Action
In this step the speaker asks the audience for a specific action—to vote in favor of the youth center—and urges listeners to influence others to do the same. The speaker also reiterates the main theme of the speech; namely, that the youth center will help reduce juvenile crime.

---

presentation outline: an outline that will assist rather than hinder your delivery of the speech. Here are some guidelines to follow in preparing this delivery outline.

- Be brief. Try to limit yourself to one side of one sheet of paper.

- Be clear. Be sure that you can see the outline while you're speaking. Use different colored inks, underlining, or whatever system will help you communicate your ideas.

- Be delivery minded. Include any guides to delivery that will help while you're speaking. Note in the outline when you'll use your presentation aid and when you'll remove it. A simple "show PA" or "remove PA" should suffice. You might also wish to note some speaking cues, such as "slow down" when reading a poetry excerpt, or perhaps a place where an extended pause might help.

- Rehearse with the presentation outline. In your rehearsals, use the delivery outline only. Remember, the objective is to make rehearsals as close to the real thing as possible.

The Public Speaking Sample Assistant box shows a sample presentation outline constructed from the preparation outline on self-disclosure. Note that the outline is brief enough so that you'll be able to use it effectively without losing eye contact with the audience. It uses abbreviations (for example, S-D for self-disclosure) and phrases rather than complete sentences. And yet it's detailed enough to include all essential parts of your speech, including transitions. It contains delivery notes specifically tailored to your own needs, such as pause suggestions and guides to using visual aids. Note also that it's clearly divided into introduction, body, and conclusion and uses the same numbering system as the preparation outline.

Public Speaking Sample Assistant

A Template Outline

This template outline would be appropriate for a speech using a temporal, spatial, or topical organization pattern. Note that in this template outline there are three main points (I, II, and III in the body). These correspond to the III A, B, and C in the introduction (where you'd orient the audience) and to the A, B, and C in the conclusion (where you'd summarize your main points). Once again, the transitions are signaled by square brackets. As you review this outline, the phrases printed in light ink will remind you of the functions of each outline item. Additional template outlines are available at MyCommunicationLab (**www.mycommunicationlab.com**).

Title: [short, relevant, and attention-getting]
General purpose: your general aim (to inform, to persuade, to entertain)
Specific purpose: what you hope to achieve from this speech
Thesis: your main assertion: the core of your speech

Introduction

I. gain attention

II. establish S-A-T connection

III. orient audience

    A. first main point; same as I in body

    B. second main point; same as II in body

    C. third main point; same as III in body

connect the introduction to the
[Transition: body]

Body

I. first main point

    A. support of I (the first main point)

    B. further support for I

connect the first main point to
[Transition: the second]

II. second main point

    A. support for II (the second main point)

    B. further support for II

connect the second main point
[Transition: to the third]

III. third main point

    A. support for III (the third main point)

    B. further support for III

connect the third main point (or
[Transition: all main points) to the conclusion]

Conclusion

I. summary

    A. first main point; same as I in body

    B. second main point; same as II in body

    C. third main point; same as III in body

II. motivation

III. closure

References

Alphabetical list of sources cited

STEP 9: WORD YOUR SPEECH

You're a successful public speaker when your listeners create in their minds the meanings you want them to create. You're successful when your listeners adopt the attitudes and behaviors you want them to adopt. The language choices you make—the words you select and the sentences you form—will greatly influence the meanings your listeners receive and, thus, how successful you are.

Oral Style

Oral style is the quality of spoken language that differentiates it from written language. You do not speak as you write (Akinnaso, 1982). The words and sentences you use differ. The major reason for this difference is that you compose speech instantly. You select your words and construct your sentences as you think your thoughts. There's very little time between the thought and the utterance. When you

Public Speaking Sample Assistant

A Phrase/Key-Word Presentation Outline

Self-Disclosure

PAUSE!
LOOK OVER THE AUDIENCE!

Introduction

  I. We've heard them:
    A. I'm in love with my nephew.
    B. My husband is not my baby's father.
    C. I'm really a woman.
  II. We've all S-D.
    A. Sometimes +, −, significant
    B. consequences = better decisions.
  III. 3 parts: (WRITE ON BOARD)
    A. 1. nature of S-D
    B. 2. rewards
    C. 3. risks
[1st = type of communication.]
PAUSE, STEP FORWARD

Body

  I. S-D: communication
    A. about self
    B. new
    C. hidden information
[Knowing what self-disclosure is, now
    rewards.]
  II. 3 rewards.
    A. self-knowledge
    B. communication effectiveness
    C. physiological health

[Benefits substantial, there are also risks.]
PAUSE!
III. 3 risks
    A. personal
    B. relationship
    C. professional
[Summarize: S-D]

Conclusion

  I. S-D = communication.
    A. about self, new, and usually hidden
    B. rewards: increased self-knowledge,
      better communication, and improved
      health
    C. risks: personal, relational, and profes-
      sional
  II. S-D, not only interesting, it's vital
    A. Explore further "S-D" on www
    B. Scholarly: Sandra Petronio's
      Boundaries.
  III. Should you S-D?
    A. Yes
    B. No
    C. Maybe
PAUSE!
ANY QUESTIONS?

---

write, however, you compose your thoughts after considerable reflection. Even then you probably often rewrite and edit as you go along. Because of this, written language has a more formal tone. Spoken language is more informal, more colloquial.

Generally, spoken language consists of shorter, simpler, and more familiar words than does written language. Also, there's more qualification in speech than in writing. For example, when speaking you probably make greater use of such expressions as *although, however, perhaps*, and the like. When writing, you probably edit these out.

Spoken language has a greater number of self-reference terms (terms that refer to the speaker herself or himself): *I, me, our, us*, and *you*. Spoken language

also has a greater number of "allness" terms such as *all, none, every, always*, and *never*. When you write, you're probably more careful to edit out such allness terms, realizing that such terms often are not very descriptive of reality.

Spoken language has more pseudo-quantifying terms (for example, *many, much, very, lots*) and terms that include the speaker as part of the observation (for example, *It seems to me that* or *As I see it*). Further, speech contains more verbs and adverbs; writing contains more nouns and adjectives.

Spoken and written language not only *do* differ, they *should* differ. The main reason why spoken and written language should differ is that the listener hears speech only once; therefore, speech must be

ASK THE RESEARCHER

Making Myself Clear

I notice that some people are very good at getting their ideas across clearly, while others are quite confusing. I'd like to know some things the clear speakers are doing that confusing speakers often fail to do.

It's important to recognize that your listeners view your topic differently than you do. Your picture is clear, while theirs is blurry. So first, give listeners a general sense or overview of your topic. Tell them in general terms what you'll be discussing. Second, condense your topic to three or four main points—too many main points will only confuse an audience, especially if the topic is new to them.

Then, to truly make your topic clear and vivid to listeners, give examples, tell stories as illustrations, and use analogies, for example. Audiences like this, and it will enhance clarity, as long as listeners can see how these supporting materials relate to your topic. Third, begin with terms that are familiar to your audience before introducing terms or concepts that are new or unique to your topic. By the end of the speech, your audience's blurry sense of the topic will become clearer.

For further information: Chesebro, J. L. (2002). Teaching clearly. In J. L. Chesebro & J. C. McCroskey (Eds.), *Communication for teachers*. Boston: Allyn & Bacon. Also Civikly, J. M. (1992). Clarity: Teachers and students making sense of instruction. *Communication Education, 41*, 138-152. And Rowan, K. E. (2003). Informing and explaining skills: Theory and research on informative communication. In J. Green & B. Burleson (Eds.), *Handbook of communication and social interaction skills* (pp. 403-438). Mahwah, NJ: Erlbaum.

Joseph Chesebro (Ed.D., West Virginia University) is an assistant professor of communication at the State University of New York at Brockport. He teaches courses in interpersonal and organizational communication and conducts research on clear teaching and conversational sensitivity as an aspect of listening. He also plays drums.

instantly intelligible. The reader can reread an essay or look up an unfamiliar word; the reader can spend as much time as he or she wishes with the written page. The listener, in contrast, must move at the pace set by the speaker. The reader may reread a sentence or paragraph if there's a temporary attention lapse. The listener doesn't have this option.

Choosing Words

Choose carefully the words you use in your public speeches. Choose words to achieve clarity, vividness, appropriateness, a personal style, and forcefulness. At the same time that you work to achieve these qualities, be careful to avoid the common fallacies of language (see Table 1).

Clarity

Clarity in speaking style should be your primary goal. Here are some guidelines to help you make your speech clear.

Be Economical. Don't waste words. Notice the wasted words in such expressions as "at nine *a.m. in*

the morning," "we *first* began the discussion," "I *myself personally*," and "blue *in color*." By withholding the italicized terms you eliminate unnecessary words and move closer to a more economical and clearer style.

Use Specific Terms and Numbers. As we get more and more specific, we get a clearer and more detailed picture. Be specific. Don't say "dog" when you want your listeners to picture a St. Bernard. Don't say "car" when you want them to picture a limousine. The same is true of numbers. Don't say "earned a good salary" if you mean "earned $90,000 a year." Don't say "taxes will go up" when you mean "taxes will increase 7 percent."

Use Guide Phrases. Use guide phrases to help listeners see that you're moving from one idea to another—phrases such as "now that we have seen how . . . , let us consider how . . . ," and "my next argument. . . ." Terms such as *first, second, and also, although,* and *however* will help your audience follow your line of thinking.

Use Short, Familiar Terms. Generally, favor the short word over the long one. Favor the familiar

Table 1 Fallacies of Language

In listening to and critically evaluating speeches, look carefully for language fallacies—ways of using language that subvert instead of clarify truth and accuracy. In discussion of verbal messages, five such barriers to language accuracy were identified: polarization, fact–inference confusion, allness, static evaluation, and indiscrimination. Here are additional language fallacies, these focusing on words that mislead and give listeners the wrong impression. After you read these several fallacies, review some commercial websites for vitamins, clothing, books, music, or any such topic you're interested in and try to find examples of misleading language. It won't be difficult.

Fallacy	Examples	Critical Response
Weasel words are words whose meanings are slippery and difficult to pin down (Hayakawa & Hayakawa, 1990).	The medicine that claims to "work better than Brand X" doesn't specify how much better or in what respect it performs better. "Better" is a weasel word, as are "help," "virtually," "as much as," "like" (as in "it will make you feel like new"), and "more economical."	Ask yourself: Exactly what is being claimed? For example, "What does 'may reduce cholesterol' mean? What exactly is being asserted?"
Euphemisms make the negative and unpleasant appear positive and appealing. Often this inflated language makes the mundane seem extraordinary, the common seem exotic.	Euphemisms are all around, as in calling the firing of 200 workers "downsizing" or "reallocation of resources" or trumpeting "the vacation of a lifetime" or "unsurpassed vistas."	Don't let words get in the way of accurate firsthand perception. The word is *not* the thing; words merely symbolize the thing (sometimes inaccurately).
Jargon, the specialized language of a professional class, becomes a problem when used with those who are not professionals in the field.	The specialized languages of communication, computer, and psychology professionals offer clear examples of jargon: terms such as *content and relationship messages, blogosphere,* and *attribution*.	Don't be intimidated by jargon; ask questions when you don't understand.
Doublespeak is language used to confuse rather than inform.	Doublespeak is evident when someone uses technical or little-known words that confuse people who don't know the meanings of these words without defining them.	As with jargon, don't allow words to intimidate you; when in doubt, find out.
Gobbledygook is overly complex language that overwhelms the listener instead of communicating meaning.	Big and relatively uncommon words and foreign terms (especially Latin or French) are examples of gobbledygook.	Don't confuse complex language with truth or accuracy; ask for simplification when appropriate.

word over the unfamiliar word. Favor the more commonly used term over the rarely used term.

Here are a few examples:

Poor Choices	Better Choices
innocuous	*harmless*
elucidate	*clarify*
utilize	*use*
ascertain	*find out*
erstwhile	*former*
eschew	*avoid*
expenditure	*cost or expense*

Carefully Assess Idioms. Idioms are expressions that are unique to a specific language and whose meaning cannot be deduced from the individual words used. Expressions such as "kick the bucket," or "doesn't have a leg to stand on" are idioms: Either you know the meaning of the expression or you don't; you can't figure it out from only a knowledge of the individual words.

The positive side of idioms is that they give your speech a casual and informal air; they make your speech sound like a speech and not like a written essay. The negative side of idioms is that they create problems for listeners who are not native speakers of your language. Many non-native speakers will simply not understand the meaning of your idioms. This problem is especially important because audiences are becoming increasingly intercultural and because the number of idioms we use is extremely high.

Distinguish between Commonly Confused Words. Many words, because they sound alike or are used in similar situations, are commonly confused. Try the self-test below, which covers 10 of the most frequently confused words.

TEST YOURSELF

Can You Distinguish between Commonly Confused Words?

Underline the word in parentheses that you would use in each sentence.

_____ 1. She (accepted, excepted) the award and thanked everyone (accept, except) the producer.

_____ 2. The teacher (affected, effected) his students greatly and will now (affect, effect) an entirely new curriculum.

_____ 3. Are you deciding (between, among) red and green or (between, among) red, green, and blue?

_____ 4. I've scaled higher mountains than this, so I'm sure I (can, may) scale this one; I and a few others know the hidden path, but I (can, may) not reveal this.

_____ 5. The table was (cheap, inexpensive) but has great style; the chairs cost a fortune but look (cheap, inexpensive).

_____ 6. We (discover, invent) uncharted lands but (discover, invent) computer programs.

_____ 7. He was direct and (explicit, implicit) in his denial of the crime but was vague and only (explicit, implicit) concerning his whereabouts.

_____ 8. She (implied, inferred) that she'd seek a divorce; we can only (imply, infer) her reasons.

_____ 9. The wedding was (tasteful, tasty) and the food (tasteful, tasty).

_____ 10. The student seemed (disinterested, uninterested) in the lecture. The teacher was (disinterested, uninterested) in who received what grades.

HOW DID YOU DO? Here are the principles that govern correct usage: (1) Use *accept* to mean "receive" and *except* to mean with "the exclusion of." (2) Use *to affect* to mean "to have an effect on or to influence," and *to effect* to mean "to produce a result." (3) Use *between* when referring to two items and *among* when referring to more than two items. (4) Use *can* to refer to ability and *may* to refer to

permission. (5) Use *cheap* to refer to something that is inferior and *inexpensive* to something that costs little. (6) Use *discover* to refer to the act of finding something out or learning something previously unknown, but use *invent* to refer to the act of originating something new. (7) Use *explicit* to mean "directly stated" and *implicit* to indicate the act of expressing something without actually stating it. (8) Use *imply* to mean "state indirectly" and *infer* to mean "draw a conclusion." (9) Use *tasteful* to refer to good taste, but use *tasty* to refer to something that tastes good. (10) Use *uninterested* to indicate a lack of interest and use *disinterested* to mean "objective" or "unbiased."

WHAT WILL YOU DO? Your use of language can greatly enhance (or detract from) your persuasiveness. A word used incorrectly can lessen your credibility and general persuasiveness. Review your English handbook and identify other commonly confused words. Get into the habit of referring to a good dictionary whenever you have doubts about which word is preferred.

Vividness

Select words to make your ideas vivid and to help your arguments come alive in the minds of your listeners. To achieve **vividness**, use active verbs, strong verbs, figures of speech, and imagery.

Use Active Verbs. Favor verbs that communicate activity rather than passivity. The verb *to be*, in all its forms—*is, are, was, were, will be*—is relatively inactive. Try using verbs of action instead. Rather than saying "The teacher was in the middle of the crowd," say "The teacher stood in the middle of the crowd." Instead of saying "The report was on the president's desk for three days," try "The report rested [or slept] on the president's desk for three days." Instead of saying "Management will be here tomorrow," consider "Management will descend on us tomorrow" or "Management jets in tomorrow."

Use Strong Verbs. The verb is the strongest part of your sentence. Choose verbs carefully, and choose them so they accomplish a lot. Instead of saying "He walked through the forest," consider such terms as *wandered, prowled, rambled,* or *roamed.* Consider whether one of these might not better suit your intended meaning. Consult a thesaurus for any verb you suspect might be weak.

Use Figures of Speech. Figures of speech help achieve vividness, in addition to making your speech more memorable and giving it a polished, well-crafted tone. **Figures of speech** are stylistic devices that have been a part of rhetoric since ancient times. Here are some of the major figures of speech; you may wish to incorporate a few of these into your next speech.

- *Alliteration* is the repetition of the same initial sound in two or more words, as in "fifty famous flavors" or the "cool, calculating leader."

- *Hyperbole* is the use of extreme exaggeration, as in "He cried like a faucet" or "I'm so hungry I could eat a whale."

- *Irony* is the use of a word or sentence whose literal meaning is the opposite of the message actually conveyed; for example, a teacher handing back failing examinations might say, "So pleased to see how many of you studied so hard."

- *Metaphor* compares two unlike things by stating that one thing "is" the other, as in "She's a lion when she wakes up" or "He's a real bulldozer."

- *Synecdoche* is the use of a part of an object to stand for the whole object, as in "All hands were on deck" (where "hands" stands for "sailor" or "crew member") or "green thumb" for "expert gardener."

- *Metonymy* is the substitution of a name for a title with which it's closely associated, as in "City Hall issued the following news release," in which "City Hall" stands for "the mayor" or "the city council."

- *Antithesis* is the presentation of contrary ideas in parallel form, as in "My loves are many, my enemies are few." Charles Dickens's opening words in *A Tale of Two Cities* are a famous antithesis: "It was the best of times; it was the worst of times."

- *Simile*, like metaphor, compares two unlike objects; but simile explicitly uses the words *like* or *as*; for example, "The manager is as gentle as an ox."

- *Personification* is the attribution of human characteristics to inanimate objects, as in "This room cries for activity" or "My car is tired and wants a drink."

- *Rhetorical questions* are questions used to make a statement or to produce a desired effect rather than to secure an answer, as in "Do you want to be popular?" "Do you want to get well?"

Use Imagery. Appeal to the senses, especially your listeners' visual, auditory, and tactile senses. Make your audience see, hear, and feel what you're talking about.

In describing people or objects, create word "pictures" or *visual imagery*. When appropriate, describe such visual qualities as height, weight, color, size, shape, length, and contour. Let your audience see the sweat pouring down the faces of the coal miners; let them see the short, overweight, cigar-smoking executive in his pin-striped suit.

Use *auditory imagery* to describe sounds; let your listeners hear the car's tires screeching, the wind whistling, the bells chiming, the angry professor roaring.

Use terms referring to temperature, texture, and touch to create *tactile imagery*. Let your listeners feel the cool water running over their bodies or the punch of the prizefighter; let them feel the smooth skin of the newborn baby.

Appropriateness

Use language that is appropriate to you as the speaker—and that is appropriate to your audience, the occasion, and the speech topic. Here are some general guidelines to help you achieve **appropriateness**.

Speak on the Appropriate Level of Formality.
The most effective public speaking style is less formal than the written essay, but more formal than conversation. One way to achieve an informal style is to use contractions. Say *don't* instead of *do not*, *I'll* instead of *I shall*, and *wouldn't* instead of *would not*. Contractions give a public speech the sound and rhythm of conversation, a quality that most listeners react to favorably. Also, use personal pronouns rather than impersonal expressions. Say "I found" instead of "It has been found," or "I will present three arguments" instead of "Three arguments will be presented."

Avoid Unfamiliar Terms.
Avoid using terms the audience doesn't know. Avoid foreign and technical terms unless you're certain the audience is familiar with them. Similarly, avoid **jargon** (the technical vocabulary of a specialized field) unless you're sure the meanings are clear to your listeners. Some acronyms (such as NATO, UN, NOW, and CORE) are probably familiar to most audiences; many, however, are not. When you wish to use any specialized terms or abbreviations, explain their meaning fully to the audience.

Avoid Slang.
Slang is language that is used by special groups but is generally considered impolite or not quite proper. *Webster's New World College Dictionary* defines *slang* as "highly informal speech that is outside conventional or standard usage and consists both of coined words and phrases and of new or extended meanings attached to established terms." Generally, it's best to avoid slang, which may offend or embarrass your audience. Although your listeners may use slang interpersonally, they probably don't want to hear it in a relatively formal situation such as public speaking. If you're in doubt about whether a word is considered slang, consult a dictionary; usually, dictionaries identify slang terms as "informal."

MEDIA WATCH
HATE SPEECH

It is not only true that the language we use puts words in our mouths; it also puts notions in our heads.

—*Wendell Johnson*

Hate speech is speech that is hostile, offensive, degrading, or intimidating to a particular group of people. Women, African Americans, Muslims, Jews, Asians, Hispanics, and gay men and lesbians are among the major targets in the United States.

Hate speech occurs in all forms of human communication; it occurs when people utter insults to someone passing by; when posters and fliers degrade specific groups; when radio talk shows denigrate members of certain groups; when computer games are reconfigured to target members of certain groups; or when websites insult, demean, and encourage hostility toward certain groups. Because the media reach so many people and are so powerful in influencing opinions, the issue of hate speech in the media takes on special importance (Ruscher, 2001).

One of the difficulties in attacking hate speech is that it's often difficult to draw a clear line between speech that is protected by the First Amendment right to freedom of expression but is simply at odds with the majority viewpoint and speech that is designed to denigrate members of

certain groups and encourage hostility against them.

Some colleges are instituting hate speech codes—written statements of what constitutes hate speech as well as enumerations of the penalties for hate speech. Proponents of such codes argue that they teach students that hate speech is unacceptable, is harmful to all people (but especially to those who are the targets of such attacks), and may be curtailed in the same way as other undesirable acts (such as child pornography or rape). Opponents argue that such codes do not address the underlying prejudices and biases that give rise to hate speech and that the codes stifle free expression and may be used unfairly by the majority to silence minority opinion and dissent.

Increasing Media Literacy

Search for "hate speech" and "campus codes," or take a look at "The Price of Free Speech" at **www.scu.edu/ethics/ publications/iie/v5n2/codes.html**, *for a review of the arguments for and against hate speech codes. After reading about hate speech and hate codes, formulate your own position on campus codes for hate speech. With this position in mind, examine a few media in terms of their own policies regarding hate speech.*

Avoid Ethnic Expressions (Generally). Racist, heterosexist, ageist, or sexist terms can only insult the audience members themselves or people they know and care about. So avoid these terms at all costs. In addition, however, avoid ethnic expressions, at least generally. Ethnic expressions are words and phrases that are peculiar to a particular ethnic group. At times these expressions are known only by members of the ethnic group; at other times they may be known more widely but still recognized as ethnic expressions.

When you are speaking to a multicultural audience, it's generally best to avoid ethnic expressions unless they're integral to your speech and you explain them. Such expressions are often interpreted as exclusionist; they highlight the connection between the speaker and the members of that particular ethnic group and the lack of connection between the speaker and all others who are not members of that ethnic group. And, of course, ethnic expressions should never be used if you're not a member of the ethnic group.

If, on the other hand, you're speaking to people who all belong to one ethnic group and if you're also a member, then such expressions are fine. In fact, they may well prove effective; being part of the common language of speaker and audience, they can help you stress your own similarities with the audience.

Personal Style

Audiences favor speakers who speak in a personal rather than an impersonal style, who speak with them rather than at them. You can achieve a more **personal style** by using personal pronouns, asking questions, and creating immediacy.

Use Personal Pronouns. Say *I*, *me*, *he*, *she*, and *you*. Avoid impersonal expressions such as *one* (as in "One is led to believe . . ."), *this speaker*, or *you, the listeners*. These expressions distance the audience and create barriers rather than bridges.

Use Questions. Ask the audience questions to involve them. In a small audience, you might even briefly entertain responses. In larger audiences, you might ask the question, pause to allow the audience time to consider their responses, and then move on. When you direct questions to your listeners, they feel a part of the public speaking transaction.

Create Immediacy. Immediacy is a connectedness, a relatedness with one's listeners. Immediacy is the opposite of disconnectedness and separation. Here are some suggestions for creating immediacy through language:

- Use personal examples.
- Use terms that include both you and the audience; for example, *we* and *our*.
- Address the audience directly; say *you* rather than *students*; say "You'll enjoy reading" instead of "Everyone will enjoy reading"; say "I want you to see" instead of "I want people to see."
- Use specific names of audience members when appropriate.
- Express concern for the audience members.
- Reinforce or compliment the audience.
- Refer directly to commonalities between you and the audience; for example, "We are all children of immigrants" or "We all want to see our team in the playoffs."
- Refer to shared experiences and goals; for example, "We all want, we all need, a more responsive PTA."
- Recognize audience feedback and refer to it in your speech. Say, for example, "I can see from your expressions that we're all anxious to get to our immediate problem."

Forcefulness/Power

Forceful or powerful language will help you achieve your purpose, whether it be informative or persuasive. **Forcefulness** in language enables you to direct the audience's attention, thoughts, and feelings. To make your speech more forceful, eliminate weakeners, vary intensity, and avoid overused expressions.

Eliminate Weakeners. Delete **weakeners**, or phrases that weaken your sentences. Among the major weakeners are uncertainty expressions and weak modifiers. Uncertainty expressions such as "I'm not sure of this, but"; "Perhaps it might"; or "Maybe it works this way" communicate a lack of commitment and conviction and will make your audience wonder if you're worth listening to. Weak modifiers such as "It works pretty well," "It's kind of like," or "It may be the one we want" make you seem unsure and indefinite about what you're saying.

Cut out any unnecessary verbiage that reduces the impact of your meaning. Instead of saying "There are lots of things we can do to help," say "We can do lots of things to help." Instead of saying "I'm sorry to be so graphic, but Senator Bingsley's proposal . . . ," say "We need to be graphic. Senator Bingsley's proposal. . . ." Instead of saying, "It should be observed in this connection that, all things considered, money is not productive of happiness," say "Money doesn't bring happiness."

Here are a few additional suggestions—which, of course, are not limited in application to public speaking but relate as well to interpersonal and small group communication.

- Avoid hesitations ("I, er, want to say that, ah, this one is, er, the best, you know"); they make you sound unprepared and uncertain.
- Avoid using too many intensifiers ("Really, this was the greatest; it was truly phenomenal"); audiences will begin to doubt the speaker who goes overboard with the superlatives.
- Avoid tag questions ("I'll review the report now, okay?" "That is a great proposal, don't you think?"); they signal your need for approval and your own uncertainty and lack of conviction.
- Avoid self-critical statements ("I'm not very good at this," "This is my first speech"); they signal a lack of confidence and make public your sense of inadequacy.
- Avoid slang and vulgar expressions; they may signal low social class and hence little power.

Table 2 identifies a variety of suggestions for nonverbal action that will also help you to communicate forcefulness and power.

Vary Intensity as Appropriate. Just as you can vary your voice in intensity, you can also phrase your ideas with different degrees of stylistic intensity. You can, for example, refer to an action as "failing to support our position" or as "stabbing us in the back"; you can say that a new proposal will "endanger our goals" or will "destroy us completely"; you can refer to a child's behavior as "playful," "creative," or "destructive." Vary your language to express different degrees of intensity—from mild through neutral to extremely intense.

Avoid Bromides and Clichés. Bromides are trite sayings that are worn out because of constant usage. A few examples:

- Honesty is the best policy.
- If I can't do it well, I won't do it at all.
- I don't understand modern art, but I know what I like.

Table 2 Powerful Bodily Action

Here are some nonverbal behaviors that are likely to help you communicate power in public speaking (Lewis, 1989; Burgoon & Bacue, 2003; Burgoon & Hoobler, 2002; Guerrero, DeVito, & Hecht, 1999):

Suggestions for Communicating Power with Bodily Action	Reasons
While speaking, avoid self-manipulations (playing with your hair or touching your face, for example); avoid leaning backward.	These signals communicate a lack of comfort and an ill-at-ease feeling and are likely to damage your persuasiveness.
Walk slowly and deliberately to and from the podium.	To appear hurried is to appear powerless, as if you were rushing to meet the expectations of those who have power over you.
Use facial expressions and gestures as appropriate.	These help you express your concern for the audience and for the interaction and help you communicate your comfort and control of the situation.
Use consistent packaging; be careful that your verbal and nonverbal messages do not contradict each other.	Inconsistency between verbal and nonverbal messages will be seen as uncertainty and a lack of conviction.

When we hear these hackneyed statements, we recognize them as unoriginal and uninspired.

Clichés are phrases that have lost their novelty and part of their meaning through overuse. Clichés call attention to themselves because of their overuse. Here are some examples of clichés to avoid:

- in this day and age
- tell it like it is
- free as a bird
- in the pink
- no sooner said than done
- it goes without saying
- few and far between
- over the hill
- no news is good news
- the life of the party
- keep your shirt on

Phrasing Sentences

Give the same careful consideration that you give to words to the sentences of your speech as well. Some guidelines follow.

Use Short Sentences

Short sentences are more forceful and economical. They are also easier for your audience to comprehend and remember. Listeners don't have the time or the inclination to unravel long and complex sentences. Help them to listen more efficiently. Use short rather than long sentences.

Use Direct Sentences

Direct sentences are easier to understand. They are also more forceful. Instead of saying "I want to tell you of the three main reasons why we should not adopt Program A," say "We should not adopt Program A. There are three main reasons."

Use Active Sentences

Active sentences—that is, sentences whose verbs are in the active voice—are easier to understand than passive ones. They also make your speech seem livelier and more vivid. Instead of saying "The lower court's decision was reversed by the Supreme Court," say "The Supreme Court reversed the lower court's decision." Instead of saying "The proposal was favored by management," say "Management favored the proposal."

Use Positive Sentences

Sentences phrased positively are easier to comprehend and remember than sentences phrased negatively. Notice how sentences *a* and *c* are easier to understand than sentences *b* and *d*:

a. The committee rejected the proposal.
b. The committee did not accept the proposal.
c. This committee works outside the normal company hierarchy.
d. This committee does not work within the normal company hierarchy.

Vary the Types of Sentences

The preceding advice to use short, direct, active, positive sentences is valid most of the time. Yet too many sentences of the same type or length will make your speech sound boring. So follow (generally) the preceding advice, but add variations as well.

STEP 10: REHEARSE AND PRESENT YOUR SPEECH

Your last step is to rehearse and present your speech. Let's look first at rehearsal.

Rehearsal

Use your rehearsal time effectively and efficiently for the following purposes:

- To develop a delivery that will help you achieve the objectives of your speech.
- To time your speech; if you time your rehearsals, you'll be able to see if you can add material or if you have to delete something.
- To see how the speech will flow as a whole and to make any changes and improvements you think necessary.
- To test the presentation aids, and to detect and resolve any technical problems.
- To learn the speech thoroughly.
- To reduce any feelings of apprehension and gain confidence.

The following procedures should assist you in achieving these goals.

Rehearse the Speech as a Whole

Rehearse the speech from beginning to end, not in parts. Rehearse it from getting out of your seat through the introduction, body, and conclusion, to returning to your seat. Be sure to rehearse the speech with all the examples and illustrations (and any audiovisual aids) included. This will enable you to connect the parts of the speech and see how they interact.

Time the Speech

Time the speech during each rehearsal. Make the necessary adjustments on the basis of this timing. If you're using computer presentation software, you'll be able to time your speech very precisely. Also time the individual parts of your speech so you can achieve the balance you want—for example, you might want to spend twice as much time on the solutions as on the problems, or you might want to balance the introduction and conclusion so that each portion constitutes about 10 percent of your speech.

Approximate the Actual Speech Situation

Rehearse the speech under conditions as close as possible to those under which you'll deliver it. If possible, rehearse the speech in the same room in which you'll

© image100/age fotostock

TIME PROBLEM

Your speech has run overtime and you've been given the 30-second stop signal. You wonder if it would be best to ignore the signal and just continue your speech or if you should wrap up in 30 seconds? In either case,

WHAT DO YOU SAY?

present it. If this is impossible, try to simulate the actual conditions as closely as you can—even in your living room or bathroom. If possible, rehearse the speech in front of a few supportive listeners. It's always helpful (and especially for your beginning speeches) that your listeners be supportive rather than too critical. Merely having listeners present during your rehearsal will further simulate the conditions under which you'll eventually speak. Get together with two or three other students in an empty classroom where you can take turns as speakers and listeners.

See Yourself as a Speaker

Rehearse the speech in front of a full-length mirror. This will enable you to see yourself and see how you'll appear to the audience. This may be extremely difficult at first, and you may have to force yourself to watch. After a few attempts, however, you'll begin to see the value of this experience. Practice your eye contact, your movements, and your gestures in front of the mirror.

Incorporate Changes and Make Delivery Notes

Make any needed changes in the speech between rehearsals. Do not interrupt your rehearsal to make notes or changes; if you do, you may never experience the entire speech from beginning to end. While making these changes note any words whose pronunciation you wish to check. Also, insert pause notations, "slow down" warnings, and other delivery suggestions into your outline.

If possible, record your speech (ideally, on videotape) so you can hear exactly what your listeners will hear: your volume, rate, pitch, pronunciation, and pauses. You'll thus be in a better position to improve these qualities.

Rehearse Often

Rehearse the speech as often as seems necessary. Two useful guides are: (1) Rehearse the speech at least three or four times; less rehearsal than this is sure to be too little. (2) Rehearse the speech as long as your rehearsals continue to result in improvements in the speech or in your delivery. Some suggestions for a long-term delivery improvement program are presented next.

Undertake a Long-Term Delivery Improvement Program

To become a truly effective speaker, you may need to undertake a long-term delivery improvement program. Approach this project with a positive attitude: Tell yourself that you can do it and that you will do it.

1. First, seek feedback from someone whose opinion and insight you respect. Your public speaking instructor may be a logical choice, but someone majoring in communication or working in a communication field might also be appropriate. Get an honest and thorough appraisal of both your voice and your bodily action.

2. Learn to hear, see, and feel the differences between effective and ineffective patterns. For example, is your pitch too high or your volume too loud? A tape recorder will be very helpful. Learn to feel your rigid posture or your lack of arm and hand gestures. Once you've perceived these voice and/or body patterns, concentrate on learning more effective habits. Practice a few minutes each day. Avoid becoming too conscious of any source of ineffectiveness. Just try to increase your awareness and work on one problem at a time. Do not try to change all your patterns at once.

3. Seek additional feedback on the changes. Make certain that listeners agree that the new patterns you're practicing really are more effective. Remember that you hear yourself through bone conduction as well as through air transmission. Others hear you only through air transmission. So what you hear and what others hear will be different.

4. For voice improvement, consult a book on voice and diction for practice exercises and for additional information on the nature of volume, rate, pitch, and quality.

5. If difficulties persist, see a professional. For voice problems, see a speech clinician. Most campuses have a speech clinic, and you can easily avail yourself of its services. For bodily action difficulties, talk with your public speaking instructor.

6. Seek professional help if you're psychologically uncomfortable with any aspect of your voice or bodily action. It may be that all you have to do is to hear yourself or see yourself on a videotape—as others hear and see you—to convince yourself that you sound and look just fine. Regardless of what is causing this discomfort, however, if you're uncomfortable, do something about it. In a college community there's more assistance available to you at no cost than you'll ever be offered again. Make use of it.

Presenting Your Speech

If you're like most students, presenting your speech creates more anxiety for you than any other aspect of public speaking. Few speakers worry about organization or audience analysis or style. Many worry about presentation, so you have lots of company. In this section we'll examine general methods and principles of effectiveness in presentation that you can adapt to your own personality.

Methods of Presentation

Speakers vary widely in their methods of presentation. Some speak off-the-cuff, with no apparent preparation; others read their speeches from manuscript. Some memorize their speeches word for word; others construct a detailed outline, rehearse often, then speak extemporaneously.

Speaking Impromptu. In an **impromptu speech** you talk without any specific preparation. You and the topic meet for the first time and immediately the speech begins. On some occasions you will not be able to avoid speaking impromptu. For example, in a classroom, after someone has spoken, you might give a brief impromptu speech of evaluation. In asking or answering questions in an interview situation, you're giving impromptu speeches, albeit extremely short ones. At a meeting, you may find yourself explaining a proposal or defending a plan of action; these too are impromptu speeches. Of course, impromptu speeches don't permit attention to the details of public speaking such as audience adaptation, research, and style.

Speaking from Manuscript. In a **manuscript speech** you read aloud the entire speech, which you've written out word for word. The manuscript

AUDIENCE INACTIVITY

You're giving a speech on the problems of teenage drug abuse and you notice that the entire back rows of your audience have totally tuned you out; they're reading, chatting, working on their laptops.

WHAT DO YOU SAY?

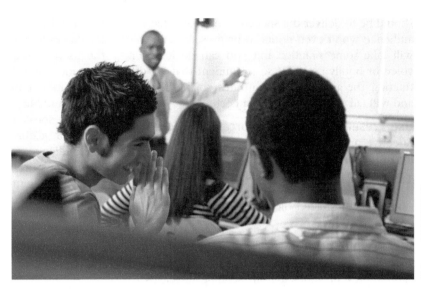

© image100/CORBIS

speech allows you to control the timing precisely—a particularly important benefit when you are delivering a speech that will be recorded (on television, for example). Also, there's no risk of forgetting, no danger of being unable to find the right word. Another feature of the manuscript method is that it allows you to use the exact wording that you (or a team of speechwriters) want. In the political arena, this is often crucial. And, of course, because the speech is already written out, you can distribute copies and are therefore less likely to be misquoted.

Many audiences, however, don't like speakers to read their speeches, except perhaps with TelePromp-Ters on television. In face-to-face situations, audiences generally prefer speakers who interact with them. Reading a manuscript makes it difficult to respond to listener feedback. You cannot easily make adjustments on the basis of feedback. And with the manuscript on a stationary lectern, as it most often is, it's impossible for you to move around.

Speaking from Memory. In a **memorized speech** you write out the speech word for word (as in the manuscript method); but instead of reading it, you then commit the speech to memory and recite it or "act it out." Speaking from memory allows you freedom to move about and otherwise concentrate on delivery. It doesn't, however, allow easy adjusting to feedback, and you thus lose one of the main advantages of face-to-face contact.

One potential problem with this method is the risk of forgetting your speech. In a memorized speech, each sentence cues the recall of the following sentence. Thus, when you forget one sentence, you may forget the rest of the speech. This danger, along with the natural nervousness that speakers feel, makes the memorizing method a poor choice in most situations.

Speaking Extemporaneously. An **extemporaneous speech** involves thorough preparation but no commitment to the exact wording to be used during the speech. It often involves memorizing your opening lines (perhaps the first few sentences), your closing lines (perhaps the last few sentences), and your main points and the order in which you'll present them. You can also, if you wish, memorize selected phrases, sentences, or quotations. Memorizing the opening and closing lines will help you to focus your complete attention on the audience and will also put you more at ease. Once you know exactly what you'll say in opening and closing the speech, you'll feel more in control.

The extemporaneous method is useful in most speaking situations. Good college lecturers use the extemporaneous method. They prepare thoroughly and know what they want to say and in what order they want to say it, but they've made no commitment to exact wording. This method allows you to respond easily to feedback. Should a point need clarification, you can elaborate on it at the moment when it will be most effective. This method makes it easy to be natural, too, because you're being yourself. It's the method that comes closest to conversation. With the extemporaneous method, you can move about and interact with the audience.

Making Your Presentation More Effective

Strive for a presentation that is natural, reinforces the message, is varied, and has a conversational tone.

Be Natural. Listeners will enjoy and believe you more if you speak naturally, as if you were conversing with a small group of people. Don't allow your delivery to call attention to itself. Your ultimate aim

169

should be to deliver the speech so naturally that the audience won't even notice your presentation. This will take some practice, but you can do it. When voice or bodily action is so prominent that it's distracting, the audience concentrates on the delivery and will fail to attend to your speech.

Use Presentation to Reinforce Your Message.
Effective presentation should aid instant intelligibility. Your main objective is to make your ideas understandable to an audience. A voice that listeners have to strain to hear, a decrease in volume at the ends of sentences, or slurred diction will obviously hinder comprehension.

Dress Appropriately.
When you give a public speech, everything about you communicates. You cannot prevent yourself from sending messages to others. The way in which you dress is no exception. In fact, your attire will figure significantly in the way your audience assesses your credibility and even the extent to which they give you attention. In short, the way you present yourself physically will influence your effectiveness in all forms of persuasive and informative speaking. Unfortunately, there are no rules that will apply to all situations for all speakers. Thus, only general guidelines are offered here. Modify and tailor these for yourself and for each unique situation.

- Avoid extremes: Don't allow your clothes, hairstyle, and so on to detract attention from what you're saying.
- Dress comfortably: Be both physically and psychologically comfortable with your appearance so that you can concentrate your energies on what you're saying.
- Dress appropriately: Your appearance should be consistent with the specific public speaking occasion.

Vary Your Presentation.
Listening to a speech is hard work for the audience. Flexible and varied presentation eases the listeners' task. Be especially careful to avoid **monotonous patterns** and **predictable patterns**.

Speakers who are monotonous keep their voices at the same pitch, volume, and rate throughout the speech. The monotonous speaker maintains a uniform level from the introduction to the conclusion. Like the drone of a motor, this easily puts the audience to sleep. Vary your pitch levels, your volume, and your rate of speaking. In a similar way, avoid monotony in bodily action. Avoid standing in exactly the same position throughout the speech. Use your body to express your ideas, to communicate to the audience what is going on in your head.

A predictable vocal pattern is a pattern in which, for example, the volume levels vary but always in the same sequence. Through repetition, the sequence soon becomes predictable. For example, each sentence may begin loud and then decline to a barely audible volume. In bodily action, the predictable speaker repeatedly uses the same movements or gestures. For example, a speaker may scan the audience from left to right to left to right throughout the entire speech. If the audience can predict the pattern of your voice or your bodily action, your speech will almost surely be ineffective. A patterned and predictable delivery will draw the audience's attention away from what you're saying.

Be Conversational.
Although more formal than conversation, presentation in public speaking should have some of the most important features of conversation. These qualities include immediacy, eye contact, expressiveness, and responsiveness to feedback.

Just as you can create a sense of immediacy through language, as discussed earlier, you can also create it with your presentation. Make your listeners feel that you're talking directly and individually to each of them. You can communicate immediacy through delivery in a number of ways:

- Maintain appropriate eye contact with the audience members.
- Maintain a physical closeness that reinforces a psychological closeness; don't stand behind a desk or lectern.
- Smile.
- Move around a bit; avoid the appearance of being too scared to move.
- Stand with a direct and open body posture.
- Talk directly to your audience, not to your notes or to your visual aids.

When you maintain eye contact, you make the public speaking interaction more conversational (in addition to communicating immediacy). Look directly into your listeners' eyes. Lock eyes with different audience members for short periods.

When you're expressive, you communicate genuine involvement in the public speaking situation. You can communicate this quality of expressiveness, of involvement, in several ways:

- Express responsibility for your own thoughts and feelings.
- Vary your vocal rate, pitch, volume, and rhythm to communicate involvement and interest in the audience and in the topic.

- Allow your facial muscles and your entire body to reflect and echo this inner involvement.

- Use gestures appropriately; too few gestures may signal lack of interest, but too many can communicate uneasiness, awkwardness, or anxiety.

Read carefully the feedback signals sent by your audience. Then respond to these signals with verbal, vocal, and bodily adjustments. For example, respond to audience feedback signals communicating lack of comprehension or inability to hear with added explanation or increased volume.

Avoid Common Mistakes. Be sure to avoid the frequently made mistakes that detract from the power of your speech. Here are a few:

- Don't start your speech immediately. Instead, survey your audience; make eye contact and engage their attention. Stand in front of the audience with a sense of control. Pause briefly, then begin speaking.

- Don't display any discomfort or displeasure. When you walk to the speaker's stand, display enthusiasm and your desire to speak. People much prefer listening to a speaker who seems to enjoy speaking to them.

- Don't race away from the speaker's stand once you've finished your presentation. After your last statement, pause, maintain audience eye contact, and then walk (don't run) to your seat. Show no signs of relief; focus your attention on whatever activity is taking place, glance over the audience, and sit down. If a question period follows your speech and you're in charge of this, pause after completing your conclusion. Ask audience members in a direct manner if they have any questions. If there's a chairperson who will ask for questions, pause after your conclusion, then nonverbally signal to the chairperson that you're ready.

Use Notes Appropriately. For many speeches, it may be helpful to use notes. A few simple guidelines may help you avoid some of the common errors made in using notes.

- Keep notes to a minimum. The fewer notes you take with you, the better off you will be. The reason so many speakers bring notes with them is that they want to avoid the face-to-face interaction required. With experience, however, you should find this face-to-face interaction the best part of the public speaking experience.

- Resist the normal temptation to bring with you the entire speech outline. You may rely on it too heavily and lose the direct contact with the audi-

ence. Instead, compose a delivery outline, as discussed earlier in this unit, using only key words. Bring this to the lectern with you—one side of an index card or at most an 8 1/2-by-11-inch sheet should be sufficient. This will relieve any anxiety over the possibility of forgetting your speech but will not be extensive enough to interfere with direct contact with your audience.

- Don't make your notes more obvious than necessary, but at the same time don't try to hide them. For example, don't gesture with your notes—but don't turn away from the audience to steal glances at them, either. Use them openly and honestly but gracefully, with "open subtlety." To do this effectively, you'll have to know your notes intimately. Rehearse with the same notes that you will take with you to the speaker's stand.

- When referring to your notes, pause to examine them; then regain eye contact with the audience and continue your speech. Don't read from your notes, just take cues from them. The one exception to this guideline is an extensive quotation or complex set of statistics that you have to read; immediately after reading, however, resume direct eye contact with the audience.

Voice

Three dimensions of voice are significant to the public speaker: volume, rate, and pitch. Your manipulation of these elements will enable you to control your voice to maximum advantage.

Vocal Volume. *Vocal volume* is the relative intensity of the voice. (Loudness, on the other hand, refers to hearers' perception of that relative intensity.) In an adequately controlled voice, volume will vary according to several factors. For example, the distance between speaker and listener, the competing noise, and the emphasis the speaker wishes to give an idea will all influence volume.

Problems with volume are easy to identify in others, though difficult to recognize in ourselves. One obvious problem is a voice that is too soft. When speech is so soft that listeners have to strain to hear, they will soon tire of expending so much energy. A voice that is too loud can also prove disturbing, because it intrudes on our psychological space. However, it's interesting to note that a voice louder than normal communicates assertiveness (Page & Balloun, 1978) and will lead people to pay greater attention to you (Robinson & McArthur, 1982). On the other hand, it can also communicate aggressiveness and give others the impression that you'd be difficult to get along with.

171

The most common problem is too little volume variation. Also, as mentioned earlier, a related problem is a volume pattern that, although varied, varies in an easily predictable way. If the audience can predict the pattern of volume changes, they will focus on that pattern and not on what you're saying.

A speaker who tends to fade away at the end of sentences is particularly disturbing to the audience. Here the speaker uses a volume that is largely appropriate but speaks the last few words of sentences at an extremely low volume. Be particularly careful when finishing sentences; make sure the audience is able to hear you without difficulty.

If you're using a microphone, test it first. Whether it's the kind that clips around your neck, the kind you hold in your hand, or the kind that is stationed at the podium, try it out first. Some speakers use the hand microphone as a prop and flip it in the air or from hand to hand as they emphasize a particular point. For your beginning speeches, it's probably best to avoid such techniques and to use the microphone as unobtrusively as you can.

Vocal Rate. Your *vocal rate* is the speed at which you speak. About 150 words per minute seems average for speaking as well as for reading aloud. Rate problems include speaking too fast, too slowly, with too little variation, or with too predictable a pattern. If you talk too fast, you deprive your listeners of time

they need to understand and digest what you're saying. If the rate is extreme, the listeners will simply not be willing to expend the energy needed to understand your speech.

If your rate is too slow, it will encourage your listeners' thoughts to wander to matters unrelated to your speech. Be careful, therefore, neither to bore the audience by presenting information at too slow a rate, nor to set a pace that is too rapid for listeners to absorb. Strike a happy medium. Speak at a pace that engages the listeners and allows them time for reflection but without boring them.

As with volume, rate variations may be underused or totally absent. If you speak at the same rate throughout the entire speech, you're not making use of this important speech asset. Use variations in rate to call attention to certain points and to add variety. For example, if you describe the dull routine of an assembly line worker in a rapid and varied pace or evoke the wonder of a circus in a pace with absolutely no variation, you're surely misusing this important vocal dimension. Again, if you're interested in and conscious of what you're saying, your rate variations should flow naturally and effectively. Too predictable a pattern of rate variations is sometimes as bad as no variation at all. If the audience can predict—consciously or unconsciously—your rate pattern, you're in a vocal rut. You're not communicating ideas but reciting words you've memorized.

Theory and Research   Speech Rate

UNDERSTANDING

You've probably noticed that advertisers and salespeople generally talk at a rate faster than normal speech. But is this effective? Are people who speak faster more persuasive? The answer is: It depends (Smith & Shaffer, 1991, 1995). The rapid speaker who speaks *against* your existing attitudes is generally more effective than the speaker who speaks at a normal rate. But the rapid speaker who speaks *in favor of* your existing attitudes (say, in an attempt to strengthen them) is actually less effective than the speaker who speaks at a normal rate. The reason for this is quite logical. In the case of the speaker speaking against your existing attitudes, rapid speech doesn't give you the time you need to think of counterarguments to rebut the speaker's position. So you're more likely to be persuaded, because you don't have time to consider why the speaker may be incorrect. In the case of the speaker speaking in favor of your existing attitudes, rapid speech doesn't give you time to mentally elaborate on the speaker's arguments; consequently, they don't carry as much persuasive force as they would if you had the time to add the speaker's arguments to those you already have.

Working with Theories and Research

With specific reference to your next speech, how might you apply this research to increase your own persuasiveness?

Building Communication SKILLS — Checking Your Pronunciation

Here are some words that are often mispronounced. Consult a print or online dictionary (ideally, one with audio capabilities) and record the correct pronunciations here.

Words Often Mispronounced	Correct Pronunciation	Words Often Mispronounced	Correct Pronunciation
abdomen	_____	herb	_____
accessory	_____	hierarchy	_____
arctic	_____	library	_____
ask	_____	nausea	_____
buffet	_____	nuclear	_____
cavalry	_____	probably	_____
clothes	_____	prostate	_____
costume	_____	realtor	_____
diagnosis	_____	relevant	_____
especially	_____	repeat	_____
espresso	_____	salmon	_____
et cetera	_____	sandwich	_____
February	_____	similar	_____
foliage	_____	substantive	_____
forte	_____	xenophobia	_____

Mispronouncing words in public speaking may significantly damage your credibility. Feeling unsure about how to pronounce any word or words in your speech is also likely to contribute to your communication apprehension.

Vocal Pitch. *Vocal pitch* is the relative highness or lowness of your voice as perceived by your listener. More technically, pitch results from the rate at which your vocal folds vibrate. If they vibrate rapidly, listeners will perceive your voice as having a high pitch. If they vibrate slowly, listeners will perceive your voice as having a low pitch.

Pitch changes often signal changes in the meanings of sentences. The most obvious is the difference between a statement and a question. Thus, vocal inflection or pitch makes the difference between the declarative sentence "So this is the proposal you want me to support" and the question "So this is the proposal you want me to support?"

The obvious problems that arise in relation to pitch are levels that are too high, too low, and too patterned. Neither of the first two problems is common in speakers with otherwise normal voices, and with practice you can correct a pitch pattern that is too predictable or monotonous. With increased

speaking experience, pitch changes will come naturally from the sense of what you're saying. After all, each sentence is somewhat different from every other sentence, so there should be a normal variation—a variation that results not from some conscious or predetermined pattern but rather from the meanings you wish to convey to the audience.

Pauses

Pauses come in two basic types: filled and unfilled. Filled pauses are pauses in the stream of speech that we fill with vocalizations such as *er*, *um*, *ah*, and the like. Even expressions such as *well* and *you know*, when used to fill up silence, are called filled pauses. These pauses are ineffective and weaken the strength of your message. They will make you appear hesitant, unprepared, and unsure of yourself.

Unfilled pauses, in contrast, are silences interjected into the normally fluent stream of speech. Unfilled pauses can be extremely effective if used

© Barbara Stitzer/PhotoEdit

correctly. Here are just a few examples of places where unfilled pauses—silences of a few seconds—should prove effective.

- Pause at transitional points. This will signal that you're moving from one part of the speech to another or from one idea to another. It will help the listeners separate the main issues you're discussing.

- Pause at the end of an important assertion. This will allow the audience time to think about the significance of what you're saying.

- Pause after asking a rhetorical question. This will give your listeners time to think about how they would answer the question.

- Pause before an important idea. This will help signal that what comes next is especially significant.

Bodily Action

Your body is a powerful instrument in your speech. You speak with your body as well as with your mouth. The total effect of the speech depends not only on what you say but also on the way you present it. It depends on your movements, gestures, and facial expressions as well as your words.

Six aspects of bodily action are especially important in public speaking: eye contact, facial expression, posture, gestures, movement, and proxemics.

Eye Contact. The most important single aspect of bodily communication is eye contact. The two major problems with eye contact in public speaking are not enough eye contact and eye contact that does not cover the audience fairly. Speakers who do not maintain enough eye contact appear distant and unconcerned and may be seen as less trustworthy than speakers who look directly at their audience. And, of course, without eye contact, you will not be able to secure that all-important audience feedback.

Maintain eye contact with the entire audience. Involve all listeners in the public speaking transaction. Communicate equally with the members on the left and on the right, in both the back and the front.

Use eye contact to secure audience feedback. Are they interested? Bored? Puzzled? In agreement? In disagreement? Use your eyes to communicate your commitment to and interest in what you're saying. Communicate your confidence and commitment by making direct eye contact; avoid staring blankly through your audience or gazing over their heads, down at the floor, or out the window.

Facial Expression. Facial expressions are especially important in communicating **emotions**—your anger or fear, boredom or excitement, doubt or surprise. If you feel committed to and believe in your thesis, you'll probably display your emotional messages appropriately and effectively.

Nervousness and anxiety, however, can sometimes prevent you from relaxing enough so that your emotions come through. Fortunately, time and practice will allow you to relax, and the emotions you feel will reveal themselves appropriately and automatically.

Generally, members of one culture will be able to recognize the emotions displayed facially by members of other cultures. But there are differences in what each culture considers appropriate to display. Each culture has its own "display rules" (Ekman, Friesen, & Ellsworth, 1972). For example, Japanese Americans watching a stress-inducing film spontaneously displayed the same facial emotions as did other Americans when they thought they were unobserved. But when an observer was present, the Japanese Americans masked (tried to hide) their emotional expressions more than did the other Americans (Gudykunst & Kim, 1992).

Posture. When presenting your speech, stand straight but not stiff. Try to communicate command of the situation without communicating the discomfort that is actually quite common for beginning speakers.

Avoid the common posture mistakes: putting your hands in your pockets or leaning on the desk, the podium, or the chalkboard. With practice, you'll come to feel more at ease and will communicate this by the way you stand before the audience.

Gestures. Gestures in public speaking help illustrate your verbal messages. We do this regularly in conversation. For example, when saying "Come here," you probably move your head, hands, arms, and perhaps your entire body to motion the listener in your direction. Your body and your verbal message say "Come here."

Avoid using your hands to preen; for example, restrain yourself from fixing your hair or adjusting your clothing. Avoid fidgeting with your watch, ring, or jewelry. Also avoid keeping your hands in your pockets or clasped in front of you or behind your back.

Effective gestures help you as the speaker, your relationship with the audience, and the subject matter of your speech seem spontaneous and natural. If gestures look planned or rehearsed, they'll appear phony and insincere. As a general rule, don't do anything with your hands that doesn't feel right for you; the audience will recognize it as unnatural. If you feel relaxed and comfortable with yourself and your audience, you'll generate natural bodily action without conscious or studied attention.

Movement. Even when speaking behind a lectern, you can give the illusion of movement. You can step back or forward or flex your upper body so you appear to be moving more than you are. It helps to move around a bit. It keeps both the audience and you more alert.

Avoid three potential problems of movement: too little, too much, and too patterned. Speakers who move too little often appear strapped to the podium,

afraid of the audience, or too detached to involve themselves fully. At the other extreme, when there's too much movement, the audience begins to concentrate on the movement itself, wondering where the speaker will wind up next. With movement that is too patterned, the audience may become bored—too steady and predictable a rhythm quickly becomes tiring. The audience will often view the speaker as nonspontaneous and uninvolved.

Use whole-body movements to emphasize transitions or to emphasize the introduction of a new and important assertion. Thus, when making a transition, you might take a step forward to signal that something new is coming. Similarly, this type of movement might signal the introduction of an important assumption, a key piece of evidence, or a closely reasoned argument.

If you're using a lectern, you may wish to signal transitions by stepping to the side or in front of it and then behind it again as you move from one point to another. As always, it's best to avoid the extremes; too much movement around the lectern and no movement from the lectern are both to be avoided. You may wish to lean over the lectern when, say, posing a question to your listeners or advancing a particularly important argument. But never lean on the lectern; never use it as support.

Proxemics. Proxemics is the study of how you use space in communication. In public speaking the amounts of space between you and your listeners and among the listeners themselves are often a crucial factor. If you stand too close to the people in the audience, they may feel uncomfortable, as if their personal space is being violated. If you stand too far away from your audience, you may be perceived as uninvolved, uninterested, and uncomfortable. Watch where your instructor and other speakers stand, and adjust your own position accordingly.

Answering Questions

In many public speaking situations, a question-and-answer period will follow the speech. So be prepared to answer questions. Here are a few suggestions for making this Q&A session more effective.

- If you wish to encourage questions, preface the question period with some kind of encouraging statement; for example, "I know you've lots of questions—especially on how the new health program will work and how we'll finance it. I'll be happy to respond to your questions. Anyone?"

- Maintain eye contact with the audience. Let the audience know that you're still speaking with them.

Building Communication Skills

Responding Strategically and Ethically

Consider the following situations that might arise in a public speaking situation. How would you respond to achieve your purpose and yet not violate any of your own ethical standards?

1. You've just given a speech to a racially diverse high school class on why they should attend your college. One audience member asks how racially diverse your faculty and students are. Your faculty is 94 percent European American, 4 percent Asian American, and 2 percent African American. You do know that the administration aims to recruit a more diverse faculty, but so far no action has been taken. Your student population is approximately 40 percent European American, 40 percent African American, 10 percent Hispanic, and 10 percent Asian American. What do you say?

2. You've just given a speech advocating banning alcohol on campus. In the speech you claimed that more than 70 percent of the students favor banning alcohol. At the end of the speech, you realize that you made a mistake and that only 30 percent favor banning alcohol; you were nervous and mixed up the figures. There's a question-and-answer period, but no one asks about the figures. What do you say?

3. You represent the college newspaper and are asking the student government to increase the paper's funding. The student government objects to giving extra money, because the paper has taken up lots of unpopular causes. You feel that it's essential for the paper to give visibility to minority views and fully expect to continue to do exactly as you have in the past. But if you say this, you won't get the added funding—and the paper won't be able to survive without increased funds. You will get the funding if you say you'll give primary coverage to majority positions. What do you say?

Because public speeches have effects, they need to be ethically grounded.

- After you hear a question, pause to think about the question and about your answer. If you suspect that some members of the audience didn't hear the question, repeat it; then begin your answer.

- Control defensiveness. Don't assume that a question is a personal attack. Assume, instead, that the question is an attempt to secure more information or perhaps to challenge a position you've taken.

- If appropriate, thank the questioner or note that it's a good question. This will encourage others also to ask questions.

- Don't bluff. If you're asked a question and you don't know the answer, say so.

- Consider the usefulness of a persuasive answer. Question-and-answer sessions often give you opportunities to further advance your purpose by connecting the question and its answer with one or more of your major points: "I'm glad you asked about child care, because that's exactly the

difference between the two proposals we're here to vote on. The plan I'm proposing. . . ."

All of these suggestions are based on the assumption that you want to encourage questions and dialogue. And generally speakers want audience questions, because the dialogue gives them an opportunity to talk more about something they're interested in. In some cases, too, there seems an ethical obligation for the speaker to entertain questions; after all, if the audience sat through what the speaker wanted to say, the speaker should listen to what they want to say.

CRITICIZING SPEECHES

In learning the art of public speaking, you can gain much insight from the criticism offered by others as well as from your own efforts to critique others' speeches. This section considers the nature of criticism in a learning environment, the influence of culture on criticism, and the standards and principles for evaluating a speech and for making criticism easier and more effective.

What Is Criticism?

Critics and criticism are essential parts of any art. The word *criticism* comes into English from the Latin *criticus*, which means "able to discern," "able to judge." In the context of public speaking, therefore, **criticism** is the process of evaluating a speech, of rendering a judgment of its value. Note that there is nothing inherently negative about criticism; criticism may be negative, but it also may be positive.

Perhaps the major value of criticism in the classroom is that it helps you improve your public speaking skills. Through the constructive criticism of others, you'll learn the principles of public speaking more effectively. You'll be shown what you do well; what you could improve; and, ideally, how to improve. As a listener–critic, you'll also learn the principles of public speaking through assessing the speeches of others. Just as you learn when you teach, you also learn when you criticize.

When you give criticism—as you do in a public speaking class—you're telling the speaker that you've listened carefully and that you care enough

about the speech and the speaker to offer suggestions for improvement.

Of course, criticism can be difficult—for the critic (whether student or instructor) as well as for the person criticized. As a critic, you may feel embarrassed or uncomfortable about offering evaluation. After all, you may think, "Who am I to criticize another person's speech? My own speech won't be any better." Or you may be reluctant to offend, fearing that your criticism may make the speaker feel uncomfortable. Or you may view criticism as a confrontation that will do more harm than good.

But reconsider this view. By offering criticism, you're helping the speaker; you're giving the speaker another perspective that should prove useful in future speeches. When you offer criticism, you're not claiming to be a better speaker; you're simply offering another point of view. It's true that by offering criticism, you're stating a position with which others may disagree. That's one of the things that will make the study of public speaking exciting and challenging.

Criticism is also difficult to receive. After working on a speech for a week or two and dealing with the normal anxiety that comes with giving a speech, the last thing you want is to stand in front

REFLECTIONS ON ETHICS

Criticizing Ethically

Just as speakers and listeners have ethical obligations, so do critics. To be an ethical critic, keep in mind these guidelines:

- Separate personal feelings about the speaker from your evaluations. Liking the speaker should not lead you to evaluate a speech positively, nor should disliking the speaker lead you to evaluate a speech negatively.

- Separate personal feelings about the issues from your evaluation of the validity of the arguments. Recognize the validity of an argument even if it contradicts a deeply held belief; by the same token, recognize the fallaciousness of an argument even if it supports a deeply held belief.

- Demonstrate cultural sensitivity and be conscious of your own ethnocentrism. Beware of evaluating customs and forms of speech negatively simply because they differ from your own. Conversely, be careful not to evaluate a speech positively just

because it supports your own cultural beliefs and values. Avoid any inclination to discriminate for or against speakers simply because they're of a particular gender, race, nationality, religion, age group, or affectional orientation.

Ethical Choice Point

You and your best friend are taking this course together. Your friend just gave a pretty terrible speech, and unfortunately, the instructor has asked you to offer a critique. The wrinkle here is that the instructor's grades seem to be heavily influenced by what student critics say. So in effect your critique will largely determine your friend's grade. You'd like to give your friend a positive critique so he can earn a good grade—which he badly needs—and you figure you can always tell him the truth later and even help him to improve. What is your ethical obligation in this situation? What would you do?

© Barbara Stitzer/PhotoEdit

of the class and hear others say what you did wrong. Public speaking is ego-involving, and it's normal to take criticism personally. But if you learn how to give and how to receive criticism, it will help you improve your public speaking skills. Constructive criticism also can serve as an important support mechanism for the developing public speaker, a way of patting the speaker on the back for all the positive effort.

Culture and Criticism

There are vast cultural differences in what is considered proper when it comes to criticism. For example, criticism will be viewed very differently depending on whether members come from an individualist culture (which emphasizes the individual, placing primary value on the individual's goals) or a collectivist culture (which emphasizes the group, placing primary value on the group's goals).

Those who come from cultures that are highly individualist and competitive (the United States, Germany, and Sweden are examples) may find public criticism a normal part of the learning process. Those who come from cultures that are more collectivist and therefore emphasize the group rather than the individual (Japan, Mexico, and Korea are examples) are likely to find giving and receiving public criticism uncomfortable. Thus, people from individualist cultures may readily criticize speakers and are likely to expect the same "courtesy" from listeners. "After all," such a person might reason, "if I'm going to criticize your skills to help you improve, I expect you to help me in the same way." Persons from collectivist cultures, on the other

hand, may feel that it's more important to be polite and courteous than to help someone learn a skill. Cultural rules that maintain peaceful relations among the Japanese (Midooka, 1990) and norms of politeness among many Asian cultures (Fraser, 1990) may conflict with the classroom cultural norm that promotes the expression of honest criticism. In some cultures, being kind to the person is more important than telling the truth, so members may say things that are complimentary but that are untrue in a strict literal sense.

Collectivist cultures place a heavy emphasis on face-saving—on allowing people always to appear in a positive light (James, 1995). In these cultures people may prefer not to say anything negative in public. In fact, they may even be reluctant to say anything positive, lest any omission be construed as negative. Japanese executives, for instance, are reluctant to say no in a business meeting for fear of offending the other person. But their yes, properly interpreted in light of the context and the general discussion, may mean no. In cultures in which face-saving is especially important, communication rules such as the following tend to prevail:

- Don't express negative evaluation in public; instead, compliment the person.

- Don't prove someone wrong, especially in public; express agreement even if you know the person is wrong.

- Don't correct someone's errors; don't even acknowledge them.

- Don't ask difficult questions, lest the person not know the answer and lose face or be embarrassed; generally, avoid asking questions.

The difficulties that these differences may cause may be lessened if they're discussed openly. Some people may become comfortable with public criticism once it's explained that the cultural norms of most public speaking classrooms include public criticism, just as they incorporate informative and persuasive speaking and written outlines. Others may feel more comfortable offering written criticism as a substitute for oral and public criticism. Or perhaps private consultations can be arranged.

Guidelines for Criticizing More Effectively

A useful standard to use in evaluating a classroom speech is the speech's degree of conformity to the principles of the art. Using this standard, you'll evaluate a speech positively when it follows the principles of public speaking established by the critics, theorists, and practitioners of public speaking and evaluate it negatively if it deviates from these principles. These principles include, for example, speaking on a subject that is worthwhile, relevant, and interesting to listeners; designing a speech for a specific audience; and constructing a speech that is based on sound research.

Before reading the specific suggestions for making critical evaluations a more effective part of the total learning process and avoiding some of the potentially negative aspects of criticism, take the following self-test, which asks you to identify what's wrong with selected critical comments.

TEST YOURSELF

What's Wrong with These Critical Evaluations?

For the purposes of this exercise, assume that each of the following 10 comments represents the critic's complete criticism. What's wrong with each?

_____ 1. I loved the speech. It was great. Really great.

_____ 2. The introduction didn't gain my attention.

_____ 3. You weren't interested in your own topic. How do you expect us to be interested?

_____ 4. Nobody was able to understand you.

_____ 5. The speech was weak.

_____ 6. The speech didn't do anything for me.

_____ 7. Your position was unfair to those of us on athletic scholarships; we earned those scholarships.

_____ 8. I found four things wrong with your speech. First, . . .

_____ 9. You needed better research.

_____ 10. I liked the speech; we need more police on campus.

HOW DID YOU DO? Before reading the discussion that follows, try to explain why each of these statements is ineffective. Visualize yourself as the speaker receiving such comments, and ask yourself if these comments would help you in any way. If not, then they are probably not very effective critical evaluations.

WHAT WILL YOU DO? To help you improve your criticism, try to restate the basic meaning of each of these comments but in a more constructive manner.

The following guidelines will help you become a more constructive critic.

Stress the Positive

Egos are fragile, and public speaking is extremely personal. Speakers understand what Noel Coward meant when he said, "I love criticism just as long as it's unqualified praise." Part of your function as a critic is to strengthen the already positive aspects of someone's public speaking performance. Positive criticism is particularly important in itself, but it's almost essential as a preface to negative comments. There are always positive characteristics about any speech, and it's more productive to concentrate on these first. Thus, instead of saying (as in the self-test), "The speech didn't do anything for me," tell the speaker what you liked first, then bring up a weak point and suggest how it might be improved.

When criticizing a person's second or third speech, it's especially helpful if you can point out specific improvements ("You really held my attention in this speech," "I felt you were much more in control of the topic today than in your first speech").

Remember, too, that communication is irreversible. Once you say something, you can't take it back. Remember this when offering criticism, especially criticism that may be negative. If in doubt, err on the side of gentleness.

Be Specific

Criticism is most effective when it's specific. General statements such as "I thought your presentation was bad," "I thought your examples were good," or, as in the self-test, "I loved the speech.... Really great" or "The speech was weak" are poorly expressed criticisms. These statements don't specify what the speaker might do to improve his or her presentation or to capitalize on the examples used. In commenting on presentation, refer to such specifics as eye contact, vocal volume, or whatever else is of consequence. In commenting on the examples, tell the speaker why they were good. Were they realistic? Were they especially interesting? Were they presented dramatically?

In giving negative criticism, specify and justify—to the extent that you can—positive alternatives. Here's an example.

> I thought the way you introduced your statistics was vague. I wasn't sure where the statistics came from or how recent or reliable they were. It might have been better to say something like "The U.S. Census figures for 2000 show...." That way we would know that the statistics were as recent as possible and the most reliable available.

Be Objective

In criticizing a speech, transcend your own biases as best you can, unlike the self-test's example ("Your position was unfair . . . ; we earned those scholarships"). See the speech as objectively as possible. Suppose, for example, that you're strongly for a woman's right to an abortion and you encounter a speech diametrically opposed to your position. In this situation, you'll need to take special care not to dismiss the speech because of your own biases. Examine the speech from the point of view of a detached critic; evaluate, for example, the validity of the arguments and their suitability to the audience, the language, and the supporting materials. Conversely, take special care not to evaluate a speech positively because it presents a position with which you agree, as in "I liked the speech; we need more police on campus."

Be Constructive

Your primary goal should be to provide the speaker with insight that will prove useful in future public speaking transactions. For example, to say that "The introduction didn't gain my attention" doesn't tell the speaker how he or she might have gained your attention. Instead, you might say, "The example about the computer crash would have more effectively gained my attention in the introduction."

Another way you can be constructive is to limit your criticism. Cataloging a speaker's weak points, as in "I found four things wrong with your speech," will

overwhelm, not help, the speaker. If you're the sole critic, your criticism naturally will need to be more extensive. But if you're one of many critics, limit your criticism to one or perhaps two points. In all cases, your guide should be the value your comments will have for the speaker.

Focus on Behavior

Focus criticism on what the speaker said and did during the actual speech. Try to avoid the very natural tendency to read the mind of the speaker—to assume that you know why the speaker did one thing rather than another. Compare the critical comments presented in Table 3. Note that those in the first column, "Criticism as Attack," try to identify the reasons the speaker did as he or she did; they try to read the speaker's mind. At the same time, they blame the speaker for what happened. Those in the second column, "Criticism as Support," focus on the specific behavior. Note, too, that those in the first column are likely to encourage defensiveness; you can almost hear the speaker saying, "I was so interested in the topic." Those in the second column are less likely to create defensiveness and are more likely to be appreciated as honest reflections of how the critic perceived the speech.

Own Your Criticism

In giving criticism, own your comments; take responsibility for them. The best way to express this ownership is to use "I-messages" rather than "you-messages." Instead of saying, "You needed better research," say, "I would have been more persuaded if you had used more recent research."

Avoid attributing what you found wrong to others. Instead of saying, "Nobody was able to understand you," say, "I had difficulty understanding you. It would have helped me if you had spoken more slowly." Remember that your criticism is important precisely because it's your perception of what the speaker did and what the speaker could have done more effectively. Speaking for the entire audience ("We couldn't hear you clearly" or "No one was convinced by your arguments") will not help the speaker, and it's likely to prove demoralizing.

Employing I-messages also will prevent you from using "should messages," a type of expression that almost invariably creates defensiveness and resentment. When you say "You should have done this" or "You shouldn't have done that," you assume a superior position and imply that what you're saying is correct and that what the speaker did was incorrect. On the other hand, when you own your evaluations and use I-messages, you're giving your perceptions; it's then up to the speaker to accept or reject them.

Table 3 Criticism as Attack and as Support

Can you develop additional examples to illustrate criticism as attack and as support?

Criticism as Attack	Criticism as Support
"You weren't interested in your topic."	"I would have liked to see greater variety in your presentation. It would have made me feel that you were more interested."
"You should have put more time into the speech."	"I think it would have been more effective if you had looked at your notes less."
"You didn't care about your audience."	"I would have liked it if you had looked more directly at me while speaking."

SUMMARY: STYLE AND DELIVERY IN PUBLIC SPEAKING

This unit focused on outlining, style, rehearsal, and presentation. The unit offered suggestions for using preparation, template, and presentation outlines; choosing words and phrasing sentences; and rehearsing and presenting your speech. In addition, this unit discussed guidelines for giving and receiving criticism.

1. An outline is a blueprint that helps you organize and evaluate your speech. The preparation outline is extremely detailed and includes all of your main points, supporting materials, introduction, conclusion, transition, and references. The skeletal outline is a kind of template that can help you see where certain material can be placed. The presentation outline is a brief version of your preparation outline that you use as a guide when presenting your speech.

2. Compared with written style, oral style contains shorter, simpler, and more familiar words; greater qualification; and more self-referential terms.

3. Effective public speaking style is clear (be economical and specific; use guide phrases; and stick to short, familiar, and commonly used terms), vivid (use active verbs, strong verbs, figures of speech, and imagery), appropriate to audience (speak on a suitable level of formality; avoid jargon and technical expressions; avoid slang, vulgarity, and offensive terms), personal (use personal pronouns, ask questions, and create immediacy), and forceful (eliminate weakeners, vary intensity, and avoid trite expressions).

4. In constructing sentences for public speeches, favor short, direct, active, and positively phrased sentences. Vary the type and length of sentences.

5. Use rehearsal to time your speech; perfect your volume, rate, and pitch; incorporate pauses and other delivery notes; and perfect your bodily action.

6. There are four basic methods of presenting a public speech. The impromptu method involves speaking without any specific preparation. The manuscript method involves writing out the entire speech and reading it to the audience. Memorized delivery involves writing out the speech, memorizing it, and reciting it. The extemporaneous method involves thorough preparation and memorizing of the main ideas and their order of appearance but no commitment to exact wording.

7. Effective presentation is natural, reinforces the message, is varied, and has a conversational quality. When you present your speech, regulate your voice for greatest effectiveness. Adjust your vocal volume, rate, and pitch as appropriate.

8. Use unfilled pauses to signal a transition between the major parts of the speech, to allow the audience time to think, to allow the audience to ponder a rhetorical question, or to signal the approach of a particularly important idea. Avoid filled pauses; they weaken your message.

9. Effective body action involves maintaining eye contact with your entire audience, allowing your facial expressions to convey your feelings, using your posture to communicate command of the public speaking interaction, gesturing naturally, and moving around a bit.

10. In answering sessions after the speech, encourage questions, maintain eye contact, repeat the question if necessary, avoid any signs of defensiveness, express thanks for the question (if appropriate), don't bluff, and consider the usefulness of a persuasive answer.

11. Criticism, a process of judging and evaluating a work, is crucial to mastering the principles of public speaking.

12. Criticism can (1) identify strengths and weaknesses and thereby help you improve as a public speaker, (2) identify standards for evaluating all sorts of public speeches, and (3) show that the audience is listening and is concerned about the speaker's progress.

13. Cultures differ in their views of criticism and in the rules they consider appropriate. For example, members of individualist cultures may find public criticism easier and more acceptable than people from collectivist cultures.

14. Among the guidelines for effective criticism are these: Stress the positive, be specific, be objective, be constructive, focus on behavior, and own your criticism.

KEY TERMS IN STYLE AND DELIVERY IN PUBLIC SPEAKING

appropriateness	forcefulness	outline	template outline
clarity	impromptu speech	pauses	vividness
clichés	jargon	personal style	weakeners
criticism	manuscript speech	predictable patterns	
emotions	memorized speech	preparation outline	
extemporaneous speech	monotonous patterns	presentation outline	
figures of speech	oral style	slang	

THINKING CRITICALLY ABOUT STYLE AND DELIVERY IN PUBLIC SPEAKING

1. **Wording the Speech for Different Audiences.** Francisco is scheduled to give two speeches, one to a predominantly female audience of health professionals and one to a predominantly male audience of small business owners. His topic for both groups is the same: neighborhood violence. What advice—if any—would you give Francisco for tailoring his speech to the two different audiences? If you would not offer advice, why not?

2. **Using Humor.** John has this great joke that is only tangentially related to his speech topic. But the joke is so great that it will immediately get the audience actively involved in his speech; this, John thinks, outweighs the fact that the joke isn't integrally related to the speech. John asks your advice; what do you suggest?

3. **Projecting an Image.** Michael has a very formal type of personality; he's very restrained in everything he does. But he wants to try to project a different image—a much more personable, friendly, informal quality—in his speeches. What advice would you give Michael?

4. **E-Talk and Public Speaking.** How would you describe your language—word and sentence choices—in online and in public speaking communication? How would you describe the "rehearsal" you go through in online messages and in public speeches? How would you compare your willingness to criticize, say, an acquaintance in an e-mail as opposed to a public setting? Would the substance of the criticism change? Would the way you expressed it change? More generally, what are the major differences between online and public communication?

5. **The Two-Minute Speech.** Prepare and deliver a two-minute speech in which you do one of the following:
   - describe the language of a noted personality
   - introduce an excerpt from literature and read the excerpt as you might a manuscript speech
   - analyze an advertisement in terms of one or two of the characteristics of effective style: clarity, vividness, appropriateness, personal style, or forcefulness
   - describe an object in the room using visual, auditory, and tactile imagery

LOGON! MYCOMMUNICATIONLAB
WWW.MYCOMMUNICATIONLAB.COM

Visit MCL for 13 template outlines to help you outline a wide variety of speeches. There are also extended discussions of Oral and Written Style, Making Your Speech Easy to Remember, Humor in Public Speaking, and Using Visual Aspects to Reflect Your Organization. Exercises include Organizing a Scrambled Outline, Rephrasing Clichés, Making Concepts Specific, Undertaking a Long-Term Delivery Improvement Program, and Communicating Vocally but Nonverbally. Watch one or more of the speeches; they will help illustrate in concrete fashion the elements of style and techniques of presentation. Also visit the Allyn & Bacon public speaking website (**www.ablongman.com/pubspeak**) for guidance on delivering the speech and criticizing the speech.

REFERENCES

Akinnaso, F. N. (1982). On the differences between spoken and written language. *Language and Speech, 25* (Part 2), 97-125.

Burgoon, J. K., & Bacue, A. E. (2003). Nonverbal communication skills. In J. O. Greene & B. R. Burleson (Eds.), *Handbook of communication and social interaction skills* (pp. 179-220). Mahwah, NJ: Lawrence Erlbaum.

Burgoon, J. K., & Hoobler, G. D. (2002). Nonverbal signals. In M. L. Knapp & J. A. Daly (Eds.), *Handbook of interpersonal communication* (3rd ed., pp. 240-299). Thousand Oaks, CA: Sage.

Ekman, P., Friesen, W. V., & Ellsworth, P. (1972). *Emotion in the human face: Guidelines for research and an integration of findings.* New York: Pergamon Press.

Fraser, B. (1990). Perspectives on politeness. *Journal of Pragmatics, 14* (April), 219-236.

Gudykunst, W. B., & Kim, Y. Y. (1992). *Communicating with strangers: An approach to intercultural communication* (2nd ed.). New York: Random House.

Guerrero, L. K., DeVito, J. A., & Hecht, M. L. (Eds.). (1999). *The nonverbal communication reader: Class and contemporary readings* (2nd ed.). Prospect Heights, IL: Waveland Press.

James, D. L. (1995). *The executive guide to Asia-Pacific communications.* New York: Kodansha International.

Lewis, D. (1989). *The secret language of success.* New York: Carroll & Graf.

Midooka, K. (1990). Characteristics of Japanese style communication. *Media, Culture and Society, 12* (October), 477-489.

Page, R. A., & Balloun, J. L. (1978). The effect of voice volume on the perception of personality. *Journal of Social Psychology, 105*, 65-72.

Robinson, J., & McArthur, L. Z. (1982). Impact of salient vocal qualities on casual attribution for a speaker's behavior. *Journal of Personality and Social Psychology, 43*, 236-247.

Ruscher, J. B. (2001). *Prejudiced communication: A social psychological perspective.* New York: Guilford.

Smith, S. M., & Shaffer, D. R. (1991). Celerity and cajolery: Rapid speech may promote or inhibit persuasion through its impact on message elaboration. *Personality and Social Psychology Bulletin, 17* (December), 663-669.

Smith, S. M., & Shaffer, D. R. (1995). Speed of speech and persuasion: Evidence for multiple effects. *Personality and Social Psychology Bulletin, 21* (October), 1051-1060.

183

Chapter 7

The Persuasive Speech

MAJOR TOPICS

Goals of Persuasive Speaking

Principles of Persuasive Speaking

Persuasive Speeches on Questions of Fact

Persuasive Speeches on Questions of Value

Persuasive Speeches on Questions of Policy

Special Features

Age and Credibility: Jon F. Nussbaum

How Credible Are You?

The Spiral of Silence

The Ethics of Emotional Appeals

 Balance Theories

 Credibility Impressions

Finding the Available Means of Persuasion

Constructing Logical, Motivational, and Credibility Appeals

 A Poorly Constructed Persuasive Speech

 An Excellent Persuasive Speech

© Marilyn Humphries/The Image Works

In addition to informing others, you'll also be called upon to deliver speeches of persuasion—speeches that aim to influence the attitudes and beliefs and sometimes the behaviors of your listeners.

In this unit you'll learn about:
- the nature and goals of persuasion and how attitudes, beliefs, values, and behaviors are influenced.
- the major types of persuasive speeches.

You'll learn to:
- use the strategies of persuasion in a variety of communication contexts.
- prepare a variety of effective persuasive speeches on questions of fact, value, and policy.
- prevent yourself from being unfairly or unethically persuaded.

This unit looks at persuasive speaking: the goals of persuasive speaking, essential principles of persuasion, and the varied types of persuasive speeches you might give.

GOALS OF PERSUASIVE SPEAKING

Persuasion is the process of influencing another person's attitudes, beliefs, values, and/or behaviors. Here is a brief glossary of the terms in this definition:

- *Attitude:* The tendency to behave in a certain way. For example, if your audience has a positive attitude toward the current administration, then they're likely to favor the policies, proposals, and values of the administration. If they have a negative attitude, they're likely to oppose administration policies and the like.

- *Belief:* The conviction in the existence or reality of something or in the truth of some assertion. For example, if your audience believes that soft drugs lead to hard drugs, then they're likely to oppose legalizing marijuana and perhaps to favor harsher penalties for soft drug use.

- *Value:* An indicator of what people feel is good or bad, ethical or unethical, just or unjust. For example, if your audience positively values "free speech," then they'll likely oppose increased restrictions on what can and cannot be said publicly and will likely oppose increased surveillance of their e-mail or phone calls.

- *Behavior:* Overt, observable actions, such as voting for increased funding for education or for a particular electoral candidate, contributing money to the Red Cross, or buying a Ford.

Your persuasive speeches may focus on influencing listeners' attitudes, beliefs, values, and/or behaviors. You may want to accomplish any one of the following three general goals of persuasive speaking:

- *To strengthen or weaken attitudes, beliefs, or values.* Persuasion often aims to strengthen audience views. For example, religious sermons usually seek to strengthen the existing beliefs of the congregation. Similarly, many public service announcements try to strengthen existing beliefs about, say, recycling, smoking, or safe sex. At times, however, you may want to weaken the existing beliefs of the audience—to suggest that what they currently believe may not be entirely true. For example, you might want to weaken the favorable attitudes people might have toward a particular political party or policy.

- *To change attitudes, beliefs, or values.* Sometimes you'll want to change how your audience feels. You might want to change their attitudes to the college's no-smoking rules, to change their beliefs about television's influence on viewer violence, or to change their values about the efficacy of war.

- *To motivate to action.* Ultimately, your goal is to get people to do something—for example, to vote for one person rather than another, to donate money to a fund for the homeless, or to take a course in personal finance.

It's useful to view the effects of persuasion as a continuum ranging from one extreme to another. Let's say, to take one issue currently in the news, that you want to give a persuasive speech on same-sex marriage. You might visualize your audience as existing on

CHANGING BEHAVIOR

You're supervising a small work force. Your problem is that some members are just not doing their job and you've been assigned the task of making sure they start working. You decide to tackle this in your weekly meeting with the workers.

WHAT DO YOU SAY?

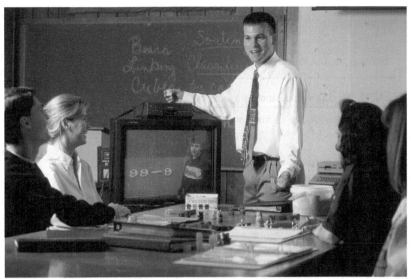

© K. Shamsi-Basha/The Image Works

a continuum ranging from strongly in favor to strongly opposed, as shown in Figure 1. Your task is to move your audience in the direction of your persuasive purpose, which you can do in any of three ways (corresponding to the goals of persuasion identified above). You can design your persuasive speech to attempt to:

- Strengthen or weaken your listeners' attitudes, beliefs, or values about same-sex marriage.

- Change your listeners' attitudes, beliefs, or values about same-sex marriage.

- Move your listeners to act—to protest, write letters, or sign a petition.

If your purpose is to persuade the audience to *oppose* same-sex marriage, then in Figure 1 any movement toward the right will be successful persuasion; if your purpose is to persuade listeners to *support* same-sex marriage, then any movement toward the left will be successful persuasion. Notice, however, that it's quite possible to give a speech in which you hope to move your listeners in one

Theory and Research — UNDERSTANDING **Balance Theories**

An especially interesting group of theories of persuasion go under the general term *balance theories*. The general assumption of balance theories is that people strive to maintain consistency between their beliefs and their behaviors. For example, if you believe that people should exercise regularly (because you believe it's the healthy thing to do) but you don't exercise (because you feel exercise is difficult and boring), then you'll be in a state of imbalance or dissonance. According to balance theory, you will then strive either to change your beliefs about exercise (to make them consistent with your behavior) or to change your behavior (to make it consistent with your beliefs).

Applied to persuasion, balance theories claim that people look for information that will maintain or restore balance or consonance. For example, if you as a speaker demonstrate that you offer an easy and enjoyable (not difficult and boring) exercise plan, you stand a good chance of influencing the audience—because they are looking for the very means to restore balance that you are now providing. Conversely, of course, you might assert that exercise is unhealthy; the belief that exercise is unhealthy would be consistent with their no-exercise behavior and also would restore balance.

Working with Theories and Research

How might you use the insights of balance theories in preparing a speech on why the audience should start investing, give up junk food, or quit smoking?

| Strongly in favor of same-sex marriage | ___:___:___:___:___:___:___ | Strongly opposed to same-sex marriage |

FIGURE 1 The Persuasion Continuum

Any movement along the continuum would be considered persuasion.

direction but actually move them in the other direction. This "negative persuasion" effect can occur, for example, if the audience members perceive you as dishonest or self-promoting or if they feel you presented biased evidence or faulty reasoning.

PRINCIPLES OF PERSUASIVE SPEAKING

To succeed in strengthening or changing attitudes or beliefs and in moving your listeners to action, follow these guidelines for persuasive speaking.

Anticipate Selective Exposure

Listeners follow the "law of selective exposure." This principle has two parts: (1) Listeners actively seek out information that supports their opinions, beliefs, values, decisions, and behaviors; and (2) listeners actively avoid information that contradicts their existing opinions, beliefs, attitudes, values, decisions, and behaviors.

Of course, if people are very sure that their opinions and attitudes are logical and valid, then they may not bother to seek out supporting information or to avoid contradictory messages. People exercise selective exposure most often when their confidence in their opinions and beliefs is weak.

So if you want to persuade an audience that holds attitudes different from your own, anticipate selective exposure operating and proceed inductively; that is, hold back on your thesis until you've given them your evidence and argument. Only then relate this evidence and argument to your initially contrary thesis.

If you were to present your listeners with your thesis first, they might tune you out without giving

THE SPIRAL OF SILENCE

I have noticed that nothing I have never said ever did me any harm.

—Calvin Coolidge

The spiral of silence theory argues that you're more likely to voice agreement than disagreement (Noelle-Neumann, 1973, 1980, 1991; Windahl, Signitzer, & Olson, 1992). The theory claims that when a controversial issue arises, you try to estimate public opinion on the issue and figure out which views are popular and which are not, largely by attending to the media (Gonzenbach, King, & Jablonski, 1999; Jeffres, Neuendorf, & Atkin, 1999). At the same time, you also judge the likelihood and the severity of punishment for expressing minority opinions. You then use these estimates to regulate your expression of opinions.

The theory continues: When you agree with the majority, you're more likely to voice your opinions than when you disagree. You may avoid expressing minority opinions because you don't want to be isolated from the majority or confront the unpleasant possibility of being proven wrong. Or, you may assume that the majority, because they're a majority, are right.

Not all people seem affected equally by this spiral (Noelle-Neumann, 1991). For example, younger people and men are more likely to express minority opinions than are older people and women. Educated people are more likely to express minority opinions than are those who are less educated. Similarly, the tendency to voice minority opinions will vary from one culture to another (Scheufele & Moy, 2000).

In any case, the "spiral" effect occurs when, as people with minority views remain silent, the media position gets stronger (because those who agree with it are the only ones speaking). As the media's position grows stronger, the voice of the opposition also gets weaker. Thus, the situation becomes an ever-widening spiral of silence.

Increasing Media Literacy

In what ways does the spiral of silence operate in your own media life? For example, do you contribute to this spiral of silence? Under what conditions are you most likely to conform to the predictions of this theory? What are its effects on your self-image and on your popularity with peers?

your position a fair hearing. So become thoroughly familiar with the attitudes of your audience if you want to succeed in making these necessary adjustments and adaptations.

Let's say you're giving a speech on the need to reduce spending on college athletic programs. If your audience is composed of listeners who agree with you and want to cut athletic spending, you might lead with your thesis. Your introduction might go something like this:

> Our college athletic program is absorbing money that we can more profitably use for the library, science labs, and language labs. Let me explain how the money now going to unnecessary athletic programs could be better spent in these other areas.

On the other hand, suppose you're addressing alumni who strongly favor the existing athletic programs. In this case, you may want to lead with your evidence and hold off stating your thesis until the end of your speech.

Ask for Reasonable Amounts of Change

The greater and more important the change you want to encourage in your audience, the more difficult your task will be. The reason is simple: We normally demand a greater number of reasons and a lot more evidence before we make important decisions such as, say, changing careers, moving to another state, or investing in stocks. On the other hand, we may be more easily persuaded (and demand less evidence) on relatively minor issues—whether to take "Small Group Communication" rather than "Persuasion" or whether to give to the United Heart Fund instead of the American Heart Fund.

Generally, people change gradually, in small degrees over a long period of time. Persuasion, therefore, is most effective when it strives for small changes and works over a period of time. For example, a persuasive speech stands a better chance when it tries to get an alcoholic to attend just one AA meeting rather than asking the person to give up alcohol for life. If you try to convince your audience to change their attitudes radically or to engage in behaviors to which they're initially opposed, your attempts may backfire. In this type of situation, the audience may tune you out, closing its ears to even the best and most logical arguments.

In your classroom speeches, set reasonable goals for what you want the audience to do. Remember that you have only perhaps 10 minutes; in that time you cannot move the proverbial mountain. So ask your listeners for small, easily performed behaviors—

signing a petition, voting in the next election, donating a small amount of money.

When you're addressing an audience that is opposed to your position and you're trying to change their attitudes and beliefs, be especially careful to seek change in small increments. Let's say, for example, that your ultimate goal is to get an antiabortion group to favor abortion on demand. Obviously, this goal is too great to achieve in one speech. Therefore, strive for small changes. For example, in the following excerpt the speaker attempts to get an audience that opposes legalized abortion to agree that at least some abortions should be legalized. The speaker begins:

> One of the great lessons I learned in college was that most extreme positions are wrong. Most of the important truths lie somewhere between the extreme opposites. And today I want to talk with you about one of these truths. I want to talk with you about rape and the problems faced by the mother carrying a child conceived in this most violent of all violent crimes we can imagine.

Notice that the speaker does not state a totally pro-choice position, but instead focuses on one area of the abortion issue and attempts to get the audience to ask themselves, "What if my daughter was raped and abortion was unavailable?" and perhaps ultimately to agree that in some cases the possibility of abortion should be available.

When you have the opportunity to persuade your audience on several occasions (rather than simply delivering one speech), two strategies will prove helpful: the foot-in-the-door and door-in-the-face techniques.

Foot-in-the-Door Technique

As its name implies, the **foot-in-the-door technique** involves requesting something small, something that your audience will easily agree to. Once they agree to this small request, you then make your real request (Cialdini, 1984; Dejong, 1979; Freedman & Fraser, 1966; Pratkanis & Aronson, 1991). People are more apt to comply with a large request after they have complied with a similar but much smaller request. For example, in one study the objective was to get people to put a "Drive Carefully" sign on their lawn (a large request). When this (large) request was made first, only about 17 percent of the people were willing to agree. However, when this request was preceded by a much smaller request (to sign a petition), between 50 and 76 percent granted permission to install the sign. Agreement with the smaller request paves the way for the larger request and puts the audience into an agreeable mood.

A Poorly Constructed Persuasive Speech

This speech was written by the author to illustrate some really broad as well as some rather subtle errors that a beginning speaker might make in constructing a persuasive speech.

XXX Has Got to Go

You probably didn't read the papers this weekend, but there's a XXX movie, I mean video, store that moved in on Broad and Fifth Streets. My parents, who are retired teachers, are protesting it, and so am I. My parents are organizing a protest for next weekend.

What do you think of the title of the speech? Visualizing yourself as a listener, how would the opening comment make you feel? Does the speaker gain your attention? What thesis do you think the speaker will support? Does mentioning "my parents" help or hurt the speaker's credibility?

There must be hundreds of XXX video stores in the country, and they all need to be closed down. I have a lot of reasons.

What is the speaker's thesis? What impression are you beginning to get of the speaker?

First, my parents think it should be closed down. My parents are retired teachers and have organized protests over the proposed new homeless shelter and to prevent the city from making that park on Elm Street. So they know what they're doing.

How do the speaker's parents sound to you? Do they sound like credible leaders with a consistent cause? Professional protesters (with perhaps a negative agenda)? What evidence is offered to support the assertion that we should believe the speaker's parents? Is this adequate? What would you need to know about people before believing them?

The XXX video place is irreligious. No good person would ever go there. Our minister is against it and is joining in the protest.

What does this statement assume about the audience? How would this statement be responded to by your public speaking class? What are some reasons why the speaker might not have explained how XXX video stores are against religion?

These stores bring crime into the neighborhood. I have proof of that. Morristown's crime increased after the XXX video store opened. And in Martinsville, where they got rid of the video store, crime did not increase. If we allow the video store in our own town, then we're going to be like Morristown and our crime is going to increase.

What do you think of the reasoning used here? Are there other factors that could have influenced Morristown's crime increase? Is there any evidence that getting rid of the video store resulted in the stable crime rate in Martinsville? What assumption about the audience does the speaker make in using Martinsville and Morristown as analogies?

These stores make lots of garbage. The plastic wrappings from the videos will add to our already overextended and overutilized landfill. And a lot of them are going to wind up as litter on the streets.

Do you agree with this argument about the garbage? Is this argument in any way unique to the video store? Is it likely that people will open the wrappers and drop them on the street?

The XXX Video House stays open seven days a week, 24 hours a day. People will be forced to work at all hours and on Sunday, and that's not fair. And the store will increase the noise level at night with the cars pulling up and all.

What validity do you give to each of these arguments? Given the 24-hour policy, how might you construct an argument against the video store? Are there advantages of a neighborhood store's 24-hour policy that the audience may be thinking of and thus countering the speaker's argument? If there are, how should the speaker deal with them?

The XXX Video House—that's its name, by the way—doesn't carry regular videos that most people want. So, why do we want them?

Upon hearing this, would you be likely to extend this argument and start asking yourself, "Do we now close up all stores that most people don't want?"

The XXX Video House got a lease from an owner who doesn't even live in the community, someone by the name of, well, it's an organization called XYX Management. And their address is Carlson Place in Jeffersonville. So, they don't even live here.

Is there a connection between who the owner is and whether the video store should or shouldn't be closed? Could the speaker have effectively used this information in support of the thesis to close the video store?

Public Speaking Sample Assistant

A Poorly Constructed Persuasive Speech (Continued)

A neighboring store owner says he thinks the store is in violation of several fire laws. He says they have no sprinkler system and no metal doors to prevent the spread of a fire. So, he thinks they should be closed down, too.

Last week on *Oprah* three women were on and they were in the XXX movie business and they were all on drugs and had been in jail and they said it all started when they went into the porno business. One woman wanted to be a teacher, another wanted to be a nurse, and the other wanted to be a beautician. If there weren't any XXX video stores then there wouldn't be a porn business and, you know, pornography is part of organized crime, and so if you stop pornography you take a bite out of crime.

One of the reasons I think it should be closed is that the legitimate video stores—the ones that have only a small selection of XXX movies somewhere in the back—will lose business. And if they continue to lose business, they'll leave the neighborhood and we'll have no video stores.

That's a lot of reasons against XXX movie houses. I have a quote here: Reason is "a portion of the divine spirit set in a human body." Seneca.

In conclusion and to wrap it up and close my speech, I want to repeat and say again that the XXX video stores should all be closed down. They corrupt minors. And they're offensive to men and women and especially women. I hope you'll all protest with the Marshalls—my mother and father—and there'll be lots of others there too.

What credibility do you ascribe to the "neighboring store owner"? Do you begin to wonder if the speaker would simply agree to have the store brought up to the fire code laws?

What is the cause and what is the effect that the speaker is asserting? How likely is it that the proposed cause actually produced the effect? Might there have been causes other than working in pornography that might have led these women into drugs? What credibility do you give to people you see on talk shows? Does it vary with the specific talk show? Do you accept the argument that there would be no pornography business without video stores? What would have to be proved to you before you accepted this connection? How do you respond to the expression "Take a bite out of crime"?

Is the speaker implying that this is the real reason against XXX video stores? Do you start wondering if the speaker is against XXX video stores—as it seemed in the last argument—or only against stores that sell XXX material exclusively? What effect does this impression have on your evaluation of the speaker's credibility and the speaker's thesis?

How do you feel about the number of "reasons"? Would you have preferred fewer reasons or reasons more fully developed or more reasons? What purpose does this quotation serve?

Might the speaker have introduced this conclusion differently? What is the speaker's thesis now? What do you think of the arguments that XXX video stores are offensive? What is the effect of this argument's being introduced here in the conclusion? Do you think you'd go to the protest? Why or why not?

Door-in-the-Face Technique

With the **door-in-the-face technique**, the opposite of foot-in-the-door, you first make a large request that you know will be refused and then follow it with a more moderate request. For example, your large request might be "We're asking people to donate $100 for new school computers." When this is refused, you make a more moderate request, the one you really want your listeners to comply with (for example, "Might you be willing to contribute $10?"). In changing from the large to the more moderate request, you demonstrate your willingness to compromise and your sensitivity to your listeners. The general idea here is that your listeners will feel that since you've made concessions, they should also make concessions and at least contribute something. Listeners will probably also feel that $10 is actually quite a small amount considering the initial request and are more likely to donate the $10 (Cialdini, 1984; Cialdini & Ascani, 1976).

Identify with Your Audience

If you can show your audience that you and they share important attitudes, beliefs, and values you'll clearly advance your persuasive goal. Other similarities are also important in **identification**. For example, in some cases similarity of cultural, educational, or social background may help you identify yourself with your audience. Be aware, however, that insincere or dishonest identification is likely to backfire and create problems for the speaker. So avoid even implying similarities between yourself and your audience that don't exist.

Similarly, as a general rule, never ask the audience to do what you have not done yourself. So demonstrate your own willingness to do what you want the audience to do. If you don't, the audience will rightfully ask, "Why haven't *you* done it?" In addition to making it clear that you have done what you want your listeners to do, show them that you're happy about it. Tell them of the satisfaction you have derived from, for example, donating blood or reading to students with visual difficulties.

Use Logical Appeals

Logical, emotional, and credibility appeals are all effective tools in persuasion, and we will examine all three. However, it is persuasion from logical argument that proves to be the most effective. When the speaker persuades listeners with **logic**, the listeners are more likely to remain persuaded over time and are more likely to resist counterarguments that may come up in the future (Petty & Wegener, 1998). Let's look at three kinds of reasoning that you can use in logical appeals.

Reasoning from Specific Instances and Generalizations

In **reasoning from specific instances** (or examples), you examine several specific instances and then arrive at a generalization about the whole. This form of reasoning, known as induction, is useful when you want to develop a general principle or conclusion but cannot examine the whole. For example, you sample a few communication courses and conclude something about communication courses in general; you visit several Scandinavian cities and conclude something about the whole of Scandinavia. Critically analyze reasoning from specific instances by asking the following questions.

Were enough specific instances examined? Two general guidelines may help you decide how many instances are enough. First, the larger the group you wish covered by your conclusion, the greater the number of specific instances you should examine. If you wished to draw conclusions about members of an entire country or culture, you'd have to examine a considerable number of people before drawing even tentative conclusions. On the other hand, if you were attempting to draw a conclusion about a bushel of apples, sampling a few apples probably would be sufficient.

Second, the greater the diversity of items in the class, the more specific instances you will have to examine. Some classes or groups of items are relatively homogeneous, whereas others are more heterogeneous; this will influence how many specific instances constitute a sufficient number. Pieces of spaghetti in boiling water are all about the same; thus, sampling one usually tells you something about all the others. On the other hand, communication courses probably differ widely, so valid conclusions about communication courses as a group will require a much larger sample.

Are there significant exceptions? When you examine specific instances and attempt to draw a conclusion about the whole, take into consideration the exceptions. Thus, if you examine the GPA of computer science majors and discover that 70 percent have GPAs above 3.5, you may be tempted to draw the conclusion that computer science majors are especially bright. But what about the 30 percent who have lower GPAs? How much lower are these scores? This may be a significant exception that you'll need to take into account and may require you to qualify your conclusion in significant ways. Exactly how many exceptions will constitute "significant exceptions" will depend on the unique situation.

Reasoning from Causes and Effects

In **reasoning from causes and effects**, you may go in either of two directions. You may reason from cause to effect (from observed cause to unobserved effect) or from effect to cause (from observed effect to unobserved cause). In testing reasoning from cause to effect or from effect to cause, ask yourself the following questions.

Might other causes be producing the observed effect? If you observe a particular effect (say, high crime or student apathy), you need to ask if causes other than the one you're postulating might be producing these effects. For example, you might postulate that poverty leads to high crime, but there might be other factors actually causing the high crime rate. Or poverty might be one cause, but it might not be the most important cause. Therefore, explore the possibility of other causes' producing the observed effects.

Is the causal direction accurate? If two things occur together, it's often difficult to determine which is the cause and which is the effect. For example, a lack of interpersonal intimacy and a lack of self-confidence are often seen in the same person. The person who lacks self-confidence seldom has intimate relationships with others. But which is the cause and which is the effect? It might be that the lack of intimacy "causes" low self-confidence; it might also be, however, that low self-confidence "causes" a lack of intimacy. Of course, it might also be that some other cause (a history of negative criticism, for example) might be producing both the lack of intimacy and the low self-confidence.

Reasoning from Sign

Reasoning from sign involves drawing a conclusion on the basis of the presence of signs because they frequently occur together. Medical diagnosis is a good example of reasoning by sign. The general procedure is simple. If a sign and an object, event, or condition are frequently paired, the presence of the sign is taken as proof of the presence of the object, event, or condition. For example, fatigue, extreme thirst, and overeating are signs of hyperthyroidism, because they frequently accompany the condition. In reasoning from sign, ask yourself these questions.

Do the signs necessitate the conclusion drawn? Given fatigue, extreme thirst, and overeating, how certain can you be of the "hyperthyroid" conclusion? With most medical and legal matters we can never be absolutely certain, but we can be certain beyond a reasonable doubt.

Are there other signs that point to the same conclusion? In the thyroid example, the extreme thirst could have been brought on by any number of factors. Similarly, the fatigue and the overeating could have been attributed to other causes. Yet, taken together they seemed to point to only one reasonable diagnosis. Generally, the more signs that point toward the conclusion, the more confidence you can have that it's valid.

Are there contradictory signs? Are there signs pointing toward contradictory conclusions? For example, if the butler had a motive and a history of violence (signs supporting the conclusion that the butler was the murderer), but also had an alibi (a sign pointing to the conclusion of innocence), then the conclusion of guilt would have to be reconsidered or discarded.

Fallacies in Reasoning

Another useful way to approach logical appeals is to become aware of various fallacies you'll want to avoid in your own reasoning and will want to identify in the speeches you hear. Here are 10 such fallacies along with some examples (Lee & Lee 1972, 1995; Pratkanis & Aronson, 1991; Herrick, 2004). As you read these, try to think of examples you've heard or read recently.

- *Anecdotal evidence:* Often you'll hear people use anecdotes to "prove" a point: "Women are like that; I have three sisters" or "That's the way Japanese managers are; I've seen plenty of them." One reason **anecdotal evidence** is inadequate is that it relies on too few observations; it's usually a clear case of overgeneralizing on the basis of too little evidence. A second reason is that one person's observations may be unduly clouded by his or her own attitudes and beliefs; your attitudes toward women or the Japanese, for example, may influence your perception of their behaviors.

- *Straw man:* A **straw man** argument (like a man made of straw) is an argument that's set up merely to be knocked down. In this fallacy a speaker creates an easy-to-destroy oversimplification or distortion of the opposing position (that is, a "straw man") and then proceeds to demolish it. But, of course, if the opposing case were presented fairly and without bias, it wouldn't be so easy to destroy.

- *Appeal to tradition:* Speakers often argue against change by using **appeals to tradition**—that is, by claiming that something is wrong or some change should not be adopted because it was never done before. But, of course, not all tradition is good; in addition, the fact that something has not been done before says nothing about its value or whether it should be done now.

- *Bandwagon:* **Bandwagon** appeals, often referred to as appeals *ad populum* (appeals to the people), attempt to persuade the audience to accept or reject an idea or proposal because "everybody's doing it" or because the "right" people support it. The speaker tries to suggest that you should jump on this large and popular bandwagon—or be left out by yourself. This is a popular technique in political elections, in which campaigns use results of polls to get undecided voters to jump on candidates' bandwagons. After all, you don't want to vote for a loser. Fortunately, mindfulness is a good defense against bandwagon appeals (Fiol & O'Connor, 2003).

- *Testimonial:* The **testimonial** technique involves using the image associated with some person to gain your approval (if you respect the person) or your rejection (if you don't respect the person). This is the technique of advertisers who use people dressed up to look like doctors or plumbers or chefs to sell their products. Sometimes testimonial appeals cite only vague and general "authorities," as in "Experts agree," "Scientists say," "Good cooks know," or "Dentists advise."

- *Transfer:* In **transfer** appeals the speaker associates her or his idea with something you respect (to gain your approval) or with something you detest (to gain your rejection). For example, a speaker might characterize a proposal for condom distribution in schools as "saving our children from AIDS" (to encourage acceptance) or as "promoting sexual promiscuity" (to encourage disapproval). Sports car manufacturers try to get you to buy their cars by associating them with high status and sex appeal; exercise clubs and diet plans suggest associations with health, self-confidence, and interpersonal appeal.

- *Plain folks:* Using the **plain folks** approach, the speaker identifies himself or herself with the audience. The speaker is good—the "reasoning" goes—because he or she is one of the people, just "plain folks" like everyone else. Of course, the speaker who presents himself or herself as one of the plain folks is often not. And even if he or she is one of the plain folks, it has nothing to do with the issue under discussion.

- *Card stacking:* In **card stacking** the speaker selects only the evidence and arguments that support his or her case and may even falsify evidence or distort facts to better fit the case. Despite these misrepresentations, the speaker presents the supporting materials as "fair" and "impartial."

- *Thin entering wedge:* In another type of pseudo-argument, a speaker argues against a position on the grounds that it is a **thin entering wedge** that will open the floodgates to all sorts of catastrophes (Chase, 1956). People have used this argument throughout history to argue against change—contending, for example, that school integration and interracial marriage are just the start of the collapse of American education and society, same-sex marriage will destroy the family, computers will lead to mass unemployment, and banning smoking in public places will lead to the collapse of the restaurant industry.

- *Agenda setting:* In **agenda setting** a speaker indicates that X is the issue and that all others are unimportant and insignificant. This kind of fallacious appeal is heard frequently: "Balancing the budget is the key to the city's survival," or "There's only one issue confronting elementary education in our largest cities, and that is violence." In almost all situations, however, there are many issues and many sides to each issue. Often the person proclaiming that X is the issue really means, "I'll be able to persuade you if you focus solely on X and ignore the other issues."

Use Emotional Appeals

Emotional appeals—appeals to feelings, needs, desires, and wants—can be powerful means of persuasion (Wood, 2000). When you use motivational appeals, you appeal to those forces that energize, move, or motivate people to develop, change, or strengthen their attitudes or ways of behaving. For

example, one motive might be the desire for status. This desire might motivate you to enter a high-status occupation or to dress a certain way.

Developed more than 30 years ago, one of the most useful analyses of motives remains Abraham Maslow's fivefold **hierarchy of needs**, reproduced in Figure 2 (Bailey & Pownell, 1998; Kiel, 1999; Maslow, 1970). The theory proposes that you seek to fulfill the needs at the lowest level first and that only when those needs are satisfied do the needs at the next level begin to exert influence on your behavior. For example, you would not concern yourself with the need for security or freedom from fear if you were starving (if your need for food had not been met). Similarly, you would not be concerned with friendship if your need for protection and security had not been fulfilled. The implication for you as a speaker is that you have to know what needs of your audience are unsatisfied. These are the needs you can appeal to in motivating them. Let's look in detail at Maslow's model.

Physiological Needs

In many parts of the world, and even in parts of the United States, the physiological needs of the people are not fully met and thus, as you can appreciate, are powerful motivating forces. Lech Walesa, former leader of the Polish Solidarity Party, recognized this when he wrote: "He who gives food to the people will win." In many of the poorest countries of the world, the speaker who promises to meet these basic physiological needs is the one the people will follow. Most college students in the United States, however, have their physiological needs for food, water, and air well satisfied—so these needs will not help motivate them. People who already have sufficient food won't be motivated to get more.

Safety Needs

Those who do not have their basic safety and freedom-from-fear needs met will be motivated by appeals to security, protection, and freedom from physical and psychological distress. You see appeals to this need in advertisements for burglar protection devices for home and car, in political speeches promising greater police protection on the streets and in schools, and in speeches by motivational gurus who promise psychological safety and freedom from anxiety. This freedom from anxiety also seems to be the motive used in the advertisements of psychic services that promise to tell you what is really going on (with, say, your romantic partner) as well as what will happen in the future. With this information, they imply, you'll be free of the anxiety that a lack of knowledge brings. You'll also learn

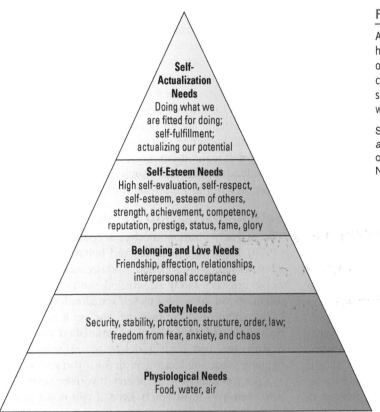

FIGURE 2 Maslow's "Hierarchy of Needs"

Abraham Maslow's model of lower-order and higher-order needs has long influenced theories of persuasion. As you read about these needs, consider which would work best with your specific class members. Are there some that would not work, at least generally?

Source: Maslow & Frager (1987). *Motivation and Personality*, 3rd ed. Adapted by permission of Pearson Education, Inc. Upper Saddle River, New Jersey.

what you should do—break off your relationship, move to the West Coast, or take that new job. The fact that this information is totally without any factual basis seems not to deter people from spending millions of dollars on psychics.

Sometimes the safety motive takes the form of a desire for order, structure, and organization—motives seen clearly in the advertisements for personal data assistants like the Blackberry, cell phones, and information management software. Many people fear what is unknown, and order and structure make things predictable and, hence, safe.

Belonging and Love Needs

Belonging and love needs are extremely powerful and comprise a variety of specific motives. For example, most people are motivated to love and be loved. For most persons, love and its pursuit occupy a considerable amount of time and energy. If you can teach your audience how to be loved and how to love, you'll have not only an attentive audience but a grateful one as well.

We also want affiliation—friendship and companionship. We want to be a part of a group, despite our equally potent desire for independence and individuality. Notice how advertisements for singles clubs, cruises, and dating services appeal to this

need for affiliation. On this basis alone they successfully gain the attention, interest, and participation of countless people. Again, such affiliation seems to assure us that we are in fact worthy creatures. If we have friends and companions, surely we are people of some merit.

Self-Esteem Needs

"In his private heart," wrote Mark Twain, "no man much respects himself." And perhaps because of this, we need to develop a positive self-image, to see ourselves in the best possible light. We want to see ourselves as self-confident, worthy, and contributing human beings. Inspirational speeches, speeches of the "you're the greatest" type, never seem to lack receptive and suggestible audiences.

Self-esteem comes, at least in part, from the approval of others (something that is important in all cultures but especially in collectivist cultures). Most people are concerned with peer approval but also want approval from family, teachers, elders, and even children. The approval of others contributes to positive self-esteem. Approval from others also ensures the attainment of related goals. For example, if you have peer approval, you probably also have influence. If you have approval, you're likely to have status. But in relating your propositions to your audience's desire for approval, avoid being too obvious. Few people want to be told that they need or desire approval.

People also want power, control, and influence. They want to have power over their own lives—to be in control of their own destiny, to be responsible for their own successes. As Emerson put it, "Can anything be so elegant as to have few wants, and to serve them one's self?"

Many people also want to have power over other persons, to be influential. Similarly, they may want to increase control over the environment and over events and things in the world. Because of this you'll motivate your listeners when you make them see that they can increase their power, control, and influence as a result of their learning what you have to say or doing as you suggest.

People want to achieve in whatever they do. As a student you want to be a successful student. You also want to achieve as a friend, as a parent, as a lover. This is why books and speeches that purport to tell people how to be better achievers are so successful. At the same time, of course, you also want others to recognize your achievements as real and valuable. In using the achievement motive, be explicit in stating how your speech, ideas, and recommendations will contribute to the listeners' achievements. At the same time, recognize that different cultures will view achievement very differently. To some achievement may mean financial success; to others, group popularity; to still others,

security. Show your audience how what you have to say will help them achieve these goals, and you'll likely have an active and receptive audience.

Although they often deny it, most people are motivated to some extent by the desire for financial gain—for what money can buy, for what it can do. Concerns for lower taxes, for higher salaries, and for fringe benefits are all related to the money motive. Show the audience that what you're saying or advocating will make them money, and they'll listen with considerable interest—much as they read the get-rich-quick books that flood the bookstores.

Self-Actualization Needs

The self-actualization motive, according to Maslow (1970), influences attitudes and behaviors only after all other needs are satisfied. And because these other needs are very rarely all satisfied, the time a speaker might spend appealing to self-actualization might be better spent on other motives. And yet it seems that, regardless of how satisfied or unsatisfied your other desires are, you have a desire to self-actualize, to become what you feel you're fit for. If you see yourself as a poet, you must write poetry. If you see yourself as a teacher, you must teach. Even if you don't pursue these as occupations, you nevertheless have a desire to write poetry or to teach. Appeals to self-actualization—"to be the best you can be"—encourage listeners to strive for their highest ideals and often are welcomed by the audience.

REFLECTIONS ON ETHICS

The Ethics of Emotional Appeals

Emotional appeals are all around. Persons who want to restrict the media's portrayal of violence may appeal to your fear of increased violence in your community; the real estate broker may appeal to your desire for status; the friend who wants a favor may appeal to your desire for social approval; the salesperson may appeal to your desire for sexual rewards. But are such appeals ethical?

Most communication theorists would argue that emotional appeals are ethical when, for example, they are used in combination with logical appeals, used in moderation, and directed at our better selves. Emotional appeals are considered unethical when, for example, they're used instead of logical evidence, directed at our baser selves, or aimed at children. In actual practice,

however, it's often difficult to distinguish between the ethical and unethical use of emotional appeals.

Ethical Choice Point

You want to dissuade your teenaged sons and daughters from engaging in sexual relationships. Would it be ethical to use emotional appeals to scare them so that they'll avoid sexual relationships? Would it be ethical to use the same appeals to get them to avoid associating with teens of other races? What ethical obligations do you have in using emotional appeals in these situations? What would you do?

© Jim Franco/Getty Images

INTRODUCING CREDIBILITY

You need a brief introduction (about 1 minute in length or about 150 words) about yourself for someone else to use to introduce you and your next speech. You want to use this introduction to establish your competence, character, and charisma.

WHAT DO YOU SAY?

Use Credibility Appeals

Your **credibility** is the degree to which your audience sees you as a believable spokesperson. If your listeners see you as competent and knowledgeable, of good character, and charismatic or dynamic, they will think you credible. As a result, you'll be more effective in changing their attitudes or in moving them to do something. Credibility is not something you have or don't have in any objective sense; rather, it's what the audience thinks of you.

What makes a person credible will vary from one culture to another. In some cultures, people would claim that competence is the most important factor in, say, the choice of a teacher for their preschool children. In other cultures, the most important factor might be the goodness or morality of the teacher or perhaps the reputation of the teacher's family.

At the same time, each culture may define each of the characteristics of credibility differently. For example, in defining "character" some cultures may emphasize the rules of a specific religion, whereas others may stress the individual conscience. The

---

Theory and Research   Credibility Impressions

UNDERSTANDING

You form a credibility impression of a speaker on the basis of two sources of information. First, you assess the reputation of the speaker as you know it. This is initial—or what theorists call "extrinsic"—credibility. Second, you evaluate the degree to which that reputation is confirmed or refuted by what the speaker says and does during the speech. This is derived—or "intrinsic"—credibility. In other words, you merge what you know about the speaker's reputation with the more immediate information you get from present interactions in order to form a combined final assessment of credibility.

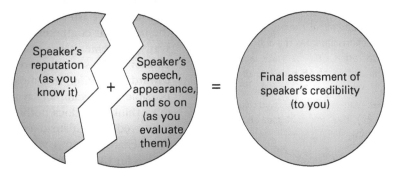

Working with Theories and Research

Does this model adequately explain how you form credibility impressions of others? Can you derive from this model any practical advice for increasing your own credibility?

Quran, the Torah, and the New Testament, for example, will all have very different levels of credibility ascribed to them depending on the religious beliefs of the audience. And this will be true even when all three religious books say essentially the same thing.

Before reading any further about the ways to establish your credibility, you may wish to take the self-test "How Credible Are You?"

TEST YOURSELF

How Credible Are You?

Respond to each of the following phrases to indicate how you think members of your class see you when you deliver a public speech. Use the following scale: Definitely true = 5; probably true = 4; neither true nor untrue = 3; probably untrue = 2; and definitely untrue = 1.

_____ 1. Knowledgeable about the subject matter

_____ 2. Experienced

_____ 3. Informed about the subject matter

_____ 4. Fair in the presentation of material (evidence and argument)

_____ 5. Concerned with the audience's needs

_____ 6. Consistent over time on the issues addressed in the speech

_____ 7. Assertive in personal style

_____ 8. Enthusiastic about the topic and in general

_____ 9. Active rather than passive

HOW DID YOU DO? This test focuses on the three qualities of credibility—competence, character, and charisma—and is based on a large body of research (for example, McCroskey, 1997; Riggio, 1987). Items 1 to 3 refer to your perceived competence: How competent or capable does the audience see you when you give a public speech? Items 4 to 6 refer to your perceived character: Does the audience see you as a person of good and moral character? Items 7 to 9 refer to your perceived charisma: Does the audience see you as dynamic and active rather than as static and passive? Scores will range from a high of 45 to a low of 9. If you scored relatively high (say around 32 or higher), then you feel your audience sees you as credible. If you scored relatively low (say below 27), then you feel your audience sees you as lacking in credibility.

WHAT WILL YOU DO? Think about how you might go about increasing your credibility. What specific steps can you take to change any audience perception with which you may be unhappy? Are there specific things you can do to strengthen your competence, character, and charisma? A good source to consult is Ronald Riggio's 1987 book *The Charisma Quotient* (New York: Dodd, Mead).

Competence

Competence includes both knowledge and expertise. The more knowledge and expertise the audience sees you as having, the more likely the audience will believe you. Similarly, you're likely to believe a teacher or doctor if you think he or she is knowledgeable on the subject. You can demonstrate your competence to your audience in a variety of ways.

Tell Listeners of Your Competence. Let the audience know of any special experience or training that qualifies you to speak on this specific topic. If you're speaking on communal living and you've lived on a commune yourself, then say so in your speech. Tell the audience of your unique and personal experiences when these contribute to your credibility.

This recommendation to tell listeners of your competence generally applies to most audiences you'll encounter in the United States. But in some cultures—notably collectivist cultures such as those of Japan, China, and Korea, for example—stressing your own competence or that of your corporation may be taken to mean that your audience members are inferior or that their corporations are not as good as yours. In other cultures—notably individualist cultures such as those of Scandinavia, the United States, and western Europe, for example—if you don't stress your competence, your listeners may assume it's because you don't have any.

Cite a Variety of Research Sources. Make it clear to your audience that you've thoroughly researched your topic. Do this by mentioning some of the books you've read, the persons you've interviewed, the articles you've consulted. Weave these throughout your speech. Don't bunch them together at one time.

Stress the Competencies of Your Sources. If your audience isn't aware of them, then emphasize the particular competencies of your sources. In this way, it becomes clear to the audience that you've chosen your sources carefully and with a view toward providing the most authoritative sources possible. For example, saying simply, "Senator Cardova thinks . . ." does nothing to establish the senator's credibility. Instead, consider saying something like "Senator Cardova, who headed the finance committee for three years and was formerly a professor of economics at MIT, thinks. . . ."

Character

An audience will see you as credible if they perceive you as having high moral **character**: as someone who is honest and someone they can trust. When an audience perceives your intentions as

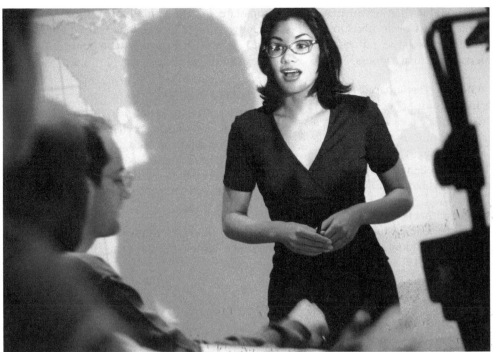

© Stockbyte/Getty Images

ESTABLISHING CREDIBILITY

You're planning a speech on baseball. The problem is that you're a woman and this audience is not going to perceive you as credible, despite your knowing more about baseball that any other person in the room.

WHAT DO YOU SAY?

good for them (rather than for your own personal gain), they'll think you credible and they'll believe you. You can establish your high moral character in several ways.

Stress Fairness. In your persuasive speech, show your fairness; stress that you've examined both sides of the issue (if indeed you have). If you're presenting both sides, then make it clear that your presentation is accurate and fair. Be particularly careful not to omit any argument the audience may already have thought of—this is a sure sign that your presentation isn't fair and balanced. Tell the audience that you would not advocate a position if you did not base it on a fair evaluation of the issues.

Stress Concern for Audience. Make it clear to the audience that you're interested in their welfare rather than seeking self-gain. If the audience feels that you're "out for yourself," they'll justifiably downgrade your credibility. Make it clear that the audience's interests are foremost in your mind. Tell your audience how the new legislation will reduce *their* taxes, how recycling will improve *their* community, how a knowledge of sexual harassment will make *their* workplace more comfortable and stress free.

Stress Concern for Enduring Values. We view speakers who are concerned with small and insignif-

icant issues as less credible than speakers who demonstrate a concern for lasting truths and general principles. Thus, make it clear to the audience that your position—your thesis—is related to higher-order values; show them exactly how this is true.

Charisma

Charisma is a combination of your personality and dynamism as seen by the audience. An audience will perceive you as credible (and believable) if they like you, and if they see you as friendly and pleasant rather than aloof and reserved. Similarly, audiences favor the dynamic speaker over the hesitant, nonassertive individual. They'll perceive you as less credible if they see you as shy, introverted, and soft-spoken rather than as extroverted and forceful. Perhaps people feel that dynamic speakers are open and honest in presenting themselves, whereas shy, introverted individuals may be hiding something. As a speaker there's much that you can do to increase your charisma and hence your perceived credibility.

Demonstrate a Positive Outlook. Show the audience that you have a positive orientation to the public speaking situation and to the entire speaker-audience encounter. We see positive and forward-looking people as more credible than negative and backward-looking people. Stress your pleasure at addressing the audience. Stress hope rather than despair; stress happiness rather than sadness.

Demonstrate Enthusiasm. The lethargic speaker who somehow plods through the speech is the very opposite of the charismatic speaker. Try viewing a film of Martin Luther King Jr. or Billy Graham speaking—they're totally absorbed with the speech and with the audience. They're excellent examples of the enthusiasm that makes a charismatic speaker.

Be Emphatic. Use language that is emphatic rather than colorless and indecisive. Use gestures that are clear and decisive rather than random and hesitant.

Demonstrate a firm commitment to the position you're advocating; the audience will be much more likely to agree with a speaker who believes firmly in the thesis of the speech.

Credibility Errors

Some speakers try to raise their own credibility by unfairly attacking another's character. For example, here are three types of such attacks. You'll want to avoid using these tactics as a speaker, and you'll want to be alert for these tactics as you listen to others (Lee & Lee, 1972, 1995; Pratkanis & Aronson, 1991; Herrick, 2004).

- *Personal interest:* **Personal interest** attacks may take either of two forms. In one form, the

THE RESEARCHER

Age and Credibility

I'm a returning student and the oldest (by about 30 years) in the class. The other students seem to regard my views as outdated even before I've explained them, and I fear it's due to my being from their parents' generation. What can I do to enhance my credibility with my classmates and with younger people generally?

College classrooms in the United States are age-segregated environments. The great majority of students are between 18 and 28 and don't expect to find students from a different age group in the classroom. Therefore, numerous age-related stereotypes will exist. The good news is that time and positive interactions can change these often negative stereotypes. First, it's important to accept that you'll be perceived as significantly different from your younger classmates. Second, it's important to realize that your life experiences, learning styles, cultural likes and dislikes, and responsibilities outside the classroom will not be similar to those of the other students. But these differences can be turned into positives. Listen to the younger students, empathize with their life issues, engage their concerns, accommodate to their styles of interaction, and find interactive strategies that are far from aggressive and "all-knowing." As the course progresses, the negative stereotypes that are evident at initial encounters will disappear, and your credibility as a student will increase.

For further information: Nussbaum, J. F., Thompson, T. L., & Robinson, J. D. (2000). *Communication and aging* (2nd ed.). Mahwah, NJ: Erlbaum. And Baringer, D. K., Kundrat, A. L., & Nussbaum, J. F. (2004). Instructional communication and older adults. In J. F. Nussbaum & J. Coupland (Eds.), *Handbook of communication and aging research* (2nd ed., pp. 543–562). Mahwah, NJ: Erlbaum.

Jon F. Nussbaum (Ph.D., Purdue University) is a professor of communication arts and sciences and human development and family studies at Pennsylvania State University. He conducts research and teaches courses on the communicative world of older adults across numerous social contexts. He has recently been elected president of the International Communication Association.

speaker disqualifies someone because he or she isn't directly affected by the issue or doesn't have firsthand knowledge, as would be the case if a speaker dismissed an argument on abortion because it was made by a man. In another form, the speaker disqualifies someone because he or she will benefit in some way from a proposal. But arguing that, for example, someone is rich, middle class, or poor and thus will benefit from a proposed tax cut does not mean that the tax cut proposal is invalid. The legitimacy of an argument can never depend on the gender (or socioeconomic status or culture) of its proponents. Nor can it depend on any gain that a person may derive from the position advocated. The legitimacy of an argument can be judged only on the basis of the evidence and reasoning presented.

■ *Character attacks:* **Character attacks**, often referred to as ad hominem attacks, involve accusing another person (usually an opponent) of some serious wrongdoing or of some serious character flaw. The purpose of this kind of fallacious appeal is to discredit the person or to divert attention from the issue under discussion. Remarks such as "How can we support a candidate who has smoked pot (or avoided the military)?" or "Do you want to believe someone who has been unfaithful on more than one occasion?" are often heard in political discussions but probably have little to do with the logic of the argument.

■ *Name calling:* In **name calling**, often referred to as "poisoning the well," the speaker calls an idea, a group of people, or a political philosophy a bad name ("atheist," "anti-American") to try to get listeners to condemn the idea without analyzing the argument and evidence. The opposite of name calling is the use of the **glittering generality**, in which the speaker tries to make listeners accept some idea by associating it with things they value highly ("democracy," "free speech," "academic freedom"). By using such "virtue words," the speaker tries to lead listeners to ignore the evidence and simply approve of the idea.

Building Communication   **Finding the Available Means of Persuasion**

What persuasive strategies would you use to convince your class of the validity of either side in any of the following points of view? For example, what persuasive strategies would you use to persuade your class members that interracial adoption should be encouraged? What strategies would you use to persuade them that interracial adoption should be discouraged?

1. *Point of View: Interracial Adoption.* Those in favor of interracial adoption argue that adoption (regardless of race) is good for the child and that the welfare of the child—who might not get adopted if not by someone of another race—must be considered first. Those opposed to interracial adoption argue that children need to be raised in a family of the same race if the child is to develop self-esteem and become a functioning member of his or her own ethnic group.

2. *Point of View: Same-Sex Marriage.* Those in favor of same-sex marriage argue that gay men and lesbians should be accorded exactly the same rights and responsibilities as heterosexuals—no more, no less. Those opposed argue that same-sex marriage will undermine the concept of marriage.

3. *Point of View: Affirmative Action.* Those in favor of affirmative action argue that because of injustices in the way certain groups (racial, national, gender) were treated, they should now be given preferential treatment to correct the imbalance caused by the earlier social injustices. Those opposed argue that merit must be the sole criterion for promotion, jobs, entrance to graduate schools, and so on, and that affirmative action is just reverse discrimination.

Working with a variety of persuasive strategies will increase your public speaking competence as both speaker and listener.

Motivate Your Listeners

If you want to persuade your listeners, you have to motivate them to believe or to act in some way. One way to motivate is to use the *motivated sequence*: Gain your audience's attention, demonstrate that a need exists, demonstrate how that need can be satisfied when they believe or do what you say, show them what things will be like once the need is satisfied, and urge them to do something to solve the problem.

Table 1 summarizes the motivated sequence as a persuasive strategy and will help you develop your persuasive speeches, whether they deal with questions of fact, value, or policy—the topics to which we now turn.

PERSUASIVE SPEECHES ON QUESTIONS OF FACT

Questions of fact concern what is or is not true, what does or does not exist, what did or did not happen. Some questions of fact are easily answered. These include many academic questions you're familiar with: Who was Aristotle? How many people use the Internet to get news? When was the first satellite launched? Questions of fact also include more mundane questions like: What's on television? When is the meeting? What's Jenny's e-mail address? You can easily find answers to these questions by looking at some reference book, finding the relevant website, or asking someone who knows the answer.

The questions of fact that we deal with in persuasive speeches are a bit different. Although these questions also have answers, the answers are not that easy to find and in fact may never be found. The questions concern controversial issues for which different people have different answers. Daily newspapers and Internet websites abound in questions of fact. For example, on July 21, 2007, Google News (www.googlenews.com) contained articles suggesting such questions of fact as these: Is Iran supporting the militias in Iraq? Did Attorney General Alberto Gonzales pressure then-Attorney General John Ashcroft to recertify President Bush's domestic surveillance program? Has North Korea complied with its promise to dismantle its nuclear plant? Is National Basketball referee Tim Donaghy guilty of betting on the games and providing information to others? Will no-smoking rules save lives? Did FEMA fail in New Orleans? Are the courts in the United States being politicized? Is human activity altering the world's rainfall patterns? Is Apple's iPhone vulnerable to hackers?

Thesis

For a persuasive speech on a question of fact, you'll formulate a thesis on the basis of a factual statement such as:

- This company has a glass ceiling for women.
- The plaintiff was slandered (or libeled or defamed).
- The death was a case of physician-assisted suicide.
- Gay men and lesbians make competent military personnel.
- Television violence leads to violent behavior in viewers.

Table 1   The Motivated Sequence as a Persuasive Strategy

Step	Purpose	Audience Question Speaker Should Answer	Audience Response You Want to Avoid
Attention	Focus listeners' attention on you and your message.	Why should I listen? Why should I use my time listening?	This is boring. This is irrelevant. This is of no interest to me.
Need	Demonstrate that there is a problem that affects them.	Why do I need to know or do anything?	I don't need to hear this. Things are fine now. This won't benefit me.
Satisfaction	Show listeners how they can satisfy the need (solve the problem).	Can I do anything about this?	I really can't do anything. It's beyond my control.
Visualization	Show listeners what their lives will be like with the need satisfied.	How would anything be different or improved?	I can't see how anything would be different. Nothing's going to change.
Action	Urge listeners to do something to solve the problem.	What can I do to effect this change?	I can't do anything. I'll be wasting my time and energy.

If you were preparing a persuasive speech on the first example given above, you might phrase your thesis as "This company discriminates against women." Whether or not the company does discriminate is a question of fact; clearly the company either does or does not discriminate. Whether you can prove it does discriminate or it doesn't, however, is another issue.

Main Points

Once you've formulated your thesis, you can generate your main points by asking the simple question "How do you know this?" or "Why would you believe this is true (factual)?" The answers to one of these questions will enable you to develop your main points. The essential components of your speech might then look something like this:

General purpose: To persuade.

Specific purpose: To persuade my listeners that this company discriminates against women.

Thesis: This company discriminates against women. (How can we tell that this company discriminates against women?)

    I. Women earn less than men.
   II. Women are hired less often than men.
  III. Women occupy fewer managerial positions than men.

Make sure that you clearly connect your main points to your thesis in your introduction, when introducing each of the points, and again in your summary. Don't allow the audience to forget that the lower salaries that women earn directly supports the thesis that this company discriminates against women.

Support

Having identified your main points, begin searching for information to support them. Taking the first point, you might develop it something like this:

  I. Women earn less than men.
     A. Over the past five years, the average salary for editorial assistants was $6,000 less for women than it was for men.
     B. Over the past five years, the entry-level salaries for women averaged $4,500 less than the entry-level salaries for men.
     C. Over the past five years, the bonuses earned by women were 20 percent below the bonuses earned by men.

The above speech focuses entirely on a question of fact; the thesis itself is a question of fact. In other speeches, however, you may want just one of your main points to center on a question of fact. So, for example, let's say you're giving a speech advocating that the military give gay men and lesbians full equality. In this case, one of your points might focus on a question of fact: You might seek to establish that gay men and lesbians make competent military personnel. Once you've established that, you'd then be in a better position to argue for equality in military policy.

In a speech on questions of fact, you want to emphasize logical proof. Facts are your best support. The more facts you have, the more persuasive you'll be in dealing with questions of fact. For example, the

Ideal Audience Response	Speech Materials to Use	Cautions to Observe
This sounds interesting. Tell me more.	Attention-gaining materials.	Make attention relevant to speech topic.
OK, I understand; there's a problem.	Supporting materials (examples, statistics, testimony).	Don't overdramatize the need.
I can change things.	Supporting materials; logical, emotional, and credibility appeals.	Answer any objections listeners might have to your plan.
Wow! Things look a lot better this way.	Emotional appeals. Illustrations and language high in imagery.	Be realistic; don't visualize the world as perfect once your listeners do as you suggest.
Let me sign up. Here's my contribution. I'll participate in the effort.	Emotional appeals. Specific language.	Be specific. Ask for small attitude changes and easily performed behaviors.

more evidence you can find that women earn less than men, the more convincing you will be in proving that women do in fact earn less and, ultimately, that women are discriminated against.

Use the most recent materials possible. The more recent your materials, the more relevant they will be to the present time and the more persuasive they're likely to be. Notice, in our example, that if you said that in 1980 women earned on average $13,000 less than men, that fact would be meaningless in relation

to the question of whether the company discriminates against women *now*.

Organization

Speeches on questions of fact probably fit most readily into a topical organizational pattern, in which each reason for your thesis is given approximately equal weight. Notice, for example, that the outline of the speech under "Main Points" uses a topic order in

An Excellent Persuasive Speech

Untitled [False Confessions]

Jessy Ohl

Kansas State University

Coached by Craig Brown, Bobby Imbody, and Erica Imbody

Assuming I don't violate the rules, I get 1,800 words to try and change the way you think and feel about some issue. My goal, in a sense, is to get you to confess that my point of view is the "truth" and to do so in around 10 minutes. But what if I really had no time limit, and could speak for say—20 hours? Twenty hours where you had to listen to me. I'd get to badger you, yell at you, no breaks, no judges' lounge, just 20 hours of me. I'm not that bad to listen to for around 10 minutes, but after 20 hours, you'd be ready to sign whatever petition I put in front of you, or confess to practically any crime just to get me to shut up. And I wouldn't blame you. And neither would Kevin Fox. He cracked after only 14 hours. Kevin Fox wasn't a judge in a seriously overtime speech round. Instead, on December 13, 2004, he was a suspect in the murder of his three-year-old daughter Riley. After 14 straight hours of "aggressive persuasion," as the June 21, 2005, *Chicago Tribune* reported, he confessed. The problem is—he didn't do the crime. Only after DNA evidence surfaced did anyone take seriously his claim that he had been coerced into giving a false confession.

There is a fatal flaw with the U.S. legal system—it's too easy to promote and create false confessions. The *Journal of Psychological Science* of August 2005 found that as many as 1 in 5 faulty convictions are from false confessions. Now, you might think, I'm never even going to be in a position to be arrested, let alone give a false confession. OK, but every time someone else is convicted on the basis of a false confession, that means that you and I are still threatened by the real guilty party. It's time to stop the promotion of and abuse of false confessions. And to do so, in what I promise will take a lot less than 20 hours, we must first examine the damage created by

Here the speaker refers to the immediate occasion—the speech contest the speaker is now in—and then relates this situation to the topic of the speech; namely, coerced confessions. After you read the entire speech, return to this introduction and consider in what other ways the speaker might gain audience attention and introduce the topic of the speech.

Here the speaker clearly identifies the thesis: The legal system is flawed because it's too easy to create false confessions. The speaker then reinforces this thesis with the finding from a current article in the *Journal of Psychological Science* that 1 out of 5 confessions may be faulty—a statistic that gains our attention. If you were listening to this speech, would you accept this statistic, or would you want more evidence that this large a number of confessions are in fact false? If you would want additional evidence, what would that look like?

Notice how the speaker makes sure that the listeners understand the importance of this topic to them—the topic is not

Public Speaking Sample Assistant

An Excellent Persuasive Speech *(Continued)*

false confessions, second, explain why anybody would admit to a crime they didn't commit, and finally, discover solutions to get our legal system back on track.

OK, there are going to be the occasional mistakes. But unfortunately, with false confessions they're more than occasional and they're creating damage throughout the process. The *Denver Post* of April 18, 2006, concludes that gross misjudgments in convictions due to coerced confessions create illegitimacy in all prosecutions. And these occurrences are unfortunately far from rare. So let's first look at the scope and then the damage created. The June 4, 2005, issue of *Psychology Today* finds that although it is nearly impossible to determine the exact number of false confessions nationwide, a 2003 review discovered 247 such instances in a single Illinois county over the past 10 years. The *Baltimore Sun* of April 26, 2005, points out that examples range from the juvenile, to adult, to mentally disabled. But the real damage is what happens to those unjustly convicted and to the public; we think we are being protected. For example, Jon Kogut was sentenced to life in prison in 1985 when he confessed to murder. Mr. Kogut spent 17 years before forensic evidence cleared his name. That "solved case" is now a cold case.

An erroneous and problematic legal system that violates the rights of innocent people puts us in danger. The *Chicago Tribune* of June 18, 2005, claims that the United States' prosecution system is constructed in a way that rushes to conviction. But these hasty decisions are threatening the very fabric of justice. As Dr. Joseph Unekis put it in his 2005 book *People, Problems and Power*, the basic principle of the American legal system is the presumed innocence of the accused. You are innocent until proven guilty, not innocent until forced to confess.

I'm sure by now you're wondering one thing about false confessions. Why would you ever admit to a crime that you didn't commit? But remember, what if I had that 20 hours? How we think an interrogation works isn't what really happens. There are two explanations for false confessions: first, interrogation techniques, and second, human tolerance to persuasion. First, police officers are effectively trained to extract confessions, truthful or not. The *Wall Street Journal* of April 15, 2005, reports that "standard interrogation techniques are masterfully designed to leave people with almost no rational choice but confess." The *Christian Science Monitor* of July 20, 2005, explains that "Police can legally lie to suspects, claiming to have physical evidence or witnesses that don't exist." This explains the *Milwaukee Journal Sentinel*'s November 7, 2004, account of the interrogation of a 14-year-old murder suspect. He was told by police that they had witnesses and if

merely important in the abstract, but it's important to these specific audience members. If you were giving this speech to the members of your class, how would you establish the importance of the topic to them? Put differently, how would you answer their question, "Why should I listen to this speech?"

Here the speaker gives an orientation as to the major ideas to be discussed: the damage created by false confessions (the problem), why anyone would admit to a crime he or she didn't commit (some causes that help create the problem), and the ways to get the legal system back on track (the solution). Might this speech have been organized in another pattern? How might you reorganize this speech into the motivated sequence pattern?

This first point explains the problem the frequency of false confessions and the damage that false confessions do to everyone. As a listener, are you convinced? If not, what would convince you?

Here the speaker provides a transition to the second point, namely why anyone would falsely confess to a crime—a question the speaker already began to answer in the introduction. This transition, as all the transitions in this speech, cue the audience into what will be discussed next. Can you identify places in the speech where additional transitions might have been effective?

This second major idea is itself divided into two parts: interrogation techniques and human tolerance.

The argument that interrogation techniques are responsible for these false confessions is supported by the strength and credibility of the *Wall Street Journal* and the *Christian Science Monitor*, two highly respected newspapers. Would members of your class agree that these are respectable and credible sources of such information?

An Excellent Persuasive Speech *(Continued)*

he didn't confess, he would be raped in prison and given the chair. After six hours with no parent or lawyer, he did confess. Only later was he found innocent.

The second cause for false confessions is the human tolerance to persuasion. Professor Saul Kassin from Williams College in Massachusetts told the *Wall Street Journal* on April 15, 2005, that under traumatic circumstances an individual will confess in order to ensure survival. Being innocent does not protect you from these limits. An experiment published in the winter 2005 edition of *Justice Denied* concluded that 69 percent of participants in the study signed a false confession that they destroyed a government property when confronted with fictitious evidence of their wrongdoing. Despite popular belief, we can all be coaxed into giving a false confession. Richard Ofshe, a sociology professor at the University of California at Berkeley, explained in *Newsday* of May 24, 2005, "most people believe that the innocent won't falsely confess unless they're tortured," but that "psychological coercion" can reduce you to "a state of hopelessness" where you believe confessing is the only alternative.

For example, after 50 hours of interrogation in a small windowless room, Corinthian Bell confessed to murder because he thought that if he told the police what they wanted to hear, they would release him. In the same way, if I legitimately threatened you with a 20-hour persuasion, you'd probably give me a good rank just to shut me up. The *St. Petersburg Times* of December 25, 2005, estimates that nearly 600 Floridians are wrongfully imprisoned, with false confession being both a leading and a preventable cause.

We need to do more to protect the innocent, and get truth back in our legal system. Therefore we will examine solutions on both the federal and personal level. First, on the federal level actions must be taken in order to make interrogations credible. The answer, according to the *New York Times* of April 11, 2006, is mandatory legislation that would require all interrogations to be recorded. Thus, Congress should pass the New York Bar Association's proposed legislation that would give all courtrooms a working history of the interrogation process. Our government must follow the example of Illinois, which as of August 2005 required all interrogations be recorded.

The good news is, cops actually like the idea. A 2004 survey by the Center of Wrongful Convictions found a 98 percent approval rating from the police department using this system. The bad news is that less than 1 percent of interrogation rooms across the country employ such technology. Once implemented this would allow jury members to judge the validity of the remarks and protect police officers who are merely trying to put criminals behind bars. Additionally, modifications must be made to the

The story of the 14-year-old boy is a particularly dramatic, example of how unethical interrogation techniques can produce false confessions. Would you have liked to hear more about this particular case? If so, what else might the speaker have included? As you read and respond to comments like this, however, remember the time limits the speaker is up against. If this example were to be increased in length, something else from the speech would have to be deleted. What might that be?

Notice that the next cause of false confessions, human tolerance, is clearly introduced. The audience knows to expect a discussion of how the limits of tolerance can produce such confessions.

This speech contains a particularly good mixture of abstract and general information (for example, the statistic that 69 percent of participants in a study signed false confessions and the fact that a sociologist argued that this can happen to most people) along with specific and concrete examples (for example, the confession of Corinthian Bell). After presenting the specific example, the speaker then returns to more general statistics, noting that in Florida alone some 600 people are wrongfully imprisoned, often based on false confessions.

The speaker here returns to the thesis of the speech—the need to get the legal system back on track—and provides a transition to the third major point, the solution to this clearly demonstrated problem.

The speaker proposes several solutions to the problem. The first solution proposed is that all interrogations be recorded. Another solution is to modify the interrogation training of police officers. Notice, below, that the speaker doesn't leave the audience with solutions that they can do little about but instead suggests that they raise the issue with relevant candidates and contribute to the Center on Wrongful Convictions.

Public Speaking Sample Assistant

An Excellent Persuasive Speech *(Continued)*

interrogation training received by police officers. In nearly all cases false confessions are the product not of bad cops, but rather of good cops wielding bad techniques. The *Boston Globe* of November 27, 2005, believes that requiring interrogators to remain truthful can prevent false confessions and still trap guilty suspects. To help make this a reality, when election time rolls around, raise this issue with candidates running for District Attorney offices in your area. And you don't have to wait for an election to help. Make a tax-deductible donation to the Center on Wrongful Convictions at Northwestern University via their website. Your contributions support the center's mission to identify and rectify wrongful convictions.

On the personal level, you should also be ready to take steps to protect yourself. If you are ever arrested or even a suspect, realize, your best defense is to know your rights. In honor of the movie *Fight Club*, the rules of interrogation are as follows: Rule 1: Don't talk; rule 2: DON'T TALK. Don't say a word without a lawyer. The police can legally lie and attempt to deceive you. So don't talk. And finally, if you're on the other side of this situation, as a jury member, help eliminate the stereotype that a confession is synonymous with truth. If this were true, I would merely confess to being the sexiest speaker in the world.

Today we examined the problem and causes of false confessions in America, and discovered solutions to get truth back in our legal system. If after only 10 minutes of my persuasion you feel like you're ready to crack, think about what Kevin Fox went through before he signed a paper saying he murdered his daughter. And remember that a confessed "truth" will not necessarily set you free.

Source: This speech is an edited version of the copy printed in Winning Orations of the Interstate Oratorical Association (Mankata, MN: Interstate Oratorical Association, 2006, pp. 25–27).

Notice that the speaker uses a variety of newspapers, newsmagazines, and professional journals along with testimony from various people. What other supporting materials might the speaker have included?

Additional solutions on a more personal level also are suggested in the event that the audience member ever finds himself or herself a suspect or a juror. Did the inclusion of this personal-level material make you feel that the topic was really important to you? If not, what additional arguments would you have wanted?

Here the speaker wraps up the speech by summarizing the three major ideas discussed (the problem, its causes, and proposed solutions) and closes by recalling the example used in the introduction.

which all of the reasons pointing to discrimination are treated as equal main points.

PERSUASIVE SPEECHES ON QUESTIONS OF VALUE

Questions of value concern what people consider good or bad, moral or immoral, just or unjust. Google News (July 21, 2007), for example, identified such questions of value as these: Are the proposed changes to Medicare beneficial? What should be the legacy of Tammy Faye [Bakker] Messner? What is the value of stopping North Korea's nuclear program? Should the Food and Drug Administration have approved the

new breast cancer drug? Was Tony Blair a good choice for Mideast envoy? Will increasing the minimum wage help workers (or businesses)? Should safeguards be developed to protect consumer privacy on the Internet? Should circumcision be promoted to slow the spread of AIDS? Should Cindy Sheehan have been arrested during her call for President Bush's impeachment? Should the state of Washington have instituted the Domestic Partnership Law? Should Calgary paramedics be permitted to strike? Is funding faith-based education a good idea?

Speeches on questions of value will seek to strengthen audiences' existing attitudes, beliefs, or values. This is true of much religious and political speaking; for example, people who listen to religious speeches usually are already believers, so these speeches strive to strengthen the beliefs and values the people already hold. In a religious setting, the listeners already share the speaker's values and are willing to listen. Speeches that seek to change audience values are much more difficult to construct. Most people resist change. When you try to get people to change their values or beliefs, you're fighting an uphill (though not necessarily impossible) battle.

Be sure that you define clearly the specific value on which you're focusing. For example, let's say that you're developing a speech to persuade high school students to attend college. You want to stress that college is of value, but what type of value do you focus on? The financial value (college graduates earn more money than nongraduates)? The social value (college is a lot of fun and a great place to make friends)? The intellectual value (college will broaden your view of the world and make you a more critical and creative thinker)? Once you clarify the type of value on which you'll focus, you'll find it easier to develop the relevant points. You'll also find it easier to locate appropriate supporting materials.

Thesis

Theses devoted to questions of value might look something like this:

- The death penalty is unjustifiable.
- Bullfighting is inhumane.
- Discrimination on the basis of affectional orientation is wrong.
- Chemical weapons are immoral.
- Human cloning is morally justified.
- College athletics minimize the importance of academics.

Main Points

As with speeches on questions of fact, you can generate the main points for a speech on a question of value by asking a strategic question of your thesis, such as "Why is this good?" or "Why is this immoral?" For example, you can take the first thesis given above and ask, "Why is the death penalty unjustifiable?" The answers to this question will give you the speech's main points. The body of your speech might then look something like this:

General purpose: To persuade.

Specific purpose: To persuade my listeners that the death penalty is unjustifiable.

Thesis: The death penalty is unjustifiable. (Why is the death penalty unjustifiable?)

I. The criminal justice system can make mistakes.
II. The death penalty constitutes cruel and unusual punishment.
III. No one has the moral right to take another's life.

Support

To support your main points, search for relevant evidence. For example, to show that mistakes have been made, you might itemize three or four high-profile cases in which people were put to death and later, through DNA, found to have been innocent.

At times, and with certain topics, it may be useful to identify the standards you would use to judge something moral or justified or fair or good. For example, in the "bullfighting is inhumane" speech, you might devote your first main point to defining when an action can be considered inhumane. In this case, the body of your speech might look like this:

I. An inhumane act has two qualities.
   A. It is cruel and painful.
   B. It serves no human necessity.
II. Bullfighting is inhumane.
   A. It is cruel and painful.
   B. It serves no necessary function.

Notice that in the example of capital punishment, the speaker aims to strengthen or change the listeners' beliefs about the death penalty. The speaker is not asking the audience to do anything about capital punishment, but merely to believe that it's not justified. However, you might also use a question of value as a first step toward persuading your audience to take some action. For example, once you got your listeners to see the death penalty as unjustified, you might then ask them to take certain actions—perhaps in your next speech—to support an anti-death penalty politician, to vote for or against a particular proposition, or to join an organization fighting against the death penalty.

Organization

Like speeches on questions of fact, speeches on questions of value often lend themselves to topical organization. For example, the speech on capital punishment cited earlier uses of topical order. But even within this topical order there is another level of organization, an organization that begins with those items on which there is least disagreement or opposition and moving on to the items on which your listeners are likely to have very different ideas. It's likely that even people in favor of the death penalty would agree that mistakes can be made; and they probably would be willing to accept evidence that mistakes have in fact been made, especially if you cite reliable statistical evidence and expert testimony. By starting

Building Communication

Constructing Logical, Motivational, and Credibility Appeals

Below are statements suitable as theses for a variety of persuasive speeches. Select any one statement (or its opposite) and construct (a) a logical appeal, (b) an emotional appeal, and (c) a credibility appeal that would prove effective in persuading your class.

1. Sports involving cruelty to animals—such as bullfighting, cockfighting, and foxhunting—should (not) be universally condemned and declared illegal.
2. Gay men and lesbians should (not) be allowed to serve in the military on the same conditions as heterosexuals.
3. Retirement should (not) be mandatory at age 65 for all government employees.
4. The death penalty is (not) morally wrong.
5. Too little (too much) government money is spent on accommodating people with disabilities.

Practicing the art of persuasion will prove useful in a wide variety of communication situations.

with this issue, you secure initial agreement and can use that as a basis for approaching areas where you and the audience are more likely to disagree.

PERSUASIVE SPEECHES ON QUESTIONS OF POLICY

When you move beyond a focus on value to urging your audience to do something about an issue, you're then into a question of policy. For example, in a speech designed to convince your listeners that bullfighting is inhumane, you'd be focusing on a question of value. If you were to urge that bullfighting should therefore be declared illegal, you'd be urging the adoption of a particular policy. Items on Google News (July 21, 2007) that suggested questions of policy included these: How can flooding be prevented? What should be the policy of search engines regarding behaviorally targeted ads? How can prison overcrowding best be reduced? What can be done to improve communication between medical professionals and their older patients? What should be the policy concerning paramedics going on strike? What policy should the National Basketball Association adapt regarding betting by members? How should the United States treat Iran (North Korea)? What safeguards should be developed to protect consumer privacy on the Internet?

Questions of policy concern what should be done, what procedures should be adopted, what laws should be changed; in short, what policy should be followed. In some speeches you may want to propose a new policy or to defend an existing policy; in others you may wish to argue that a current policy should be discontinued.

Thesis

Persuasive speeches frequently revolve around questions of policy and may use theses such as the following:

- Hate speech should be banned in colleges.
- Our community should adopt a zero tolerance policy for guns in schools.
- Abortion should be available on demand.
- Music CDs should be rated for violence and profanity.
- Medical marijuana should be legalized.
- Smoking should be banned from all public buildings and parks.

As you can tell from these examples, questions of policy almost invariably involve questions of values. For example, the argument that hate speech should be banned in colleges is based on the value judgment that hate speech is wrong. To argue for a zero tolerance policy on guns in schools implies that you think it's wrong for students or faculty to carry guns to school.

Main Points

You can develop your speech on a question of policy by asking a strategic question of your thesis. With policy issues the question will be "Why should the policy be adopted?" or "Why should this policy be

© Bob Daemmrich Photography

PERSUASIVE APPEALS

You want to give a speech urging your listeners to vote in favor of establishing a hate speech code at the college. You want to use both logical and emotional appeals.

WHAT DO YOU SAY?

discontinued?" or "Why is this policy better than what we now have?" Taking our first example, we might ask, "Why should hate speech be banned on campus?" From the answers to this question, you would develop your main points, which might look something like this:

    I. Hate speech encourages violence against women and minorities.
    II. Hate speech denigrates women and minorities.
    III. Hate speech teaches hate instead of tolerance.

SUMMARY: THE PERSUASIVE SPEECH

This unit focused on persuasive speeches and examined the goals of persuasion, several principles of persuasion, and three types of persuasive speeches.

1. Persuasive speeches may have one of three main goals: (1) to strengthen or weaken the attitudes, beliefs, or values of your listeners; (2) to change their attitudes, beliefs, or values; and (3) to motivate them to act in some way, to do something.

2. Among the guidelines for preparing persuasive speeches are the following:
   - Anticipate selective exposure.
   - Ask for reasonable amounts of change.
   - Identify with your audience.
   - Use logical appeals.
   - Use emotional appeals.

Support

Having chosen your main points, you then support each point with a variety of supporting materials that will help convince your audience that hate speech should be banned from college campuses. For example, you might cite the websites put up by certain groups that advocate violence against women and minority members, or quote from the lyrics of performers who came to campus. Or you might cite examples of actual violence that had been accompanied by hate speech or hate literature.

In some speeches on questions of policy, you may simply want your listeners to agree that the policy you're advocating is a good idea. In other cases you may want them to do something about the policy— to vote for a particular candidate, to write to their elected officials, to participate in the walkathon, to wear an AIDS awareness ribbon, and so on.

Organization

Speeches on questions of policy may be organized in a variety of ways. For example, if you're comparing two policies, consider the comparison-and-contrast method. If the existing policy is doing harm, consider using a cause-to-effect pattern. If your policy is designed to solve a problem, consider the problem-solution pattern. For example, in a speech advocating zero tolerance for guns in school, the problem-solution pattern would seem appropriate; your speech would thus be divided into two basic parts:

    I. Guns are destroying our high schools. (problem)
    II. We must adopt a zero tolerance policy. (solution)

   - Use credibility appeals.
   - Motivate your listeners.

3. Several logical fallacies are especially widespread and should be avoided by speakers and recognized by listeners: anecdotal evidence, straw man, appeal to tradition, bandwagon, testimonial, transfer, plain folks, card stacking, thin entering wedge, and agenda setting.

4. Attacks on another's credibility also should be avoided; these include attacks on the grounds of personal interest, character attacks, and name calling.

5. Persuasive speeches can be classified in various ways. One way is in terms of the major question a persuasive speech addresses:
   - Questions of fact focus on what is or is not.
   - Questions of value focus on what is good or bad.
   - Questions of policy focus on what should be done.

KEY TERMS IN THE PERSUASIVE SPEECH

agenda setting
anecdotal evidence
appeal to tradition
bandwagon
card stacking
character
character attacks
charisma
competence
credibility

door-in-the-face technique
emotional appeals
foot-in-the-door technique
glittering generality
hierarchy of needs
identification
logic
name calling
personal interest
persuasion

plain folks
questions of fact
questions of policy
questions of value
reasoning from causes and
   effects
reasoning from sign
reasoning from specific
   instances
straw man

testimonial
thin entering wedge
transfer

THINKING CRITICALLY ABOUT THE PERSUASIVE SPEECH

1. **Gender and Persuasion.** You're planning to give a speech urging more conscientious recycling to two separate audiences. One audience will be composed solely of women and the other audience solely of men. Otherwise the audience members will be similar: college-educated professionals about 30 years old. In what ways would you make the two speeches differ? What general principles or assumptions about gender are you making as you differentiate these two speeches?

2. **Foot-in-the-Door or Door-in-the-Face.** You want to get your listeners to contribute one hour a week to your college's program of helping high school students prepare for college. You're considering using the foot-in-the-door or the door-in-the-face technique. How would you develop each of these strategies? Which would you eventually use?

3. **Fact, Value, and Policy in the News.** Examine one issue of a national newspaper. What are the questions of fact, value, and policy that this newspaper edition covers? Then read the editorials. What types of questions do the editorial address?

4. **The Persuasiveness of Blogs.** Visit a few blogs and analyze them in terms of the principles of persuasion discussed in this unit. How are blogs like persuasive speeches? How are they different?

5. **The Two-Minute Speech.** Prepare and deliver a two-minute speech in which you do one of the following:
   • Explain an interesting attitude, belief, or value that you have come across.
   • Explain how a speech strengthened or changed one of your attitudes or beliefs.
   • Explain an advertisement in terms of the principles of persuasion.

LOGON! MYCOMMUNICATIONLAB
WWW.MYCOMMUNICATIONLAB.COM

Visit MCL and take the self-test on the ethics of persuasion, When Is Persuasion Unethical? Also, read the discussion Motivational Principles, and try the exercises Analyzing Arguments: The Toulmin Model and Gender, Credibility, and the Topics of Persuasive Speaking.

Take a look at the video clip on Credibility and the clips War Posters, Responsibility, and Talk to the Elderly and examine these in terms of the principles of persuasion. Also take a look at some of the explore exercises, for example, Proposition Me.

REFERENCES

Bailey, G., & Pownell, D. (1998). Technology staff-development and support programs: Applying Abraham Maslow's hierarchy of needs. *Learning and Leading with Technology, 26* (November), 47-51.

Chase, S. (1956). *Guides to straight thinking: With 13 common fallacies.* New York: Harper & Brothers.

Cialdini, R. T. (1984). *Influence: How and why people agree to things.* New York: Morrow.

Cialdini, R. T., & Ascani, K. (1976). Test of a concession procedure for inducing verbal, behavioral, and further compliance with a request to give blood. *Journal of Applied Psychology, 61,* 295-300.

DeJong, W. (1979). An examination of self-perception mediation of the foot-in-the-door effect. *Journal of Personality and Social Psychology, 37,* 2221-2239.

Fiol, C. M., & O'Connor, E. J. (2003). Waking up! Mindfulness in the face of bandwagons. *Academy of Management Review, 28* (January), 54-70.

Freedman, J., & Fraser, S. (1966). Compliance without pressure: The foot-in-the-door technique. *Journal of Personality and Social Psychology, 4,* 195-202.

Gonzenbach, W. J., King, C., & Jablonski, P. (1999). Homosexuals and the military: An analysis of the spiral of silence. *Howard Journal of Communication, 10* (October-December), 281-296.

Herrick, J. A. (2004). *Argumentation: Understanding and shaping arguments* (updated edition). State College, PA: Strata.

Jeffres, L. W., Neuendorf, K. A., & Atkin, D. (1999). Spirals of silence: Expressing opinions when the climate of opinion is unambiguous. *Political Communication, 16* (April-June), 115-131.

Kiel, J. M. (1999). Reshaping Maslow's hierarchy of needs to reflect today's education and managerial philosophies. *Journal of Instructional Psychology, 26* (September), 167-168.

Lee, A. M., & Lee, E. B. (1972). *The fine art of propaganda.* San Francisco: International Society for General Semantics.

Lee, A. M., & Lee, E. B. (1995). The iconography of propaganda analysis. *Etc.: A Review of General Semantics, 52* (Spring), 13-17.

Maslow, A. (1970). *Motivation and personality.* New York: HarperCollins.

McCroskey, J. C. (1997). *Introduction to rhetorical communication* (7th ed.). Englewood Cliffs, NJ: Prentice-Hall.

Noelle-Neumann, E. (1973). Return to the concept of powerful mass media. In H. Eguchi & K. Sata (Eds.), *Studies in broadcasting: An international annual of broadcasting science* (pp. 67-112). Tokyo: Nippon Hoso Kyokai.

Noelle-Neumann, E. (1980). Mass media and social change in developed societies. In G. C. Wilhoit & H. de Bock (Eds.), *Mass communication review yearbook* (Vol. 1, pp. 657-678). Thousand Oaks, CA: Sage.

Noelle-Neumann, E. (1991). The theory of public opinion: The concept of the spiral of silence. In J. A. Anderson (Ed.), *Communication yearbook 14* (pp. 256-287). Thousand Oaks, CA: Sage.

Pratkanis, A. R., & Aronson, E. (1991). *Age of propaganda: The everyday use and abuse of persuasion.* New York: W. H. Freeman.

Riggio, R. E. (1987). *The charisma quotient.* New York: Dodd, Mead.

Scheufele, D. A., & Moy, P. (2000). Twenty-five years of the spiral of silence: A conceptual review and empirical outlook. *International Journal of Public Opinion Research, 12* (Spring), 3-28.

Windahl, S., & Signitzer, B. (with Olson, J. T.). (1992). *Using communication theory: An introduction to planned communication.* Thousand Oaks, CA: Sage.

Wood, W. (2000). Attitude change: Persuasion and social influence. *Annual Review of Psychology, 51,* 539-570.

Chapter 8

Verbal Messages

Verbal Messages

MAJOR TOPICS

Principles of Verbal Messages
Disconfirmation and Confirmation
Using Verbal Messages Effectively

Special Features

Family and Cultural Differences:
Richard Fiordo

Can You Distinguish Facts from
Inferences?

The Media and Disconfirmation

Lying

Understanding Theories of Gender
Differences

Understanding The Verb "To Be"

Skills Confirming, Rejecting, or
Disconfirming

Skills Talking about the Middle

Y ou can use language to communicate your thoughts and feelings and to create meaningful and lasting relationships. But you can just as easily use language to distort and prevent meaningful dialogue and destroy relationships.

In this unit you'll learn about:
- how language works.
- the nature of disconfirmation and confirmation.

You'll learn to:
- express confirmation when appropriate.
- use verbal messages more effectively.

A s you communicate, you use two major signal systems—the verbal and the nonverbal. *Verbal messages* are messages sent with words. It's important to remember that the word *verbal* refers to *words*, not to *orality*; verbal messages consist of both oral and written words. In contrast, verbal messages do not include laughter; vocalized pauses you make when you speak (such as *er*, *hmm*, and *ah*); and responses you make to others that are oral but don't involve words (such as *ha ha*, *aha*, and *ugh*!). These vocalizations are considered *nonverbal*—as are, of course, facial expressions, eye movements, gestures, and so on.

Your messages normally occur in "packages" consisting of both verbal and nonverbal signals that occur simultaneously. Usually, verbal and nonverbal behaviors reinforce or support each other. For example, you don't usually express fear with words while the rest of your body relaxes. You don't normally express anger with your body posture while your face smiles. Your entire being works as a whole—verbally and nonverbally—to express your thoughts and feelings.

This unit focuses on the verbal system (the next will examine the nonverbal system) and discusses the principles of verbal messages, the concepts of confirmation and disconfirmation, and the ways you can use verbal messages most effectively.

PRINCIPLES OF VERBAL MESSAGES

As you grew up, you learned the language spoken by the people around you. You learned its phonological, or sound, system; its semantic system, or system of word meanings; and its syntactic system, which enabled you to put words into meaningful sentence patterns. Our concern in this unit is not with the grammatical structure of language (that's the linguist's job), but with the verbal messages you speak and hear. These verbal messages, of course, rely on the rules of grammar; you can't just make up sounds or words or string words together at random and expect to be understood. But, as we'll see, following the rules of grammar is not enough to achieve effective communication. For this we need to understand five key principles of verbal messages: (1) meanings are in people, (2) meanings depend on context, (3) language is denotative *and* connotative, (4) language varies in directness, and (5) messages are influenced by culture and gender.

Meanings Are in People

If you wanted to know the meaning of the word *love*, you'd probably turn to a dictionary. There you'd find a definition such as Webster's: "the attraction, desire, or affection felt for a person who arouses delight or admiration or elicits tenderness, sympathetic interest, or benevolence." But where would you turn if you wanted to know what Pedro means when he says, "I'm in love"? Of course, you'd ask Pedro to discover his meaning. It's in this sense that meanings are not in words but in people. Consequently, to uncover meaning, you need to look into people and not merely into words.

Also recognize that as you change, you also change the meanings you created out of past messages. Thus, although the message sent may not have changed, the meanings you created from it yesterday and the meanings you create today may be quite different. Yesterday, when a special someone said, "I love you," you created certain meanings. But today, when you learn that the same "I love you" was said to three other people, or when you fall in love with

215

someone else, you drastically change the meanings you perceive from those three words.

This principle is especially important in intercultural communication, as meanings for the same words are often drastically different between members of different cultures. This became especially obvious after the tragedy of the World Trade Center attack: Terms like *justice*, *suicide*, and *terrorism* were given totally different meanings by many in Afghanistan and in the United States.

A failure to recognize this important principle is at the heart of a common pattern of miscommunication called bypassing. **Bypassing** is "the miscommunication pattern which occurs when the sender (speaker, writer, and so on) and the receiver (listener, reader, and so forth) miss each other with their meanings" (Haney, 1973). Bypassing can take either of two forms.

Bypassing: Different Words, Same Meaning

One type of bypassing occurs when two people use different words but give them the same meaning; on the surface there's disagreement, but at the level of meaning there's agreement. The two people actually agree but assume, because they use different words (some of which may actually never be verbalized), that they disagree. Here's an example:

PAT: I'm not interested in one-night stands. I want a permanent relationship. [Meaning: I want an exclusive dating relationship.]

CHRIS: I'm not ready for that. [Meaning: I'm not ready for marriage.]

Bypassing: Same Words, Different Meaning

The second type of bypassing is more common and occurs when two people use the same words but give the words different meanings. On the surface it looks like the two people agree (simply because they're using the same words). But if you look more closely, you see that the apparent agreement masks real disagreement, as in this example:

PAT: I don't really believe in religion. [Meaning: I don't really believe in God.]

CHRIS: Neither do I. [Meaning: I don't really believe in organized religions.]

Here Pat and Chris assume that they agree, but actually they disagree. At some later date the implications of these differences may well become crucial.

Numerous other examples could be cited. Couples who say they're "in love" may mean very different things; one person may be thinking about "a permanent and exclusive commitment," whereas the other may be referring to "a sexual involvement." "Come home early" may mean one thing to an anxious parent and quite another to a teenager.

Because of bypassing it is a mistake to assume that when two people use the same word, they mean the same thing, or that when they use different words, they mean different things. Words in themselves don't have meaning; meaning is in the people who use those words. Therefore, people can use different words but mean the same thing or use the same words but mean different things.

Meanings Depend on Context

Verbal and nonverbal communications exist in a context, and that context to a large extent determines the meaning of any verbal or nonverbal behavior. The same words or behaviors may have totally different meanings when they occur in different contexts. For example, the greeting "How are you?" means "Hello" to someone you pass regularly on the street but means "Is your health improving?" when said to a friend in the hospital. A wink to an attractive person on a bus means something completely different from a wink that says "I'm kidding."

Similarly, the meaning of a given signal depends on the other behavior it accompanies or is close to in time. Pounding a fist on the table during a speech in support of a politician means something quite different from that same gesture in response to news of a friend's death. Focused eye contact may signify openness and honesty in one culture and defiance in another. In isolation from the context, it's impossible to tell what meaning was intended by merely examining the signals. Of course, even if you know the context in detail, you still may not be able to decipher the meaning of the message.

Language Is Denotative *and* Connotative

Denotation refers to the meaning you'd find in a dictionary; it's the meaning that members of the culture assign to a word. **Connotation** refers to the emotional meaning that specific speakers–listeners give to a word. Words have both kinds of meaning. Take as an example the word *death*. To a doctor this word might mean (or denote) the time when brain activity ceases. This is an objective description of a particular event. In contrast, when a mother is informed of her child's death, the word means (or connotes) much more. It recalls her child's youth, ambition, family, illness, and so on. To her it's a highly emotional, subjective, and personal word. These emotional, subjective, or personal reactions are the word's connotative meaning.

Take another example: Compare the term *migrants* (used to designate Mexicans coming into the United States to better their economic condition) with the term *settlers* (used to designate Europeans who came to the United States for the same reason) (Koppelman, 2005). Though both terms describe essentially the same activity (and are essentially the same denotatively), the former is often negatively evaluated and the latter often positively valued—so the two words differ widely in their connotations.

Semanticist S. I. Hayakawa (Hayakawa & Hayakawa, 1990) coined the terms "snarl words" and "purr words" to clarify further the distinction between denotative and connotative meaning. **Snarl words** are highly negative ("She's an idiot," "He's a pig," "They're a bunch of losers"). Sexist, racist, and heterosexist language and hate speech provide lots of other examples. **Purr words** are highly positive ("She's a real sweetheart," "He's a dream," "They're the greatest"). Although they may sometimes seem to have denotative meaning and to refer to the "real world," snarl and purr words are purely connotative in meaning. They don't describe people or events; rather, they reveal the speaker's feelings about these people or events.

Language Varies in Directness

Direct speech communicates your meaning explicitly and leaves little doubt as to the thoughts and feelings you want to convey. **Indirect speech**, on the other hand, communicates your meaning in a roundabout way. In indirect speech you don't really say what you mean, but you imply it. Indirect messages have both advantages and disadvantages.

One of the advantages of indirect speech is that it allows you to express a desire without insulting or offending anyone; it allows you to observe the rules of polite interaction. So instead of saying, "I'm bored with this group," you say, "It's getting late and I have to get up early tomorrow," or you look at your watch and pretend to be surprised by the time. In this way you state a preference but express it indirectly so as to avoid offending someone. Sometimes indirect messages allow you to ask for compliments in a socially acceptable manner; for example, a person who says, "I was thinking of getting a nose job" may hope to get a response such as "A nose job? You? Your nose is perfect."

Indirect messages can also create problems, however. For example, meanings that are expressed too indirectly may be misunderstood; the other person may simply not grasp your implied meaning. When this happens, you may come to resent the other person for not seeing beneath the surface—and yourself for not being more up-front. Another disadvantage is that you

may be seen as manipulative; that is, as trying to get someone to do something without really saying it. For example, you might tell a friend, "I really could use a loan until payday, but I really don't want to ask anyone."

Messages Are Influenced by Culture and Gender

Your verbal messages are influenced in large part by your culture and gender. Let's look first at some of the cultural influences.

Cultural Influences

Your culture teaches you that certain ways of using verbal messages are acceptable and certain ways are not. For example, you may have learned to address older people by Title + Last Name (Ms. Winter), as with professors and doctors, but to address peers or people much younger than you by their first names. When you follow such cultural principles in communicating, you're seen as a properly functioning member of the culture. When you violate the principles, you risk being seen as deviant or perhaps as insulting. Here are a variety of such principles:

The Principle of Cooperation. The principle of **cooperation** holds that in any communication interaction, both parties will make an effort to help each other understand each other. That is, we assume cooperation. The ways in which we assume cooperation are identified in the principle's four corollaries or maxims. As you read down the list, ask yourself how you follow these maxims in your everyday conversation:

- **The maxim of quality:** Say what you know or assume to be true, and do not say what you know to be false.
- **The maxim of relation:** Talk about what is relevant to the conversation.
- **The maxim of manner:** Be clear, avoid ambiguities (as much as possible), be relatively brief, and organize your thoughts into a meaningful pattern. In e-mail and instant messaging, brevity is especially important, and as a result acronyms have become popular. Table 1 identifies some of the more popular acronyms.
- **The maxim of quantity:** Be as informative as necessary to communicate the information.

The Principle of Peaceful Relations. This principle holds that when you communicate your primary goal is to maintain peaceful relationships. This means that you would never insult anyone and you may even express agreement with someone when you really disagree, a principle that violates

Table 1   Some Popular Acronyms

Here are some popular acronyms used widely in computer-mediated communication. For an ever-increasing list of acronyms see Net Lingua's website at www.fun-with-words.com/acronyms.html.

Acronym	Meaning
BTW	By the way
IMHO	In my humble opinion
IMNSHO	In my not so humble opinion
NP	No problem
OTT	Over the top
OTOH	On the other hand
RUOK	Are you okay?
TIC	Tongue in cheek
TTYL	Talk to you later
TVM	Thanks very much

the principle of cooperation and the maxim of quality (Midooka, 1990).

The Principle of Face-Saving.

Face-saving messages are those that preserve the image of the other person and do nothing to insult the person or make him or her appear in a negative light. The principle holds that you should never embarrass anyone, especially in public. Always allow people to save face, even if this means avoiding the truth—as when you tell someone he or she did good work although the job was actually poorly executed. Many Asian and Latin American cultures stress the value of indirectness because it helps people avoid overt criticism and the loss of face.

The Principle of Self-Denigration.

The principle of self-denigration advises you to avoid taking credit for accomplishments and to minimize your abilities or talents in conversation. At the same time, you would raise the image of the people with whom you're talking.

The Principle of Directness.

As discussed earlier, directness and indirectness communicate different impressions. Levels of directness also vary greatly from culture to culture. A somewhat different kind of indirectness is seen in the greater use of intermediaries to resolve conflict among the Chinese than among North Americans, for example (Ma, 1992). In most of the United States, directness is the preferred style. "Be up front" and "Tell it like it is" are commonly

heard communication guidelines. Contrast these with the following two principles of indirectness found in the Japanese language (Tannen, 1994a):

- *Omoiyari*, close to our concept of empathy, says that listeners need to understand the speaker without the speaker's being specific or direct. This style places a much greater demand on the listener than would a direct speaking style.

- *Sassuru* advises listeners to anticipate a speaker's meanings and to use subtle cues from the speaker to infer his or her total meaning.

The Principle of Politeness.

Most cultures have a politeness principle, but cultures differ in the way they define politeness and in how much they emphasize politeness compared with, say openness or honesty (Mao, 1994; Strecker, 1993). Asian people, especially the Chinese and Japanese, are often singled out because they emphasize politeness more and mete out harsher social punishments for violations than would people in the United States or western Europe (Fraser, 1990). Politeness also varies with the type of relationship, as depicted in Figure 1.

A somewhat different type of culture is the Internet culture, which also has its rules for politeness (see Table 2).

Cultural differences can often create misunderstanding. For example, a person from a culture that values an indirect style of speech may be speaking indirectly in order to be polite. If, however, you're from a culture that values a more direct style of

POLITENESS

After interacting with a person you're meeting for the first time and whom you want to impress, you quickly and mentally review the rules of politeness. Unfortunately, you violated just about every one. You need to correct this impression of yourself as impolite.

WHAT DO YOU SAY?

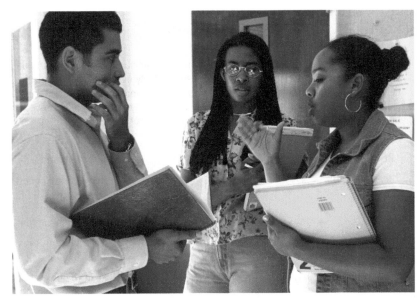

© Gary Conner/PhotoEdit

speech, you may assume that the person is using indirectness to be manipulative, because this may be how your culture regards indirectness.

Gender Influences

Gender also influences our verbal communication. For example, studies from different cultures show that women's speech is generally more polite than men's speech, even on the telephone (Brown, 1980; Wetzel, 1988; Holmes, 1995; Smoreda & Licoppe,

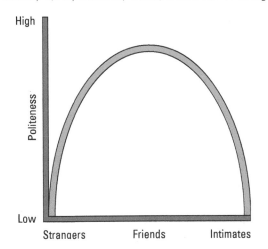

FIGURE 1 **Wolfson's Bulge Model of Politeness**

This figure depicts a proposed relationship between levels of politeness and degrees of intimacy. Politeness, according to this inverted U model, is greatest with friends and significantly less with strangers and intimates. Can you build a case for an opposite theory—that politeness is especially high with both strangers and intimates and least with friends?

Source: *Second Language Discourse: A Textbook of Current Research*, J. Fine. Copyright © 1988. Reproduced with permission of Greenwood Publishing Group, Inc., Westport, CT.

2000). Women seek areas of agreement in conversation and in conflict situations more often than men do. Similarly, young girls are more apt to try to modify disagreements, whereas young boys are more apt to express more "bald disagreements" (Holmes, 1995). Women also use more polite speech when seeking to gain another person's compliance than men do (Baxter, 1984).

The popular stereotype in much of the United States holds that women tend to be indirect in making requests and in giving orders, and that this indirectness communicates a powerlessness and discomfort with their own authority. Men, the stereotype continues, tend to be direct, sometimes to the point of being blunt or rude. This directness communicates men's power and comfort with their authority. Deborah Tannen (1994a) provides an interesting perspective on these stereotypes. Women are, it seems, more indirect in giving orders; they are more likely to say, for example, "It would be great if these letters could go out today" than "Have these letters out by three." But, Tannen (1994a, p. 84) argues, "issuing orders indirectly can be the prerogative of those in power" and does not necessarily show powerlessness. Power, to Tannen, is the ability to choose your own style of communication.

Men also can be indirect, and they are more likely to use indirectness when they express weakness, reveal a problem, or admit an error (Rundquist, 1992; Tannen, 1994a, 1994b). Men are more likely to speak indirectly when expressing emotions (other than anger). They are also more indirect when they refuse expressions of increased romantic intimacy. Men are thus indirect, the theory goes, when they are saying something that goes against the masculine stereotype.

Table 2   The Rules of Netiquette

Much as the rules of etiquette provide guidance for communicating in social situations, the rules of **netiquette** provide guidance for communicating politely over the Net. These rules, as you'll see, are helpful for making Internet communication easier and more pleasant, facilitating greater personal efficiency, and putting less strain on the system and on other users. Here are several guidelines suggested by most computer researchers; also see www.albion.com/netiquette.

Rule of Netiquette	Suggestions
Read the FAQs.	Before asking questions about the system, read the Frequently Asked Questions; your question has probably been asked before, and you'll put less strain on the system and on yourself.
Don't shout.	Don't write in caps (it's perceived as shouting). Use caps only for emphasis.
Lurk before speaking.	Read the posted notices and the conversations before contributing anything yourself; in this way you'll avoid violating any rule of the group.
Be brief.	Follow the maxim of quantity by communicating only the needed information; follow the maxim of manner by communicating clearly, briefly, and in an organized way. These suggestions are even more important in business and organizational communication.

REFLECTIONS ON ETHICS

Lying

Lying is the act of sending messages designed to make others believe what you know to be untrue (Ekman, 1985; Burgoon & Hoobler, 2002). You can lie by *commission* (making explicitly false statements or deliberately being evasive or misleading) or by *omission* (omitting relevant information and thus allowing others to draw incorrect inferences). Similarly, you can lie *verbally* (in speech or writing) or *nonverbally* (with an innocent facial expression despite the commission of some wrong, or with a knowing nod instead of the honest expression of ignorance). Lies may range from "white lies" and truth stretching to lies that form the basis of infidelity in a relationship, of libel, and perjury. Not surprisingly, lies have ethical implications.

- Some lies are considered innocent, acceptable, and ethical, such as lying to a child to protect a fantasy belief in Santa Claus or the Tooth Fairy or publicly agreeing with someone to enable the person to save face.

- Some lies may be considered not merely ethical but required, such as saying your friend looks good to make him or her feel better.

- Other lies are considered unacceptable and unethical, such as lying to defraud investors or making false accusations.

Ethical Choice Point

You've been asked to serve as a witness in the trial of a suspect in the robbery of a local grocery store. You really don't want to get involved; in fact, you're afraid to get involved. Yet you wonder if you can ethically refuse and say you didn't see anything (although you did). There are other witnesses, and your testimony is not likely to make a significant difference. What is your ethical obligation in this situation? What would you do?

There are also gender similarities. For example, in both the United States and New Zealand, men and women seem to pay compliments in similar ways (Manes & Wolfson, 1981; Holmes, 1995), and both men and women use politeness strategies when communicating bad news in an organization (Lee, 1993). A few theories of gender differences are highlighted in the accompanying Understanding Theory and Research box.

DISCONFIRMATION AND CONFIRMATION

The terms *confirmation* and *disconfirmation* refer to the extent to which you acknowledge another person. Consider this situation. You've been living with someone for the last six months and you arrive home late one night. Your partner, let's say Pat, is angry and complains about your being so late. Which of the following is most likely to be your response?

1. Stop screaming. I'm not interested in what you're babbling about. I'll do what I want, when I want. I'm going to bed.
2. What are you so angry about? Didn't you get in three hours late last Thursday when you went to that office party? So knock it off.

3. You have a right to be angry. I should have called to tell you I was going to be late, but I got involved in a serious debate at work, and I couldn't leave until it was resolved.

In response 1, you dismiss Pat's anger and even indicate dismissal of Pat as a person. In response 2, you reject the validity of Pat's reasons for being angry but do not dismiss either Pat's feelings of anger or Pat as a person. In response 3, you acknowledge Pat's anger and the reasons for it. In addition, you provide some kind of explanation and, in doing so, show that both Pat's feelings and Pat as a person are important and that Pat has the right to know what happened. The first response is an example of disconfirmation, the second of rejection, and the third of confirmation.

Psychologist William James once observed that "no more fiendish punishment could be devised, even were such a thing physically possible, than that one should be turned loose in society and remain absolutely unnoticed by all the members thereof." In this often-quoted observation, James identifies the essence of disconfirmation (Watzlawick, Beavin, & Jackson, 1967; Veenendall & Feinstein, 1995). **Disconfirmation** is a communication pattern in which we ignore someone's presence as well as that person's communications. We say, in effect, that this

Theory and Research UNDERSTANDING   Theories of Gender Differences

Gender differences are discussed in a wide variety of contexts. One researcher distinguishes three perspectives on gender differences in communication (Holmes, 1995):

- Gender differences are due to innate biological differences. Thus, gender differences in communication, such as differences in politeness or in listening behavior, are the result of these biological differences.

- Gender differences are due to different patterns of socialization, which lead to different forms of communication. Thus, the gender differences that you observe are due to the different ways boys and girls are raised and taught when growing up and throughout life—by being rewarded for "appropriate" gender communication and being punished for "inappropriate" gender communication.

- Gender differences are due to the inequalities in social power. For example, because of women's lesser social power, they're more apt to communicate with greater deference and politeness than are men.

Working with Theories and Research

What arguments could you offer in support of or in opposition to any of these positions? How might you go about conducting research to test any one of these hypotheses?

person and what this person has to say are not worth serious attention or effort—that this person and this person's contributions are so unimportant or insignificant that there is no reason to concern ourselves with her or him. The Amish community practices an extreme form of disconfirmation called "shunning," in which the community members totally ignore a person who has violated one or more of their rules. The specific aim of shunning is to get the person to repent and to reenter the community of the faithful. But it seems that all cultures practice some form of exclusion for those who violate important cultural rules.

Note that disconfirmation is not the same as **rejection.** In rejection, you disagree with the person; you indicate your unwillingness to accept something the other person says or does. In disconfirming someone, however, you deny that person's significance; you claim that what this person says or does simply does not count.

Confirmation is the opposite communication pattern. In confirmation you not only acknowledge the presence of the other person but also indicate your acceptance of this person, of this person's self-definition, and of your relationship as defined or viewed by this other person.

Disconfirmation and confirmation may be communicated in a wide variety of ways. Table 3 shows just a few examples and the accompanying Building Communication Skills box invites additional examples.

You can gain insight into a wide variety of offensive language practices by viewing them as types of disconfirmation—as language that alienates and separates. Four obvious practices, which we'll consider here, are racism, heterosexism, ageism, and sexism. Extremes of these are often termed *hate speech*.

Another-ism is *ableism*—discrimination against people with disabilities:

Table 3 Confirmation and Disconfirmation

As you review this table, try to imagine a specific illustration for each of the ways of communicating disconfirmation and confirmation (Pearson, 1993; Galvin, Bylund, & Brommel, 2004).

Confirmation

1. Acknowledge the presence and the contributions of the other by either supporting or taking issue with what the other says.

2. Make nonverbal contact by maintaining direct eye contact, touching, hugging, kissing, or otherwise demonstrating acknowledgment of the other; engage in dialogue—communication in which both persons are speakers and listeners, both are involved, and both are concerned with each other.

3. Demonstrate understanding of what the other says and means, and reflect these feelings to confirm your understanding.

4. Ask questions of the other concerning both thoughts and feelings, and acknowledge the questions of the other; return phone calls; answer e-mail and letters.

5. Encourage the other to express thoughts and feelings, and respond directly and exclusively to what the other says.

Disconfirmation

1. Ignore the presence and the messages of the other person; ignore or express (nonverbally and verbally) indifference to anything the other says.

2. Make no nonverbal contact; avoid direct eye contact; avoid touching the other person. Engage in monologue—communication in which one person speaks and one person listens, there is no real interaction, and there is no real concern or respect for each other.

3. Jump to interpretation or evaluation rather than working at understanding what the other means; express your own feelings, but ignore the feelings of the other or give abstract, intellectualized responses.

4. Make statements about yourself; ignore any lack of clarity in the other's remarks; ignore the other's requests; fail to answer questions, return phone calls, or answer e-mails and letters.

5. Interrupt or otherwise make it difficult for the other to express him- or herself; respond only tangentially or by shifting the focus in another direction.

Building Communication — Confirming, Rejecting, or Disconfirming

Here are three practice situations. For each situation, (a) write the three potential responses as indicated; then, (b) after completing all three situations, indicate what effects each type of response is likely to generate.

1. Enrique receives this semester's grades in the mail; they're a lot better than previous semesters' grades but are still not great. After opening the letter, Enrique says: "I really tried hard to get my grades up this semester." Enrique's parents respond:

   With disconfirmation
   With rejection
   With confirmation

2. Elizabeth, who has been out of work for the past several weeks, says: "I feel like such a failure; I just can't seem to find a job. I've been pounding the pavement for the last five weeks and still nothing." Elizabeth's friend responds:

   With disconfirmation
   With rejection
   With confirmation

3. Candi's colleague at work comes to her overjoyed and tells her that she was just promoted to vice president of marketing, skipping three steps in the hierarchy and tripling her salary. Candi responds:
   With disconfirmation
   With rejection
   With confirmation

Each type of response communicates a different message; generally, however, confirming message are likely to increase relationship satisfaction and disconfirming messages are likely to decrease relationship satisfaction.

- between blind and sighted people
- between people with and without disabilities
- between deaf and hearing people
- between people with and without speech and language disorders

Racism

According to Andrea Rich (1974), "any language that, through a conscious or unconscious attempt by the user, places a particular racial or ethnic group in an inferior position is racist." **Racist language** expresses racist attitudes. It also, however, contributes to the development of racist attitudes in those who use or hear the language. Even when racism is subtle, unintentional, or even unconscious, its effects are systematically damaging (Dovidio, Gaertner, Kawakami, & Hodson, 2002).

Racism exists on both individual and institutional levels, a distinction made by educational researchers and used throughout this discussion (Koppelman, 2005). The term *individual racism* refers to the negative attitudes and beliefs that people hold about specific races. Assumptions such as the idea that certain races are intellectually inferior to others or that certain races are incapable of certain achievements are clear examples of individual racism. Prejudice against American Indians, African Americans, Hispanics, and Arabs have been with us throughout history and are still a part of many people's lives today. Such racism is seen in the negative terms people use to refer to members of other races and to disparage their customs and accomplishments.

Institutionalized racism is seen in de facto school segregation, in companies' reluctance to hire members of minority groups, in banks' unwillingness

THE RESEARCHER

Family and Cultural Differences

I'm in a serious romantic relationship with someone who is my cultural opposite. We differ in race, religion, and nationality. Our problem, however, is not with us; rather, it is with our families. Both of our families are narrow-minded, bigoted, and culturally insensitive. What can we do to get our families to accept our relationship and to demonstrate some cultural sensitivity?

Your complex situation should challenge all of you. An easy answer could be offered but would be wrong. You have communication options for easing the tensions. You may try to see yourself as they see you. Rethink your negative view of them. Ask how your families may actually care about you, despite your disapproving their way of showing it. Do you see them merely as objects to be manipulated? If they are insensitive, do you want to be like them? Assuming they have shortcomings, can you change their attitudes as you would bicycle tires? To harmonize the conflict, you might modify your communication with them in hopes of improving your relationship. Focusing on your relationship, you may be able to model the caring communication you wish them to practice. You might use different communication channels to reduce disharmony. Rather than employing face-to-face communication only, you might also share your tender differences through letters, tapes, computer-mediated messages, and even go-betweens.

For further information: Barnes, S. (2003). *Computer-mediated communication*. Boston: Allyn & Bacon. Also Hall, B. J. (2005). *Among cultures: The challenge of communication*. Belmont, CA: Thompson, and Travis, L., & Violato, C. (2001). *Advances in adolescent psychology*. Calgary, AB: Detselig.

Richard Fiordo (Ph.D., University of Illinois–Urbana) is a professor of communication at the University of North Dakota, where he teaches communication courses that strive to reduce individual, group, and cultural conflict (richard.fiordo@und.edu). Much of his research applies to international and multicultural issues. He is a board member for the Society for Adolescentology (which studies diverse aspects of adolescence, including its psychological presence in adulthood) at Ambrosiana University in Milan, Italy (www.adolescence.it).

to extend mortgages and business loans to members of some races, or in lenders' charging higher interest rates to members of certain groups.

Examine your own language in regard to racism; do you

- avoid using derogatory terms for members of a particular race?

- avoid interacting with members of other races through stereotypes perpetuated by the media?

- make sure not to refer to race when it's irrelevant, as in "an African American surgeon" or "an Asian athlete"?

- avoid attributing economic or social problems to the race of the individuals rather than to institutionalized racism or to general economic problems that affect everyone?

Heterosexism

Heterosexism also exists on both an individual and an institutional level. *Individual heterosexism* involves attitudes, behaviors, and language that disparage gay men and lesbians as well as a belief that all sexual behavior that is not heterosexual is unnatural and deserving of criticism and condemnation. These beliefs are at the heart of antigay violence and "gay bashing." Individual heterosexism also includes such beliefs as the notions that homosexuals are more likely than heterosexuals to commit crimes (there's actually no difference) or to molest children (actually, heterosexual, married men are overwhelm-ingly the child molesters) (Koppelman, 2005). It also includes the belief that homosexuals cannot maintain stable relationships or effectively raise children, a belief that contradicts research evidence (Fitzpatrick, Jandt, Myrick, & Edgar, 1994).

Institutional heterosexism is easy to identify. For example, the ban on gay marriage in many states and the fact that at this time only one state (Massachusetts) allows gay marriage is a good example of institutional heterosexism. Other examples include the Catholic Church's ban on homosexual priests, the United States military's prohibiting openly gay people from serving in the armed forces, and the many laws that prohibit adoption of children by gay people. In some cultures homosexual relations are illegal (for example, in India, Malaysia, Pakistan, and Singapore); penalties range from a "misdemeanor" conviction in Liberia, to life in jail in Singapore, to death in Pakistan.

Heterosexist language includes derogatory terms used for lesbians and gay men. For example, surveys in the military showed that 80 percent of those surveyed heard "offensive speech, derogatory names, jokes or remarks about gays" and that 85 percent believed that such derogatory speech was "tolerated" (*New York Times*, March 25, 2000, p. A12). You also see heterosexism in more subtle forms of language usage; for example, when you qualify a reference to a professional—as in "gay athlete" or "lesbian doctor"—and, in effect, say that athletes and doctors are not normally gay or lesbian.

Still another instance of heterosexism is the presumption of heterosexuality. Usually, people assume the person they're talking to or about is heterosexual. And usually they're correct, because most people are heterosexual. At the same time, however, this presumption denies the lesbian or gay identity a certain legitimacy. The practice is very similar to the presumptions of whiteness and maleness that we have made significant inroads in eliminating. Here are a few additional suggestions for avoiding heterosexist (or what some call homophobic) language. Do you:

- avoid offensive nonverbal mannerisms that parody stereotypes when talking about gay men and lesbians? Do you use the "startled eye blink" with which some people react to gay couples?

- avoid "complimenting" gay men and lesbians by saying that they "don't look it"? To gay men and lesbians, this is not a compliment. Similarly, expressing disappointment that a person is gay—often thought to be a compliment, as in comments such as "What a waste!"—is not really a compliment.

- avoid making the assumption that every gay or lesbian knows what every other gay or lesbian is thinking? It's very similar to asking a Japanese person why Sony is investing heavily in the United States or, as one comic put it, asking an African American, "What do you think Jesse Jackson meant by that last speech?"

- avoid denying individual differences? Comments like "Lesbians are so loyal" or "Gay men are so open with their feelings," which ignore the reality of wide differences within any group, are potentially insulting to all members of the group.

- avoid overattribution, the tendency to attribute just about everything a person does, says, and believes to the fact that the person is gay or lesbian? This tendency helps to activate and perpetuate stereotypes.

- remember that relationship milestones are important to all people? Ignoring anniversaries or birthdays of, say, a relative's partner makes a statement that is resented by everyone.

HOMOPHOBIA

You're bringing your college roommate home for the holidays; she's an outspoken lesbian while your family is extremely homophobic. You want to prepare your family and your roommate for their holiday get-together.

WHAT DO YOU SAY?
To whom? Through what channel?

225

THE MEDIA AND DISCONFIRMATION

Whoever controls the media—the images—controls the cultures.

—Allen Ginsberg

In all forms of communication, be especially careful not to rely on media stereotypes. The media are responsible for propagating many discriminatory stereotypes, and a media-literate individual needs to be able to recognize these and to see that such stereotypes are not reality but extreme examples, often created for comic effect or to maintain a viewer's attention. Men and women on comedy shows are often seen in an unpleasant light; most men on television are portrayed as incompetent, relationally inept, absorbed with sports, and ignorant of the important things in life. Men will never learn how to relate to women and are doomed to be insensitive clods. And women are portrayed as complaining, never satisfied, and abnormally thin. Old folks are portrayed

as inept, complaining, loud, and offensive. And of course old people have lost and will never again find romance; for older people the kisses, for example, have to be nonsexual.

Racism is rampant in the media's portrayal of Muslims; almost all the Muslims on television are negatively constructed and are much more likely to be terrorists than they are to be teachers or lawyers or store owners or carpenters. Also, consider the negative stereotypes of gay men and lesbians; they're extremes that you rarely see in real life.

Increasing Media Literacy

No specific examples were given here to support the accusation of media stereotypes. Examine the current lineup of television situation comedies and dramas and try to identify examples that support or contradict the idea that media engage in stereotyping.

As you think about heterosexism, recognize that heterosexist language will create barriers to communication, whereas its absence will foster more meaningful communication: greater comfort, an increased willingness to disclose personal information, and a greater willingness to engage in future interactions.

Ageism

Although used mainly to refer to prejudice against older people, the term *ageism* can also refer to prejudice against other age groups. For example, if you describe all teenagers as selfish and undependable, you're discriminating against a group purely because of their age, and thus are using **ageist language**. In some cultures—some Asian and some African cultures, for example—the old are revered and respected. Younger people seek them out for advice on economic, ethical, and relationship issues.

Individual ageism is seen in negative stereotypes and in the general disrespect many have for older people. *Institutional ageism* is seen in mandatory retirement laws and age restrictions in certain occupations (as opposed to requirements based on demonstrated competence). In less obvious forms, ageism is seen in the media's portrayal of old people

as incompetent, complaining, and, perhaps most clearly evidenced in both television and films, without romantic feelings. Rarely, for example, does television or film show older people working productively, being cooperative and pleasant, and engaging in romantic and sexual relationships.

Popular language is replete with examples of linguistic ageism; terms like "little old lady," "old hag," "old-timer," "over the hill," "old coot," and "old fogy" are a few examples. As with sexism, qualifying a description of someone in terms of his or her age demonstrates ageism. For example, if you refer to "a quick-witted 75-year-old" or "an agile 65-year-old" or "a responsible teenager," you're implying that these qualities are unusual in people of these ages and thus need special mention. You're saying that "quick-wittedness" and "being 75" do not normally go together. The problem with this kind of stereotyping is that it's simply wrong. There are many 75-year-olds who are extremely quick-witted (and many 30-year-olds who aren't).

You also communicate ageism when you speak to older people in overly simple words or explain things that don't need explaining. Nonverbally, you demonstrate ageist communication when, for example, you avoid touching an older person but touch others, or when you avoid making direct eye contact with the older person but readily do so with others, or when you speak at an overly high volume (suggesting that all older people have hearing difficulties).

One useful way to avoid ageism is to recognize and avoid the illogical stereotypes that ageist language is based on. Do you:

- avoid talking down to a person because he or she is older? Older people are not mentally slow; most people remain mentally alert well into old age.

- refrain from refreshing an older person's memory each time you see the person? Older people can and do remember things.

- avoid implying that relationships are no longer important? Older people continue to be interested in relationships.

- speak at a normal volume and maintain a normal physical distance? Being older does not mean being hard of hearing or being unable to see; most older people hear and see quite well, sometimes with hearing aids or glasses.

- engage older people in conversation as you would wish to be engaged? Older people are interested in the world around them.

Even though you want to avoid ageist communication, there are times when you may wish to make adjustments when talking with someone who does have language or communication difficulties. The American Speech and Hearing Association offers several useful suggestions (www.asha.org/public/speech/development/communicating-better-with-older-people.htm, accessed June 3, 2006):

- Reduce as much background noise as you can.

- Ease into the conversation by beginning with casual topics and then moving into more familiar topics. Stay with each topic for a while; avoid jumping too quickly from one topic to another.

- Speak in relatively short sentences and questions.

- Give the person added time to respond. Some older people react more slowly and need extra time.

- Listen actively. Practice the skills of active listening.

Sexism

Sexism—like all the -isms discussed here—exists on both an individual and institutional level. *Individual sexism* consists of prejudicial attitudes and beliefs about men or women based on rigid beliefs about gender roles. These might include beliefs such as the ideas that women should be caretakers, should be sensitive at all times, and should acquiesce to a man's decisions concerning political or financial matters. Sexist attitudes would also include beliefs

that men are insensitive, interested only in sex, and incapable of communicating feelings.

Institutional sexism, on the other hand, involves customs and practices that discriminate against people because of their gender. Two very clear examples are the widespread practice of paying women less than men for the same job and the discrimination against women in the upper levels of management. Another clear example of institutionalized sexism is seen in the divorce courts' practice of automatically or near-automatically granting child custody to the mother rather than the father.

Of particular interest here is **sexist language**: language that puts down someone because of his or her gender (a term usually used to refer to language derogatory toward women). The National Council of Teachers of English has proposed guidelines for nonsexist (gender-free, gender-neutral, or sex-fair) language. These guidelines concern the use of the generic word *man*, the use of generic *he* and *his*, and sex-role stereotyping (Penfield, 1987). Consider your own communication behavior. Do you

- avoid using *man* generically? Using the term to refer to both men and women emphasizes maleness at the expense of femaleness. Gender-neutral terms can easily be substituted. Instead of *mankind*, say *humanity*, *people*, or *human beings*. Similarly, the use of terms such as *policeman* or *fireman* and other terms that presume maleness as the norm—and femaleness as a deviation from this norm—are clear and common examples of sexist language.

- refrain from using *he* and *his* as generic? Instead, you can alternate pronouns or restructure your sentences to eliminate any reference to gender. For example, the NCTE Guidelines (Penfield, 1987) suggest that instead of saying, "The average student is worried about his grades," you say, "The average student is worried about grades."

- stay away from sex-role stereotyping? When you make the hypothetical elementary school teacher female and the college professor male or refer to doctors as male and nurses as female, you're sex-role stereotyping; the same is true when you identify the sex of a professional in phrases such as *woman doctor* or *male nurse*.

Racist, Heterosexist, Ageist, and Sexist Listening

Just as racist, heterosexist, ageist, and sexist attitudes will influence your language, they can also influence your listening. In this disconfirming type of listening, you hear what the speaker is saying through the

© Rosa & Rosa/CORBIS

MISUSING CULTURAL IDENTIFIERS

During a conversation, your classmates all use negative self-reference terms. Trying to be one of the group, you too use these terms and almost immediately realize that the linguistic privilege allowing insiders to use [self] derogatory names, does not apply to outsiders. You don't want anyone to think that you normally talk this way.

WHAT DO YOU SAY?

stereotypes you hold. Disconfirmation in listening occurs when you listen differently to a person because of his or her gender, race, affectional orientation, or age even though these characteristics are irrelevant to the message.

Racist, heterosexist, ageist, and sexist listening occurs in lots of situations. For example, when you dismiss a valid argument—or attribute validity to an invalid argument—because the speaker is of a particular race, affectional orientation, age group, or gender, you're listening with prejudice.

But there also are many instances when these characteristics are relevant and pertinent to your evaluation of the message. For example, the sex of a person who is talking about pregnancy, fathering a child, birth control, or surrogate motherhood is, most would agree, probably relevant to the message. So in these cases it is not sexist listening to take the sex of the speaker into consideration. It is, however, sexist listening to assume that only one sex can be

an authority on a particular topic or that one sex's opinions are without value. The same is true in relation to listening through a person's race, affectional orientation, or age.

Cultural Identifiers

Perhaps the best way to develop nonsexist, non-heterosexist, nonracist, and nonageist language is to examine the preferred cultural identifiers to use in talking to and about members of different groups. Remember, however, that preferred terms frequently change over time, so keep in touch with the most current preferences. The preferences and many of the specific examples identified here are drawn largely from the findings of the Task Force on Bias-Free Language of the Association of American University Presses (Schwartz, 1995).

Race and Nationality

Generally, most African Americans prefer *African American* to *black* (Hecht, Collier, & Ribeau, 1993), although *black* is often used with *white*, as well as in a variety of other contexts (for example, Department of Black and Puerto Rican Studies, the *Journal of Black History*, and Black History Month). The American Psychological Association recommends that both terms be capitalized, but the *Chicago Manual of Style* (the manual used by most newspapers and publishing houses) recommends using lowercase. The terms *Negro* and *colored*, although used in the names of some organizations (for example, the United Negro College Fund and the National Association for the Advancement of Colored People), are not used outside these contexts.

White is generally used to refer to those whose roots are in European cultures and usually does not include Hispanics. Analogous to *African American* (which itself is based on a long tradition of terms such as *Irish American* and *Italian American*) is the phrase *European American*. Few European Americans, however, call themselves that; most prefer their national origins emphasized, as in, for example, *German American* or *Greek American*. This preference may well change as Europe moves toward becoming a more cohesive and united entity. *People of color*—a more literary-sounding term appropriate perhaps to public speaking but awkward in most conversations—is preferred to *nonwhite*, which implies that whiteness is the norm and nonwhiteness is a deviation from that norm. The same is true of the term *non-Christian*: It implies that people who have other beliefs deviate from the norm.

Generally, the term *Hispanic* refers to anyone who identifies himself or herself as belonging to a Spanish-speaking culture. *Latina* (female) and *Latino* (male) refer to persons whose roots are in one of the Latin American countries, such as Haiti, the Dominican Republic, Nicaragua, or Guatemala. *Hispanic American* refers to United States residents whose ancestry is in a Spanish culture; the term includes people from Mexico, the Caribbean, and Central and South America. In emphasizing a Spanish heritage, however, the term is really inaccurate, because it leaves out the large numbers of people in the Caribbean and in South America whose origins are African, Native American, French, or Portuguese. The words *Chicana* (female) and *Chicano* (male) refer to persons with roots in Mexico, although these terms often connote a nationalist attitude (Jandt, 2004) and are considered offensive by many Mexican Americans. *Mexican American* is generally preferred.

Inuk (plural *Inuit*), also spelled with two n's (*Innuk* and *Innuit*), is preferred to *Eskimo* (a term the United States Census Bureau uses), which was applied to the indigenous peoples of Alaska and Canada by Europeans and literally means "raw meat eaters."

The word *Indian* technically refers only to someone from India, not to citizens of other Asian countries or to the indigenous peoples of North America. *American Indian* or *Native American* is preferred, even though many Native Americans do refer to themselves as *Indians* and *Indian people*. The word *squaw*, used to refer to a Native American woman and still used in the names of some places in the United States and in some textbooks, is clearly a term to be avoided; its usage is almost always negative and insulting (Koppelman, 2005).

In Canada indigenous people are called *first people* or *first nations*. The term *native American* (with a lowercase n) is most often used to refer to persons born in the United States. Although technically the term could refer to anyone born in North or South America, people outside the United States generally prefer more specific designations such as *Argentinean*, *Cuban*, or *Canadian*. The term *native* describes an indigenous inhabitant; it is not used to indicate "someone having a less developed culture."

Muslim (rather than the older *Moslem*) is the preferred form to refer to a person who adheres to the religious teachings of Islam. *Quran* (rather than *Koran*) is the preferred term for the scriptures of Islam. *Jewish people* is often preferred to *Jews*, and *Jewess* (a Jewish female) is considered derogatory.

When history was being written from a European perspective, Europe was taken as the focal point and the rest of the world was defined in terms of its location relative to that continent. Thus, Asia became the East or the Orient, and *Asians* became *Orientals*—a term that is today considered inappropriate or Eurocentric. Thus, people from Asia are *Asians*, just as people from Africa are *Africans* and people from Europe are *Europeans*.

Affectional Orientation

Generally, *gay* is the preferred term to refer to a man who has an affectional orientation toward other men, and *lesbian* is the preferred term for a woman who has an affectional orientation toward other women (Lever, 1995). (*Lesbian* means "homosexual woman," so the term *lesbian woman* is redundant.) *Homosexual* refers to both gays and lesbians, but more often to a sexual orientation to members of one's own sex. *Gay* and *lesbian* refer to a lifestyle and not merely to sexual orientation. *Gay* as a noun, although widely used, may prove offensive in some contexts, as in "We have two gays on the team." Because most scientific thinking holds that sexuality is not a matter of choice, the terms *sexual orientation* and *affectional orientation* are preferred to *sexual preference* or *sexual status* (for example, **www.apa.org/topies/orientation.html**; **www.pflagatl.org/FandFarticles/APA.htm**).

Age

Older person is preferred to *elder, elderly, senior*, or *senior citizen* (which last term technically refers to someone older than 65). Usually, however, language designating age is unnecessary. There are times, of course, when you'll need to refer to a person's age group, but most of the time age is beside the point—in much the same way that racial or affectional orientation terms are usually irrelevant.

Sex

Generally, the term *girl* should be used only to refer to very young females and is equivalent to *boy*. Neither term should be used for people older than age 17 or 18. *Girl* is never used to refer to a grown woman, nor is *boy* used to refer to people in blue-collar positions, as it once was. *Lady* is negatively evaluated by many because it connotes the stereotype of the prim and proper woman. *Woman* or *young woman* is preferred.

Let's turn now from issues of confirmation to some guidelines for using language effectively by avoiding common mistakes and applying some simple principles.

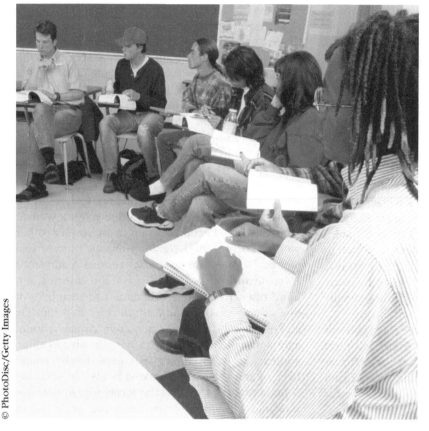

© PhotoDisc/Getty Images

OBJECTING TO DISCONFIRMATION

One of your instructors persists in using all of the inappropriate and culturally insensitive sexist, heterosexist, racist, and ageist language. You want to object to this type of talk.

WHAT DO YOU SAY?
To whom? Through what channel?
What do you say?

USING VERBAL MESSAGES EFFECTIVELY

A chief concern in using verbal messages is to recognize what critical thinking theorists call "conceptual distortions"; that is, mental mistakes, misinterpretations, or reasoning fallacies. Avoiding these distortions and substituting a more critical, more realistic analysis is probably the best way to improve your own use of verbal messages (DeVito, 1974). Let's look at several principles of language that are often ignored or misunderstood along with the conceptual distortions that result from such misunderstandings (Korzybski, 1933).

Language Symbolizes Reality (Partially)

Language symbolizes reality; it's not the reality itself. Of course, this is obvious. But consider: Have you ever reacted to the way something was labeled or described rather than to the actual item? Have you ever bought something because of its name rather than because of the actual object? If so, you were probably responding as if language were the reality, a distortion called intensional orientation.

Intensional Orientation

Intensional orientation (the *s* in *intensional* is intentional) is the tendency to view people, objects, and events according to the way they're talked about—the way they're labeled. For example, if Sally were labeled "uninteresting," you would, responding intensionally, evaluate her as uninteresting even before listening to what she had to say. You'd see Sally through a filter imposed by the label "uninteresting." **Extensional orientation**, on the other hand, is the tendency to look first at the actual people, objects, and events and only afterwards at their labels. In this case, it would mean looking at Sally without any preconceived labels, guided by what she says and does, not by the words used to label her.

To avoid intensional orientation, extensionalize. Never give labels greater attention than the actual thing. Give your main attention to the people, things, and events in the world as you see them and not as they're presented in words. For example, when you meet Jack and Jill, observe and interact with them. Then form your impressions. Don't respond to them as "greedy, money-grubbing landlords" because Harry labeled them this way. Don't respond to George as "lazy" just because Elaine told you he was.

The accompanying Understanding Theory and Research box explores the concept of intensional orientation and its connection with the verb "to be."

Allness

A related distortion is **allness**: forgetting that language symbolizes only a portion of reality, never the whole. When you assume that you can know all or say all about anything, you're into allness. In reality, you never can see all of anything. You never can experience anything fully. You see a part, then conclude what the whole is like. You have to draw conclusions on the basis of insufficient evidence (because you always have insufficient evidence). A useful **extensional device** to help combat the tendency to think that all can or has been said about anything is to end each statement mentally with **et cetera**—a reminder that there's more to learn, more to know, and more to say and that every statement is inevitably incomplete. Instead of saying, for example, "I wouldn't like her; I saw the way she treated her father," you'd say, "I don't think I'd like her; I saw the way she treated her father,

but I haven't seen her with other people, and I really don't know her father, et cetera." Of course, some people overuse the "et cetera." They use it not as a mental reminder but as a substitute for being specific. This obviously is to be avoided and merely adds to conversational confusion.

To avoid allness, recognize that language symbolizes only a part of reality, never the whole. Whatever someone says—regardless of what it is or how extensive it is—represents only part of the story.

Language Expresses Both Facts and Inferences

Language enables you to form statements of both facts and inferences without making any linguistic distinction between the two. Similarly, in speaking and listening you often don't make a clear distinction between statements of fact and statements of inference. Yet there are great differences between the two. Barriers to clear thinking can be created when inferences are treated as facts, a tendency called **fact–inference confusion**.

For example, you can say, "She's wearing a blue jacket," and you can say, "He's harboring an illogical hatred." Although the sentences have

---

Understanding Theory and Research   **The Verb "To Be"**

The theory of **E-prime** (or E') argues that if you wrote and spoke English without the verb *to be*, you'd describe events more accurately (Bourland, 1965–1966; Wilson, 1989; Klein, 1992). For example, when you say, "Johnny is a failure," the verb *is* implies that "failure" is in Johnny rather than in your observation or evaluation of Johnny. The verb *to be* (in forms such as *is*, *are*, and *am*) also implies permanence; the implication is that because failure is in Johnny, it will always be there; Johnny will always be a failure. A more accurate and descriptive statement might be "Johnny failed his last two math exams."

Consider this theory as applied to your thinking about yourself. When you say, for example, "I'm not good at public speaking" or "I'm unpopular" or "I'm lazy," you imply that these qualities are in you. But these are simply evaluations that may be incorrect or, if at least partly accurate, may change over time (Joyner, 1993).

Working with Theories and Research

How might you apply the E-prime principle to gain greater understanding of the ways in which you view yourself? To answer this question you might try first to identify your self (who you are, what you are) in a few sentences using forms of the verb to be *and then to rephrase these same sentences in E-prime. What different perspectives do these two versions give you?*

---

similar structures, they're different. You can observe the jacket and its color, but how do you observe "illogical hatred"? Obviously, this is not a **factual statement** but an **inferential statement**. It's a statement you make on the basis not only of what you observe, but of what you infer. For a statement to be considered factual, it must be made by the observer after observation and must be limited to what is observed (Weinberg, 1958).

There is nothing wrong with making inferential statements. You must make them in order to talk about much that is meaningful to you. The problem arises when you act as if those inferential statements were factual. You can test your ability to distinguish facts from inferences by taking the fact-inference self-test below (based on the tests constructed in Haney, 1973).

TEST YOURSELF

Can You Distinguish Facts from Inferences?

Carefully read the following report and the observations based on it. Indicate whether you think the observations are true, false, or doubtful on the basis of the information presented in the report. Write T if the observation is definitely true, F if the observation is definitely false, and ? if the observation may be either true or false. Judge each observation in order. Don't reread the observations after you've indicated your judgment, and don't change any of your answers.

A well-liked college teacher had just completed making up the final examinations and had turned off the lights in the office. Just then a tall, broad figure with dark glasses appeared and demanded the examination. The professor opened the drawer. Everything in the drawer was picked up and the individual ran down the corridor. The dean was notified immediately.

_____ **1.** The thief was tall and broad and wore dark glasses.

_____ **2.** The professor turned off the lights.

_____ **3.** A tall figure demanded the examination.

_____ **4.** The examination was picked up by someone.

_____ **5.** The examination was picked up by the professor.

_____ **6.** A tall, broad figure appeared after the professor turned off the lights in the office.

_____ **7.** The man who opened the drawer was the professor.

_____ **8.** The professor ran down the corridor.

_____ **9.** The drawer was never actually opened.

_____ **10.** Three persons are referred to in this report.

HOW DID YOU DO? Number 3 is true, number 9 is false, and all the rest are "?" Review your answers by referring back to the story. To get you started, consider: Is there necessarily a thief? Might the dean have demanded to see the instructor's examination (statement 1)? Did the examination have to be in the drawer (statements 4 and 5)? How do you know it was the professor who turned off the lights (statement 6)? Need the professor have been a man (statement 7)? Do the instructor and the professor have to be the same person (statement 10)?

WHAT WILL YOU DO? Again, recognize that there's nothing wrong with making inferences. When you hear inferential statements, however, treat them as inferences and not as facts. Be mindful of the possibility that such statements may prove to be wrong. As you read this chapter, try to formulate specific guidelines that will help you distinguish facts from inferences.

To avoid fact–inference confusion, phrase inferential statements in such a way as to show that they are tentative. Inferential statements should leave open the possibility of alternatives. If, for example, you treat the statement "Our biology teacher was fired for poor teaching" as factual, you eliminate any alternatives. But if you preface your statement with, say, "Pat told me . . ." or "I'm wondering if . . .," the inferential nature of your statement will be clear. Be especially sensitive to this distinction when you're listening. Most talk is inferential. Beware of the speaker who presents everything as fact. Analyze closely and you'll uncover a world of inferences.

Language Is Relatively Static

Language changes only very slowly, especially when compared to the rapid change in people and things. **Static evaluation** is the tendency to retain evaluations without change while the reality to which they refer is changing. Often a verbal statement you make about an event or person remains static ("That's the way he is; he's always been that way") while the event or person may change enormously. Alfred Korzybski (1933) used an interesting illustration.

In a tank you have a large fish and many small fish, the natural food for the large fish. Given freedom in the tank, the large fish will eat the small fish. If you partition the tank, separating the large fish from the small fish by a clear piece of glass, the large fish will continue to attempt to eat the small fish but will fail, knocking instead into the glass partition.

Eventually, the large fish will learn the futility of attempting to eat the small fish. If you now remove the partition, the small fish will swim all around the big fish, but the big fish will not eat them. In fact, the large fish will die of starvation while its natural food swims all around. The large fish has learned a pattern or "map" of behavior, and even though the actual territory has changed, the map remains static.

The mental **date** is an extensional device that helps you keep your language (and your thinking) up to date and helps you guard against static evaluation. The procedure is simple: date your statements and especially your evaluations. Remember that Pat Smith$_{1995}$ is not Pat Smith$_{2008}$; academic abilities$_{2004}$ are not academic abilities$_{2008}$. T. S. Eliot, in *The Cocktail Party*, said, "What we know of other people is only our memory of the moments during which we knew them. And they have changed since then ... at every meeting we are meeting a stranger." In listening, look carefully at messages that claim that what was true still is. It may or may not be. Look for change.

Language Can Obscure Distinctions

Language can obscure distinctions among people or events that are covered by the same label but are really quite different (indiscrimination); it can also make it easy to focus on extremes rather than on the vast middle ground between opposites (polarization).

Indiscrimination

Indiscrimination is the failure to distinguish between similar but different people, objects, or events. This error occurs when you focus on categories or classes and fail to see that each phenomenon is unique and needs to be looked at individually.

Everything is unlike everything else. Our language, however, provides you with common nouns, such as *teacher*, *student*, *friend*, *enemy*, *war*, *politician*, and *liberal*. These lead you to focus on similarities—to group together all teachers, all students, and all politicians. At the same time, the terms divert attention away from the uniqueness of each person, each object, and each event.

Building Communication Skills   Talking about the Middle

Fill in the word that would logically go where the question mark appears, a word that is the opposite of the term on the left.

hot _____?
high _____?
good _____?
popular _____?
sad _____?

Filling in these opposites was probably easy—the words you supplied were probably short, and, if various different people supplied opposites, you'd probably find a high level of agreement among them.

Now fill in the middle positions with words meaning, for example, "midway between hot and cold," "midway between high and low." Do this before reading further.

You probably had greater difficulty here. You probably took more time to think of these middle terms, and you also probably used multiword phrases. Further, you would probably find less agreement among different people completing this same task. From this brief experience what implications can you draw about polarization?

Although most things, people, and events fall between extremes, the common but illogical tendency is to concentrate on the extremes and ignore the middle.

This misevaluation is at the heart of stereotyping on the basis of nationality, race, religion, sex, and affectional orientation. A stereotype, as you know, is a fixed mental picture of a group that is applied to each individual in the group without regard to his or her unique qualities. Whether stereotypes are positive or negative, they create the same problem: They provide you with shortcuts that are often inappropriate.

A useful antidote to indiscrimination (and stereotyping) is another extensional device called the **index.** This mental subscript identifies each individual as an individual even though both may be covered by the same label. Thus, politician$_1$ is not politician$_2$, teacher$_1$ is not teacher$_2$. The index helps you to discriminate among without discriminating against. Although the label ("politician," for example) covers all politicians, the index makes sure that each is thought about as an individual. The index would, for example, prevent you from grouping all Muslims or all Christians or all Jews in the same category. Each Muslim, each Christian, and each Jew is unique and needs a unique index number. So at the same time that you have to generalize and appreciate similarities, the index reminds you also to look at differences. Instead of saying, for example, "I don't want you to hang around with Muslims," a parent would discriminate *among* (rather than *against*) Muslims and say something like "I don't want you to hang around with Abdul or with Said."

Polarization

Another way in which language can obscure differences is in its preponderance of extreme terms and its relative lack of middle terms, a characteristic that often leads to polarization. **Polarization** is the tendency to look at the world in terms of opposites and to describe it in extremes—good or bad, positive or negative, healthy or sick, intelligent or stupid. Polarization is often referred to as the fallacy of "either/or" or "black or white." Most people exist somewhere between the extremes. Yet there's a strong tendency to view only the extremes and to categorize people, objects, and events in terms of polar opposites.

Problems are created when opposites are used in inappropriate situations. For example, "So-and-so is either for us or against us." These options don't include all possibilities. The person may be for us in some things and against us in other things, or may be neutral.

To correct this polarizing tendency, beware of implying (and believing) that two extreme classes include all possible classes—that an individual must be one or the other, with no alternatives ("Are you pro-choice or pro-life?"). Most people, most events, most qualities exist between polar extremes. When others imply that there are only two sides or alternatives, look for the middle ground.

The Building Communication Skills box explores the ease of polarizing and the difficulty of talking about the middle.

SUMMARY: VERBAL MESSAGES

This unit focused on verbal messages, and specifically on the nature of language and the ways language works; the concept of disconfirmation and how it relates to racism, heterosexism, ageism, and sexism; and the ways in which language can be used more effectively.

1. Meanings are in people, not in things.

2. Meanings are context based; the same message in a different context will likely mean something different.

3. Language is both denotative (objective and generally easily agreed upon) and connotative (subjective and generally highly individual in meaning).

4. Language varies in directness; through language you can state exactly what you mean or you can hedge and state your meaning very indirectly.

5. Meanings are influenced by culture and gender; each culture has its own rules identifying the ways in which language should be used, and in some respects males and females use language differently.

6. Disconfirmation is the process of ignoring the presence and the communications of others. Confirmation is accepting, supporting, and acknowledging the importance of the other person.

7. Racist, heterosexist, ageist, and sexist language puts down and negatively evaluates members of various groups.

8. Using language effectively involves eliminating conceptual distortions and substituting more accurate assumptions about language.

9. Language symbolizes reality; it's not the reality itself, so avoid intensional orientation and allness.

10. Language can express both facts and inferences, so learn to make distinctions between them.

11. Language is relatively static, but reality changes rapidly; try to constantly revise the way you talk about people and things.

12. Language can obscure distinctions in its use of general terms and in its emphasis on extreme rather than middle terms, so be careful to avoid indiscrimination and polarization.

KEY TERMS IN VERBAL MESSAGES

ageist language	direct speech	heterosexist language	polarization
allness	disconfirmation	index	purr words
bypassing	E-prime	indirect speech	racist language
confirmation	et cetera	indiscrimination	rejection
connotation	extensional device	inferential statement	sexist language
cooperation	extensional orientation	intensional orientation	snarl words
date	fact–inference confusion	lying	static evaluation
denotation	factual statement	netiquette	

THINKING CRITICALLY ABOUT VERBAL MESSAGES

1. **Changing Communication Styles.** When researchers asked men and women what they would like to change about the communication style of the opposite sex, most men said they wanted women to be more direct, and most women said they wanted men to stop interrupting and offering advice (Noble, 1994). What one change would you like to see in the communication style of the opposite sex? Of your own sex?

2. **Importance of a Concept.** A widely held assumption in anthropology, linguistics, and communication is that the importance of a concept to a culture can be measured by the number of words the language has for talking about the concept. So, for example, in English there are lots of words for money, transportation, or communication, as all these concepts are important in English-speaking cultures. With this principle in mind, consider the findings of Julia Stanley, for example, who researched terms indicating sexual promiscuity. Stanley found 220 English-language terms referring to a sexually promiscuous woman but only 22 terms for a sexually promiscuous man (Thorne, Kramarae, & Henley, 1983). What does this suggest about cultural attitudes and beliefs about promiscuity in men and women?

3. **From Negative to Positive.** It's interesting to note that terms denoting some of the major movements in art—for example, impressionism and cubism—were originally applied negatively. The terms were then adopted by the artists themselves and eventually became positive. A parallel can be seen in the use of the word *queer* by some lesbian and gay organizations. The purpose of these groups in using the term is to cause it to lose its negative connotation. One possible problem, though, is that such terms may not lose their negative connotations and may simply reinforce the negative stereotypes that society has already assigned to certain groups. By using these terms, members may come to accept the labels with their negative connotations and thus contribute to their own stereotyping. What's been your experience with people who refer to themselves with negative terms? How do you feel about this?

4. **Directness.** How would you describe the level of directness you use when talking face-to-face versus the level you use in e-mail and chat rooms? If you do notice differences, to what do you attribute them?

5. **Cell Phone Politeness.** Among the rules of cell phone etiquette are these don'ts: (1) Don't intrude on others with your cell conversations; (2) don't take a cell call during a business meeting; (3) don't use your cell in elevators, libraries, or theaters; and (4) don't use loud or annoying ring tones (see, for example, **www.microsoft.com/smallbusiness/resources/ technology/communications/cell_phone**, accessed June 3, 2006, or **www.infoworld.com/articles/op/ xml/00/05/26/000526opwireless.html**, accessed June 3, 2006; or search for "cell phone etiquette"). What rule do you wish people would follow more often? What is your own code for cell phone etiquette?

LogOn! MyCommunicationLab

WWW.MYCOMMUNICATIONLAB.COM

Visit MCL for self-tests that measure how confirming, polite, and direct you are—and for a variety of exercises and discussions on verbal messages (Men and Women Talking, Talking with the Grief Stricken, Integrating Verbal and Nonverbal Messages, Using the Abstraction Ladder as a Creative Thinking Tool, Varying Directness, Identifying the Barriers to Communication, "Must Lie" Situations, What Do You Mean? Biased Language Survey, What's in a Name? and Semiotics for Beginners (on connotation and denotation). Also watch the video Having a Baby on supportive communication and Verbal Pitfalls.

While online visit the Institute of General Semantics website, www.time-binding.org. General semantics is an approach to language that emphasizes the connection between the way you speak (on the one hand) and the way you think and behave (on the other). This unit's discussion of Using Verbal Messages Effectively rests on the principles of general semantics.

References

Baxter, L. A. (1984). An investigation of compliance-gaining as politeness. *Human Communication Research, 10,* 427–456.

Bourland, D. D., Jr. (1965–66). A linguistic note: Writing in E-prime. *General Semantics Bulletin, 32–33,* 111–114.

Brown, P. (1980). How and why are women more polite: Some evidence from a Mayan community. In S. McConnell-Ginet, R. Borker, & M. Furman (Eds.), *Women and language in literature and society* (pp. 111–136). New York: Praeger.

Burgoon, J. K., & Hoobler, G. D. (2002). Nonverbal signals. In M. L. Knapp & J. A. Daly (Eds.), *Handbook of interpersonal communication* (3rd ed., pp. 240–299). Thousand Oaks, CA: Sage.

DeVito, J. A. (1974). *General semantics: Guide and workbook* (Rev. ed.). DeLand, FL: Everett/Edwards.

Dovidio, J. F., Gaertner, S. E., Kawakami, K., & Hodson, G. (2002). Why can't we just get along? Interpersonal biases and interracial distrust. *Cultural Diversity and Ethnic Minority Psychology, 8,* 88–102.

Ekman, P. (1985). *Telling lies: Clues to deceit in the market-place, politics, and marriage.* New York: Norton.

Fitzpatrick, M. A., Jandt, F. E., Myrick, F. L., & Edgar, T. (1994). Gay and lesbian couple relationships. In Ringer, R. J. (Ed.), *Queer words, queer images: Communication and the construction of homosexuality* (pp. 265–285). New York: New York University Press.

Fraser, B. (1990). Perspectives on politeness. *Journal of Pragmatics, 14* (April), 219–236.

Galvin, K., Bylund, C., & Brommel, B. J. (2004). *Family communication: Cohesion and change* (6th ed.). Boston: Allyn & Bacon.

Haney, W. (1973). *Communication and organizational behavior: Text and cases* (3rd ed.). Homewood, IL: Irwin.

Hayakawa, S. I., & Hayakawa, A. R. (1990). *Language in thought and action* (5th ed.). New York: Harcourt Brace Jovanovich.

Hecht, M. L., Collier, M. J., & Ribeau, S. (1993). *African American communication: Ethnic identity and cultural interpretation.* Thousand Oaks, CA: Sage.

Holmes, J. (1995). *Women, men and politeness.* New York: Longman.

Joyner, R. (1993). An auto-interview on the need for E-prime. *Etc.: A Review of General Semantics, 50* (Fall), 317–325.

Klein, J. (Ed.). (1992). The E-prime controversy: A symposium [Special issue]. *Etc.: A Review of General Semantics, 49*(2).

Knapp, M. L., & Hall, J. (1997). *Nonverbal behavior in human interaction* (4th ed.). New York: Holt, Rinehart & Winston.

Koppelman, K. L., with Goodhart, R. L. (2005). *Understanding human differences: Multicultural education for a diverse America.* Boston: Allyn & Bacon.

Korzybski, A. (1933). *Science and sanity.* Lakeville, CT: International Non-Aristotelian Library.

Lee, F. (1993). Being polite and keeping MUM: How bad news is communicated in organizational hierarchies. *Journal of Applied Social Psychology, 23,* 1124–1149.

Lever, J. (1995, August 22). The 1995 *Advocate* survey of sexuality and relationships: The women, lesbian sex survey. *The Advocate, 687/688,* pp. 22–30.

Ma, R. (1992). The role of unofficial intermediaries in interpersonal conflicts in the Chinese culture. *Communication Quarterly, 40* (Summer), 269–278.

Manes, J., & Wolfson, N. (1981). The compliment formula. In F. Coulmas (Ed.), *Conversational routines* (pp. 115–132). The Hague: Mouton.

Mao, L. R. (1994). Beyond politeness theory: "Face" revisited and renewed. *Journal of Pragmatics, 21* (May), 451–486.

Midooka, K. (1990). Characteristics of Japanese style communication. *Media, Culture and Society, 12* (October), 477–489.

Noble, B. P. (1994, August 14). The gender wars: Talking peace. *New York Times,* p. 21.

Pearson, J. C. (1993). *Communication in the family* (2nd ed.). New York: Harper & Row.

Penfield, J. (Ed.). (1987). *Women and language in transition.* Albany, NY: State University of New York Press.

Rich, A. L. (1974). *Interracial communication.* New York: Harper & Row.

Rundquist, S. (1992). Indirectness: A gender study of Fluting Grice's maxims. *Journal of Pragmatics, 18* (November), 431–449.

Schwartz, M., and the Task Force on Bias-Free Language of the Association of American University Presses. (1995). *Guidelines for bias-free writing.* Bloomington, IN: Indiana University Press.

Smoreda, Z., & Licoppe, C. (2000). Gender-specific use of the domestic telephone. *Social Psychology Quarterly, 63,* 238–252.

Strecker, I. (1993). Cultural variations in the concept of "face." *Multilingua 12,* 119–141.

Tannen, D. (1994a). *Gender and discourse*. New York: Oxford University Press.

Tannen, D. (1994b). *Talking from 9 to 5: How women's and men's conversational styles affect who gets heard, who gets credit, and what gets done at work*. New York: Morrow.

Thorne, B., Kramarae, C., & Henley, N. (Eds.). (1983). *Language, gender and society*. Rowley, MA: Newbury House.

Veenendall, T. L., & Feinstein, M. C. (1995). *Let's talk about relationships: Cases in Study* (2nd ed.). Prospect Heights, IL: Waveland Press.

Watzlawick, P., Beavin, J. H., & Jackson, D. D. (1967). *Pragmatics of human communication: A study of interactional patterns, pathologies, and paradoxes*. New York: Norton.

Weinberg, H. L. (1958). *Levels of knowing and existence*. New York: Harper & Row.

Wetzel, P. J. (1988). Are "powerless" communication strategies the Japanese norm? *Language in Society, 17*, 555-564.

Wilson, R. A. (1989). Toward understanding E-prime. *Etc.: A Review of General Semantics, 46*, 316-319.

Chapter 9

Nonverbal Messages

MAJOR TOPICS

The Functions of Nonverbal Communication

The Channels of Nonverbal Communication

Culture and Nonverbal Communication

Special Features

Cues for Success: Don W. Stacks

Do You Avoid Touch?

What Time Do You Have?

Legible Clothing

Silence

The Facial Feedback Hypothesis

Space Violations

Choosing a Seat

Expressing Praise and Criticism

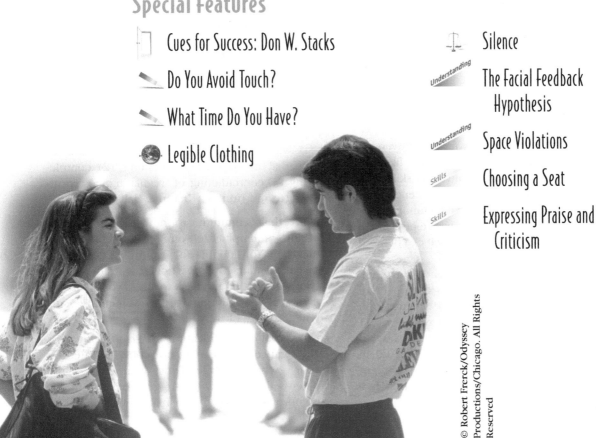

From *Human Communication: The Basic Course*, Eleventh Edition. Joseph A. DeVito. Copyright © 2009 by Pearson Education, Inc. Published by Pearson Allyn and Bacon. All rights reserved.

When you smile, nod your head in agreement, or wave your hand to someone, you're communicating nonverbally. In fact, some researchers argue that you actually communicate more information nonverbally than you do with words.

In this unit you'll learn about:

- the functions nonverbal communication serves and how nonverbal communication interacts with your verbal messages.
- the channels of nonverbal communication.
- the role of culture and gender in nonverbal communication.

You'll learn to:

- communicate more effectively with nonverbal messages.
- respond appropriately to the nonverbal messages of others.
- communicate with an awareness of cultural and gender influences and differences in nonverbal communication.

Nonverbal communication is communication without words. You communicate nonverbally when you gesture, smile or frown, widen your eyes, move your chair closer to someone, wear jewelry, touch someone, raise your vocal volume, or even say nothing. The crucial aspect of nonverbal communication is that the message you send is in some way received by one or more other people. If you gesture while alone in your room and no one is there to see you, then, most theorists would argue, communication has not taken place. The same, of course, is true of verbal messages; if you recite a speech and no one hears it, then communication has not taken place.

Using nonverbal communication effectively can yield two major benefits (Burgoon & Hoobler, 2002). First, the greater your ability to send and receive nonverbal signals, the higher your attractiveness, popularity, and psychosocial well-being are likely to be. Second, the greater your nonverbal skills, the more successful you're likely to be at influencing (or deceiving) others. Skilled nonverbal communicators are highly persuasive, and this persuasive power can be used to help or support another or it can be used to deceive and fool.

Research shows that of the two genders, women are the better senders and receivers of nonverbal messages in most contexts (Hall, 1998; Burgoon & Hoobler, 2002). For example, in a review of 21 research studies, 71 percent of the findings showed women to be superior nonverbal senders. And in a review of 61 studies on decoding, 84 percent showed women to be superior receivers (Hall, 1998).

THE FUNCTIONS OF NONVERBAL COMMUNICATION

Let's consider the functions of nonverbal communication by looking at (1) the ways in which nonverbal messages are integrated with verbal messages, and (2) the functions that researchers have focused on most extensively.

Integrating Nonverbal and Verbal Messages

In face-to-face communication you blend verbal and nonverbal messages to best convey your meanings. While speaking, you also smile, frown, or gesture, for example. It's this combination of verbal and nonverbal signals that communicates your meanings. Here are six ways in which nonverbal messages interact with verbal messages: (1) accenting, (2) complementing, (3) contradicting, (4) regulating, (5) repeating, and (6) substituting (Knapp & Hall, 1997):

- Nonverbal communication often serves to *accent* or emphasize some part of the verbal message. You might, for example, raise your voice to underscore a particular word or phrase; bang your fist on the desk to stress your commitment; or look longingly into someone's eyes when saying, "I love you."

- Nonverbal communication may *complement* or add nuances of meaning not communicated by your verbal message. Thus, you might smile when telling a story (to suggest that you find it humorous), or frown and shake your head when recounting someone's deceit (to suggest your disapproval).

- You may deliberately *contradict* your verbal messages with nonverbal movements—for example, by crossing your fingers or winking to indicate that you're lying.

- Movements may be used to *regulate*—to control or indicate your desire to control—the flow of verbal messages, as when you purse your lips, lean forward, or make hand gestures to indicate that you want to speak. You might also put up your hand or vocalize your pauses (for example, with "um" or "ah") to indicate that you have not finished and are not ready to relinquish the floor to the next speaker.

- You can *repeat* or restate the verbal message nonverbally. You can, for example, follow your verbal "Is that all right?" with raised eyebrows and a questioning look, or motion with your head or hand to repeat your verbal "Let's go."

- You may also use nonverbal communication to *substitute for* or take the place of verbal messages. For instance, you can signal "OK" with a hand gesture. You can nod your head to indicate yes or shake your head to indicate no.

Serving Varied Communication Functions

Although nonverbal communication serves the same functions as verbal communication, nonverbal researchers have singled out several specific functions as especially significant (Burgoon, Buller, & Woodall, 1996; Burgoon & Hoobler, 2002).

To Manage Self-Impression

It is largely through the nonverbal communications of others that you form impressions of them. Based

THE RESEARCHER

Cues for Success

I'm running for office in a class election, and I want to know what I can do nonverbally to make myself more likable and more credible and hence more likely to be elected. Any suggestions?

In a campaign speech enhance your physical appearance (if female, moderate makeup; if male, shave) and dress slightly better than expected at your school. You should engage in pleasant facial expressions, use a slightly faster speech rate with a good range of inflection, and speak from your diaphragm. Engage in a moderate amount of gestures, but keep them between your neck and waist and spread them away from your body. Engage your audience with a slight forward lean to show interest in them.

In interpersonal contexts where you have already enhanced your physical appearance, close your distance slightly if your listener agrees with you, but increase your distance slightly if s/he disagrees with you. If you have not enhanced your appearance, maintain your initial distance. Allow your natural emotions to flow (provide positive feedback, unless you totally disagree with the point), reduce your range of gestures, and speak with a confident, slightly faster than normal rate, but at a conversational volume.

For further information: Hickson, M. L., Stacks, D. W., & Moore, N. J. (2003). *Nonverbal communication: Studies and applications*. Los Angeles: Roxbury. And Richmond, V. P., & McCroskey, J. C. (2003). *Nonverbal behavior in interpersonal relations*. Boston: Allyn & Bacon.

Don W. Stacks (Ph.D., University of Florida) is a professor of advertising and public relations at the University of Miami. He teaches courses in public relations, research methods, nonverbal communication, persuasion, and communication theory and directs the undergraduate and graduate programs in advertising and public relations.

on a person's body size, skin color, and dress as well as on the way the person smiles, maintains eye contact, and expresses himself or herself facially, you form impressions—you judge who the person is and what the person is like. Nonverbal researchers group these impressions into five categories (Leathers, 1997; Mehrabian, 1976).

- credibility, or how competent and believable you find the person
- likability, or how much you like or dislike the person
- attractiveness, or how attractive you find the person
- dominance, or how powerful the individual is
- status, or relative rank or standing of the person; a relaxed rather than a tense posture and large gestures contribute to an impression of higher status

And, of course, you reveal yourself largely through the same nonverbal signals you use to size up others. But not only do you communicate your true self nonverbally; you also strive to manage the impression that you give to others. For example, you may do your best to appear brave when you're really scared, or to appear happy when you're really sad.

To Define Relationships

Much of your relationship life is lived nonverbally: Largely through nonverbal signals, you communicate your relationship to another person and that person communicates to you. Holding hands, gazing into each other's eyes, and even dressing alike are ways in which you communicate closeness in your interpersonal relationships.

You also use nonverbal signals to communicate your relationship dominance and status (Knapp & Hall, 1997). The large corner office with the huge desk communicates high status, just as the basement cubicle communicates low status.

To Structure Interaction

When you're in conversation, you give and receive cues—to speak, to listen, to comment on what the speaker just said. Turn-taking cues regulate and structure the interaction. These turn-taking cues may be verbal (as when you say, "What do you think?"), but most often they're nonverbal—a nod of the head in the direction of someone else, for example, signals that you're ready to give up your speaking turn and want this other person to say something.

You also show that you're listening and that you want the conversation to continue (or that you're not listening and want the conversation to end) largely through nonverbal signals.

To Influence

Much as you influence others by what you say, you also influence others by your nonverbal signals. A focused glance that says you're committed, gestures that further explain what you're saying, and appropriate dress signaling that "I'll easily fit in with this company" are a few examples of how you influence others with nonverbal signals.

And, of course, with the ability to influence comes the ability to deceive—to lie, to mislead another person into thinking something is true when it's false or that something is false when it's true. Using your eyes and facial expressions to communicate a liking for other people when you're really just interested in gaining their support for your promotion is an often-seen example of nonverbal deception.

Not surprisingly, you also may try to use nonverbal signals to detect deception in others. For example, you may suspect a person of lying if he or she avoids eye contact, fidgets, or sends verbal and nonverbal messages that are inconsistent. But be careful. Research shows that it is much more difficult to tell when someone is lying than you probably think it is. Using nonverbal cues in an effort to detect lying is likely to get you into trouble by leading you to formulate incorrect conclusions (Burgoon & Hoobler, 2002; Burgoon & Bacue, 2003; Knapp & Hall, 1997). For example, you may judge a person who avoids eye contact as lying when the eye avoidance may really be due to shyness or to a cultural rule that discourages eye contact, as does Japanese culture (Axtell, 1993).

To Communicate Emotion

Although people often explain and reveal emotions verbally, nonverbal expressions communicate a great part of emotional experience. It is largely through facial expressions that you reveal your level of happiness or sadness or confusion, for example. Of course, you also reveal your feelings by posture (for example, whether tense or relaxed), gestures, and eye movements and even by the extent to which your pupils dilate.

Nonverbal messages often serve to communicate unpleasant messages—messages you might feel uncomfortable saying in words (Infante, Rancer, & Womack, 2002). For example, you might avoid eye contact and maintain large distances between yourself and someone with whom you don't want to interact, or with whom you want to decrease the intensity of your relationship.

THE CHANNELS OF NONVERBAL COMMUNICATION

Nonverbal communication is probably most easily explained in terms of the various channels through which messages pass. Here we'll survey 10 channels: (1) body, (2) face, (3) eye, (4) space, (5) artifactual, (6) touch, (7) paralanguage, (8) silence, (9) time, and (10) smell.

The Body

Two areas of the body are especially important in communicating messages. First, the movements you make with your body communicate; second, the general appearance of your body communicates.

Body Movements

Researchers in **kinesics**, or the study of nonverbal communication through face and body movements, identify five major types of movements: emblems, illustrators, affect displays, regulators, and adaptors (Ekman & Friesen, 1969; Knapp & Hall, 1997).

Emblems. **Emblems** are body gestures that directly translate into words or phrases; for example, the OK sign, the thumbs-up for "good job," and the V for victory. You use these consciously and purposely to communicate the same meaning as the words. But emblems are culture specific, so be careful when using your culture's emblems in other cultures. For example, when President Nixon visited Latin America and gestured with the OK sign, intending to communicate something positive, he was quickly informed that this gesture was not universal. In Latin America the gesture has a far more negative meaning. Here are a few cultural differences in the emblems you may commonly use (Axtell, 1993):

- In the United States, to say "hello" you wave with your whole hand moving from side to side, but in a large part of Europe that same signal means "no." In Greece such a gesture would be considered insulting.

- The V for victory is common throughout much of the world; but if you make this gesture in England with the palm facing your face, it's as insulting as the raised middle finger is in the United States.

- In Texas the raised fist with little finger and index finger held upright is a positive expression of support, because it represents the Texas longhorn steer. But in Italy it's an insult that means "Your spouse is having an affair with someone else." In parts of South America it's a gesture to ward off evil, and in parts of Africa it's a curse: "May you experience bad times."

- In the United States and in much of Asia, hugs are rarely exchanged among acquaintances; but among Latins and southern Europeans, hugging is a common greeting gesture, and failing to hug someone may communicate unfriendliness.

Illustrators. **Illustrators** enhance (literally "illustrate") the verbal messages they accompany. For example, when referring to something to the left, you might gesture toward the left. Most often you illustrate with your hands, but you can also illustrate with head and general body movements. You might, for example, turn your head or your entire body toward the left. You might also use illustrators to communicate the shape or size of objects you're talking about. Research points to an interesting advantage of illustrators: They increase your ability to remember. In one study people who illustrated their verbal messages with gestures remembered some 20 percent more than those who didn't gesture (Goldin-Meadow, Nusbaum, Kelly, & Wagner, 2001).

Affect Displays. **Affect displays** are movements of the face (smiling or frowning, for example) but also of the hands and general body (body tension or relaxation, for example) that communicate emotional meaning. Often affect displays are unconscious; you smile or frown, for example, without awareness. At other times, however, you may smile consciously, trying to convey your pleasure or satisfaction. Not surprisingly, people who smile spontaneously are judged to be more likable and more approachable than people who don't smile or people who pretend to smile (Gladstone & Parker, 2002).

Regulators. **Regulators** are behaviors that monitor, control, coordinate, or maintain the speaking of another individual. When you nod your head, for example, you tell the speaker to keep on speaking; when you lean forward and open your mouth, you tell the speaker that you would like to say something.

Adaptors. **Adaptors** are gestures that satisfy some personal need, such as scratching to relieve an itch or moving your hair out of your eyes. **Self-adaptors** are self-touching movements (for example, rubbing your nose). **Alter-adaptors** are movements directed at the person with whom you're speaking, such as removing lint from someone's jacket or straightening a person's tie or folding your arms in front of you to keep others a comfortable distance from you. **Object-adaptors** are gestures focused on objects, such as doodling on or shredding a Styrofoam coffee cup.

Body Appearance

Your general body appearance also communicates. Height, for example, has been shown to be significant in a wide variety of situations. Tall presidential candidates have a much better record of winning the election than do their shorter opponents. Tall people seem to be paid more and are favored by interviewers over shorter job applicants (Keyes, 1980; Guerrero, DeVito, & Hecht, 1999; Knapp & Hall, 1997). Taller people also have higher self-esteem and greater career success than do shorter people.

Your body also reveals your ethnicity (through skin color and tone) and may also give clues as to your more specific nationality. Your weight in proportion to your height will also communicate messages to others, as will the length, color, and style of your hair.

Your general **attractiveness** is also a part of body communication. Attractive people have the advantage in just about every activity you can name. They get better grades in school, are more valued as friends and lovers, and are preferred as coworkers (Burgoon, Buller, & Woodall, 1996). Although we normally think that attractiveness is culturally determined—and to some degree it is—research seems to indicate that definitions of attractiveness are universal (Brody, 1994). A person rated as attractive in one culture is likely to be rated as attractive in other cultures—even in cultures whose people are widely different in appearance.

Facial Communication

Throughout your interactions, your face communicates various messages, especially your emotions. Facial movements alone seem to communicate the degree of pleasantness, agreement, and sympathy felt; the rest of the body doesn't provide any additional information. But for other emotional messages—for example, the intensity with which an emotion is felt—both facial and bodily cues send messages (Graham, Bitti, & Argyle, 1975; Graham & Argyle, 1975).

So important are these cues in communicating your full meaning that graphic representations are commonly used in Internet communication. In graphic user interface chat groups, buttons are available to help you encode your emotions graphically. Table 1 identifies some of the more common "emoticons," icons that communicate emotions.

Some researchers in nonverbal communication claim that facial movements may express at least the following eight emotions: happiness, surprise, fear, anger, sadness, disgust, contempt, and interest (Ekman, Friesen, & Ellsworth, 1972). Facial expressions of these emotions are generally called primary affect displays: They indicate relatively pure, single emotions. Other emotional states and other facial displays are combinations of these various primary emotions and are called affect blends. You communicate these blended feelings with different parts of your face. Thus, for example, you may experience both fear and disgust at the same time. Your

---

Table 1 Some Popular Emoticons

Here are a few of the many popular emoticons used in computer communication. The first six are popular in the United States; the last three are popular in Japan and illustrate how culture influences such symbols. That is, because Japanese culture considers it impolite for women to show their teeth when smiling, the emoticon for a woman's smile shows a dot signifying a closed mouth. Two excellent websites that contain extensive examples of smileys, emoticons, acronyms, and shorthand abbreviations are www.netlingo.com/smiley.cfm and www.netlingo.com/emailsh.cfm.

Emoticon	Meaning	Emoticon	Meaning
:-)	Smile; I'm kidding	*This is important*	Substitutes for underlining or italics
:-(	Frown; I'm feeling down	<G>	Grin; I'm kidding
*	Kiss	<grin>	Grin; I'm kidding
{}	Hug	^.^	Woman's smile
{*****}	Hugs and kisses	^_^	Man's smile
This is important	Gives emphasis, calls special attention to	^o^	Happy

244

eyes and eyelids may signal fear, and movements of your nose, cheek, and mouth area may signal disgust.

Facial Management

As you learned your culture's nonverbal system of communication, you also learned certain **facial management techniques** that enable you to communicate your feelings to achieve the effect you want—for example, ways to hide certain emotions and to emphasize others. Consider your own use of such techniques. As you do so, think about the types of interpersonal situations in which you would use each of the following facial management techniques (Malandro, Barker, & Barker, 1989; Metts & Planalp, 2002). Would you

- *Intensify?* For example, would you exaggerate surprise when friends throw you a party to make your friends feel better?

- *Deintensify?* Would you cover up your own joy about a successful outcome in the presence of a friend who didn't receive such good news?

- *Neutralize?* Would you cover up your sadness to keep from depressing others?

- *Mask?* Would you express happiness in order to cover up your disappointment at not receiving the gift you expected?

- *Simulate?* Would you express an emotion you don't feel?

These tactics of facial management help you display emotions in socially acceptable ways. For example, when someone gets bad news in which you may secretly take pleasure, the cultural display rule dictates that you frown and otherwise nonverbally signal your displeasure. If you place first in a race and your best friend barely finishes, the display rule requires that you minimize your expression of pleasure in winning and avoid any signs of gloating. If you violate these display rules, you'll seem insensitive. So although facial management techniques may be deceptive, they're also expected—in fact required—by the rules of polite interaction.

Encoding–Decoding Accuracy

One popular question concerns the accuracy with which people can encode and decode emotions through facial expressions. It can be difficult to separate the ability of the encoder from the ability of the decoder, however. Thus, a person may be quite adept at communicating emotions nonverbally, but the receiver may prove insensitive. On the other hand, the receiver may be good at deciphering emotions, but the sender may be inept. For example, introverts are not as accurate at decoding nonverbal cues as are extroverts (Akert & Panter, 1988).

© Steven Begleiter/Pictor/ImageState

SMILING

Sam smiles almost all the time. Even when he criticizes or reprimands a subordinate, he ends with a smile and this dilutes the strength of his message. As Sam's supervisor, you need him to realize what he's doing and to change his nonverbals.

WHAT DO YOU SAY?
Through what channel?
In what context?

Despite this difficulty, research in 11 different countries shows that women are better than men at both encoding and decoding nonverbal cues (Rosenthal & DePaulo, 1979). It may be argued that because men and women play different roles in society, they've learned different adaptive techniques and skills to help them perform these roles. Thus, in most societies women are expected to be more friendly, nurturing, and supportive and so learn these skills (Eagly & Crowley, 1986).

Accuracy in decoding also varies with the emotions themselves. Some emotions are easier to encode and decode than others. In one study, for example, people judged facial expressions of happiness with an accuracy ranging from 55 to 100 percent, surprise from 38 to 86 percent, and sadness from 19 to 88 percent (Ekman, Friesen, & Ellsworth, 1972).

Eye Communication

Research on the messages communicated by the eyes (a study known technically as oculesis) shows that these messages vary depending on the duration, direction, and quality of the eye behavior. For example, in every culture there are strict, though unstated, rules for the proper duration for eye contact. In U.S. culture the average length of gaze is 2.95 seconds. The average length of mutual gaze (two persons gazing at each other) is 1.18 seconds (Argyle & Ingham, 1972; Argyle, 1988). When eye contact falls short of this amount, you may think the person is uninterested, shy, or preoccupied. When

Theory and Research   UNDERSTANDING   The Facial Feedback Hypothesis

The **facial feedback hypothesis** holds that your facial expressions influence physiological arousal (Lanzetta, Cartwright-Smith, & Kleck, 1976; Zuckerman, Klorman, Larrance, & Spiegel, 1981). In one study, for example, participants held a pen in their teeth to simulate a sad expression and then rated a series of photographs. Results showed that mimicking sad expressions actually increased the degree of sadness the subjects reported feeling when viewing the photographs (Larsen, Kasimatis, & Frey, 1992). Further support for this hypothesis comes from a study that compared (1) participants who felt emotions such as happiness and anger with (2) participants who both felt and expressed these emotions. In support of the facial feedback hypothesis, people who felt and expressed the emotions became emotionally aroused faster than did those who only felt the emotion (Hess, Kappas, McHugo, & Lanzetta, 1992).

Generally, research finds that facial expressions can produce or heighten feelings of sadness, fear, disgust, and anger. But this effect does not occur with all emotions; smiling, for example, doesn't seem to make us feel happier (Burgoon & Bacue, 2003). Further, it has not been demonstrated that facial expressions can eliminate one feeling and replace it with another. So if you're feeling sad, smiling will not eliminate the sadness and replace it with gladness. A reasonable conclusion seems to be that your facial expressions can influence some feelings, but not all (Burgoon & Bacue, 2003).

Working with Theories and Research

What effect do you observe when you express your emotions? Do your feelings get stronger? Weaker?

the appropriate amount of time is exceeded, you may perceive the person as showing unusually high interest.

The direction of the eye also communicates. In much of the United States, you're expected to glance alternately at the other person's face, then away, then again at the face, and so on. The rule for the public speaker is to scan the entire audience, not focusing for too long on or ignoring any one area of the audience. When you break these directional rules, you communicate different meanings—abnormally high or low interest, self-consciousness, nervousness over the interaction, and so on. The quality of eye behavior—how wide or how narrow your eyes get during interaction—also communicates meaning, especially interest level and such emotions as surprise, fear, and disgust. Some researchers note that eye contact serves to enable gay men and lesbians to signal their homosexuality and perhaps their interest in the other person—an ability referred to as "gaydar".

Eye Contact and Eye Avoidance

Eye contact can serve a variety of functions. One such function is to seek feedback. In talking with someone, we look at her or him intently, as if to say, "Well, what do you think?" As you might predict,

listeners gaze at speakers more than speakers gaze at listeners. In public speaking, you may scan hundreds of people to secure this feedback.

A second function is to inform the other person that the channel of communication is open and that he or she should now speak. You see this regularly in conversation, when one person asks a question or finishes a thought and then looks to you for a response. And one study found that eye contact was the most frequently noted nonverbal behavior used to tell library users that the librarian was approachable (Radford, 1998).

Eye movements may also signal the nature of a relationship, whether positive (an attentive glance) or negative (eye avoidance). You can also signal your power through **visual dominance** behavior (Exline, Ellyson, & Long, 1975). The average person, for example, maintains a high level of eye contact while listening and a lower level while speaking. When people want to signal dominance, they may reverse this pattern—maintaining a high level of eye contact while talking but a much lower level while listening.

By making eye contact you psychologically lessen the physical distance between yourself and another person. When you catch someone's eye at a party, for example, you become psychologically close though physically far apart.

Eye avoidance, too, can serve several different functions. When you avoid eye contact or avert your glance, you may help others maintain their privacy. For example, you may do this when you see a couple arguing in public. You turn your eyes away (though your eyes may be wide open) as if to say, "I don't mean to intrude; I respect your privacy," a behavior referred to as **civil inattention** (Goffman, 1971).

Eye avoidance can also signal lack of interest—in a person, a conversation, or some visual stimulus. At times, too, you may hide your eyes to block out unpleasant stimuli (a particularly gory or violent scene in a movie, for example) or close your eyes to block out visual stimuli and thus heighten other senses. For example, you may listen to music with your eyes closed. Lovers often close their eyes while kissing, and many prefer to make love in a dark or dimly lit room.

Pupil Dilation

In the fifteenth and sixteenth centuries, Italian women put drops of belladonna (which literally means "beautiful woman") into their eyes to enlarge the pupils so that they would look more attractive. Contemporary **pupillometrics** research supports the intuitive logic of these women; dilated pupils are judged more attractive than constricted ones (Hess, 1975; Marshall, 1983). In one study, researchers retouched photographs of women; in half they enlarged the pupils, and in the other half they made them smaller (Hess, 1975). Men were then asked to judge the women's personalities from the photographs. The photos of women with small pupils drew responses such as "cold," "hard," and "selfish"; those with dilated pupils drew responses such as "feminine" and "soft." Interestingly, the male observers could not verbalize the reasons for their different perceptions. Pupil dilation and our reactions to changes in the pupil size of others may function below the level of conscious awareness.

Pupil size also reveals your interest and level of emotional arousal. Your pupils enlarge when you're interested in something or when you are emotionally aroused. When homosexuals and heterosexuals were shown pictures of nude bodies, the homosexuals' pupils dilated more when they viewed same-sex bodies, whereas the heterosexuals' pupils dilated more when they viewed opposite-sex bodies (Hess, Seltzer, & Schlien, 1965). These pupillary responses are also observed in persons with profound mental retardation (Chaney, Givens, Aoki, & Gombiner, 1989). Perhaps we judge dilated pupils as more attractive because we respond to them as indicative of a person's interest in us. And that may be the reason why both models and fuzzy beanbag toys have exceptionally large pupils.

Space Communication

Space is an especially important factor in interpersonal communication, although we seldom think

---

Building Communication Skills   Choosing a Seat

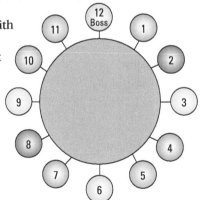

Look at the diagram here, which represents a table with 12 chairs, one of which is already occupied by the "boss." Below are listed five messages you might want to communicate. For each of these messages, indicate (a) where you would sit to communicate the desired message, and (b) any other messages that your seating position will make it easier for you to communicate.

1. You want to polish the apple and ingratiate yourself with your boss.

2. You aren't prepared and want to be ignored.

3. You want to challenge your boss on a certain policy that will come up for a vote.

4. You want to be accepted as a new (but important) member of the company.

5. You want to get to know the person already seated at position number 5.

Every nonverbal (and verbal) message that you send has an impact, even the seat you select at a meeting. Your messages always reveal (to some extent) who you are and what others will think of you.

about it. Edward T. Hall (1959, 1963, 1976) pioneered the study of spatial communication and called this research area **proxemics**. We can examine this broad area by looking at (1) proxemic distances and (2) territoriality.

Proxemic Distances

Edward Hall (1959, 1963, 1976) distinguishes four **proxemic distances**, or **spatial distances**: the physical distances that define the types of relationships between people and the types of communication in which they are likely to engage (see Table 2).

Intimate Distance. In **intimate distance**, ranging from actual touching to 18 inches, the presence of the other individual is unmistakable. Each person experiences the sound, smell, and feel of the other's breath. You use intimate distance for lovemaking, comforting, and protecting. This distance is so short that most people don't consider it proper in public.

Personal Distance. **Personal distance** refers to the protective "bubble" that defines your personal space, ranging from 18 inches to 4 feet. This imaginary bubble keeps you protected and untouched by others. You can still hold or grasp another person at this distance, but only by extending your arms; this allows you to take certain individuals such as loved ones into your protective bubble. At the outer limit of personal distance, you can touch another person only if both of you extend your arms. This is the distance at which you conduct most of your interpersonal interactions; for example, talking with friends and family.

Social Distance. At **social distance**, ranging from 4 to 12 feet, you lose the visual detail you have at personal distance. You conduct impersonal business and interact at a social gathering at this social distance. The more distance you maintain in your interactions, the more formal they appear. In offices of high officials, the desks are positioned so the official is assured of at least this distance from clients.

Public Distance. **Public distance**, from 12 to more than 25 feet, protects you. At this distance you could take defensive action if threatened. On a public bus or train, for example, you might keep at least this distance from a drunken passenger. Although at this distance you lose fine details of the face and eyes, you're still close enough to see what is happening.

The specific distances that we maintain between ourselves and other people depend on a wide variety of factors (Burgoon, Buller, & Woodall, 1996; Burgoon & Bacue, 2003). Among the most significant are *gender* (in same-sex dyads women sit and stand closer to each other than do men, and people approach women more closely than they approach men); *age*

Table 2   Relationships and Proxemic Distances

Note that these four distances can be further divided into close and far phases and that the far phase of one level (say, personal) blends into the close phase of the next level (social). Do your relationships also blend into one another? Or are, say, your personal relationships totally separate from your social relationships?

Relationship		Distance
Intimate relationship		Intimate distance
		0 —————————— 18 inches
		close phase far phase
Personal relationship		Personal distance
		1 —————————— 4 feet
		close phase far phase
Social relationship		Social distance
		4 —————————— 12 feet
		close phase far phase
Public relationship		Public distance
		12 —————————— 25+ feet
		close phase far phase

PROXEMICS

Like the close-talker in an episode of Seinfeld, one of your team members at work maintains an extremely close distance when talking. Coupled with the fact that this person is a heavy smoker and reeks of smoke, you need to say something.

WHAT DO YOU SAY?
Through what channel?

© Zefa RF/Alamy

(people maintain closer distances with similarly aged others than they do with those much older or much younger); and *personality* (introverts and highly anxious people maintain greater distances than do extroverts). Not surprisingly, we maintain shorter distances with people we're familiar with than with strangers and with people we like than with those we don't like. One theoretical explanation of the dynamics of spatial distances is discussed in the accompanying Understanding Theory and Research box.

Territoriality

One of the most interesting concepts in ethology (the study of animals in their natural surroundings) is **territoriality**, a possessive or ownership reaction to an area of space or to particular objects. Two interesting dimensions of territoriality are territory types and territorial markers.

Territory Types. Three types of territory are often distinguished: primary, secondary, and public (Altman, 1975). **Primary territories** are your exclusive preserve: your desk, room, house, or backyard, for example. In these areas you're in control. The effect is similar to the **home field advantage** that a sports team has when playing in its own ballpark. When you're in these home territories, you generally have greater influence over others than you would in someone else's territory. For example, in their own home or office, people generally take on a kind of leadership role; they initiate conversations, fill in silences, assume relaxed and comfortable postures, and maintain their positions with greater conviction. Because the territorial owner is dominant, you stand a better chance of getting your raise approved, your point accepted, or a contract resolved in your favor if you're in your own primary territory (home, office) rather than in someone else's (Marsh, 1988).

Secondary territories, although they don't belong to you, are associated with you—perhaps because you've occupied them for a long time or they were assigned to you. For example, your desk in a classroom may become a secondary territory if it is assigned to you or if you regularly occupy it and others treat it as yours. Your neighborhood turf, a cafeteria table where you usually sit, or a favorite corner of a local coffee shop may be secondary territories. You feel a certain "ownership-like" attachment to the place, even though it's really not yours in any legal sense.

Public territories are areas that are open to all people, such as a park, movie house, restaurant, or beach. European cafés, food courts in suburban malls, and the open areas in large city office buildings are public spaces that bring people together and stimulate communication.

The electronic revolution, however, may well change the role of public space in stimulating communication (Drucker & Gumpert, 1991; Gumpert & Drucker, 1995). For example, home shopping clubs make it less necessary for people to go downtown or to the mall, and shoppers consequently have less opportunity to run into other people and to talk and exchange news. Similarly, electronic mail permits us to communicate without talking and without leaving the house to mail a letter. Perhaps the greatest change is telecommuting (Giordano, 1989), in which workers can go to work without leaving their homes. The face-to-face communication that normally takes place in an office is replaced by communication via computer.

Territoriality is closely linked to **status**. Generally, the size and location of your territories signal your status within your social group. For example, male animals will stake out a particular territory and consider it their own. They will allow prospective mates

249

Theory and Research · Understanding · Space Violations

Expectancy violations theory, developed by Judee Burgoon, explains what happens when you increase or decrease the distance between yourself and another person in an interpersonal interaction (Burgoon, 1978; Burgoon & Bacue, 2003). Each culture has certain expectancies for the distance that people are expected to maintain in their conversations. And, of course, each person has certain idiosyncrasies. Together, these determine expected distance. If you violate the expected distance to a great extent (small violations most often go unnoticed), the relationship itself comes into focus; the other person begins to turn attention away from the topic of conversation to you and to your relationship with him or her.

If this other person perceives you positively—for example, if you're a high-status person or you're particularly attractive—then you'll be perceived even more positively if you violate the expected distance. If, on the other hand, you're perceived negatively and you violate the norm, you'll be perceived even more negatively.

Working with Theories and Research

Do your own experiences support this theory of space expectancy violations? What do you see happening when space expectations are violated?

---

to enter but will defend the territory against entrance by others, especially by other males of the same species. The larger the animal's territory, the higher the status of animal within the herd. The size and location of human territories also say something about status (Mehrabian, 1976). An apartment or office in midtown Manhattan or downtown Tokyo, for example, is extremely high-status territory. The cost of the territory restricts it to those who have lots of money.

Territory Markers. Much as animals mark their territory, humans mark theirs with three types of **markers**: central markers, boundary markers, and earmarkers (Hickson, Stacks, & Moore, 2003). **Central markers** are items you place in a territory to reserve it. For example, you place a drink at the bar, books on your desk, or a sweater over the chair to let others know that these territories belong to you.

Boundary markers set boundaries that divide your territory from "theirs." In the supermarket checkout line, the bar placed between your groceries and those of the person behind you is a boundary marker. Similarly, the armrests separating your seat from those of the people on either side at a movie theater and the molded plastic seats on a bus or train are boundary markers.

Earmarkers—a term taken from the practice of branding animals on their ears—are those identifying marks that indicate your possession of a territory or object. Trademarks, nameplates, and initials on a shirt or attaché case are all examples of earmarkers. Some teenagers, for example, perhaps because they can't yet own territories, often use markers to indicate a kind of pseudo-ownership or appropriation of someone else's or a public territory for their own use. Examples of graffiti and the markings of gang boundaries come quickly to mind.

Artifactual Communication

Artifactual communication is communication via objects made by human hands. Thus, color, clothing, jewelry, and the decoration of space would be considered artifactual. Let's look at each of these briefly.

Color Communication

There is some evidence that colors affect us physiologically. For example, respiratory movements increase with red light and decrease with blue light. Similarly, eye blinks increase in frequency when eyes are exposed to red light and decrease when exposed to blue. These responses seem consistent with our intuitive feelings about blue being more soothing and red more arousing. When a school changed the color of its walls from orange and white to blue, the blood pressure of the students decreased and their academic performance increased (Ketcham, 1958; Malandro, Barker, & Barker, 1989).

Color communication also influences perceptions and behaviors (Kanner, 1989). People's acceptance of a product, for example, is largely determined by its packaging, especially its color. In one study the very same coffee taken from a yellow can was described as weak, from a dark brown can as too strong, from a red can as rich, and from a blue can as mild. Even your acceptance of a person may depend on the colors he or she wears. Consider, for example, the comments of one color expert (Kanner, 1989): "If you have to pick the wardrobe for your defense lawyer heading into court and choose anything but blue, you deserve to lose the case." Black is so powerful it could work against the lawyer with the jury. Brown lacks sufficient authority. Green would probably elicit a negative response.

Clothing and Body Adornment

People make inferences about who you are, at least in part, from the way you dress. Whether these inferences are accurate or not, they will influence what people think of you and how they react to you. Your socioeconomic class, your seriousness, your attitudes (for example, whether you're conservative or liberal), your concern for convention, your sense of style, and perhaps even your creativity will all be judged in part by the way you dress (Molloy, 1975, 1977, 1981; Burgoon, Buller, & Woodall, 1996; Knapp & Hall, 1997). In the business world, your clothing may communicate your position within the hierarchy and your willingness and desire to conform to the norms of the organization. It also may communicate your professionalism, which seems to be the reason why some organizations favor dress codes. On campus, college students will perceive an instructor dressed informally as friendly, fair, enthusiastic, and flexible; they will see the same instructor dressed formally as prepared, knowledgeable, and organized (Malandro, Barker, & Barker, 1989).

Try personalizing this brief discussion by considering, for example, how you'd dress in each of such situations as these:

- to interview for a job at a prestigious and conservative law firm

- to appear friendly but serious as you teach your first college class

- to appear as the trendiest partygoer at the trendiest spot in town

- to make your romantic partner's parents (you've been dating about six months), about whom you know very little, think you're absolutely wonderful

- to attend a parent-teacher conference (you're the parent) at your child's preschool and appear very

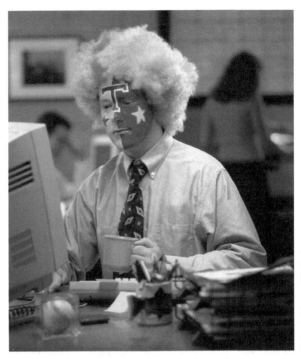

Robert Mizono/Getty Images

CLOTHING COMMUNICATION

One of your friends has been passed over for promotion several times and you think you know the reason: Your friend dresses inappropriately, though generally not as bad as the guy in the photo. You want to help your friend.

WHAT DO YOU SAY?
Through what channel? In what context?

concerned and involved, though in truth you've not participated in any of the school's activities

Very likely you'd dress very differently in each of these situations, attesting to the importance of clothing in impression formation.

The way you wear your hair says something about your attitudes—from a concern about being up to date, to a desire to shock, to perhaps a lack of interest in appearances. Men with long hair will generally be judged as less conservative than those with shorter hair. Your jewelry also communicates about you. Wedding and engagement rings are obvious examples that communicate specific messages. College rings and political buttons likewise communicate specific messages. If you wear a Rolex watch or large precious stones, others are likely to infer that you're rich. Men who wear earrings will be judged differently from men who don't. What judgments are made will depend on who the receiver is, the communication context, and all the factors identified throughout this text.

Body piercings are now common, especially among the young. Nose, nipple, tongue, and belly button jewelry (among other piercings) send a variety of messages. Although people wearing such jewelry may wish to communicate positive meanings, research indicates that those interpreting these messages seem to infer that the wearer is communicating an unwillingness to conform to social norms and a willingness to take greater risks than people without such piercings (Forbes, 2001). It's worth noting that in a study of employers' perceptions, applicants with eyebrow piercings were rated and ranked significantly lower than those without such piercings (Acor, 2001). In another study, nose-pierced job candidates were scored lower on measures of credibility such as character and trust as well as sociability and hirability (Seiter & Sandry, 2003). And in health care situations, tattoos and piercings may communicate such undesirable traits as impulsiveness, unpredictability, and a tendency toward being reckless or violent.

Tattoos, whether temporary or permanent, likewise communicate a variety of messages—often the name of a loved one or some symbol of allegiance or affiliation. Tattoos also communicate to the wearers themselves. For example, tattooed students see themselves (and perhaps others do as well) as more adventurous, creative, individualistic, and risk-prone than those without tattoos (Drews, Allison, & Probst, 2000).

The accompanying Media Watch box continues this discussion of clothing by looking at clothing with specific verbal messages.

Space Decoration

The way you decorate your private spaces also communicates about you. The office with a mahogany desk and bookcases and oriental rugs communicates your importance and status within an organization, just as a metal desk and bare floor indicate a worker much farther down in the hierarchy.

Similarly, people will make inferences about you based on the way you decorate your home. The expensiveness of the furnishings may communicate your status and wealth; their coordination may convey your sense of style. The magazines may reflect your interests, and the arrangement of chairs around a television set may reveal how important watching television is to you. The contents of bookcases lining the walls reveal the importance of reading in your life. In fact, there's probably little in your home that will not send messages from which others will draw inferences about you. Computers, wide-screen televisions, well-equipped kitchens, and oil paintings of great-grandparents, for example,

MEDIA WATCH

LEGIBLE CLOTHING

Legible clothing is anything that you wear that displays some verbal message; it's clothing that literally can be read. In some instances the message proclaims status; it tells others that you are, for example, rich or stylish or youthful. The Gucci or Louis Vuitton logos on your luggage communicate your financial status. In a similar way your sweatshirt with the word "Bulls" or "Pirates" emblazoned across it communicates your interest in sports and your favorite team.

Legible clothing is being bought and worn in record numbers. Many designers and manufacturers have their names integrated into the design of the clothing: DKNY, Calvin Klein, Armani, L. L. Bean, the Gap, and Old Navy are just a few examples. At the same time that you're paying extra to buy the brand name, you're also providing free advertising for the designer.

T-shirts and sweatshirts are especially popular as message senders. One study surveyed 600 male and female students as to the types of T-shirt messages they preferred (Sayre, 1992). Four messages were cited most often:

- Affiliation messages, such as a club or school name, communicate that you're a part of a larger group.
- Trophy names, such as those of a high-status concert or perhaps a ski lodge, say that you were in the right place at the right time.
- Metaphorical expressions, such as pictures of rock groups or famous athletes, reveal that you're part of a current trend.
- Personal messages, such as statements of beliefs or philosophies, tell others that you're willing to express your beliefs publicly.

Increasing Media Literacy

Affiliation messages may create problems when they identify the wearer as a member of a gang, because wearing gang colors can contribute to violence, especially in schools (Burke, 1993; Zimmerman, 2000). How do you feel about these and other provocative types of clothing messages? Do you feel that some clothing messages should be prohibited? If so, which ones? Or do you feel that such messages should be protected by the First Amendment to the Constitution, which guarantees freedom of speech?

TOUCH BOUNDARIES

A colleague at work continually touches you in passing—your arm, your shoulder, your waist. These touches are becoming more frequent and more intimate. You want this touching to stop.

WHAT DO YOU SAY?
To whom? Through what channel?

© Photolibrary

all say something about the people who live in the home.

Similarly, the absence of certain items will communicate something about you. Consider what messages you'd get from a home where no television, phone, or books could be seen.

People will also make judgments as to your personality on the basis of room decorations. Research finds, for example, that people will make judgments about your openness to new experiences (distinctive decorating usually communicates this, as would different types of books and magazines and travel souvenirs) and even about your conscientiousness, emotional stability, degree of extroversion, and agreeableness. Not surprisingly, bedrooms prove more revealing of personality than offices (Gosling, Ko, Mannarelli, & Morris, 2002).

Touch Communication

The study of **touch communication**, technically referred to as **haptics**, suggests that touch is perhaps the most primitive form of communication (Montagu, 1971). Developmentally, touch is probably the first sense to be used. Even in the womb the child is stimulated by touch. Soon after birth the child is fondled, caressed, patted, and stroked. In turn, the child explores its world through touch. In a short time the child learns to communicate many different meanings through touch.

The Meanings of Touch

Touch communicates a wide range of messages (Jones & Yarbrough, 1985). Here are five major types of messages that will illustrate this great variety.

- Touch communicates positive feelings; for example, support, appreciation, inclusion, sexual interest or intent, composure, immediacy, affection,

trust, similarity and quality, and informality (Jones & Yarbrough, 1985; Burgoon, 1991). Touch also stimulates self-disclosure (Rabinowitz, 1991).

- Touch often communicates your intention to play, either affectionately or aggressively.

- Touch may control the behaviors, attitudes, or feelings of other people. To obtain compliance, for example, you touch a person to communicate "move over," "hurry," "stay here," or "do it." You might also touch a person to gain his or her attention, as if to say "look at me" or "look over here." In some situations touching can even amount to a kind of **nonverbal dominance** behavior. Touch even seems to increase a waitperson's tips. Researchers found that people who were touched by a female waitperson on the hand or shoulder tipped more than those who weren't touched (Crusco & Wetzel, 1984; Stephen & Zweigenhaft, 1986).

- Ritualistic touching centers on greetings and departures; examples are shaking hands to say "hello" or "good-bye," hugging, kissing, or putting your arm around another's shoulder when greeting or saying farewell.

- Task-related touching is associated with the performance of some function, as when you remove a speck of dust from another person's coat, help someone out of a car, or check someone's forehead for fever.

Touch Avoidance

Much as you have a need and desire to touch and be touched, you also have a tendency to avoid touch from certain people or in certain circumstances (Andersen & Leibowitz, 1978). You may wish to examine your own **touch avoidance** tendency by taking the self-test on the following page.

253

TEST **YOURSELF**

Do You Avoid Touch?

This test is composed of 18 statements concerning how you feel about touching other people and being touched. Please indicate the degree to which each statement applies to you according to the following scale: 1 = strongly agree; 2 = agree; 3 = undecided; 4 = disagree; and 5 = strongly disagree.

_____ **1.** A hug from a same-sex friend is a true sign of friendship.

_____ **2.** Opposite-sex friends enjoy it when I touch them.

_____ **3.** I often put my arm around friends of the same sex.

_____ **4.** When I see two friends of the same sex hugging, it revolts me.

_____ **5.** I like it when members of the opposite sex touch me.

_____ **6.** People shouldn't be so uptight about touching persons of the same sex.

_____ **7.** I think it is vulgar when members of the opposite sex touch me.

_____ **8.** When a member of the opposite sex touches me, I find it unpleasant.

_____ **9.** I wish I were free to show emotions by touching members of the same sex.

_____ **10.** I'd enjoy giving a massage to an opposite-sex friend.

_____ **11.** I enjoy kissing a person of the same sex.

_____ **12.** I like to touch friends that are the same sex as I am.

_____ **13.** Touching a friend of the same sex does not make me uncomfortable.

_____ **14.** I find it enjoyable when my date and I embrace.

_____ **15.** I enjoy getting a back rub from a member of the opposite sex.

_____ **16.** I dislike kissing relatives of the same sex.

_____ **17.** Intimate touching with members of the opposite sex is pleasurable.

_____ **18.** I find it difficult to be touched by a member of my own sex.

HOW DID YOU DO? To score your touch avoidance questionnaire:

1. Reverse your scores for items 4, 7, 8, 16, and 18. Use these reversed scores in all future calculations.

2. To obtain your same-sex touch avoidance score (the extent to which you avoid touching members of your sex), total the scores for items 1, 3, 4, 6, 9, 11, 12, 13, 16, and 18.

3. To obtain your opposite-sex touch avoidance score (the extent to which you avoid touching members of the opposite sex), total the scores for items 2, 5, 7, 8, 10, 14, 15, and 17.

4. To obtain your total touch avoidance score, add the subtotals from steps 2 and 3.

The higher the score, the higher the touch avoidance—that is, the greater your tendency to avoid touch. In studies by Andersen and Leibowitz (1978), who constructed this test, average opposite-sex touch avoidance scores were 12.9 for males and 14.85 for females. Average same-sex touch avoidance scores were 26.43 for males and 21.70 for females. How do your scores compare with those of the college students in Andersen and Leibowitz's study? Is your touch avoidance likely to be higher when you are interacting with persons who are culturally different from you? Can you identify types of people and types of situations in which your touch avoidance would be especially high? Especially low?

WHAT WILL YOU DO? Are you satisfied with your score? Would you like to change your touch avoidance tendencies? What might you do about them?

Source: From "The Development and Nature of the Construct Touch Avoidance" by Andersen et al., _Journal of Nonverbal Behavior_, 3(2) 89–106. With kind permission from Springer Science and Business Media.

Researchers using the self-test presented here have found several interesting connections between touch avoidance and other factors (Andersen & Liebowitz, 1978). For example, touch avoidance is positively related to communication apprehension. If you have a strong fear of oral communication, then you probably also have strong touch avoidance tendencies. Touch avoidance is also high in those who self-disclose less.

Both touch and self-disclosure are intimate forms of communication. People who are reluctant to get close to another person by self-disclosing also seem reluctant to get close by touching.

Older people avoid touch with opposite-sex persons more than younger people do. As people get older they're touched less by members of the opposite sex; this decreased frequency of touching may lead them to avoid touching.

Not surprisingly, touch also varies with your relationship stage. In the early stages of a relationship, you touch little; in intermediate stages (involvement and intimacy), you touch a great deal; and at stable or deteriorating stages, you again touch little (Guerrero & Andersen, 1991, 1994).

Paralanguage: The Vocal Channel

Paralanguage is the vocal but nonverbal dimension of speech. It has to do not with what you say but with how you say it. A traditional exercise students use to increase their ability to express different emotions, feelings, and attitudes is to repeat a sentence while accenting or stressing different words. One popular sentence is, "Is this the face that launched a thousand ships?" Significant differences in meaning are easily communicated depending on where the speaker places the stress. Consider the following variations:

- Is *this* the face that launched a thousand ships?
- Is this the *face* that launched a thousand ships?
- Is this the face that *launched* a thousand ships?
- Is this the face that launched a *thousand ships*?

Each sentence communicates something different; in fact, each asks a different question, even though the words are exactly the same. All that distinguishes the sentences is stress, one aspect of paralanguage. In addition to stress and **pitch** (highness or lowness), paralanguage includes such **voice qualities** as **rate** (speed), **volume** (loudness), rhythm, and pauses or hesitations as well as the vocalizations you make in crying, whispering, moaning, belching, yawning, and yelling (Trager, 1958, 1961; Argyle, 1988). A variation in any of these features communicates. When you speak quickly, for example, you communicate something different from when you speak slowly. Even though the words may be the same, if the speed (or volume, rhythm, or pitch) differs, the meanings people receive will also differ. The Building Communication Skills exercise, "Expressing Praise and Criticism," explores the different meanings that variations in paralanguage (and other nonverbal signals) can communicate.

Judgments about People

Paralanguage cues are often used as a basis for judgments about people; for example, evaluations of their emotional state or even their personality. A listener can accurately judge the emotional state of a speaker from vocal expression alone if both speaker and listener speak the same language. Paralanguage cues are not so accurate when used to communicate emotions to those who speak a different language (Albas, McCluskey, & Albas, 1976). Also, some emotions are easier to identify than others; it's easy to distinguish between hate and sympathy but more difficult to distinguish between fear and anxiety. And, of course, listeners vary in their

---

B u i l d i n g   C o m m u n i c a t i o n   Expressing Praise and Criticism

Consider how nonverbal messages can communicate praise and criticism by reading each of the following statements, first to communicate praise and second, criticism. In the second and third columns, record the nonverbal signals you used to help you communicate these differences in meaning between praise and criticism.

Message	Nonverbal cues to communicate praise	Nonverbal cues to communicate criticism
You lost weight.		
You look happy.		
You're an expert.		
Your parents are something else.		

You cannot speak a sentence without using nonverbal signals, and these signals influence the meaning the receiver gets. Acquiring the skills of nonverbal communication will help you communicate your meanings more effectively whether in interpersonal, small group, or public speaking.

ability to decode, and speakers in their ability to encode emotions (Scherer, 1986).

Judgments about Communication Effectiveness

In one-way communication (when one person is doing all or most of the speaking and the other person is doing all or most of the listening), those who talk fast (about 50 percent faster than normal) are more persuasive (MacLachlan, 1979). People agree more with a fast speaker than with a slow speaker and find the fast speaker more intelligent and objective.

When we look at comprehension, rapid speech shows an interesting effect. When the speaking rate is increased by 50 percent, the comprehension level drops by only 5 percent. When the rate is doubled, the comprehension level drops only 10 percent. These 5 and 10 percent losses are more than offset by the increased speed; thus, the faster rates are much more efficient in communicating information. If speeds are more than twice the rate of normal speech, however, comprehension begins to fall dramatically.

Do exercise caution in applying this research to all forms of communication (MacLachlan, 1979). For example, if you increase your rate to increase efficiency, you may create an impression so unnatural that others will focus on your speed instead of your meaning.

Silence

Like words and gestures, **silence**, too, communicates important meanings and serves important functions (Johannesen, 1974; Jaworski, 1993). Silence allows the speaker *time to think*, time to formulate and organize his or her verbal communications. Before messages of intense conflict, as well as before those confessing un-dying love, there's often silence. Again, silence seems to prepare the receiver for the importance of these future messages.

Some people use silence as a *weapon* to hurt others. We often speak of giving someone "the silent treatment." After a conflict, for example, one or both individuals may remain silent as a kind of punishment. Silence used to hurt others may also take the form of refusing to acknowledge the presence of another person, as in disconfirmation (see Unit 5); here silence is a dramatic demonstration of the total indifference one person feels toward the other.

Sometimes silence is used as a *"response to personal anxiety,"* shyness, or threats. You may feel anxious or shy among new people and prefer to remain silent. By remaining silent you preclude the chance of rejection. Only when you break your silence and make an attempt to communicate with another person do you risk rejection.

Silence may be used to *prevent communication* of certain messages. In conflict situations silence is sometimes used to prevent certain topics from surfacing and to prevent one or both parties from saying things they may later regret. In such situations silence often allows us time to cool off before expressing hatred, severe criticism, or personal attacks—which, as we know, are irreversible.

Like the eyes, face, and hands, silence can also be used to *communicate emotional responses* (Ehrenhaus, 1988). Sometimes silence communicates a determination to be uncooperative or defiant; by refusing to engage in verbal communication, you defy the authority or the legitimacy of the other person's position. Silence is often used to communicate annoyance, particularly when accompanied by a pouting expression, arms crossed in front of the chest, and nostrils flared. Silence may express affection or love, especially when coupled with long and longing gazes into each other's eyes.

Of course, you may also use silence when you simply have *nothing to say*, when nothing occurs to you, or when you don't want to say anything. James Russell Lowell expressed this best: "Blessed are they who have nothing to say, and who cannot be persuaded to say it." Silence may also be used to avoid responsibility for any wrongdoing (Beach, 1990-91).

Time Communication

The study of **temporal communication**, known technically as **chronemics**, concerns the use of time—how you organize it, react to it, and communicate messages through it (Bruneau, 1985, 1990). Consider, for example, your **psychological time** orientation; the emphasis you place on the past, present, and future. In a past orientation, you have special reverence for the past. You relive old times and regard old methods as the best. You see events as circular and recurring, so the wisdom of yesterday is applicable also to today and tomorrow. In a present orientation, however, you live in the present: for now, not tomorrow. In a future orientation, you look toward and live for the future. You save today, work hard in college, and deny yourself luxuries because you're preparing for the future. Before reading more about time, take the following self-test.

TEST YOURSELF

What Time Do You Have?

For each statement, indicate whether the statement is true (T) or false (F) in relation to your general attitude and behavior. (A few statements are purposely repeated to facilitate scoring and analysis of your responses.)

_____ 1. Meeting tomorrow's deadlines and doing other necessary work comes before tonight's partying.

_____ 2. I meet my obligations to friends and authorities on time.

_____ 3. I complete projects on time by making steady progress.

_____ 4. I am able to resist temptations when I know there is work to be done.

_____ 5. I keep working at a difficult, uninteresting task if it will help me get ahead.

_____ 6. If things don't get done on time, I don't worry about it.

_____ 7. I think that it's useless to plan too far ahead, because things hardly ever come out the way you planned anyway.

_____ 8. I try to live one day at a time.

_____ 9. I live to make better what is rather than to be concerned about what will be.

_____ 10. It seems to me that it doesn't make sense to worry about the future, since fate determines that whatever will be, will be.

_____ 11. I believe that getting together with friends to party is one of life's important pleasures.

_____ 12. I do things impulsively, making decisions on the spur of the moment.

_____ 13. I take risks to put excitement in my life.

_____ 14. I get drunk at parties.

_____ 15. It's fun to gamble.

_____ 16. Thinking about the future is pleasant to me.

_____ 17. When I want to achieve something, I set sub-goals and consider specific means for reaching those goals.

_____ 18. It seems to me that my career path is pretty well laid out.

_____ 19. It upsets me to be late for appointments.

_____ 20. I meet my obligations to friends and authorities on time.

_____ 21. I get irritated at people who keep me waiting when we've agreed to meet at a given time.

_____ 22. It makes sense to invest a substantial part of my income in insurance premiums.

_____ 23. I believe that "A stitch in time saves nine."

_____ 24. I believe that "A bird in the hand is worth two in the bush."

_____ 25. I believe it is important to save for a rainy day.

_____ 26. I believe a person's day should be planned each morning.

_____ 27. I make lists of things I must do.

_____ 28. When I want to achieve something, I set sub-goals and consider specific means for reaching those goals.

_____ 29. I believe that "A stitch in time saves nine."

HOW DID YOU DO? This time test measures seven different factors. If you selected true (T) for all or most of the statements within any given factor, you are probably high on that factor. If you selected false (F) for all or most of the statements within any given factor, you are probably low on that factor.

The first factor, measured by items 1–5, is a future, work motivation, perseverance orientation. These people have a strong work ethic and are committed to completing a task despite difficulties and temptations. The second factor (items 6–10) is a present, fatalistic, worry-free orientation. High scorers on this factor live one day at a time, not necessarily to enjoy the day but to avoid planning for the next day or anxiety about the future.

The third factor (items 11–15) is a present, pleasure-seeking, partying orientation. These people enjoy the present, take risks, and engage in a variety of impulsive actions. The fourth factor (items 16–18) is a future, goal-seeking, planning orientation. These people derive special pleasure from planning and achieving a variety of goals.

The fifth factor (items 19–21) is a time-sensitivity orientation. People who score high are especially sensitive to time and its role in social obligations. The sixth factor (items 22–25) is a future, practical action orientation. These people do what they have to do—take practical actions—to achieve the future they want.

The seventh factor (items 26–29) is a future, somewhat obsessive daily planning orientation. High scorers on this factor make daily "to do" lists and devote great attention to specific details.

WHAT WILL YOU DO? Now that you have some idea of how you treat time, consider how these attitudes and behaviors work for you. For example, will your time orientations help you achieve your social and professional goals? If not, what might you do about changing these attitudes and behaviors?

Source: From "Time in Perspective" by Alexander Gonzalez and Philip G. Zimbardo in *Psychology Today*, V. 19, pp. 20–26. Reprinted with permission of *Psychology Today* magazine, Copyright © 1985.

REFLECTIONS ON ETHICS

Silence

Remaining silent is at times your right. For example, you have the right to remain silent so as not to incriminate yourself. You have a right to protect your privacy —to withhold information that has no bearing on the matter at hand. And thus, your previous relationship history, affectional orientation, or religion is usually irrelevant to your ability to function in a job, and thus may be kept private in most job-related situations. On the other hand, these issues may be relevant when, for example, you're about to enter a more intimate phase of a relationship—then there may be an obligation to reveal information about yourself that could have been kept hidden at earlier relationship stages.

At other times, however, you have an obligation *not to* remain silent; and in fact in some cases it may be unlawful to say nothing. For example, you do not have the right to remain silent and to refuse to reveal information about crimes you've seen others commit. You have a

legal obligation to report such crimes and in some cases even suspicions of crime. Psychiatrists, clergy, and lawyers—fortunately or unfortunately—are often exempt from this requirement to reveal information about criminal activities when the information had been gained through privileged communication with clients.

Ethical Choice Point

On your way to work, you witness a father verbally abusing his three-year-old child. You worry that he might psychologically harm the child, and your first impulse is to speak up and tell this man that verbal abuse can have lasting effects on the child and often leads to physical abuse. At the same time, you don't want to interfere with his right to speak to his child, and you certainly don't want to make him angrier. What is your ethical obligation in this case? What would you do in this situation?

The time orientation you develop depends largely on your socioeconomic class and your personal experiences (Gonzalez & Zimbardo, 1985). For example, parents with unskilled and semiskilled occupations are likely to teach their children a present-orientated fatalism and a belief that enjoying yourself is more important than planning for the future. Parents who are teachers, managers, and in other professions, teach their children the importance of planning and preparing for the future, along with strategies for success.

Different **cultural time** perspectives also account for much intercultural misunderstanding, as different cultures often teach their members drastically different time orientations. For example, members of some Latin cultures would rather be late for an appointment than end a conversation abruptly or before it has come to a natural end. So the Latin may see lateness as a result of politeness. But others may see this as impolite to the person with whom he or she had the appointment (Hall & Hall, 1987).

Smell Communication

Smell communication, or **olfactory communication**, is extremely important in a wide variety of situations and is now big business. For example, there's some evidence (though clearly not very conclusive evidence) that the smell of lemon contributes to a perception of health, the smells of lavender and

eucalyptus increase alertness, and the smell of rose oil reduces blood pressure. Findings such as these have contributed to the growth of aromatherapy and to a new profession of aromatherapists (Furlow, 1996). Because humans possess "denser skin concentrations of scent glands than almost any other mammal," it has been argued that it only remains for us to discover how we use scent to communicate a wide variety of messages (Furlow, 1996, p. 41). Research also finds that smells can influence your body's chemistry, which in turn influences your emotional state. For example, the smell of chocolate results in the reduction of theta brain waves, which produces a sense of relaxation and a reduced level of attention (Martin, 1998).

Here are some of the most important messages scent seems to communicate.

- *Attraction messages.* Humans use perfumes, co-lognes, after-shave lotions, powders, and the like to enhance their attractiveness to others and to themselves. After all, you also smell yourself. When the smells are pleasant, you feel better about yourself. Women, research finds, prefer the scent of men who bear a close genetic similarity to themselves; this finding may account in part for our attraction to people much like ourselves (Ober, Weitkamp, Cox, Dytch, Kostyu, & Elias, 1997). And although we often think of women as the primary users of perfumes and scents, increasingly men are using them as well—not only the cologne and aftershave lotions they have long used but also, more recently, body sprays, which have become big business with a market estimated at $180 million.

- *Taste messages.* Without smell, taste would be severely impaired. For example, without smell it would be extremely difficult to taste the difference between a raw potato and an apple. Street vendors selling hot dogs, sausages, and similar foods are aided greatly by the smells, which stimulate the appetites of passersby.

- *Memory messages.* Smell is a powerful memory aid; you often recall situations from months and even years ago when you encounter a similar smell.

- *Identification messages.* Smell is often used to create an image or an identity for a product. Advertisers and manufacturers spend millions of dollars each year creating scents for cleaning products and toothpastes, for example, which have nothing to do with their cleaning power. There's also evidence that we can identify specific significant others by smell. For example, young children were able to identify the T-shirts of their brothers and sisters solely on the basis of smell (Porter & Moore, 1981).

CULTURE AND NONVERBAL COMMUNICATION

This chapter has already noted a few cultural and gender differences in nonverbal communication. The importance of culture in certain areas of nonverbal communication, however, has become the focus of sustained research. Here we consider just a sampling of research on gesture, facial expression, eye communication, colors, touch, silence, and time.

Culture and Gesture

There is much variation in gestures and their meanings among different cultures (Axtell, 1993). Consider a few common gestures that you might use even without thinking, but that could easily get you into trouble if you used them in another culture (also, take a look at Figure 1):

- Folding your arms over your chest would be considered defiant and disrespectful in Fiji.
- Waving your hand would be insulting in Nigeria and Greece.
- Gesturing with the thumb up would be rude in Australia.
- Tapping your two index fingers together would be considered an invitation to sleep together in Egypt.

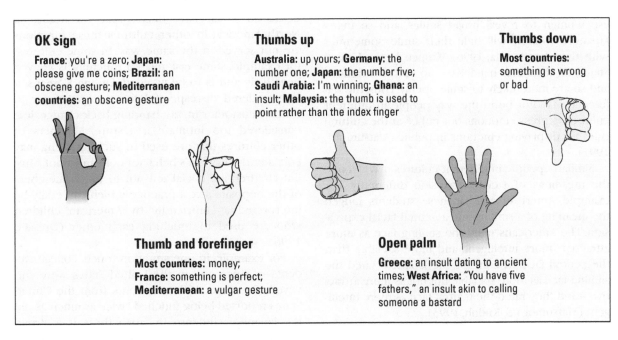

OK sign

France: you're a zero; **Japan:** please give me coins; **Brazil:** an obscene gesture; **Mediterranean countries:** an obscene gesture

Thumbs up

Australia: up yours; **Germany:** the number one; **Japan:** the number five; **Saudi Arabia:** I'm winning; **Ghana:** an insult; **Malaysia:** the thumb is used to point rather than the index finger

Thumbs down

Most countries: something is wrong or bad

Thumb and forefinger

Most countries: money; **France:** something is perfect; **Mediterranean:** a vulgar gesture

Open palm

Greece: an insult dating to ancient times; **West Africa:** "You have five fathers," an insult akin to calling someone a bastard

FIGURE 1   **Some Cultural Meanings of Gestures**

Cultural differences in the meanings of nonverbal gestures are often significant. The over-the-head clasped hands that signify victory to an American may signify friendship to a Russian. To an American, holding up two fingers to make a V signifies victory or peace. To certain South Americans, however, it is an obscene gesture that corresponds to the American's extended middle finger. This figure highlights some additional nonverbal differences. Can you identify others?

- Pointing with your index finger would be impolite in many Middle Eastern countries.
- Bowing to a lesser degree than your host would be considered a statement of your superiority in Japan.
- Inserting your thumb between your index and middle finger in a clenched fist would be viewed as a wish that evil fall on the person in some African countries.
- Resting your feet on a table or chair would be insulting and disrespectful in some Middle Eastern cultures.

Culture and Facial Expression

The wide variations in facial communication that we observe in different cultures seem to reflect different attitudes about what reactions are permissible in public rather than differences in the way humans show emotions. For example, Japanese and American students watched a film of a surgical operation (Ekman, 1985). The students were videotaped both in an interview situation about the film and alone while watching the film. When alone the students showed very similar reactions; in the interview, however, the American students displayed facial expressions indicating displeasure, whereas the Japanese students did not show any great emotion. Similarly, it's considered "forward" or inappropriate for Japanese women to reveal broad smiles, and so many Japanese women will hide their smile, sometimes with their hands (Ma, 1996). Women in the United States, on the other hand, have no such restrictions and so are more likely to smile openly. Thus, the difference may not be in the way people in different cultures express emotions but rather in the cultural rules for displaying emotions in public (Matsumoto, 1991).

Similarly, people in different cultures may decode the meanings of facial expression differently. For example, American and Japanese students judged the meaning of a smiling and a neutral facial expression. The Americans rated the smiling face as more attractive, more intelligent, and more sociable than the neutral face. In contrast, the Japanese rated the smiling face as more sociable but not as more attractive—and they rated the neutral face as more intelligent (Matsumoto & Kudoh, 1993).

Culture and Eye Communication

Not surprisingly, eye messages vary with both culture and gender. Americans, for example, consider direct eye contact an expression of honesty and forthrightness, but the Japanese often view this as a lack of respect. A Japanese person will glance at the other person's face rarely, and then only for very short periods (Axtell, 1990). Interpreting another's eye contact messages with your own cultural rules is a risky undertaking; eye movements that you may interpret as insulting may have been intended to show respect.

Women make eye contact more and maintain it longer (both in speaking and in listening) than men. This holds true whether women are interacting with other women or with men. This difference in eye behavior may result from women's greater tendency to display their emotions. When women interact with other women, they display affiliative and supportive eye contact, whereas when men interact with other men, they avert their gaze.

Culture and Colors

Colors vary greatly in their meanings from one culture to another. Some of these cultural differences are summed up in Table 3; but before looking at the table, think about the meanings given to such colors as red, green, black, white, blue, yellow, and purple in your own culture or cultures.

Culture and Touch

The several functions and examples of touching discussed so far have been based on studies in North America; in other cultures these functions are not served in the same way. In some cultures, for example, some task-related touching is viewed negatively and is to be avoided. Among Koreans, it is considered disrespectful for a store owner to touch a customer in, say, handing back change; it is considered too intimate a gesture. Members of other cultures that are used to such touching may consider the Korean's behavior cold and aloof. Muslim children are socialized not to touch members of the opposite sex, a practice which can easily be interpreted as unfriendly by American children who are used to touching each other (Dresser, 1996).

For example, in one study on touch, college students in Japan and in the United States were surveyed (Barnlund, 1989). Students from the United States reported being touched twice as much as did the Japanese students. In Japan there is a strong taboo against touching between strangers, and the Japanese are therefore especially careful to maintain sufficient distance.

Some cultures—including many in southern Europe and the Middle East—are contact cultures; others are noncontact cultures, such as those of

Table 3 Cultural Meanings and Color

This table, constructed from research reported by various culture watchers, illustrates only some of the different meanings that colors may communicate and especially how they are viewed in different cultures (Dreyfuss, 1971; Hoft, 1995; Dresser, 1996; Singh & Pereira, 2005). As you read this table consider the meanings you give to these colors and where your meanings came from.

Color	Cultural Meanings and Comments
Red	In China red signifies prosperity and rebirth and is used for festive and joyous occasions; in France and the United Kingdom it indicates masculinity, in many African countries blasphemy or death, and in Japan anger and danger. Red ink, especially among Korean Buddhists, is used only to write a person's name at the time of death or on the anniversary of the person's death; this can create problems when American teachers use red ink to mark homework.
Green	In the United States green signifies capitalism, go ahead, and envy; in Ireland patriotism; among some Native Americans femininity; to the Egyptians fertility and strength; and to the Japanese youth and energy.
Black	In Thailand black signifies old age, in parts of Malaysia courage, and in much of Europe death.
White	In Thailand white signifies purity, in many Muslim and Hindu cultures purity and peace, and in Japan and other Asian countries death and mourning.
Blue	In Iran blue signifies something negative, in Ghana joy; among the Cherokee it signifies defeat, for the Egyptian virtue and truth, and for the Greek national pride.
Yellow	In China yellow signifies wealth and authority; in the United States caution, cowardice, and support for troops; in Egypt happiness and prosperity; and in many countries throughout the world femininity.
Purple	In Latin America purple signifies death, in Europe royalty, in Egypt virtue and faith, in Japan grace and nobility, in China barbarism, and in the United States nobility and bravery.

northern Europe and Japan. Members of contact cultures maintain close distances, touch one another in conversation, face one another more directly, and maintain longer and more focused eye contact. Members of noncontact cultures maintain greater distance in their interactions, touch one another rarely (if at all), avoid facing one another directly, and maintain much less direct eye contact. As a result, southern Europeans may perceive northern Europeans and Japanese as cold, distant, and uninvolved. Southern Europeans may in turn be perceived as pushy, aggressive, and inappropriately intimate.

Culture, Paralanguage, and Silence

Cultural differences also need to be taken into consideration is evaluating the results of the studies on speech rate, as different cultures view speech rate differently. For example, in one study Korean male speakers who spoke rapidly were given unfavorable credibility ratings, as opposed to the results obtained by Americans who spoke rapidly (Lee & Boster, 1992). Researchers have suggested that in individualistic societies a rapid-rate speaker is seen as more competent than a slow-rate speaker, whereas in collectivist cultures a speaker who uses a slower rate is judged as more competent.

Similarly, all cultures do not view silence as functioning in the same way. In the United States, for example, silence is often interpreted negatively. At a business meeting or even in an informal social group, the silent member may be seen as not listening, having nothing interesting to add, not understanding the issues, being insensitive, or being too self-absorbed to focus on the messages of others. Other cultures, however, view silence more positively. In many situations in Japan, for example, silence is a response that is considered more appropriate than speech (Haga, 1988).

The traditional Apache, to take another example, regard silence very differently than do European Americans (Basso, 1972). Among the Apache, mutual friends do not feel the need to introduce strangers who may be working in the same area or on the same project. The strangers may remain silent for several days. This period enables them to observe and to form judgments about each other. Once this assessment is made, the individuals talk. When courting, especially during the initial stages, the Apache remain silent for hours; if they do talk, they generally talk very little. Only after a couple has been dating for several months will they have lengthy conversations. These periods of silence are generally attributed to shyness or self-consciousness; but the use of silence is explicitly taught to Apache women, who are especially discouraged from engaging in long discussions with their dates. Silence during courtship is a sign of modesty to many Apache.

Culture and Time

People in different cultures view time very differently. Here are three aspects of time and some cultural differences: the social clock, formal and informal time, and monochronism versus polychronism.

The Social Clock

Your culture maintains an implicit "schedule" for the right time to do a variety of important things; for example, the right time to start dating, to finish college, to buy your own home, or to have a child. This unspoken timetable provides you with a **social clock**, a schedule that tells you if you're keeping pace with your peers, are ahead of them, or are falling behind (Neugarten, 1979). On the basis of this social clock, which you learned as you grew up, you evaluate your own social and professional development. If you're in synch with the rest of your peers—for example, if you started dating at the "appropriate" age or if you're finishing college at the "appropriate" age—then you'll feel well adjusted, competent, and a part of the group. If you're late, you'll probably experience feelings of dissatisfaction. And although in some cultures the social clock is becoming more flexible and more tolerant of deviations from the conventional timetable, it still exerts pressure to keep pace with your peers (Peterson, 1996).

Formal and Informal Time

Days are astronomically determined by the earth's rotation on its axis, months by the moon's movement around the earth, and years by the earth's rotation around the sun. But the rest of our time divisions are cultural (largely religious) in origin.

In the United States and in most of the world, formal time divisions include seconds, minutes, hours, days, weeks, months, and years. Some cultures, however, may use phases of the moon or the seasons to delineate their most important time periods. Other formal time units exist, too. For example, in the United States, if your college is on the semester system, your courses are divided into 50- or 75-minute periods that meet two or three times a week for 14-week periods. Eight semesters of 15 or 16 periods per week equal a college education. As these examples illustrate, formal time units are arbitrary. The culture establishes them for convenience.

Informal time terms are more hazy and subject to interpretation—terms such as "forever," "immediately," "soon," "right away," or "as soon as possible." This type of time creates the most communication problems, because the terms have different meanings for different people.

Attitudes toward both formal and informal time vary from one culture to another. One study, for example, measured the accuracy of clocks in six cultures—those of Japan, Indonesia, Italy, England, Taiwan, and the United States. Japan had the most accurate and Indonesia had the least accurate clocks. The researchers also measured the speed at which people in these six cultures walked, and results showed that the Japanese walked the fastest, the Indonesians the slowest (LeVine & Bartlett, 1984).

Table 4 Monochronic and Polychronic Time

As you read down this table, based on Hall and Hall (1987), note the potential for miscommunication that these differences might create when M-time and P-time people interact. Have any of these differences ever created interpersonal misunderstandings for you?

The Monochronic-Time Person	The Polychronic-Time Person
does one thing at a time	does several things at once
treats time schedules and plans very seriously; feels they may be broken only for the most serious of reasons	treats time schedules and plans as useful (not sacred); feels they may be broken for a variety of causes
considers the job the most important part of life, ahead of even family	considers the family and interpersonal relationships more important than the job
considers privacy extremely important; seldom borrows or lends to others; works independently	is actively involved with others; works in the presence of and with lots of people at the same time

Monochronism and Polychronism

Another important distinction is that between **monochronic** and **polychronic time orientations** (Hall, 1959, 1976; Hall & Hall, 1987). Monochronic people or cultures—such as those of the United States, Germany, Scandinavia, and Switzerland—generally schedule one thing at a time. In these cultures time is compartmentalized and there is a time for everything. Polychronic people or cultures, on the other hand—groups such as Latin Americans, Mediterranean people, and Arabs—tend

to schedule more than one thing at the same time. Eating, conducting business with several different people, and taking care of family matters may all be conducted simultaneously. No culture is entirely monochronic or polychronic; rather, these are general tendencies that are found across a large part of the culture. Some cultures combine both time orientations; in Japan and in some American groups, for example, both orientations are found. Table 4 on previous page identifies some of the distinctions between these two time orientations.

SUMMARY: NONVERBAL MESSAGES

In this unit we explored nonverbal communication—communication without words. We considered body movements, facial and eye movements, spatial and territorial communication, artifactual communication, touch communication, paralanguage, silence, time communication, and smell communication. Finally, we looked at cultural variations in many types of nonverbal communication.

1. Nonverbal messages may accent or emphasize a part of a verbal message; complement or add nuances of meaning not communicated by a verbal message; contradict verbal messages (for example, when you cross your fingers or wink to indicate that you're lying); regulate, control, or show a wish to control the flow of verbal messages; repeat or restate a verbal message; or substitute for or take the place of verbal messages.

2. Nonverbal messages serve important communications functions: They help us form and manage impressions, form and define relationships, structure conversation and social interaction, influence others, and express emotions.

3. The five categories of body movements are emblems (nonverbal behaviors that directly translate words or phrases); illustrators (nonverbal behaviors that accompany and literally "illustrate" verbal messages); affect displays (nonverbal movements that communicate emotional meaning); regulators (nonverbal movements that coordinate, monitor, maintain, or control the speaking of another individual); and adaptors (nonverbal behaviors that are emitted without conscious awareness and that usually serve some kind of need, as in scratching an itch).

4. Facial movements may communicate a variety of emotions. The most frequently studied are happiness, surprise, fear, anger, sadness, disgust, and contempt. Facial management techniques enable you to control the extent to which you reveal the emotions you feel.

5. The facial feedback hypothesis claims that facial display of an emotion can lead to physiological and psychological changes.

6. Through eye contact you may seek feedback, signal others to speak, indicate the nature of a relationship, or compensate for increased physical distance. Eye avoidance may help you avoid prying or may signal a lack of interest.

7. Pupil enlargement shows a person's level of interest and positive emotional arousal.

8. Proxemics is the study of the communicative functions of space and spatial relationships. Four major proxemic distances are (1) intimate distance, ranging from actual touching to 18 inches; (2) personal distance, ranging from 18 inches to 4 feet; (3) social distance, ranging from 4 to 12 feet; and (4) public distance, ranging from 12 to more than 25 feet.

9. Your treatment of space is influenced by such factors as status, culture, context, subject matter, gender, age, and positive or negative evaluation of the other person.

10. Territoriality has to do with your possessive reaction to an area of space or to particular objects.

11. Artifactual communication consists of messages conveyed through human-made articles; for example, communication through color, clothing and body adornment, and space decoration.

12. The study of haptics indicates that touch may convey a variety of meanings, the most important being positive affect, playfulness, control, ritual, and task-relatedness. Touch avoidance is the desire to avoid touching and being touched by others.

13. Paralanguage involves the vocal but nonverbal dimensions of speech. It includes rate, pitch, volume, rhythm, and vocal quality as well as pauses and hesitations. Paralanguage helps us make judgments about people, their emotions, and their believability.

14. Silence may communicate a variety of meanings, from messages aimed at hurting another (the silent treatment) to deep emotional responses.

15. The study of time communication (chronemics) explores the messages communicated by our treatment of time.

16. Smell can communicate messages of attraction, taste, memory, and identification.

17. Among the cultural differences that researchers have focused on are facial expressions and displays, eye communication, the meanings of color, the appropriateness and uses of touch, the uses of silence, and the ways in which different cultures treat time.

KEY TERMS IN NONVERBAL MESSAGES

adaptors
affect displays
alter-adaptors
artifactual communication
attractiveness
boundary marker
central marker
chronemics
civil inattention
color communication
cultural time
earmarker
emblems
expectancy violations
 theory

facial feedback hypothesis
facial management
 techniques
haptics
home field advantage
illustrators
informal time
intimate distance
kinesics
markers
monochronic time
 orientation
nonverbal communication
nonverbal dominance
object-adaptors

olfactory communication
paralanguage
personal distance
pitch
polychronic time
 orientation
primary territories
proxemic distances
proxemics
psychological time
public distance
public territories
pupillometrics
rate
regulators

secondary territories
self-adaptors
silence
social clock
social distance
spatial distance
status
temporal communication
territoriality
touch avoidance
touch communication
visual dominance
voice qualities
volume

THINKING CRITICALLY ABOUT NONVERBAL MESSAGES

1. **Physical Appearance.** On a 10-point scale, with 1 indicating "not at all important" and 10 indicating "extremely important," how important is body appearance to your own romantic interest in another person? Do the men and women you know conform to the stereotypes of males being more concerned with physical appearance and females more concerned with personality?

2. **Status and Invasion.** One signal of status is an the unwritten "law" granting the right of invasion. Higher-status individuals have more of a right to invade the territory of others than vice versa. The boss, for example, can invade the territory of junior executives by barging into their offices, but the reverse would be unacceptable. In what ways do you notice this "right" of territorial invasion in your workplace?

3. **Blaming the Victim.** A popular defense tactic in criminal trials for sex crimes against women, gay men, and lesbians is to blame the victim by implying that the way the victim was dressed provoked the attack. Currently, New York and Florida are the only states that prohibit defense attorneys from referring to the way a sex-crime victim was dressed at the time of the attack (*New York Times*, July 30, 1994, p. 22). What do you think of this?

If you don't live in New York or Florida, have there been proposals in your state to similarly limit this popular defense tactic?

4. **Gender and Nonverbal Communication.** Here is a brief summary of findings from research on gender differences in nonverbal expression (Burgoon, Buller, & Woodall, 1996; Eakins & Eakins, 1978; Pearson, West, & Turner, 1995; Arliss, 1991; Shannon, 1987): (1) Women smile more than men; (2) women stand closer to one another than do men and are generally approached more closely than men; (3) both men and women, when speaking, look at men more than at women; (4) women both touch and are touched more than men; (5) men extend their bodies, taking up greater areas of space, more than women. What problems might these differences create when men and women communicate with each other?

5. **Liking Cues.** What nonverbal cues should you look for in judging whether someone likes you? List cues in the order of their importance, beginning with 1 for the cue that is of most value in making your judgment. Do you really need two lists? One for judging a woman's liking and one for a man's?

LogOn! MyCommunicationLab
WWW.MYCOMMUNICATIONLAB.COM

Several exercises and self-tests will help you better understand how nonverbal communication works and will give you opportunities to practice the skills of nonverbal communication: Facial Expressions, Eye Contact, Interpersonal Interactions and Space, Artifacts and Culture: The Case of Gifts, Communicating Vocally but Nonverbally, Communicating Emotions Nonverbally, Recognizing Verbal and Nonverbal Message Functions, Coloring Meanings, Deciphering Paralanguage Cues, Do You Avoid Touch? Also take the monochronic and polychronic time test and explore the activities on the human face, the human voice, and spatial communication. Recognizing Facial Expressions of Emotions is an interesting and instructive simulation.

An interesting blog dealing with nonverbal communication is available at **www.geocities .com/marvin_hecht/nonverbal.html** (accessed June 3, 2006).

References

Acor, A. A. (2001). Employers' perceptions of persons with body art and an experimental test regarding eyebrow piercing. (Doctoral dissertation, Marquette University, 2001). *Dissertation Abstracts International, 61,* 3885B.

Akert, R. M., & Panter, A. T. (1988). Extraversion and the ability to decode nonverbal communication. *Personality & Individual Differences, 9,* 965-972.

Albas, D. C., McCluskey, K. W., & Albas, C. A. (1976). Perception of the emotional content of speech: A comparison of two Canadian groups. *Journal of Cross-Cultural Psychology, 7* (December), 481-490.

Altman, I. (1975). *The environment and social behavior.* Monterey, CA: Brooks/Cole.

Andersen, P. A., & Leibowitz, K. (1978). The development and nature of the construct touch avoidance. *Environmental Psychology and Nonverbal Behavior, 3,* 89-106.

Argyle, M. (1988). *Bodily communication* (2nd ed.). New York: Methuen.

Argyle, M., & Ingham, R. (1972). Gaze, mutual gaze, and distance. *Semiotica, 1,* 32-49.

Arliss, L. P. (1991). *Gender communication.* Englewood Cliffs, NJ: Prentice-Hall.

Axtell, R. E. (1990). *Do's and taboos of hosting international visitors.* New York: Wiley.

Axtell, R. E. (1993). *Do's and taboos around the world* (3rd ed.). New York: Wiley.

Barnlund, D. C. (1989). *Communicative styles of Japanese and Americans: Images and realities.* Belmont, CA: Wadsworth.

Basso, K. H. (1972). To give up on words: Silence in Apache culture. In P. P. Giglioli (Ed.), *Language and social context.* New York: Penguin.

Beach, W. A. (1990-91). Avoiding ownership for alleged wrongdoings. *Research on Language and Social Interaction, 24,* 1-36.

Brody, J. E. (1994, March 21). Notions of beauty transcend culture, new study suggests. *New York Times,* p. A14.

Burgoon, J. K. (1978). A communication model of personal space violations: Explication and an initial test. *Human Communication Research, 4,* 129-142.

Burgoon, J. K. (1991). Relational message interpretations of touch, conversational distance, and posture. *Journal of Non-verbal Behavior, 15* (Winter), 233-259.

Burgoon, J. K., & Bacue, A. E. (2003). Nonverbal communication skills. In J. O. Greene & B. R. Burleson (Eds.), *Handbook of communication and social interaction skills* (pp. 179-220). Mahwah, NJ: Lawrence Erlbaum.

Burgoon, J. K., Buller, D. B., & Woodall, W. G. (1996). *Nonverbal communication: The unspoken dialogue* (2nd ed.). New York: McGraw-Hill.

Burgoon, J. K., & Hoobler, G. D. (2002). Nonverbal signals. In M. L. Knapp & J. A. Daly (Eds.), *Handbook of interpersonal communication* (3rd ed., pp. 240-299). Thousand Oaks, CA: Sage.

Burke, N. D. (1993). Restricting gang clothing in the public schools. *West's Education Law Quarterly, 2* (July), 391-404.

Chaney, R. H., Givens, C. A., Aoki, M. F., & Gombiner, M. L. (1989). Pupillary responses in recognizing awareness in persons with profound mental retardation. *Perceptual and Motor Skills, 69* (October), 523-528.

Crusco, A. H., & Wetzel, C. G. (1984). The Midas touch: The effects of interpersonal touch on restaurant tipping. *Personality and Social Psychology Bulletin, 10* (December), 512-517.

Dresser, N. (1996). *Multicultural manners: New rules of etiquette for a changing society.* New York: Wiley.

Drews, D. R., Allison, C. K., & Probst, J. R. (2000). Behavioral and self-concept differences in tattooed and nontattooed college students. *Psychological Reports, 86,* 475-481.

Dreyfuss, H. (1971). *Symbol sourcebook.* New York: McGraw-Hill.

Drucker, S. J., & Gumpert, G. (1991). Public space and communication: The zoning of public interaction. *Communication Theory, 1* (November), 294-310.

Eagly, A. H., & Crowley, M. (1986). Gender and helping behavior: A meta-analytic review of the social psychological literature. *Psychological Bulletin, 100* (November), 283-308.

Eakins, B., & Eakins, R. G. (1978). *Sex differences in communication.* Boston: Houghton Mifflin.

Ehrenhaus, P. (1988). Silence and symbolic expression. *Communication Monographs, 55* (March), 41-57.

Ekman, P. (1985). *Telling lies: Clues to deceit in the marketplace, politics, and marriage.* New York: Norton.

Ekman, P., & Friesen, W. V. (1969). The repertoire of nonverbal behavior: Categories, origins, usage, and coding. *Semiotica, 1,* 49-98.

Ekman, P., Friesen, W. V., & Ellsworth, P. (1972). *Emotion in the human face: Guidelines for research and an integration of findings.* New York: Pergamon Press.

Exline, R. V., Ellyson, S. L., & Long, B. (1975). Visual behavior as an aspect of power role relationships. In P. Pliner, L. Krames, & T. Alloway (Eds.), *Nonverbal communication of aggression*. New York: Plenum Press.

Forbes, G. B. (2001). College students with tattoos and piercings: Motives, family experiences, personality factors, and perception by others. *Psychological Reports, 89*, 774-786.

Furlow, F. B. (1996). The smell of love. *Psychology Today* (March/April), 38-45.

Giordano, J. (1989). *Telecommuting and organizational culture: A study of corporate consciousness and identification*. Unpublished doctoral dissertation, University of Massachusetts, Amherst.

Gladstone, G. L., & Parker, G. B. (2002). When you're smiling, does the whole world smile for you? *Australasian Psychiatry, 10* (June), 144-146.

Goffman, E. (1971). *Relations in public: Microstudies of the public order*. New York: HarperCollins.

Goldin-Meadow, S., Nusbaum, H., Kelly, S. D., & Wagner, S. (2001). Gesture—Psychological aspects. *Psychological Science, 12*, 516-522.

Gonzalez, A., & Zimbardo, P. G. (1985). Time in perspective. *Psychology Today, 19*, 20-26.

Gosling, S. D., Ko, S. J., Mannarelli, T., & Morris, M. E. (2002). A room with a cue: Personality judgments based on offices and bedrooms. *Journal of Personality and Social Psychology, 82* (March), 379-398.

Graham, J. A., & Argyle, M. (1975). The effects of different patterns of gaze, combined with different facial expressions, on impression formation. *Journal of Human Movement Studies, 1* (December), 178-182.

Graham, J. A., Bitti, P. R., & Argyle, M. (1975). A Cross-cultural study of the communication of emotion by facial and gestural cues. *Journal of Human Movement Studies, 1* (June), 68-77.

Guerrero, L. K., & Andersen, P. A. (1991). The waxing and waning of relational intimacy: Touch as a function of relational stage, gender and touch avoidance. *Journal of Social and Personal Relationships, 8*, 147-165.

Guerrero, L. K., & Andersen, P. A. (1994). Patterns of matching and initiation: Touch behavior and touch avoidance across romantic relationship stages. *Journal of Nonverbal Behavior, 18* (Summer), 137-153.

Guerrero, L. K., DeVito, J. A., & Hecht, M. L. (Eds.). (1999). *The nonverbal communication reader: Class and contemporary readings* (2nd ed.). Prospect Heights, IL: Waveland Press.

Gumpert, G., & Drucker, S. J. (1995). Place as medium: Exegesis of the cafe drinking coffee, the art of watching others, civil conversation—with excursions into the effects of architecture and interior design. *The Speech Communication Annual, 9* (Spring), 7-32.

Haga, Y. (1988). Traits de langage et caractere Japonais. *Cahiers de Sociologie Economique et Culturelle, 9*, 105-109.

Hall, E. T. (1959). *The silent language*. Garden City, NY: Doubleday.

Hall, E. T. (1963). A system for the notation of proxemic behavior. *American Anthropologist, 65*, 1003-1026.

Hall, E. T. (1976). *Beyond culture*. Garden City, NY: Doubleday.

Hall, E. T., & Hall, M. R. (1987). *Hidden differences: Doing business with the Japanese*. New York: Doubleday.

Hall, J. A. (1998). How big are nonverbal sex differences? The case of smiling and sensitivity to nonverbal cues. In D. J. Canary & K. Dindia (Eds.), *Sex differences and similarities in communication: Critical essays and empirical investigations of sex and gender in interaction* (pp. 155-178). Mahwah, NJ: Lawrence Erlbaum.

Hess, E. H. (1975). *The tell-tale eye*. New York: Van Nostrand Reinhold.

Hess, E. H., Seltzer, A. L., & Schlien, J. M. (1965). Pupil response of hetero- and homosexual males to pictures of men and women: A pilot study. *Journal of Abnormal Psychology, 70*, 165-168.

Hess, U., Kappas, A., McHugo, G. J., Lanzetta, J. T., et al. (1992). The facilitative effect of facial expression on the self-generation of emotion. *International Journal of Psychophysiology, 12* (May), 251-265.

Hickson, M. L., Stacks, D. W., & Moore, N. J. (2003). *Nonverbal communication: Studies and applications*. Los Angeles: Roxbury.

Hoft, N. L. (1995). *International technical communication: How to export information about high technology*. New York: Wiley.

Infante, D. A., Rancer, A. S., & Womack, D. F. (2002). *Building communication theory* (4th ed.). Prospect Heights, IL: Waveland Press.

Jaworski, A. (1993). *The power of silence: Social and pragmatic perspectives*. Thousand Oaks, CA: Sage.

Johannesen, R. L. (1974). The functions of silence: A plea for communication research. *Western Speech, 38* (Winter), 25-35.

Jones, S., & Yarbrough, A. E. (1985). A naturalistic study of the meanings of touch. *Communication Monographs, 52*, 19-56. A version of this paper appears in DeVito and Hecht (1990).

Kanner, B. (1989, April 3). Color schemes. *New York Magazine*, pp. 22-23.

Ketcham, H. (1958). *Color planning for business and industry*. New York: Harper.

Keyes, R. (1980). *The height of your life*. New York: Warner Books.

Knapp, M. L., & Hall, J. (1997). *Nonverbal behavior in human interaction* (4th ed.). New York: Holt, Rinehart & Winston.

Lanzetta, J. T., Cartwright-Smith, J., & Kleck, R. E. (1976). Effects of nonverbal dissimulations on emotional experience and autonomic arousal. *Journal of Personality and Social Psychology, 33*, 354-370.

Larsen, R. J., Kasimatis, M., & Frey, K. (1992). Facilitating the furrowed brow: An unobtrusive test of the facial feedback hypothesis applied to unpleasant affect. *Cognition and Emotion, 6* (September), 321-338.

Leathers, D. G. (1997). *Successful nonverbal communication: Principles and applications* (3rd ed.). New York: Macmillan.

Lee, H. O., & Boster, F. J. (1992). Collectivism-individualism in perceptions of speech rate: A cross-cultural comparison. *Journal of Cross-Cultural Psychology, 23*, 377-388.

LeVine, R., & Bartlett, K. (1984). Pace of life, punctuality, and coronary heart disease in six countries. *Journal of Cross-Cultural Psychology, 15*, 233-255.

Ma, K. (1996). *The modern Madame Butterfly: Fantasy and reality in Japanese cross-cultural relationships*. Rutland, VT: Charles E. Tuttle.

MacLachlan, J. (1979). What people really think of fast talkers. *Psychology Today, 13* (November), 113-117.

Malandro, L. A., Barker, L., & Barker, D. A. (1989). *Nonverbal communication* (2nd ed.). New York: Random House.

Marsh, P. (1988). *Eye to eye: How people interact*. Topfield, MA: Salem House.

Marshall, E. (1983). *Eye language: Understanding the eloquent eye*. New York: New Trend.

Martin, G. N. (1998). Human electroencephalographic (EEG) response to olfactory stimulation: Two experiments using the aroma of food. *International Journal of Psychophysiology, 30*, 287-302.

Matsumoto, D. (1991). Cultural influences on facial expressions of emotion. *Southern Communication Journal, 56* (Winter), 128-137.

Matsumoto, D., & Kudoh, T. (1993). American-Japanese cultural differences in attributions of personality based on smiles. *Journal of Nonverbal Behavior, 17*, 231-243.

Mehrabian, A. (1976). *Public places and private spaces.* New York: Basic Books.

Metts, S., & Planalp, S. (2002). Emotional communication. In M. L. Knapp & J. A. Daly (Eds.), *Handbook of interpersonal communication* (3rd ed., pp. 339-373). Thousand Oaks, CA: Sage.

Molloy, J. (1975). *Dress for success.* New York: P. H. Wyden.

Molloy, J. (1977). *The woman's dress for success book.* New York: Warner Books.

Molloy, J. (1981). *Molloy's live for success.* New York: Bantam.

Montagu, A. (1971). *Touching: The human significance of the skin.* New York: Harper & Row.

Neugarten, B. (1979). Time, age, and the life cycle. *American Journal of Psychiatry, 136*, 887-894.

Ober, C., Weitkamp, L. R., Cox, N., Dytch, H., Kostyu, D., & Elias, S. (1977). HLA and mate choice in humans. *American Journal of Human Genetics, 61*, 494-496.

Pearson, J. C., West, R., & Turner, L. H. (1995). *Gender and communication* (3rd ed.). Dubuque, IA: William C. Brown.

Peterson, C. C. (1996). The ticking of the social clock: Adults' beliefs about the timing of transition events. *International Journal of Aging and Human Development, 42*, 189-203.

Porter, R. H., & Moore, J. D. (1981). Human kin recognition by olfactory cues. *Physiology and Behavior, 27*, 493-495.

Rabinowitz, F. E. (1991). The male-to-male embrace: Breaking the touch taboo in a men's therapy group. *Journal of Counseling and Development, 69* (July-August), 574-576.

Radford, M. L. (1998). Approach or avoidance? The role of nonverbal communication in the academic library user's decision to initiate a reference encounter. *Library Trends, 46* (Spring), 699-717.

Rosenthal, R., & DePaulo, B. M. (1979). Sex differences in accommodation in nonverbal communication. In R. Rosenthal (Ed.), *Skill in nonverbal communication: Individual differences* (pp. 68-103). Cambridge, MA: Oelgeschlager, Gunn & Hain.

Sayre, S. (1992). T-shirt messages: Fortune or folly for advertisers? In S. R. Danna (Ed.), *Advertising and popular culture* (pp. 73-82). Bowling Green, OH: Bowling Green State University Popular Press.

Scherer, K. R. (1986). Vocal affect expression. *Psychological Bulletin, 99*, 143-165.

Seiter, J. S., & Sandry, A. (2003). Pierced for success?: The effects of ear and nose piercing on perceptions of job candidates' credibility, attractiveness, and hirability. *Communication Research Reports, 20* (Fall), 287-298.

Shannon, J. (1987). Don't smile when you say that. *Executive Female, 10*, 33, 43.

Singh, N., & Pereira, A. (2005). *The culturally customized Web site.* Oxford, UK: Elsevier Butterworth-Heinemann.

Stephen, R., & Zweigenhaft, R. L. (1986). The effect on tipping of a waitress touching male and female customers. *Journal of Social Psychology, 126* (February), 141-142.

Trager, G. L. (1958). Paralanguage: A first approximation. *Studies in Linguistics, 13*, 1-12.

Trager, G. L. (1961). The typology of paralanguage. *Anthropological Linguistics, 3*, 17-21.

Zimmerman, A. (2000, November 10). If boys just want to have fun, this may bring them down. *Wall Street Journal*, pp. A1, A12.

Zuckerman, M., Klorman, R., Larrance, D. T., & Spiegel, N. H. (1981). Facial, autonomic, and subjective components of emotion: The facial feedback hypothesis versus the externalizer-internalizer distinction. *Journal of Personality and Social Psychology, 41*, 929-944.

267

Chapter 10

Listening in Human Communication

UNIT CONTENTS

The Importance of Listening: Task and Relationship Benefits

The Listening Process

Listening, Culture, and Gender

Styles of Effective Listening

Special Features

 Not Listening: Judi Brownell

How Do You Listen?

 Principles of Media Literacy Listening

 Listening Ethicall

 Reconstructing Memory

 Cues to Lying

 Expressing Empathy

 Regulating Your Listening Style

© Walter Hodges/CORBIS

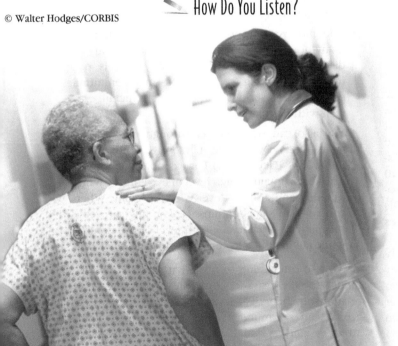

There can be little doubt that you listen a great deal. On waking, you listen to the radio or television. On the way to school, you listen to friends, people around you, screeching cars, singing birds, or falling rain. In school, you listen to the instructors, to other students, and to yourself. You listen to friends at lunch and return to class to listen to more instructors. You arrive home and again listen to family and friends. Perhaps you listen to CDs, radio, or television. All in all, you listen for a good part of your waking day.

In this unit you'll learn about:
- the benefits of listening.
- how listening works and how it varies with gender and culture.
- the styles of listening you can use.

You'll learn to
- avoid the barriers to effective listening.
- adjust your listening so that it's most effective for the specific situation.

According to the International Listening Association, **listening** is "the process of receiving, constructing meaning from, and responding to spoken and/or nonverbal messages" (Emmert, 1994 and cited in Brownell, 2006).

In this unit we will look at the importance of listening, the nature of the listening process, some cultural and gender differences in listening, and the varied styles of listening you might use in different situations. Throughout this unit, we'll identify ways to avoid the major barriers to listening and guidelines for more effective listening.

THE IMPORTANCE OF LISTENING: TASK AND RELATIONSHIP BENEFITS

Regardless of what you do, listening will prove a crucial communication component and will serve both task and relationship functions. For example, one study concluded that in this era of technological transformation, employees' interpersonal skills are especially significant; workers' advancement will depend on their ability to speak and write effectively, to display proper etiquette, and *to listen attentively*. And in a revealing survey of 40 CEOs of Asian and Western multinational companies, respondents cited a lack of listening skills as *the major shortcoming* of top executives (Witcher, 1999).

An important task benefit of listening is to establish and communicate power. In much the same way that you communicate power verbally and nonverbally you also can communicate your power through listening. Here are a few suggestions on how to listen with power.

- Respond visibly, but in moderation. Too little response says you aren't listening, and too much response says you aren't listening critically. Backchanneling cues—head nods and brief oral responses that say you're listening—are especially helpful in communicating power.

- Avoid "adaptors"—behaviors such as playing with your hair or drawing pictures on a Styrofoam cup. Adaptors signal discomfort and hence a lack of power. The absence of adaptors, on the other hand, makes you appear in control of the situation and comfortable in the role of listener.

- Maintain an open posture. When around a table or in an audience, resist covering your face, chest, or stomach with your hands. These postures are often interpreted as signaling defensiveness or vulnerability and hence powerlessness.

- Take modest notes when appropriate. Taking too many notes may communicate a lack of ability to distinguish between what is and what is not important. Taking too few notes may communicate a lack of serious purpose or a reluctance to deal with the material.

- You also can signal power through visual dominance behavior (Exline, Ellyson, & Long, 1975; Burgoon & Bacue, 2003). For example, the average speaker maintains a high level of eye contact while listening and a lower level while speaking. When you want to signal dominance, you might reverse this pattern—maintain a high level of eye contact while talking but a lower level while listening.

It's also interesting to note that the effective listener—to take just a few examples of both task and relationship benefits—is more likely to emerge as group leader, a more effective salesperson, a more attentive and effective health-care worker, and a more effective manager (Johnson & Bechler, 1998; Kramer, 1997; Castleberry & Shepherd, 1993; Lauer, 2003; Stein & Bowen, 2003; Levine, 2004). Recently medical educators, claiming that doctors are not trained to listen to their patients, have introduced what they call "narrative medicine" to teach doctors how to listen to their patients and to help doctors recognize how their perceptions of their patients are influenced by their own emotions (Smith, 2003).

Another way to appreciate the importance of listening is to consider its many benefits. Here are some, built around the purposes of human communication:

- **Learning:** Listening enables you to acquire knowledge of others, the world, and yourself, so as to avoid problems and make better-informed decisions. For example, hearing Peter tell about his travels to Cuba will help you learn more about Peter and about life in another country. Listening to the difficulties of your sales staff may help you offer more pertinent sales training.

- **Relating:** Through attentive and supportive listening you can gain social acceptance and popularity. Others will increase their liking of you once they see your genuine concern for them.

- **Influencing:** Listening can help you change the attitudes and behaviors of others. For example, workers are more likely to follow your advice once they feel you've really listened to their insights and concerns.

- **Playing:** Listening can be enjoyable, letting you share pleasurable thoughts and feelings. Really listening to the anecdotes of coworkers will allow you to balance the world of work and the world of play.

- **Helping:** Listening often is vital in efforts to assist others. For example, listening to your child's complaints about her teacher will increase your ability to help your child cope with school and her teacher.

THE LISTENING PROCESS

Before reading about the process of listening, examine your own listening habits and tendencies by taking the following self-test.

TEST YOURSELF

How Do You Listen?

Respond to each question with the following scale: 1 = always, 2 = frequently, 3 = sometimes, 4 = seldom, and 5 = never.

_____ **1.** I listen actively, communicate acceptance of the speaker, and prompt the speaker to further explore his or her thoughts.

_____ **2.** I listen to what the speaker is saying and feeling; I try to feel what the speaker feels.

_____ **3.** I listen without judging the speaker.

_____ **4.** I listen to the literal meanings that a speaker communicates; I don't look too deeply into hidden meanings.

_____ **5.** I listen without active involvement; I generally remain silent and take in what the other person is saying.

_____ **6.** I listen objectively; I focus on the logic of the ideas rather than on the emotional meaning of the message.

_____ **7.** I listen critically, evaluating the speaker and what the speaker is saying.

_____ **8.** I look for the hidden meanings: the meanings that are revealed by subtle verbal or nonverbal cues.

HOW DID YOU DO? These statements focus on the ways of listening discussed in this unit. All of these ways are appropriate at some times but not at other times. It depends. So the only responses that are really inappropriate are "always" and "never." Effective listening is listening that is tailored to the specific communication situation.

WHAT WILL YOU DO? Consider how you might use these statements to begin to improve your listening effectiveness. A good way to start is to review these listening behaviors and try to identify situations in which each behavior would be appropriate and situations in which each behavior would be inappropriate.

The process of listening can be described as a series of five steps: (1) receiving (hearing and attending to the message), (2) understanding (deciphering meaning from the message you hear), (3) remembering (retaining what you hear in memory), (4) evaluating (thinking critically about and judging the message), and (5) responding (answering or giving feedback to the speaker). The process is visualized in Figure 1.

Note that the listening process is circular. The responses of person A serve as the stimuli for person B, whose responses in turn serve as the stimuli for person A, and so on. As will become clear in the following discussion of the five steps, listening is not a

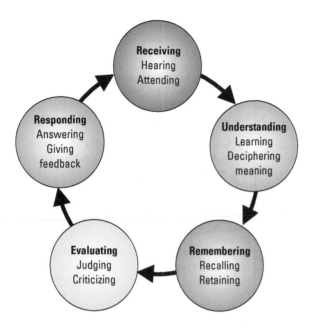

FIGURE 1 **A Five-Stage Model of Listening**

At each stage of listening there will be lapses. Thus, for example, at the receiving stage, a listener receives part of the message but because of noise (and perhaps for other reasons) fails to receive other parts. Similarly, at the stage of understanding, a listener understands part of the message but because of the inability to share another's meanings exactly fails to understand other parts. The same is true for remembering, evaluating, and responding. This model draws on a variety of previous models that listening researchers have developed (e.g., Alessandra, 1986; Barker & Gaut, 2002; Brownell, 1987; Steil, Barker, & Watson, 1983).

process of transferring an idea from the mind of a speaker to the mind of a listener. Rather, it is a process in which speaker and listener work together to achieve a common understanding.

As you read this discussion of the five stages of listening, realize that listening can go wrong at any of the five stages. At the same time, you can enhance your listening ability by strengthening the skills needed at each listening stage.

Receiving

Unlike listening, hearing begins and ends with this first stage—receiving. Hearing is something that just happens when you open your ears or when you get within earshot of auditory stimuli.

Listening is quite different. Listening begins, but does not end, with receiving messages the speaker sends. In listening you receive both the verbal and the nonverbal messages—not only the words but also the gestures, facial expressions, variations in

volume and rate, and lots more, as you'll discover when we discuss messages in more detail for improved reception:

- **Focus attention** on the speaker's verbal and nonverbal messages, on both what is said and what is not said.
- **Look for feedback** in response to previous messages as well as feedforward, which can reveal how the speaker would like his or her message viewed.
- **Avoid distractions** in the environment and focus attention on the speaker rather than on what you'll say next.
- **Maintain your role as listener** and avoid interrupting the speaker until he or she is finished.

In this brief discussion of receiving (and in this entire unit on listening), the unstated assumption is that both individuals can receive auditory signals without difficulty. But for the many people who have hearing impairments, listening presents a variety of problems. Table 1 provides tips for communication between those with and those without hearing problems.

Understanding

Understanding is the stage at which you learn what the speaker means. This understanding must take into consideration both the thoughts that are expressed and the emotional tone that accompanies them—the urgency or the joy or sorrow expressed in the message. For improved understanding:

- **Relate new information** to what you already know.
- **See the speaker's messages** from the speaker's point of view. Avoid judging the message until you've fully understood it—as the speaker intended it.
- **Ask questions** to clarify or to secure additional details or examples if necessary.
- **Rephrase (paraphrase)** the speaker's ideas in your own words.

Remembering

Messages that you receive and understand need to be remembered for at least some period of time. In some small group and public speaking situations, you can augment your memory by taking notes or by tape-recording the messages. In most interpersonal communication situations, however, such note taking would be considered inappropriate—although you often do write down a phone number, an appointment, or directions.

Table 1   Interpersonal Communication Tips

Between People with and without Hearing Impairment

People differ greatly in their hearing ability: Some are totally deaf and can hear nothing; others have some hearing loss and can hear some sounds; still others have impaired hearing but can hear most speech. Although people with profound hearing loss can speak, their speech may appear labored and may be less clear than the speech of those with unimpaired hearing. Here are some suggestions for more effective communication between deaf and hearing people.

If you have unimpaired hearing:

1. *Set up a comfortable context.* Reduce the distance between yourself and the person with a hearing impairment. Reduce the background noise. Turn off the television or even the air conditioner.

2. *Avoid interference.* Make sure the visual cues from your speech are clearly observable; for example, face the person squarely and avoid smoking, chewing gum, or holding your hand over your mouth. Make sure the lighting is adequate.

3. *Speak at an adequate volume.* But avoid shouting, which can distort your speech and may insult the person. Be careful to avoid reducing volume at the ends of your sentences.

4. *Phrase ideas in different ways.* Because some words are easier to lip-read than others, it often helps if you rephrase your ideas in different ways.

5. *Avoid overlapping speech.* In group situations only one person should speak at a time. Similarly, don't talk to a person with a hearing impairment through a third party; direct your comments to the person himself or herself. Elementary school teachers, for example, have been found to direct fewer comments to deaf children than to hearing students (Cawthon, 2001).

6. *Ask for additional information.* Ask the person if there is anything you can do to make it easier for him or her to understand you.

7. *Don't avoid common terms.* Use terms like "hear," "listen," "music," or "deaf" when they're relevant to the conversation. Trying to avoid these common terms will make your speech sound artificial.

8. *Use nonverbal cues.* These can help communicate your meaning; gestures indicating size or location and facial expressions indicating emotions and feelings are often helpful.

If you have impaired hearing:

1. *Do your best to eliminate background noise.*

2. *Move closer to the speaker if this helps you hear better.* Alert the speaker that this closer distance will help you hear better.

3. *Ask for adjustments.* If you feel the speaker can make adjustments to ease your comprehension, ask. For example, ask the speaker to repeat a message, to speak more slowly or more distinctly, or to increase his or her volume.

4. *Position yourself for best reception.* If you hear better in one ear than another, position yourself accordingly; if necessary, clue the speaker in to this fact.

5. *Ask for additional cues.* If necessary, ask the speaker to write down certain information, such as phone numbers or website addresses. Carrying a pad and pencil will prove helpful for this and in the event that you wish to write something down for others.

These suggestions were drawn from a variety of sources: *Tips for Communicating with Deaf People* (Rochester Institute of Technology, National Technical Institute for the Deaf, Division of Public Affairs), www.his.com/∼lola/deaf.html, www.zak.co.il/deaf-info/old/comm_strategies.html, and www.agbell.org/information/brochures_communication.cfm (all websites accessed October 23, 2004).

What you remember of a message is not an exact recording of what you hear; your memory doesn't just reproduce what you hear. Rather, your memory *reconstructs* the messages you hear and read, a process considered in more detail in the Understanding Theory and Research box (Reconstructing Memory) on the next page.

You can improve your message memory by:

- **identifying the central ideas** in a message and the major support advanced for them;
- **summarizing the message** in a more easily retained form, being careful not to ignore crucial details or qualifications;
- **repeating names and key concepts** to yourself or, if appropriate, aloud; and
- **asking questions** when in doubt.

Theory and Research | Reconstructing Memory

UNDERSTANDING

When you remember a message, do you remember it as it was spoken, or do you remember what you think you heard? The commonsense response, of course, would be that you remember what was said. But before accepting this simple explanation, try to memorize the list of 12 words presented below, modeled on an idea from a research study (Glucksberg & Danks, 1975). Don't worry about the order of the words; only the number of words remembered counts. Take about 20 seconds to memorize as many words as possible. Then close the book and write down as many words as you can remember.

dining room	table	milk
cafeteria	shopping	hungry
green beans	steak	saucer
satisfied	knife	menu

Don't read any further until you've tried to memorize and reproduce the list of words.

If you're like most people, you not only remembered a good number of the words on the list, but also "remembered" at least one word that was not on the list: *eat*. Most people would recall the word as being on the list (whether they read the list as you've done here or hear it spoken)—but, as you can see, it wasn't. What happens is that in remembering you don't simply reproduce the list; you reconstruct it. In this case you gave the list meaning, and part of that meaning included the word *eat*. Memory for speech, then, is not reproductive—you don't simply reproduce in your memory what the speaker said. Rather, memory is reconstructive: You reconstruct the messages you hear into a system that makes sense to you but, in the process, often remember distorted versions of what was said.

Working with Theories and Research

Log on to your favorite database or search engine and search for articles dealing with false memory. In what types of situations is false memory found? What are some of its implications for communication?

Evaluating

Evaluating consists of judging messages in some way. At times, you may try to evaluate the speaker's underlying intent. Often this evaluation process goes on without much conscious thought. For example, Elaine tells you that she is up for a promotion and is really excited about it. You may then try to judge her intention. Does she want you to use your influence with the company president? Is she preoccupied with her accomplishment and thus telling everyone about it? Is she looking for a pat on the back? Generally, if you know the person well, you'll be able to identify the intention and therefore be able to respond appropriately.

In other situations, evaluation is more in the nature of critical analysis. For example, in listening to proposals advanced in a business meeting, you will at this stage evaluate them. Is there evidence to show that these proposals are practical and will increase productivity? Is there contradictory evidence? Are there alternative proposals that would be more practical and more productive?

In evaluating, try to

- **resist evaluation** until you fully understand the speaker's point of view;

- **assume that the speaker is a person of goodwill**, and give the speaker the benefit of any doubt by asking for clarification on issues that you feel you must object to (are there any other reasons for accepting this new proposal?);

- **distinguish facts from inferences**, opinions, and personal interpretations by the speaker; and

- **identify any biases, self-interests, or prejudices** that may lead the speaker to slant unfairly what is presented

Responding

Responding occurs in two phases: (1) responses you make while the speaker is talking and (2) responses you make after the speaker has stopped talking. These responses are feedback—information that you send back to the speaker and that tells the speaker how you feel and think about

ASK THE RESEARCHER

Not Listening

I appreciate all these suggestions for listening, but what if you don't want to listen? For example, I don't want to hear about my colleagues' relationships, my neighbor's tax problems, or even my partner's frequent and detailed sports updates.
Any suggestions?

It's not unusual to find yourself in a situation where someone is speaking and you don't want to listen. The speaker isn't thinking about you—he or she is talking to sort out a problem or to express an enthusiasm. The way you respond is always your judgment call. Consider whether listening in this case is something that the speaker would greatly appreciate before you take the risk of offending your partner by cutting them off.

If you decide not to listen, take a deep breath and interrupt. Politely. Change the subject by recognizing the speaker's concern and then move on to a different topic: "I'm amazed that Jim hasn't responded. I realize it's very stressful. You know, there's something that I need to discuss with you...." Don't hang in the middle. There's nothing worse than giving the impression that you're listening when you're not. Either listen, or be assertive and change the subject.

For further information: Brownell, J. (2006). *Listening: Attitudes, principles and skills* (3rd ed.). Boston: Allyn & Bacon.

Judi Brownell (Ph.D., Syracuse University) is dean of students and a professor of organizational communication in the School of Hotel Administration at Cornell University, where she teaches managerial communication and organizational behavior. Professor Brownell is a past president of the International Listening Association and was inducted into the Listening Hall of Fame.

his or her messages. Responses made while the speaker is talking should be supportive and should acknowledge that you're listening. These include what researchers on nonverbal communication call **backchanneling cues**: "I see," "yes," "uh-huh," and similar signals that let the speaker know you're attending to the message.

Responses made after the speaker has stopped talking are generally more elaborate and might include expressing empathy ("I know how you must feel"), asking for clarification ("Do you mean that this new health plan is to replace the old one, or will it just be a supplement?"), challenging ("I think your evidence is weak here"), and agreeing ("You're absolutely right on this, and I'll support your proposal when it comes up for a vote"). For effective responding:

- **Be supportive** of the speaker throughout the speaker's talk by using and varying backchanneling cues; using only one backchanneling cue—for example, saying "uh-huh" throughout—may make it appear that you're not really listening.

- **Express support** for the speaker in your final responses.

- **Be honest**; the speaker has a right to expect honest responses, even if these express anger or disagreement.

- **State your thoughts and feelings** as your own, using I-messages. For example, say "I think the new proposal will entail greater expense than you outlined" rather than "Everyone will object to the plan for costing too much."

Table 2 identifies some types of difficult listeners—listeners who don't follow the suggestions for each of the five listening stages—and their problem-causing ways of responding.

LISTENING, CULTURE, AND GENDER

Listening is difficult, in part, because of the inevitable differences in the communication systems between speaker and listener. Because each person has had a

Table 2   Some Problem-Causing Ways of Responding in Listening

Review this table and try to see if it includes some of your own listening behaviors.

Listener Type	Listening (Responding) Behavior	(Mis)interpreting Thoughts
Static	Gives no feedback, remains relatively motionless, reveals no expression.	Why isn't she reacting? Am I not producing sound?
Monotonous	Seems responsive, but the responses never vary; regardless of what you say, the response is the same.	Am I making sense? Why is he still smiling? I'm being dead serious.
Overly expressive	Reacts to just about everything with extreme responses.	Why is she so expressive? I didn't say anything that provocative. She'll have a heart attack when I get to the punch line.
Reader/writer	Reads or writes while "listening" and only occasionally glances up.	Am I that boring? Is last week's student newspaper more interesting than me?
Eye avoider	Looks all around the room and at others but never at you.	Why isn't he looking at me? Do I have spinach on my teeth?
Preoccupied	Listens to other things at the same time, often with headphones turned up so loud that the sound interferes with your own thinking.	When is she going to shut that music off and really listen? Am I so boring that my talk needs background music?
Waiting	Listens for a cue to take over the speaking turn.	Is he listening to me or rehearsing his next interruption?
Thought-completing	Listens a little and then finishes your thought.	Am I that predictable? Why do I bother saying anything? He already knows what I'm going to say.

unique set of experiences, each person's communication and meaning system is going to be different from each other person's. When speaker and listener come from different cultures or are of different genders, the differences and their effects are naturally so much greater. Let's look first at culture.

Listening and Culture

In a global environment in which people from very different cultures work together, it's especially important to understand the ways in which cultural differences can influence listening. Four of these listening influences include: (1) language and speech, (2) nonverbal behaviors, (3) feedback, and (4) credibility.

Language and Speech

Even when speaker and listener speak the same language, they speak it with different meanings and different accents. No two speakers speak exactly the same language. Speakers of the same language will, at the very least, have different meanings for the same terms because they have had different experiences.

Speakers and listeners who have different native languages and who may have learned English as a second language will have even greater differences in meaning. Translations are never precise and never fully capture the meaning in the other language. If your meaning for "house" was learned in a culture in which everyone lived in their own house with lots of land around it, then talking about houses with someone whose meaning was learned in a neighborhood of high-rise tenements is going to be difficult. Although you'll each hear the same word, the meanings you'll each develop will be drastically different. In adjusting your listening—especially in an intercultural setting—understand that the speaker's meanings may be very different from yours even though you're speaking the same language.

In many classrooms throughout this country, there will be a wide range of **accents**. Those whose native language is a tonal one such as Chinese (in which differences in pitch signal important meaning differences) may speak English with variations in pitch that may seem puzzling to their hearers. Those whose native language is Japanese may have trouble distinguishing *l* from *r*, as Japanese does not include this distinction. The native language acts as a filter and influences the accent given to the second language.

PRINCIPLES OF MEDIA LITERACY LISTENING

In a day of virtual reality and computer simula-tions "seeing is NOT believing."

—*David Considine*

Here are a few basic principles to illustrate the importance of listening in media literacy.

1. Media messages are value-laden, meaning that the media contain the values of the producer and often of the primary audience. And these messages ethicize and socialize you—they give you an ethical standard and teach you the social rules you should follow. Because media messages are (generally) expensive to produce (feature films, television shows), they are likely to reflect the values of the rich and powerful. In contrast, electronic media—blogs, websites, and social networks such as MySpace or Friendster—are free or relatively inexpensive, and through these media people normally without influence voice opinions and send out persuasive messages. So listen to television programs, for example, with a consciousness of the values that are embedded in the production—the sitcom as well as the news broadcast—and how might these influence your thoughts and behaviors.

2. Media messages are informative and persua-sive. They inform you of the news and at the same time persuade you that this is in fact the news; that is, that what the newspaper covers are in fact the significant events of the day. And of course media persuade you, on a more obvious level, with advertising. Almost all media messages have some persuasive aim. As a literate media consumer, see these persuasive messages clearly so that you can analyze them and test their validity, rather than letting them influence you without your awareness.

3. Media help construct your view of reality: What you know of the world and its people you probably learned largely from the media. Some media messages are accurate, and some are not; some messages are slanted, and most of them are overly simplified. Listen to the ways in which the media influence how you see the world and to the ways they present distorted pictures of what is supposed to be reality.

Increasing Media Literacy

In what ways have the media influenced your beliefs about, for example, the war in Iraq, the economy, or reli-gion in government? How have the media influenced your peers' beliefs about these same issues? What specific media have the most influence on you? Why?

Nonverbal Behaviors

Speakers from different cultures have different display rules—cultural rules that govern which non-verbal behaviors are appropriate and which are inap-propriate in a public setting. As you listen to other people, you also "listen" to their nonverbal cues. If these are drastically different from what you expect on the basis of the verbal message, you may see them as a kind of noise or interference or even as contra-dictory messages. Also, of course, different cultures may give very different meanings to the same non-verbal gesture; for example, the thumb and forefinger forming a circle means "OK" in most of the United States, but it means "money" in Japan, "zero" in some Mediterranean countries, and "I'll kill you" in Tunisia.

Feedback

Members of some cultures give very direct and hon-est feedback. Speakers from these cultures—the United States is a good example—expect the feed-back to be a forthright reflection of what their listeners are feeling. In other cultures—Japan and Korea are good examples—it's more important to be positive than to be truthful, so people may respond with positive feedback (say, in commenting on a business colleague's proposal) even though they don't actually feel positive. Listen to feedback, as you would all messages, with a full recognition that vari-ous cultures view feedback very differently.

Credibility

What makes a speaker credible, or believable, also will vary from one culture to another. In some cul-tures people would claim that competence is the most important factor in, say, the choice of a teacher for their preschool children. In other cultures the most important factor might be the goodness or morality of the teacher. Similarly, members of different cultures may perceive the credibility of various media very differently. For example, members of a repres-sive society in which the government controls televi-sion news may come to attribute little credibility to

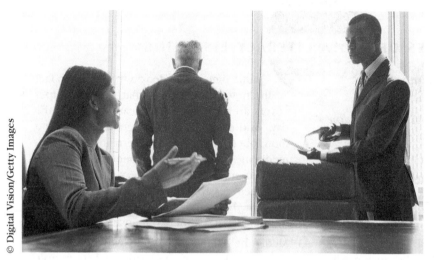

© Digital Vision/Getty Images

LISTENING THROUGH GENDER

Your supervisor just doesn't seem to listen to your ideas and your feedback and you have the strong suspicion that it's because of your gender. You want to be listened to more fairly and yet you don't want to alienate your supervisor.

WHAT DO YOU SAY?
Through what channel?

such broadcasts. After all, these listeners might reason, television news is simply what the government wants you to know. This reaction may be hard to understand or even recognize for someone raised in the United States, for example, where traditionally the media have been largely free of such political control.

Listening and Gender

Deborah Tannen opens her chapter on listening in her best-selling *You Just Don't Understand: Women and Men in Conversation* (1990) with several anecdotes illustrating that when men and women talk, men lecture and women listen. The lecturer is positioned as the superior: as the teacher, the expert.

The listener is positioned as the inferior: as the student, the nonexpert.

Women, according to Tannen, seek to build rapport and establish a closer relationship, and so use listening to achieve these ends. For example, women use more listening cues (such as interjecting "yeah," or "uh-huh," nodding in agreement, or smiling) to let the other person know they're paying attention and are interested. Women also make more eye contact when listening than do men, who are more apt to look around and often away from the speaker (Brownell, 2006). Men not only use fewer listening cues but interrupt more, and they will often change the topic to a subject they know more about or that is less relational or people oriented or

REFLECTIONS ON ETHICS

Listening Ethically

Most often discussions of ethics in communication focus on the speaker. But listeners, too, have ethical obligations.

- Give the speaker an honest hearing. Avoid prejudging the speaker before hearing her or him. Try to put aside prejudices and preconceptions so you can understand and then evaluate the speaker's message fairly.
- Empathize with the speaker. You don't have to agree with the speaker, but try to understand emotionally as well as intellectually what the speaker means. In this way, you'll come to understand the speaker more fully.
- Give the speaker honest responses and feedback. In a learning environment such as a communication class, this means giving honest and constructive criticism to help the speaker improve.

- Reflect honestly on the questions the speaker raises. Much as the listener has a right to expect an active speaker, the speaker has the right to expect a listener who will actively deal with, rather than just passively hear, the message.

Ethical Choice Point

You're teaching a class in communication. In the public speaking segment, one of your students, a sincere and devout Iranian Muslim, gives a speech on "why women should be subservient to men." After the first two minutes of the speech, half the class walks out. During the next class you plan to give a lecture on the ethics of listening. What is your ethical obligation in this situation? What would you say?

Theory and Research UNDERSTANDING   Cues to Lying

In listening, you normally assume that the speaker is telling the truth and seldom even ask yourself if the speaker is lying. When you do wonder about a speaker's truthfulness, research shows, it may be because the speaker exhibits behaviors that often accompany lying. Here are some verbal and nonverbal behaviors that are associated with lying (Knapp & Hall, 1997; O'Hair, Cody, Goss, & Krayer, 1988; Bond & Atoum, 2000; Al-Simadi, 2000; Burgoon & Bacue, 2003). As you review these behaviors, ask yourself if you use these cues in making assumptions about whether or not people are telling the truth. Be careful that you don't fall into the trap of thinking that just because someone emits these cues, he or she is therefore lying; these cues are often used by truth-tellers as well and are not 100 percent reliable in indicating lying. In fact, in one study participants who held stereotypical views of how liars behave (for example, liars don't look at you, or liars fidget) were less effective in detecting lying than were those who did not hold such beliefs (Vrij & Mann, 2001). Generally, however, research finds that liars

- smile less
- respond with shorter answers, often simple yes or no responses
- use fewer specifics and more generalities; for example, "we hung out"
- shift their posture more
- use more self-touching movements
- use more and longer pauses
- avoid direct eye contact with the listener and blink more often than normal
- appear less friendly and attentive
- make more speech errors

Working with Theories and Research

Can you recall a situation in which you made the assumption that someone was lying on the basis of such cues (or others)? What happened? Should you want to learn more about lying, search for such terms as "lying," "deception," "poker tells," and "falsehood." It's a fascinating subject of study.

that is more factual, such as sports statistics, economic developments, or political problems. Men, research shows, tend to play up their expertise, emphasize it, and use it in dominating the conversation. Women often play down their expertise.

Now, you might be tempted to conclude from this that women play fair in conversation and that men don't; for example, that men consistently seek to put themselves in a position superior to women. But that may be too simple an explanation. Research shows that men communicate this way not only with women but with other men as well. Men are not showing disrespect for their female conversational partners but are simply communicating as they normally do. Women, too, communicate as they do not only with men but also with other women.

Tannen argues that the goal of a man in conversation is to be accorded respect. Therefore, a man seeks to display his knowledge and expertise, even if to do this he has to change the topic to one he

knows a great deal about. Women, on the other hand, seek to be liked; so they express agreement, rarely interrupt in order to take their turn as speaker, and give lots of cues (verbally and nonverbally) to indicate that they are listening.

There's no evidence to show that these differences represent any negative motives—for example, motives on the part of men to prove themselves superior or on the part of women to ingratiate themselves. Rather, these differences in listening are largely the result of the ways in which men and women have been socialized.

It should be mentioned that not all researchers agree that there is sufficient evidence to make the claims that Tannen and others make about gender differences in listening (Goldsmith & Fulfs, 1999). Gender differences are changing in today's world, and it's best to take generalizations about gender as starting points for investigation and not as airtight conclusions.

STYLES OF EFFECTIVE LISTENING

As stressed throughout this unit, listening is situational; the type of listening that is appropriate will vary with the situation, and each situation will call for a somewhat different combination of listening styles. The art of effective listening largely consists of making appropriate choices along the following four dimensions:

- empathic and objective listening
- nonjudgmental and critical listening
- surface and depth listening
- active and inactive listening

Let's take a look at each of these dimensions.

Empathic and Objective Listening

To understand what a person means and feels, listen with **empathy** (Rogers, 1970; Rogers & Farson, 1981). To empathize with others is to feel with them, to see the world as they see it, to feel what they feel. Empathy will enable you to understand other people's meanings, and it will also enhance your relationships (Barrett & Godfrey, 1988; Snyder, 1992).

Empathy is best understood as having two distinct parts: thinking empathy and feeling empathy (Bellafiore, 2005). In *thinking empathy* you express an understanding of what the person means. For example, when you paraphrase someone's comment, showing that you understand the meaning the person is trying to communicate, you're communicating *thinking empathy*. The second part is *feeling empathy*; here you express your feeling of what the other person is feeling. You demonstrate a similarity between what you're feeling and what the other person is feeling. Often you'll respond with both thinking and feeling empathy in the same brief response; for example, when a friend tells you of problems at home, you may respond by saying, for example, *Your problems at home do seem to be getting worse. I can imagine how you feel so angry at times.*

Empathic listening is the preferred mode of responding in most communication situations, but there are times when you need to go beyond it to measure meanings and feelings against some objective reality. It's important to listen to Peter tell you how the entire world hates him and to understand how Peter feels and why he feels this way. But then you need to look more objectively at Peter and perhaps see the paranoia or the self-hatred behind his

© Chuck Savage/CORBIS

EMPATHIC LISTENING

Your neighbors who've avoided work all their lives and lived off unfairly obtained government disability payments have just won the lottery for $86 million. They want you to share their joy, and they invite you over for a champagne toast and tell you about their plan to move into a mansion.

WHAT DO YOU SAY?

complaints. Sometimes, in other words, you have to put your empathic responses aside and listen with objectivity and detachment.

In adjusting your empathic and objective listening focus, keep the following recommendations in mind:

- **Punctuate from the speaker's point of view**. If you want to understand the speaker's perspective, see the sequence of events as the speaker does, and try to figure out how this can influence what the speaker says and does. Keep your focus (your thoughts and your messages) on the speaker.

- **Engage in equal, two-way conversation**. To encourage openness and empathy, try to eliminate any physical or psychological barriers to equality (for example, step out from behind the large desk separating you from your employee). Avoid interrupting the speaker—a sign that what you have to say is more important.

- **Seek to understand both thoughts and feelings**. Don't consider your listening task finished until you've understood what the speaker is feeling as well as what he or she is thinking.

- **Avoid "offensive listening,"** the tendency to listen to bits and pieces of information that will enable you to attack the speaker or find fault with something the speaker has said.

- **Strive especially to be objective in listening to friends and foes alike**. Be aware that your attitudes may lead you to distort messages—for example, to block out positive messages about a foe or negative messages about a friend. Guard against "expectancy hearing," in which you fail to hear what the speaker is really saying and instead hear what you expect.

- **Avoid trying to solve the problem** or even giving advice when trying to achieve empathy. Being empathic is hard enough, and at this point it's better to communicate your support and understanding rather than your evaluation of the situation.

- **Encourage the speaker to explore his or her feelings further** by demonstrating a willingness to listen and an interest in what the speaker is saying.

The accompanying Building Communication Skills box provides a few situations for you to practice your empathic skills (below).

Nonjudgmental and Critical Listening

Effective listening includes both nonjudgmental and critical responses. Listen nonjudgmentally (with an open mind and with a view toward understanding) and listen critically (with a view toward making some kind of evaluation or judgment). Listen first for understanding; only when you understand should you be willing to evaluate or judge the messages.

Listening with an open mind will help you understand messages better; listening with a critical mind

© Richard Lord/PhotoEdit

ADJUSTING LISTENING

Your friend has just broken up a love affair and is telling you about it. "I can't seem to get Chris out of my mind," he says. "All I do is daydream about the stuff we used to do, and all the fun we used to have."

WHAT DO YOU SAY?

will help you analyze and evaluate the messages. In adjusting your nonjudgmental and critical listening, focus on the following guidelines:

- **Keep an open mind**. Avoid prejudging. Delay your judgments until you fully understand the intention and the content the speaker is communicating. Avoid both positive and negative evaluation until you have a reasonably complete understanding.

- **Avoid filtering out or oversimplifying difficult or complex messages**. Similarly, avoid filtering out

---

B u i l d i n g   C o m m u n i c a t i o n   S k i l l s   Expressing Empathy

For any one or two of the following situations, indicate in one sentence (or more) how you'd respond to the speaker with *thinking empathy* and in one sentence (or more) how you'd respond with *feeling empathy*. Assume that all three people are your peers.

1. "I've never felt so alone in my life. Chris left last night and said it was all over. We were together for three years and now—after a 10-minute argument—everything is lost."

2. "I just got $20,000 from my aunt's estate. She left it to me! Twenty thousand! Now I can get that car and buy some new clothes!"

3. "A Camry! My parents bought me a Camry for graduation. What a bummer. They promised me a Lexus."

Expressing empathy is crucial to meaningful communication, but it is not an easily acquired skill; it takes practice.

undesirable messages. Clearly, you don't want to hear that something you believe in is untrue, that people you care for are unkind, or that ideals you hold are self-destructive. Yet it's important that you reexamine your beliefs by listening to such messages.

- **Recognize your own biases**. These may interfere with accurate listening and cause you to distort message reception through the process of **assimilation**—the tendency to integrate and interpret what you hear or think you hear to conform to your own biases, prejudices, and expectations. For example, are your ethnic, national, or religious biases preventing you from appreciating a speaker's point of view?

- **Avoid uncritical listening when you need to make evaluations and judgments**. Recognize and resist the normal tendency to sharpen—a process in which one or two aspects of a message become highlighted, emphasized, and perhaps embellished. Often the concepts that are sharpened are incidental remarks that somehow stand out from the rest of the message.

- **Recognize fallacies**—ways of using language to subvert instead of clarify truth and accuracy—and don't be persuaded by their pseudo-logic. Table 3 identifies some popular language fallacies. In "The Persuasive Speech," we'll consider additional fallacies that are closely related to persuasion.

Surface and Depth Listening

In Shakespeare's *Julius Caesar*, Marc Antony, in giving the funeral oration for Caesar, says: "I come to bury Caesar, not to praise him. / The evil that men do lives after them; / The good is oft interred with

---

Table 3 Listening to Fallacies of Language

Here are four language fallacies that often get in the way of meaningful communication and that need to be identified in critical listening. After reviewing these fallacies, take a look at some of the commercial websites for clothing, books, music, or any such product you're interested in. Can you find examples of these fallacies?

Fallacy	Example	Notes
Weasel words are terms whose meanings are slippery and difficult to pin down (Hayakawa & Hayakawa, 1990).	A commercial claiming that Medicine M works "better" than Brand X but failing to specify how much or in what respect Medicine M performs better. It's quite possible that Medicine M performs better in one respect but less effectively according to nine other measures.	Other weasel words are *help, virtually, as much as, like* (as in "it will make you feel like new"), and *more economical*. Ask yourself, "Exactly what is being claimed?" For example, "What does 'may reduce cholesterol' mean? What exactly is being asserted?"
Euphemisms make the negative and unpleasant appear positive and appealing.	An executive's reference to the firing of 200 workers as "downsizing" or "reallocation of resources"; Justin Timberlake's reference to the highly publicized act with Janet Jackson during the 2004 Super Bowl as a "wardrobe malfunction."	Often euphemisms take the form of inflated language designed to make the mundane seem extraordinary, the common seem exotic ("the vacation of a lifetime," "unsurpassed vistas"). Don't let words get in the way of accurate firsthand perception.
Jargon is the specialized language of a professional class.	The language of the computer hacker, the psychologist, or the advertiser.	When used to intimidate or impress, as when used with people who aren't members of the profession, jargon prevents meaningful communication. Don't be intimidated by jargon; ask questions when you don't understand.
Gobbledygook is overly complex language that overwhelms the listener instead of communicating meaning.	Extra-long sentences, complex grammatical constructions, and rare or unfamiliar words.	Some people just normally speak in complex language. But others use complexity to confuse and mislead. Ask for simplification when appropriate.

B u i l d i n g   C o m m u n i c a t i o n   Regulating Your Listening Style

With specific reference to the four dimensions of effective listening discussed here, what styles would you use in each of the following situations? What types of listening would be obviously inappropriate in each situation?

1. Your steady dating partner for the last five years tells you that spells of depression are becoming more frequent and more long lasting.
2. Your history instructor lectures on the contributions of the ancient Greeks to modern civilization.
3. Your brother tells you he's been accepted into Harvard's MBA program.
4. Your supervisor explains the new computerized mail system.
5. A newscaster reports on a recent Arab-Israeli meeting.

Regulate your listening on the basis of the specific situation in which you find yourself.

---

their bones." And later: "For Brutus is an honourable man; / So are they all, all honourable men." But if we listen beyond the surface of Marc Anthony's words, we can see that he does indeed come to praise Caesar, and to convince the crowd that Brutus was dishonorable—despite the fact that at first glance his words seem to say quite the opposite.

In most messages there's an obvious meaning that you can derive from a literal reading of the words and sentences. But there's often another level of meaning. Sometimes, as in these famous lines from *Julius Caesar*, the deeper level is the opposite of the literal meaning. At other times it seems totally unrelated. In reality, most messages have more than one level of meaning. For example, suppose Carol asks you how you like her new haircut. On one level, the meaning is clear: Do you like the haircut? But there's also another, perhaps a more important level: Carol is asking you to say something positive about her appearance. In the same way, the parent who complains about working hard at the office or in the home may, on a deeper level, be asking for an expression of appreciation. The child who talks about the unfairness of the other children in the playground may be asking for comfort and love, for some expression of caring.

To appreciate these other meanings, engage in depth listening. If you respond only to the surface-level communication (the literal meaning), you miss the opportunity to make meaningful contact with the other person's feelings and needs. If you say to the parent, "You're always complaining. I bet you really love working so hard," you fail to respond to the call for understanding and appreciation. In regulating your surface and depth listening, consider the following guidelines:

■ **Focus on both verbal and nonverbal messages**. Recognize both consistent and inconsistent

"packages" of messages, and use these as guides for drawing inferences about the speaker's meaning. Ask questions when in doubt. Listen also to what is omitted. Remember that speakers communicate by what they leave out as well as by what they include.

■ **Listen for both content and relational messages**. The student who constantly challenges the instructor is, on one level, communicating disagreement over content. However, on another level—the relationship level—the student may be voicing objections to the instructor's authority or authoritarianism. The instructor needs to listen and respond to both types of messages.

■ **Make special note of statements that refer back to the speaker**. Remember that people inevitably talk about themselves. Whatever a person says is, in part, a function of who that person is. Attend carefully to those personal, self-reference messages.

■ **Don't disregard the literal meaning of messages in trying to uncover the more hidden meanings**. Balance your listening between surface and the underlying meanings. Respond to the different levels of meaning in the messages of others, as you would like others to respond to yours—sensitively but not obsessively, readily but not overambitiously.

Active and Inactive Listening

One of the most important communication skills you can learn is active listening. Consider the following interaction. You say: "I can't believe I have to redo this entire budget report. I really worked hard on this project, and now I have to do it all over again." To this, you get three different responses.

ANDY: That's not so bad; most people find they have to redo their first reports. That's the norm here.

CONNIE: You should be pleased that all you have to do is a simple rewrite. Peggy and Michael both had to completely redo their entire projects.

GREG: You have to rewrite that report you've worked on for the last three weeks? You sound really angry and frustrated.

All three listeners are probably trying to make you feel better. But they go about it in very different ways—and surely with very different results. Andy tries to lessen the significance of the rewrite. This well-intended and extremely common response does little to promote meaningful communication and understanding. Connie tries to give the situation a positive spin. In their responses, however, both Andy and Connie are also suggesting that you should not be feeling the way you do; they're saying that your feelings are not legitimate and should be replaced with more logical feelings.

Greg's response, however, is different from the others. Greg uses active listening. **Active listening** owes its development to Thomas Gordon (1975), who made it a cornerstone of his P.E.T. (parent effectiveness training) technique. It is a process of sending back to the speaker what you as a listener think the speaker meant—both in content and in feelings. Active listening, then, is not merely repeating the speaker's exact words, but rather putting together into some meaningful whole your understanding of the speaker's total message. And, incidentally, when combined with empathic listening, it proves the most effective mode for success as a salesperson (Comer & Drollinger, 1999).

Active listening helps you check your understanding of what the speaker said and, more importantly, of what he or she meant. Reflecting back perceived meanings to the speaker gives the speaker an opportunity to offer clarification and to correct any misunderstandings. Active listening also lets the speaker know that you acknowledge and accept his or her feelings. In the sample responses given above, Greg listened actively and reflected back what he thought you meant while accepting what you were feeling. Note too that he also explicitly identified the feelings ("You sound angry and frustrated"), allowing you the opportunity to correct his interpretation. Still another function of active listening is that it stimulates the speaker to explore feelings and thoughts. Greg's response encourages you to elaborate on your feelings and perhaps to understand them better as you talk them through.

Three simple techniques may help you master the process of active listening: paraphrasing the

Jim Whitmer

ACTIVE LISTENING

Your life partner comes from work visibly upset, and clearly has a need to talk about what happened . . . but simply says, "Work sucks!" You're determined to use active listening techniques.

WHAT DO YOU SAY?
Through what channel?

speaker's meaning, expressing understanding, and asking questions.

- **Paraphrase the speaker's meaning**. Stating in your own words what you think the speaker means and feels helps ensure understanding and demonstrates your interest. Paraphrasing gives the speaker a chance to extend what was originally said. In paraphrasing, be objective; be especially careful not to lead the speaker in the direction you think he or she should go. Also, don't overdo paraphrasing. Paraphrase when you feel there's a chance for misunderstanding or when you want to express support for the other person and keep the conversation going.

- **Express understanding of the speaker's feelings**. In addition to paraphrasing the content, echo the feelings the speaker expressed or implied ("You must have felt horrible"). This expression of feelings will help you further check your perception of the speaker's feelings and will allow the speaker to see his or her feelings more objectively (especially helpful when they're feelings of anger, hurt, or depression) and the opportunity to elaborate on these feelings.

- **Ask questions**. Asking questions ensures your own understanding of the speaker's thoughts and feelings and secures additional information ("How did you feel when you read your job appraisal report?"). Ask questions to provide just enough stimulation and support so that the speaker feels he or she can elaborate on these thoughts and feelings.

Table 4 presents a summary of some of the major themes presented in the above suggestions for listening more effectively.

Table 4   Listening Barriers and What to Do about Them

Here are a few general barriers to listening and some suggestions for dealing with these barriers as a listener and as a speaker.

Barriers	Correctives	
	For Listener	**For Speaker**
Physical barriers; for example, a chalkboard with a previous speaker's notes; defective hearing	Focus on the speaker; you can look at the room and the audience later.	Try—whenever possible—to remove potential distractions.
Mental distractions; for example, thinking about your upcoming Saturday night date or becoming too emotional to think (and listen) clearly	Recognize that you can think about your date later; get back to listening.	Make what you say compelling and so relevant to the listener.
Closed-mindedness; for example, refusing to hear any feminist argument or anything about gay marriage	Assume that what the speaker is saying will be useful in some way.	Anticipate this and ask for openness—"I know this seems contrary to what many people think, but let's look at this logically."
Biases and prejudices; for example, a gender bias that assumes that only one sex has anything useful to say about certain topics	Be willing to subject your biases and prejudices to contradictory information; after all if they're worth having, they should stand up to differences of opinion.	When you feel that your listener(s) may be biased, ask for a suspension of bias—"I know you don't like the XXX, and I can understand that. But just listen to. . . ."
Rehearsing responses; for example, anticipating what you're going to say and how you're going to phrase your response or even interrupting the speaker	Make a mental note of something and then get back to listening.	When you feel the audience is preparing to argue with you, tell them that you'll return to this point later.
Dismissing the speaker; for example, because of the way the speaker is dressed, or because of his or her accent, or because his or her last speech was dull, or because the Dems (Reps) are just telling us what we want to hear—therefore, there's no sense listening	Assume that everyone has something of value to say to you; in fact, people who are most unlike you probably have the most to tell you.	Stress the importance of what you will say; dress so as not to detract from your message.
Focusing on irrelevancies; for example, an especially vivid example	When encountering a particularly vivid example, recall the point, the main idea, that it refers to; don't get hung up on red flags.	Repeat the main points and connect them to your examples and illustrations. Try to avoid language or examples that may divert attention from your main ideas
Excessive self-focus; for example, listening only to those ideas that have direct relevance to you	Think about how this topic relates to others or to some larger picture. Not everything is about you; avoid interpreting everything in terms of what it means to you; see other perspectives.	Include all listeners; make what you say relevant to everyone.
Faulty assumptions; for example, assuming you know what the speaker is going to say so there's no need to listen	Let the speaker guide your listening.	If you suspect that listeners will make faulty assumptions, make it clear that what you're saying will be unexpected.
Drawing too-early conclusions or judgments; for example, not listening after you hear an idea with which you disagree (not waiting for the evidence or argument)	Avoid making judgments before you gather all the information; listen before judging.	Consider giving part of the evidence before stating any idea to which you anticipate serious objection from listeners.

SUMMARY: LISTENING IN HUMAN COMMUNICATION

This unit discussed the importance of listening, the process of listening, the influence of culture and gender on the way people listen, and the principles for listening more effectively.

1. Effective listening yields a wide variety of benefits, including more effective learning, relating, influencing, playing, and helping.

2. Listening is a five-part process that begins with receiving, and continues through understanding, remembering, evaluating, and responding.

3. Receiving consists of hearing the verbal signals and perceiving the nonverbal signals.

4. Understanding involves learning what the speaker means, not merely what the words mean.

5. Remembering involves retaining the received message, a process that involves considerable `reconstruction.

6. Evaluating consists of judging the messages you receive.

7. Responding involves giving feedback while the speaker is speaking and taking your turn at speaking after the speaker has finished.

8. Listening is influenced by a wide range of cultural factors, such as differences in language and speech, nonverbal behaviors, credibility criteria, and feedback approaches.

9. Listening is influenced by gender: Men and women seem to view listening as serving different purposes.

10. Effective listening involves adjusting our behaviors on the basis of at least four dimensions: empathic and objective listening, nonjudgmental and critical listening, surface and depth listening, and active and inactive listening.

11. The empathic–objective dimension involves the degree to which the listener focuses on feeling what the speaker is feeling versus grasping the objective message.

12. The nonjudgmental–critical dimension involves the degree to which the listener evaluates what is said.

13. The surface–depth dimension has to do with the extent to which the listener focuses on literal or obvious meanings versus hidden or less obvious meanings.

14. The active–inactive dimension involves the extent to which the listener reflects back and expresses support for the speaker.

KEY TERMS IN LISTENING IN HUMAN COMMUNICATION

accent	assimilation	empathy
active listening	backchanneling cues	listening

THINKING CRITICALLY ABOUT LISTENING IN HUMAN COMMUNICATION

1. **Your Listening Self.** Using the four dimensions of listening effectiveness discussed here (empathic–objective, nonjudgmental–critical, surface–depth, and active–inactive), how would you describe yourself as a listener when listening in class? When listening to your best friend? When listening to a romantic partner? When listening to your parents? When listening to your superiors at work?

2. **Listening to Complaints.** Would you find it difficult to listen to friends who were complaining that the insurance premium on their Bentley was going up? Would you find it difficult to listen to unemployed friends complain that their rent was going up and that they feared becoming homeless? If there is a difference, why?

3. **Selling by Listening.** Researchers have argued that effective listening skills are positively associated with salespeople's effectiveness in selling (Castleberry & Shepherd, 1993). Can you think of examples from your own experience that would support this positive association between effective listening and effective selling?

4. **Men and Women Listening.** The popular belief, as noted in this unit, is that men listen the way they do to prove themselves superior and that women listen as they do to ingratiate themselves. Although there is no evidence to support this belief, it persists in the assumptions people make about the opposite sex. What do you believe accounts for the differences in the way men and women listen?

5. **Cell Phone Annoyances.** Some researchers have argued that listening to the cell phone conversations of others is particularly annoying because you can hear only one side of the conversation; cell phone conversations were rated as significantly more intrusive than two people talking face-to-face (Monk, Fellas, & Ley, 2004). Do you find the cell phone conversations of people near you on a bus or in a store annoying, perhaps for the reason given here? For other reasons?

LogOn! MyCommunicationLab

Visit MCL and take a look at the self-test [When] Is Lying Unethical? and the exercises Passing Information from One Person to Another, Listening Like a Man and a Woman, Reducing Listening Barriers, Practicing Active Listening, and Listening. Also listen to Taking Lessons from a Guru of Listening and participate in the simulation How Good Is Your Memory for Stories.

While you're online visit The International Listening Association, a professional association of people interested in the study and teaching of effective listening (www.listen.org) and check out the Listening Resources. What can you add to the discussion presented in this unit?

REFERENCES

Alessandra, T. (1986). *How to listen effectively, speaking of success* (Video Tape Series). San Diego, CA: Levitz Sommer Productions.

Al-Simadi, F. A. (2000). Detection of deception behavior: A cross-cultural test. *Social Behavior & Personality, 28,* 455–461.

Barker, L. L., & Gaut, D. (2002). *Communication* (8th ed.). Boston: Allyn & Bacon.

Barrett, L., & Godfrey, T. (1988). Listening. *Person-Centered Review, 3* (November), 410–425.

Bellafiore, D. (2005). *Interpersonal conflict and effective communication.* Retrieved May 7, 2006, from http://www.drbalternatives.com/articles/cc2.html.

Bond, C. F., Jr., & Atoum, A. O. (2000). International deception. *Personality & Social Psychology Bulletin, 26* (March), 385–395.

Brownell, J. (1987). Listening: The toughest management skill. *Cornell Hotel and Restaurant Administration Quarterly, 27,* 64–71.

Brownell, J. (2006). *Listening: Attitudes, principles, and skills* (3rd ed.). Boston: Allyn & Bacon.

Burgoon, J. K., & Bacue, A. E. (2003). Nonverbal communication skills. In J. O. Greene & B. R. Burleson (Eds.), *Handbook of communication and social interaction skills* (pp. 179–220). Mahwah, NJ: Lawrence Erlbaum.

Castleberry, S. B., & Shepherd, D. D. (1993). Effective interpersonal listening and personal selling. *Journal of Personal Selling and Sales Management, 13,* 35–49.

Comer, L. B., & Drollinger, T. (1999). Active emphatic listening and selling success: A conceptual framework. *Journal of Personal Selling and Sales Management, 19,* 15–29.

Emmert P. (1994). A definition of listening. *Listening Post, 51,* 6.

Exline, R. V., Ellyson, S. L., & Long, B. (1975). Visual behavior as an aspect of power role relationships. In P. Pliner, L. Krames, & T. Alloway (Eds.), *Nonverbal communication of aggression.* New York: Plenum Press.

Glucksberg, S., & Danks, J. H. (1975). *Experimental psycholinguistics: An introduction.* Hillsdale, NJ: Erlbaum.

Goldsmith, D. J., & Fulfs, P. A. (1999). "You just don't have the evidence": An analysis of claims and evidence. In M. E. Roloff (Ed.), *Communication yearbook, 22* (pp. 1–49). Thousand Oaks, CA: Sage.

Gordon, T. (1975). *P.E.T.: Parent effectiveness training.* New York: New American Library.

Hayakawa, S. I., & Hayakawa, A. R. (1990). *Language in thought and action* (5th ed.). New York: Harcourt Brace Jovanovich.

Johnson, S. D., & Bechler, C. (1998). Examining the relationships between listening effectiveness and leadership emergence: Perceptions, behaviors, and recall. *Small Group Research, 29* (August), 452–471.

Knapp, M. L., & Hall, J. (1997). *Nonverbal behavior in human interaction* (4th ed.). New York: Holt, Rinehart & Winston.

Kramer, R. (1997). Leading by listening: An empirical test of Carl Rogers's theory of human relationship using interpersonal assessments of leaders by followers. *Dissertation Abstracts International: Section A. Humanities and Social Sciences, 58* (August), 0514.

Lauer, C. S. (2003). Listen to this. *Modern Healthcare, 33* (February 10), 34.

Levine, M. (2004, June 1). Tell the doctor all your problems, but keep it to less than a minute. *New York Times,* F6.

Monk, A., Fellas, E., & Ley, E. (2004). Hearing only one side of normal and mobile phone conversations. *Behaviour & Information Technology 23* (September/October), 301–306.

O'Hair, D., Cody, M. J., Goss, B., & Krayer, K. J. (1988). The effect of gender, deceit orientation and communicator style on macro-assessments of honesty. *Communication Quarterly, 36,* 77–93.

Rogers, C. (1970). *Carl Rogers on encounter groups.* New York: Harrow Books.

Rogers, C., & Farson, R. (1981). Active listening. In J. A. DeVito (Ed.), *Communication: Concepts and processes* (3rd ed., pp. 137–147). Englewood Cliffs, NJ: Prentice-Hall.

Smith, D. (2003, December 2). Doctors cultivate a skill: Listening. *New York Times,* p. 6.

Snyder, M. (1992). A gender-informed model of couple and family therapy: Relationship enhancement therapy. *Contemporary Family Therapy: An International Journal, 14* (February), 15–31.

Steil, L. K., Barker, L. L., & Watson, K. W. (1983). *Effective listening: Key to your success.* Reading, MA: Addison-Wesley.

Stein, M. M., & Bowen, M. (2003). Building a customer satisfaction system: Effective listening when the customer speaks. *Journal of Organizational Excellence, 22* (Summer), 23–34.

Tannen, D. (1990). *You just don't understand: Women and men in conversation.* New York: Morrow.

Vrij, A., & Mann, S. (2001). Telling and detecting lies in a high-stake situation: The case of a convicted murderer. *Applied Cognitive Psychology, 15* (March–April), 187–203.

Witcher, S. K. (1999, August 9–15). Chief executives in Asia find listening difficult. *Asian Wall Street Journal Weekly, 21,* p. 11.

Chapter 11

Small Group Communication

Small Group Communication

MAJOR TOPICS

Small Groups
Idea-Generation Groups
Personal Growth Groups
Information-Sharing Groups
Problem-Solving Groups

Special Features

Team Problems: Carole A. Barbato

How Powerful Are You?

The Third-Person Effect

Telling Secrets

Understanding Group Power

Understanding Group Polarization

Skills Combating Idea Killers

Skills Listening to New Ideas

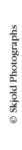

© Skjold Photographs

A great deal of your social and professional life will revolve around your participation in groups—groups for developing ideas, increasing self-awareness, learning, and solving problems. Understanding the nature and functions of small groups and learning to use these groups effectively and efficiently will help you throughout your social and professional career.

In this unit, you'll learn about:
- the nature and types of small groups.
- the stages and formats of small groups.
- the structure and functions of idea-generation, personal growth, information-sharing, and problem-solving groups.

You'll learn to:
- use small groups to achieve a variety of personal, social, and professional goals.
- participate effectively in a variety of small groups.

SMALL GROUPS

A **group** is (1) a collection of individuals who (2) are connected to one another by some common purpose, (3) are interdependent, (4) have some degree of organization among them, and (5) see themselves as a group. For small groups in particular, each of these characteristics needs to be explained a bit further.

- *Collection of Individuals.* A **small group** is, first, a collection of individuals few enough in number so that all members may communicate with relative ease as both senders and receivers. Generally, a small group consists of approximately 3 to 12 people. The important point to keep in mind is that each member should be able to function as both source and receiver with relative ease. If the group gets much larger than 12, this becomes difficult.

- *Common Purpose.* Second, the members of a group must be connected to one another through some common purpose. People on a bus normally do not constitute a group, because they're not working at some common purpose. But if the bus gets stuck in a ditch, the riders may quickly become a group and work together to get the bus back on the road. This does not mean that all members must have exactly the same purpose in being part of the group. But generally there must be some similarity in the individuals' reasons for interacting.

- *Interdependence.* Third, in a small group, members are interdependent, meaning that the behavior of one member is significant for and has an impact on all other members. When one member attacks or supports the ideas of another member, that behavior influences the other members and the group as a whole. When one member proposes a great idea, that behavior has an effect on all group members.

- *Organizing Rules.* Fourth, members of small groups must be connected by some organizing rules or structure. At times the structure is rigid—as in groups operating under parliamentary procedure, in which each comment must follow prescribed rules. At other times, as in a social gathering, the structure is very loose. Yet in both instances there's some organization and some structure: Two people don't speak at the same time, comments or questions by one member are responded to by others rather than ignored, and so on.

- *Self-Perception as a Group.* Fifth, members of small groups feel they are, in fact, members of this larger whole. This doesn't mean that individuality is ignored or that members do not see themselves as individuals; it simply means that each member thinks, feels, and acts as a part of the group. The more members see themselves as part of the group, the greater the group cohesion (or sense of "groupness"); the more they see themselves as individuals, separate from the group, the less the group cohesion. Members in high-cohesive groups are usually more satisfied and more productive than members of low-cohesive groups.

Basic Types of Groups

A good way to begin the study of small group communication is to look at the various types of groups in which we all participate: relationship and task groups and reference and membership groups.

Relationship and Task Groups

You can look at groups as serving two broad and overlapping purposes: social or relationship purposes on the one hand and work or task purposes on the other. Social or relationship groups are what sociologists call **primary groups**. These are the groups in which you participate early in life and include, for example, your immediate family, your group of friends at school, and perhaps your neighbors. Usually these groups serve your relationship needs for affiliation, affirmation, and affection. Some of these groups, like family, are extremely long lasting; some, like friends at college, may last only a year or two. It is largely through participating in primary groups and through your strong identification with other group members that you develop your self-concept.

Task groups, which sociologists call **secondary groups**, are groups formed to accomplish something. Some task groups are put together to solve a specific problem; for example, a committee of college professors might be formed to hire a new faculty member, select a textbook, or serve on a graduate student's dissertation committee. Once the specific task is accomplished, the group is dissolved. Other task groups have more long-range concerns; for example, a committee to oversee diversity in the workplace, to monitor fairness in advertising, or to rate feature films may be an ongoing, permanent group.

Unlike relationship groups, which are informal and in which the reward of participation consists simply of being together, task groups are more formal, and the reward of participation comes from accomplishing the specific task. Another interesting difference between relationship and task groups is that in relationship groups each member is irreplaceable and unique. In task groups, in contrast, each member plays a role but can be replaced by a similarly competent individual. For example, in a group formed to develop a core curriculum for undergraduates, the professor representing the sciences could easily be replaced by another science professor and the group would remain essentially the same.

Relationship and task functions often overlap. In fact, it would be difficult to find a group in which these two functions were not combined in some way at some times. The coworkers who bowl together or the two chemistry professors who begin dating are clear examples of how functions can overlap. Not surprisingly, when groups normally devoted to one function start serving another function, they often encounter difficulties. For example, the much-in-love couple who are effective at home may find their relationship under stress when they open a business together.

Reference and Membership Groups

A **reference group** is a group from which you derive your values and norms of behavior. It is a group you use as a standard and against which you compare yourself; in other words, you judge your successes and failures in comparison with the outcomes of other members of reference groups. Reference groups may be primary or secondary. For example, early in life you may compare yourself with and measure your successes against those of your siblings or cousins (primary groups); later you may look to classmates or coworkers (generally secondary groups) as reference groups.

A **membership group** is a group you participate in but do not use as a guide or to measure yourself. Reference and membership groups are often the same. For the most part you participate in the groups whose values you share, and, at the same time, you acquire the values of the groups in which you participate. In some cases, however, reference and membership groups may differ. For example, if you are a student in medical school, you are not yet a member of the "doctor group," but you certainly will have learned the group's norms and values. As such, you probably emulate doctors in your preparation to be an MD and would likely view the "doctor group" as your reference group.

Small Group Stages

The small group develops in much the same way that a conversation develops. As in conversation, there are five **small group stages**: (1) opening, (2) feedforward, (3) business, (4) feedback, and (5) closing.

A small group's *opening stage* is usually a getting-acquainted time in which members introduce themselves and engage in social small talk, or phatic communication. After this preliminary get-together, there's usually *a feedforward stage* in which members make some attempt to identify what needs to be done, who will do it, and so on. In formal business groups, the meeting agenda (which is a perfect example of feedforward) may be reviewed and the tasks of the group identified. In informal social groups, the feedforward may consist simply of introducing a topic of conversation or talking about what the group's members should do.

The *business stage* is the actual work on the tasks—the problem solving, the sharing of information, or whatever else the group needs to do. At the *feedback stage*, the group may reflect on what it has done and perhaps on what remains to be done. Some groups may even evaluate their performance at this stage. At the *closing stage*, the group members again return to their focus on individuals and will perhaps exchange closing comments—"Good seeing you again," and the like.

These stages are rarely distinct from one another. Rather, they blend into one another. For example, the opening stage is not completely finished before the feedforward begins. Rather, as the opening comments are completed, the group begins to introduce feedforward; as the feedforward begins to end, the business starts.

Small Group Formats

Small groups serve their functions in a variety of formats. Among the most popular **small group formats** for relatively formal functions are the round table, the panel, the symposium, and the symposium–forum (Figure 1).

The Round Table

In the **round table** format, group members arrange themselves in a circular or semicircular pattern. They share the information or solve the problem without any set pattern of who speaks when. Group interaction is informal, and members contribute as they see fit. A leader or moderator may be present; he or she may, for example, try to keep the discussion on the topic or encourage more reticent members to speak up.

The Panel

In the **panel**, group members are "experts" but participate informally and without any set pattern of who speaks when, as in a round table. The difference is that there's an audience whose members may interject comments or ask questions. Many talk shows, such as the Jerry Springer and Oprah Winfrey shows, use this format.

A variation is the two-panel format, with an expert panel and a lay panel. The lay panel discusses the topic but may turn to the expert panel members when in need of technical information, additional data, or direction.

The Symposium

In the **symposium**, each member delivers a prepared presentation much like a public speech. All speeches are addressed to different aspects of a single topic. A symposium leader introduces the speakers, provides transitions from one speaker to another, and may provide periodic summaries.

The Symposium–Forum

The symposium–forum consists of two parts: a symposium, with prepared speeches, and a **forum**, with questions from the audience and responses by the speakers. The leader introduces the speakers and moderates the question-and-answer session.

Small Groups Online

Small groups use a wide variety of channels. Often, of course, they take place face-to-face; this is the channel that probably comes to mind when you think of group interaction. But today much small group interaction also takes place online, where groups serve both relationship or social purposes on the one hand and business and professional purposes on the other. **Virtual groups** are groups that rarely meet face-to-face but instead carry on their work through computer-mediated communication (Roebuck, 2001; Kelly, 2006). As you know, more and more work groups are virtual groups; members may work in their offices that are separated geographically or they may work from home.

The advantages of such virtual teams, of course, is that the members may communicate with one another without the expenses of traveling or of establishing office space for meetings. Another advantage is that members may be drawn from an ever-widening pool of competent workers spanning the entire globe. Members from India, Germany, and the United States can communicate in virtual groups just as easily as can members from New York, Connecticut, and New Jersey. An organization need not restrict its membership to those who live close by.

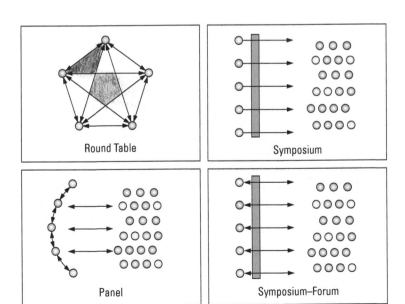

FIGURE 1 Small Group Formats

These four formats are general patterns that may describe a wide variety of groups. Within each type there will naturally be considerable variation. For example, in the symposium–forum there's no set pattern for how much time will be spent on the symposium part and how much time will be spent on the forum part. Similarly, combinations may be used. Thus, for example, group members may each present a position paper (basically a symposium) and then participate in a round table discussion.

As technology becomes more sophisticated and less expensive, virtual teams will become even more prevalent and more productive.

Of course, there are also disadvantages. Members may not feel as connected to the organization when they're not "at the office," and much of the interpersonal interaction that is so vital to many undertaking may be missing.

Two major types of online groups may be noted here: the mailing list group and the chat group. In conjunction with the following discussions, take a look at the "Credo for Free and Responsible Use of Electronic Communication Networks" at www .natcom.org. It's one attempt by a national communication association to articulate some of the ethical issues in electronic group communication.

Mailing List Groups

Mailing list groups are groups of people interested in particular topics who communicate with one another through e-mail. Generally, you subscribe to a list and communicate with all other members by addressing your mail to the group e-mail address. Any message you send to this address will be sent to all members who subscribe to the list at the same time; there are no asides to the person sitting next to you (as in face-to-face groups). Several websites provide extensive lists of listservs or mailing group lists; for example, L-Soft at www.isolft.com/lists/ listref.html and Cool List at www.coollist.com. A list of frequently asked questions and mailing list addresses can be found at www.intuitive.com/social-faq.html. Of course you could also go to one of the search engines and search for mailing lists.

Communication through mailing lists does not take place in real time. It's like regular e-mail; you may send your message today, but it may not be read until next week and you may not get an answer for another week. Much of the spontaneity created by real-time communication is lost. For example, you may be very enthusiastic about a topic when you send your e-mail but may practically forget about it by the time someone responds.

Chat Groups

Chat groups have proliferated across the Internet. These groups enable members to communicate with one another in real time and are now extremely popular. Social networking websites such as MySpace (www.myspace.com) and Facebook (www.facebook .com) are especially popular among college students.

Unlike mailing lists, chat groups let communication take place in real time; you see and in many cases hear a member's message as it's being sent, with virtually no delay. As in mailing lists and face-to-face conversation, the purposes of chat groups vary from communication that simply maintains connection with others (what many would call "idle chatter" or phatic communication) to extremely significant interchanges of ideas.

Communication in a chat group resembles the conversation you would observe at a large party. The total number of guests divide up into small groups varying from two on up, and members of each subgroup discuss their own topic or their own aspect of a general topic. For example, in a group about food, 10 people may be discussing food calories, 8 people may be discussing restaurant food preparation, and 2 people may be discussing the basic food groups, all on this one channel. So although you may be communicating in one primary group (say, dealing with restaurant food), you also have your eye trained to pick up something particularly interesting in another group, much as you do at a party. Like mailing lists, chat groups have the great advantage that they enable you to communicate with people you would never meet or interact with otherwise. Because such groups are international, they provide excellent exposure to other cultures, other ideas, and other ways of communicating.

Small Group Culture

Small groups, especially those of long standing, develop their own culture. Especially relevant to understanding this cultural dimension of small groups are the group norms and the high or low context with which the group operates. Let's look at each in turn.

Small Group Norms

In much the same way as a society establishes norms—rules for acceptable and unacceptable social behavior concerning everything from cell phone etiquette to child discipline or relationship fidelity—small groups establish group norms. **Group norms** are rules or standards of behavior identifying which behaviors are considered appropriate (for example, being willing to take on added tasks or directing conflict toward issues rather than toward people) and which are considered inappropriate (for example, coming in late or not contributing actively). Sometimes these rules for appropriate behavior are *explicit*; they're clearly stated in a company contract or policy, such as "All members must attend department meetings." Sometimes the rules are *implicit*: "Members should be well groomed." Regardless of whether norms are spelled out or not, they're powerful regulators of members' behaviors.

Small group norms may apply to individual members as well as to the group as a whole and, of course, will differ from one society to another (Axtell, 1993). For example, in the United States men and women in business are expected to interact when making business decisions as well as when socializing. In Muslim and Buddhist societies, however, religious restrictions

GROUP NORMS

Your manager wastes the first twenty minutes of just about every meeting at work with talk of his weekend or his personal life. You could really put this time to much better use.

WHAT DO YOU SAY?
To whom? Through what channel?

© Walter Hodgers/Getty Images

prevent mixed-gender groups. In groups in some societies, including those of the United States, Bangladesh, Australia, Germany, Finland, and Hong Kong, punctuality for business meetings is very important. But in Morocco, Italy, Brazil, Zambia, Ireland, and Panama, time is less highly regarded; being late is no great insult and is even expected. In the United States and in much of Asia and Europe, meetings are typically held between two parties at a time. In many Persian Gulf states, however, the business executive is likely to conduct meetings with several different people—sometimes dealing with totally different issues—at the same time. In this situation you have to expect to share what in the United States would be "your time" with these other parties. In the United States very little interpersonal touching goes on during business meetings; in Arab countries, however, touching (for example, hand holding) is common and is a gesture of friendship.

Norms that regulate a particular group member's behavior, called **role** expectations, identify what each person in an organization is expected to do; for example, Pat is great at formatting and editing and so should play the role of secretary.

You're more likely to accept the norms of your group's culture when you feel your group membership is important and want to continue your membership in the group. You're also more likely to accept these norms when your group is cohesive. **Cohesiveness** means that you and the other members are closely connected, are attracted to one another, and depend on one another to meet your needs. Lastly, you're more apt to accept these norms if you'd be punished by negative reactions or exclusion from the group for violating them (Napier & Gershenfeld, 1992).

High- and Low-Context Cultures

A cultural distinction has special relevance to small group communication (and to public speaking) the distinction between high- and low-context cultures. A high-context culture, you'll recall, is a culture in which much of the information in communication is in the context or in the person rather than explicitly coded in the verbal messages. In a high-context culture people have lots of information in common, so it does not have to be made explicit. A low-context culture, on the other hand, is a culture in which most of the information in communication is explicitly stated in the verbal messages. In a low-context culture people do not assume they share certain information and so make all crucial details explicit.

As you might expect, group members in high-context cultures spend a lot of time getting to know one another before engaging in any important transactions. Because of this prior personal knowledge, a great deal of information is shared and therefore does not have to be explicitly stated in the group's deliberations. Members of low-context cultures, on the other hand, spend less time getting to know one another and therefore do not have that shared knowledge. As a result everything has to be stated explicitly during the group's discussions. When this simple difference is not taken into account, misunderstandings can easily result. For example, the directness and explicitness characteristic of the low-context culture may prove insulting, insensitive, or unnecessary to members of a high-context culture. Conversely, to members of a low-context culture, someone from a high-context culture may appear vague, underhanded, even dishonest in his or her reluctance to be explicit or to engage in communication that a low-context culture would consider open and direct.

Members of high-context cultures also are reluctant to question the judgments of their superiors. So, for example, if a group leader or manager in a high-context culture proposes something that is obviously in error, group members may be reluctant to express disagreement or to correct the error (Gross, Turner, & Cederholm, 1987).

Power in the Small Group

Power permeates all small groups and all relationships. It influences what you do, when, and with whom. It influences the employment you seek and the employment you get. It influences the friends you choose and don't choose and those who choose you and those who don't. It influences your romantic and family relationships—their success, failure, and level of satisfaction or dissatisfaction.

Power is what enables one person (the one with power) to control the behaviors of others. Thus, if A has power over B and C, then A, by virtue of this power and through the exercise of this power

(or the threat of exercising it), can control the behaviors of B and C. Differences in individuals' amounts and types of power influence who makes important decisions, who will prevail in an argument, and who will control the finances.

Although all relationships involve power, they differ in the types of power that the people use and to which they respond. The self-test will help you identify the six major types of power.

The six types of power covered in the self-test are (1) legitimate, (2) referent, (3) reward, (4) coercive, (5) expert, and (6) information or persuasion power (French & Raven, 1968; Raven, Centers, & Rodrigues, 1975). You have **legitimate power** (self-test statement 1) over another person when this person believes you have a right by virtue of your position (for example, you're the appointed group leader) to influence or control his or her behavior. Legitimate power usually comes from the leadership roles people occupy. Teachers are often seen to have legitimate power, and this is doubly true for religious teachers. Parents are seen as having legitimate power over their children. Employers, judges, managers, doctors, and police officers are others who may hold legitimate power.

REFLECTIONS ON ETHICS

Telling Secrets

In groups of close friends, among family members, or in standing workplace committees, people often exchange secrets with the explicit or only implied assumption that these secrets will not be revealed to outsiders. Revealing or not revealing such secrets often has ethical implications.

In *Secrets* (1983) ethicist Sissela Bok identifies three types of situations in which she argues it would be *unethical* to reveal the secrets of another person. These conditions aren't always easy to identify in any given instance, but they do provide excellent starting points for asking whether or not it's ethical to reveal what we know about another person. And, of course, for any situation, there may be legitimate exceptions.

- It's unethical *to reveal information that you have promised to keep secret.*

- It's unethical *to say things about another person when you know the information to be false.*

- It's unethical *to invade the privacy to which everyone has a right*—to reveal information that no one else has a right to know.

In other situations, however, you may actually have *an obligation* to reveal a secret. For example, Bok (1983) argues that you have an obligation to reveal a secret when keeping the information hidden will do more harm than good. For example, if a teenager confided in you that he or she intended to commit suicide, you'd have an ethical obligation to say something.

Ethical Choice Point

How would you handle the following situations? (1) An instructor who supervises your study group confides that she is a confirmed racist and proud of it. (2) A 16-year-old member of the wilderness group you're leading confides that she's having unprotected sex with her supervisor at work, a married man. (3) A community religious leader confides that he's skimming a portion of the members' contributions to fund his retirement.

TEST YOURSELF

How Powerful Are You?

For each statement, indicate which of the following descriptions is most appropriate, using the following scale: 1 = true of 20 percent or fewer of the people I know; 2 = true of about 21 to 40 percent of the people I know; 3 = true of about 41 to 60 percent of the people I know; 4 = true of about 61 to 80 percent of the people I know; and 5 = true of 81 percent or more of the people I know.

_____ 1. My position is such that I often have to tell others what to do. For example, a mother's position demands that she tell her children what to do, a manager's position demands that he or she tell employees what to do, and so on.

_____ 2. People wish to be like me or identified with me. For example, high school football players may admire the former professional football player who is now their coach and want to be like him.

_____ 3. People see me as having the ability to give them what they want. For example, employers have the ability to give their employees increased pay, longer vacations, or improved working conditions.

_____ 4. People see me as having the ability to administer punishment or to withhold things they want. For example, employers have the ability to reduce voluntary overtime, shorten vacation time, or fail to improve working conditions.

_____ 5. Other people realize that I have expertise in certain areas of knowledge. For example, a doctor has expertise in medicine and so others turn to the doctor to tell them what to do. Someone knowledgeable about computers similarly possesses expertise.

_____ 6. Other people realize that I possess the communication ability to present an argument logically and persuasively.

HOW DID YOU DO? These statements refer to the six major types of power, as described in the text following this self-test. Low scores (1s and 2s) indicate your belief that you possess little of these particular types of power, and high scores (4s and 5s) indicate your belief that you possess a great deal of these particular types of power.

WHAT WILL YOU DO? How satisfied are you with your level of power? If you're not satisfied, what might you do about it? A good starting place, of course, is to learn the skills of communication—interpersonal, small group, and public speaking—discussed in this text. Consider the kinds of communication patterns that would help you communicate power and exert influence in group situations.

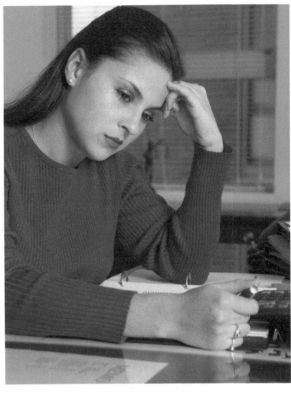

© David Young-Wolff/PhotoEdit

GROUP PRESSURE

Everyone at your new job pads their expense accounts. You don't want to go along with this but, if you don't, everyone else will be found out. You don't want to make waves and yet you don't want to do something unethical.

WHAT DO YOU SAY?
To whom? Through what channel?

You have **referent power** (statement 2) over another person when that person wishes to be like you or identified with you. For example, an older brother may have referent power over a younger brother because the younger sibling wants to be like his older brother. Your referent power over another person increases when you're well liked and well respected, when you're seen as attractive and prestigious, when you're of the same gender, and when you have attitudes and experiences similar to those of the other person. This is why role models are so important: By definition, role models (sports figures are probably the best examples) possess referent power and exert great influence on those looking up to them.

You have **reward power** (statement 3) over a person if you have the ability to give that person rewards—either material (money, promotions, jewelry) or social (love, friendship, respect). Reward power increases attractiveness; we like those who have the power to reward us and who do in fact give us rewards.

UNDERSTANDING

Theory and Research   Group Power

High-power-distance cultures are those in which power is concentrated in the hands of a few and there's a great difference between the power held by these people and the power held by the ordinary citizen; in contrast, in low-power-distance cultures power is more evenly distributed throughout the citizenry (Hofstede, 1997). Groups also may be viewed in terms of high and low power distance. In high-power-distance groups, the leader is far more powerful than the members. In low-power-distance groups, leaders and members differ much less in their power.

Of the groups in which you'll participate—as a member or as a leader—some will be high in power distance and others will be low. The skill is to recognize which is which, to follow the rules generally, and to break the rules only after you've thought through the consequences. For example, in low-power-distance groups, you're expected to confront a group leader (or friend or supervisor) assertively; acting assertively denotes a general feeling of equality (Borden, 1991). In high-power-distance groups, direct confrontation and assertiveness toward the leader (or toward any person in authority, such as a teacher or doctor) may be viewed negatively (Westwood, Tang, & Kirkbride, 1992; also see Bochner & Hesketh, 1994).

Working with Theories and Research

Visit one of the online databases to which you have access—for example, Research Navigator at www.researchnavigator.com—*and search the communication and sociology databases for "power." What types of questions engage the attention of researchers?*

Conversely, you have **coercive power** (statement 4) if you have the ability to remove rewards or to administer **punishments**. Usually, the two kinds of power go hand in hand; if you have reward power, you also have coercive power. For example, parents may grant as well as deny privileges to their children.

You possess **expert power** (statement 5) if group members regard you as having expertise or knowledge—whether or not you truly possess such expertise. Expert power increases when you are seen as being unbiased and having nothing to gain personally from influencing others. It decreases if you are seen as biased and as having something to gain from securing the compliance of others.

You have **information power**, or persuasion power (statement 6), if you're seen as someone who can communicate logically and persuasively. Generally, persuasion power is attributed to people who are seen as having significant information and the ability to use that information in presenting a well-reasoned argument.

Now that the general nature of the small group is clear, let's look at several of the more important types of small groups you'll encounter: idea-generation groups, personal growth groups, information-sharing groups, and problem-solving groups.

IDEA-GENERATION GROUPS

Idea-generation groups are small groups that exist solely to generate ideas and often follow a formula called brainstorming (Osborn, 1957; Beebe & Masterson, 2006; DeVito, 1996). **Brainstorming** is a technique for bombarding a problem and generating as many ideas as possible. This technique involves two stages. The first is the brainstorming period proper; the second is the evaluation period.

The procedures are simple. A problem is selected that is amenable to many possible solutions or ideas. Group members are informed of the problem to be brainstormed before the actual session so that they can think about the topic. When the group meets, each person contributes as many ideas as he or she can think of. All ideas are recorded either in writing or on tape. During this idea-generating session, four general rules are followed.

- *Brainstorm Rule 1: Don't Criticize.* In a brainstorming session all ideas are recorded. They're not evaluated, nor are they even discussed. Any negative criticism—whether verbal or nonverbal—is itself criticized by the leader or the members. This is a good general rule to follow in all creative thinking: Allow your idea time to develop before you look for problems with it. At the same time, don't praise the ideas either. All evaluations should be suspended during the brainstorming session.

■ *Brainstorm Rule 2: Strive for Quantity.* Linus Pauling, Nobel Prize winner for chemistry in 1954 and for peace in 1962, once said, "The best way to have a good idea is to have lots of ideas." This second rule of brainstorming embodies this concept. If you need an idea, you're more likely to find it in a group of many than in a group of few. Thus, in brainstorming, the more ideas the better.

■ *Brainstorm Rule 3: Combine and Extend Ideas.* Although you may not criticize a particular idea, you're encouraged to extend it or combine it in some way. The value of a particular idea may be the way it stimulates someone to combine or extend it. Even if your modification seems minor or obvious, say it. Don't censor yourself.

■ *Brainstorm Rule 4: Develop the Wildest Ideas Possible.* The wilder the idea, the better. It's easier to tone an idea down than to build it up. A wild idea can easily be tempered, but it's not so easy to elaborate on a simple or conservative idea.

Sometimes a brainstorming session may break down, with members failing to contribute new ideas. At this point the moderator may prod the members with statements such as the following:

■ Let's try to get a few more ideas before we close this session.

■ Can we piggyback any other ideas or add extensions on the suggestion to ...

■ Here's what we have so far. As I read the list of contributed suggestions, additional ideas may come to mind.

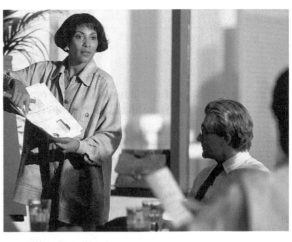

© Dan Bosler/Getty Images

BRAINSTORMING

You're in charge of a brainstorming group to generate ideas for improving the company website. On the basis of past experiences, you anticipate that a few of the members will just sit there, afraid to offer any suggestions. You need to combat this.

WHAT DO YOU SAY?
To whom?

■ Here's an aspect we haven't focused on. Does this stimulate any ideas?

After all the ideas are generated—a period lasting no longer than 15 or 20 minutes—the group evaluates the entire list of ideas, using the critical thinking skills developed throughout this text. The ideas that are unworkable are thrown out; those that show promise are retained and evaluated. During this stage negative criticism is allowed.

Building Communication Skills   Combating Idea Killers

Think about how you can be on guard against negative criticism and how you can respond to "idea killers" or "killer messages." Some expressions, such as those listed below, aim to stop an idea from being developed—to kill it in its tracks before it can even get off the ground. As you read down the list of these commonly heard killer messages, formulate at least one response you might give if someone used one of these on you or if you yourself used it to censor your own creative thinking.

1. It'll never work.
2. No one would vote for it.
3. It's too complex.
4. It's too simple.
5. It would take too long.

6. It's too expensive.
7. It's not logical.
8. What we have is good enough.
9. It just doesn't fit us.
10. It's impossible.

Creativity needs a great deal of freedom to develop; try not to stifle it by allowing ideas to be put down before you have a chance to examine them carefully.

Building Communication Skills Listening to New Ideas

A useful skill for listening to new ideas is PIP'N, a technique that derives from Carl Rogers's (1970) emphasis on paraphrasing as a means for ensuring understanding and Edward deBono's (1976) PMI (*plus*, *minus*, and *interesting*) technique. PIP'N involves four steps:

P = Paraphrase. State in your own words what you think the other person is saying. This will ensure that you and the person proposing the idea are talking about the same thing. Your paraphrase also will provide the other person with the opportunity to elaborate or clarify his or her ideas.

I = Interesting. State something interesting that you find in the idea. Say why you think this idea might be interesting to you, to others, to the organization.

P = Positive. Say something positive about the idea. What is good about it? How might it solve a problem or make a situation better?

N = Negative. State any negatives that you think the idea might entail. Might it prove expensive? Difficult to implement? Is it directed at insignificant issues?

Try using PIP'N the next time you hear about a new idea; say, in conversation or in a small group. For practice, try PIP'N on the PIP'N technique itself: (1) Paraphrase the PIP'N technique; (2) say why the technique is interesting; (3) say something positive about it; and (4) say something negative about it.

It's often easier to analyze an idea when you follow specific steps; in this way there's less likelihood that you'll omit some crucial element in the process.

PERSONAL GROWTH GROUPS

Some **personal growth groups**, sometimes referred to as support groups, aim to help members cope with particular difficulties—such as drug addiction, not being assertive enough, having an alcoholic parent, being an ex-convict, or having a hyperactive child or a promiscuous spouse. Other groups are more clearly therapeutic and are designed to change significant aspects of an individual's personality or behavior. Still other groups are devoted to making healthy individuals function even more effectively.

Personal growth groups vary widely in the procedures they follow, so it's not possible to provide a standard pattern that all such groups follow (as is the case with brainstorming or with problem-solving groups, discussed later in this chapter). But let's look briefly at three well-known types of personal growth groups: the encounter group, the assertiveness training group, and the consciousness-raising group.

The Encounter Group

Encounter groups, also known as "sensitivity groups" or "T [Training]-groups," for example, constitute a form of psychotherapy; these groups try to facilitate members' personal growth and foster their ability to deal effectively with other people (Rogers, 1970; Hirsch, Kett, & Trefil, 2002). One of the encounter group's assumptions is that the members

will be more effective, both psychologically and interpersonally, if they get to know and like themselves better. Consequently, members are encouraged to look at themselves and their relationships honestly and in depth and to react to others in the group openly and honestly. Members are encouraged to express their inner thoughts, fears, and doubts in the encounter group, in which interactions are always characterized by total acceptance and support.

The Assertiveness Training Group

The **assertiveness training group** aims to increase the willingness of its members to stand up for their rights and to act more assertively in a wide variety of situations (Adler, 1977; Bishop, 2006). Distinctions are made between being assertive (which is good and effective); being nonassertive (which is ineffective, because your own wants and needs are unlikely to be met); and being aggressive (which also is ineffective, because it contributes to escalating the conflict and causing resentment). The group aims to increase the assertiveness skills of its members, who are likely to be people who feel they are not assertive enough.

The Consciousness-Raising Group

The **consciousness-raising group** aims to help people cope with the problems society confronts them with. The members of a consciousness-raising group

THE THIRD-PERSON EFFECT

The *third-person effect* concept is a theory of media influence claiming that people routinely believe they are influenced less by the media than their peers are. So, according to this theory, you tend to believe that your friends, neighbors, and coworkers are influenced more by the media than you are; you believe yourself to be the most resistant to media influence. A variety of studies conducted on college students have supported this idea (Davison, 1983). Whether the topic was political advertising, rap music, or pornography, students felt they were less susceptible to media influence than were their peers (Hoffner et al., 2001). This belief, research finds, is especially strong when the media message is a negative or socially unacceptable one; for example, people think that messages of violence, racism, or sexism influence them much less than their peers. The effect is weakened but still present when the message is a more acceptable one (for example, public service announcements).

Increasing Media Literacy

Visit one of the online databases to which you have access and search the communication and psychology databases for "third-person effect." What can you add to the brief discussion presented here? You also might wish to try testing out this theory. For example, survey 10 or 20 people and ask them how influenced they feel they are by, say, media violence or racism. Then ask them if their friends and relatives are influenced by such media messages more than they are. Then conduct the same type of two-step survey with a more socially acceptable message, such as a media campaign on the value of education or the importance of proper diet. On the basis of your research, what can you add to this discussion?

all have one characteristic in common (for example, they may all be women, unwed mothers, gay fathers, or recently unemployed executives). It's this commonality that leads the members to join together and help one another. In the consciousness-raising group the assumption is that similar people are best equipped to assist one another's personal growth. The procedures generally followed are simple: A topic is selected, and each member speaks on the topic as it relates to the general group topic. For example, if the group consists of unwed mothers, then whatever the topic (taxes, children, school, prejudice), the members address it in the context of the group's focus on unwed motherhood. No interruptions are allowed. After each member has finished, the other group members may ask questions of clarification. The feedback from other members is to be totally supportive. After the last member has spoken, a general discussion follows. This procedure is designed to help raise members' consciousness by giving them an opportunity to formulate and verbalize their thoughts on a particular topic, hear how others feel and think about the same topic, and formulate and answer questions of clarification.

INFORMATION-SHARING GROUPS

The purpose of **information-sharing groups** is to enable members to acquire new information or skills through a sharing of knowledge. In most information-sharing groups, all members have something to teach and something to learn. In some, however, the interaction takes place because some members have information and some don't.

Educational or Learning Groups

In *educational or learning groups*, the members pool their knowledge to the benefit of all, as in the popular law and medical student learning groups. Members may follow a variety of discussion patterns. For example, a historical topic might be developed chronologically, with the discussion progressing from the past into the present and perhaps predicting the future. Issues in developmental psychology, such as physical maturity or language development in the child, also might be discussed chronologically. Some topics lend themselves to spatial development. For example, study of the development of the United States might take either a spatial pattern, going from east to west, or a chronological pattern, going from 1776 to the present. Other suitable patterns, depending on the nature of the topic and the needs of the discussants, might be developed in terms of causes and effects, problems and solutions, or structures and functions.

Perhaps the most popular is the topical pattern. A group might discuss the challenges of raising a hyperactive child by itemizing and discussing each of the major problems. The structure of a corporation might also be considered in terms of its major divisions. As can be appreciated, topical approaches may be further systematized; for instance, a learning group might rank the problems of hyperactivity in

THE RESEARCHER

Team Problems

My professor placed us in teams to work on a project for the whole semester. Our group is having problems with several members' dominating the team, especially when we need to make a "team decision." These people just assume we all accept their decisions because we don't say anything different. We want to say something, but if we are going to work with them all semester, we don't want to get them mad at us or hurt their feelings. What can we do to survive this team experience and still get our voices heard?

Teams and small groups all have their own personalities. Your team is made up of individuals! It is common for some members to dominate or talk all the time—perhaps even to argue for arguing's sake. You can use idea-generating techniques to enable all members to have a voice in the decisions being made by your team. Your team needs to try out the nominal group technique described in this unit. It enables all members to participate by writing and presenting their ideas one at a time in a round-robin fashion. The technique even has a rank-ordering procedure to let the team members understand how important each suggestion was to the majority of its members. Try it! I think it will work for your team. Sometimes talking can be hazardous to a team's health. The technique will enable all members to participate whether they like to talk or not. It also takes the personality out of decision suggestions.

For further information: Moore, C. M. (1994). *Group techniques for idea building* (2nd ed.). Thousand Oaks, CA: Sage. Also Gorden, W. I., Nagel, E. L., Myers, S. A., and Barbato, C. A. (1996). *The team trainer: Winning tools and tactics for successful workouts*. Chicago, IL: Irwin.

Carole A. Barbato (Ph.D., Kent State University) is a professor of communication studies and graduate faculty member at Kent State. She teaches classes in public speaking and in small group and interpersonal communication. Her research interests include small group communication, communication motives, and communication and aging. Carole (cbarbato@kent.edu) has provided team training to numerous organizations and small businesses.

terms of their importance or complexity or might order the major structures of the corporation in terms of decision-making power.

Focus Groups

A different type of learning group is the **focus group**, a small group assembled for a kind of in-depth interview. The aim here is to discover what people think about an issue or product; for example, what do men between 18 and 25 think of the new aftershave lotion and its packaging? What do young executives earning more than $100,000 think about buying a foreign luxury car?

In the focus group, a leader tries to discover the beliefs, attitudes, thoughts, and feelings that members have so as to help an organization make decisions on changing the scent or redesigning the packaging or constructing advertisements for luxury cars. It is the leader's task to prod members to analyze their thoughts and feelings on a deeper level

and to use the thoughts of one member to stimulate the thoughts of others.

Generally, approximately 12 people are assembled. The leader explains the process, the time limits, and the general goal of the group—let's say, for example, to discover why these 12 individuals requested information on the XYZ health plan but purchased a plan from another company. The idea, of course, is that these 12 people are representing a wider population. The leader, who is usually a professional focus group facilitator rather than a member of the client organization itself, asks a variety of questions such as: How did you hear about the XYZ health plan? What other health plans did you consider before making your actual purchase? What influenced you to buy the plan you eventually bought? Were any other people influential in helping you make your decision? Through the exploration of these and similar questions, the facilitator and the relevant members of the client organization (who may be seated behind a one-way mirror, watching the discussion) may put together a more effective health plan or more effective advertising strategies.

PROBLEM-SOLVING GROUPS

A **problem-solving group** is a collection of individuals who meet to solve a problem or to reach a decision. In one sense this is the most exacting kind of group to participate in. It requires not only a knowledge of small group communication techniques, but also a thorough knowledge of the particular problem. And it usually demands faithful adherence to a somewhat rigid set of rules. We'll look at this group first in terms of the classic and still popular problem-solving approach, whereby we identify the steps to go through in solving a problem. In the context of this sequence, we'll consider the major decision-making methods. Finally, we'll survey some types of groups that are popular in organizations today: the nominal group, the Delphi method, quality circles, and improvement groups.

The Problem-Solving Sequence

The approach developed by philosopher John Dewey (1910), the **problem-solving sequence**, is probably the technique used most often. The six steps of the sequence (see Figure 2 on next page) are designed to make problem solving more efficient and effective: (1) Define and analyze the problem, (2) establish criteria, (3) identify possible solutions, (4) evaluate solutions, (5) select the best solution(s), and (6) test the selected solution(s).

Define and Analyze the Problem

In many instances the nature of the problem is clearly specified. For example, a group of designers might discuss how to package a new soap product. In other instances, however, the problem may be vague, and it may remain for the group to define it in concrete terms. Thus, for example, the general problem may be that your company is losing money, and the solution that needs to be found is a way to make the company profitable. But such a broad and general topic is difficult to tackle in a single problem-solving discussion, so it may be helpful to specify the problem in more specific and limited terms. Perhaps this hypothetical problem will need to be dealt with in a series of problem-solving discussions on "How to reduce waste," "How to increase market visibility," and/or "How to attract bright college graduates to join the firm."

Define the problem as an open-ended question ("How can we improve the company website?") rather than as a statement ("The company website needs to be improved") or a yes/no question ("Does the website need improvement?"). The open-ended question allows greater freedom of exploration.

Appropriate questions for most problems revolve around the following issues:

- *Duration*: How long has the problem existed? Is it likely to continue in the future? What is the predicted course of the problem? For example, will it grow or lessen in impact?

- *Causes*: What are the major causes of the problem? How certain can we be that these are the actual causes?

- *Effects*: What are the effects of the problem? How significant are they? Who is affected by this problem? How significantly are they affected? Is this problem causing other problems? How important are these other problems?

Establish Criteria for Evaluating Solutions

Before any solutions are proposed, you need to decide how to evaluate them. At this stage you identify the standards or criteria that you'll use in evaluating solutions or in selecting one solution over another. Generally, two types of criteria need to be

CRITICAL THINKING

You're on a team charged with designing the packaging for a new shampoo and you want to use the six critical thinking hats technique to evaluate the proposed solutions.

WHAT DO YOU SAY (FOR EACH HAT)?

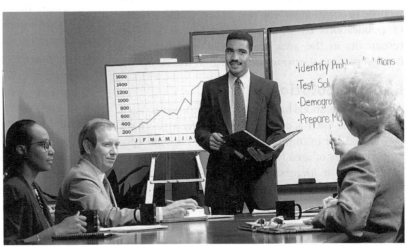

© David Young-Wolff/PhotoEdit

FIGURE 2 **Steps in Problem-Solving Discussion**

Although most small group theorists would advise you to follow the problem-solving pattern as presented here, others would alter it somewhat. For example, the pattern here advises you first to define the problem and then to establish criteria for identifying possible solutions. You would then keep these criteria in mind as you generated possible solutions (step 3). Another school of thought, however, would advise you to generate solutions first and to consider how they will be evaluated only after these solutions are proposed (Brilhart & Galanes, 1992). The advantage of this second approach is that you may generate more creative solutions if you're not restricted by standards of evaluation. The disadvantage is that you may spend a great deal of time generating impractical solutions that would never meet the standards you'll eventually propose.

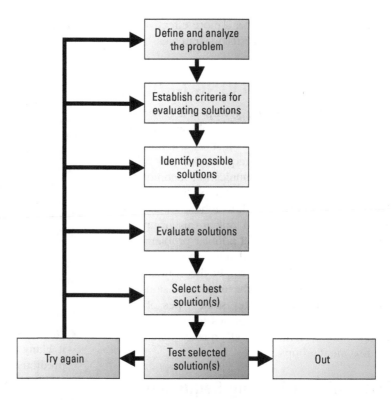

considered. First, there are the practical criteria. For example, you might decide that solutions to the website problem must not increase the budget, must lead to a higher volume of business, must be constructed in-house, must load almost immediately, and so on. Second, there are the value criteria. These are more difficult to identify. These might include, for example, requirements that the website reflect the culture of the company or that it represent the company's commitment to multiculturalism.

Identify Possible Solutions

At this stage identify as many solutions as possible. Focus on quantity rather than quality. Brainstorming may be particularly useful at this point (see the earlier discussion of idea-generation groups). Solutions to the website problem might include incorporating reviews of publications by company members, reviews of restaurants in the area, recruitment guidelines, and new employment opportunities within the company.

Evaluate Solutions

After all the solutions have been proposed, you go back and evaluate each according to the criteria you have established. For example, to what extent does incorporating reviews of area restaurants meet the evaluation criteria? Will it increase the budget? Each potential solution should be matched against the criteria.

An especially insightful technique for evaluating solutions (or gaining a different perspective on a problem) was offered by **critical thinking** pioneer

Edward deBono (1987). DeBono's **critical thinking hats technique** involves thinking with six different "hats" and, in doing so, subjecting an issue to a six-part analysis.

- The *fact hat* focuses attention on the data—the facts and figures that bear on the problem. For example: What are the relevant data on the website? How much does it cost to establish and maintain a website? How much advertising revenue can we get?

- The *feeling hat* focuses attention on your feelings, emotions, and intuitions concerning the problem. How do we feel about the website and about making major changes?

- The *negative argument hat* asks that you become the devil's advocate. Why might this proposed solution fail? What is the worst-case scenario?

- The *positive benefits hat* asks that you look at the upside. What opportunities will a new format open up? What benefits will this website provide for employees? What would be the best thing that could happen?

- The *creative new idea hat* focuses attention on new ways of looking at the problem and can be easily combined with the techniques of brainstorming discussed earlier in this unit. In what other ways can we look at this problem? How can the website provide a service to the community?

- The *control of thinking hat* helps you analyze what you have done and are doing. It asks that you reflect on your own thinking processes and synthesize the results of your thinking. Have we adequately defined the problem? Are we focusing too much on insignificant issues? Have we given enough attention to possible negative effects?

Select the Best Solution(s)

At this stage the best solution or solutions are selected and put into operation. For instance, in the company website example, if "reviews of area restaurants" and "listings of new positions" best met the evaluation criteria, the group might then incorporate these two new items in the redesign of the website.

Groups may use different decision-making methods in deciding, for example, which criteria to use or which solutions to accept. Generally, groups use one of three methods: decision by authority, majority rule, or consensus.

Decision by Authority. In decision by authority, members voice their feelings and opinions, but the leader, boss, or CEO makes the final decision. This is surely an efficient method; it gets things done quickly, and the amount of discussion can be limited as desired. Another advantage is that experienced and informed members (for example, those who have been with the company longest) will probably exert a greater influence on the final decision. The great disadvantage is that group members may not feel the need to contribute their insights and may become distanced from the power within the group or organization. Another disadvantage is that this method may lead members to tell the decision maker what they feel she or he wants to hear, a condition that can easily lead to groupthink.

Decision by Majority Rule. With this method the group members agree to abide by the majority decision and may vote on various issues as the group works toward solving its problem. Majority rule is efficient, as there's usually the option of calling for a vote when the majority is in agreement. One disadvantage of this method is that it can lead to factioning, in which various minorities align against the majority. The method may also lead to limiting discussion once a majority has agreed and a vote is called.

Decision by Consensus. In some situations *consensus* means unanimous agreement; for example, a criminal jury must reach a unanimous decision to convict or acquit a defendant. In most business groups, however, consensus means that members agree that they can live with the solution; they agree that they can do whatever the solution requires (Kelly, 1994). Consensus is especially important when the group wants each member to be satisfied with and committed to the decision and the decision-making process as a whole (DeStephen & Hirokawa, 1988; Beebe & Masterson, 2006). The consensus method obviously takes the longest, and it

---

Theory and Research   Group Polarization

UNDERSTANDING

Groups frequently make more extreme decisions than individuals—a tendency known as *group polarization* (Brauer, Judd, & Gliner, 1995; Friedkin, 1999; Bullock, et al., 2003). For example, a group will take greater risks if the individual members are already willing to take risks (a condition known as the "risky shift phenomenon"), or will become more cautious if the members are already cautious. What seems to happen is that as a group member you estimate how others in the group feel about risk taking. If you judge the group as one of high risk takers, you're likely to become more willing to take risks than you were before the group interaction. Similarly, if you judge the group members as cautious and as low risk takers, you'll become even more cautious than you were before the interaction. In other words—and not surprisingly—your own attitudes toward risk will be heavily influenced by the attitudes you think the group possesses, and you're likely to change your attitudes to more closely match those of the group.

Working with Theories and Research

Have you ever observed group polarization? What happened? What implications does this theory have for, say, gang members, professors joining a new faculty, or investment analysts?

can lead to a great deal of wasted time if members wish to prolong the discussion process needlessly or selfishly.

Test Selected Solution(s)

After solutions are put into operation, test their effectiveness. The group might, for example, poll employees about the website changes, examine the number of hits, or analyze the advertising revenue.

If the solutions you have adopted prove ineffective, you will need to go back to one of the previous stages and repeat part of the process. Often this takes the form of selecting other solutions to test. But it may also involve going further back—to, for example, a reanalysis of the problem, an identification of other solutions, or a restatement of evaluation criteria.

Problem-Solving Groups at Work

The problem-solving sequence discussed here is used widely in business in a variety of different types of groups. Let's examine three group approaches popular in business that rely largely on the problem-solving techniques just discussed: the nominal group technique, the Delphi method, and quality circles.

As you read these discussions, realize that the available technology will dictate some of the ways in which these groups operate. If all the members have is a chalkboard, then much will be recorded on the board. If all members have laptops connected to the company website, then much of the record keeping will go onto the website and at the same time into each laptop.

The Nominal Group Technique

The **nominal group** technique is a method of problem solving that uses limited discussion and confidential voting to obtain a group decision. It's especially helpful when some members may be reluctant to voice their opinions in a regular problem-solving group or when the issue is controversial or sensitive. With this technique, each member contributes equally and each contribution is treated equally. Another advantage of the nominal group process is that it can be accomplished in a relatively short period of time. The nominal group approach can be divided into seven steps (Kelly, 1994):

1. The problem is defined and clarified for all members.
2. Each member writes down (without discussion or consultation with others) his or her ideas on or possible solutions to the problem.

3. Each member—in sequence—states one idea from his or her list, which is recorded on a board or flip chart so everyone can see it. This process is repeated until all suggestions are stated and recorded. Duplicates are then eliminated. Group agreement is secured before overlapping ideas are combined.
4. Each suggestion is clarified (without debate). Ideally, each suggestion is given equal time.
5. Each member rank-orders the suggestions in writing.
6. The rankings of the members are combined to get a group ranking, which is then written on the board.
7. Clarification, discussion, and possible reordering may follow.
8. The highest-ranking solution may then be selected to be tested, or perhaps several high-ranking solutions may be put into operation.

The Delphi Method

In the **Delphi method** a group of "experts" is established, but there's no interaction among them; instead, they communicate by repeatedly responding to questionnaires (Tersine & Riggs, 1980; Kelly, 1994). The Delphi method is especially useful when you want to involve people who are geographically distant from one another, when you want all members to become part of the solution and to uphold it, or when you want to minimize the effects of dominant members or even of peer pressure. The method is best explained as a series of steps (Kelly, 1994):

1. The problem is defined (for example, "We need to improve intradepartmental communication"). What each member is expected to do is specified (for example, each member should contribute five ideas on this specific question).
2. Each member then anonymously contributes five ideas in writing. This step used to be completed through questionnaires sent through traditional mail but now is more frequently done through e-mail, which greatly increases the speed with which this entire process can be accomplished.
3. The ideas of all members are combined, written up, and distributed to all members.
4. Members then select the three or four best ideas from this composite list and submit these.
5. From these responses another list is produced and distributed to all members.
6. Members then select the one or two best ideas from the new list and submit these.

7. From these responses another list is produced and distributed to all members. The process may be repeated any number of times, but usually three rounds are sufficient for achieving a fair degree of agreement.

8. The "final" solutions are identified and are communicated to all members.

Quality Circles

A **quality circle** is a group of workers (usually about 6 to 12) whose task it is to investigate and make recommendations for improving the quality of some organizational function. The members are drawn from the workers whose area is being studied; for example, if the problem were how to improve advertising on the Internet, then the quality circle membership would be drawn from the advertising and technology departments. The basic assumption is that people who work on similar tasks will be better able to improve their departments or jobs by pooling their insights and working through problems they share.

Generally, the motivation for establishing quality circles is economic; the company's aim is to improve profitability. Another related goal is to improve worker morale: Because quality circles involve workers in decision making, workers may feel empowered and see themselves as more essential to the organization (Gorden & Nevins, 1993).

Quality circle members investigate problems using any method they feel might be helpful; for example, they may form face-to-face problem-solving groups or use nominal groups or Delphi methods. The group then reports its findings and its suggestions to those who can implement the proposals.

SUMMARY: SMALL GROUP COMMUNICATION

This unit introduced the nature of the small group and discussed four major types of groups and their functions.

1. A small group is a collection of individuals who are connected to one another by some common purpose, are interdependent, have some degree of organization among them, and see themselves as a group.

2. Relationship groups (primary groups) generally serve relationship needs for affiliation, affirmation, and affection and include family and friendship networks. Task groups (secondary groups) are formed to accomplish something, often work related, and may then be disbanded.

3. Reference groups are groups from which you derive your values and norms of behavior; membership groups are groups in which you participate but whose values you don't necessarily adopt.

4. Small groups make use of four major formats: the round table, the panel, the symposium, and the symposium–forum.

5. Online groups, such as mailing lists and chat groups, serve both relationship and professional purposes.

6. Most small groups develop norms or rules that operate much like cultural norms, identifying what is considered appropriate behavior for the group members.

7. Power operates in all groups. Six types of power may be identified: legitimate, referent, reward, coercive, expert, and information or persuasion.

8. The idea-generation or brainstorming group attempts to generate as many ideas as possible.

9. The personal growth group helps members to deal with personal problems and to function more effectively. Popular types of personal growth groups are the encounter group, the assertiveness training group, and the consciousness-raising group.

10. Information-sharing groups attempt to enable members to acquire new information or skill through a mutual sharing of knowledge or insight. In educational or learning groups, the members pool their knowledge to the benefit of all. The focus group aims to discover what people think about an issue or product through a kind of in-depth group interview.

11. The problem-solving group attempts to solve a particular problem, or at least to reach a decision that may cause the problem to solve itself.

12. The six steps in the problem-solving sequence are: Define and analyze the problem; establish criteria for evaluating solutions; identify possible solutions; evaluate solutions; select best solution(s); and test solution(s).

13. The six critical thinking hats technique is especially useful in analyzing problems and evaluating solutions. This technique consists of focusing on different aspects of the issue: facts, feelings, negative arguments, positive benefits, creative or new ways of viewing problems, and control of thinking processes.

14. Decision-making methods include decision by authority, decision by majority rule, and decision by consensus.

15. Small group approaches that are widely used in business today include the nominal group, the Delphi method, and quality circles.

KEY TERMS IN SMALL GROUP COMMUNICATION

assertiveness training group	encounter group	membership group	referent power
brainstorming	expert power	nominal group	reward power
chat groups	focus group	panel	role
coercive power	forum	personal growth groups	round table
cohesiveness	group	power	secondary groups
consciousness-raising group	group norms	primary groups	small group
critical thinking	idea-generation group	problem-solving group	small group formats
critical thinking hats technique	information power	problem-solving sequence	small group stages
Delphi method	information-sharing groups	punishment	symposium
	legitimate power	quality circle	virtual groups
	mailing list group	reference group	

THINKING CRITICALLY ABOUT SMALL GROUP COMMUNICATION

1. **Small Group Creativity.** Studies find that persons high in communication apprehension are generally less effective in idea-generation groups than those who are low in apprehension (Jablin, 1981; Comadena, 1984; Cragan & Wright, 1990). Why do you think this is so?

2. **Group Norms.** What norms govern your class in human communication? What norms govern your family? Your place of work? Do you have any difficulty with these norms?

3. **Chat Groups.** In research on chat groups, it was found that people were more likely to comment on a participant's message when that message was negative than when it was positive (Rollman, Krug, & Parente, 2000). Do you find this to be true? If so, why do you think this occurs?

4. **Developing Criteria.** What type of criteria would an advertising agency use in evaluating a campaign to sell soap? A university, in evaluating a new multicultural curriculum? Parents, in evaluating a preschool for their children?

5. **Uses and Gratifications.** One study identified seven gratifications you derive from online communication: being in a virtual community, seeking information, aesthetic experience, financial compensation, diversion, personal status, and maintaining relationships (Song, LaRose, Eastin, & Lin, 2004). How would you describe the gratifications you receive from online groups?

LOGON! MYCOMMUNICATIONLAB
WWW.MYCOMMUNICATIONLAB.COM

Visit MCL for a variety of video clips on small group communication and for a variety of exercises and study aids. Watch the video Team Project Conflict and analyze the conflict in terms of the principles discussed in this unit. Also, try the web activity Technology and Groups. Another website devoted to small group communication, maintained by the publisher of this book, provides a wealth of additional insights into why people join groups, types of groups, decision making, roles in groups, and mediated groups: www.abacon.com/commstudies/groups/group.html.

While you're online and in connection with brainstorming, take a look at the Creativity Web at http://members/optusnet.com.au/~charles57/creative/index2.html for a wealth of links to all aspects of creativity—quotations, affirmations, humor, discussions of the brain and the creative process, and more.

REFERENCES

Adler, R. B. (1977). *Confidence in communication: A guide to assertive and social skills.* New York: Holt, Rinehart & Winston.

Axtell, R. E. (1993). *Do's and taboos around the world* (3rd ed.). New York: Wiley.

Beebe, S. A., & Masterson, J. T. (2006). *Communicating in small groups: Principles and practices* (8th ed.). Boston: Allyn & Bacon.

Bishop, S. (2006). *Develop your assertiveness.* London: Kogan Page.

Bochner, S., & Hesketh, B. (1994). Power, distance, individualism/collectivism, and job-related attitudes in a culturally diverse work group. *Journal of Cross-Cultural Psychology, 25* (June), 233–257.

Bok, S. (1983). *Secrets.* New York: Vintage.

Borden, G. (1991). *Cultural orientation: An approach to understanding intercultural communication.* Englewood Cliffs, NJ: Prentice-Hall.

Brauer, M., Judd, C. M., & Gliner, M. D. (1995). The effects of repeated expressions on attitude polarization during group discussions. *Journal of Personality and Social Psychology, 68* (June), 1014–1029.

Brilhart, J., & Galanes, G. (1992). *Effective group discussion* (7th ed.). Dubuque, IA: Brown & Benchmark.

Bullock, C., McCluskey, M., Stamm, K., Tanaka, K., Torres, M. & Scott, C. (2003). Group affiliations, opinion polarization, and global organization: Views of the World Trade Organization before and after Seattle. *Mass Communication & Society, 5*(4), 433–450.

Comadena, M. E. (1984). Brainstorming groups: Ambiguity tolerance, communication apprehension, task attraction, and individual productivity. *Small Group Behavior, 15,* 251–254.

Cragan, J. F., & Wright, D. W. (1990). Small group communication research of the 1980s: A synthesis and critique. *Communication Studies, 41* (Fall), 212–236.

Davison, W. P. (1983). The third-person effects and the differential impact in negative political advertising. *Journalism Quarterly, 68,* 680–688.

deBono, E. (1976). *Teaching thinking.* New York: Penguin.

deBono, E. (1987). *The six thinking hats.* New York: Penguin.

DeStephen, R., & Hirokawa, R. (1988). Small group consensus: Stability of group support of the decision, task process, and group relationships. *Small Group Behavior 19,* 227–239.

DeVito, J. A. (1996). *Brainstorms: How to think more creatively about communication (or about anything else).* New York: Longman.

Dewey, J. (1910). *How we think.* Boston: Heath.

French, J. R. P., Jr., & Raven, B. (1968). The bases of social power. In D. Cartwright & A. Zander (Eds.), *Group dynamics: Research and theory* (3rd ed., pp. 259–269). New York: Harper & Row.

Friedkin, N. E. (1999). Choice shift and group polarization. *American Sociological Review, 64* (December), 856–875.

Gorden, W. I., & Nevins, R. J. (1993). *We mean business: Building communication competence in business and professions.* New York: Longman.

Gross, T., Turner, E., & Cederholm, L. (1987, June). Building teams for global operation. *Management Review,* 32–36.

Hirsch, E. D., Jr., Kett, J. F., & Trefil, J. (Eds.). (2002). *The new dictionary of cultural literacy.* Boston: Houghton Mifflin.

Hoffner, C., Plotkin, R. S., Buchanan, M., Anderson, J. D., Kamigaki, S. K., Hubbs, L. A., Kowalczyk, L., Silberg, K., & Pastoret, A. (2001). The third-person effect in perceptions of the influence of television violence. *Journal of Communication, 51* (June), 283–299.

Hofstede, G. (1997). *Cultures and organizations: Software of the mind.* New York: McGraw-Hill.

Jablin, F. M. (1981). Cultivating imagination: Factors that enhance and inhibit creativity in brainstorming groups. *Human Communication Research, 7,* 245–258.

Kelly, M. S. (2006). *Communication@work: Ethical, effective, and expressive communication in the workplace.* Boston: Allyn & Bacon.

Kelly, P. K. (1994). *Team decision-making techniques.* Irvine, CA: Richard Chang Associates.

Napier, R. W., & Gershenfeld, M. K. (1992). *Groups: Theory and experience* (5th ed.). Boston: Houghton Mifflin.

Osborn, A. (1957). *Applied imagination* (Rev. ed.). New York: Scribners.

Raven, R., Centers, C., & Rodrigues, A. (1975). The bases of conjugal power. In R. E. Cromwell & D. H. Olson (Eds.), *Power in families* (pp. 217–234). New York: Halsted Press.

Roebuck, D. B. (2001). *Improving business communication skills* (3rd ed.). Upper Saddle River, NJ: Prentice-Hall.

Rogers, C. (1970). *Carl Rogers on encounter groups.* New York: Harrow Books.

Rollman, J. B., Krug, K., & Parente, F. (2000). The chat room phenomenon: Reciprocal communication in cyberspace. *CyberPsychology and Behavior, 3* (April), 161–166.

Song, I, LaRose, R., Eastin, M. S., & Lin, C. A. (2004). Internet gratifications Internet addiction: On the uses and abuses of new media. *CyberPsychology & Behavior 7* (August), 384–394.

Tersine, R. J., & Riggs, W. E. (1980). The Delphi technique: A long-range planning tool. In S. Ferguson & S. D. Ferguson (Eds.), *Intercom: Readings in organizational communication* (pp. 366–373). Rochelle Park, NJ: Hayden Books.

Westwood, R. I., Tang, F. F., & Kirkbride, P. S. (1992). Chinese conflict behavior: Cultural antecedents and behavioral consequences. *Organizational Development Journal, 10* (Summer), 13–19.

Chapter 12

Members and Leaders

MAJOR TOPICS

Members in Small Group Communication
Leaders in Small Group Communication
Membership, Leadership, and Culture

Special Features

Becoming a Leader: Katherine Hawkins

What Kind of Group Member Are You?

What Kind of Leader Are You?

Gatekeeping

The Leader's Ethical Responsibilities

Understanding Styles of Leadership

Understanding Attila's Theory of Leadership

Skills Combating Groupthink

Skills Empowering Others

© Helen King/CORBIS

From *Human Communication: The Basic Course*, Eleventh Edition. Joseph A. DeVito. Copyright © 2009 by Pearson Education, Inc. Published by Pearson Allyn and Bacon.

Throughout your life, you'll participate in a wide variety of groups—as a member of a work group, as a part of a social or neighborhood group, or as a player on a team. Probably you'll also lead some of these social or work groups, and your leadership responsibilities are likely to increase as you rise in the group hierarchy.

In this unit, you'll learn about:
- the kinds of roles members play in groups.
- the types and styles of leadership.

You'll learn to:
- participate more effectively as a group member.
- lead a wide variety of groups effectively and efficiently.

MEMBERS IN SMALL GROUP COMMUNICATION

You can view membership in small group communication situations from a variety of perspectives—in terms of the roles that members serve, the types of contributions they make, and the principles for more effective participation.

Member Roles

Before reading about the roles of members in small groups, take the following self-test, which encourages you to look at your own small group membership behavior.

TEST YOURSELF

What Kind of Group Member Are You?

For each statement below, respond with T for true if the statement is often true of your group behavior or F for false if the statement generally does not apply to your group behavior.

_____ **1.** I present new ideas and suggest new strategies.

_____ **2.** I ask for facts and opinions.

_____ **3.** I stimulate the group.

_____ **4.** I give examples and try to look for positive solutions.

_____ **5.** I positively reinforce group members.

_____ **6.** I try to reconcile differences.

_____ **7.** I go along with the other members.

_____ **8.** I offer compromises as ways of resolving conflict.

_____ **9.** I express negative evaluation of the actions and feelings of the group members.

_____ **10.** I try to run the group.

_____ **11.** I express personal perspectives and feelings.

_____ **12.** I express confusion or deprecate myself.

HOW DID YOU DO? As you'll see as you read further, these behaviors are characteristic of the three general types of group member roles. The first four statements refer to your taking on group task roles, and the next four refer to your taking on group building and maintenance roles. Both of these types of roles are productive. The final four refer to your taking an individual rather than a group focus; these are the behaviors that often work against the group's achieving its goals.

WHAT WILL YOU DO? As you read the following sections on member roles, try to relate these roles to your own behavior or to group behavior you've witnessed. Then ask yourself what worked and what didn't work. What roles were productive, and what roles were unproductive?

As mentioned in the preceding self-test, group member roles fall into three general classes—group task roles, group building and maintenance roles, and individual roles—a classification introduced in early research (Benne & Sheats, 1948) and still widely used today (Lumsden & Lumsden, 1996; Beebe & Masterson, 2006). These roles are, of course, frequently served by leaders as well.

Group Task Roles

Group task roles are those that help the group focus more specifically on achieving its goals. In serving any of these roles, you act not as an isolated individual but rather as a part of the larger whole. The needs and goals of the group dictate the task roles you serve. As an effective group member you would serve several of these functions.

Some people, however, lock into a few specific roles. For example, one person may almost always seek the opinions of others; another may concentrate on elaborating details; still another, on evaluating suggestions. Usually this kind of single focus is counterproductive. It's usually better for group task roles to be spread more evenly so that each member may serve many roles. The 12 specific group task roles include:

- The *initiator-contributor* presents new ideas or new perspectives on old ideas, suggests new goals, or proposes new procedures or organizational strategies.

- The *information seeker* asks for facts and opinions and seeks clarification of the issues being discussed.

- The *opinion seeker* tries to discover the values underlying the group's task.

- The *information giver* presents facts and opinions to the group members.

- The *opinion giver* presents values and opinions and tries to spell out what the values of the group should be.

- The *elaborator* gives examples and tries to work out possible solutions, trying to build on what others have said.

- The *coordinator* spells out relationships among ideas and suggested solutions and coordinates the activities of the different members.

- The *orienter* summarizes what has been said and addresses the direction the group is taking.

- The *evaluator-critic* evaluates the group's decisions, questions the logic or practicality of the suggestions, and thus provides the group with both positive and negative feedback.

- The *energizer* stimulates the group to greater activity.

- The *procedural technician* takes care of various mechanical duties such as distributing group materials and arranging seating.

- The *recorder* writes down the group's activities, suggestions, and decisions; he or she serves as the memory of the group.

Group Building and Maintenance Roles

Most groups focus not only on the task to be performed but also on interpersonal relationships among members. If the group is to function effectively, and if members are to be both satisfied and productive, these relationships must be nourished. When these needs are not met, group members may become irritable when the group process gets bogged down, may engage in frequent conflicts, or may find the small group process as a whole unsatisfying. The group and its members need the same kind of support that individuals need. The **group building and maintenance roles** serve this general function. Group building and maintenance functions are broken down into seven specific roles:

- The *encourager* supplies members with positive reinforcement in the form of social approval or praise for their ideas.

- The *harmonizer* mediates differences among group members.

- The *compromiser* offers compromises as a way to resolve conflicts between his or her ideas and those of others.

- The *gatekeeper-expediter* keeps the channels of communication open by reinforcing the efforts of others.

- The *standard setter* proposes standards for the functioning of the group or for its solutions.

- The *group observer and commentator* keeps a record of the proceedings and uses this in the group's evaluation of itself.

- The *follower* goes along with the members of the group, passively accepts the ideas of others, and functions more as an audience than as an active member.

Individual Roles

The group task and group building and maintenance roles just considered are productive roles; they aid the group in achieving its goals. **Individual roles**, on the other hand, are counterproductive; they hinder the group's productivity and member satisfaction, largely because they focus on serving individual rather than group needs. As you read about these eight specific types, consider what you'd say to each of them if you were a member or a leader of the group and wanted to deal with this dysfunctional role playing but, at the same time, didn't want to alienate the individual or the group.

- The *aggressor* expresses negative evaluation of the actions or feelings of the group members; he or she attacks the group or the problem being considered.

- The *blocker* provides negative feedback, is disagreeable, and opposes other members or suggestions regardless of their merit.

- The *recognition seeker* tries to focus attention on himself or herself rather than on the task at hand, boasting about his or her own accomplishments.

- The *self-confessor* expresses his or her own feelings and personal perspectives rather than focusing on the group.

- The *playboy/playgirl* jokes around without any regard for the group process.

- The *dominator* tries to run the group or the group members by pulling rank, flattering members of the group, or acting the role of the boss.

- The *help seeker* expresses insecurity or confusion or deprecates himself or herself and thus tries to gain sympathy from the other members.

- The *special interest pleader* disregards the goals of the group and pleads the case of some special group.

As you might expect, your tendency to play group versus individual roles will be influenced by your culture—and especially by your individualist or collectivist orientation, and your power orientation.

Interaction Process Analysis

Another way of looking at the contributions group members make is through **interaction process analysis** (IPA), developed by Robert Bales (1950). In this system you analyze the contributions of members under four general categories: (1) social-emotional positive contributions, (2) social-emotional negative

contributions, (3) attempted answers, and (4) questions. Each of these four areas contains three subdivisions, yielding a total of 12 categories into which you can classify group members' contributions (Table 1). Note that the categories under social-emotional positive are the natural opposites of those under social-emotional negative, and those under attempted answers are the natural opposites of those under questions. You may want to try out Bales's IPA system by listening to a small group discussion or a televised situation comedy or drama and recording the interactions using Table 1.

Both the three-part member role classification and the IPA categories are useful for analyzing the contributions members make in small group situations. When you look at member contributions through these systems, you can see, for example, if one member is locked into a particular role or if the group process is breaking down because too many people are serving individual rather than group goals or because social-emotional negative comments dominate the discussion. You should also be in a better position to offer improvement suggestions for individual members based on this analysis.

Member Participation

For another perspective on group membership, let's consider the recommendations for effective participation in small group communication. Look at these

Table 1 Interaction Process Analysis Form

The names of participants appear in the top spaces, as shown by the examples here. In the column under each participant's name, you place a slash mark for each contribution in each of the 12 categories.

		Joe	Judy	Liz	Mike	Peg
Social-Emotional Positive Contributions	Shows solidarity					
	Shows tension release					
	Shows agreement					
Social-Emotional Negative Contributions	Shows disagreement					
	Shows tension					
	Shows antagonism					
Attempted Answers	Gives suggestions					
	Gives opinions					
	Gives information					
Questions	Asks for suggestions					
	Asks for opinions					
	Asks for information					

INDIVIDUAL ROLES

In a group of workers you're leading, one member consistently plays the role of blocker, objecting to everything anyone says. Another member plays the role of self-confessor, revealing feelings no one wants to hear. You need to lessen these comments if your group is to succeed.

WHAT DO YOU SAY?
To whom? Through what channel?

© PhotoDisc/Getty Images

suggestions as an elaboration and extension of the characteristics of effective conversation.

Be Group or Team Oriented

In the small group you're a member of a team, a larger whole. As a group your task is to pool your talents, knowledge, and insights so as to arrive at a better solution than any one person could have developed. This call for group orientation is not to be taken as a suggestion that members abandon their individuality or give up their personal values or beliefs for the sake of the group, however. Individuality with a group orientation is what is advocated here.

Center Conflict on Issues

It's particularly important in the small group to center conflict on issues rather than on personalities. When you disagree, make it clear that your disagreement is with the solution suggested or with the ideas expressed, not with the person who expressed them. Similarly, when someone disagrees with what you say, don't take it as a personal attack. Instead, view this as an opportunity to discuss issues from an alternative point of view.

Be Critically Open-Minded

Because the most effective and creative solutions often emerge from a combination of ideas, approach small group situations with flexibility; come to the group with ideas and information but without firmly formulated conclusions. Advance any solutions or conclusions tentatively rather than with certainty.

Be willing to alter your suggestions and revise them in light of the discussion.

Ensure Understanding

Make sure that your ideas are understood by all participants. If something is worth saying, it's worth saying clearly. When in doubt, ask: "Is that clear?" "Did I explain that clearly?" Make sure, too, that you understand fully the contributions of other members, especially before you take issue with them. In fact, it's often wise to preface any extended disagreement with some kind of paraphrase to give the other person the opportunity to clarify, deny, or otherwise alter what was said. For example, you might say, "As I understand it, you want to exclude freshmen from playing on the football team. Is that correct? I disagree with that idea and I'd like to explain why I think that would be a mistake."

Beware of Groupthink

Groupthink is a way of thinking that people use when agreement among members has become excessively important. Groupthink is most likely to occur when there is high stress, when like-minded individuals are isolated from others, and when there is an especially strong and opinionated leader. Overemphasis on agreement among members tends to shut out realistic and logical analysis of a problem or of possible alternatives (Janis, 1983; Mullen, Tara, Salas, & Driskell, 1994). The term *groupthink* itself is meant to signal a "deterioration of mental efficiency, reality testing, and moral judgment that results from in-group pressures" (Janis, 1983, p. 9).

The following symptoms should help you recognize groupthink in groups you observe or participate in (Janis, 1983; Schafer & Crichlow, 1996; Richmond, McCroskey, & McCroskey, 2005):

- *Illusion of invulnerability.* Group members think the group and its members are invulnerable, that they are virtually beyond being harmed.

- *Avoidance.* Members create rationalizations to avoid dealing with warnings or threats.

- *Assumption of morality.* Members believe their group is moral and, often, that any opposition is immoral.

- *Intolerance of differences of opinion.* Those opposed to the group are perceived in simplistic, stereotyped ways, and group pressure is applied to any member who expresses doubts or questions the group's arguments or proposals.

- *Self-censorship.* Members censor their own doubts.

- *Assumption of unanimity.* Group members believe that all members are in unanimous agreement, whether this is stated or not. This belief is encouraged, of course, by members censoring their own doubts and not allowing differences of opinion to be discussed.

- *Gatekeeping.* Group members emerge whose function it is to guard the information that gets to other members, especially when it may create diversity of opinion.

- *Peer pressure.* Groupthinkers pressure others to go along with the group and not to express any disagreement.

Here are three suggestions for combating groupthink.

1. When too-simple solutions are offered to problems, try to illustrate (with specific examples, if possible) for the group members how the complexity of the problem is not going to yield to the solutions offered.

2. When you feel that members are not expressing their doubts about the group or its decisions, encourage members to voice disagreement. Ask members to play devil's advocate, to test the adequacy of the solution. Or, if members resist, do it yourself. Similarly, if you feel there is unexpressed disagreement, ask specifically if anyone disagrees. If you still get no response, it may be helpful to ask everyone to write his or her comments anonymously, then read them aloud to the group.

3. To combat the group pressure toward agreement, reward members who do voice disagreement or doubt. Say, for example, "That's a good argument; we need to hear more about the potential problems of this proposal. Does anyone else see any problems?"

LEADERS IN SMALL GROUP COMMUNICATION

Leadership is defined in two very different ways in research and theory:

- Leadership is the process of influencing the thoughts, feelings, and behaviors of group members and establishing the direction that others follow; leadership and influence are parts of the same skill.

- Leadership is the process of empowering others; the leader is the person who helps others to maximize their potential and to take control of their lives.

© Sotograph/Getty Images

ASSERTING YOURSELF IN A GROUP

In your casual conversations with friends as well as at work meetings, people consistently ignore your cues that you want to say something. And when you do manage to say something, no one reacts. You're determined to change this situation.

WHAT DO YOU SAY?
To whom? Through what channel?

Building Communication Skills — Combating Groupthink

Develop specific messages you might use as a member or a leader of a group in which you see the signs of groupthink noted on the left and you wish to use the combat tactic noted in the center column.

Suspected problem	Combat tactic	Messages to accomplish your combat goal
Group members assume there's unanimous agreement.	Ask for a poll of opinion; survey the group members.	_____
Members are not expressing their doubts about the group or its decisions.	Encourage members to voice disagreement, or ask if anyone disagrees.	_____
There's lots of group pressure toward agreement.	Reward members who voice disagreement, or voice it yourself.	_____

Groupthink prevents creativity and logical analysis; watch out for it and try to reduce its influence whenever you can.

These two definitions are not mutually exclusive; in fact, most effective leaders do both; they influence and they empower. As you read the remaining discussion of leadership, keep these two definitions in mind and see leadership as embodying both power and empowerment.

In many small groups one person serves as leader. In other groups leadership may be shared by several persons.

In some cases a person may be appointed the leader or may serve as leader because of her or his position within the company or hierarchy. In other cases the leader may emerge as the group proceeds in fulfilling its functions or may be elected leader by the group members. Two significant factors exert considerable influence on who emerges as group leader. One is the extent of active participation: The person who talks the most is more likely to emerge as leader (Mullen, Salas, & Driskell, 1989; Shaw & Gouran, 1990). The second factor is effective listening: Members who listen effectively will emerge as leaders more often than those who don't (Johnson & Bechler, 1998; Bechler & Johnson, 1995).

The **emergent leader** performs the duties of leadership, though not asked or expected to, and gradually becomes recognized by the members as the group's leader. And because this person has now proved herself or himself an effective leader, it's not surprising that this emergent leader often becomes the designated leader for future groups.

The role of the leader or leaders is vital to the well-being and effectiveness of the group. Even in leaderless groups in which all members are equal, leadership functions must still be served.

Myths about Leadership

As with many important concepts, beliefs about leadership have grown. Some of these beliefs are erroneous and need to be recognized as such. Here are just three myths about leadership offered by—and here paraphrased from—small group theorists (Bennis & Nanus, 1985):

- *Myth: The skills of leadership are rare.* Actually, all of us have the potential for leadership; and, of course, there are millions of leaders throughout the world who are serving a variety of functions in government, business, education, and countless other fields.

- *Myth: Leaders are born.* Actually, the major leadership skills can be learned by just about everyone. No specific genetic endowment is necessary. We all can improve our leadership abilities.

- *Myth: Leaders are all charismatic.* Actually, only some leaders are. According to one survey of leaders (Bennis & Nanus, 1985, p. 208): "Our leaders were all 'too human'; they were short and tall, articulate and inarticulate, dressed for success and dressed for failure, and there was virtually nothing in terms of physical appearance, personality, or style that set them apart from their followers."

THE RESEARCHER

Becoming a Leader

I'm going to start a new job—a great position at a large investment firm. I'm very focused on rising in the organization (yes, I want status and money), and I want to know what I can do to establish myself as someone who has leadership potential. Are there any communication skills that are absolutely essential and that I should concentrate on?

There are a number of things you can do to establish yourself as having leadership potential. First and foremost, demonstrate task-relevant expertise. Don't be a know-it-all, but do share accurate information and insightful interpretations of complex data when you have the opportunity to do so. If you don't know the answer to a question, say so, but show initiative by offering to find the answer for the person who posed the question. Then be sure to follow up with a correct, detailed response in a timely way.

Second, demonstrate relational competence. Always be civil and pleasant to your colleagues, regardless of the circumstances. Don't engage in political squabbles with your peers, but do work to maintain productive lines of communication between conflicted persons or groups.

Finally, let your word be your bond. Credibility is your most precious possession. Always be authentic in your dealings with others. If you want to be a leader, your colleagues must trust you.

For further information: Frey, L. R., & Barge, J. K. (1997). *Managing group life: Communicating in decision-making groups*. Boston: Houghton Mifflin. Also Hawkins, K. W., & Fillion, B. (1999). Perceived communication skill needs for work groups. *Communication Research Reports, 16*, 167–174.

Katherine Hawkins (Ph.D., University of Texas) is a professor of communication studies at Clemson University. She teaches courses in communication theory and research methods. She also serves as department chair and is a past president of the Southern States Communication Association.

Approaches to Leadership

Not surprisingly, leadership has been the focus of considerable attention from theorists and researchers, who have used numerous approaches to understand this particular communication behavior. Before reading about these approaches, you may wish to take the self-test below to examine yourself as a leader.

TEST YOURSELF

What Kind of Leader Are You?

This self-test is designed to stimulate you to think about yourself in the role of leader. Respond to the following statements in terms of how you perceive yourself and how you think others perceive you, using a 10-point scale ranging from 10 (extremely true) to 1 (extremely false).

Others see me as	I see myself as	Perceptions
_____ 1.	_____ 1.	Generally popular with group members
_____ 2.	_____ 2.	Knowledgeable about the topics and subjects discussed
_____ 3.	_____ 3.	Dependable
_____ 4.	_____ 4.	Effective in establishing group goals
_____ 5.	_____ 5.	Competent in giving directions
_____ 6.	_____ 6.	Capable of energizing group members
_____ 7.	_____ 7.	Charismatic (dynamic, engaging, powerful)

_____ 8. _____ 8. Empowering of group members

_____ 9. _____ 9. Moral and honest

_____ 10. _____ 10. Skilled in balancing the concerns of getting the task done and satisfying the group members' personal needs

_____ 11. _____ 11. Flexible in adjusting leadership style on the basis of the unique situation

_____ 12. _____ 12. Able to delegate responsibility

HOW DID YOU DO? This test was designed to encourage you to look at yourself in terms of the four approaches to leadership that will be discussed in the following text. Phrases 1–3 refer to the traits approach to leadership, which defines a leader as a person who possesses certain qualities. Phrases 4–6 refer to the functional approach, which defines a leader as a person who performs certain functions. Phrases 7–9 refer to the transformational approach, which defines a leader as a person who inspires the group members to become the best they can be. Phrases 10–12 refer to the situational approach, which defines a leader as someone who can adjust his or her style to balance the needs of the specific situation.

To compute your scores:

1. Add your scores for statements 1–3: _____.
   This will give you an idea of how you and others see you in terms of the leadership qualities identified by the *traits approach*.

2. Add your scores for statements 4–6: _____.
   This will give you an idea of how you and others see you in relation to the varied leadership functions considered in the *functional approach*.

3. Add your scores for statements 7–9: _____.
   This will give you an idea of how you and others see you as a *transformational leader*.

4. Add your scores for statements 10–12: _____.
   This will give you an idea of how you and others see you as a *situational leader*.

WHAT WILL YOU DO? As you read the remainder of this unit and the rest of the book, try to identify specific skills and competencies you might learn that would enable you to increase your scores on all four approaches to leadership. Also, try searching the Web for information on "leadership" as well as, say, "business leadership" and "political leaders."

Traits Approach

The **traits approach to leadership** argues that leaders must possess certain qualities if they're to function effectively. Some of the traits found to be associated with leadership are intelligence, dominance, honesty, foresight, altruism, popularity, sociability, cooperativeness, knowledge, and dependability (Hackman & Johnson, 1991). The problem with the traits approach is that the specific qualities called for will vary with the situation, with the members, and with the culture in which the leader functions. Thus, for example, the leader's knowledge and personality are generally significant factors; but for some groups a knowledge of financial issues and a serious personality might be effective, whereas for other groups a knowledge of design and a more humorous personality might be effective.

Functional Approach

The **functional approach to leadership** focuses on what the leader should do in a given situation. We have already considered some of these functions in the discussion of group membership, which identified group roles. Other functions found to be associated with leadership are setting group goals, giving direction to group members, and summarizing the group's progress (Schultz, 1996). Still other functions are identified in the section entitled "Functions of Leadership," later in this unit.

Transformational Approach

In the **transformational approach to leadership** the leader elevates the group's members, enabling them not only to accomplish the group task but also to emerge as more empowered individuals (Li & Shi, 2003). At the center of the transformational approach is the concept of charisma, that quality of an individual that makes us believe in or want to follow him or her. Gandhi, Martin Luther King Jr., and John F. Kennedy may be cited as examples of transformational leaders. These leaders were seen as role models of what they asked of their members, were perceived as extremely competent and able leaders, and articulated moral goals (Northouse, 1997).

Situational Approach

The **situational approach to leadership** focuses on the two major responsibilities of the leader—accomplishing the task at hand and ensuring the satisfaction of the members—and recognizes that the leader's style must vary on the basis of the

SITUATIONAL LEADERSHIP

You're in an advanced Internet design team whose leader uses a telling style, creating resentment among members. You've been elected to clue the leader into appropriate and inappropriate styles.

WHAT DO YOU SAY?
Through what channels?

specific situation. Just as you adjust your interpersonal style in conversation or your motivational appeals in public speaking on the basis of the particular situation, so you must adjust your leadership style. Leadership effectiveness, then, depends on combining the concerns for task and people according to the specifics of the situation. Some situations will call for high concentration on task issues but will need little in the way of people encouragement. For example, a group of scientists working on AIDS research would probably need a leader primarily to provide them with the needed information to accomplish their task. They would be self-motivating and would probably need little in the way of social and emotional encouragement. On the other hand, a group of recovering alcoholics might require leadership that stressed the social and emotional needs of the members.

An interesting extension of the situational approach portrays four basic leadership styles, as illustrated in Figure 1 (Hersey, Blanchard, & Johnson, 2001). This model claims that groups differ in their degree of readiness. A group that contains members who are knowledgeable, experienced, and demonstrating that skill at a sustained and acceptable level have a high degree of readiness. Because of that readiness, group members are able to set realistic and attainable goals. Continued success and supportive behavior from others tends to build confidence which leads to higher levels of readiness where group members are willing to appropriately take responsibility for their decisions. A group this high in readiness is characterized by members who are both willing and able to perform the task in question. This is a critical point. A group or individual's readiness varies with the task; an individual may be

FIGURE 1 A Model of Situational Leadership

This figure depicts four different styles of leadership that differ in the degree to which they are supportive (relationship oriented) or directive (task oriented). Are there any leadership styles with which you're uncomfortable? What skills can you acquire to help you feel more comfortable and competent with these styles?

Source: "Model of Situational Leadership" by Paul Hersey and Kenneth Blanchard in *Management of Organizational Behavior*, p. 277. Copyright © 2006. Reprinted with permission of the Center for Leadership Studies, Inc. Escondido, CA 92025. All rights reserved.

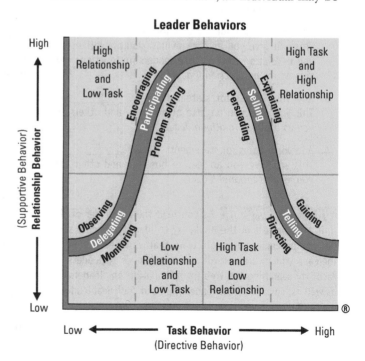

skilled at, and more than happy to engage in, discussions about food and exercise, but less than amenable when it comes to talking about their finances.

Effective leadership, then, depends on the leader's assessment of the group's ability and willingness to do the task. To complicate matters even more, the readiness of the group will also change as the group develops or regresses over time—so the style of leadership will have to change in response to the changes in the group. The Situational Leadership Model identifies four different leadership styles that provide the highest probability of successfully and effectively influencing the behaviors of others based on their level of readiness for a specific task:

- The **telling style** of leadership is appropriate for a group that lacks knowledge of the issues involved and needs the direct guidance of the telling leader, the leader who tells the members what they should do. The telling style focuses almost exclusively on the task; this leader offers little if any relationship support.

- The **selling style** is appropriate for a group that is trying hard but still lacks the needed skills or information to accomplish their task. The selling style is a persuasive strategy; it is high in both directiveness and in relationship support. Here the leader seeks to gain the group members' psychological support (to get them to "buy into" the ideas) and so does lots of explaining. At the same time, however, this leader provides direct guidance for what the group should do.

- The **participating style** is appropriate for groups that know what to do but may not be so willing to do it. This leader, therefore, relies heavily on communicating, facilitating, and encouraging group members. This leader participates in the group's problem solving but, because group members already know what to do, provides little direction.

- The **delegating style** is appropriate for groups that know what to do and are eager to do it. Here the leader need not provide extensive direction or relationship support but instead monitors and observes.

Theory and Research   Styles of Leadership

UNDERSTANDING

Small group communication researchers distinguish three basic types of group leaders: *laissez-faire, democratic,* and *authoritarian* (Bennis & Nanus, 1985; Hackman & Johnson, 1991).

The **laissez-faire leader** takes no initiative in directing or suggesting alternative courses of action. Rather, this leader allows the group to develop and progress on its own, even allowing it to make its own mistakes. The laissez-faire leader answers questions and provides information only when specifically asked. During the group interaction, this leader neither compliments nor criticizes the group's members or their progress. Generally, this type of leadership results in a satisfied but inefficient group.

The **democratic leader** provides direction but allows the group to develop and progress the way its members wish. This leader encourages group members to determine their own goals and procedures and works to stimulate the self-direction and self-actualization of group members. Unlike the laissez-faire leader, the democratic leader does contribute suggestions and does comment on member and group performance. Generally, this form of leadership results in both satisfaction and efficiency.

The **authoritarian leader**, the opposite of the laissez-faire leader, determines group policies and makes decisions without consulting or securing agreement from the members. This leader discourages member-to-member communication but encourages communication from member to leader. The authoritarian leader is concerned with getting the group to accept his or her decisions rather than making its own. If the authoritarian leader is competent, the group may be highly efficient, but its members are likely to be less personally satisfied.

Working with Theories and Research

Which leadership style—say, in a work situation with colleagues—are you likely to feel most comfortable using? Most comfortable working with as a group member?

MEDIA WATCH
GATEKEEPING

The concept of "gatekeeping," introduced by Kurt Lewin in his *Human Relations* (1947), has to do with both *the process* by which a message passes through various gates and *the people or groups*, or gatekeepers, that allow the message to pass.

As you were growing up, your parents—your first gatekeepers—gave you certain information and withheld other information. For example, depending on the culture in which you were raised, you may have been told about Santa Claus and the tooth fairy but not about cancer or mutual funds. When you went to school, your teachers served a similar gatekeeping function. They taught you about certain historical events, for example, but not others. Textbook authors also serve as gatekeepers (Robinson, 1993). Editors of newspapers and magazines; television producers, writers, and advertisers; and those who regulate and monitor Internet messages are all gatekeepers: They allow certain information to come through and other information to be filtered out (Lewis 1995; Bodon, Powell, & Hickson, 1999).

Often the media gatekeeps to increase profits, as when they emphasize (open the gates for) stories of celebrities, violence, and sex—because these sell—and deemphasize (close the gates on) minority issues, classical drama, or antireligious statements. At times they may gatekeep because of legal restrictions.

So, when you hear a news broadcast, read an article, or listen to a commentator, ask yourself if you're seeing or hearing an incomplete or unrealistic picture. Ask yourself, what might not have passed through the gate?

Increasing Media Literacy

How do one, two, or three of the following people function as gatekeepers in relation to your ability to acquire information: the editor of your local or college newspaper, Oprah Winfrey, your romantic partner (past or present), the president of the United States, network news shows, or the advertising department of a large corporation?

As you can tell from these descriptions, the leader exerts more control with immature groups (telling and selling) and less control with mature groups (participating and delegating). As groups become more mature, members assume greater responsibility and control and leaders' control diminishes.

Functions of Leadership

In relatively formal small group situations, as when politicians plan a strategy, advertisers discuss a campaign, or teachers consider educational methods, the leader has several specific functions. These functions—a mixture of task and people functions—are not the exclusive property of the leader. Nevertheless, when there's a specific leader, he or she is expected to perform them.

As you read these functions, keep in mind that an effective leader needs not only knowledge of the topic of the discussion but also communication competence—the ability to effectively use the group process as well as to use mindfulness, flexibility, and cultural sensitivity plus more specific skills of openness, empathy, positiveness, immediacy, interaction management, expressiveness, and other-orientation.

Still another skill the leader needs is the ability to manage any group conflict that might arise.

Prediscussion Functions

It often falls to the leader to provide members with necessary materials prior to the meeting. Prediscussion functions may include, for example, arranging a convenient meeting time and place; informing members of the purposes and goals of the meeting; providing them with materials they should read or view; and recommending that they come to the meeting with, for example, general ideas or specific proposals.

Similarly, groups form gradually and need to be eased into meaningful discussion. Diverse members should not be expected to sit down and discuss a problem without becoming familiar with one another. Put more generally, the leader is responsible for any preparations and preliminaries necessary to ensure an orderly and productive group experience.

Activating the Group Agenda

Most groups have an agenda. An **agenda** is simply a list of the tasks the group wishes to complete. It's an itemized listing of what the group should devote its attention to. In some cases the supervisor or consultant or CEO prepares the agenda and simply presents it to the group; the group is then expected to follow the agenda item by item. In other cases the group will develop its own agenda, usually as its first or second order of business.

Generally, the more formal the group, the more important the agenda becomes. In informal groups the agenda may simply consist of general ideas in the minds of the members (for example, "We'll review the class assignment and then make plans for the weekend"). In formal business groups the agenda will be much more detailed and explicit. Some agendas specify not only the items that must be covered but also the order in which they should be covered and even the amount of time that should be devoted to each item.

Promoting Group Interaction

Many groups need some prodding to interact. Perhaps the group is newly formed and the members feel a bit uneasy with one another. One of the leader's functions is to stimulate the members to interact. A leader also serves this function when members act as individuals rather than as a group. In this instance the leader needs to focus the members on their *group* task.

Maintaining Effective Interaction

Suppose that you are leading a group and have successfully stimulated group interaction, but now the discussion begins to drag. Your job is to prod the group to maintain effective interaction: "Do we have any additional comments on the proposal to eliminate required courses?" "What do those of you who are members of the college curriculum committee think about the English Department's proposal to restructure required courses?" "Does anyone want to make any additional comments on eliminating the minor area of concentration?" As the leader, you must strive to ensure that all members have an opportunity to express themselves.

Empowering Group Members

An important function in at least some leadership styles (though not limited to leadership) is to empower others—to help other group members (but also your relational partner, coworkers, employees, other students, or siblings) to gain increased power over themselves and their environment. Some ways to empower others include the following:

- Raise the person's self-esteem. Compliment, reinforce. Resist faultfinding; it doesn't benefit anyone and in fact disempowers.

- Share skills as well as decision-making power and authority.

- Be constructively critical. Be willing to offer your perspective, to lend an ear to an intern's first proposal, for example. Be willing to react honestly to suggestions from all group members and not just those in high positions.

- Encourage growth in all forms: academic, relational, and professional, among others. The growth and empowerment of the other person enhances your own growth and power.

LEADER GUIDANCE

Members of your group are not participating equally. Of the five members, two monopolize the discussion while three say as little as possible. You want greater participation from the silent ones and less from the monopolizers.

WHAT DO YOU SAY?
To whom?

323

Building Communication Skills — Empowering Others

As Bennis and Nanus (1985, p. 209) argue, "leadership is not so much the exercise of power itself as the empowerment of others." For each situation below, indicate what you might say to help empower the other person(s), using such strategies as (a) raising the other person's self-esteem; (b) listening actively and supportively; (c) being open, positive, and empathic; and (d) avoiding verbal aggressiveness or any unfair conflict strategies.

1. Your partner is having lots of difficulties—recently he lost his job, received poor grades in a night class, and started gaining a lot of weight. At the same time, you're doing extremely well. You want to give your partner back his confidence. What do you say?

2. You're managing four college interns who are redesigning your company's website, three men and one woman. The men are extremely supportive of one another and regularly contribute ideas. Although equally competent, the woman doesn't contribute; she seems to lack confidence. But the objective of this redesign is to increase the number of female visitors, so you really need her input and want to empower her. What do you say?

3. You're a third-grade teacher. Most of the students are from the same ethnic–religious group; three, however, are from a very different group. The problem is that these three have not been included in the social groupings of the students; they're considered outsiders. As a result these children stumble when they have to read in front of the class and make a lot of mistakes at the chalkboard (though they consistently do well in private). You want to empower these students. What do you say?

Empowering others, far from reducing your own power, actually increases it.

Keeping Members on Track

Many individuals are egocentric and will pursue only their own interests and concerns, even in a group setting. Your task as the leader is to keep all members reasonably on track. Here are a few ways you might accomplish this:

- Ask questions that focus on the specific topic at hand, especially of those who seem to be wandering off in other directions.

- Interject internal summaries in which you briefly identify what has been accomplished and what the group needs to move on to next.

- Consider setting a formal agenda and sticking to it.

- Focus your own attention on the topics at hand; your example will influence the behavior of the other members.

Ensuring Member Satisfaction

Group members have different psychological needs and wants; in fact, many people enter groups primarily to satisfy these personal concerns. Even though a group may, for example, deal with political issues, the members may have come together for reasons that are more psychological than political. If a group is to be effective, it must meet not only the surface purposes of the group but also the underlying or interpersonal purposes that motivated many of the members to come together in the first place.

Depending on the specific people involved, special adjustments may have to be made to accommodate group members with disabilities. You can easily adapt to group situations the principles that deal with communication between people with and without disabilities.

Encouraging Ongoing Evaluation

Most groups could profit from improving their techniques. If any group is to improve, it must focus on itself. Along with trying to accomplish some objective task, it must try to solve its own internal problems as well: issues such as personal conflicts, the failure of members to meet on time, or the tendency of some members to come unprepared. As the leader, try to identify any such difficulties and encourage and help the group to analyze and resolve them.

Managing Conflict

When there is small group conflict—whether openly expressed or hidden in subtle nonverbal cues—the leader needs to address it. The conflict management techniques that are useful in small groups are the same techniques that are useful in an interpersonal interaction.

Postdiscussion Functions

Just as the leader is responsible for prediscussion functions, the leader also is responsible for postdiscussion functions. Such functions might include summarizing the group's discussion, organizing future meetings, or presenting the group's decisions to some other group. All in all, the leader is responsible

for doing whatever needs to be done to ensure that the group's experience is productive.

MEMBERSHIP, LEADERSHIP, AND CULTURE

Most research on and theories about small group communication, membership, and leadership have emerged from universities in the United States and reflect U.S. culture. For example, in the United States—and in individualist cultures generally—each group member is important. But in collectivist cultures the individual is less important; it's the *group* that is the significant entity. In Japan, for example, group researchers find that "individual fulfillment of self is attained through finding and maintaining one's place within the group" (Cathcart & Cathcart, 1985, p. 191). In the United States, in contrast, individual fulfillment of self is attained by the individual and through his or her own efforts, not by the group.

REFLECTIONS
ON ETHICS

The Leader's Ethical Responsibilities

In addition to mastering the skills of effective and efficient leadership, the leader needs also to consider the ethical issues involved in leading a group or an organization. Since the leader is often a chair, CHAIR seems an appropriate acronym to help identify at least some of the characeristics of the ethical leader:

Concern for the welfare of their members. Leaders who are more concerned with their own personal interests, rather than with the group task or the interpersonal needs of the members, would clearly be acting unethically.

Honesty. Leaders should be honest with the group members by, for example, revealing any hidden agendas and presenting information fairly.

Accountability. Leaders should take responsibility for their actions and decisions, admit making mistakes, and take corrective action when necessary.

Integrity. Leaders have integrity; they take the high road. They don't lie or deceive. And they avoid any actions that might violate the basic rights of others.

Responsiveness. The leader must be responsive to all members of the group or the organization.

Ethical Choice Point

You're leading a discussion among a group of high school freshmen whom you're mentoring. The topic turns to marijuana, and the students ask you directly if you smoke pot. The truth is that on occasion you do—but it's a very controlled use, and you feel that it would only destroy your credibility and lead the students to experiment with or continue smoking pot if they knew you did (something you do not want to do). At the same time, you wonder if you can ethically lie to them and tell them that you do not smoke. What is your ethical obligation in this situation? What would you do?

© David Joel/Getty Images

SMALL GROUP CONFLICTS

You're leading a group of graduate and undergraduate students, charged with evaluating the core curriculum. The problem is that neither the graduate students nor the undergraduates want to listen fairly to each other.

WHAT DO YOU SAY?
To whom? Through what channel?

It's often thought that because group membership and group identity are so important in collectivist cultures, it's the group that makes important decisions. Actually, this does not seem to be the case. In fact, a study of 48 (highly collectivist) Japanese organizations found that participating in decision-making groups did not give the members decision-

making power. Group members were encouraged to contribute ideas, but the decision-making power was reserved for the CEO or for managers higher up the organizational ladder (Brennan, 1991).

The discussion of member roles earlier in this unit devoted an entire category to individual roles: roles adopted by individuals to satisfy individual

Theory and Research — Attila's Theory of Leadership
UNDERSTANDING

From a totally different perspective, consider these leadership qualities, paraphrased from Wes Roberts's *Leadership Secrets of Attila the Hun* (1987), a study of the warrior who united many of the nomadic tribes in first-century Asia.

- *Empathy:* Leaders must develop an appreciation for and an understanding of other cultures and the values of their group members.

- *Courage:* Leaders should be fearless and should have the courage to complete their assignments; they must not complain about obstacles or be discouraged by adversity.

- *Dependability:* Leaders must be dependable in carrying out their responsibilities; leaders must also be willing to depend on their group members to accomplish matters they themselves can't oversee.

- *Credibility:* Leaders must be seen as believable by both friends and enemies; they must possess the integrity and intelligence needed to secure and communicate accurate information.

- *Stewardship:* Leaders must be caretakers of their group members' interests and well-being; they must guide and reward subordinates.

Working with Theories and Research

Of these five qualities, which do you see as being the most important to you in your personal and social life? In your business and professional life?

rather than group goals. In other cultures (notably collectivist cultures) these roles probably would not even be mentioned—simply because they wouldn't be acted out often enough to deserve such extended discussion. For example, in many collectivist cultures the group orientation is too pervasive for individuals to violate it by acting as the blocker, the recognition seeker, or the dominator.

In a similar way, each culture's belief system influences group members' behavior. For example, members of many Asian cultures, influenced by Confucian principles, believe that "the protruding nail gets pounded down" and are therefore not likely to voice disagreement with the majority of the group. Americans, on the other hand, influenced by the belief that "the squeaky wheel gets the grease," are more likely to voice disagreement or to act differently from other group members in order to get what they want.

Also, each culture has its own rules of preferred and expected leadership style. In the United States the general and expected style for a group leader is democratic. Our political leaders are elected by a democratic process; similarly, boards of directors are elected by the shareholders of a corporation. In other situations, of course, leaders are chosen by those in authority. The directors choose the president of a company, and the president will normally decide who will supervise and who will be supervised within the organization. Even in this situation, however, we expect the supervisor to behave democratically—to listen to the ideas of employees, to take their views into consideration when decisions are to be made, to keep them informed of corporate developments, and generally to respect their interests. Also, we expect that leaders will be changed fairly regularly, much as we elect a president every four years and company directors each year.

The important point to realize is that your membership and leadership styles are influenced by the culture in which you were raised. Consequently, when in a group with members of different cultures, consider the differences in both membership and leadership styles that individuals bring with them. For example, a member who plays individual roles may be tolerated in many groups in the United States and in some cases may even be thought amusing and different. That same member playing the same roles in a group with a more collectivist orientation is likely to be evaluated much more negatively. Multicultural groups may find it helpful to discuss members' views of group membership and leadership and what constitutes comfortable interaction for them.

SUMMARY: MEMBERS AND LEADERS

This unit examined the roles of members and leaders of small groups and the principles that govern effective small group interaction.

1. A popular classification of small group member roles divides them into group task roles, group building and maintenance roles, and individual roles.

2. Twelve group task roles are: initiator–contributor, information seeker, opinion seeker, information giver, opinion giver, elaborator, coordinator, orienter, evaluator–critic, energizer, procedural technician, and recorder.

3. Seven group building and maintenance roles are: encourager, harmonizer, compromiser, gatekeeper-expediter, standard setter, group observer and commentator, and follower.

4. Eight individual roles are: aggressor, blocker, recognition seeker, self-confessor, playboy/playgirl, dominator, help seeker, and special interest pleader.

5. Interaction process analysis categorizes group members' contributions into four areas: social–emotional positive contributions, social–emotional negative contributions, attempted answers, and questions.

6. Member participation should be group oriented, should center conflict on issues, should be critically open-minded, and should ensure understanding.

7. Groupthink is a way of thinking that develops when concurrence seeking in a cohesive group overrides realistic appraisal of alternative courses of action.

8. Among the major myths about leadership are that leaders are rare, that leaders are born, and that all leaders are charismatic.

9. The traits approach to leadership focuses on personal characteristics that contribute to leadership; the functional approach centers on what the leader does (the functions the leader serves); and the transformational approach focuses on the leader's empowerment of the group members.

10. In the situational theory of leadership, leadership is seen as concerned with both accomplishing the task and serving the interpersonal needs of the members.

The degree to which either concern is emphasized should depend on the specific group and the unique situation.

11. An extension of this situational approach to leadership identifies four leadership styles: the telling style, the selling style, the participating style, and the delegating style. The appropriate style to use depends on the group's level of task and relationship maturity.

12. Among the leader's functions are to activate the group agenda, activate group interaction, maintain effective interaction, empower group members, keep members on track, ensure member satisfaction, encourage ongoing evaluation and improvement, and wrap up the discussion (with summaries or notices of future meetings, for example). In addition, the leader is responsible for appropriate pre- and post-discussion functions.

13. The culture in which people are raised will greatly influence the ways in which members and leaders interact in small groups.

KEY TERMS IN MEMBERS AND LEADERS

agenda
authoritarian leader
delegating style
democratic leader
emergent leader

functional approach to leadership
group building and maintenance roles
group task roles
groupthink

individual roles
interaction process analysis
laissez-faire leader
leadership
participating style
selling style

situational approach to leadership
telling style
traits approach to leadership
transformational approach to leadership

THINKING CRITICALLY ABOUT MEMBERS AND LEADERS

1. **Group Roles in Interpersonal Relationships.** Can you identify roles that you habitually serve in certain groups? Do you serve these roles in your friendship, love, and family relationships as well?

2. **Groupthink.** Have you ever been in a group when groupthink was operating? If so, what were its symptoms? What effect did groupthink have on the process and conclusions of the group?

3. **Leadership Style.** How would you characterize the leadership style of one of your local politicians, religious leaders, college instructors, or talk show hosts? How would you characterize your own leadership style? For example, are you usually more concerned with people or with tasks? Are you more likely to be a laissez-faire, democratic, or authoritarian leader?

4. **The Emergent Leader.** It's been found that the group member with the highest rate of participation is the person most likely to be chosen leader (Mullen, Salas, & Driskell, 1989). Do you find this to be true of the groups in which you have participated? Why do you suppose this relationship exists?

5. **Gender Differences.** Do you find that women and men respond similarly to the different leadership styles? Do women and men exercise the different leadership styles with equal facility, or are women more comfortable and more competent in certain leadership styles and men more comfortable and competent in other styles?

LOGON! MYCOMMUNICATIONLAB
WWW.MYCOMMUNICATIONLAB.COM

Visit MCL and take the self-tests on the kind of leader you are and on your Machiavellian tendencies. Also explore the videos depicting leadership styles and try the Web activity on groupthink. In addition, visit the Small Group Communication website at www.abacon.com/commstudies/groups/group.html for discussions of groupthink, leadership, and group conflict.

REFERENCES

Bales, R. F. (1950). *Interaction process analysis: A method for the study of small groups.* Cambridge, MA: Addison-Wesley.

Bechler, C., & Johnson, S. D. (1995). Leadership and listening: A study of member perceptions. *Small Group Research, 26,* 77-85.

Beebe, S. A., & Masterson, J. T. (2006). *Communicating in small groups: Principles and practices* (8th ed.). Boston: Allyn & Bacon.

Benne, K. D., & Sheats, P. (1948). Functional roles of group members. *Journal of Social Issues, 4,* 41-49.

Bennis, W., & Nanus, B. (1985). *Leaders: The strategies for taking charge.* New York: Harper & Row.

Bodon, J., Powell, L., & Hickson, M., III. (1999). Critiques of gatekeeping in scholarly journals: An analysis of perceptions and data. *Journal of the Association for Communication Administration, 28* (May), 60-70.

Brennan, M. (1991). Mismanagement and quality circles: How middle managers influence direct participation. *Employee Relations, 13,* 22-32.

Cathcart, D., & Cathcart, R. (1985). Japanese social experience and concept of groups. In L. A. Samovar & R. E. Porter (Eds.), *Intercultural communication: A reader* (4th ed., pp. 190-197). Belmont, CA: Wadsworth.

Hackman, M. Z., & Johnson, C. E. (1991). *Leadership: A communication perspective.* Prospect Heights, IL: Waveland Press.

Hersey, P., Blanchard, K. H., & Johnson, D. E. (2001). *Management of organizational behavior: Leading human resources* (8th ed.). Upper Saddle River, NJ: Prentice-Hall.

Janis, I. (1983). *Victims of group thinking: A psychological study of foreign policy decisions and fiascoes* (2nd ed.). Boston: Houghton Mifflin.

Johnson, S. D., & Bechler, C. (1998). Examining the relationships between listening effectiveness and leadership emergence: Perceptions, behaviors, and recall. *Small Group Research, 29* (August), 452-471.

Lewin, K. (1947). *Human relations.* New York: Harper & Row.

Lewis, P. H. (1995, November 13). The new Internet gatekeepers. *New York Times,* pp. D1, D6.

Li, C., & Shi, K. (2003). Transformational leadership and its relationship with leadership effectiveness. *Psychological Science, 26* (January), 115-117.

Lumsden, G., & Lumsden, D. (1996). *Communicating in groups and teams* (2nd ed.). Belmont, CA: Wadsworth.

Mullen, B., Tara, A., Salas, E., & Driskell, J. E. (1994). Group cohesiveness and quality of decision making: An integration of tests of the groupthink hypothesis. *Small Group Research, 25,* 189-204.

Mullen, B., Salas, E., & Driskell, J. (1989). Salience, motivation, and artifact as contributions to the relation between participation rate and leadership. *Journal of Experimental Social Psychology, 25* (November), 545-559.

Northouse, P. G. (1997). *Leadership: Theory and practice.* Thousand Oaks, CA: Sage.

Richmond, V. P., McCroskey, J. C., & McCroskey, L. L. (2005). *Organizational communication for survival: Making work, work.* Boston: Allyn & Bacon.

Roberts, W. (1987). *Leadership secrets of Attila the Hun.* New York: Warner.

Robinson, W. P. (1993). Lying in the public domain. *American Behavioral Scientist, 36* (January), 359-382.

Schafer, M., & Crichlow, S. (1996). Antecedents of groupthink. *Journal of Conflict Resolution, 40* (September), 415-435.

Schultz, B. G. (1996). *Communicating in the small group: Theory and practice* (2nd ed.). New York: HarperCollins.

Shaw, M. E., & Gouran, D. S. (1990). Group dynamics and communication. In G. Dahnke & G. W. Clatterbuck (Eds.), *Human communication: Theory and research.* Belmont, CA: Wadsworth.

329

Chapter 13

Interpersonal and Small Group Conflict

MAJOR TOPICS

Interpersonal and Small Group Conflict

Types of Conflict

Conflict Management Strategies

Special Features

Verbal Aggressiveness:
Charles J. Wigley III

How Verbally Aggressive Are You?

How Argumentative Are You?

Violence and the Media

Ethical Fighting

Understanding Conflict Issues

Understanding Conflict and Gender

Skills Managing Conflicts Early

Skills Finding Win–Win Solutions

© Dirk Anschutz/Getty Images

No matter how effective a communicator you are, you'll still experience conflict and disagreements in interpersonal relationships and in the social and work groups of which you are a part. At some point you are bound to find yourself in conflict with another person or even with an entire group. Because conflict is an inevitable part of interpersonal and group life, it's essential to learn how it works, how it can go wrong, and what you can do to resolve conflicts effectively.

In this unit, you'll learn about:
- the nature of conflict.
- the types of conflict.
- the strategies that people use to manage conflict.

You'll learn to:
- approach conflict positively and realistically.
- engage in interpersonal and group conflict using productive conflict management strategies.

INTERPERSONAL AND SMALL GROUP CONFLICT

Pat wants to go to the movies with Chris; Chris wants to stay home. Pat's insisting on going to the movies interferes with Chris's staying home, and Chris's determination to stay home interferes with Pat's going to the movies. Carl is a member of a work team and wants to convince the group to change advertising agencies; other members don't want any change. Each person in these scenarios has goals that interfere with someone else's desired goals.

Interpersonal and small group conflicts may concern goals to be pursued (for example, parents get upset that their child wants to become an actor instead of a doctor); the allocation of resources such as money or time (for example, group members differ on how to spend the advertising dollar); decisions to be made (for example, some people want a holiday party and others want a cash bonus); or behaviors that are considered appropriate or desirable by one person but inappropriate or undesirable by the other (for example, two people disagree over whether one of them was flirting or drinking or not working at full speed).

As these examples illustrate, interpersonal and small group **conflict** occurs (Hocker & Wilmot, 1985; Folger, Poole, & Stutman, 1997) when people:

- are interdependent; what one person does has an effect on the other person.

- perceive their goals to be incompatible; if one person's goal is achieved, the other's cannot be (for example, if one person wants to buy a new car and the other person wants to save the money for a house).

- see each other as interfering with the attainment of their own goals.

Myths about Conflict

One of the problems many people have in dealing with conflict is that they may be operating on the basis of false assumptions about what conflict is and what it means. Think about your own assumptions about interpersonal and small group conflict, which were probably derived from the communications you witnessed in your family and in your social interactions. For example, do you think the following are true or false?

- Conflict is best avoided.

- If two people are in a relationship conflict, it means they have a bad relationship.

- Conflict damages an interpersonal relationship or small group.

- Conflict is bad because it reveals our negative selves—our pettiness, our need to be in control, our unreasonable expectations.

Simple answers are usually wrong. In this case, each of the four assumptions above may be true or may be false. It depends. In and of itself, conflict is neither good nor bad. Conflict is a part of every interpersonal relationship—of relationships between parents and children, brothers and sisters, friends, lovers, coworkers. If it isn't, then the interaction is probably dull, irrelevant, or insignificant. Conflict seems inevitable.

It's not so much conflict that creates problems as the way in which you approach and deal with the conflict. Some ways of approaching conflict can resolve difficulties and actually improve a relationship. Other ways can hurt the relationship; they can destroy self-esteem, create bitterness, and foster suspicion. Your task, therefore, is not to try to create relationships or groups that will be free of conflict but rather to learn appropriate and productive ways of managing conflict.

Theory and Research   Conflict Issues
UNDERSTANDING

Think about your own interpersonal conflicts, and particularly about the issues you fight over. What exactly do you fight about? Here are the results of two studies that investigated what couples fight about. One study focused on heterosexual couples and identified the four conditions that most often led up to a couple's "first big fight" (Siegert & Stamp, 1994): uncertainty over commitment, jealousy, violation of expectations, and personality differences.

Another study asked what heterosexual, gay, and lesbian couples argued about most and found that all three types of couples were amazingly similar in their conflict issues. All three types argued primarily about these six issues (Kurdek, 1994):

- *Intimacy* issues such as affection and sex
- *Power* issues such as excessive demands or possessiveness, lack of equality in the relationship, friends, and leisure time
- *Personal flaws* issues such as drinking or smoking, personal grooming, and driving style
- *Personal distance* issues such as frequently being absent and school or job commitments
- *Social issues* such as politics, friendships, parents, and personal values
- *Distrust issues* such as previous lovers and lying

Working with Theories and Research

Log on to an online database (for example, Research Navigator at **www.researchnavigator.com***) and search the New York Times archives for recent articles dealing with world conflict. How much of the conflict in the world can be interpreted in communication terms?*

Similarly, it's not the conflict (the disagreement itself) that will reveal your negative side but the fight strategies you use. Thus, if you attack other people, use force, or use personal rejection or manipulation, you will reveal your negative side. But in fighting you can also reveal your positive self—your willingness to listen to opposing points of view, your readiness to change unpleasant behaviors, your willingness to accept imperfection in others.

The Context of Conflict

Conflict, like any form of communication, takes place in a context that is physical, sociopsychological, temporal, and—perhaps most important—cultural.

The Physical, Sociopsychological, and Temporal Contexts

The *physical context*—for example, whether you engage in conflict privately or publicly, alone or in front of children or relatives—will influence the way the conflict is conducted as well as the effects that this conflict will have.

The *sociopsychological context* also will influence the conflict. If the atmosphere is one of equality, for example, the conflict is likely to progress very differently than it would in an atmosphere of inequality. A friendly or a hostile context will exert different influences on the conflict.

The *temporal context* will likewise prove important to understand. A conflict that follows a series of similar conflicts will be seen differently than a conflict that follows a series of enjoyable experiences and an absence of conflict. A conflict immediately after a hard day of work will engender feelings different from a conflict after an enjoyable dinner.

The Cultural Context

Culture influences not only the issues that people fight about, but also what is considered appropriate and inappropriate in terms of dealing with conflict. Researchers have found, for example, that cohabiting 18-year-olds are more likely to experience conflict with their parents about their living style if they live in the United States than if they live in Sweden, where cohabitation is much more accepted. Similarly, male infidelity is more likely to cause conflict between American spouses than in southern European couples. Students from the United States are more likely to engage in conflict with another U.S. student than with someone from another culture. Chinese students, on the other hand, are more likely to engage in a conflict with a non-Chinese student than with another Chinese (Leung, 1988).

The types of conflicts that arise depend on the cultural orientation of the individuals involved. For example, in collectivist cultures, such as those of Ecuador, Indonesia, and Korea, conflicts are more likely to center on violations of collective or group norms and values. Disagreeing in public or proving a colleague wrong in front of others and causing this person to lose face (and violate important cultural norms) is likely to create conflict. Conversely, in individualist cultures, such as those of the United States, Canada, and western Europe, conflicts are more likely to occur when people violate individual norms; for example, if bonuses are not distributed according to merit (Ting-Toomey, 1985).

Americans and Japanese differ in their view of the aim or purpose of conflict. The Japanese (a collectivist culture) tend to see conflicts and conflict resolution in terms of compromise; each side gains something and each side gives up something. Americans (an individualist culture), on the other hand, often see conflict in terms of winning; it's an "I win, you lose" approach (Gelfand, et al., 2001). Also, different cultures seem to teach their members different views of conflict strategies (Tardiff, 2001). For example, in Japan it's especially important that you not embarrass the person with whom you are in conflict, especially if the disagreement occurs when others are present. This face-saving principle prohibits the use of such strategies as personal rejection or verbal aggressiveness. In another example, many Middle Eastern and Pacific rim cultures discourage women from direct and forceful expressions; rather, these societies expect more agreeable and submissive postures on the part of women. Also, in general, members of collectivist cultures tend to avoid conflict more than members of individualist cultures (Dsilva & Whyte, 1998; Haar & Krabe, 1999; Cai & Fink, 2002).

Even within a given general culture, more specific cultures differ from one another in their methods of conflict management. African American men and women and European American men and women, for example, engage in conflict in very different ways (Kochman, 1981). The issues that cause conflict and aggravate conflict, the conflict strategies that are expected and accepted, and the entire attitude toward conflict vary from one group to the other (Collier, 1991; Hecht, Jackson, & Ribeau, 2003).

The cultural norms of organizations also influence the types of conflicts that occur and the ways people may deal with them. Some work environments, for example, would not tolerate the expression of disagreement with high-level management; others might welcome it. In individualist cultures there is greater tolerance for conflict, even when it involves different levels of an organizational hierarchy. In collectivist cultures, there's less tolerance. And, not surprisingly, the culture influences how the conflict will be resolved. For example, managers in the United States (an individualist culture) deal with workplace conflict by seeking to integrate the demands of the different sides; managers in China (a collectivist culture) are more likely to call on higher management to make decisions—or not to resolve the conflict at all (Tinsley & Brett, 2001).

The Negatives and Positives of Conflict

The kind of conflict we are considering here is conflict among or between "connected" individuals, whether in a primary relationship or in a small group. Such conflict occurs frequently between lovers, best friends, siblings, and parent and child; it also occurs within the extended family as well as in workplaces or on sports teams. Such conflict is all the more difficult because, unlike many other conflict situations, interpersonal and small group disagreements often involve people you care for, like, even love. At the very least, these are people with whom you're going to have to interact—so even if there were no other reason, you might as well make conflict as pleasant and productive as you can. There are both negative and positive aspects or dimensions to conflict; let's look at each of these.

Some Negatives of Conflict

Conflict often leads to increased negative regard for the opponent; when this opponent is someone you love or work with on a daily basis, it can create serious problems for the relationship. One reason is that many conflicts involve unfair fighting methods that aim largely to hurt the other person. When one person hurts the other, increased negative feelings are inevitable; even the strongest relationship has limits.

Conflict frequently leads to a depletion of energy better spent on other areas. This is especially true in the small group context; days and even weeks of 10 or 12 people's time can be wasted on conflicts instead of being devoted to solving the problem at hand.

At times, conflict leads you to close yourself off from the other people involved. In an intimate

Theory *and* Research — UNDERSTANDING — Conflict and Gender

Not surprisingly, there are significant gender differences in interpersonal conflict. For example, men are more apt to withdraw from a conflict situation than are women. It's been argued that this may be due to the fact that men become more psychologically and physiologically aroused during conflict (and retain this heightened level of arousal much longer) than do women and so may try to distance themselves and withdraw from the conflict to prevent further arousal (Gottman & Carrere, 1994; Canary, Cupach, & Messman, 1995; Goleman, 1995). Women, on the other hand, want to get closer to the conflict; they want to talk about it and resolve it. Even adolescents reveal these differences; in a study of boys and girls aged 11 to 17, boys withdrew more than girls (Lindeman, Harakka, & Keltikangas-Jarvinen, 1997; Heasley, Babbitt, & Burbach, 1995).

Other research finds that women are more emotional and men are more logical when they argue (Schaap, Buunk, & Kerkstra, 1988; Canary, Cupach, & Messman, 1995). Women have been defined as conflict "feelers" and men as conflict "thinkers" (Sorenson, Hawkins, & Sorenson, 1995). Another difference is that women are more apt to reveal their negative feelings than are men (Schaap, Buunk, & Kerkstra, 1988; Canary, Cupach, & Messman, 1995).

It should be noted, however, that much research fails to support the gender "differences" in conflict style that cartoons, situation comedies, and films portray so readily and so clearly. For example, numerous studies of both college students and men and women in business found no significant differences in the ways men and women engage in conflict (Wilkins & Andersen, 1991; Canary & Hause, 1993; Gottman & Levenson, 1999).

Working with Theories and Research

Log on to an online database and search the communication, psychology, and sociology databases for research on gender and conflict. What can you add to the discussion presented here?

---

relationship, for example, you may hide your true self on the theory that it would not be to your advantage to reveal your weaknesses to your "enemy." But at the same time, closing yourself off may also prevent meaningful communication from taking place. One possible consequence is that one or both parties may seek intimacy elsewhere. This often leads to further conflict, mutual hurt, and resentment—all of which can add heavily to the costs carried by the relationship. As these costs increase, exchanging rewards may become difficult, perhaps impossible. The result is a situation in which the costs increase and the rewards decrease—a situation that often results in relationship deterioration and eventual dissolution.

Some Positives of Conflict

The major value of interpersonal and small group conflict is that it forces you to examine a problem and work toward a potential solution. If people use productive conflict strategies, the relationship or group may well emerge from the encounter stronger, healthier, and more satisfying than before.

Conflict enables each of you to state what you want and—if the conflict is resolved effectively—perhaps to get it. In fact, a better understanding of each other's feelings has been found to be one of the main results of the "first big fight" (Siegert & Stamp, 1994).

Conflict also prevents hostilities and resentments from festering. Suppose you're annoyed at your partner for e-mailing colleagues from work for two hours instead of giving that time to you. If you say nothing, your annoyance and resentment are likely to grow. Further, by saying nothing you implicitly approve of the e-mailing and so make it more likely that such behavior will be repeated. In contrast, through conflict and its resolution you can stop resentment from increasing. In the process you each can let your own needs be known—for example, that you need lots of attention when you come home from work and that your partner needs to review and get closure on the day's work. If you both can appreciate the legitimacy of each other's needs, then solutions may be easily identified. Perhaps the e-mailing can be done after your attention needs are met, or perhaps you can delay your need for attention until your partner gets closure about work. Or perhaps you can learn to provide for your partner's closure needs—and in doing so also get the attention you need.

Consider, too, that when you try to resolve conflict within an interpersonal or small group situation, you're saying in effect that the relationship or group is worth the effort; otherwise you'd walk away from such a conflict. Although there may be exceptions—as when you engage in conflict to save face or to gratify some ego need—usually confronting a conflict indicates concern, commitment, and a desire to improve the relationship or group.

TYPES OF CONFLICT

Conflict can occur in many situations and may be of varied types. Especially important to understand are the differences between (1) content and relationship conflicts, (2) online and workplace conflicts, and (3) the various conflict styles that individuals have.

Content and Relationship Conflicts

Using concepts developed, we may distinguish between content conflict and relationship conflict. **Content conflicts** center on objects, events, and persons in the world that are usually, though not always, external to the parties involved in the conflict. These include the millions of issues that you argue and fight about every day—the value of a particular movie, what to watch on television, the fairness of the last examination or job promotion, the way to spend your savings.

Relationship conflicts are equally numerous and include such conflict situations as a younger brother who does not obey his older brother, group members who all want the final say in what the group decides, and the mother and daughter who each want to have the final word concerning the daughter's lifestyle. Here the conflicts are concerned not so much with some external object as with the relationships between the individuals—with such issues as who is in charge, how equal the partners in a primary relationship are, the importance of each group member, or who has the right to set down rules of behavior.

Content conflicts are usually *manifest*; that is, they're clearly observable and identifiable. Relationship conflicts are often *latent*; they tend to be hidden and much more difficult to identify. Thus, a conflict over where you should vacation may on the surface, or manifest, level center on the advantages and disadvantages of Mexico versus Hawaii. On a relationship and often latent level, however, the conflict may be about who has the greater right to select the place to vacation, who should win the argument, who is the decision maker in the relationship, and so on.

Online and Workplace Conflicts

Two special conflict situations should be noted. The first is online conflict. Just as you can experience disagreement in face-to-face communication, you can experience conflict online; but there are a few conflict situations that are unique to online communication, and we'll look at them here. The second is conflict in the workplace or formal group—in any group that consists of a leader and various members of the organization.

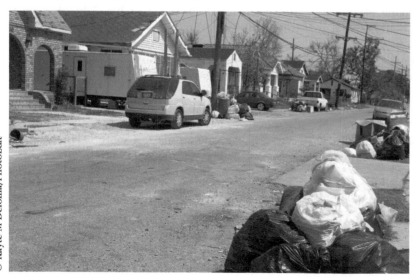

© Kayte M Deioma/PhotoEdit

CONFRONTING A PROBLEM

Your neighbor never puts out the garbage in time for pickup and so the garbage—often broken into by stray animals—remains until the next pickup. You're fed up with the rodents the garbage draws, the smell, and the horrible appearance. You're determined to stop this problem and yet not have your next door neighbor hate you.

WHAT DO YOU SAY?
To whom? Through what channel?

Online Conflicts

Sending commercial messages to those who didn't request them often creates conflict. Junk mail is junk mail; but on the Internet, junk mail slows down the entire Internet system, as well as the individual who has to sit through the downloading of unwanted messages. In many cases (when you access your e-mail from an Internet café, for example), you have to pay for the time it takes to download junk mail.

Spamming often causes conflict. *Spamming* is sending someone unsolicited mail, repeatedly sending the same mail, or posting the same message on lots of bulletin boards, even when the message is irrelevant to the focus of the group. One of the very practical reasons spamming is frowned upon is that it generally costs people money. And even if the e-mail is free, it takes up valuable time and energy to read something you didn't want in the first place. Another reason, of course, is that spam clogs the system, slowing it down for everyone.

Flaming, especially common in newsgroups, is sending messages that personally attack another user. Flaming frequently leads to flame wars, in which everyone in the group gets into the act and attacks other users. Generally, flaming and flame wars prevent us from achieving our goals and so are counterproductive.

Workplace and Formal Group Conflicts

Unlike conflicts that might occur in an informal group of friends or in a family, which are more similar to interpersonal encounters, disagreements in the workplace group present a specific set of issues.

In formal groups it's often the leader's responsibility to manage conflict. Small group communication researchers distinguish between procedural and people conflicts and offer a wide variety of conflict management strategies (Patton, Giffin, & Patton, 1989; Folger, Poole, & Stutman, 1997; Kindler, 1996).

Procedural conflicts involve disagreements over who is in charge (who is the leader or who should be the leader), what the agenda or task of the group should be, and how the group should conduct its business. The best way to deal with procedural problems is to prevent them from occurring in the first place by establishing early in the group's interaction who is to serve as leader and what the agenda should be. If procedural problems arise after these agreements are reached, the leader or members can refer the conflicting participants to the group's earlier decisions. When members oppose or become dissatisfied with these early decisions, however, they may become negative or antagonistic and cease to participate in the discussion. If this happens (or if members want to change procedures), a brief discussion on the procedures can be held. The important point is to deal with procedural conflicts as procedural conflicts and not allow them to escalate into something else.

People conflicts can occur when one member dominates the group, when several members battle for control, or when some members refuse to participate. The leader should try to secure the commitment of all members and to convince them that the progress of the group depends on everyone's contributions. At times, it may be necessary to concentrate on people needs—on the importance of satisfying members' needs for group approval, for periodic rewards, or for encouragement. People conflicts also can develop in the course of debate if members attack people rather than ideas. The leader needs to ensure that attacks and disagreements are clearly focused on ideas, not people. If a personal attack does get started, the leader should step in to refocus the discussion to the idea and away from the person.

The conflict management strategies presented later in this unit are applicable to the workplace or formal group situation. In addition, here are four principles that have special relevance to conflict in this type of group (Kindler, 1996):

- *Preserve the dignity and respect of all members.* Assume, for example, that each person's disagreement is legitimate and stems from a genuine concern for the good of the group. Therefore, treat disagreements kindly; even if someone attacks you personally, it's generally wise not to respond in kind but to redirect the criticism to the issue at hand.

- *Listen empathically.* See the perspectives of the other members; try to feel what they're feeling without making any critical judgments. Try to ask yourself why others see the situation differently from the way you see it.

- *Seek out and emphasize common ground.* Even in the midst of disagreement, there are areas of common interest, common beliefs, and common aims. Find these and build on them.

- *Value diversity and differences.* Creative solutions often emerge from conflicting perspectives. So don't gloss over differences; instead, explore them for the valuable information they can give you.

Conflict Styles

Figure 1 illustrates an approach to conflict that identifies five basic styles or ways of engaging in conflict and is especially helpful in relation to interpersonal and small group conflicts (Blake & Mouton, 1984). The five-styles model, plotted along the dimensions of "concern for oneself" and "concern for the other person," provides considerable insight into the ways people engage in conflict and some of the advantages and disadvantages of each approach. As you read through these styles, try to identify the conflict style you generally use as well as the styles of those with whom you have close relationships.

Competing

The competitive style reflects great concern for your own needs and desires and little for those of others. As long as your needs are met, the conflict has been dealt with successfully. In conflict motivated by competitiveness, you'd be likely to be verbally aggressive while blaming the other person. This style represents an *I win, you lose* philosophy.

Avoiding

The avoider fails to address his or her own or the other's needs or desires. This person avoids any real communication about the problem, changes the topic when the problem comes up, and generally withdraws from the scene both psychologically and physically. As you can appreciate, this style does little to resolve any conflicts and may be viewed as an *I lose, you lose* philosophy.

Accommodating

In accommodating you sacrifice your own needs for the needs of the other person. Your major purpose is to maintain harmony and peace in the relationship or group. This style may help you achieve the immediate goal of maintaining peace and perhaps may satisfy the other person; but it does little to meet your own needs, which are unlikely to go away. This style represents an *I lose, you win* philosophy.

Collaborating

In collaborating you focus on both your own and the other person's needs. This style, often considered the ideal, takes time and a willingness to communicate, and especially a readiness to listen to the perspectives and needs of the other person. Ideally, this style of conflict resolution results in each person's needs being satisfied, an *I win, you win* situation.

Compromising

The compromising style is in the middle; there is some concern for your own needs and some concern for the other's needs. It's the kind of strategy

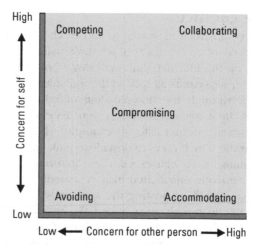

FIGURE 1   Five Conflict Styles

This figure is adapted from Blake and Mouton's (1984) approach to managerial leadership and conflict. Try to locate your usual conflict style on this grid. How well does this style work for you?

Source: An adaptation of The Managerial Grid®, Blake and Mouton's approach to managerial and leadership styles from *The Managerial Grid III*, 3rd Ed. by Blake & Mouton, p. 12. Permission granted by Grid International Inc., copyright owners.

you might refer to as "meeting each other halfway," "horse trading," or "give and take." Compromising is likely to help you maintain peace but to involve some dissatisfaction over the inevitable losses that have to be endured. It results in an *I win and lose and you win and lose* outcome.

CONFLICT MANAGEMENT STRATEGIES

In managing conflict, you can choose from a variety of strategies, which this section will describe. Before getting to the specific conflict management strategies, however, we need to consider some preliminaries.

Preliminaries to Conflict Management Skills

You're more likely to select appropriate strategies if you prepare for and follow up the conflict appropriately, understand the influences on your choice of conflict strategies, and apply the stages of conflict management.

Before the Conflict

Try to fight in private—within the relationship or within the group. When you air your conflicts in front of others, you create a wide variety of other problems. You may not be willing to be totally honest when third parties are present; you may feel you

---

Building Communication Skills — Managing Conflicts Early

This exercise helps you look at your own way of dealing with conflict starters—something someone says that signals to you that this is the start of an interpersonal conflict. For each situation, (a) write an *un*productive response (a response that is likely to cause the conflict to escalate); (b) write a productive response (a response that will likely lessen the potential conflict); and (c) in one sentence explain the major difference that you see between the productive and the unproductive responses.

1. You're late again. You're always late. Your lateness is so inconsiderate!

2. I just can't bear another weekend of sitting home watching cartoon shows with the kids.

3. Well, there goes another anniversary that you forgot.

4. You think I'm fat, don't you?

5. You never want to do what I want. We always have to do what you want.

Impending conflicts are often signaled at a stage when they can be confronted and relatively easily resolved. If they aren't caught early, they may escalate and prove a lot more difficult to resolve later.

---

have to save face and therefore must win the fight at all costs. This may lead you to use strategies aimed at winning the argument rather than strategies aimed at resolving the conflict. Also, of course, you run the risk of embarrassing or upsetting others, which will cause resentment and hostility.

Be sure everyone is ready to fight. Although conflicts arise at the most inopportune times, you can choose the time when you will try to resolve them. The moment when your partner comes home after a hard day of work may not be the right time for a confrontation. When a group is completing the company's most important project on a deadline, it may not be the wisest time to raise minor conflict issues. In general, make sure that all individuals are relatively free of other problems and ready to deal with the conflict at hand.

Know what you're fighting about. Sometimes people in a relationship or in a close-knit group become so hurt and angry that they lash out at the other person just to vent their own frustration. The "content" of the conflict is merely an excuse to express anger. Any attempt at resolving such a "problem" will of course be doomed to failure, because the problem addressed is not what really gave rise to the conflict. Instead, it may be underlying hostility, anger, and frustration that need to be dealt with.

At other times, people argue about general and abstract issues that are poorly specified; for example, a friend's or colleague's lack of consideration or failure to accept responsibility. Only when you define your differences in specific terms can you begin to understand them and thus resolve them.

Fight about problems that can be solved. Fighting about past behaviors or about family members or situations over which you have no control solves nothing; instead, it creates additional difficulties. Any attempt at resolution is doomed, because by their nature such problems can't be solved. Often such conflicts are concealed attempts at expressing frustration or dissatisfaction.

Consider what beliefs you hold that may need to be reexamined. Unrealistic beliefs are often at the heart of interpersonal and group conflicts. Such beliefs include ideas like "If my partner really cared, he or she would do what I ask," "If people really cared about the success of the group, they'd devote 100 percent of their time to the project," or "People don't listen to what I have to say."

After the Conflict

After the conflict is resolved, there's still work to be done. Often, after one conflict is supposedly settled, another conflict will emerge—because, for example, one person may feel harmed and may feel the need to retaliate and take revenge in order to restore self-worth (Kim & Smith, 1993). So it's especially important that the conflict be resolved in such a way that it does not generate other, perhaps more significant, conflicts.

Learn from the conflict and from the process you went through in trying to resolve it. For example, can you identify the fight strategies that aggravated the situation? Do some people need a cooling-off period? Do you need extra space when upset? Can you identify when minor issues are going to escalate into major arguments? Does avoidance make matters worse? What issues are particularly disturbing and likely to cause difficulties? Can these be avoided?

Keep the conflict in perspective. Be careful not to blow it out of proportion—to define your relationship or your social or work group in terms of the conflict. Also, avoid the tendency to see disagreement as inevitably leading to major blowups. Conflicts in most interpersonal and group situations actually occupy a very small percentage of real time, even though in recollection they often loom extremely large.

Negative feelings frequently arise after a conflict, most often because unfair fight strategies were used—strategies such as personal rejection, manipulation, or force. Resolve to avoid such unfair tactics in the future, but at the same time let go of guilt and blame for yourself and others. If you think it would help, discuss these feelings with your partner, your group members, or even a therapist.

Increase the exchange of rewards and cherishing behaviors to demonstrate your positive feelings and to show that you're over the conflict. It's a good way of saying you want the relationship or the group to survive and to flourish.

Influences on Your Choice of Conflict Strategies

A variety of factors will influence the strategies you choose to manage your interpersonal conflicts (Koerner & Fitzpatrick, 2002):

- the goals to be achieved
- your emotional state
- your cognitive assessment of the situation
- your personality and communication competence
- your family history

Understanding these factors may help you select more appropriate and more effective strategies to manage conflict with success (Weitzman & Weitzman, 2000; Weitzman, 2001; Neff & Harter, 2002).

The *goals* (short-term and long-term) you wish to achieve will influence what strategies seem appropriate to you. If you just want to enjoy the moment, you might want to simply "give in" and ignore the difficulty. On the other hand, if you want to build a long-term relationship, you might want to fully analyze the cause of the problem and look for strategies that will enable both parties to win.

Your *emotional state* will influence your strategies; you're not likely to select the same strategies when you're sorry as when you're angry. When sorry, you're likely to use conciliatory strategies designed to make peace; but when you're angry, you're more likely to use strategies that attack the other person.

Your *cognitive assessment* of the situation will exert powerful influence on your selection of strategies. For example, your attitudes and beliefs about what is fair and equitable will influence your readiness to acknowledge the fairness in the other person's position. Your own assessment of who (if anyone) is the cause of the problem also will influence your conflict style. You may also assess the likely effects of your various strategies. For example, what do you risk if you fight with your boss by using blame or personal rejection? As a parent, do you risk alienating your teenager if you use force?

Your *personality and communication competence* will influence the way you engage in conflict. For example, if you're shy and unassertive, you may want to avoid conflict rather than fighting actively. If you're extroverted and have a strong desire to state your position, you may be more likely to fight actively and to argue forcefully.

Your *family history* influences the strategies you use, the topics you choose to fight about, and perhaps your tendencies to obsess or forget about interpersonal conflicts. People often imitate their parents; if your parents argued about money or gave each other the silent treatment when conflict arose, you may repeat these patterns yourself.

The Stages of Conflict Management

If you make the assumption that a conflict is a problem to be resolved, then the steps you go through in managing interpersonal and small group conflict will (generally at least) follow the problem-solving stages. In brief review, you'll recall that these:

- Define and analyze the problem—just what is causing the conflict?

- Establish criteria for evaluating solutions—what will a productive resolution look like?

- Identify possible solutions—what changes will help resolve or manage the conflict?

- Evaluate solutions—which solutions seem to best meet the criteria already identified and thus go furthest in managing the conflict?

- Select the best solution—what solution seems to satisfy all sides the most?

- Test the selected solution—how does the relationship do under this new solution?

With these preliminary guidelines in mind, let's turn now to several different conflict strategies, both productive and unproductive.

Building Communication Skills — Finding Win–Win Solutions

As this section explains, win-win conflict strategies are preferable to win-lose approaches, at least when the conflict is interpersonal. Often, however, people fail even to consider what possible win-win solutions might exist. To get into the habit of looking for these types of solutions, try generating as many win-win solutions as possible (that you feel the individuals could reasonably accept) for the following scenarios. Give yourself two minutes for each case. If possible, share your win-win solutions with other individuals or groups; also, consider ways in which you might incorporate win-win strategies into your own conflict management behavior.

1. Pat and Chris plan to take a two-week vacation in August. Pat wants to go to the shore and relax by the water. Chris wants to go the mountains and go hiking and camping.

2. Pat recently got a totally unexpected $3,000 bonus. Pat wants to buy a new computer and printer for the home office; Chris wants to take a much-needed vacation.

3. Philip has recently come out as gay to his parents. He wants them to accept him and his life (which includes a committed relationship with another man). His parents want him to seek religious counseling for help in changing his orientation.

Win-win solutions exist for most but probably not all conflict situations. Whether you find them or not, it's generally worth looking for them.

Win–Lose and Win–Win Strategies

If you look at interpersonal and small group conflict in terms of winning and losing, you'll see that there are four potential outcomes: (1) A wins, B loses; (2) A loses, B wins; (3) A loses, B loses; and (4) A wins, B wins.

In managing conflict you have a choice and can seek to achieve any one of those combinations of winning and losing. You can look for solutions in which one person or one side wins (usually you or your side) and the other person or other side loses: **win–lose solutions**. Or you can look for solutions in which both you and the other person or side win: **win–win solutions**.

Obviously, win-win solutions are the most desirable. Perhaps the most important reason is that win-win solutions lead to mutual satisfaction and prevent the resentment that win-lose solutions often engender. Looking for and developing win-win solutions makes the next conflict less unpleasant; the participants can more easily view conflict as "solving a problem" rather than as "fighting." Still another advantage is that win-win solutions promote mutual face-saving: Both parties can feel good about themselves. Also, people are more likely to abide by the decisions reached in a win-win conflict than they are in win-lose or lose-lose situations. For all these reasons, win-win solutions are worth seeking whenever possible.

Take an interpersonal example: Let's say that I want to spend our money on a new car (my old one is unreliable) and you want to spend it on a vacation (you're exhausted and feel the need for a rest). Through our conflict and its resolution, ideally we learn what each of us really wants. We may then be able to figure out a way for each of us to get what we want. I might accept a good used car and you might accept a less expensive vacation. Or we might buy a used car and take an inexpensive road trip. Each of these win-win solutions will satisfy both of us; each of us wins, each of us gets what we wanted.

Avoidance and Active Fighting

One nonproductive conflict strategy is **avoidance**. Avoidance may involve actual physical flight: You may leave the scene (walk out of the apartment or meeting room). Or you may simply psychologically tune out all incoming arguments or problems. In the United States men are more likely to use avoidance than women (Markman, Silvern, Clements, & Kraft-Hanak, 1993; Oggins, Veroff, & Leber, 1993), often additionally denying that anything is wrong (Hafer-kamp, 1991-92).

Nonnegotiation is a special type of avoidance. Here you refuse to discuss the conflict or to listen to the other person's argument. At times, nonnegotiation takes the form of hammering away at your point

© CORBIS

of view until the other person gives in, a method referred to as steamrolling.

Instead of avoiding the issues, take an active role in your conflicts. Don't close your ears (or mind) or walk out during an argument. This does not mean that taking time out to cool off is not a useful first strategy. Sometimes it is. In an e-mail conflict, for example, a cooling-off period is an easy-to-use and often effective strategy. By delaying your response until you've had time to think things out more logically and calmly, you'll be better able to respond constructively and to address possible ways to resolve the conflict and get the relationship back to a less hostile stage.

To take an active role, involve yourself on both sides of the communication exchange. That is, participate actively as a speaker-listener; voice your own feelings and listen carefully to the voicing of your opponent's feelings. Be willing to communicate as both sender and receiver—to say what is on your mind and to listen to what the other person is saying.

Another part of active fighting involves taking responsibility for your thoughts and feelings. For example, when you disagree with your partner or with other group members, say, "I disagree with . . ." or "I don't like it when you . . ." Avoid statements that deny your responsibility, as in, "Everybody thinks you're wrong about . . ." or "Even the photography department thinks we shouldn't. . . ."

Force and Talk

When confronted with conflict, many people prefer not to deal with the issues but rather to force their position on the other person. **Force** may be emotional or physical. In either case, it is an unproductive strategy: The issues are avoided and the person who

"wins" is merely the combatant who exerts the most force. This is the technique used by warring nations, children, and even some normally sensible and mature adults. It seems also to be the technique of some persons who are dissatisfied with the power they perceive themselves to have in a relationship, as research shows that perpetrators of violence against both men and women often are motivated to gain control or to defend their own image (Ronfeldt, Kimerling, & Arias, 1998; Felson, 2002).

The use of force is surely one of the most serious problems confronting relationships today, although many approach it as if it were a minor—or even humorous—issue. Researchers found that more than 50 percent of both single and married couples reported that they had experienced physical violence in their relationship. If we add symbolic violence (for example, threatening to hit the other person or throwing something), the percentages are above 60 percent for singles and above 70 percent for marrieds (Marshall & Rose, 1987). In a study of divorced couples, 70 percent reported at least one episode of violence in their premarital, marital, or postmarital relationship. Violence during marriage was higher than for pre- or postmarital relationships (Olday & Wesley, 1990). In another study, 47 percent of a sample of 410 college students reported some experience with violence in a dating relationship (Deal & Wampler, 1986). In most cases the violence was reciprocal—each person in the relationship used violence. In cases in which only one person was violent, the research results were conflicting. For example, in cases in which only one partner was violent, the aggressor was significantly more often the female partner (Deal & Wampler, 1986). Earlier research found similar gender differences (for example, Cate et al., 1982). Other research, however, has tended to confirm the widespread view that men are more likely to use force than women (DeTurck, 1987). Still other research shows that both men and women are likely to use violence but that women are more likely to be injured (Frieze, 2000).

Findings such as these point to problems well beyond the prevalence of unproductive conflict strategies that we want to identify and avoid. They demonstrate the existence of underlying pathologies that we are discovering are a lot more common than were thought previously, when issues like these were never mentioned in college textbooks or lectures. Awareness, of course, is only a first step in understanding and eventually combating such problems.

The only real alternative to force is talk. Instead of using force, you need to talk and listen. The qualities of empathy, openness, and positiveness, for example, are suitable starting points.

Blame and Empathy

Conflict is rarely caused by a single, clearly identifiable problem or by only one of the parties. Usually, conflict occurs because of a wide variety of factors, and all concerned play a role. Any attempt to single out one person for **blame** is sure to be unproductive. Even so, a frequently used fight strategy is to blame another person. Consider, for example, the couple who fight over their child's getting into trouble with the police. Instead of dealing with the conflict itself, the parents may blame each other for the child's troubles. Such blaming, of course, does nothing to resolve the problem or to help the child.

Often, when you blame someone, you attribute motives to the person, a process often referred to as "mind reading." Thus, if the person forgot your birthday and this disturbs you, tackle the actual behavior—the forgetting of the birthday. Try not to presuppose motives: "Well, it's obvious you just don't care about me. If you really cared, you could never have forgotten my birthday!"

Empathy is an excellent alternative to blame. Try to feel what the other person is feeling and to see the situation as the other person does. Try to see the situation as punctuated by the other person, and think about how this differs from your own punctuation.

MEDIA WATCH
VIOLENCE AND THE MEDIA

Most research on media violence has focused on television and, to a lesser extent, on films. But increasingly researchers are examining video games, music, and Internet entertainment for their violent content and potential influence on children. For example, a study of Nintendo and Sega Genesis video games showed that approximately 80 percent of the games included aggression or violence as an essential part of the strategy (Dietz, 1998).

Generally, research finds that media violence can contribute to a variety of effects (Rodman, 2001; Bok, 1998):

- The viewing of violence can teach young people how to be violent; it can teach them the techniques of violence.

- Media violence often gives people (and children especially) role models to emulate (Derne, 1999).

- Because media violence is so prevalent, it can desensitize people to real-life violence around them, which often is not as extreme as they regularly see on television and in the movies.

Media violence can make viewers afraid of becoming victims of violence. The extent to which watching media violence contributes to actual viewer violence, however, has not been determined. In its latest study, unfortunately already more than 20 years old, the National Institute of Mental Health (1982) reported that heavy viewing of violence is related to aggressive behavior and that the greater the viewing of violence, the more likely the person is to be aggressive. But there are probably other factors that lead some people to watch violent films, and these factors may well contribute—in large or small part—to aggressive behavior. Family and social factors, developmental and affective disorders, substance abuse, experience with crime, and the motivation to watch violence, for example, interact with exposure to media violence to produce violent behavior (Withecomb, 1997; Haridakis & Rubin, 2003).

Increasing Media Literacy

How do you feel about violence in the media? If you're unhappy with the current state of media violence, what would you like to see changed? How might you go about effecting these changes?

Demonstrate empathic understanding. Once you have empathically understood the feelings of the other person or group members, validate those feelings as appropriate. If your partner is hurt or angry and you feel that such feelings are legitimate and justified (from the other person's point of view), say so; say, "You have a right to be angry; I shouldn't have said what I did. I'm sorry. But I still don't want to go on vacation with your college roommate." In expressing validation you're not necessarily expressing agreement on the point at issue; you're merely stating that your partner's feelings are legitimate and that you recognize them as such.

Gunnysacking and Present Focus

A *gunnysack* is a large bag, usually made of burlap. The unproductive conflict strategy known as **gunnysacking** is the practice of storing up grievances so as to unload them at another time (Bach & Wyden, 1968). The occasion for unloading may be relatively minor (or so it might seem at first); for example, you come home late without calling, or you fail to fulfill your assigned task before a meeting at work. Instead of addressing the immediate problem, the gunnysacker unloads all past grievances. The birthday you forgot, the times you were absent from meetings, the hotel reservations you forgot to make. As you probably know from experience, gunnysacking begets gunnysacking. When one person gunnysacks, the other person gunnysacks. The result is that both sides dump their stored-up grievances on each other. Frequently, the trigger problem never gets addressed. Instead, resentment and hostility escalate.

Focus your conflict on the here and now rather than on issues that occurred two months ago. Similarly, focus your conflict on the person with whom you're fighting, not on the person's mother, child, or friends.

Manipulation and Spontaneity

Manipulation involves an avoidance of open conflict. The manipulative individual tries to divert conflict by being especially charming (disarming, actually). The manipulator gets the other individual into a receptive and noncombative frame of mind, then presents his or her demands to a weakened opponent. The manipulator relies on our tendency to give in to people who are especially nice to us.

Instead of manipulating, try expressing your feelings with **spontaneity** and honesty. Remember that in conflict situations there's no need to plan a strategy to win a war. The objective is not to win but to increase mutual understanding and to reach a decision that both parties can accept.

Personal Rejection and Acceptance

A person practicing **personal rejection** withholds approval and affection from his or her opponent in conflict, seeking to win the argument by getting the other person to break down in the face of this withdrawal. The individual acts cold and uncaring in an effort to demoralize the other person. In a group situation a person might practice rejection by not listening, not giving any positive feedback, or perhaps even giving negative feedback, making you think everything you're saying is gibberish. In withdrawing positive messages, the rejecting individual hopes to make the other person question his or her own self-worth. Once the other is demoralized and feels less than worthy, it's relatively easy for "rejectors" to get their way. They hold out the renewal of approval and affection as a reward for a resolution in their own favor.

Instead of rejection, express positive feelings for the other person and for the relationship or group. Throughout any conflict, harsh words will probably be exchanged, later to be regretted. The words cannot be unsaid or uncommunicated, but they can be partially offset by the expression of positive statements.

Fighting below and above the Belt

Much like boxers in a ring, each of us has a "belt line." When you hit someone below the emotional belt line, a tactic called **beltlining,** you can inflict serious injury. When you hit above the belt, however, the person is able to absorb the blow. With most interpersonal relationships, especially those of long standing, we know where the belt line is. You know, for example, that to hit Pat with the inability to have children is to hit below the belt. You know that to hit Chris with the failure to get a permanent job is to hit below the belt. You know that to stress the number of years your colleague has been in the same position without a promotion is to hit below the belt. Hitting below the belt line causes everyone involved added problems. Keep blows to areas your opponent can absorb and handle.

Remember that the aim of interpersonal and small group conflict is not to win and have your opponent lose. Rather, it's to resolve a problem and strengthen the relationship or group. Keep this ultimate goal always in clear focus, especially when you're angry or hurt.

Face-Detracting and Face-Enhancing Strategies

Another dimension of conflict strategies is that of *face orientation*. Face-detracting or face-attacking

REFLECTIONS ON ETHICS

Ethical Fighting

This unit emphasizes the differences between effective and ineffective conflict strategies. But every conflict strategy also has an ethical dimension. Consider just a few examples:

- Does conflict avoidance have an ethical dimension? For example, is it unethical for one romantic partner to refuse to discuss issues of disagreement with the other?

- Is it ever ethical to force someone to accept your position? Can you identify situation in which it would be appropriate for someone with greater physical strength to overpower another person to enforce his or her point of view?

- Is it ever ethical to use face-detracting strategies? Are face-detracting strategies inherently unethical, or might it be appropriate to use them in certain situations? Can you identify such situations?

- What are the ethical implications of verbal aggressiveness? Why might it be argued that argumentativeness is more ethical than verbal aggressiveness?

Ethical Choice Point

At your high-powered and highly stressful job you sometimes use coke with your colleagues. This happens several times a month. You don't use drugs of any kind at any other times. Your partner—who you know hates drugs and despises people who use any recreational drug—asks you if you take drugs. Because your use is so limited, but mostly because you know that admitting it will cause a huge conflict in a relationship that's already having difficulties, you wonder if you can ethically lie about this. What is your ethical obligation in this situation? What would you say?

---

strategies involve treating the other person as incompetent or untrustworthy, as unable or bad (Donohue, 1992). Such attacks can vary from mildly embarrassing to severely damaging to the other person's ego or reputation (Imahori & Cupach, 1994). When such attacks become extreme, they may be similar to verbal aggressiveness—another unproductive tactic that we'll consider shortly. Protecting our image (or face), especially in the midst of conflict, is important to everyone, but especially important to members of the collectivist cultures of Asia (Zane & Yeh, 2002).

Face-enhancing techniques, in contrast, help the other person maintain a positive image—an image as competent and trustworthy, able and good. There's some evidence to show that even when, say, you get what you want in a bargaining situation, it is wise to help the other person retain positive face. This makes it less likely that future conflicts will arise (Donohue, 1992).

Not surprisingly, people are more likely to make a greater effort to support their opponent's "face" if they like the opponent than if they don't (Meyer, 1994). So be especially careful to avoid "fighting words"—words that are sure to escalate the conflict rather than to help resolve it. Words like *stupid*, *liar*, and *bitch*, as well as words like *always* and *never* (as in "you always" or "you never"), invariably create additional problems. In contrast, confirming the other person's definition of self, avoiding attack

and blame, and using excuses and apologies as appropriate are some generally useful face-positive strategies.

Nonassertive and Assertive Strategies

Nonassertiveness can be unproductive, because it involves the failure to express your thoughts and feelings in certain or all communication situations. Nonassertive people often fail to assert their rights. In many instances these people do what others tell them to do—parents, employers, and the like—without questioning. They operate with a "you win, I lose" philosophy, giving others what they want without concern for themselves (Lloyd, 2001). Nonassertive people often ask permission from others to do what is their perfect right. They are often anxious in social situations and their self-esteem is likely to be low.

Assertiveness means acting in your own best interests *without* denying or infringing on the rights of others. Not surprisingly, assertiveness can be especially helpful in conflict situations (Fodor & Collier, 2001). Assertive people operate with an "I win, you win" philosophy; they assume that both parties can gain something from conflict. Assertive people speak their minds and welcome others' doing likewise. Assertive people also tend to be more positive and generally score higher on measures of hopefulness than nonassertive individuals (Velting, 1999).

There are wide cultural differences in assertiveness. For example, individualist cultures are more likely to value assertiveness than are collectivist cultures. That is, cultures that stress competition, individual success, and independence also will admire assertiveness; cultures that stress cooperation, group success, and the interdependence of all members will value assertiveness much less. American students, for example, are found to be significantly more assertive than Japanese or Korean students (Thompson, Klopf, & Ishii, 1991; Thompson & Klopf, 1991). Thus, in conflict situations assertiveness may prove an effective strategy in one culture but may create problems in another culture.

Here are a few suggestions to help you communicate more assertively:

- *Describe the problem; don't evaluate or judge it:* "We both want what's right for the kids, but we haven't gotten together to discuss the problems." Be sure to use I-messages and to avoid messages that accuse or blame the other person.

- *State how this problem affects you:* "I'm worrying about this during the day and it's affecting my job."

- *Propose solutions that are workable and that allow the person to save face:* "Let's make some time tomorrow to discuss how we want to handle things."

- *Confirm understanding:* "Would that be okay? Say, about eight?"

Aggressiveness and Argumentativeness

An especially interesting perspective on conflict has emerged from researchers' work on verbal aggressiveness and argumentativeness (Infante, 1988; Rancer, 1998; Wigley, 1998). Understanding these two concepts will help you understand some of the reasons why things go wrong and some of the ways in which you can use conflict to actually improve your relationships.

Verbal Aggressiveness

Verbal aggressiveness is an unproductive conflict strategy in which one person tries to win an argument by inflicting psychological pain, by attacking the other person's self-concept. The technique relies on many of the other unproductive conflict strategies we've already considered. It's a type of disconfirmation in that it seeks to discredit the individual's view of self. To explore this tendency further, take the following self-test of verbal aggressiveness.

TEST YOURSELF

How Verbally Aggressive Are You?

This scale measures how people try to obtain compliance from others. For each statement, indicate the extent to which you feel it's true for you in your attempts to influence others. Use the following scale: 5 = strongly agree, 4 = agree, 3 = undecided, 2 = disagree, and 1 = strongly disagree.

_____ **1.** If individuals I am trying to influence really deserve it, I attack their character.

_____ **2.** When individuals are very stubborn, I use insults to soften their stubbornness.

_____ **3.** When people behave in ways that are in very poor taste, I insult them in order to shock them into proper behavior.

_____ **4.** When people simply will not budge on a matter of importance, I lose my temper and say rather strong things to them.

_____ **5.** When individuals insult me, I get a lot of pleasure out of really telling them off.

_____ **6.** I like poking fun at people who do things that are stupid in order to stimulate their intelligence.

_____ **7.** When people do things that are mean or cruel, I attack their character in order to help correct their behavior.

_____ **8.** When nothing seems to work in trying to influence others, I yell and scream in order to get some movement from them.

_____ **9.** When I am unable to refute others' positions, I try to make them feel defensive in order to weaken their positions.

_____ **10.** When people refuse to do a task I know is important without good reason, I tell them they are unreasonable.

HOW DID YOU DO? To compute your verbal aggressiveness score, simply add up your responses. A total score of 30 would indicate the neutral point, not especially aggressive but not especially confirming of the other either. If you scored about 35, you would be considered moderately aggressive; and if you scored 40 or more, you'd be considered very aggressive. If you scored below the neutral point, you'd be considered less verbally aggressive and more confirming when interacting with others. In looking over your responses, take special note of the behaviors identified in the 10 statements, all of which indicate a tendency to act verbally aggressive. Note any inappropriate behaviors that you're especially prone to commit.

WHAT WILL YOU DO? Because verbal aggressiveness is likely to seriously reduce communication effectiveness, you probably want to reduce your tendencies to respond aggressively. Review the times when you acted verbally aggressive toward another person. What effect did such actions have on your subsequent interaction? What effect did they have on your relationship with the other person? What alternative ways of getting your point across might you have used? Might these have proved more effective? Perhaps the most general suggestion for reducing verbal aggressiveness is to increase your argumentativeness, as will be discussed below.

Source: From a 20-item scale developed by Infante and Wigley (1986) and factor analyzed by Beatty, Rudd, and Valencic (1999). Also see Dominic Infante & C. J. Wigley, "Verbal Aggressiveness," *Communication Monographs, 53*, 1986; Michael J. Beatty, Jill E. Rudd, & Kristin Marie Valencic, "A Re-evaluation of the Verbal Aggressiveness Scale: One Factor or Two?" *Communication Research Reports, 16*, 10–17, 1999; and T. R. Levine, M. J. Beatty, S. Limon, M. A. Hamilton, R. Buck, & R. M. Chory-Assad, "The Dimensionality of the Verbal Aggressiveness Scale," *Communication Monographs, 71*, 245–268, September 2004. Copyright © 1986 by the National Communication Association. Reprinted by permission of the publisher and authors.

ASK THE RESEARCHER

Verbal Aggressiveness

My boyfriend is really sweet, and I know he really loves me. But at times, he's verbally aggressive. Sometimes he gets really angry (like when I do something wrong) and says really hurtful things. He's asked me to move in with him, and I'm not sure what to do. Any ideas?

Can a sweet guy be hurtful? Some people attack so often, they become less sensitive to their hurtfulness. Tell him what made you feel badly. If he was more aware of his unfriendly language, maybe he'd curtail it.

When you "do something wrong," he gets angry. Is his behavior justified? Most people believe justified aggression is okay (like shooting back!) but that aggression without justification is bad. Maybe you said something "well-intended" to him that made him feel attacked. Maybe your words served as a Verbal Trigger Event, a catalyst to a verbal "shooting back." He might think he's justified, even though it's just misplaced defensiveness.

Is aggression ever justified? Here's a simple test: If his boss made the "mistake," would he react the same way? I'll bet he wouldn't! Assertiveness, constructive arguing, and, sometimes, silence are nice alternatives.

Remember, words can't hurt you, only people can hurt you. Should you move in? Harry Connick Jr. sings, never "build a house in a hurricane."

For further information: Venable, K. V., & Martin, M. M. (1997). Argumentativeness and verbal aggressiveness in dating relationships. *Journal of Social Behavior and Personality, 12*(4), 955–964. Also Rancer, A. S., & Avtgis, T. A. (2006). *Argumentative and aggressive communication: Theory, research, and application*, pp. 87–108. Thousand Oaks, CA: Sage.

Charles J. Wigley III (Ph.D., Kent State University; J.D., University of Akron) is a professor of communication at Canisius College and teaches research methods and training and development (wigley@canisius.edu). An experienced defense attorney, he studies the role of communication in jury selection.

Argumentativeness

Contrary to popular usage, argumentativeness is a quality to be cultivated rather than avoided. The term **argumentativeness** in this context refers to your willingness to argue for a point of view, your tendency to speak your mind on significant issues. It's the mode of dealing with disagreements that is the preferred alternative to verbal aggressiveness (Infante & Rancer, 1995). Assess your own degree of argumentativeness by taking the self-test below.

TEST YOURSELF

How Argumentative Are You?

This questionnaire contains statements about controversial issues. Indicate how often each statement is true for you personally according to the following scale: 1 = almost never true, 2 = rarely true, 3 = occasionally true, 4 = often true, and 5 = almost always true.

_____ **1.** While in an argument, I worry that the person I am arguing with will form a negative impression of me.

_____ **2.** Arguing over controversial issues improves my intelligence.

_____ **3.** I enjoy avoiding arguments.

_____ **4.** I am energetic and enthusiastic when I argue.

_____ **5.** Once I finish an argument, I promise myself that I will not get into another.

_____ **6.** Arguing with a person creates more problems for me than it solves.

_____ **7.** I have a pleasant, good feeling when I win a point in an argument.

_____ **8.** When I finish arguing with someone, I feel nervous and upset.

_____ **9.** I enjoy a good argument over a controversial issue.

_____ **10.** I get an unpleasant feeling when I realize I am about to get into an argument.

_____ **11.** I enjoy defending my point of view on an issue.

_____ **12.** I am happy when I keep an argument from happening.

_____ **13.** I do not like to miss the opportunity to argue a controversial issue.

_____ **14.** I prefer being with people who rarely disagree with me.

_____ **15.** I consider an argument an exciting intellectual challenge.

_____ **16.** I find myself unable to think of effective points during an argument.

_____ **17.** I feel refreshed and satisfied after an argument on a controversial issue.

_____ **18.** I have the ability to do well in an argument.

_____ **19.** I try to avoid getting into arguments.

_____ **20.** I feel excitement when I expect that a conversation I am in is leading to an argument.

HOW DID YOU DO? To compute your score follow these steps:

1. Add your scores on items 2, 4, 7, 9, 11, 13, 15, 17, 18, and 20.

2. Add 60 to the sum obtained in step 1.

3. Add your scores on items 1, 3, 5, 6, 8, 10, 12, 14, 16, and 19.

4. Subtract the total obtained in step 3 from the total obtained in step 2.

Your score will range between a low of 20 to a high of 100. Scores between 73 and 100 indicate high argumentativeness; scores between 56 and 72 indicate moderate argumentativeness; and scores between 20 and 55 indicate low argumentativeness.

WHAT WILL YOU DO? The researchers who developed this test note that both high and low argumentatives may experience communication difficulties. The high argumentative, for example, may argue needlessly, too often, and too forcefully. The low argumentative, on the other hand, may avoid taking a stand even when it seems necessary. Persons scoring somewhere in the middle are probably the more interpersonally skilled and adaptable, arguing when it is necessary but avoiding arguments that are needless and repetitive. Does your experience support this observation? What specific actions might you take to improve your level of argumentativeness?

Source: From Dominic Infante and Andrew Rancer, "A Conceptualization and Measure of Argumentativeness," *Journal of Personality Assessment, 46* (1982), 72–80. Copyright © 1982 Lawrence Erlbaum Associates, Inc. Reprinted by permission of Lawrence Erlbaum Associates, Inc., and the authors.

Differences between Argumentativeness and Verbal Aggressiveness.

As you can appreciate, there are numerous differences between argumentativeness and verbal aggressiveness. Here are just a few (Infante & Rancer, 1995; Rancer & Atvgis, 2006):

Argumentativeness	Verbal Aggressiveness
Is *constructive*; the outcomes are positive in a variety of communication situations (interpersonal, group, organizational, family, and intercultural).	Is destructive; the outcomes are negative in a variety of communication situations (interpersonal, group, organizational, family, and intercultural).
Leads to relationship *satisfaction*.	Leads to relationship dissatisfaction, not surprising for a strategy that aims to attack another's self-concept.
May prevent *relationship violence*, especially in domestic relationships.	May lead to relationship violence.
Enhances *organizational life*; for example, subordinates prefer supervisors who encourage argumentativeness.	Damages organizational life and demoralizes workers on varied levels.
Enhances *parent–child communication* and enables parents to gain greater compliance.	Prevents meaningful parent–child communication and makes corporal punishment more likely.
Increases the user's *credibility*; argumentatives are seen as trustworthy, committed, and dynamic.	Decreases the user's credibility, in part because it's seen as a tactic to discredit the person rather than address the argument.
Argumentativeness increases the user's *power of persuasion* in varied communication contexts; argumentatives are more likely to be seen as leaders.	Decreases the user's power of persuasion.

© Bob Daemmrich Photography

TALKING AGGRESSIVELY

Your partner is becoming more and more verbally aggressive and you're having trouble with this new communication pattern. Regardless of what the conflict is about, your self-concept is attacked. You've had enough and you want to stop this kind of attack.

WHAT DO YOU SAY?
Through what channel?

Strategies for Becoming More Argumentative.

Here are some suggestions for developing argumentativeness—and for preventing it from degenerating into aggressiveness (Infante, 1988).

- Treat disagreements as objectively as possible; avoid assuming that because someone takes issue with your position or your interpretation, they're attacking you as a person.

- Center your arguments on issues rather than personalities. Avoid attacking a person (rather than the person's arguments), even if this would give you a tactical advantage—it will probably backfire at some later time and make your relationship or group participation more difficult.

- Reaffirm the other person's sense of competence; compliment the other person as appropriate.

- Allow the other person to state her or his position fully before you respond; avoid interrupting.

- Stress equality, and stress the similarities that you have with the other person or persons; stress your areas of agreement before attacking the disagreements.

- Express interest in the other person's position, attitude, and point of view.

- Avoid getting overemotional; using an overly loud voice or interjecting vulgar expressions will prove offensive and eventually ineffective.

- Allow people to save face; never humiliate another person.

SUMMARY: INTERPERSONAL AND SMALL GROUP CONFLICT

This unit has explored interpersonal and small group conflict: the types of conflicts that occur, the don'ts and dos of conflict management, and what to do before and after the conflict.

1. Relationship and small group conflict occurs among people who are connected but who have opposing goals that interfere with others' desired goals. Conflicts may occur face-to-face or on the Internet, through e-mail, in newsgroups, and in other contexts.

2. Interpersonal conflicts may yield both positive and/or negative results.

3. Content conflicts center on objects, events, and persons in the world that are usually, though not always, external to the parties involved.

4. Relationship conflicts are concerned not so much with some external object as with relationships between individuals—with such issues as who is in charge, how equal the partners are in a primary relationship, or who has the right to set down rules of behavior.

5. In preparation for conflict, try to fight in private and when all are ready to fight. Have a clear idea of what you want to fight about, and be specific; fight about things that can be solved; and reexamine beliefs that may be unrealistic. Consider, too, the value of following a standard sequence of steps in dealing with the conflict.

6. After the conflict, assess what you've learned, keep the conflict in perspective, let go of negative feelings, and increase positiveness.

7. Among the conflict styles are competing, avoiding, accommodating, collaborating, and compromising.

8. Unproductive and productive conflict strategies include: win–lose and win–win approaches, avoidance and fighting actively, force and talk, blame and empathy, gunnysacking and present focus, manipulation and spontaneity, personal rejection and acceptance, fighting below and above the belt, face-detracting and face-enhancing tactics, nonassertive and assertive approaches, and fighting aggressively and argumentatively.

9. To cultivate constructive argumentativeness, treat disagreements objectively and avoid attacking the other person, reaffirm the other's sense of competence, avoid interrupting, stress equality and similarities, express interest in the other's position, avoid presenting your arguments too emotionally, and allow the other to save face.

KEY TERMS IN INTERPERSONAL AND SMALL GROUP CONFLICT

argumentativeness	conflict	nonnegotiation	win–lose solution
assertiveness	content conflict	personal rejection	win–win solution
avoidance	force	relationship conflict	
beltlining	gunnysacking	spontaneity	
blame	manipulation	verbal aggressiveness	

THINKING CRITICALLY ABOUT INTERPERSONAL AND SMALL GROUP CONFLICT

1. **Gender Differences.** Why do you think men are more likely to withdraw from conflict than women? For example, what arguments can you present for or against any of these reasons (Noller, 1993): Because men have difficulty dealing with conflict? Because the culture has taught men to avoid it? Because withdrawal is an expression of power?

2. **Culture and Conflict.** What does your own culture teach about conflict and its management? What strategies does it prohibit? Are some strategies prohibited in conflicts with certain people (say, your parents) but not in conflicts with others (say, your friends)? Does your culture prescribe certain ways of dealing with conflict? Does it have different expectations for men and for women? To what degree have you internalized these teachings? What effect do these teachings have on your actual conflict behaviors?

3. **Conflict Style.** How would you describe your conflict style in your own close relationships in terms of the competing/avoiding/accommodating/collaborating/compromising model?

4. **E-mail and Interpersonal Conflict.** In what ways do you find that e-mail can escalate interpersonal conflict? In what ways might e-mail help resolve conflict?

5. **Positiveness.** One study found that, at least in general, people are more positive in dealing with conflict in face- to-face situations than in computer-mediated communication (Zornoza, Ripoll, & Peiró, 2002). Do you find this to be true? If so, why do you think it's true?

LogOn! MyCommunicationLab
WWW.MYCOMMUNICATIONLAB.COM

Visit MCL and take the self-test to measure your own assertiveness. Try also working with the exercises and reading the additional discussions: Managing Power Plays, Assertiveness, The Influence of Culture on Conflict: An Example, Analyzing a Conflict Episode and How Do You Fight? Like a Man? Like a Woman? Explore the video on conflict among prom planners and listen to the brief discussions on Domestic Violence against Men and The Reunion. Also take a look at the Small Group Communication website at **www.abacon.com/commstudies/groups** and read about conflict in groups.

References

Bach, G. R., & Wyden, P. (1968). *The intimate enemy*. New York: Avon.

Blake, R. R., & Mouton, J. S. (1984). *The managerial grid III* (3rd ed.). Houston, TX: Gulf Publishing.

Bok, S. (1998). *Mayhem: Violence as public entertainment*. Reading, MA: Perseus Books.

Cai, D. A., & Fink, E. L. (2002). Conflict style differences between individualists and collectivists. *Communication Monographs, 69* (March), 67-87.

Canary, D. J., Cupach, W. R., & Messman, S. J. (1995). *Relation ship conflict*. Thousand Oaks, CA: Sage.

Canary, D. J., & Hause, K. S. (1993). Is there any reason to research sex differences in communication? *Communication Quarterly, 41* (Spring), 129-144.

Cate, R., Henton, J., Koval, J., Christopher, R., & Lloyd, S. (1982). Premarital abuse: A social psychological perspective. *Journal of Family Issues, 3*, 79-90.

Collier, M. J. (1991). Conflict competence within African, Mexican, and Anglo-American friendships. In S. Ting-Toomey & F. Korzenny (Eds.), *Cross-cultural interpersonal communication* (pp. 132-154). Thousand Oaks, CA: Sage.

Deal, J. E., & Wampler, K. S. (1986). Dating violence: The primacy of previous experience. *Journal of Social and Personal Relationships, 3*, 457-471.

Derne, S. (1999). Making sex violent: Love as force in recent Hindi films. *Violence against Women, 5* (May), 548-575.

DeTurck, M. A. (1987). When communication fails: Physical aggression as a compliance-gaining strategy. *Communication Monographs, 54*, 106-112.

Dietz, T. L. (1998). An examination of violence and gender role portrayals in video games: Implications for gender socialization and aggressive behavior. *Sex Roles, 38* (March), 425-442.

Donohue, W. A. (with Kolt, R.). (1992). *Managing interpersonal conflict*. Thousand Oaks, CA: Sage.

Dsilva, M. U., & Whyte, L. O. (1998). Cultural differences in conflict styles: Vietnamese refugees and established residents. *The Howard Journal of Communications, 9* (January-March), 57-68.

Felson, R. B. (2002). Violence and gender reexamined. *Law and public policy*. Washington, DC: American Psychological Association.

Fodor, I. G., & Collier, J. C. (2001). Assertiveness and conflict resolution: An integrated Gestalt/cognitive behavioral model for working with urban adolescents. In M. McConville & G. Wheeler (Eds.), *The heart of development: Vol. II: Adolescence: Gestalt approaches to working with children, adolescents and their worlds* (pp. 214- 252). Cambridge, ME: Analytic Press.

Folger, J. P., Poole, M. S., & Stutman, R. K. (1997). *Working through conflict: A communication perspective* (3rd ed.). New York: Longman.

Frieze, I. H. (2000). Violence in close relationships—development of a research area: Comment on Archer (2000). *Psychological Bulletin, 126* (September), 681-684.

Gelfand, M. J., Nishii, L. H., Holcombe, K. M., Dyer, N., Ohbuchi, K., & Fukuno, M. (2001). Cultural influences on cognitive representations of conflict: Interpretations of conflict episodes in the United States and Japan. *Journal of Applied Psychology, 86*, 1059-1074.

Goleman, D. (1995, February 14). For man and beast, language of love shares many traits. *New York Times*, pp. C1, C9.

Gottman, J. M., & Carrere, S. (1994). Why can't men and women get along? Developmental roots and marital inequities. In D. J. Canary & L. Stafford (Eds.), *Communication and relational maintenance* (pp. 203-229). San Diego, CA: Academic Press.

Gottman, J. M., & Levenson, R. W. (1999). Dysfunctional marital conflict: Women are being unfairly blamed. *Journal of Divorce and Remarriage, 31*, 1-17.

Haar, B. F., & Krabe, B. (1999). Strategies for resolving interpersonal conflicts in adolescence: A German-Indonesian comparison. *Journal of Cross-Cultural Psychology, 30* (November), 667-683.

Haferkamp, C. J. (1991-92). Orientations to conflict: Gender, attributions, resolution strategies, and self-monitoring. *Current Psychology Research and Reviews, 10* (Winter), 227-240.

Haridakis, P. M., & Rubin, A. M. (2003). Motivation for watching television violence and viewer aggression. *Mass Communication and Society, 6* (February), 29-56.

Heasley, J. B., Babbitt, C. E., & Burbach, H. J. (1995). Gender differences in college students' perceptions of "fighting words." *Sociological Viewpoints, 11* (Fall), 30-40.

Hecht, M. L., Jackson, R. L., & Ribeau, S. (2003). *African American communication: Exploring identity and culture* (2nd. ed.). Mahwah, NJ: Erlbaum.

Hocker, J. L., & Wilmot, W. W. (1985). *Interpersonal conflict* (2nd ed.). Dubuque, IA: William C. Brown.

Imahori, T. T., & Cupach, W. R. (1994). A cross-cultural comparison of the interpretation and management of face: U.S. American and Japanese responses to embarrassing predicaments. *International Journal of Intercultural Relations, 18* (Spring), 193-219.

Infante, D. A. (1988). *Arguing constructively*. Prospect Heights, IL: Waveland Press.

Infante, D. A., & Rancer, A. S. (1995). Argumentativeness and verbal aggressiveness: A review of recent theory and research. In B. R. Burleson (Ed.), *Communication Yearbook 19*. Thousand Oaks, CA: Sage.

Kim, S. H., & Smith, R. H. (1993). Revenge and conflict escalation. *Negotiation Journal, 9* (January), 37-43.

Kindler, H. S. (1996). *Managing disagreement constructively* (Rev. ed.). Menlo Park, CA: Crisp Publications.

Kochman, T. (1981). *Black and white: Styles in conflict.* Chicago, IL: University of Chicago Press.

Koerner, A. F., & Fitzpatrick, M. A. (2002). You never leave your family in a fight: The impact of family of origin on conflict behavior in romantic relationships. *Communication Studies 53* (fall), 234-252.

Kurdek, L. A. (1994). Areas of conflict for gay, lesbian, and heterosexual couples: What couples argue about influences relationship satisfaction. *Journal of Marriage and the Family, 56* (November), 923-934.

Leung, K. (1988). Some determinants of conflict avoidance. *Journal of Cross-Cultural Psychology, 19* (March), 125-136.

Lindeman, M., Harakka, T., & Keltikangas-Jarvinen, L. (1997). Age and gender differences in adolescents' reactions to conflict situations: Aggression, prosociality, and withdrawal. *Journal of Youth and Adolescence, 26* (June), 339-351.

Lloyd, S. R. (2001). *Developing positive assertiveness* (3rd ed.). Menlo Park, CA: Crisp Publications.

Markman, H. J., Silvern, L., Clements, M., & Kraft-Hanak, S. (1993). Men and women dealing with conflict in heterosexual relationships. *Journal of Social Issues, 49* (Fall), 107-125.

Marshall, L. L., & Rose, P. (1987). Gender, stress, and violence in the adult relationships of a sample of college students. *Journal of Social and Personal Relationships, 4*, 299-316.

Meyer, J. R. (1994). Effect of situational features on the likelihood of addressing face needs in requests. *Southern Communication Journal, 59* (Spring), 240-254.

National Institute of Mental Health. (1982). *Television and behavior: Ten years of scientific progress and implications for the eighties.* Rockville, MD: National Institute of Mental Health.

Neff, K. D., & Harter, S. (2002). The authenticity of conflict resolutions among adult couples: Does women's other oriented behavior reflect their true selves? *Sex Roles, 47* (November), 403-417.

Noller, P. (1993). Gender and emotional communication in marriage: Different cultures or differential social power? In *Emotional communication, culture, and power* [Special issue]. *Journal of Language and Social Psychology, 12* (March-June), 132-152.

Oggins, J., Veroff, J., & Leber, D. (1993). Perceptions of marital interaction among black and white newlyweds. *Journal of Personality and Social Psychology, 65* (September), 494-511.

Olday, D., & Wesley, B. (1990). Intimate relationship violence among divorcees. *Free Inquiry in Creative Sociology, 18* (May), 63-71.

Patton, B. R., Giffin, K., & Patton, E. N. (1989). *Decision-making group interaction* (3rd ed.). New York: HarperCollins.

Rancer, A. S. (1998). Argumentativeness. In J. C. McCroskey, J. A. Daly, M. M. Martin, & M. J. Beatty (Eds.), *Communication and personality: Trait perspectives* (pp. 149-170). Cresskill, NJ: Hampton Press.

Rancer, A. S., & Avtgis, T. A. (2006). *Argumentative and aggressive communication: Theory, research, and application.* Thousand Oaks, CA: Sage.

Rodman, G. (2001). *Making sense of media: An introduction to mass communication.* Boston: Allyn & Bacon.

Ronfeldt, H. M., Kimerling, R., & Arias, I. (1998). Satisfaction with relationship power and the perpetration of dating violence. *Journal of Marriage & the Family, 60* (February), 70-78.

Schaap, C., Buunk, B., & Kerkstra, A. (1988). Marital conflict resolution. In P. Noller & M. A. Fitzpatrick (Eds.), *Perspectives on marital interaction* (pp. 203-244). Philadelphia: Multilingual Matters.

Siegert, J. R., & Stamp, G. H. (1994). "Our first big fight" as a milestone in the development of close relationships. *Communication Monographs, 61* (December), 345-360.

Sorenson, P. S., Hawkins, K., & Sorenson, R. L. (1995). Gender, psychological type and conflict style preferences. *Management Communication Quarterly, 9* (August), 115-126.

Tardiff, T. (2001). Learning to say "no" in Chinese. *Early Education and Development 12*, 303-323.

Thompson, C. A., & Klopf, D. W. (1991). An analysis of social style among disparate cultures. *Communication Research Reports, 8*, 65-72.

Thompson, C. A., Klopf, D. W., & Ishii, S. (1991). A comparison of social style between Japanese and Americans. *Communication Research Reports, 8*, 165-172.

Ting-Toomey, S. (1985). Toward a theory of conflict and culture. *International and Intercultural Communication Annual, 9*, 71-86.

Tinsley, C. H., & Brett, J. M. (2001). Managing workplace conflict in the United States and Hong Kong. *Organizational Behavior and Human Decision Processes 85*, 360-381.

Weitzman, P. F., & Weitzman, E. A. (2000). Interpersonal negotiation strategies in a sample of older women. *Journal of Clinical Geropsychology, 6*, 41-51.

Weitzman, P. F. (2001). Young adult women resolving interpersonal conflicts. *Journal of Adult Development, 8*, 61-67.

Wigley, C. J., III. (1998). Verbal aggressiveness. In J. C. McCroskey, J. A. Daly, M. M. Martin, & M. J. Beatty (Eds.), *Communication and personality: Trait perspectives* (pp. 191-214). Cresskill, NJ: Hampton Press.

Wilkins, B. M., & Andersen, P. A. (1991). Gender differences and similarities in management communication: A meta-analysis. *Management Communication Quarterly, 5* (August), 6-35.

Withecomb, J. L. (1997). Causes of violence in children. *Journal of Mental Health, 5* (October), 433-442.

Zane, N., & Yeh, M. (2002). The use of culturally-based variables in assessment: Studies on loss of face. In K. S. Kurasaki (Ed.), *Asian American mental health: Assessment theories and methods* (pp. 123-138). New York: Kluwer Academic/Plenum Publishers.

Zornoza, A., Ripoll, P., & Peiró, J. M. (2002). Conflict management in groups that work in two different communication contexts: Face-to-face and computer-mediated communication. *Small Group Research 33* (October), 481-508.